Discrimination in Employment

a claims handbook

 **Cloisters** is a leading employment, discrimination and equality chambers, recognised as such by the *Legal 500* and *Chambers UK*. Cloisters barristers have been at the heart of virtually all major equality and discrimination developments, both through their work in the tribunals and courts, and in their contributions to legislation, guidance and policy.

Members of chambers act in cases that set the terms of equality law, and have recently helped to bring about the end of the default retirement age (*Heyday/Age Concern*); to extend discrimination law to cover carers of disabled people (*Coleman v Attridge Law*); to establish the scope of the protection to be given to volunteers under discrimination law (*X v Mid-Sussex CAB*); to extend pension provision to part-time judges (*O'Brien v Ministry of Justice*) and to establish the limits on justification of direct age discrimination (*Seldon v Clarkson Wright and Jakes*).

Cloisters barristers regularly advise and act on behalf of the Equality and Human Rights Commission. During the passage of the Equality Act 2010, Cloisters was involved in drafting amendments and briefings, as well as advising several NGOs and statutory bodies on the implications of the Act for future policy and practice. Members of chambers also drafted the statutory Code of Practice on Services, Public Functions and Associations, and are currently engaged in producing a supplement to that Code relating to the prohibition on age discrimination in goods, facilities and services. Many Cloisters barristers undertake Direct Public Access work.

Available as an ebook at www.lag.org.uk/ebooks

The purpose of the Legal Action Group is to promote equal access to justice for all members of society who are socially, economically or otherwise disadvantaged. To this end, it seeks to improve law and practice, the administration of justice and legal services.

Discrimination in Employment

a claims handbook

Edited by Declan O'Dempsey, Catherine Casserley, Sally Robertson and Anna Beale

 Legal Action Group
2013

This edition published in Great Britain 2013
by LAG Education and Service Trust Limited
242 Pentonville Road, London N1 9UN
www.lag.org.uk

British Library Cataloguing in Publication Data
a CIP catalogue record for this book is available from the British Library.

Print ISBN 978 1 903307 82 3
ebook ISBN 978 1 908407 23 8

Typeset by Regent Typesetting, London
Printed in Great Britain by Hobbs the Printers, Totton, Hampshire

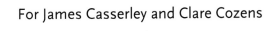
For James Casserley and Clare Cozens

Foreword

Explaining discrimination law in a comprehensive and comprehensible way is not easy, yet it is vitally important if its provisions are to be fairly and fully applied. The authors of *Discrimination in Employment: a claims handbook* have met that challenge fully. This reflects the fact that they work at the coal face, making the law work each day. It reflects also the fact that they have been involved in explaining, justifying and applying its provisions at every appellate level in the largest, most complex and most important cases.

At Cloisters we are very proud of the commitment the authors have made to this substantial project, and the support it will give to the Discrimination Law Association. It has involved over 15 members of our chambers.

The law in this area changes frequently and our website www.cloisters.com will carry developments so that readers can keep up to date with them. The reader will therefore find a very practical book which is easy to navigate and easy to understand and use. I have no doubt that it will become the companion to all lawyers and advisers undertaking employment discrimination and equality law work and will be used by judges, lay tribunal members, barristers and other advocates alike.

The previous, more general, *Discrimination Law Handbook* achieved almost biblical authority among discrimination law practitioners. I am sure that this book will too. I will use it constantly.

Robin Allen QC
Cloisters
March 2013

Acknowledgements

This book has had a very long gestation period. It was begun in 2009 and was overtaken by events specific to its then two editors in 2010. Since then it has been through a number of transformations and much updating and there are now four editors. It is, as a result, we hope, an extremely useful work which will enable both litigants in person and those representing claimants to navigate the Byzantine maze that is the Equality Act 2010 with some degree of confidence and which will help them to put forward the best case possible. We have attempted to state the law as at 28 February 2013.

The landscape surrounding discrimination law and practice is changing rapidly. The Equality Act 2010, like many pieces of social legislation recently, has suffered from a change of political perspective on its fundamental values. It appears that a change of culture is being encouraged by the Coalition Government in particular in the case of the use of the public sector equality duty. Previously equality and the means to equality were regarded as a necessity, but now equality is, perhaps, regarded as a luxury reserved for economically prosperous times. For those who need to use a book such as this, we are convinced that the latter perspective can never be correct.

We would like to thank those in Cloisters who have written chapters for the book and who may have thought their work would never see the light of day: Tom Brown, Olivia-Faith Dobbie, Danny Dyal, Sarah Fraser Butlin, Yvette Genn, Schona Jolly, Claire McCann, David Massarella, Dee Masters, Caroline Musgrave and Adam Ohringer.

We would also like to thank others in Cloisters who have made this work possible, including Robin Allen QC, Daphne Romney QC, Jacques Algazy QC, and our former colleague Damian McCarthy.

Many have contributed, but any errors are ours.

We would like also to thank our colleagues in Cloisters for their support of this project. The authors' royalties will go to the Discrimination Law Association. Our colleagues (barristers and clerks) in chambers have actively supported the many days taken out of practice necessary to produce this handbook. We are proud to belong to a set of chambers that takes pro bono commitments of all sorts as seriously as Cloisters does.

In addition, we must express our immense gratitude to our publisher, Esther Pilger, and all those at Legal Action Group (LAG), for their unfailing patience and understanding, and for the fantastic work that LAG does. They have had to draw on those virtues frequently and deeply.

We would also like to thank Alex Dunn, Will Garrood, and Pip Jones for their patience and support.

Finally, this book is dedicated both to the memory of James Casserley and to that of Declan's wife, Clare Cozens, who died suddenly on 27 July 2010. Clare was a committed equality campaigner who contributed much to equality and human rights, the *Discrimination Law Review* and ultimately to the Equality Act 2010.*

Declan O'Dempsey, Catherine Casserley, Sally Robertson, Anna Beale
Cloisters
March 2013

* See Clare's obituary: *The Guardian*, Sunday 15 August 2010, Trevor Phillips.

Contributors

Anna Beale has a prolific appellate practice and extensive experience of lengthy discrimination and equal pay litigation. Her reported cases include *Wong v Igen Ltd* (leading authority on the burden of proof in discrimination claims) and *Elstone v BP* (establishing the scope of the whistleblowing legislation). Anna co-authored (with Declan O'Dempsey) a report on Age and Employment, published by the European Commission in 2011, and (with Robin Allen QC and Rachel Crasnow) *Employment Law and Human Rights* (2nd ed, OUP, 2007).

Tom Brown was called to the Bar in 2000. He previously worked at the UN International Criminal Tribunal for Rwanda. Tom was a judicial assistant to the late Lord Bingham of Cornhill and worked at the Federal Court of Australia. He specialises in employment, discrimination and human rights law and has written and lectured widely on discrimination law, as well as appearing in leading cases in the EAT and Court of Appeal.

Sarah Fraser Butlin is an experienced employment law practitioner with particular expertise in multi-ground discrimination claims and appellate work. She has a particular interest in healthcare related work. In addition to her private practice, Sarah teaches at the University of Cambridge and has contributed to numerous publications including the *Industrial Law Journal*.

Catherine Casserley specialises in employment, human rights and discrimination law. She has considerable expertise in the Equality Act 2010 and its predecessor legislation and in disability discrimination litigation in particular, appearing, for example in *Boyle v SCA Packaging Ltd (Equality and Human Rights Commission intervening)* – the first case in which the Lords considered the definition of disability for the purposes of section 1 of the Disability Discrimination Act in any detail. She has appeared in the Employment Tribunal, County Courts, Employment Appeal Tribunal, Court of Appeal, House of Lords and Supreme Court.

Olivia-Faith Dobbie appears in discrimination cases at all levels and in a variety of forums, including workplace disputes in the Employment Tribunal, judicial review in the High Court, and appeals in the EAT, Court of Appeal and Supreme Court. In recent years, she has appeared in several high-profile cases, including *X v Mid-Sussex CAB* and *British Gurkha Welfare Society & Others v Ministry of Defence*.

Daniel Dyal is an employment and equality law specialist. He litigates claims at first instance and at appellate level. He is highly regarded for his appellate work and his ability to craft creative and persuasive legal arguments on difficult points of law. Daniel has appeared in numerous reported cases. He is a former director of the Discrimination Law Association.

Yvette Genn specialises in all types of discrimination litigation. She is particularly known for her expertise in equal pay, having acted as leading counsel in the high profile litigation in the North East and Scotland on behalf of thousands of women in the NHS and local government. She is recognised as an expert in this area by regular requests across a range of organisations for training and regular presentation of the workshop on equal pay to judges from across Europe at the Academy of European Law in Trier. Yvette sits as a Deputy District Judge and Recorder in civil and private family law matters, and this experience informs all aspects of her practice.

Schona Jolly has an extensive domestic and international equalities, employment and human rights law practice. Her most recent notable successes include the Supreme Court crossover employment/ commercial case *Jivraj v Hashwani* and *Singh v France* before the UNHRC.

Claire McCann is a highly regarded employment law practitioner who also specialises in non-employment discrimination claims, both judicial reviews and county court proceedings. She often works at the cutting edge of equality law: she was instructed by the successful claimant in one of the first reported cases concerning the public sector race equality duty (*Elias v Secretary of State for Defence*) and acted for the successful female claimants in the seminal equal pay case,

Surtees v Middlesbrough County Council. She has recently advised transsexual and intersex clients on their rights under domestic and international discrimination and human rights law. She writes and lectures extensively on employment and equality issues.

David Massarella appears for both claimants and respondents across all types of discrimination claims. He has particular expertise in disability discrimination (*Meikle v Nottinghamshire County Council*) and sexual orientation discrimination (*Bivonas LLP v Bennett*). His recent tribunal cases have included two high-profile pregnancy discrimination cases against the RAF (*Gregory v RAF*) and a leading city law firm (*Tantum v Travers Smith Braithwaite*). Before coming to the Bar he worked for ten years as a director in theatre and opera, including work for the Royal Opera House. He is a trustee of Southwark CAB and Actors Touring Company.

Dee Masters is an employment law barrister who specialises in discrimination. She has appeared in numerous reported cases such as *Seldon v Clarkson Wright and Jakes* and *Wilson v HSE*. She is currently drafting a supplement to the statutory Code of Practice relating to the prohibition on age discrimination in goods, facilities and services on behalf of the Equality and Human Rights Commission.

Caroline Musgrave joined Cloisters following a career in international relief and development work in the charity sector. Caroline maintains a healthy balance of work representing both claimants and respondents and, as shown in her capacity as junior counsel in the equal pay litigation of *Brennan v Sunderland City Council*, is experienced and capable in her handling of complex and lengthy discrimination litigation.

Declan O'Dempsey has specialised in discrimination, human rights and administrative law for many years. He has been involved in many of the leading age discrimination and disability discrimination employment cases (eg *Seldon, Homer, Heyday, Coleman*). He has previously co-written LAG's *Age Discrimination Handbook*. Declan was vice chair of the Bar Standards Board's equality and diversity Committee, and has co-written the EHRC's Services, Public Functions and Associations Statutory Code of Practice, the Public Sector Equality Duty Guidance, and the Age Supplement to the Services etc Code.

Adam Ohringer is an employment specialist who still maintains a broader civil law practice. He represents claimants, respondents and union clients at all levels. Adam is particularly known for his strategic approach to litigation as well as his ability to deal with 'difficult' witnesses. He is frequently instructed on multi-day discrimination cases involving complex issues of fact and law.

Sally Robertson specialises in multi-factorial employment and discrimination cases, often in the context of whistleblowing, safeguarding children, mental health issues and dismissals that are potentially career ending. Reported cases include *Saini v All Saints Haque Centre* on associative religious discrimination. She brings to her practice experience of working within and managing organisations in the not-for-profit sector, a background that includes writing 13 editions of the *Disability Rights Handbook*.

Contents

Table of cases

Table of statutes

Table of statutory instruments

Table of European and international legislation

Employment General Framework Directive (General Framework in
  Employment and Occupation) (2000/78/EC) *continued*

Art 2(2)(b)	2.85
Art 2(2)(b)(i)	19.69
Art 2(2)(b)(ii)	4.11, 19.118
Art 2(3)	19.121
Art 2(4)	19.121
Art 2(5)	2.86, 19.122, 19.124
Art 3	10.28, 10.29
Art 3(1)	19.126
Art 3(1)(a)	13.5, 19.128
Art 3(2)	19.125
Art 3(3)	19.126
Art 4	13.4, 13.5, 13.8, 13.17, 13.36, 13.47, 19.61
Art 4(1)	2.86, 13.4, 13.37, 13.47, 19.127
Art 4(2)	13.6, 13.36, 13.37, 13.40, 19.129
Art 5	4.51
Art 6	2.85, 19.69, 19.70
Art 6(1)	2.85, 2.86, 13.91, 19.66, 19.69, 19.71, 19.73, 19.74, 19.131
Art 6(2)	15.62–15.64
Art 7	19.110, 19.132
Art 9(2)	19.134
Art 8	13.12, 19.133
Art 8(2)	19.133
Art 9(2)	19.134
Art 10	19.135
Art 11	19.136
Art 12	19.138
Art 13	19.138
Art 14	19.138
Art 16	8.48
Art 17	18.15, 19.140
Equal Pay Directive (75/117/EC)	7.5, 18.22, 19.15
Equal Treatment Between Men and Women Engaged in an Activity, Including Agriculture, in a Self-Employed Capacity, and on the Protection of Self-Employed Women During Pregnancy and Motherhood Directive (86/613/EEC)	19.25
Equal Treatment Between Men and Women Engaged in an Activity in a Self-Employed Capacity Directive 2010/41/EU	19.25

United Nations Legislation

Abbreviations

AAL	Additional adoption leave
ACAS	Advisory, Conciliation and Arbitration Service
AML	Additional maternity leave
APL	Additional paternity leave
AVC	Additional voluntary contributions
CEDAW	Convention (UN) Eliminating all forms of Discrimination against Women
Charter	Charter of the Fundamental Rights of the European Union
CJEU	Court of Justice of the European Union
DDA 1995	Disability Discrimination Act 1995
EAT	Employment Appeal Tribunal
ECHR	European Convention on Human Rights and Fundamental Freedoms
ECJ	European Court of Justice
ECtHR	European Court of Human Rights
EEA	European Economic Area
EERBR	2003 Employment Equality (Religion and Belief) Regulations 2003
EHRC	Equality and Human Rights Commission
Employment Code	Equality Act 2010 Code of Practice: employment statutory code of practice
EPC	Equal Pay Statutory Code of Practice
EqA 2010	Equality Act 2010
ERA 1996	Employment Rights Act 1996
ET	Employment Tribunal
ETA 1973	Employment and Training Act 1973
ETD	Equal Treatment Directive 2006/54
EU	European Union
EWC	Expected week of childbirth
FED	Framework Employment Directive 2000/78
GOR	Genuine occupational requirement
HRA 1998	Human Rights Act 1998
HSE	Health and Safety Executive
LLP	Limited liability partnership
MAPLE 1999	Maternity and Parental Leave Regulations 1999
MEC	Maternity equality clause

MHSW 1999	Management of Health and Safety at Work Regulations 1999
OAL	Ordinary adoption leave
OML	Ordinary maternity leave
OPS	Occupational pension scheme
PAL 2002	Paternity and Adoption Leave Regulations 2002
PCP	Provision, criterion or practice
PHA 1997	Protection from Harassment Act 1997
PSED	Public sector equality duty
PTW 2000	Part time Workers Regulations 2000
PTWD	Part time workers Directive 97/81
PWD	Pregnant Workers Directive 92/85
Recast Directive	Directive 2006/54/EC: the Gender Recast Directive
RRA 1976	Race Relations Act 1976
SDA 1975	Sex Discrimination Act 1975
SEC	Sex equality clause
SERPS	State earnings-related pension scheme
SMP	Statutory maternity pay
TFEU	Treaty on the Functioning of the European Union
TULRCA 1992	Trade Union and Labour Relations (Consolidation) Act 1992
TUPE	Transfer of Undertakings (Protection of Employment) Regulations 2006
UNCRPD	United Nations Convention on the Rights of Persons with Disabilities

Protected characteristics

> **Key points**
> - The Equality Act (EqA) 2010 requires an understanding of what the protected characteristics are.
> - Direct discrimination is triggered by less favourable treatment because of one or more of these protected characteristics.
> - The definition of many of the protected characteristics will vary from case to case and attention must be given to the nature of the protected characteristic in the particular case at every stage of the case.
> - The definition of the protected characteristic may make a difference to the potential comparators for any case.
> - The definition will also be relevant for the purposes of indirect discrimination, when considering a group sharing a protected characteristic.

Introduction

1.1   Part 2 of the Equality Act (EqA) 2010 contains the key concepts of equality. It deals with the types of unlawful conduct[1] and protected characteristics.[2] 'Protected characteristics' are the characteristics that trigger the prohibition against discrimination in the Act. They are defined in EqA 2010 s4 as:

- age;
- disability;
- gender reassignment;
- marriage and civil partnership;
- pregnancy and maternity;
- race;
- religion or belief;
- sex;
- sexual orientation.[3]

1.2   Protected characteristics play an important role in the Act, and their scope can sometimes be understood by reference to the international law on which they are based.[4] Unlawful discrimination will occur

---

1 EqA 2010 ss13–27.
2 EqA 2010 ss2–12.
3 EqA 2010 s4.
4 See chapter 19.

where the prohibited conduct is connected with the protected characteristic in the ways set out in the Act. As discussed in chapter 3, the
characteristic does not need to be that of the complainant.[5]

Protected characteristics

Age[6]

1.3   Age is defined by reference to a person's age group which, in turn, is
defined as a reference to a particular age or to a range of ages.[7] Where
people fall within the same age group, they share the protected characteristic of age. Age means a person's chronological age, and it can
mean their relative age, or an age group characteristic (such as being
'middle aged'). The age group must, however, be defined by reference to a chronological age or range of ages. It can be defined by
reference to a series of ages or more than one range of ages.

1.4   It is important to be clear as to the formulation of the protected
characteristic of age and be prepared to apply this analytic approach
in each case. Sometimes the adviser will have to deal with a stereotype that is applied to everyone in a very broad and ill-defined age
related band. In those circumstances the age group may appear to be
defined by reference to vague concepts such as old age, middle age
and youth. Yet these are age groups within the Act because they can
be defined by reference to a range (or more than one range) of ages.
The context of the case may mean that a very small difference in age
is relevant to reveal the comparator. Thus in one Irish case a benefit
was significantly greater by reference to a date of birth. Clearly a comparison between a person with that date of birth and a person born
two days later could reveal the differential treatment based on age.[8]
Thus age groups can be relatively narrow (such as '21-year-olds') or
very wide (such as 'over 50s'). An age group can also be defined in

5 Direct discrimination can occur therefore because of (a) the complainant's
   characteristics, (b) the complainant's perceived characteristics, (c) a
   characteristic with which the complainant is associated (which may be that of
   another person) or (d) a perceived characteristic of a person with whom the
   complainant is associated.
6 See Equality Act 2010 Code of Practice: Employment Statutory Code of Practice
   (Equality and Human Rights Commission 2011) ('the Employment Code')
   paras 2.3–2.7 and examples.
7 See EqA 2010 s5.
8 *Perry v The Garda Commissioner* DEC-E/2001/29, 24 September 2001: two days
   difference either side of 60.

a relative way (for example, 'older than you'). Consequently, claims can be pursued on grounds of youth as well as on grounds of old age, depending on the circumstances.

1.5   Sometimes tribunals find this flexibility of definition troubling. However, race and ethnicity may be determined by reference to negatively defined groups (eg non-Africans) or by relative group references (non-English Europeans) or by references such as 'lighter skinned than Somalians'. The fact that one person may fall into many different protected characteristic categories does not create difficulties in defining the characteristic for the purposes of the particular case. What is important is to see the context of the case. In age cases the use of genuine occupational requirements makes understanding what is an age-related characteristic particularly important.[9]

1.6   Some age-related terms derive their meaning from their context and it is an area in which stereotyping can lead quickly into difficulties. The use of intuition in discrimination cases is unsafe because it leads to such stereotyping. For example, a person might have a stereotype whereby a youthful travel representative is more likely to denote a younger person by reference to chronological age than would a youthful managing director. Although these appear to be age-related terms, in fact they rely on age stereotypes relative to the expectations we have in respect of travel representatives and managing directors.[10]

1.7   In the same way that the Act does not prescribe the racial group to which the person seeks to compare themselves, the Act does not specify the age group with which comparison should be made in respect of age. So, for example, a 25-year-old victim of discrimination who was not promoted because she was thought to be too 'youthful'

9 See *Wolf v Stadt Frankfurt am Main* [2010] IRLR 244 and EqA 2010 Sch 9 Pt 1 para 1 and chapter 19.

10 *Wilkinson v Springwell Engineering Ltd* ET/2507420/07: an employer had made stereotypical assumptions about ability based on age that were not borne out by the evidence of the employee's work. In the Northern Irish Industrial Tribunal: *McCoy v James McGregor & Sons Ltd, Dixon and Aitken* 00237/07IT, an advert used the words 'youthful enthusiasm' for a job. The employer's focus on 'drive' and 'motivation' pointed towards a stereotypical view of the attributes to be associated with youth. The employer had rejected the 58-year-old claimant (with over 30 years' relevant experience), offering the jobs to significantly less experienced applicants, aged 15 years younger. The IT said that using 'youthful enthusiasm', in the whole context, raised a prima facie case of direct discrimination. The burden shifted to the employer. The other evidence included challenging drive and motivation in the claimant's interview and doing the scoring on an ad hoc basis.

might compare herself to 'over 25s' or 'over 35s' or 'older workers'. What matters is that there should be a proper basis for comparison.

1.8 The use of 'because of' in the formulation of direct discrimination in EqA 2010 s13, means that there is no longer any need to stipulate, as was done in the Employment Equality (Age) Regulations 2006 that reference to an individual's age includes reference to that person's 'apparent age'.[11]

1.9 The Court of Appeal has rejected any difference of approach except in the ways in which the legislation makes plain between age and the other protected characteristics.[12]

Disability

1.10 UK law sets out a specific definition of disability in EqA 2010 s6. An individual will need to meet that definition in order to claim discrimination arising from disability (s15), failure to comply with the duty to make reasonable adjustments (ss20 and 21) and indirect discrimination (s19). Direct discrimination and harassment (ss13 and 26), however, do not require the person claiming a breach to have a disability themselves – the treatment must be 'because of' disability. This is based on the wording of the Employment Framework Directive. It remains to be seen how courts will approach claims based on treatment because an employer perceives an individual to have a disability when they have a condition that does not meet the definition of disability set down in the Act. See further chapter 2 on direct discrimination.

1.11 In *Sonia Chacón Navas v Eurest Colectividades SA ('Chacón Navas')*[13] – the first case in which the Court of Justice of the European Union (CJEU) considered the definition of disability for the purposes of the Directive – the CJEU stated that despite the absence of a definition of disability in Directive 2000/78, it was not for the Member States to determine independent definitions. There must be a uniform interpretation across the States. The concept of 'disability' within the meaning of Directive 2000/78 is set out as:[14]

> ... a limitation which results in particular from physical, mental or psychological impairments and which hinders the participation of the person concerned in professional life ... In order for the limitation to

---

11 See paras 2.54–2.66.
12 See *Homer v Chief Constable of West Yorkshire* [2010] EWCA 419, [2010] ICR 987, [2010] IRLR 619 at paras [35]–[36] and see [2012] UKSC 15.
13 C-13/05, [2006] ECR I-06467, 11 July 2006.
14 *Chacón Navas* [2006] IRLR 706 at paras 43–45.

fall within the concept of 'disability', it must ... be probable that it will last for a long time.

1.12   'Disability' and 'sickness' are distinct concepts and the Directive did not require the protection of a person from the moment they develop any kind of sickness. The Court said that the Directive:[15]

> ... precludes dismissal on grounds of disability which, in the light of the obligation to provide reasonable accommodation for people with disabilities, is not justified by the fact that the person concerned is not competent, capable and available to perform the essential functions of his post.

1.13   The *Chacón Navas* definition of disability should, however, be regarded as being displaced by the definition of disability provided in the United Nations Convention on the Rights of Persons with Disabilities (UNCRPD)[16] as the latter definition is more inclusive. On 6 December 2012, Advocate General (AG) Kokott's Opinion in *335/11 HK Danmark, acting on behalf of Jette Ring v Dansk Almennyttigt Boligselskab DAB* was published. Paragraphs 23ff discuss the impact of the UNCRPD definition of disability on the definition in Directive 2000/78 and the distinction between illness and disability. Noting that *Coleman v Attridge Law*[17] explained that *Chacón Navas* did not mean that the concept of disability in the Directive was to be narrowly interpreted, the AG recommended to the CJEU, in para 46 of the Opinion, that the concept of 'disability' must be understood as referring to a limitation which results in particular from physical, mental or psychological impairments and which hinders (ie restricts) the participation of the person concerned in professional life. For the purposes of the definition of disability, it is irrelevant that the impairment has originated in a disease. The only decisive question is whether the restriction is lengthy. The use of special equipment is not part of the definition. If a person is not able to work full time they will fall within the notion of the disability within the meaning of Directive 2000/78. It remains to be seen whether the CJEU with follow this Opinion.

1.14   Under EqA 2010 s6 a person has a disability if they have a physical or mental impairment that has a long-term and substantial adverse effect on their ability to carry out normal day-to-day

---

15   *Chacón Navas* at para 51.
16   Persons with disabilities include those who have long-term physical, mental, intellectual or sensory impairments which in interaction with various barriers may hinder their full and effective participation in society on an equal basis with others (Art 1). See chapter 19.
17   (Case C-303/06), [2008] ICR 1128.

activities. 'Substantial' is defined in the Act as meaning more than minor or trivial (s212). Physical or mental impairment includes sensory impairments, such as those affecting sight or hearing. Schedule 1 to the Act sets out the definition of some of these terms, such as long term, which means that the impairment has lasted or is likely to last for the rest of the affected person's life (Sch 1 para 2(1)). Of critical importance is the fact that where a person is taking measures to treat or correct an impairment (other than by using spectacles or contact lenses) and, but for those measures, the impairment would be likely to have a substantial adverse effect on the ability to carry out normal day-to-day activities, it is still to be treated as though it does have such an effect (Sch 1 para 5). This means that 'hidden' impairments, for example mental health conditions, or those such as diabetes and epilepsy, may be disabilities within the meaning of the Act.

1.15   Cancer, HIV infection and multiple sclerosis are deemed to be disabilities under EqA 2010 (Sch 1 para 6). Where an individual is certified as blind, severely sight impaired, sight impaired or partially sighted by a consultant ophthalmologist, they are also deemed to have a disability.[18]

1.16   An impairment that consists of a severe disfigurement is treated as having a substantial adverse effect on the ability of a person to carry out normal day-to-day activities (Sch 1 para 3), meaning that they have simply to show that it is long term in order to meet the definition of disability.

1.17   Where an impairment ceases to have a substantial adverse effect, it will be treated as continuing to have that effect if the effect is likely to recur. Thus those with recurring, or fluctuating, conditions are covered (Sch 1 para 2(2)).

1.18   Where an individual has a progressive condition, which has some effect on their ability to carry out normal day-to-day activities but the effect is not, or was not, substantial, it will taken to be substantial if it is likely to become substantial at some point (Sch 1 para 8).

1.19   Taking each of these aspects in turn, a body of case-law now gives a settled approach to the recognition of disability. The burden of proving disability is on the claimant.[19] In many cases the employer will initially query whether the claimant has a disability. In an obvious case, denying or not admitting disability may be an unreasonable way of conducting the case. If the employer denies that there is a

18 Equality Act 2010 (Disability) Regulations 2010 SI No 2128 reg 7.
19 *Kapadia v Lambeth LBC* [2000] IRLR 699.

disability, particulars should be sought of that denial. Point out that there should be some basis for it, otherwise the employer may simply 'not admit' that there is a disability and await the evidence supporting the assertion of disability.[20] In the normal such case it is important to obtain medical evidence.[21] If an employer obtains medical reports that purport to deal with the question of whether the person is a disabled person for the purposes of the Act, point out that the issue of disability is one solely for the court or tribunal to decide on all the evidence, including any expert medical evidence. However, medical evidence cannot usurp the evidence of the claimant about how the impairment affects normal day-to-day activities (and whether it actually has a more than minor or trivial effect on ability to carry them out).[22]

1.20   EqA 2010 s6(5) provides the secretary of state with power to issue guidance about the matters to be taken into account in deciding the question of disability under section 6(1) – referred to here as 'the Guidance'. The Guidance (in this context) has a similar status to the Codes of Practice on Employment issued by the Equality and Human Rights Commission. While it does not by itself impose any legal obligations, a court or tribunal must take into account any aspect of the guidance which appears to be relevant.[23]

1.21   The components of disability under the EqA 2010 must be understood in the light of the Guidance:

- impairment;[24]
- substantial adverse effect;[25]

---

20 Expert evidence, particularly expert medical evidence, is always likely to be necessary in a case where a person's disability is not accepted and may be useful in any event to identify impairments which contribute to disadvantage.

21 An example of what can go wrong at first instance is illustrated by *F v Cleveland Police* [2012] UKEAT 10586/11, 14 March 2012, in which the claimant did not support her claim with medical evidence, materially affecting the ET's view of her credibility.

22 *Abadeh v British Telecommunications plc* [2001] IRLR 23. The adviser should always therefore take a witness statement dealing with the effects of the impairment on the person with disabilities in these cases.

23 The importance of the Code of Practice and Guidance as a source of assistance in identifying whether someone is disabled has been strongly emphasised: see *Goodwin v Patent Office* [1999] ICR 302. However, if the Guidance has misstated or misapplied the legislation, then it should not be followed: see *SCA Packaging Ltd v Boyle* [2009] ICR 1056.

24 See paras A3 to A8 *Guidance on matters to be taken into account in determining questions relating to the definition of disability* ('Guidance').

25 See Guidance section B.

- normal day-to-day activities;[26]
- a long term effect.[27]

Impairment

1.22   The threshold for establishing an impairment is very low, putting aside cases in which the claimant is simply lying about his or her impairment. The Guidance states that it is not necessary to categorise a condition as either a physical or a mental impairment. The underlying cause of the impairment may be hard to establish. There may be adverse effects that are both physical and mental in nature. Furthermore, effects of a mainly physical nature may stem from an underlying mental impairment, and vice versa.[28] The dictionary definition[29] of impairment is 'the fact of being impaired; deterioration; injurious lessening or weakening' and 'impair' in turn means 'to make worse, less valuable or weaker; to lessen injuriously, to damage, to injure'.[30] Thus an impairment means anything that worsens the condition of the body or mind.[31] A person has a physical impairment if they have 'something wrong with them physically'.[32] In some circumstances, it may also be worth consulting the World Health Organisation publications on disability.

---

26 See Guidance section D.
27 See Guidance section C.
28 See Guidance para A6.
29 *McNicol v Balfour Beatty* [2002] IRLR 711, CA: 'impairment' has 'its ordinary and natural meaning ... It is left to the good sense of the ET to make a decision in each case on whether the evidence available establishes that the applicant has a physical or mental impairment with the stated effects'. An individual who suffers from an impairment, or combination of impairments with different effects, to different extents over periods of time which overlapped can still be regarded as disabled within the statutory definition: *Ministry of Defence v Hay* [2008] ICR 1247.
30 The *Compact Oxford English Dictionary* (2nd edn).
31 The importance of the ordinary meaning is emphasised by para A3 in the Guidance: 'The definition requires that the effects which a person may experience must arise from a physical or mental impairment. The term mental or physical impairment should be given its ordinary meaning. It is not necessary for the cause of the impairment to be established, nor does the impairment have to be the result of an illness. In many cases, there will be no dispute whether a person has an impairment. Any disagreement is more likely to be about whether the effects of the impairment are sufficient to fall within the definition and in particular whether they are long-term. Even so, it may sometimes be necessary to decide whether a person has an impairment so as to be able to deal with the issues about its effects.'
32 *College of Ripon & St John v Hobbs* [2002] IRLR 185.

1.23   'Mental impairment' covers 'a wide range of impairments relating to mental functioning, including what are often referred to as learning disabilities'.[33] In the case of mental impairments in particular (eg depression) the extent of the effects of the impairment and the length of the effect will therefore be key.[34] There is a close, but not total, correlation between the identification of impairments such as depression and their medical diagnosis. The requirement that a mental impairment should be 'clinically well recognised' has been absent from the definition of disability since 2004 and the early case-law should not be followed in so far as it insists on this aspect. On a practical level, advisers will be concerned about the medical evidence it is necessary to obtain. The EAT helpfully has remarked that a GP,[35]

> treating a condition such as depression over a long period of time is in a very strong position to give an authoritative view of materials relevant to the assessment of disability under the Act and sometimes may be in a better position than a consultant examining a claimant on one occasion only. Those are matters of assessment for an Employment Tribunal.

The GP records may give a better idea of the effects on the ability to carry out normal day-to-day activities.

Excluded impairments

1.24   Regulations exclude certain impairments which are to be treated as not amounting to an impairment for the purposes of the Act. If an impairment is a consequence of one of the excluded conditions, it may nonetheless constitute a disability if it satisfies the other conditions.[36]

---

33 Employment Code, Appendix 1 para 6.
34 *J v DLA Piper UK LLP* UKEAT/0263/09: The ET's enquiry concerns principally the effect the impairment has on an employee's day-to-day activities. If the ET finds long-term substantial adverse effect, it normally follows 'as a matter of common sense inference' that the claimant is suffering from a condition which has produced that effect.
35 *Rayner v Turning Point* UKEAT/0397/10.
36 See the DDA case of *Power v Panasonic* [2003] IRLR 151. Depression caused by alcohol abuse was not automatically prevented from being a disability because addiction to alcohol is excluded. The EqA 2010 Guidance states that it is not necessary to consider how an impairment is caused, even if the cause is a consequence of a condition which is excluded. Thus liver disease as a result of alcohol dependency will count as an impairment (para A7).

1.25   The excluded conditions are:[37]

- addiction to alcohol, nicotine or any other substance;[38]
- a tendency to set fires;
- a tendency to steal;
- a tendency to physical or sexual abuse of other persons;
- exhibitionism;
- voyeurism;[39] and
- seasonal allergic rhinitis.[40]

1.26   Where these tendencies are a consequence of an impairment that would meet the definition of disability the tendency is likely to be excluded following the Guidance issued under the EqA 2010 which summarises, perhaps too broadly, the significance of the case-law in this area:[41]

> The exclusions apply where the tendency to set fires, tendency to steal, tendency to physical or sexual abuse of other persons, exhibitionism, or voyeurism constitute an impairment in themselves. The exclusions also apply where these tendencies arise as a consequence of, or a manifestation of, an impairment that constitutes a disability for the purposes of the Act. It is important to determine the basis for the alleged discrimination. If the alleged discrimination was a result of an excluded condition, the exclusion will apply.
>
> However, if the alleged discrimination was specifically related to the actual disability which gave rise to the excluded condition, the exclusion will not apply. Whether the exclusion applies will depend on all the facts of the individual case.

1.27   Prior to this guidance case-law had held that the condition must not be a freestanding condition in its own right.[42] It emphasised that the central issue will be causation of the less favourable treatment: was it because of the disability or the excluded condition?[43] The new

37 Equality Act 2010 (Disability) Regulations 2010 SI No 2128 from 1 October 2010.
38 However, addiction which was originally the result of administration of medically prescribed drugs or other medical treatment *will* be counted as an impairment (2010 SI No 2128 reg 3(2)).
39 Reg 4(1).
40 However, by reg 4(3) this does not prevent seasonal allergic rhinitis from being taken into account for the purposes of the Act where it aggravates the effect of any other condition. The implication of this exclusion is that all the other conditions are not to be taken into account when they appear to aggravate the effect of any other condition.
41 Guidance para A13.
42 *Murray v Newham CAB* [2003] IRLR 340.
43 See *Edmund Nuttall Ltd v Butterfield* [2006] ICR 77. The claimant's depression constituted a disability but his exhibitionism was an excluded condition. When

guidance reflects that position and does not simply exclude all manifestations of the excluded tendencies.

1.28   Other impairments are excluded by means of stipulating that they
have no effect on the ability to carry out normal day-to-day activities. Thus although a severe disfigurement can constitute an impairment, it will be considered to have no substantial adverse effect on
the ability to carry out normal day-to-day activities if it consists of
either a tattoo (which has not been removed), or a piercing of the
body for decorative or other non-medical purposes, including any
object attached through the piercing for such purposes.[44]

Deemed impairments

1.29   On the other hand some situations are included. Thus where a child
under six years of age has an impairment that does not have a substantial and long-term adverse effect on the child's ability to carry out
normal day-to-day activities, the impairment is to be taken to have
a substantial and long-term adverse effect on the child's ability to
carry out normal day-to-day activities where it would normally have
that effect on the ability of a person aged six years or over to carry
out normal day-to-day activities.[45] The inclusion of children under six
may be of significance when considering disability discrimination by
association with such a child with a disability.

1.30   As set out above, a person who is certified by a consultant ophthalmologist as blind, severely sight impaired, sight impaired or partially sighted is deemed to be a person with a disability and hence a
disabled person under the Act.[46] Similarly cancer, HIV infection and
multiple sclerosis are deemed to constitute disabilities.[47]

---

an ET finds that there is a legitimate medical impairment underlying an
excluded condition, it must consider whether the condition is the reason for
the less favourable treatment. If so then disability will not be the reason. If
the reason for the less favourable treatment was the excluded condition and
not the legitimate impairment, the claim should fail. Applying the *Nuttall*
approach, the High Court in *Governing Body of X Endowed Primary School v
Special Educational Needs and Disability Tribunal, Mr and Mrs T, The National
Autistic Society* [2009] EWHC 1842 (Admin), [2009] ACD 70, held that even
though physical abuse was a manifestation of T's ADHD it was excluded as
an impairment, and the treatment complained of (exclusion) was due to the
physical abuse, not the ADHD.

44   2010 SI No 2128 reg 5.
45   2010 SI No 2128 reg 6.
46   2010 SI No 2128 reg 7.
47   EqA 2010 Sch 1 para 6(1).

Substantial

1.31 Whether an effect is substantial is determined by considering:

- What are the actual effects? Are the effects of this impairment more than minor or trivial? If so the substantial condition is satisfied; if they are not
- Would the effects of the impairment be more than minor or trivial if 'medical' 'treatment' had not been in place at the relevant time? This requires consideration of what the effects of the impairment before treatment was sought were? Were these more than minor or trivial? If they were then it is likely that in the absence of treatment they would remain so.

1.32 The Guidance makes clear that the requirement for the effect to be a substantial adverse effect is satisfied if the effect is 'more than minor or trivial'.[48] It can be satisfied by the cumulative effect of two or more impairments.[49] The focus, when considering whether an adverse effect is more than minor or trivial must be on what the individual cannot do, and not on what they can do.[50]

1.33 The employment tribunal (ET) must establish how the individual carries out the activity compared with how they would carry it out if they did not have the impairment. As a rule of thumb, if the difference is more than the type of difference one might expect taking a cross-section of the population, the effects are substantial.[51]

1.34 In looking at the question of whether the effect is substantial the Guidance recommends that the ET looks at the following factors:

- the time taken to carry out an activity;[52]
- the way in which a person with that impairment carries out a normal day-to-day activity. The comparison should be with the way that the person might be expected to carry out the activity compared with someone who does not have the impairment;[53]

---

48 Note it was suggested in *Anwar v Tower Hamlets College* UKEAT/0091/10 that if either of these traits is missing the 'substantial' requirement is not satisfied. This must be doubted, because 'more than minor or trivial' is clearly disjunctive rather than conjunctive.
49 *Ginn v Tesco Stores* UKEAT 0917/05/MAA.
50 *Goodwin v Patent Office* [1999] ICR 302, approved in *Lewisham LBC v Malcolm* [2008] UKHL 43, [2008] 1 AC 1399 at [126]. See also *Vicary v BT* [1999] IRLR 680 and *Leonard v South Derbyshire Chamber of Commerce* [2001] IRLR 19.
51 *Paterson v Metropolitan Police Comr* [2007] ICR 1522.
52 Guidance B2.
53 Guidance B3.

- whether its effects on more than one activity, when taken together, could result in an overall substantial adverse effect;[54]
- how far a person can reasonably be expected to modify his or her behaviour;[55]
- environmental conditions that may exacerbate or lessen the effect of an impairment. When assessing whether adverse effects of an impairment are substantial, the extent to which such environmental factors, individually or cumulatively, are likely to have an impact on the effects should, therefore, also be considered.[56]
- whether an impairment is subject to treatment or correction. If so, the impairment is to be treated as having a substantial adverse effect if, but for the treatment or correction, the impairment is likely to have that effect. In this context, 'likely' should be interpreted as meaning 'could well happen'.[57]

Medical treatment

1.35   The Act stipulates that where a person is taking measures to treat or correct an impairment and, but for those measures, the impairment would have a substantial adverse effect on the ability to carry out normal day-to-day activities, then the impairment is to be treated as though it has that effect.[58] Where a person is following a course of treatment[59] on medical advice, in the absence of any indication to the contrary, the employer can assume that the impairment is likely, without treatment (a) to recur and (b) to have a substantial effect (if

---

54   Guidance B4.
55   Guidance B7: for example by use of a coping or avoidance strategy, to prevent or reduce the effects of an impairment on normal day-to-day activities. In some instances, a coping or avoidance strategy might alter the effects of the impairment to the extent that they are no longer substantial and the person would no longer meet the definition of disability. In other instances, even with the coping or avoidance strategy, there is still an adverse effect on the carrying out of normal day-to-day activities.
56   Guidance B11: factors such as temperature, humidity, lighting, the time of day or night, how tired the person is, or how much stress they are under, may have an impact on the effects.
57   Guidance B12.
58   EqA 2010 Sch 1 para 5.
59   Guidance B12 makes clear: 'medical treatments would include treatments such as counselling, the need to follow a particular diet, and therapies, in addition to treatments with drugs'.

it had a substantial effect prior to treatment).[60] The ET must judge how the impairment would affect the claimant's day-to-day activities if the medical treatment were stopped at the time of the discrimination. It should not ask itself what the position would be had the treatment never been received at all.[61] Permanent improvements from treatment are not to be excluded from consideration of the effects of the impairment.[62] The Guidance suggests that it would be reasonable to disregard such treatment if the final outcome of treatment cannot be determined, or removal of the treatment would result in a relapse or a worsened condition.[63]

1.36   The Act's approach to treatment does not apply to sight impairments to the extent that they are capable of correction by spectacles or contact lenses.[64]

Substantial adverse effects[65]

1.37   The Guidance suggests that the following should be taken into account in considering whether there is a substantial adverse effect:[66]

(a) physical impairments can result in mental effects and mental impairments can have physical manifestations;

(i) a person with a physical impairment may, because of pain or fatigue, experience difficulties in carrying out normal activities that involve mental processes;

(ii) a person with a mental impairment or learning disability may experience difficulty in carrying out normal day-to-day activities that involve physical activity.

---

60 *Boyle v SCA Packaging Ltd (ECHR intervening)* [2009] UKHL 37 at para 42. In the context of recurrence 'likely' meant that something 'could well happen'. This is an easier test than 'more probable than not'.

61 *Woodrup v Southwark LBC* [2003] IRLR 111.

62 *Abadeh v BT* [2001] IRLR 23.

63 Guidance B13. Counter-intuitive results from the *Woodrup* approach may also be avoided by addressing the commencement of disability status from a date earlier than the relevant act of discrimination.

64 EqA 2010 Sch 1 para 5(3). So the only effects on the ability to carry out normal day-to-day activities which are to be considered are those which remain when spectacles or contact lenses are used (or would remain if they were used). This does not include the use of devices to correct sight that are not spectacles or contact lenses. Guidance B15.

65 Guidance D11–19 gives examples of situations in which it would, and would not, be reasonable to regard the effect as an adverse effect on the ability to carry out normal day to day activities.

66 Guidance D15.

Normal day-to-day activities[67]

1.38   There is no definition in the Act of normal day-to-day activities. The Guidance gives examples of when it would be reasonable to regard something as having an adverse effect on the ability to carry out normal day-to-day activities. However, it states generally:

> In general, day-to-day activities are things people do on a regular or daily basis, and examples include shopping, reading and writing, having a conversation or using the telephone, watching television, getting washed and dressed, preparing and eating food, carrying out household tasks, walking and travelling by various forms of transport,

and taking part in social activities. Normal day-to-day activities can include general work-related activities, and study and education related activities, such as interacting with colleagues, following instructions, using a computer, driving, carrying out interviews, preparing written documents, and keeping to a timetable or a shift pattern.

1.39   Normal day-to-day activities do not include activities that are normal only for a particular individual or small group.[68] The question is whether an activity is normal or abnormal rather than how many people do it.[69] The fact that the activities take place at work makes no difference to whether they are normal day-to-day activities.[70] Participation in professional life may constitute a normal day-to-day activity.[71] However, participation in a specific profession will be unlikely to be a normal day-to-day activity without more.[72]

1.40   The most effective way of considering any situation that arises at work is whether it is constituted by activities that would commonly be regarded as normal day-to-day activities.[73] Thus if a person has a difficulty in communicating that is more than minor or trivial, it

---

67   Guidance Section D.

68   Guidance D4.

69   Guidance D5. Thus the fact that only some groups of people (rather than the majority of the population) perform night work does not stop night working being a normal day-to-day activity: see *Chief Constable of Dumfries and Galloway Constabulary v Adams* UKEATS/0046/08.

70   The ET should take account of the effect on an employee of circumstances which only arise at work (*Law Hospital Trust v Rush* [2001] IRLR 611 and *Cruickshank v VAW Motorcast* [2002] IRLR 24). It is sufficient if there is 'a limitation which results in particular from physical, mental or psychological impairments and which hinders the participation of the person concerned in professional life' (see *Chacón Navas* para 1.11 above).

71   *Paterson v Commissioner of Police of the Metropolis* [2007] IRLR 763.

72   *Chief Constable of Lothian and Borders Police v Cumming* EATS/0077/08.

73   See Guidance D10.

is highly likely that it will affect all activities whether carried out at work or not. It does not matter that the work requires a high level of communication at times, at other times it will only require ordinary communication. Thus the fact that the person does not tend to communicate when away from work (having modified his or her behaviour to cope with the effects of the impairment) will make no difference. It is only highly specialised activities that might be excluded. Thus if the impairment only ever had an impact on the speed with which the claimant could play virtuoso violin, it would not be regarded as having the substantial adverse effect.[74]

1.41   Normal day-to-day activities include activities required to maintain personal well-being or ensure personal (or other people's) safety. The ET should consider whether the effects of the impairment have an impact on whether the person is inclined to do or neglect basic functions (eg eating, drinking, sleeping, keeping warm or personal hygiene) or to exhibit behaviour that puts the person or other people at risk.[75]

1.42   Examples from the case-law of normal day-to-day activities include matters such as putting on makeup and[76] travelling by underground train.[77]

Long-term effects

1.43   To determine whether a person is disabled, a long-term effect of an impairment is one:

- that has lasted at least 12 months; or
- where the total period for which it lasts, from the time of the first onset, is likely to be at least 12 months; or
- that is likely to last for the rest of the life of the person affected.[78]

1.44   'Likely' in this context means 'it could well happen', rather than 'more probable than not' or 'a greater than 50 per cent probability'.[79] However, the time at which likelihood is assessed is of the time when the act of discrimination occurs rather than when the ET hears the claim.[80]

74 See also Guidance D8–D9.
75 Guidance D16.
76 *Ekpe v Metropolitan Police Comr* [2001] IRLR 605.
77 *Abadeh v BT* [2001] IRLR 23.
78 EqA 2010 Sch 1 para 2.
79 *SCA Packaging Ltd v Boyle* [2009] ICR 1056 paras 2 and 52 and see C3 Guidance.
80 Guidance C4.

1.45   When considering the length of time for which the effects have lasted, the effects of an illness or condition likely to develop or which has developed from another illness or condition can be part of the assessment of whether the effect of the original impairment is likely to last or has lasted at least 12 months.[81]

1.46   A person who has a disability has the protected characteristic of 'disability' and, where people have the same disability, they share the protected characteristic of disability. Section 6(4) of the EqA 2010 makes it clear that for all purposes (except the transport and certain housing provisions) a person will have the protected characteristic of disability even if they no longer have that disability.

Recurring or fluctuating effects

1.47   A substantial adverse effect is treated as continuing to have that effect if it could well happen that it would recur.[82] The prospects of recurrence must be ascertained as at the time of the act of discrimination.[83]

1.48   Four questions can be asked:[84]

- Was there at some stage an impairment that had a substantial adverse effect on C's ability to carry out normal day-to-day activities?
- Did the impairment cease to have such an effect and, if so, when?
- What was the substantial adverse effect?
- Is that substantial adverse effect likely to recur?

Past disability

1.49   A person who has a disability, or who had a disability in the past,[85] or who is perceived to have a disability or is associated with a disabled

---

81 *Patel v (1) Oldham MBC, (2) The Governing Body of Rushcroft Primary School* [2010] IRLR 280.

82 Guidance C5.

83 *McDougall v Richmond Adult Community College* [2008] IRLR 227: the Court of Appeal stated that the existence of a disability should be assessed, especially when determining the 'likelihood' of a substantial adverse effect lasting for 12 months, recurring or occurring in the future at the date of the act of discrimination.

84 *Swift v Chief Constable of Wiltshire Constabulary* [2004] IRLR 540: C must show that the particular effect is likely to recur on at least one occasion during C's life. C can be disabled under the Act even if the condition is not likely to recur immediately. Note that in other respects *Swift* depended on *Latchman v Reed Business Information Ltd* [2002] ICR 1453, which was overruled in *SCA Packaging Ltd v Boyle* [2009] ICR 1056.

85 EqA 2010 s6(4).

person is protected against discrimination. The EqA 2010 does not on its face extend to cases where the discriminatory conduct occurs because the person is perceived to have had a disability in the past. Section 6(4) does not expressly provide this. However, such treatment is because of the characteristic of disability and hence, taking into account the breadth of interpretation of the Directive 2000/78 in *Coleman*,[86] is actionable.

Progressive conditions

1.50   Where a person has a progressive condition that is 'likely' in his case to change over time so as substantially and adversely to affect ability to carry out normal day-to-day activities, then they are taken to have an impairment that has a substantial adverse effect before that effect is fully manifested.

1.51   Claimants will have to establish three matters:

- they have a condition; and
- as a result of the condition, they have an impairment that has or had some effect on their day-to-day activities; and
- the condition is likely[87] to result in an impairment having a substantial adverse effect.[88]

1.52   Therefore the impairment is treated as having a substantial adverse effect from the time it first has 'an effect' on the person's ability to carry out normal day-to-day activities. Whether a meaningful difference between an impairment caused by a progressive condition and an impairment that results from medical treatment for the condition can be drawn will depend on the particular facts of the progressive condition. However, an impairment will arise as a 'result' of a condition if it follows in the ordinary course of events from the disease. The likely substantial effect does not need to be of the same nature as the first insubstantial effect. In one case the claimant suffered minor incontinence resulting from a standard response to prostate cancer (a surgical procedure). The 'progressive condition' requirements were satisfied and an ET finding to the contrary erred in law.[89]

---

86   *Coleman v Attridge Law* C-303/06 [2008] IRLR 722 (ECJ).

87   'Likely' means 'it could well happen': *SCA Packaging Ltd v Boyle* [2009] ICR 1056. The suggestion that likely meant more likely than not, made in the earlier EAT case of *Mowat-Brown v University of Surrey* [2002] IRLR 235 although not explicitly overruled in *Boyle*, must be regarded as inconsistent with this approach and implicitly overruled in this respect.

88   EqA 2010 Sch 1 para 8.

89   *Kirton v Tetrosyl* [2003] ICR 1237 [2003] IRLR 353.

Gender reassignment

1.53   The Employment Code is a particularly important source of information as the concept of gender reassignment is different to the
previously used concepts in this area.[90] People who are proposing
to undergo, are undergoing or have undergone a process (or part of
a process) in order to reassign their sex by changing physiological
or other attributes of sex have the protected characteristic of 'gender reassignment'.[91] A reference to a transsexual person is a reference to a person who has the protected characteristic of gender
reassignment.[92] As such, a woman making the transition to being a
man and a man making the transition to being a woman both share
the protected characteristic of gender reassignment, as does a person
who has only just started out on the process of changing his or her
sex and a person who has fully completed the process.

1.54   The Code at para 2.23 gives the essential aspect of the characteristic: 'Under the Act "gender reassignment" is a personal process, that
is, moving away from one's birth sex to the preferred gender, rather
than a medical process.'

1.55   Thus 'the reassignment of a person's sex may be proposed but
never gone through; the person may be in the process of reassigning their sex; or the process may have happened previously. It may
include undergoing the medical gender reassignment treatments, but
it does not require someone to undergo medical treatment in order
to be protected.'[93] The Act requires that a person should have at least
proposed to undergo gender reassignment. It does not require such a
proposal to be irrevocable. People who start the gender reassignment
process but then decide to stop still have the protected characteristic
of gender reassignment.[94] So the question of whether a person has
this characteristic may depend on whether the person has 'proposed'
to undergo gender reassignment. The Code assists on this point,
stating that protection is provided where, as part of the process of
reassigning their sex, someone is driven by their gender identity to
cross-dress, but not where someone chooses to cross-dress for some

90   See para 2.21. During the passage of the Act, there was much debate on the
proper definition of 'gender reassignment'. The Code mirrors much of the
Ministerial statements that were made in parliament about the new approach.
91   EqA 2010 s7(1).
92   EqA 2010 s7(2).
93   Employment Code para 2.24.
94   Employment Code para 2.25.

other reason.[95] Note that there is no requirement for the employer to know that the person has the characteristic.[96]

1.56   Once a person can show that they have reached a definitive position and are 'proposing' to undergo gender reassignment, they are protected under the Act. Nevertheless, the Act does not require that person to have reached a decision that they will transition away from their birth sex and never turn back. There are many ways in which a person may show that they have reached a definitive position and are 'proposing' gender reassignment:

- starting to dress or behave like someone who is changing their gender or living in the new sex;
- making their intention known to someone, even if no further steps are taken at that point;
- cross-dressing, even where this is intermittent;
- attending counselling sessions related to the medical processes of gender reassignment.

1.57   The definition of 'gender reassignment' goes much wider than the precursor concept that required consideration of complex practical issues arising during the process of gender reassignment.[97]

1.58   The Employment Code examples point to a broad interpretation of the characteristic. For example, a person who was born female decides to spend the rest of life as a man. He starts to live as a man and decides not to seek medical advice as he successfully passes for a man without the need for any medical intervention. He would be afforded protection under the Act.[98] People who have started a gender reassignment process but then withdraw still have the protected characteristic because they have undergone part of a process. So, by way of example from the Employment Code, a person born male lets her friends know that she intends to reassign. She attends counselling sessions to start the process but decides to go no further. Although she no longer intends or proposes to undergo reassignment, she will remain protected against discrimination based on her

95 Employment Code para 2.26.
96 Employment Code para 2.27. However, it is plain that in certain situations alleged to involve direct discrimination it may not be possible to argue any causal link between the characteristic and the treatment if the employer knows nothing about the characteristic and it played no role in the decision-making process.
97 In effect cases such as *Croft v Royal Mail Group plc* [2003] ICR 1425, in so far as they deal with the issue of the nature of the protected characteristic are now not to be used.
98 See example in Employment Code para 2.24.

gender reassignment characteristic because she has undergone part
of a process to change attributes of sex.

1.59   As with other protected characteristics (with the exception of marriage and civil partnership and pregnancy/maternity), a person is
protected against direct discrimination and harassment because they
are perceived to be proposing, undergoing or having undergone the
process of gender reassignment or because they are associated with
someone proposing, or undergoing or who has undergone gender
reassignment. Therefore, where someone is a transvestite but is not
driven by their gender identity to cross dress, they will be protected
from direct discrimination and harassment if they are perceived to
be proposing to undergo gender reassignment. Similarly, if someone
were directly discriminated against because they lived with a transsexual, they too would be protected under the characteristic of gender
reassignment. In other cross-dressing cases the reason for the direct
discrimination may be the protected characteristic of sex, or of sexual
orientation, whether perceived, associative or actual.[99]

1.60   The existence of a condition known as 'Gender Dysphoria' or
'Gender Identity Disorder' (GID) means that it is possible sometimes
that the person will be a person with a disability if the GID has a substantial and long-term adverse impact on their ability to carry out
normal day-to-day activities. Hence the employer may need to make
adjustments and avoid other forms of discrimination in relation to
the person in respect of the additional characteristic of disability.[100]

1.61   The Code makes two other points about this characteristic. Where
a person holds a gender recognition certificate they must be treated
according to their acquired gender.[101] Transsexual people 'should not
be routinely asked to produce their gender recognition certificate as
evidence of their legal gender. Such a request would compromise a
transsexual person's right to privacy. If an employer requires proof
of a person's legal gender, then their (new) birth certificate should be
sufficient confirmation'.[102]

99 Constructing the hypothetical comparator to help tease out the operative
    'reason why' requires particular care, so as to avoid taking into account
    features associated with a different protected characteristic. For a helpful
    starting point in the context of an employer's dress code see *Smith v Safeway
    plc* [1996] ICR 868.
100 See Employment Code para 2.28.
101 Gender Recognition Act (GRA) 2004; Employment Code para 2.29.
102 Employment Code para 2.30.

Marriage and civil partnership

1.62 Persons who are married or in a civil partnership share the same protected characteristic of 'marriage and civil partnership'.[103]

1.63 Marriage is not defined in the Act but will cover any formal union of a man and a woman that is legally recognised in the United Kingdom as a marriage. A civil partnership refers to a registered civil partnership under the Civil Partnership Act 2004, including those registered outside the United Kingdom.

1.64 Only people who are actually married or in a civil partnership are protected against discrimination on this ground so the status of being unmarried or single is not protected. This asymmetrical protection, as is the case with disability, originates in the need to prohibit the historic discrimination that occurred against married women. Only people who are in fact married or civil partners are protected. So, people who are co-habiting but not legally married or civil partners are not protected, even if they are engaged to be married or are planning to become civil partners.[104] Equally, a person who is divorced or whose civil partnership has been dissolved is not protected.

1.65 Therefore, if an employer refuses to promote a woman who is about to be married, this will not be discrimination because of marital status. However, it may be an act of discrimination because of sex if the dismissal is based on sexual prejudices held by the employer.[105] Similarly, discrimination against a person who is about to enter into a civil partnership would not be unlawful discrimination because of the protected characteristic of marriage and civil partnership. However, it may well amount to unlawful discrimination because of sexual orientation. While discrimination against people because they are parents would not be direct discrimination because of marriage and civil partnership, it may constitute indirect discrimination, eg on gender grounds.[106]

1.66 Unlike the other protected characteristics discrimination based on association or perception of this characteristic is not prohibited.[107] Only discrimination because the person is actually married or in a civil partnership is protected against in the Act: 'It is the status that is

---

103 EqA 2010 s8. So a married man and a woman in a civil partnership share the protected characteristic of marriage and civil partnership: s8(2)(b).
104 EqA 2010 s13(4).
105 *McLean v Paris Travel Service Ltd* [1976] IRLR 202.
106 *Hurley v Mustoe* [1981] ICR 490.
107 The same is true of pregnancy and maternity. See para 7.65.

protected. However, the fact that I am married or civil partnered to A rather than B can, it seems, form the basis for a claim.'[108]

1.67   Note that there is no remedy under the Act for harassment because of marriage and civil partnership.[109]

Race

1.68   Race includes colour, nationality and ethnic or national origins.[110] The Act does not give an exhaustive list.[111] The term 'race' itself has not been the subject of judicial definition.

1.69   Ethnic origins are determined by reference to the individual's ethnic group. For a group to be an ethnic group it must regard itself, and be regarded by others, as a distinct community by virtue of certain characteristics.[112] It must have:

- a long, shared history, the memory of which the group keeps alive and that consciously distinguishes it from other groups; and
- a cultural tradition of its own including family and social customs and manners, often, but not necessarily, associated with religious observance.

1.70   In addition, there are other relevant characteristics, one or more of which will commonly be found and will help to distinguish the group from the larger community, either:

- a common geographical origin or descent from a small number of common ancestors;
- a common language, not necessarily peculiar to the group;
- a common literature peculiar to the group;
- a common religion different from that of the neighbouring groups or from the general community surrounding it; and/or
- a sense of being a minority or being an oppressed or dominant group within a larger community.

1.71   The definition given by the House of Lords needs revisiting in the light of the development of international law on race and in particular the inclusion of 'descent' as an aspect of race. This is because 'ethnic

108 *Dunn v The Institute of Cemetery and Crematorium Management* UKEAT/0531/2 December 2011; but see *Hawkins v Atex Group Ltd* [2012] IRLR 807 at paras 21–23.
109 EqA 2010 s26.
110 EqA 2010 s9.
111 See chapter 19 for the international materials which are available to assist in the interpretation of the term 'race'.
112 *Mandla v Lee* [1983] ICR 385. Sikhs are such an ethnic group.

origins' may include the concept of lineage or descent.[113] Discrimination based on genealogical descent from a particular ethnic group has been held capable of forming the basis of direct discrimination because of race (that is, ethnic origins).[114] A pub putting up a 'no travellers' notice could discriminate indirectly on the grounds of ethnic origin against Roma.[115] Where a characteristic is 'indissociable' from the protected characteristic, discrimination on the ground of that characteristic will be because of the protected characteristic.[116]

1.72   The significant characteristics of the racial group in question may be both ethnic and religious. Muslims are not a distinct ethnic group.[117] Refusal to permit a religious observance or a traditional practice of a religious group not amounting to an observance could amount to unlawful indirect racial discrimination.[118] Information will need to be provided on the statistical ethnic/racial makeup of the particular religious group.

1.73   Rastafarians, although a separate group with identifiable characteristics, have yet to establish a separate identity by reference to their ethnic origins.[119] Neither the English nor the Scots have the requisite racial element required for recognition as an ethnic group[120] although they may be captured under 'national origins'. Irish

---

113 See *Mandla* para 11.

114 *R (E) v The Governing Body of JFS* [2010] 2 WLR 153, where the reference to the international material on descent in ICERD was made, but the broader point was not conclusively determined. The SC concluded that there had been direct discrimination on the ground of ethnic origins because E had been refused admission to the school due to a lack of matrilineal connection to Orthodox Judaism. E's ethnic origins encompassed his paternal Jewish lineage and his descent from an Italian, Roman Catholic mother who had converted to Judaism but under the auspices of a non-Orthodox synagogue.

115 *CRE v Dutton* [1989] IRLR 8. Although the words 'Traveller' and 'Gypsy' were ambiguous, the latter constituted a racial group if defined in the narrow sense of 'Romanies'. This was the case if there remained a discernible minority of the group which adhered to the group even though a substantial proportion of it had become assimilated in the general public. NB, if the same notice were to appear today the case might have to be approached on the basis that the 'no travellers' sign was a provision criterion or practice excluding new age travellers as well as the ethnic groups Irish Travellers and Roma.

116 *Patmalniece v Secretary of State for Work and Pensions* [2011] UKSC 11, [2011] 1 WLR 783 at para 32, thus treatment because of the characteristic will be treatment because of the protected characteristic.

117 *Nyazi v Rymans Ltd*, 10 May 1988, EAT. They are of course protected due to the provisions relating to religion and belief.

118 *Hussain v J H Walker Ltd* [1996] IRLR 11.

119 *Crown Suppliers (PSA) Ltd v Dawkins* [1993] ICR 517.

120 *BBC Scotland v Souster* [2001] IRLR 150.

travellers constitute an ethnic group,[121] having their own language 'Shelta', beliefs and social customs.

Nationality and national origins

1.74   'National origins' refers only to a particular place or country of origin.[122] There is no discrimination because of national origins where the complainant is treated less favourably on the grounds that he was born abroad, without reference to any particular place or country of origin, notwithstanding that a person born in the United Kingdom would not have been treated in the same way.[123] There are clearly identifiable separate nations of the English and the Scots. Therefore there are different national origins.[124] While 'Welsh' is a group defined by national origin, the group could not be further sub-divided into Welsh speakers and English speakers.[125] The Code makes the point that national origins 'must have identifiable elements, both historic and geographic, which at least at some point in time indicate the existence or previous existence of a nation'.[126]

1.75   Nationality (or citizenship) is the specific legal relationship between a person and a state through birth or naturalisation. It is distinct from national origins.[127] If the precise nationality status is ever relevant specialist nationality books can be consulted.[128] However, for the most part the precise nationality will not be relevant as the perceived nationality or attributed nationality will be sufficient to show that the characteristic of race is involved under the Act.

121   *O'Leary v Allied Domecq Inns Ltd* CL 950275, July 2000 (unreported).

122   *Tejani v The Superintendent Registrar for the District of Peterborough* [1986] IRLR 502.

123   See *MOD v Elias* [2006] 1 WLR 3213. If discrimination is based on 'born abroad', although indirect discrimination its justification must be scrutinised rigorously.

124   *Northern Joint Police Board v Power* [1997] IRLR 610. The Employment Code now makes the point that 'A person's own national origin is not something that can be changed, though national origin can change through the generations' (Employment Code para 2.45).

125   *Gwynedd County Council v Jones* [1986] ICR 833.

126   'For example, as England and Scotland were once separate nations, the English and the Scots have separate national origins. National origins may include origins in a nation that no longer exists (for example, Czechoslovakia) or in a "nation" that was never a nation state in the modern sense.' Employment Code para 2.43.

127   Employment Code para 2.38 and at para 2.44: 'National origin is distinct from nationality. For example, people of Chinese national origin may be citizens of China but many are citizens of other countries.'

128   Such as Laurie Fransman QC, *Fransman's British Nationality Law* (Bloomsbury Professional, 3rd edn, 2011).

'Racial group' and 'Race'

1.76 A racial group is a group of people who have or share a colour, nationality or ethnic or national origins. For example, a racial group could be 'British' people. All racial groups are protected from unlawful discrimination under the Act.[129] References to someone's racial group include any racial group into which he falls and is therefore inclusive in its scope. If a racial group comprises two or more distinct racial groups it can still form a particular racial group. For example:

- the concept of 'race' includes 'African' even though it is possible that many different colours, ethnic groups and nationalities exist in Africa;[130]
- the words 'bloody foreigners' and 'get back to your own country' can racially aggravate an offence in criminal law.[131] Those who are not of British origin constitute a racial group, as do 'foreigners'. Racial groups can be defined by exclusion so discrimination against someone who is not English or who is not white or who is not of European descent is prohibited;[132]
- a Nigerian may be defined by colour, nationality, ethnic or national origin.[133]

Caste

1.77 Section 9(5) of the EqA 2010 enables the Secretary of State to amend the Act by way of secondary legislation to add 'caste' to the current definition of 'race' or to provide for exceptions to provisions of the Act so as to make particular provisions apply or not to apply in respect of 'caste'. Existing legislation has not marked the seriousness of caste discrimination by giving it a specific express status. Some have felt that the concept of 'caste' does not sit neatly into the established concepts of 'race' or 'religion or belief'. The National Institute of Economic and Social Research had conducted a study of the extent of caste discrimination in the United Kingdom. [134] The Government

---

129 Employment Code para 2.46 and EqA 2010 s9(3).
130 *R v White* [2001] EWCA Crim 216.
131 *R v Rogers* [2007] UKHL 8.
132 *Orphanos v Queen Mary College* [1985] IRLR 349 and Employment Code para 2.49.
133 Employment Code para 2.47.
134 Hilary Metcalf and Heather Rolfe, *Caste discrimination and harassment in Great Britain*, December 2010: www.homeoffice.gov.uk/publications/equalities/research/caste-discrimination/caste-discrimination?view=Binary (accessed 12 March 2012).

response indicates that it is likely to bring in legislation to deal with this.[135]

1.78   The Employment Code is silent on caste. However, the Explanatory Notes to the Act state that the term 'caste' denotes a hereditary, endogamous (that is, marrying within the group) community associated with a traditional occupation and ranked accordingly on a perceived scale of ritual purity. 'Caste' is generally, but not exclusively, associated with South Asia and its diaspora (particularly India). It can encompass the four classes (varnas) of Hindu tradition (the Brahmin, Kshatriya, Vaishya and Shudra communities); the thousands of regional Hindu, Sikh, Muslim, Christian or other religious groups known as jatis; and groups amongst South Asian Muslims called biradaris. Some jatis regarded as below the varna hierarchy (once termed, 'untouchable') are known as Dalit.

1.79   It is suggested that for the most part caste is within the concept of race. That term must be interpreted to give effect to Directive 2000/43. It, in turn, gives effect to the international law on discrimination in ICERD.[136]

Religion or belief

1.80   Religion or belief includes any religion and any religious or philosophical belief.[137] It also includes a lack of any such religion or belief so that atheists, agnostics and humanists are all protected.[138] Therefore, Christians are protected against discrimination and non-

---

135 www.homeoffice.gov.uk/publications/equalities/research/caste-discrimination/caste-discrimination-summary?view=Binary (see p 4/5 for the government's conclusions). 'The study found evidence of caste discrimination and harassment in Britain in areas relevant to the Equality Act 2010, namely in work ... The consequences of these could be severe for the victims ... Because some religions are almost wholly low caste, some cases of caste discrimination and harassment may be covered by religious discrimination provisions of the Equality Act 2010. However, for caste discrimination and harassment, religious provisions are likely to be less effective than caste-specific provisions and are unlikely to provide protection for members of a mixed-caste religion (including many Hindus, Sikhs, Christians and Muslims) or for atheists ... The Government might tackle caste discrimination and harassment through: extending anti-discrimination legislation to cover caste (ie using the power in the Equality Act 2010 to make caste an aspect of race); through educative routes ... Education without legislation could be effective in the public sector, but is unlikely to be so in the private sector.'

136 See para 1.79 and chapter 19.

137 EqA 2010 s10 and Employment Code para 2.55.

138 EqA 2010 s10(1), (2).

Christians are protected against discrimination because they are not Christians, whether they have another religion, another belief or no religion or belief.

1.81   The Employment Code states that the 'meaning of religion and belief in the Act is broad and is consistent with Article 9 of the European Convention on Human Rights (which guarantees freedom of thought, conscience and religion)'.[139]

1.82   As with the other protected characteristics (except for marriage and civil partnership and pregnancy/maternity), a person is protected against direct discrimination and harassment because of their religion or belief, their perceived religion or belief or because of the religion or belief of someone they associate with.

Religion

1.83   The Employment Code states that 'Religion' means any religion and includes a lack of religion. The term 'religion' 'includes the more commonly recognised religions in the United Kingdom such as the Baha'i faith, Buddhism, Christianity, Hinduism, Islam, Jainism, Judaism, Rastafarianism, Sikhism and Zoroastrianism. It is for the courts to determine what constitutes a religion.'[140]

1.84   A religion need not be mainstream or well known to gain protection as a religion. However, it must have a clear structure and belief system. Denominations or sects within religions, such as Methodists within Christianity or Sunnis within Islam, may be considered a religion for the purposes of the Act.[141]

1.85   How will the courts determine whether something is a religion? The religion must have a clear structure and belief system.[142] Scientology has been accepted as a religion by the European Commission

139 Employment Code para 2.52.
140 Employment Code para 2.53.
141 Employment Code para 2.54. The ECtHR or EComHR have found the following to be religions: Scientology (*X and Church of Scientology v Sweden* 16 D & R 68 (1978)), the Moon Sect (*X v Austria* 26 D & R 89 (1981)), the Divine Light Zentrum(*Omkarananda and the Divine Light Zentrum v UK* 25 D & R 105 (1981)), Druidism (*Pendragon v UK* (1998) EHRR CD 179) and Krishna Consciousness (*ISKCON v UK* 76A D&R 90 (1994)).
142 This is the main limitation according to the Act's Explanatory Notes. The ACAS Guidance issued under the previous legislation, the Employment Equality (Religion or Belief) Regulations 2003 SI No 1660, stated that a court or tribunal would be likely to consider things such as 'collective worship, a clear belief system and a profound belief affecting the way of life or view of the world'. Denominations or sects within a religion can be considered to be a religion or belief.

on Human Rights.[143] On the other hand, the European Human Rights Commission invoked the need to have clear evidence of the rules and structure to rule inadmissible a claim that 'Wicca' was a religion. The claimants could not establish a clear structure for the belief system.[144]

Religious belief or other belief

1.86   To qualify for protection a belief must have sufficient cogency, seriousness, cohesion and importance and be worthy of respect in a civilised society.[145] 'Religious belief' goes beyond beliefs about and adherence to a religion or its central articles of faith and may vary from person to person within the same religion.[146]

1.87   The Code makes clear that a 'belief which is not a religious belief may be a philosophical belief. Examples of philosophical beliefs include Humanism and Atheism'.[147]

1.88   A distinction must be drawn between beliefs which qualify for protection and opinions which are simply 'based on some real or perceived logic or based on information or lack of information available'.[148] The latter will not be protected against discrimination. The following test can be applied:[149]

- Is the belief genuinely held?
- Is it a belief and not an opinion or viewpoint based on the present state of information available?

---

143   *X and Church of Scientology v Sweden* (1979) 16 DR 68; UK courts declined to recognise Scientology as a religion, although Scientology would be likely to qualify for protection under the Act as a philosophical belief, even if not a religion or a religious belief.

144   *X v United Kingdom* 11 DR 55 (1977), EComHR.

145   See *Campbell v UK* (1982) 4 EHRR 293.

146   Employment Code para 2.56.

147   Employment Code para 2.57.

148   *McClintock v Department of Constitutional Affairs* [2008] IRLR 29. A magistrate who objected to adoptions involving same sex adoptive parents could not claim protection. He acknowledged that his objections to same sex adoptive parents were not based on matters of principle, but on an absence of cogent scientific evidence showing that same sex adoptions were in the interest of the child. How far domestic law is compatible with ECtHR cases is questionable. See *Eweida v United Kingdom* (48420/10) [2013] ECHR 37, para 81. However, systemic lack of knowledge (agnosticism) can be distinguished from ignorance of particular facts.

149   See *Grainger Plc v Nicholson* [2010] IRLR 4, where the claimant's beliefs concerning man-made climate change were philosophical beliefs and protected. Now see Employment Code para 2.59.

- Is it a belief as to a weighty and substantial aspect of human life and behaviour?
- Does it attain a certain level of cogency, seriousness, cohesion and importance?
- Is it
  - worthy of respect in a democratic society,
  - not incompatible with human dignity and
  - not in conflict with the fundamental rights of others?[150]

1.89   Thus the belief 'need not include faith or worship of a God or Gods, but must affect how a person lives their life or perceives the world'.[151] However, as the example in the Code illustrates, there is an objective judgment to be made as to conflicts with the fundamental rights of others etc that may override the subjective value to the claimant of the beliefs. Thus a woman who believes in racial superiority and makes the most important decisions in her life based on that philosophy will nonetheless not have belief as a protected characteristic.[152]

1.90   A belief based on political philosophy or on science is capable of qualifying for protection on this analysis. Political beliefs should not be excluded from protection[153] and even one-off beliefs, not shared by others, could be protected so long as the five-part test would otherwise be met.

1.91   However, caution needs to be exercised in respect of claims based on philosophical beliefs. The claimant must be prepared to adduce evidence to establish the genuineness of the belief (if this is in doubt), and to establish that the action complained about was done because of this belief. Cross-examination is likely to be needed on both of those areas. This is a different situation to that of a litigant relying

150 So a belief in the racial superiority of a particular racial group would not constitute a 'belief' under the Act for these reasons.
151 Employment Code para 2.58.
152 This approach is consistent with *Jersild v Denmark* (A/298) (1995) 19 EHRR 1; and the human rights cases dealing with abuse of the right of free expression for race hate purposes, see for example *Hennicke v Germany* Application No 34889/97. Note also in *Redfearn v United Kingdom* (47335/06) [2012] ECHR 1878, the ECtHR declared mainfestly unfounded the claim based on Article 9 ECHR, as disclosing no appearance of violation of Article 9.
153 There is a strong argument that they must be covered (a) due to the provisions of the Social Charter (see chapter 19) and (b) because they were initially excluded expressly under the precursor legislation. However, an amendment to the Employment Equality (Religion or Belief) Regulations 2003 under the Equality Act 2006 removed the requirement that beliefs needed to be 'similar' to religious beliefs. Consequently, any genuine philosophical belief, including political beliefs, must be covered, as many political beliefs meet the *Nicholson* test.

upon a religious belief. To establish a religious belief, a litigant need only show that he is an adherent to a particular religion.

Manifestation

1.92   The question of when a characteristic is indissociable from a protected characteristic is particularly sharp in the case of religion and belief. Some beliefs require behaviour. If the behaviour is indissociable from the belief, discrimination in respect of the behaviour will be discrimination because of the belief. However, the Employment Code says:[154]

> While people have an absolute right to hold a particular religion or belief under Article 9 of the European Convention on Human Rights, manifestation of that religion or belief is a qualified right which may in certain circumstances be limited. For example, it may need to be balanced against other Convention rights such as the right to respect for private and family life (Article 8) or the right to freedom of expression (Article 10).

Whilst this may be right in terms of the HRA 1998, it cannot be taken to be determinative of any aspect of belief discrimination.

1.93   Considerable case-law has examined the difference between freedom to hold a belief and freedom to express or 'manifest' a belief in the human rights context. This is because while in the ECHR, the freedom to hold a belief is absolute, the freedom to manifest a belief is qualified so that interference with that freedom is capable of being justified.[155] However, this distinction does not exist in the Act. Thus if the employer treats a Muslim less favourably for wearing hijab, than it treats a non-Muslim who also wears a head scarf, this is simply direct discrimination.[156] The question of whether one is dealing with a manifestation of a belief or a belief itself can never be determinative of whether the treatment is direct or indirect discrimination.

1.94   The Code says:[157]

> Manifestations of a religion or belief could include treating certain days as days for worship or rest; following a certain dress code; following a particular diet; or carrying out or avoiding certain practices. There is not always a clear line between holding a religion or belief and the manifestation of that religion or belief. Placing limitations on a person's right to manifest their religion or belief may amount

154 Employment Code para 2.60.
155 *Kurtulmus v Turkey* [2006] ECHR II-297.
156 See *Azmi v Kirklees* BC [2007] ICR 1154 at para 76.
157 Employment Code para 2.61.

to unlawful discrimination; this would usually amount to indirect discrimination.

1.95   Unfortunately the reason why it would usually amount to indirect discrimination needs more explanation than the Code gives to it. It is also not clear whether this analysis can be upheld in the light of the Supreme Court's judgment in *Patmalniece*.[158] There is not always a clear distinction between a religion or belief and the manifestation of that religion or belief. Thus if a woman believes that a woman should cover her face in the presence of unrelated adult men, it is a belief with a behavioural content. The woman could not be said to hold it if she did not attempt at least some times to follow that content by her behaviour. It could be argued that in such behavioural beliefs the behaviour is 'indissociable' from the characteristic of belief.

1.96   However, in practice most manifestations of religious or other beliefs are affected by neutral rules and hence the form of discrimination is indirect. For example if there is a rule banning the wearing of jewellery at work, this may prevent certain people with beliefs exhibiting the signs of those beliefs. So the rule may in effect prohibit the wearing of a particular garment or having a particular hair style.[159] Notoriously this question of manifestation has arisen from the interface of certain religious beliefs and sexuality. If a claimant is dismissed for refusing to comply with his employer's (neutral) Equal Opportunities Policy by refusing to work with homosexual couples, that is a dismissal for refusing to comply with the Equal Opportunities Policy, and is not because of his beliefs.[160]

1.97   The ECtHR in *Eweida v United Kingdom*[161] accepted that in such cases the right to manifest religious belief was in issue but held that such neutral rules are capable of being justified. The Court accepted that the prohibition on wearing a cross amounted to an interference with Ms Eweida's right to manifest her religion. The same was true of the requirement on Ms Ladele to act as registrar on civil partnerships and the requirement on Mr McFarlane to counsel same sex couples. The Court looked at whether the United Kingdom was in breach of its positive obligations arising out of Article 9 to secure that right in domestic law (ie discrimination law). The lack of specific protection

158 [2011] UKSC 11.
159 Eg the wearing of dreadlocks by Rastafarians: *Harris v NKL Automotive Ltd* UKEAT/0134/07.
160 *McFarlane v Relate Avon Ltd* [2010] ICR 507 and see *Eweida v United Kingdom* [2013] ECHR 37 paras 107–110; *Islington LBC v Ladele* [2010] ICR 532 and paras 102–106 of the ECtHR judgment in *Eweida*.
161 [2013] ECHR 37.

for Article 9 rights before the ETs was not conclusive as the uniform code and the other rules applied to the other claimants were examined in detail. The aims in each case were also considered legitimate. In Mr McFarlane and Ms Ladele's cases in particular the aims of promoting equal treatment were considered legitimate. The ECtHR then considered whether the code and rules were proportionate in each case. In *McFarlane* and *Ladele* they were considered proportionate to that aim. However, in Ms Eweida's case the aim of BA was to communicate a certain image of the company and to promote recognition of its brand and staff and the ban was not proportionate. It was not a means of protecting the rights of others. The right to manifest her religion was a fundamental right and there was no evidence that previously allowed religious symbols had affected the corporate image.[162]

1.98   There is a specific rule in respect of the wearing of turbans by Sikhs on construction sites, which provides that where an employer requires a Sikh wearing a turban to wear a safety helmet on a construction site, this is to be treated as unjustifiable and so unlawful indirect race discrimination.[163]

Sex

1.99   The protected characteristic of sex refers to a man or a woman[164] so that a reference to persons who share the protected characteristic of sex is a reference to persons of the same sex – that is, men or women.[165] Consequently, a comparator for the purposes of showing unlawful sex discrimination will be a person of the opposite sex. This is a new provision as the Sex Discrimination Act 1975 did not define 'sex' as meaning a reference to a man or a woman. Sex does not include gender reassignment, sexual orientation or pregnancy and maternity which are all dealt with separately.[166]

Pregnancy and maternity

1.100   Although pregnancy and maternity is listed as one of the 'protected characteristics' this characteristic is not further defined in Chapter 1 of Part 2.[167] It receives treatment in Chapter 2 of Part 2, which deals with

162 See paras 92–95 of the judgment.
163 Section 12 of the Employment Rights Act 1989 remains in force.
164 See Employment Code para 2.62.
165 EqA 2010 ss11 and 212(1).
166 Employment Code para 2.63.
167 EqA 2010 s4.

'prohibited conduct'. Discrimination based on pregnancy or maternity is afforded particular protection under European law, in that a woman subjected to such discrimination during the protected period is not required to compare her treatment with a man or with someone who did not have the characteristic of pregnancy/maternity.[168]

1.101   The protected period, broadly speaking, starts when a woman becomes pregnant and finishes at the end of her statutory maternity leave.[169] Sections 17 and 18 of the Act prohibit discriminatory 'unfavourable treatment' based on the protected characteristic of pregnancy and maternity, as opposed to 'less favourable treatment'.[170] So no comparison is required. The protected characteristic of pregnancy and maternity is tied up with the way in which discrimination is defined in the Act.

1.102   The Code deals with pregnancy and maternity in Chapter 8. However, some points are worth noting at this stage. First, for pregnancy and maternity discrimination, the unfavourable treatment must be because of the woman's own pregnancy. However, the Code implies that a worker treated less favourably because of association with a pregnant woman, or a woman who has recently given birth, may have a claim for sex discrimination.[171] If a man is treated less favourably because of his partner's pregnancy, then this could amount to sex discrimination by association. For example if a man and a woman expecting a child work for the same employer and bring to the attention of the employer that the woman needs to sit down at work due to her pregnancy and the man is dismissed for raising this as a health and safety issue, he could claim sex discrimination because of his association with the pregnant woman. However, the EAT rejected this argument in the case of *Kulikaoskas v MacDuff Shellfish*.[172] The Court of Session has now referred the question of whether this treatment is prohibited under the Directive to the CJEU.

1.103   Second, unfavourable treatment will only be unlawful if the employer is aware the woman is pregnant. The employer must know, believe or suspect that she is pregnant – whether this is by formal notification or through the grapevine.[173]

---

168 *Webb v EMO Air Cargo (UK) Ltd* [1994] ICR 770.
169 See para 7.57.
170 These seem to be compatible with the specific prohibition against discrimination based on pregnancy and maternity in the Equal Treatment Directive (as amended – 2002/73/EC).
171 Employment Code para 8.16.
172 [2011] ICR 48.
173 Employment Code para 8.18.

1.104   Third, if a woman is subjected to discrimination based on preg-
nancy/maternity after the end of the protected period (or before the
protected period, for example, where she tells her employer that she
intends to have a baby), then this will be considered as sex discrimination and she will then have to rely on the ordinary provisions of
direct and indirect discrimination and the comparative exercises
required by those provisions. If she experiences unfavourable treatment after the end of the protected period, but which results from
a decision taken during it, the conduct will be regarded as having
occurred during the protected period.[174]

1.105   Fourth, indirect discrimination and harassment[175] do not apply to
the protected characteristic of pregnancy and maternity. Therefore, a
woman who is indirectly discriminated against or harassed because
of pregnancy and maternity will need to bring her claims as indirect
sex discrimination and sexual harassment.

Sexual orientation[176]

1.106   Sexual orientation is defined[177] by reference to a person's sexual orientation towards:

- persons of the same sex (ie the person is a gay man or a lesbian);
- persons of the opposite sex (ie the person is a heterosexual);
- persons of either sex (ie the person is bisexual).

1.107   Sexual orientation relates to how people feel as well as their
actions.[178] So there is no requirement that a person be sexually active
in order to be regarded as being of a particular 'sexual orientation'. A
reference to people who share the protected characteristic of 'sexual
orientation' is a reference to people who are of the same sexual orientation.[179] Therefore, a gay man and a lesbian share the same sexual
orientation because they have a sexual orientation towards persons
of the same sex as them. If a gay man is treated less favourably than
a lesbian, then this might amount to direct sex discrimination, not

---

174 Case C-460/06 *Paquay v Societe d'architects Hoet + Minne SPRL* [2008] ICR 420.
   This has been given statutory effect in EqA 2010 s18(5).
175 EqA 2010 ss19 and 26 respectively.
176 The Employment Code points out that 'Gender reassignment is a separate
   protected characteristic and unrelated to sexual orientation – despite a
   common misunderstanding that the two characteristics are related': para 2.68.
177 EqA 2010 s12.
178 Employment Code para 2.65.
179 Employment Code para 2.67.

sexual orientation discrimination because they share the same sexual orientation.

1.108   Being asexual, celibate, or having particular sexual preferences (for example sadomasochism, bestiality etc) has nothing to do with sexual orientation and is not covered by the Act. However, as with religion and belief certain behaviour may be closely connected with a particular sexual orientation. Where an employer's reason for subjecting a gay man to a detriment is the employer's objection to certain forms of behaviour he assumes are prevalent in the gay community rather than any objection to homosexuality itself, this is unlikely to succeed as a defence. Moreover as with religion and belief where the treatment is given to the person as a result of a characteristic which is indissociable with the protected characteristic, that is likely to be direct discrimination.[180]

1.109   Examples are given in the Explanatory Notes to the Act. So, for example, a man who experiences sexual attraction towards both men and women is 'bisexual' even if he only has relationships with women.

1.110 Practical points

- Careful scrutiny of the basis of discrimination is always necessary. Consider whether 'multiple' discrimination is in issue.[181]
  - Is the characteristic on which the treatment is based 'indissociable' (inseparable) from a protected characteristic?
- While many advisers feel comfortable with race and sex, there are some issues surrounding other characteristics. Such as:
  - Disability needs medical evidence in many cases in relation to (a) likelihood of duration of impairment (b) the usual effects of an impairment (c) the presence of a physical or psychological impairment having some effects.
  - In age cases involving comparators it may be necessary to be precise in the description of the relevant age group, to enable a more telling comparison to be made.
  - Religion and belief cases require a careful analysis of the belief said to be the cause of the treatment. What looks like a case of discrimination because of religion may, on closer scrutiny,

180 See paras 2.15–2.26 (direct discrimination) and the discussion of *Patmalniece v Secretary of State for Work and Pensions* there.
181 See paras 2.77–2.80 for discussion.

relate to a belief held only by a subset of the relevant religion. The witness statement should carefully identify precisely what the claimant says caused the respondent to behave as it did. Assumptions about the nature of a belief due to the religious or other belief group to which the person is supposed to belong should be avoided.

- In cases involving 'manifestations' of all of the protected characteristics, it is important to ascertain whether the manifestation is 'indissociable'(ie inseparable') with the protected characteristic. Understanding and demonstrating that connection may be the difference between being able to mount a direct discrimination claim and not being able to do so.

- In none of these cases, save pregnancy, marital status and civil partnership status, is it necessary for the person to be able to show that they have the protected characteristic themselves in order to claim direct discrimination. However, the associative link should always be made clear in the direct discrimination claims in which it is used.

Direct discrimination

Key points

In practice a claim for direct discrimination should identify:

- the protected characteristic or indissociable (inseparable) characteristic said to have caused the treatment;
- the treatment (what was the detriment?);
- why the treatment was less favourable treatment:
  - the actual or hypothetical comparator relied upon (or both);
  - the material (relevant) circumstances for the comparison;
- other facts from which an inference can be drawn that direct discrimination has taken place (such as the employer's responses to questions or other secondary evidence);
- the flaws in the respondent's explanation for the treatment;
- the 'reason why' the treatment occurred: that it was because of the protected characteristic.

Direct discrimination arises where a rule or treatment is not neutral in relation to the protected characteristic (eg people must retire at age 65), or where although it seems neutral on analysis the rule is not (pensioners get in free – but there are different pension ages for men and women). If a neutral rule is applied (you must be over 6ft tall to join the police force), this may give rise to indirect discrimination unless there is an indissociable link between the rule and a characteristic.

Direct discrimination arises where because of a protected characteristic the claimant is treated less favourably than another person who (or whose situation) lacks that characteristic.

- Intention to discriminate is not necessary.
- Whether treatment is reasonable or unreasonable is no more than the start of the inquiry in many cases. The issue is whether the treatment is less favourable.
- Even reasonable treatment may constitute direct discrimination if (eg) the particular rule would not have been applied at all, or in that way, but for the protected characteristic.
- If everyone appears to be treated equally badly the treatment is unlikely to be less favourable unless either some factor indissociable from a protected characteristic means the victim is the subject of the treatment more often or that there is some respect in which the apparent equality of bad treatment is not in fact equal.

Pregnancy and maternity discrimination receives a different treatment to direct discrimination reflecting the unique features of pregnancy and maternity.

Age discrimination can be ojectively justified. Other direct discrimination cannot be justified.

Introduction

2.1   The source of the concept of equality is the idea that persons in like situations should be treated alike and that persons in unlike situations should not be treated in the same manner. 'Thus to treat unequal matters differently according to their inequality is not merely permitted but required' by the principle of equality.[1] In terms of EU law, the discrimination directives all embrace this approach to the concept of discrimination. It is also the approach adopted in European human rights law.[2]

2.2   In UK law, s13(1) of the EqA 2010 provides that direct discrimination occurs where,

- because of
- a protected characteristic,
- a person (A) treats another person (B)
- less favourably
- than A treats or would treat others.

This chapter examines this structure. The claim, applications for and compliance with disclosure, witness statements and submissions should always be referred back to it.

---

1   See *South West Africa case* (1966) ICJ Rep 4, dissenting opinion of Judge Tanaka.

2   Thus *Thlimmenos v Greece* (2000) 31 EHRR 411, ECtHR: 'The court has so far considered that the right under art 14 not to be discriminated against in the enjoyment of the rights guaranteed under the Convention is violated when states treat differently persons in analogous situations without providing an objective and reasonable justification ... However, the court considers that this is not the only facet of the prohibition of discrimination in art 14. The right not to be discriminated against in the enjoyment of the rights guaranteed under the Convention is also violated when states without an objective and reasonable justification fail to treat differently persons whose situations are significantly different.'

2.3   The Directives[3] provide that direct discrimination shall be taken to occur where one person is treated less favourably than another is, has been, or would be treated in a comparable situation on grounds of a protected characteristic.[4]

2.4   Note the following exceptions, amplifications and qualifications to this definition of direct discrimination:

- It cannot be justified save in the case of direct age discrimination.[5]
- A person can treat people who are disabled more favourably than non-disabled people without committing direct discrimination because of disability.[6]
- Direct discrimination because of marriage or civil partnership in the field of work is unlawful only if the less favourable treatment is because the recipient of the treatment is married or a civil partner.[7]
- In relation to direct race discrimination, less favourable treatment includes segregation of a person from other people.
- In relation to direct sex discrimination:
  - less favourable treatment of a woman because she is breastfeeding is not treated as less favourable treatment in relatio n to work;[8]
  - in comparing men and women, no account is to be taken of the special treatment afforded to women in connection with pregnancy and childbirth;[9]
  - unfavourable treatment because of pregnancy and maternity receives a different treatment in the Act.[10]. So the prohibition on direct discrimination does not apply to anything done in relation to a woman:
    a) because of a pregnancy of hers;[11] or

---

3 The Race Directive 2000/43/EC, the General Framework Directive 2000/78/EC and the Equal Treatment Directive 2006/54/EC, see chapter 19.

4 Race Directive 2000/43/EC Article 2(2)(a); General Framework Directive 2000/78 Article 2(2)(a) and Equal Treatment Directive 2006/54/EC Article 2(1)(a).

5 EqA 2010 s13(2); this is covered in paras 2.81–2.99.

6 EqA 2010 s13(3); this is not expressed to apply only where the s20 duty to make reasonable adjustments applies.

7 EqA 2010 s13(4).

8 EqA 2010 s13(7), although outside work it counts as less favourable treatment (EqA 2010 s13(6)(a)).

9 EqA 2010 s13(6)(b).

10 Dealt with in chapter 7.

11 EqA 2010 ss13(8) and 17(6)(a).

b) done in the 26-week week period beginning on the day on which she gives birth because she has given birth;[12]
c) done in the 'protected period' beginning when a woman's pregnancy begins and ending in accordance with her maternity leave rights[13] and done because of her pregnancy or because of illness suffered by her as a result of it;[14]
d) because she is on compulsory maternity leave or because she is exercising or seeking to exercise or has exercised or sought to exercise the right to ordinary or additional maternity leave.[15]

2.5 When comparing cases to see if there has been direct discrimination, there must be no material difference between the circumstances relating to each case.[16] Where the (or a) protected characteristic relied on is disability, the circumstances of the case include a person's abilities.[17] If the protected characteristic is sexual orientation, the fact that one person is a civil partner while another is married is not a material difference between the circumstances relating to each case.[18]

An overview of the concept of direct discrimination

2.6 Direct discrimination is perhaps the conceptually simplest form of discrimination. It occurs where two people whose circumstances (except for a protected characteristic) are the same are treated differently because of the protected characteristic.

2.7 The structure of a direct discrimination case will therefore generally take the form of ascertaining:

- the protected characteristic;
- what the treatment was;[19]
- whether there is someone to whom the claimant can be compared or whether C will have to rely on a hypothetical comparator:

---

12 EqA 2010 ss13(8) and 17(6)(b).
13 See chapter 7.
14 EqA 2010 ss13(8) and 18(7)(a).
15 EqA 2010 ss13(8) and 18(7)(b).
16 EqA 2010 s23(1).
17 EqA 2010 s23(2).
18 EqA 2010 s23(3).
19 Identifying the 'treatment' will also help in identifying the 'act' of discrimination for the purposes of determining whether the claim was presented within the time-limits (see chapter 17).

> – What are the relevant circumstances of the claimant and any comparator?
> – Are those circumstances the same or not materially different?
> • what reason is advanced by the respondent for the treatment?

2.8   The starting point for a direct discrimination case is the proper identification of the protected characteristic in question. Properly describing the characteristic in question may be of vital importance in some cases.[20]

2.9   The Employment Code[21] gives an example at para 3.4:

> At a job interview, an applicant mentions she has a same sex partner. Although she is the most qualified candidate, the employer decides not to offer her the job. This decision treats her less favourably than the successful candidate, who is a heterosexual woman. If the less favourable treatment of the unsuccessful applicant is because of her sexual orientation, this would amount to direct discrimination.

2.10   Analysing this in terms of the above scheme:

• the protected characteristic: sexual orientation;
• the treatment: not appointing the woman;
• the comparator (an actual one): the woman who was appointed:
   – the relevant circumstances: both applying for the same job; both being assessed on qualifications;
   – the circumstances are not the same, because the complainant is better qualified than the comparator, but they are not materially different.

2.11   Further examples also illustrate the way in which direct discrimination operates. Three employees (two male, one female) are considered for promotion. Their abilities are the same. The two men are promoted, but, because the employer thinks that she will probably want to have children in a year or two, the woman is not. The employer cannot produce an innocent explanation for the treatment (and the actual reason is clearly not free from the characteristic of sex). The treatment will be unlawful without more.

2.12   Another example from race relations goods and services case-law is: A pub landlord refuses entry to a customer from the traveller community because of a stereotypical assumption that such a customer is likely to cause trouble. The landlord would not have treated someone

---

20 See the discussion at para 1.86 and following for example.
21 The *Equality Act 2010 Code of Practice on Employment Equality*; see Codes of Practice (Services, Public Functions and Associations, Employment, and Equal Pay) Order 2011. The codes came into force on 6 April 2011.

who was not from the traveller community in the same way. That is direct discrimination.[22]

2.13 A school dismisses an employee when it discovers that she has schizophrenia, on the assumption that there is a risk of harm to others. That is direct discrimination.[23]

2.14 Sometimes the concept of direct discrimination is misunderstood. In *Islington London Borough Council v Ladele*[24] the council had a rule that all its registrars should perform civil partnership ceremonies. It applied this to all registrars. Ladele believed that this rule conflicted with her beliefs relating to sexual orientation. L did not want to perform civil partnership ceremonies. The ET held that requiring her to do something which conflicted with her religious beliefs, subjected her to direct discrimination on grounds of religion and belief. However, the EAT and the Court of Appeal disagreed because she had been treated in the same way as all other registrars any of whom would have been disciplined for failing to officiate at a civil partnership ceremony. The complaint was better analysed as a complaint of indirect discrimination: a provision was applied to her as to any other civil registrar – that she should officiate at civil partnership ceremonies – but the effect on her was different to the effect on others. In an indirect discrimination case the question of justification then needs to be examined.[25]

The line between indirect and direct discrimination

2.15 Sometimes the distinction between direct and indirect discrimination is unclear. It was discussed by the Supreme Court in *Patmalniece (FC) v Secretary of State for Work and Pensions*.[26] A Latvian citizen, P, worked in Latvia for 40 years and, retiring, received a Latvian state retirement pension. Her claim for asylum in the United Kingdom made in 2000 was refused in 2004 but she remained in the United Kingdom, where she never worked past May 2004 when Latvia joined the European Union. P claimed UK state pension credit. Section 1(2)(a) of the pension credit legislation required P to be 'in Great

22 See *Commission for Racial Equality v Dutton* [1989] QB 783, [1989] 2 WLR 17.
23 See *Mr A v London Borough of Hounslow* EAT/1155/98 11 July 2001, decided before the 2004 amendments to the DDA 1995.
24 [2009] EWCA Civ 1357, [2010] 1 WLR 955, [2010] ICR 532, [2010] IRLR 211.
25 See *Eweida v United Kingdom* [2013] 37; Ladele's Article 9 complaint was rejected.
26 [2011] UKSC 11 [2011] 1 WLR 783, [2011] 3 All ER 1, [2011] 2 CMLR 45.

Britain'. However, regulation 2(1) of the State Pension Credit Regulations 2002 meant that P was treated as not in Great Britain as she was not habitually resident in the common travel area of the British Isles. She was not because under regulation 2(2), P was not to be treated as habitually resident in the common travel area unless she had a right to reside there. Her claim was refused because she lacked that right. An appeal tribunal found regulation 2(2) constituted direct discrimination on grounds of nationality.[27] The social security commissioner allowed the DWP's appeal because the right to reside test was to be analysed as indirect discrimination which was justified as a proportionate means of achieving the legitimate aim of protecting the public finances of the host member state. The Court of Appeal dismissed the claimant's appeal against that decision.

2.16   The Supreme Court indicated a test for marking the difference between direct and indirect discrimination based on the Opinion of Sharpston A-G in Case C-73/08 *Bressol v Gonvernement de la Communauté Francaise.*[28]

> She said that discrimination could be considered to be direct where the difference in treatment was based on a criterion which was either explicitly that of nationality or was necessarily linked to a characteristic indissociable from nationality: para 53.

2.17   The concept of a criterion which is indissociable from a protected characteristic may perhaps be understood by considering the example from *Bressol* itself. To achieve a benefit a person had to satisfy a set of cumulative criteria: (1) that the principal place of residence of a person to receive the benefit was in Belgium. This did not give rise to direct discrimination because Belgians and non-Belgians alike could establish their principal place of residence in Belgium. (2) The person claiming the benefit had to have the right to remain permanently in Belgium. This did give rise to direct discrimination because Belgians automatically had the right to remain in Belgium, whereas non-Belgians did not and had to satisfy further criteria.

2.18   Sharpston A-G referred to the opinion of Jacobs A-G in *Schnorbus v Lind Hessen*[29]

---

27   Contrary to Article 3 of Council Regulation (EEC) No 1408/71. This provided for equality of treatment in the application of social security schemes to employed persons, including retired persons who remained insured by the social security system of an EU member state because of contributions paid during their working life.

28   [2010] 3 CMLR 559.

29   Case C-79/991 [2000] ECR I-10997 para 33.

It may be said that discrimination on grounds of sex arises where members of one sex are treated more favourably than the other. The discrimination is direct where the difference in treatment is based on a criterion which is either explicitly that of sex or necessarily linked to a characteristic indissociable from sex. It is indirect where some other criterion is applied but ... [the A-G went on to describe the then indirect discrimination test] ... is in fact affected.

2.19　Baroness Hale JSC analysed these opinions and pointed out the complaint in the *Schnorbus* case was that candidates who had completed their national service were given priority over other candidates in admission to the second stage of legal training but only men were eligible for national service.

2.20　Baroness Hale at least preferred the approach taken by Jacobs A-G in *Schnorbus*: eligibility for national service in that case was a legal requirement rather than one, such as pregnancy, based on a physical characteristic which is indissociable from sex. Baroness Hale pointed out that:

this distinction between legal requirements and physical characteristics might come as something of a surprise, for example, to readers of *James v Eastleigh Borough Council* [1990] 2 AC 751, where the discrimination between male and female swimmers was linked to a legal requirement, the statutory retirement age, which was indissociable from sex.

2.21　Baroness Hale was sceptical whether there could be direct discrimination where the provision etc disadvantaged both members of the group and non-members of the group and noted that the opinion to that effect in *Bressol* was not followed by the court. She said that Sharpston A-G had:

held it direct discrimination on grounds of nationality when both Belgians and other nationals might fulfill the requirement of a right to remain permanently in Belgium, but only Belgians could do so automatically. This may be an attractive approach: it is, of course, the exact equivalent of the situation in this case. But it is certainly a development of the principle established in the Schnorbus case.

However, it is submitted that it is not. Sharpston A-G appears to have focused on the feature of 'automatic fulfillment' of the requirements. Looked at in that way there was an exact split. Belgians could automatically qualify to remain permanently, no non-Belgian could. Hence the concept of indissociability should, it is submitted, be viewed in the following way:

- Where there is a difference in treatment based on a criterion that is either explicitly that of the protected characteristic or necessarily

linked to a characteristic inseparable from the protected characteristic there will be direct discrimination.
- Indissociability can be physical but it can also be satisfied by legal
requirements. Thus in *James* it was a legal requirement linked
to gender that created the difference in treatment amounting to
direct discrimination.
- The *Bressol* case focused on provisions criteria or practices which
were broad in scope and did not appear to make the comparison
between those who could automatically satisfy the requirement
and those who could might or might not satisfy the requirement
in practice but none of whom would satisfy it automatically.

2.22   The way in which the concept of indissociability operates can, perhaps, be seen in the reasoning of the Supreme Court in *R (E) v
Governing Body of JFS*,[30] that there was discrimination when the JFS
excluded those who were not Jewish on the basis of genetic descent by
the maternal line from a woman who is Jewish. Matrilineal descent
in this context was inextricably linked to ethnic orgins.

2.23   In *JFS* Baroness Hale noted that direct and indirect discrimination were mutually exclusive: you cannot have both at once. The
prohibition on direct discrimination seeks to establish formal equality. The prohibition on indirect discrimination looks beyond formal
equality towards a more substantive equality of results.[31]

2.24   Claimants must therefore be careful in formulating pleadings
such as the ET claim form relating to direct or indirect discrimination, because they are mutually exclusive. Plead them as alternatives if
there is any doubt whether what happened was direct or indirect.[32]

2.25   *James v Eastleigh Borough Council*[33] also illustrates the difficulties in making the distinction between direct and indirect discrimination. Mr and Mrs James were each 61. Because of the different
statutory retirement ages for men and women, Mrs James was a
pensioner but Mr James was not. The council provided free swimming for people of pensionable age, so Mrs James swam free, but
Mr James did not. The council's policy was on its face gender-neu-
tral: all pensioners could swim free. But it was based on a factor that
was directly discriminatory: the difference in pension age for men
and women. The Court of Appeal held that there was no direct sex

30 [2010] 2 WLR 153.
31 [2010] 2 WLR 153 at para 56.
32 A tribunal can only find that unlawful discrimination has taken place when the
act has been pleaded and the cause of action is properly pleaded.
33 [1990] 2 AC 751, [1990] ICR 554, [1990] IRLR 288.

discrimination: the council was simply providing free swimming to pensioners. The House of Lords disagreed: the difference in statutory pension age was an instance of direct sex discrimination, so any other differential treatment which adopted the same criterion was also direct discrimination.

2.26   It is the necessary link between pension age and sex that distinguishes a case likes *James v Eastleigh* from the classic example of indirect discrimination: a height requirement. A height requirement is likely to disadvantage more women than men, but it will not inevitably disadvantage all women and no men, whereas that was the effect of the policy under consideration in *James v Eastleigh*.[34] Indirect discrimination is considered in detail in chapter 3.

The distinction between harassment and direct discrimination

2.27   Under the EqA 2010 direct discrimination and harassment are regarded as separate concepts.[35] Under the precursor legislation, before the introduction of a concept of harassment and a specific statutory test, the ETs sought to capture harassment on protected grounds by reference to direct discrimination.[36] The cases allowing characteristic-specific discrimination (requiring no comparator) were disapproved by the House of Lords in *Macdonald v Ministry of Defence*.[37]

2.28   Lord Nicholls said[38] that the fact that the harassment is gender specific in form cannot be regarded as of itself establishing conclusively that the reason for the harassment is gender based, although it would point to the conclusion that the treatment was 'on the ground

---

34 See also *R (Elias) v Secretary of State for Defence (Commission for Racial Equality intervening)* [2005] IRLR 788 paras 45–51.

35 See chapter 5 for details of the current test for harassment.

36 Thus in *Porcelli v Strathclyde Regional Council* [1986] ICR 564, P complained about her treatment by her colleagues at work. The ET found that, although the colleagues' behaviour was unacceptable, they would have treated a male colleague they disliked just as unpleasantly. The EAT allowed an appeal by P and the Court of Session upheld the EAT's decision: part of the treatment was only meted out to P because she was a woman and, therefore, she had been treated less favourably than a man would have been treated. In *BT plc v Williams* [1997] IRLR 668, the EAT went further and held that, in complaints of sexual harassment, there was no need to look for a male comparator because the behaviour was gender-specific. See also *Sidhu v Aerospace Composite Technology Ltd* [2000] IRLR 602, CA.

37 [2003] ICR 937.

38 [2003] ICR 937 at para 17.

of her sex'. That did not dispense with the need for the ET to be satisfied that the reason why the victim was being harassed was her sex.
The gender-specific nature of the harassment would only be evidence,
whose weight will depend on the circumstances, that the reason for
the harassment was the sex of the victim. Where treatment does not
satisfy the EqA 2010's definition of harassment this comparative
approach can be considered. Caution needs to be exercised where the
reason the statutory definition is not satisfied is because it would not
be reasonable for the recipient to consider that the unwanted conduct had the proscribed effect. Note that where conduct constitutes
harassment it is not a 'detriment' under the Act.[39] If in doubt over
this issue, set out the case as direct discrimination or, in the alternative,
harassment.

What is 'less favourable' treatment?

2.29   The treatment must be less favourable. To decide whether an employer has treated a worker 'less favourably', a comparison must be made
with how they have treated another person[40] or would have[41] treated another in similar circumstances. The Employment Code states
that:

> If the employer's treatment of the worker puts the worker at a clear
> disadvantage compared with other workers, then it is more likely that
> the treatment will be less favourable: for example, where a job appli-
> cant is refused a job.[42]

2.30   The Code also makes clear that less favourable treatment could also
involve being deprived of a choice or excluded from an opportunity. Being deprived of a choice or excluded from an opportunity is

39 EqA 2010 s212(1) provides that 'detriment' does not include conduct which
amounts to harassment. However, where the Act disapplies a prohibition on
harassment in relation to a specified protected characteristic, the disapplication
does not prevent conduct relating to that characteristic from amounting to a
detriment for the purposes of discrimination within section 13 because of that
characteristic (s212(5)).
40 The Employment Code deals with this at para 3.4, by reference to the treatment
of other workers. However, the comparator does not need to be a worker if, in a
particular case, the status of worker/employee is not material to the treatment.
41 Thus permitting the claimant to ask the tribunal to examine how hypothetically
another person would be treated: this is the so-called 'hypothetical comparator'.
42 Employment Code para 3.4. However, that is tautologous: a better way to read
this is that if the treatment puts the worker at a clear comparative disadvantage
it is obvious that the treatment will be less favourable.

likely to constitute less favourable treatment if co-workers are not so excluded in the same circumstances.

2.31   The examples in the Code illustrate the broader reading of the Code.[43] Concerning less favourable treatment the Code gives the example:[44]

> At a job interview, an applicant mentions she has a same sex partner. Although she is the most qualified candidate, the employer decides not to offer her the job. This decision treats her less favourably than the successful candidate, who is a heterosexual woman. If the less favourable treatment of the unsuccessful applicant is because of her sexual orientation, this would amount to direct discrimination.

2.32   Under the EqA 2010 it is necessary to compare like with like to establish less favourable treatment. It is not possible therefore for the employer to argue that less favourable treatment in respect of one act or omission is off set by more favourable treatment in respect of another act or omission. It does not thereby lose the character of less favourable treatment. Thus the Code points out 'Under the Act, it is not possible for the employer to balance or eliminate less favourable treatment by offsetting it against more favourable treatment – for example, extra pay to make up for loss of job status.'[45]

2.33   An act is capable of being less favourable treatment if it deprives a person of a choice which, on reasonable grounds they value, even if others might take a different view.[46] So where a woman was not allowed to stand at a bar to drink, but could sit at a table and have a drink brought to her, she was subjected to less favourable treatment than a man who was allowed.[47]

---

43   The examples of how the Act is likely to work are included in the Code to 'illustrate the principles and concepts used in the legislation and should be read in that light. The examples use different protected characteristics and work-related situations to demonstrate the breadth and scope of the Act' (para 1.22). Hence when determining the scope of the Code the wording of the examples is important.

44   Employment Code para 3.4.

45   Employment Code para 3.6 and see *Ministry of Defence v Jeremiah* [1980] ICR 13 where the men were paid extra for working in the colourblasting shed, while the women avoided the irksome (but better paid) work.

46   *R v Birmingham City Council ex p Equal Opportunities Commission* [1989] 1 AC 1155 at 1194.

47   *Gill v El Vino Co Ltd* [1983] 1 QB 425.

2.34   Less favourable treatment will include disadvantages even if they do not have physically- or economically-detrimental consequences. Lord Hoffmann put it this way:[48]

> There is a distinction between the question of whether treatment is less favourable and the question of whether it has damaging consequences. Mr Khan, with full knowledge of what Chief Inspector Sidney's assessment contained, wanted it to be sent to Norfolk. His request was refused when a similar request by someone else would have been granted. That seems to me to be less favourable treatment which the tribunal found caused injury to Mr Khan's feelings. The fact that he was actually invited to an assessment showed that the less favourable treatment caused him no economic loss but does not prevent it from having been less favourable.
>
> The point is allied to the question of whether, assuming that there was discrimination [...], Mr Khan was subjected to 'detriment' [...]. Being subjected to detriment [...] is an element in the statutory cause of action additional to being treated 'less favourably' which forms part of the definition of discrimination. A person may be treated less favourably and yet suffer no detriment. But, bearing in mind that the employment tribunal has jurisdiction to award compensation for injury to feelings, the courts have given the term 'detriment' a wide meaning. In *Ministry of Defence v Jeremiah* [1980] ICR 13, 31 Brightman LJ said that 'a detriment exists if a reasonable worker would or might take the view that the [treatment] was in all the circumstances to his detriment'. Mr Khan plainly did take the view [...] that not having his assessment forwarded was to his detriment and I do not think that, in his state of knowledge at the time, he can be said to have been unreasonable.

2.35   The question whether something is less favourable is to be assessed objectively.[49] Clearly words or acts of discouragement can amount to less favourable treatment.[50] Whether an act amounts to less favourable treatment is a question solely for a tribunal of fact.[51] The significance of this is that the powers of the appeal tribunals to interfere

---

48   *Chief Constable of West Yorkshire v Khan* [2001] ICR 1065 Lord Hoffmann at paras 52–53.

49   So, where a hospital required uniforms to be worn by all nurses, but those uniforms were different for men and women, there was no less favourable treatment of a female nurse who objected to the uniform she was required to wear: *Burrett v West Birmingham Health Authority* [1994] IRLR 7. See also the Court of Appeal in *Smith v Safeway* [1996] ICR 868.

50   *Simon v Brimham Associates* [1987] IRLR 307. However, if like a sergeant major 'he's like that to everyone', less favourable treatment will not have been made out, although unfavourable treatment might exist, it is a detriment shared.

51   *Stewart v Cleveland Guest (Engineering) Ltd* [1996] ICR 535 at 542.

with a finding of fact are limited. Hence particular care should be taken to ensure that the evidence is set out clearly in the claimant's witness statement on less favourable treatment. It is important to follow the analytic structure that helps the ET to see how each element of the claim is satisfied.

'... he treats or would treat others ...' – comparators

2.36 Direct discrimination necessarily involves a comparison between actual persons and the claimant or hypothetical persons and the claimant. In some respects this is the most difficult aspect of a direct discrimination claim. It should therefore receive corresponding attention in preparation of the case. The focus should be on showing that the situation of the claimant is analogous to that of a person without the protected characteristic who was treated better.

2.37 The Code states that:[52]

> The worker does not have to experience actual disadvantage (economic or otherwise) for the treatment to be less favourable. It is enough that the worker can reasonably say that they would have preferred not to be treated differently from the way the employer treated – or would have treated – another person.

The example clarifies this passage:

> Example: A female worker's appraisal duties are withdrawn while her male colleagues at the same grade continue to carry out appraisals. Although she was not demoted and did not suffer any financial disadvantage, she feels demeaned in the eyes of those she managed and in the eyes of her colleagues. The removal of her appraisal duties may be treating her less favourably than her male colleagues. If the less favourable treatment is because of her sex, this would amount to direct discrimination.

2.38 The comparison must be between like situations:[53]

> It stands to reason that in making this comparison, with a view to deciding whether a woman who was dismissed received less favourable treatment than a man, it is necessary to compare like with like. The situations being compared must be such that, gender apart, the situation of the man and the woman are in all material respects the same.

---

52 Employment Code para 3.5.
53 Lord Nicholls of Birkenhead in *Shamoon v Chief Constable of the Royal Ulster Constabulary* [2003] ICR 337 at para 4.

2.39   However, in some circumstances, there is no need to undertake a formal, forensic, comparative process:[54]

> ... employment tribunals may sometimes be able to avoid arid and confusing disputes about the identification of the appropriate comparator by concentrating primarily on why the claimant was treated as she was. Was it on the proscribed ground which is the foundation of the application? That will call for an examination of all the facts of the case. Or was it for some other reason? If the latter, the application fails. If the former, there will be usually be no difficulty in deciding whether the treatment, afforded to the claimant on the proscribed ground, was less favourable than was or would have been afforded to others.

> The most convenient and appropriate way to tackle the issues arising on any discrimination application must always depend upon the nature of the issues and all the circumstances of the case. There will be cases where it is convenient to decide the less favourable treatment issue first. But, for the reason set out above, when formulating their decisions employment tribunals may find it helpful to consider whether they should postpone determining the less favourable treatment issue until after they have decided why the treatment was afforded to the claimant.

2.40   A comparison must take into account all of the circumstances that are relevant to the way that the complainant has been treated, including the circumstances that are relevant to the question why the complainant was treated differently.[55]

2.41   There may be an actual comparator, or it may be necessary to speculate on how a fictional 'hypothetical' comparator would be treated in the same circumstances.[56] The absence of an actual comparator is never fatal. This point sometimes needs to be made to ETs and it should be pointed out that:[57]

> In some cases a person identified as an actual comparator turns out to have circumstances that are not materially the same. Such instances can provide evidence about what the treatment of the hypothetical comparator would have been and so may help to construct a hypothetical comparator.

Plainly the more analogous the situation in which the comparator (real or hypothetical) is treated more favourably than the claimant,

---

54 [2003] ICR 337 at paras 11–12.

55 [2003] ICR 337 at paras 44, 49 and 135–6.

56 The Code points out that in practice it is not always possible to identify an actual person whose relevant circumstances are the same or not materially different to those of the claimant (para 3.24).

57 Employment Code para 3.25.

the more likely the ET will accept that the circumstances are not (or would not be) materially different.

2.42 The ET must then consider how someone would have been treated in materially identical circumstances.[58] The Code points out that identification of the hypothetical comparator may also depend on the reason why the employer treated the claimant as they did. In many cases it may be more straightforward for the ET to establish the reason for the claimant's treatment first. This could include considering the employer's treatment of a person whose circumstances are not the same as the claimant's to shed light on the reason why that person was treated in the way they were. If the reason for the treatment is found to be because of a protected characteristic, a comparison with the treatment of hypothetical comparator(s) can then be made.

2.43 So instead of constructing a hypothetical comparator the ET can ask instead why it was that a complainant was treated as they were.[59]

2.44 However, the relevant circumstances should not include any circumstances that are themselves discriminatory. So, for example, in *James v Eastleigh Borough Council* (above), the significance of the state pension age, itself a form of direct sex discrimination, could not be included as a material circumstance. In *Showboat Entertainment Centre Ltd v Owens* (below) an employee who was dismissed for refusing to obey an instruction to exclude black people fell to be compared with an employee who did not refuse the (racist) instruction, rather than with another employee who indifferently followed the instruction to discriminate.

2.45 In making a comparison it is important that the only thing that changes in the comparison is the protected characteristic of the complainant, not the characteristics of the other people involved. So, in *Grieg v Community Industry*,[60] a woman complained about her non-appointment to an all-male painting and decorating team. The employer argued that a man would not have been appointed to an

---

58 *Balamoody v UK Central Council for Nursing, Midwifery and Health Visiting* [2002] IRLR 288.
59 *Igen Ltd v Wong* [2005] IRLR 258.
60 [1979] IRLR 158. See also *Smyth v Croft Inns Ltd* [1996] IRLR 84 (NICA): A Catholic barman was told of a threat to his presence in a Protestant bar. He resigned and complained of constructive dismissal. The correct comparison, the court held, was with a Protestant barman working in the same bar, not a hypothetical Protestant barman working in a hypothetical Catholic bar. That would be to reverse the circumstances not only of the claimant but of the comparators too.

all-female team. But the EAT ruled that the question was whether a man would have been appointed to the all-male team. He would have been and so there was sex discrimination.

Hypothetical comparators

2.46   The Code states that constructing a hypothetical comparator may involve considering elements of the treatment of several people whose circumstances are similar to those of the claimant, but not the same. Looking at these elements together, the ET can conclude that the claimant was less favourably treated than a hypothetical comparator would have been treated.[61] Thus in constructing a hypothetical comparator, and considering how such a person would probably have been treated, the ET can consider evidence of how people who are not actual comparators but who bear features of a hypothetical comparator have been treated in this sense.

2.47   The Code gives the following example:[62]

> An employer dismissed a worker at the end of her probation period because she had lied on one occasion. While accepting she had lied, the worker explained that this was because the employer had undermined her confidence and put her under pressure. In the absence of an actual comparator, the worker compared her treatment to two male comparators; one had behaved dishonestly but had not been dismissed, and the other had passed his probation in spite of his performance being undermined by unfair pressure from the employer. Elements of the treatment of these two comparators could allow a tribunal to construct a hypothetical comparator showing the worker had been treated less favourably because of sex.

2.48   This approach of constructing analogoies is born out of the earlier case-law. In *Rihal v Ealing LBC*,[63] the Court of Appeal provided support for the proposition that wider circumstances may be relevant in the process of constructing a hypothetical comparison. However, the less similarity there is between circumstances, the less significance the comparison between those circumstances may have. In *Chief Constable of West Yorkshire v Vento*[64] V complained of direct sex discrimination in her non-appointment at the end of her probationary period. There were no actual comparators, but the ET, in considering how a hypothetical male comparator would have been treated, considered

---

61 Employment Code para 3.26.
62 Employment Code para 3.26..
63 [2004] IRLR 642.
64 [2001] IRLR 124.

evidence concerning four other police constables, concluding that there were elements in the treatment of the 'comparators' that led to the conclusion that there had been less favourable treatment than a man would have received in the same circumstances. The EAT held that this was not only a legally permissible approach, but that it seemed the only proper way for the ET to proceed on the evidence before it.

Comparators in complaints of disability discrimination: the significance of ability

2.49   The Code makes clear that:[65]

> The comparator for direct disability discrimination is the same as for other types of direct discrimination. However, for disability, the relevant circumstances of the comparator and the disabled person, including their abilities, must not be materially different. An appropriate comparator will be a person who does not have the disabled person's impairment but who has the same abilities or skills as the disabled person (regardless of whether those abilities or skills arise from the disability itself).

2.50   In comparing circumstances for the purposes of a complaint of direct disability discrimination, the circumstances include a person's abilities. This is because one of the main aims of the prohibition of direct discrimination is to prevent stereotypical assumption and prejudice leading to less favourable treatment. It is through the prohibition on indirect discrimination,[66] discrimination arising from disability[67] and the duty to make reasonable adjustments[68] that the particular and additional needs of people with disabilities are given legal protection.

2.51   The Court of Appeal held in *Stockton on Tees Borough Council v Aylott*[69] that in a case of direct disability discrimination, the core question was why the disabled claimant was treated less favourably than a person not having his particular disability. In making the comparison the ET is permitted, but not obliged, to consider a hypothetical comparator. In determining the characteristics of that comparator, the ET may determine the reason why the claimant received

---

65   Employment Code para 3.29.
66   EqA 2010 s19.
67   EqA 2010 s15.
68   EqA 2010 s20.
69   [2010] ICR 1278, decided before the EqA 2010.

the treatment of which complaint was made. The circumstances and attributes of an appropriate comparator should reflect those relevant to the reason for the action complained of, while omitting the complainant's particular disability. Some behavioural difficulties linked to disability, may be omitted in constructing the comparison. The Court of Appeal stressed that it was not an error of law for a ET not to consider a hypothetical comparator. Therefore if the claimant wants to rely on one, the details of the hypothetical comparator and the case for considering one should be set out by the adviser for consideration by the ET.

2.52   Sometimes the choice of comparator can be decisive. In *High Quality Lifestyles Ltd v Watts*,[70] the EAT considered the dismissal of a person with HIV+ status who worked with people with learning difficulties. Employees had been injured, bitten and scratched by service users. The EAT held that W had been dismissed not because of HIV+, but because of the risk of transmission of that condition to others. The circumstances to be compared included abilities but were not limited to them: more circumstances were relevant than just the comparator's abilities. The correct comparator was someone who had an attribute, whether caused by medical condition or otherwise, which carried the same risk of causing illness or injury to others of similar gravity to contracting HIV. If such a comparator would have been dismissed (and there was no evidence to suggest they would not have been), then there was no direct discrimination; in other words, the protected characteristic did not cause the detriment and the claimant could not in any event establish that a comparator would have been treated any better. The case turns on the question of what a relevant circumstance is for the purposes of making the comparison. It is suggested that comparisons must be able to throw light on the basis for the less favourable treatment.

2.53   For more detail on direct discrimination and disability see chapter 4 on disability discrimination.

'... because of a protected characteristic ...'

2.54   This element concerns whether a protected characteristic causes the less favourable treatment identified. The Code states:

> 3.11 'Because of' a protected characteristic has the same meaning as the phrase 'on grounds of' (a protected characteristic) in previous

equality legislation. The new wording does not change the legal meaning of what amounts to direct discrimination. The characteristic needs to be a cause of the less favourable treatment, but does not need to be the only or even the main cause.

3.12 In some instances, the discriminatory basis of the treatment will be obvious from the treatment itself ...

3.13 In other cases, the link between the protected characteristic and the treatment will be less clear and it will be necessary to look at why the employer treated the worker less favourably to determine whether this was because of a protected characteristic.

2.55　The Code goes on to point out that:[71]

Direct discrimination is unlawful, no matter what the employer's motive or intention, and regardless of whether the less favourable treatment of the worker is conscious or unconscious. Employers may have prejudices that they do not even admit to themselves or may act out of good intentions – or simply be unaware that they are treating the worker differently because of a protected characteristic.

2.56　The previous case-law forms the basis for the Code. In *R v Birmingham City Council ex p Equal Opportunities Commission*[72] a consequence of the smaller number of grammar school places for girls than boys in the city was that a girl had to achieve a higher mark in the 11+ exam to obtain a place than a boy. The House of Lords held that the council's motive or intention was irrelevant.[73] It asked: 'but for' the protected characteristic would the boys have received the same treatment as the girls?'

2.57　The protected characteristic need not be the sole, or even principal, reason for the treatment, as long as it has significantly influenced the reason for the treatment.[74]

2.58　The new formulation of the causation test should not therefore cause any difficulties. In particular the solutions reached under the precursor legislation to alleged ambiguity between motive for treatment and the factual criteria applied by the decision maker in

71　Employment Code para 3.14.
72　[1989] 1 AC 1155.
73　[1989] 1 AC 1155 at 1194: 'There is discrimination under the statute if there is less favourable treatment on the ground of sex, in other words if the relevant girl or girls would have received the same treatment as the boys but for their sex.'
74　*Nagarajan v London Regional Transport* [1999] IRLR 572.

reaching its decision should not be resurrected. Motive is irrelevant.[75] Baroness Hale said in *R (E) v JFS*:[76]

> The distinction between the two types of 'why' question is plain enough: one is what caused the treatment in question and one is its motive or purpose. The former is important and the latter is not. But the difference between the two types of 'anterior' inquiry, into what caused the treatment in question, is also plain. It is that which is also explained by Lord Phillips PSC, Lord Kerr and Lord Clarke JJSC. There are obvious cases, where there is no dispute at all about why the complainant received the less favourable treatment. The criterion applied was not in doubt. If it was based on a prohibited ground, that is the end of the matter. There are other cases in which the ostensible criterion is something else usually, in job applications, that elusive quality known as 'merit'. But nevertheless the discriminator may consciously or unconsciously be making his selections on the basis of race or sex. He may not realise that he is doing so, but that is what he is in fact doing. As Lord Nicholls went on to say in the *Nagarajan* case [2000] 1 AC 501, 512:
>
> > 'An employer may genuinely believe that the reason why he rejected an applicant had nothing to do with the applicant's race. After careful and thorough investigation of a claim members of an employment tribunal may decide that the proper inference to be drawn from the evidence is that, whether the employer realised it at the time or not, race was the reason why he acted as he did ...'

2.59   Having analysed the proper approach to the phrase 'on the ground of ...' Lord Bridge in *James v Eastleigh Borough Council* proposed the but for test: would the claimant, but for his sex, have received the same treatment as his wife? Lord Phillips PSC in *JFS* suggested that such a test was not helpful: it is better simply to ask what were the facts that the discriminator considered to be determinative when making the relevant decision.[77] In *Amnesty International v Ahmed*[78] the EAT sought to reconcile the perceived differences between the approaches taken in *James v Eastleigh Borough Council* and *Nagarajan v London Regional Transport*. No real difficulty existed provided due attention was paid to the form of discrimination alleged:[79]

---

75 See *R (E) v Governing Body of JFS* [2010] 2 WLR 153 at para 13, citing *R v Birmingham City Council ex p Equal Opportunities Commission* [1989] AC 1155 at 1194.

76 [2010] 2 WLR 153 at para 64.

77 [2010] 2 WLR 153 at para 16.

78 [2009] ICR 1450, Underhill P at para 31.

79 [2009] ICR 1450 at paras 31–36.

The first question is the ground or grounds for the treatment complained of.

That is no different to asking what the reason was for the act complained of.

In some cases the reason is obvious, for example, where the owner of premises puts up a sign saying 'no black people admitted.

In such a case it is irrelevant what is going on inside the head of the putative discriminator. The ground of his action is inherent in the act itself. No further enquiry is needed.

In other cases, the act complained of is not inherently discriminatory, but is rendered so by an allegedly discriminatory motivation. In such cases, the tribunal of fact must reach a conclusion by drawing inferences. But even in such a case, the subject of the enquiry is the reason for the putative discriminator's action, not his motive.

2.60   Thus, the EAT held, the difference between the *James* and *Eastleigh* analyses simply reflects the different ways in which conduct may be directly discriminatory. These differences are reflected in the analysis given in the Code.

2.61   The courts have emphasised the dangers of using a 'but for' approach as an all-purpose substitute for the statutory language: the fact that a protected characteristic is part of the circumstances in which the treatment complained of occurred, or of the sequence of events leading up to it, does not necessarily mean that it formed part of the reason for the treatment.[80]

2.62   The degree to which the protected characteristic must cause the less favourable treatment can sometimes be called into question. For example in *O'Neill v Governors of St Thomas More Upper School*[81] the claimant, a teacher of religious education and personal relationships, alleged that she had been dismissed because of her pregnancy and brought a claim of sex discrimination. The respondent argued that the reason for dismissal was that the child's father was a local Catholic priest, which was not a pregnancy related reason. The ET agreed. Her position had been made untenable. The EAT held that there was direct sex discrimination. The EAT said that a distinction between pregnancy itself and a pregnancy's surrounding circumstances was

---

80 See *Ahmed* para 37. See eg *Martin v Lacehawk Ltd* UKEAT/525/03, 15 January 2004, M was dismissed when an affair with the managing director came to an end. But for M's sex, there would have been no affair and therefore the reason for dismissal would not have occurred. But this did not mean that sex was the reason for the less favourable treatment.

81 [1996] IRLR 372, [1997] ICR 33.

erroneous, because a pregnancy always had surrounding circumstances. It said:[82]

> The critical question is whether, on an objective consideration of all the surrounding circumstances, the dismissal or other treatment complained of by the applicant is on the ground of pregnancy. It need not be only on that ground. It need not even be mainly on that ground. Thus, the fact that the employer's ground for dismissal is that the pregnant woman will become unavailable for work because of her pregnancy does not make it any the less a dismissal on the ground of pregnancy. She is not available because she is pregnant. Similarly, in the present case, the other factors in the circumstances surrounding the pregnancy relied upon as the 'dominant motive' are all causally related to the fact that the applicant was pregnant – the paternity of the child, the publicity of that fact and the consequent untenability of the applicant's position as a religious education teacher are all pregnancy-based or pregnancy-related grounds. Her pregnancy precipitated and permeated the decision to dismiss her. It is not possible, in our view, to say, on the facts found by the industrial tribunal, that the ground for the applicant's dismissal was anything other than her pregnancy. Indeed, there was no finding of fact by the tribunal that the applicant would have been dismissed, even if she had not become pregnant.

2.63   The EAT identified the following principles relevant to the question of causation:

> (i) The tribunal's approach to the question of causation should be ... simple, pragmatic and commonsensical.

> (ii) The question of causation has to be answered in the context of a decision to attribute liability for the acts complained of. It is not simply a matter of a factual, scientific or historical explanation of a sequence of events, let alone a matter for philosophical speculation. The basic question is: what, out of the whole complex of facts before the tribunal, is the 'effective and predominant cause' or the 'real and efficient cause' of the act complained of? As a matter of common sense not all the factors present in a situation are equally entitled to be treated as a cause of the crucial event for the purpose of attributing legal liability for consequences.

> (iii) The approach to causation is further qualified by the principle that the event or factor alleged to be causative of the matter complained of need not be the only or even the main cause of the result complained of (though it must provide more than just the occasion for the result complained of).

> ... It is enough if it is an effective cause.

---

82 [1996] IRLR 372 at para 55.

2.64   In *Serco Ltd v Redfearn*,[83] R, a bus driver and prospective BNP councillor, complained that his dismissal because of his BNP membership was on racial grounds. The Court of Appeal rejected that argument:

> ... the circumstances in which the decision to dismiss Mr Redfearn was taken included racial considerations, namely the fact that Serco's customers were mainly Asian and that a significant percentage of the workforce was Asian. Racial considerations were relevant to Serco's decision to dismiss Mr Redfearn, but that does not mean that it is right to characterise Serco's dismissal of Mr Redfearn as being 'on racial grounds'. It is a non-sequitur to argue that he was dismissed 'on racial grounds' because the circumstances leading up to his dismissal included a relevant racial consideration, such as the race of fellow employees and customers and the policies of the BNP on racial matters. Mr Redfearn was no more dismissed 'on racial grounds' than an employee who is dismissed for racially abusing his employer, a fellow employee or a valued customer. Any other result would be incompatible with the purpose of the 1976 Act to promote equal treatment of persons irrespective of race by making it unlawful to discriminate against a person on the grounds of race.

2.65   The precursor legislation contained different wording for the different tests of causation.[84] These are all replaced with a common test: 'because of a protected characteristic'. This reflects an intention by Parliament to demonstrate that the scope of the test for the causal link was the same and was as broad as the broadest 'on grounds of' test under the precursor legislation. The Directives on which the Act is based all required a broad interpretation of the concept of causation.

2.66   Thus in *P v S*,[85] the ECJ held that the prohibition on sex discrimination[86] included a prohibition on discrimination on grounds of gender reassignment: a complainant could compare her unfavourable treatment with the treatment of persons of the sex to which she was treated as belonging before reassignment.[87]

---

83 [2006] ICR 1367, [2006] IRLR 623. In *Redfearn v United Kingdom* [2012] ECHR 1878, the ECtHR held that the lack of protection during the qualifying period for unfair dismissal contravened the state's positive obligation to secure his Article 11 right to freedom of association. The Enterprise and Regulatory Reform Bill now includes a clause to disapply the qualifying period if the reason (or, if more than one, the principal reason) for the dismissal is, or relates to, the employee's political opinions or affiliation.

84 See RRA 1976 s1(1)(a); SDA 1975 s1(1)(a), (2)(a) and DDA 1995 s3A(5).

85 [1996] IRLR 347.

86 Directive 76/207.

87 But in *Grant v South West Trains Ltd* [1998] IRLR 206, the ECJ was not prepared to extend the scope of its decision in *P v S* to cover people subjected to discrimination because of their sexual orientation. The House of Lords,

Discrimination by association

2.67   Direct discrimination because of a protected characteristic can happen when the characteristic does not belong to the claimant in the case. The Code explains that 'discrimination by association' can occur in various ways – for example, where the worker has a relationship of parent, son or daughter, partner, carer or friend of someone with a protected characteristic. The association with the other person need not be a permanent one.

2.68   The Code at para 3.19 gives an example to illustrate:

A lone father caring for a disabled son has to take time off work whenever his son is sick or has medical appointments. The employer appears to resent the fact that the worker needs to care for his son and eventually dismisses him. The dismissal may amount to direct disability discrimination against the worker by association with his son.

2.69   This concept is derived from the approach adopted to the interpretation of Directive 2000/78, by the ECJ in *Coleman v Attridge Law*.[88] The prohibition on the ground of disability precludes treatment based on the disability of the child of a non-disabled claimant. It is the use of the characteristic as a relevant factor in decision-making that is prohibited. It does not matter whether the recipient has the characteristic or not.

2.70   It is therefore not necessary that the person themselves possess the characteristic, and it does not matter if the perpetrator is correct in the ascription of any protected characteristic to the claimant. Thus if A treats B less favourably because A believes that B is a US citizen, but in fact B is Canadian, race is still the basis of the less favourable treatment.

2.71   In *English v Thomas Sanderson Blinds Ltd*[89] a heterosexual man complained of sustained sexual innuendo by his colleagues at work that he was homosexual, based on the fact that he had attended boarding school and lived in Brighton. He accepted that his colleagues did not really believe that he was homosexual. The Court of Appeal held

similarly, rejected an invitation to interpret 'on grounds of her sex' in the SDA to cover sexual orientation discrimination, even where that discrimination took a sex-specific (but expressly homophobic) form: *Macdonald v Ministry of Defence* [2003] ICR 937.

88 [2008] ICR 1128. The ECJ held that the prohibition on direct disability discrimination was not limited to persons who were themselves disabled and applied to prohibit less favourable treatment of an employee based on the disability of her child for whom she was the primary carer: see para 56.

89 [2009] IRLR 206.

that, nonetheless, his treatment could amount to harassment on the grounds of sexual orientation.

Instructions to discriminate

2.72 A case that could now be dealt with under the provisions relating to 'instructions to discriminate'[90] but which could equally be dealt with under direct discrimination by association, is *Showboat Entertainment Centre Ltd v Owens*.[91] There the EAT held that the dismissal of a white manager for refusing to obey instructions not to admit black customers amounted to less favourable treatment of the manager on racial grounds. 'On racial grounds' could be read as referring either to the racial characteristics of the complainant or as applying to any case where the race of the complainant or a third party was an effective cause of the detriment that the complainant suffered. The Court of Appeal reached the same conclusion in *Weathersfield Ltd v Sargent*[92] where it held that instructing an employee to carry out a racially discriminatory trading policy was less favourable treatment on grounds of race, irrespective of the race of the complainant.

Pregnancy and maternity discrimination

2.73 Pregnancy and maternity discrimination is not a species of direct discrimination, because it does not require a comparison to be carried out. It is however a surrogate for such discrimination under the EqA 2010 in relation to pregnancy and maternity. By section 18 unfavourable treatment of a woman because of her pregnancy or maternity leave during 'the protected period' is unlawful pregnancy and maternity discrimination. By section 18(7) this cannot be treated as direct sex discrimination (for which a comparator, actual or hypothetical, is required).

2.74 The effect of the exception in section 18(7) is to avoid a particular act amounting both to direct sex discrimination and maternity or pregnancy related discrimination.

2.75 In some cases, employers have to treat workers who are pregnant or have recently given birth more favourably than other workers.

90 EqA 2010 s111.
91 [1984] ICR 65.
92 [1999] ICR 425. Pill LJ observed in passing that if a white person was refused entry to a restaurant because he had a black wife that refusal would be on racial grounds, notwithstanding that it was the race of a third party which led to the less favourable treatment: at p428.

Men cannot make a claim for sex discrimination in relation to any special treatment given to a woman in connection with pregnancy or childbirth, such as maternity leave or additional sick leave.[93]

2.76   It is not possible to define a relevant comparison for a pregnant woman in sex discrimination terms, so the EqA's approach is sensible. It was previously argued that a pregnant woman or new mother should be compared with a man who had been similarly incapacitated by illness, or a non-pregnant woman, or, most recently, with the same woman before she became pregnant. The ECJ rejected this argument. Such arguments might deprive pregnant women and new mothers of protection that they should enjoy in their unique situation. If an employer could rely on the fact that it would have treated a man off sick for several months in as detrimental a way to argue that it was treating a pregnant woman no differently to the man, it would nullify much protection for pregnant women and new mothers.[94]

Combined discrimination: dual characteristics

2.77   The Coalition Government decided not to bring into force section 14 of the EqA 2010, which provides that combined discrimination occurs where a person (A) discriminates against another (B) if, because of a combination of two relevant protected characteristics, A treats B less favourably than A treats or would treat a person who does not share either of those characteristics. Marriage and civil partnership and pregnancy and maternity were excluded as protected characteristics for these purposes. For the purpose of establishing combined discrimination B does not need to show that his treatment by A is direct discrimination because of each of the characteristics taken separately.[95] There is no combined discrimination if, in reliance on another provision in the EqA 2010 or in any other enactment, the alleged discriminator shows that his treatment of B is not direct discrimination because of either or both of the characteristics in the combination: section 14(4). The effect of section 14 is to prohibit the less favourable treatment of a black woman when compared to a white man, or the less favourable treatment of a homosexual man when compared to a heterosexual woman. It is expressly limited to a combination of two characteristics. The effect is that a claim brought by a black

---

93   But note *Eversheds Legal Services Ltd v De Belin* [2011] IRLR 448. See chapter 7 for pregnancy and maternity discrimination.

94   *Webb v EMO Cargo (UK) Ltd* [1994] IRLR 482 and see *Hardman v Mallon t/a Orchard Lodge Nursing Home* [2002] IRLR 516.

95   EqA 2010 s14(3).

woman would not be defeated by findings that a white woman and a black man would have been treated no less favourably than a complainant. Section 23(1) applies as in cases of direct discrimination, providing that a comparison of cases must be such that there is no material difference between the circumstances relating to each case. Accordingly, any actual or hypothetical comparator in a case of combined discrimination will be someone whose circumstances (but for the combination of protected characteristics) are materially the same. Then there must be two differences between the protected characteristics of the complainant and the comparator. There may be other differences (eg a black Christian woman comparing herself to a white Buddhist man), but only two of the protected characteristics can be material or in play in a case.

2.78   This provision avoids a perceived problem with the precursor legislation: a black woman might complain that she had been treated less favourably than a white man. But she would have to bring either or both of two complaints: a complaint of sex discrimination and a complaint of race discrimination. And if each of the component comparisons suggested that she had been treated no less favourably than a white woman or a black man, she would be unsuccessful in each of her claims. It was not impossible for such a claim to succeed, because prohibited discrimination need only be an effective cause of the less favourable treatment, but there could be evidential problems and where, in fact, the reason for less favourable treatment was a combination of characteristics, rather than just one, the division between two causes of action was artificial.

2.79   Section 14(4) means that an act is not combined discrimination where the alleged discriminator is able to show that less favourable treatment in at least one of the two protected characteristics is not unlawful direct discrimination. For example, where one of the combined characteristics is age and the alleged discriminator proves that less favourable treatment is justified, or where the alleged discriminator proves a genuine occupational requirement in respect of one of the protected characteristics, then there is no combined discrimination.

2.80   Given that section 14 is not to be brought into force, it may be suggested that claimants have no redress for multiple discrimination. This is not the case. Claimants confronted with a case in which a problem of multiple discrimination arises should simply set out the case for each protected characteristic in the alternative, making the point that it is not clear on which basis discrimination occurred; that it may have occurred with a combination of protected characteristics all of which may have been operative causes of the less favourable treatment, singly or in combination. Provided the case is properly set out by reference to the combined characteristics, the ET will still be able to make findings reflecting the traditional test of causation. The lack of commencement of section 14 should make no difference to this.[96] The Directives on which the Act is based require that multiple discrimination should be capable of redress, and hence the failure of the Government to bring provisions to do this into effect cannot be relied upon to prevent application of EU law.[97]

Justification of direct age discrimination

2.81   Section 13(2) permits less favourable treatment because of age to be justified. In *Seldon v Clarkson Wright Jakes* the Supreme Court[98] looked at the concept of justification in the context of direct age discrimination. The test for justification can be stated as follows:

- The burden of proof is on the employer to prove justification.
- The employer must be able to point to an aim which is in fact being pursued.
- The employer must be able to prove that the aim is (a) capable of being a legitimate aim because it has a public interest nature to it and (b) actually legitimate in particular circumstances of the employment/business/case.
- The means adopted to achieve the legitimate aim are
  - appropriate, and
  - necessary.

2.82   Each step of the process of justification must be scrutinised carefully. The new test must be seen in the context of the purpose of anti-discrimination legislation: to 'address the mismatch between reality and past assumptions or stereotypes. In the context of age discrimination these assumptions have usually concerned age as a proxy for continuing competence or capability or financial security or intentions about work'. The Supreme Court accepted that these assumptions no longer hold good and such stereotypical assumptions need to be put out of the ETs' mind.[99]

---

96 In *O' Reilly v British Broadcasting Corporation* (ET Decision) the BBC sought to argue that it did.
97 See chapter 19.
98 [2012] UKSC 16.
99 *Seldon v Clarkson Wright Jakes* [2012] UKSC 16 at para 15.

2.83   Since *R (Age UK) v Secretary of State for Business, Innovation and Skills (Equality and Human Rights Commission and another intervening)*[100] the United Kingdom has accepted that only certain kinds of aim are capable of justifying direct age discrimination and that the apparently broad terms of section 13(2) must be restrictively interpreted ('read down') accordingly.[101]

2.84   The effect of the new test is spelled out below. However, it makes justification of direct age discrimination function in a way that is much nearer to direct discrimination in relation to the other protected characteristics.

Capable of being a legitimate aim

2.85   The employer's stated aim must be carefully scrutinised. The aim must be capable of being a legitimate aim under Article 6 of the Directive 2000/78. A distinction is drawn between aims relating to 'employment policy, the labour market or vocational training', which are legitimate, and 'purely individual reasons particular to the employer's situation, such as cost reduction or improving competitiveness', which in general are not.[102] The Supreme Court surveyed the CJEU case-law and then drew up a series of points derived from the CJEU case-law:[103]

> (1) All the references to the European Court discussed above have concerned national laws or provisions in collective agreements authorised by national laws. They have not concerned provisions in individual contracts of employment or partnership, as this case does. However, the *Bartsch*[104] case, mentioned at [2] above, did concern the rules of a particular employers' pension fund; and the *Prigge*[105] case, [49] above, concerned a collective agreement governing the employees of a single employer, Deutsche Lufthansa.

> (2) If it is sought to justify direct age discrimination under article 6(1), the aims of the measure must be social policy objectives, such as those related to employment policy, the labour market or vocational training. These are of a public interest nature, which is 'distinguishable from purely individual reasons particular to the employer's situation,

100 [2009] EWHC 2336 (Admin), [2010] ICR 260.
101 [2012] UKSC 16 at para 30.
102 [2012] UKSC 16 at para 30.
103 [2012] UKSC 16 at para 50.
104 *Birgit Bartsch v Bosch und Siemens Hausgerate (BSH) Altersfursorge GmbH* [2008] ECR I-7245.
105 *Prigge v Deutsche Lufthansa AG* Case C-447 09 [2011] IRLR 1052.

such as cost reduction or improving competitiveness' (*Age Concern*,[106] *Fuchs*[107]).

(3) It would appear from that, as Advocate General Bot pointed out in *Kücükdeveci*[108], that flexibility for employers is not in itself a legitimate aim; but a certain degree of flexibility may be permitted to employers in the pursuit of legitimate social policy objectives.

(4) A number of legitimate aims, some of which overlap, have been recognised in the context of direct age discrimination claims:

(i)   promoting access to employment for younger people (*Palacios de la Villa*,[109] *Hütter*,[110] *Kücükdeveci*);

(ii)   the efficient planning of the departure and recruitment of staff (*Fuchs*);

(iii) sharing out employment opportunities fairly between the generations (*Petersen*,[111] *Rosenbladt*,[112] *Fuchs*);

(iv)   ensuring a mix of generations of staff so as to promote the exchange of experience and new ideas (*Georgiev*,[113] *Fuchs*);

(v)   rewarding experience (*Hütter, Hennigs*[114]);

(vi)   cushioning the blow for long serving employees who may find it hard to find new employment if dismissed (*Ingeniørforeningen i Danmark*[115]);

(vii) facilitating the participation of older workers in the workforce (*Fuchs*, see also *Mangold v Helm*, Case C-144/04 [2006] 1 CMLR 1132);

(viii) avoiding the need to dismiss employees on the ground that they are no longer capable of doing the job which may be humiliating for the employee concerned (*Rosenbladt*); or

(ix)   avoiding disputes about the employee's fitness for work over a certain age (*Fuchs*).

(5) However, the measure in question must be both appropriate to achieve its legitimate aim or aims and necessary in order to do

106 R *(Incorporated Trustees of the National Council on Ageing (Age Concern England)) v Secretary of State for BERR* [2009] ECR 1-1569.

107 *Fuchs v Land Hessen* Case C-159-10 [2011] 3 CMLR 47.

108 *Kücükdeveci v Swedex GmbH* Case C-555-07 [2011] 2 CMLR 27.

109 *Palacios de la Villa v Cortefiel Servicios SA* Case C-411-05 [2007] ECR I-8531.

110 *Hütter v Technische Universitat Graz* Case C-88 08 [2009] ECR I-5325.

111 *Petersen v Berufungsausschuss fur Zahnarzte fue den Bezirk Westfalen-Lippe* Case C-341 08 [2010] 2 CMLR 31.

112 *Rosenbladt v Oellerking Gmbh* Case C-45 09 [2011] 1 CMLR 32.

113 *Georgiev v Tehnicheski Universitet* Cases C-250 09 & C-268 09 [2011] 2 CMLR 7.

114 *Sabine Hennigs v Eisenbahn-Bundesamt and Land Berlin v Alexander Mai* Case C-297 10 and C-298 10 [2011] ECR.

115 *Ingeniørforeningen i Danmark v Region Syddanmark* Case C-499/08 [2011] 1 CMLR 1140.

so. Measures based on age may not be appropriate to the aims of rewarding experience or protecting long service (*Hütter, Kücükdeveci, Ingeniørforeningen i Danmark*).

(6) The gravity of the effect upon the employees discriminated against has to be weighed against the importance of the legitimate aims in assessing the necessity of the particular measure chosen (*Fuchs*).

(7) The scope of the tests for justifying indirect discrimination under article 2(2)(b) and for justifying any age discrimination under article 6(1) is not identical. It is for the member states, rather than the individual employer, to establish the legitimacy of the aim pursued (*Age Concern*).

2.86   The Supreme Court stated: 'It now seems clear that the approach to justifying direct age discrimination cannot be identical to the approach to justifying indirect discrimination and that ... section 13(2) of the Equality Act 2010 ... must be read accordingly'.[116] In *Ingeniørforeningen i Danmark*, Kokott A-G pointed out that the objectives which might be relied upon to justify direct discrimination, whether under Articles 6(1), 4(1) or 2(5), were 'fewer than those capable of justifying an indirect difference in treatment, even though the proportionality test requirements are essentially the same'.[117]

2.87   The choice of social policy aims is for the member states to make and in *Age UK* Blake J identified the state's aim, in relation to regulation 3 as being to preserve the confidence and integrity of the labour market. The Supreme Court commented that:

- This is not an easy concept to understand, and there is a risk that it might be taken as allowing employers to continue to do whatever suits them best.
- It is difficult to see how granting flexibility to employers can be a legitimate aim in itself, as opposed to a means of achieving other legitimate aims.[118]
- The Secretary of State had accepted that there is a distinction between aims such as cost reduction and improving competitiveness, which would not be legitimate, and aims relating to employment policy, the labour market and vocational training, which would.

---

116 *Seldon v Clarkson Wright Jakes* [2012] UKSC 16 at para 51.

117 *Ingeniørforeningen i Danmark v Region Syddanmark* Case C-499/08 [2011] 1 CMLR 1140 AG31.

118 See A-G Bot in *Kücükdeveci v Swedex GmbH* Case C-555-07 [2011] 2 CMLR 27.

2.88   The starting point for considering whether an aim which the employer has is capable of being a legitimate aim is that:[119]

> ... the United Kingdom has chosen to give employers and partnerships the flexibility to choose which objectives to pursue, provided always that (i) these objectives can count as legitimate objectives of a public interest nature within the meaning of the Directive and (ii) are consistent with the social policy aims of the state and (iii) the means used are proportionate, that is both appropriate to the aim and (reasonably) necessary to achieve it.

2.89   The Supreme Court went on to set out the two different kinds of legitimate objective which have been identified by the Luxembourg court:

- inter-generational fairness: It can mean a variety of things, depending upon the particular circumstances of the employment concerned: for example, it can mean facilitating access to employment by young people; it can mean enabling older people to remain in the workforce; it can mean sharing limited opportunities to work in a particular profession fairly between the generations; it can mean promoting diversity and the interchange of ideas between younger and older workers.[120]
- dignity: This has been variously put as avoiding the need to dismiss older workers on the grounds of incapacity or underperformance, thus preserving their dignity and avoiding humiliation, and as avoiding the need for costly and divisive disputes about capacity or underperformance.[121]

Actually legitimate

2.90   It is not enough that the employer shows that the aim is capable of being legitimate, it must be legitimate in the particular circumstances. The Supreme Court noted that there is a tension between the demands of individual dignity and fact that the Luxembourg court has held that the avoidance of unseemly debates about capacity can be a legitimate aim, categorised as 'dignity' above. In the latter sense it is used as a short hand for avoiding the need to dismiss older workers on the grounds of incapacity or underperformance, thus preserving their dignity and avoiding humiliation, avoiding the need for costly and divisive disputes about capacity or underperformance.

119 [2012] UKSC 16 at para 55.
120 [2012] UKSC 16 at para 56.
121 [2012] UKSC 16 at para 57.

However, the Supreme Court recognised that the dignity of each individual (the right to be treated equally irrespective of either irrational prejudice or stereotypical assumptions that may be true of some but not of others) pulls powerfully in the other direction. The demands of individual dignity and the CJEU recognition of the potentially fair aim of 'dignity', needed to be reconciled.

2.91   The Supreme Court did this by saying that 'the focus must therefore turn to whether it is a legitimate aim in the particular circumstances of the case'. Therefore the fact that a particular aim is capable of being a legitimate aim under the Directive (and therefore the domestic legislation) is only the beginning of the story. It is still necessary to inquire whether it is in fact the aim being pursued. It must be the actual objective, but this may be an ex post facto rationalisation.[122] Further:[123]

> 61. Once an aim has been identified, it has still to be asked whether it is legitimate in the particular circumstances of the employment concerned. For example, improving the recruitment of young people, in order to achieve a balanced and diverse workforce, is in principle a legitimate aim. But if there is in fact no problem in recruiting the young and the problem is in retaining the older and more experienced workers then it may not be a legitimate aim for the business concerned. Avoiding the need for performance management may be a legitimate aim, but if in fact the business already has sophisticated performance management measures in place, it may not be legitimate to avoid them for only one section of the workforce.

2.92   This principle significantly narrows the scope of justification of direct age discrimination. In practical terms it means that claimants should question not whether the business has (or can state) an aim, but whether given its circumstances the aim is a legitimate one. This means that at an early stage, questions should be asked about the business's circumstances in relation to any aim that had been asserted, and documentary evidence should be sought to demonstrate whether or not the circumstances of the business were such that their aim (eg of avoiding performance management for older workers) was necessary. If a business has performance management as part of the ordinary management of the workforce, there appears to be no reason why it should not apply to older as to younger workers. The Supreme Court has added a step into the ordinary justification process.

---

122 [2012] UKSC 16 at para 60.
123 [2012] UKSC 16 at para 61.

'... the means chosen have to be both appropriate and necessary'

2.93   In *Seldon* the Supreme Court refers to the other age discrimination case decided by it on the same day for the approach to proportionality. The Supreme Court in *Homer*[124] draws the distinction between calling a means appropriate and necessary to an aim and calling it proportionate to achieve that aim. They are not the same. The aspect of appropriateness must be attended to as must whether the aim is reasonably necessary to achieve that aim in the sense of being the least discriminatory means of achieving that aim. It is one thing to say that the aim is to achieve a balanced and diverse workforce. It is another thing to say that a mandatory retirement age of 65 is both appropriate and necessary to achieving this end. It is one thing to say that the aim is to avoid the need for performance management procedures. It is another to say that a mandatory retirement age of 65 is appropriate and necessary to achieving this end.

2.94   The means have to be carefully scrutinised in the context of the particular business concerned in order to see whether they do meet the objective and there are not other, less discriminatory, measures which would do so. The Supreme Court therefore appears to be saying that there must be some evidence produced by the employer that (a) the means actually meet the objective, (b) there are not other less discriminatory measures that would meet the objective.

2.95   The means therefore must not simply be capable of achieving the aim. Thus if the aim is encouraging loyalty of a particular age group in the employment, there must be some evidence that the means adopted (eg higher pay for that age group) actually renders the age group more loyal.

2.96   The Supreme Court considered whether the measure has to be justified, not only in general but also in its application to the particular individual. The section applies to a particular act of direct discrimination, where 'on grounds of B's age, A treats B less favourably than he treats or would treat other persons' and 'A cannot show the treatment ... to be a proportionate means of achieving a legitimate aim.' The argument on behalf of Mr Seldon, therefore, was that the partnership, A, had to show that its particular less favourable treatment of him, B, was justified. This could be another distinction between direct and indirect discrimination, because for indirect discrimination the regulation only requires A to show that the

---

124 *Homer v Chief Constable of West Yorkshire Constabulary* [2012] IRLR 601.

'provision, criterion or practice' is a proportionate means of achieving a legitimate aim. Hence, it was argued, the partnership should have to show, not only that the mandatory retirement rule was a proportionate means of achieving a legitimate aim, but also that applying it to Mr Seldon could be justified at the time.

2.97   The Supreme Court accepted that where it is justified to have a general rule, then the existence of that rule will usually justify the treatment that results from it. This represents a different position to that in the Court of Appeal or EAT (to which the Supreme Court made reference immediately prior to making this statement) where it was said that it would be extremely rare for the individual case of the application of the general rule not to be justified. The reasons why this is so are interesting.

> In the particular context of inter-generational fairness, it must be relevant that at an earlier stage in his life, a partner or employee may well have benefited from a rule which obliged his seniors to retire at a particular age. Nor can it be entirely irrelevant that the rule in question was re-negotiated comparatively recently between the partners. It is true that they did not then appreciate that the forthcoming Age Regulations would apply to them. But it is some indication that at the time they thought that it was fair to have such a rule. Luxembourg has drawn a distinction between laws and regulations which are unilaterally imposed and collective agreements which are the product of bargaining between the social partners on a presumably more equal basis (*Rosenbladt, Hennigs*).

2.98   The Supreme Court stated:[125]

> There is therefore a distinction between justifying the application of the rule to a particular individual, which in many cases would negate the purpose of having a rule, and justifying the rule in the particular circumstances of the business. All businesses will now have to give careful consideration to what, if any, mandatory retirement rules can be justified.

2.99   It is therefore the particular circumstances of the business which must be examined. This interpretation applies to all acts of direct age discrimination that it is sought to justify. The application of the general rule in the particular circumstances of the business (presumably at the time the treatment is meted out) must be considered. Nevertheless it is the rule in the circumstances of the business that must be considered.

---

125 *Seldon v Clarkson Wright & Jakes* [2012] UKSC 16, [2012] IRLR 590 at paras 65–66.

2.100 **Practical points**

- The claimant's experience of direct discrimination often takes the form of experiencing unfavourable, or less favourable, treatment and being unable to explain why it has happened.
- Much of the preparation of a claim will be devoted to looking at the reasons for the treatment (unless explicitly referring to a protected characteristic) and establishing the comparators or the comparable circumstances.
- Why is the respondent's explanation for the treatment not an 'innocent' one, in the sense of having nothing to do with the protected characteristic(s)?
- In a case of 'multiple discrimination', the same analytic process set out in this chapter should be addressed for each characteristic involved, to demonstrate that each was either a sole cause or an 'operative' cause of the treatment.
- In presenting a direct discrimination claim the effects of:
  - the rules on inference and the burden of proof; and
  - equivocal or evasive answers to requests for information (and or questionnaires) should be considered.
- Direct age discrimination can be justified only by an aim which is a social policy or employment policy aim and which is legitimate in the circumstances of the business; the means adopted to pursue that aim must be appropriate and necessary.
- At an early stage of a case in which it is asserted that there is a justification for direct age discrimination, details of that justification ought to be obtained. The claimant should point out the stringency of the test set down in the Seldon case.

Indirect discrimination

continued

Key points

- Indirect discrimination arises where an employer applies an ostensibly neutral provision, criterion or practice that places those with particular protected characteristics at a particular disadvantage (without justification).
- Intention is irrelevant to liability for indirect discrimination.
- A provision, criterion or practice does not have to be an absolute bar to employment or a benefit. The definition is, for example, wide enough to cover a 'desirable' criterion in a job advertisement.
- Some criteria will obviously be liable to place people with a protected characteristic at a particular disadvantage. Where that is not the case, claimants can rely on a wide variety of evidence, including local and national statistics, academic research and witness evidence to prove particular disadvantage. Statistics are not in this sense necessary. However, they will generally be useful.
- The claimant must also be able to show that the PCP puts, or would put, him/her at a particular disadvantage if applied to him/her.
- The burden is on the respondent to show that the disadvantaging PCP is justified.
- The respondent must show the PCP is an appropriate and necessary means of achieving a legitimate aim.
  - Claimants should make sure that the legitimate aim put forward by the employer truly is the legitimate aim being pursued and not a combination of means and aims.
  - If the aim is legitimate, the ET must determine whether the reasonable needs of the employer are outweighed by the discriminatory impact of the PCP on the claimant. Find evidence to show that there are other, less discriminatory, ways of achieving the legitimate aim, or that the impact of the means required to achieve the aim is so discriminatory that it cannot be justified by the employer. Cost alone will not be sufficient to justify a disadvantaging PCP.
- The key case on justification in indirect discrimination is *Homer v West Yorkshire Chief Constable*, which considers the effect of the new test.

Introduction

3.1   The EqA 2010 deals with indirect discrimination in section 19. The concept deals with barriers that people who have particular protected characteristics encounter as a result of the way in which work and the workplace is structured.

3.2   Indirect discrimination arises when an employer applies a particular provision, criterion or practice (generally referred to as a 'PCP') which on the face of it has nothing to do with a particular protected characteristic but in fact has the effect of placing people with that characteristic at a particular disadvantage when compared with people who do not have the characteristic. If a person with the particular protected characteristic is, or would be, disadvantaged by the application of the PCP, and the employer is unable objectively to justify its application, the person can claim indirect discrimination.

Statutory provisions

3.3   The precursor legislation[1] had a different test for indirect discrimination. This should be borne in mind when looking at earlier case-law on indirect discrimination. In their place section 19 of the EqA 2010 provides a single and largely new test which for the first time, extends to cover the characteristic of disability. Section 19 provides as follows:

(1) A person (A) discriminates against another (B) if A applies to B a provision, criterion or practice which is discriminatory in relation to a relevant protected characteristic of B's.

(2) For the purpose of subsection (1), a provision, criterion or practice is discriminatory in relation to a relevant protected characteristic of B's if –

(a) A applies, or would apply, it to persons with whom B does not share the characteristic;

(b) it puts, or would put, persons with whom B shares the characteristic at a particular disadvantage when compared with persons with whom B does not share it;

(c) it puts, or would put, B at that disadvantage, and

(d) A cannot show it to be a proportionate means of achieving a legitimate aim.

---

1   Sex Discrimination Act (SDA) 1975, Race Relations Act (RRA) 1976, Employment Equality (Sexual Orientation) Regulations (SOR) 2003, Employment Equality (Religion and Belief) Regulations (RBR) 2003 and Employment Equality (Age) Regulations 2006 (Age Regulations 2006).

(3) The relevant protected characteristics are –
>   age;
>   disability;
>   gender reassignment;
>   marriage and civil partnership;
>   race;
>   religion or belief;
>   sex;
>   sexual orientation.

The burden of proof

3.4   The burden of proof under the Act[2] is divided. The claimant (B) must show:

- B has a relevant protected characteristic (there is therefore no scope for associative discrimination);
- the respondent applies a PCP to B (and to others with whom B does not share the protected characteristic);
- the PCP puts or would put persons sharing B's protective characteristic at a particular disadvantage when compared with those with whom B does not share that characteristic (and who are in comparable circumstances);
- B was put at the same particular disadvantage as is or would be experienced by those sharing B's protected characteristic.

The respondent must justify the PCP if and only if the matters listed above are all established on a balance of probabilities by B. The respondent must prove:

- The respondent was/is pursuing an aim by using the PCP.
- The identified aim is legitimate.
- The PCP is an appropriate means of pursing the identified aim.
- The PCP is a necessary means of achieving the identified aim.

3.5   In *Nelson v Carillion Services Ltd,*[3] the Court of Appeal held that the initial burden is on the claimant (B) to prove facts from which the ET could conclude, in the absence of an adequate explanation, that B has been unlawfully discriminated against. In practice, this means that B

---

2   EqA 2010 s135. The concept is in effect the same as the equivalent provisions at SDA 1975 s63A, RRA 1976 s54A, Disability Discrimination Act (DDA) 1995 s17A(1C) and in the various Regulations, although the wording is a little different.

3   [2003] EWCA Civ 344, [2003] 1 ICR 1256.

must establish facts from which the ET could conclude that the relevant PCP places B and persons with B's protected characteristic at a particular disadvantage before the burden moves to the employer.

The role of intention

3.6   Intention is irrelevant to liability for indirect discrimination save that if a PCP is intentionally applied just to those with a particular protected characteristic, the treatment is not indirect but direct discrimination.

3.7   Neither UK nor EU law requires that any intention to discriminate be proved before indirect discrimination can be established. Such a requirement would significantly undermine the protection afforded by the indirect discrimination provisions, the whole point of which is to make it unlawful to apply an apparently neutral provision, criterion or practice that places one sector of the population at a particular disadvantage. If the purpose of applying an apparently neutral rule was to discourage persons possessing a particular protected characteristic from applying for jobs (eg the imposition of a 'no headscarves' rule intended to discourage Muslim applicants), that is likely to amount to direct discrimination, and the case should be set out in the ET forms in both ways.

3.8   Intention has some, debateable, relevance for remedies.[4]

Provision, criterion or practice

3.9   Determining whether the respondent has applied a PCP will be relatively easy in most cases.

3.10   There is no definition of any of the three terms in the Act. In most cases it will be obvious whether a PCP has been applied, and there will be no need to separate out the different concepts. However, the following suggestions as to the meaning of each word may assist.

- In *British Airways v Starmer*,[5] the EAT held that the word 'provision' was similar in meaning to a 'requirement' or 'condition'. The EAT did not consider any of these words to carry the suggestion that an absolute bar (eg on part-time working) would be required; something less than that would be sufficient. 'Provision'

---

4   See paras 18.15–18.17.
5   [2005] IRLR 862.

appears most likely to apply to a written term of a contract or a collective agreement, or an internal rule, perhaps in a handbook. It is possible that it could apply to a 'one off' decision, as appeared to be the case in *Starmer*.

- A 'criterion' is most obviously defined as a standard or principle for making a decision or judgment. Examples might include criteria for selection for a particular post, or for promotion, or for redundancy – whether written or unwritten, formal or informal. A criterion can be essential or desirable. In *Perera v Civil Service Commission (No 2)*[6] the claimant, who was rejected for a particular job because of various factors including his experience in the United Kingdom, his command of English, his nationality and his age, failed in his claim under the old indirect discrimination provisions as none of these matters were 'requirements' or 'conditions' for the post. As, however, they were all factors that the interviewing committee took into account in considering whether to select him, they would now fall within the expanded definition as 'criteria'.

- A 'practice' implies something less formal than a 'provision'. The most obvious example might be an unwritten rule or way of doing things that has developed over a period of time, but there is no reason why a practice should be long-standing in order to qualify.

3.11 The courts have shown a willingness to adopt a wide interpretation of the statutory language.

3.12 In *Starmer*,[7] the claimant, who was a female co-pilot, had asked to reduce her hours to 50 per cent of full-time hours in order to accommodate her childcare needs. British Airways refused the request, but were willing to allow her to work 75 per cent of full-time hours. The ET rejected BA's argument that this could not be a PCP because it was a discretionary, one-off management decision, and other employees had in the past been permitted to work 50 per cent of full hours. Indirect discrimination does not require the universal, general or even wide application of a PCP. It is only necessary that the provision is one that would be applied equally to a man.

3.13 The claimants in *GMB v Allen*[8] contended that they had been discriminated against by their union because it had placed a higher

---

6 [1983] IRLR 166.
7 [2005] IRLR 862 at para 18.
8 [2007] IRLR 752; see also CA judgment, overturning in part the EAT judgment, [2008] EWCA Civ 810, [2008] ICR 1407.

priority on securing pay protection for workers 'losing out' under the local authority Green Book job evaluation study than on securing back pay for female employees who had historically been underpaid as a result of past sex discrimination. The PCP on which they relied in their indirect discrimination claim was that 'in order to get full representational support from the union you must be a non back pay person'. The union argued that this was not a PCP, on the basis that it was not a 'barrier' or 'gateway' making it harder for members of one gender to qualify for a benefit than for the other.

3.14   The EAT held[9] that the union's policy did amount to a PCP. The union was not using its negotiating pressure equally for the benefit of all. It was deliberately adopting a practice or policy that focused on a characteristic that itself divided the membership into predominantly male and female groups. Although there was no 'absolute bar' to support for female claims, the EAT held that this was in essence the 'classic form' of indirect discrimination.[10] The EAT's comments imply, however, that the meaning of PCP extends beyond the classic 'requirement or condition' analysis.

3.15   The wording of the test in the Act makes it clear that something may amount to a PCP even if it has no immediate effect and will only disadvantage the complainant if certain circumstances arise in the future, as EqA 2010 s19(2)(c) covers a PCP which 'puts or would put' a person at a particular disadvantage. The Act clarifies what was in this respect already the position under the precursor legislation: see *Meade-Hill v British Council*.[11]

Multiple PCPs?

3.16   A claimant may rely on the combined effect of more than one PCP in claiming indirect discrimination. The PCP may disadvantage the claimant due to different protected characteristics. Likewise the disadvantage may arise from the action of more than one PCP.

3.17   In *MoD v DeBique*,[12] the claimant contended that she had been placed at a particular disadvantage by two PCPs (that she must be available for duty 24/7, and that she could not have a member of her extended family (a half-sister) to stay with her in the service families accommodation because she was a foreign national only entitled

9 This aspect of the EAT's judgment was not challenged in the Court of Appeal.
10 At paras 58–62.
11 [1995] ICR 847.
12 [2010] IRLR 471.

to stay in the United Kingdom for a short period). She argued that the former was indirectly discriminatory under the SDA 1975 and the latter under the RRA 1976. The EAT dismissed the Ministry of Defence's appeal, brought in part on the ground that the ET should not have conflated the two PCPs. It held that the particular disadvantage suffered by the claimant was a consequence of both of the PCPs (and thus both of her sex and of her race), and the two therefore fell to be considered together.[13] The decision in favour of the claimant appears to have been based on the conclusion that neither of the PCPs was justifiable in the light of the other.

The dividing line between direct and indirect discrimination

'Objective' test

3.18   Some PCPs are so closely linked to one of the protected characteristics that their application will in reality amount to direct rather than indirect discrimination. Here the PCP will not be neutral because it will be indissociable (or inseparable) from the protected characteristic in question.

3.19   Thus in the case of *James v Eastleigh Borough Council*[14] the claimant challenged the council's practice of allowing free entry to a swimming pool for persons who had reached the state pension age – which at that time was 60 for women, and 65 for men – on the basis that it discriminated directly on the grounds of sex. The practice was found not to be a neutral requirement or condition. Whilst the council's motive for applying the policy may well have been to ensure that benefits were given to those whose resources were more likely to have been reduced by retirement, that was not the relevant question. The objective factual criterion for the discrimination was the sex of the person seeking admission to the centre – as only women could fulfil the criterion of attaining state pensionable age at 60.

3.20   This approach was endorsed by a nine-judge panel of the Supreme Court in *R (E) v Governing Body of JFS and the Admissions Appeal Panel of JFS;*[15] see in particular the comments of Lord Kerr at paras 116 and 117.

---

13 [2010] IRLR 471 at paras 162–170.
14 [1990] 2 AC 751.
15 [2009] UKSC 15, [2010] 2 AC 728.

3.21   The Supreme Court has also considered the concept of 'indissociable' characteristics.[16] Thus a characteristic might be so linked to
a protected characteristic as to be legally or physically inseparable
from the protected characteristic. Discrimination on the basis of the
indissociable characteristic will be direct discrimination on the basis
of the protected characteristic.[17] Particular problems in differentiating between direct and indirect discrimination arise in the context of
discrimination on the ground of religion or belief.[18] On the current
state of the law, it is not clear whether some acts (such as refusing to
allow employees to wear the niqab, or dismissing employees because
they refuse to do a particular aspect of their job on religious grounds)
will amount to direct or indirect discrimination. It is always sensible
to set out in the ET forms both types of discrimination.

The comparative exercise: particular disadvantage

3.22   At the heart of EqA 2010 s19 is a comparative exercise. B must show
that the PCP on which B relies 'puts or would put persons with
whom B shares the [protected characteristic] at a particular disadvantage when compared with persons with whom B does not share it'.[19]

What is 'a particular disadvantage'?

3.23   The Employment Code suggests that 'disadvantage' can include
denial of an opportunity or choice, deterrence, rejection or exclusion.
The concept is analogous to that of 'detriment' and a disadvantage
will be something a reasonable person would complain about, so that
an unjustified sense of grievance would not qualify as a disadvantage.
A disadvantage does not have to quantifiable, or to involve actual loss;
it is sufficient that the worker can reasonably say that they would
prefer to have been treated differently.[20]

3.24   The Employment Code makes clear[21] that sometimes, a PCP is
intrinsically liable to disadvantage a group with a particular protected
characteristic. It gives the example of an employer inviting seasonal
workers employed during the previous summer to claim a bonus

16   *Patmalniece v Secretary of State for Work and Pensions* [2011] UKSC 11.
17   See paras 2.15–2.26.
18   See para 1.90–1.98.
19   Section 19(2)(b).
20   Employment Code of Practice para 4.9.
21   At para 4.10.

within a 30-day time-limit. By writing to these workers at their last-known address, the employer is liable to disadvantage migrant workers. This is because these workers normally return to their home country during the winter months, and so they are unlikely to apply for the bonus within the specified period.

3.25　　The PCP of being at the last-known address is intrinsically liable to disadvantage the migrant workers compared with those resident in the United Kingdom. Section 19 captures by these means the normal behaviour of a group (migrant seasonal workers tend to return to their country of origin) which in conjunction with PCP gives rise to disadvantage.

3.26　　There have been few decisions on the point, mainly in the context of religion and belief, but it is possible to draw some principles from those judgments.

3.27　　A claimant and/or a group may be placed at a particular disadvantage by a PCP forbidding them from holding or actioning a religious belief even if that belief is not a compulsory requirement of their religion.

3.28　　Thus in *R (Watkins-Singh) v Governing Body of Aberdare Girls' High School*,[22] the claimant argued that her school's jewellery policy, which prevented her from wearing the Sikh kara, placed her at a particular disadvantage. She did not argue that wearing the kara was a condition or requirement of her religion, but said it was 'central to her ethnic identity and religious observance as a Sikh'. Silber J found that there would be a 'particular disadvantage' where a pupil genuinely believed on reasonable grounds that wearing an item was a matter of exceptional importance to their racial identity or their religious belief, and where this could also be shown objectively.[23]

3.29　　In the important case of *Eweida v British Airways plc*, successive courts have given close consideration to the concept of particular disadvantage in the context of religion and belief.

a) The EAT[24] and Court of Appeal[25] dismissed Ms Eweida's claim of indirect discrimination, which was based on BA's refusal, under its uniform policy, to allow her to wear a plain silver cross over her uniform. Both courts suggested that what is now section 19(2)(b) requires a claimant to show that some identifiable section of a workforce, quite possibly a small one, suffers a particular

22　[2008] EWHC 1865 (Admin).
23　See para 56 of the judgment.
24　[2009] ICR 303.
25　[2010] EWCA Civ 80; [2010] ICR 890.

disadvantage in connection with possession of a protected characteristic, as does the claimant. Ms Eweida produced no evidence
to show that her own position relating to visible display of a cross
was shared by other Christians, and as a result, her claim failed.
There are obvious problems with the test apparently suggested
by the Court of Appeal, not least that it would not permit a person who is the first in a workplace to adopt a new belief to claim
indirect discrimination. However on inspection of the judgments
beyond their summary, a different picture emerges.

b)   In the Court of Appeal Sedley LJ stated:

> 17. ... [The purpose of the conditional ('would put persons ... at a
> particular disadvantage')], in my judgment, is the simple one ... to
> include in the disadvantaged group not only employees to whom the
> condition has actually been applied but those to whom it potentially
> applies. Thus, if you take facts like those in the seminal case of *Griggs
> v Duke Power Co* 401 US 424 , the group of manual workers adversely
> affected by the unnecessary academic requirement will have included
> not only those to whom it had been applied but those to whom it stood
> to be applied.

Thus the group disadvantage will only be proven if, at the very
least, there is some evidence that people from the relevant group
would be placed at a disadvantage. For this there must be evidence of people to whom the PCP potentially applies. However
the Court of Appeal did not decide the vital issue of how broadly
the idea of a 'group' which is disadvantaged should be interpreted. On this point, Sedley LJ said:

> 18. On the narrowest view, its practical application in a case like this
> would require evidence that other uniformed BA staff would, like Ms
> Eweida, have wished to wear a cross in a visible place but were deterred
> by the code from doing so: the fact that, unlike Ms Eweida, they had
> not chosen to provoke a confrontation would not count against them.
> On the widest view it would operate wherever evidence showed that
> there were in society others who shared the material religion or belief
> and so would suffer a disadvantage were they to be BA employees. On
> an intermediate view, it would operate by assuming, even if it is not
> the case, that the workforce includes such others and asking whether
> they too, or some of them, would be adversely affected by the relevant
> requirement. All three have difficulties. The narrow view excludes the
> solitary individual from the protection of the law against indirect dis-
> crimination – a result which the Disability Discrimination Act 1995
> explicitly avoids but which the 2003 Regulations do not. The wide view
> places an impossible burden on employers to anticipate and provide
> for what may be parochial or even factitious beliefs in society at large.

The intermediate view, despite its attractions, in practice risks becoming merged with the wide view by inviting proof that in the world outside the workforce are co-religionists or fellow believers, however few, who are to be assumed to have entered the same employment as the claimant and have become subject to the requirement to which the claimant objects.

19. We do not have to resolve this issue because Ms Eweida's evidence failed all three tests. It is also possible that the meaning and effect of the formula differ depending on the form of discrimination alleged: it may be relatively simple, and within the legislative purpose, to aggregate a single female employee with a hypothetical group of other female staff in order to gauge adverse impact, but forensically difficult, even impossible, to do the same for a solitary believer whose fellow-believers elsewhere in society may accord different degrees of importance to the same manifestation of faith.

c) Of course it is desirable that differences in the treatment of different protected characteristics under the same equality law should be avoided. Since the Court of Appeal's decision, the ECtHR has suggested that a broader approach to the 'particular disadvantage' question may be necessary in future. The ECtHR held[26] that Ms Eweida needed only to show that her views attained a certain level of cogency, seriousness, cohesion and importance for Article 9 to be engaged. Her desire visibly to wear a cross at work was a manifestation of her religious belief in the form of worship, practice and observance, and therefore attracted the protection of Article 9 ECHR.

d) It may be possible to reconcile the position of the Court of Appeal with that of the ECtHR if Sedley LJ's 'broad' or 'intermediate' view of group disadvantage is adopted. Where there is a well defined belief group, it will always be possible to ascertain whether anyone within that belief group would be disadvantaged by the PCP. The conceptual difficulty of Ms Eweida's case was heightened by the fact that she sought to argue disadvantage to all Christians, when the actual disadvantaged group was a small, and not well defined sub-set of that group. If there was a PCP which genuinely could affect anyone from a belief group, it is strongly arguable that particular disadvantage to the group could now be proved simply by reference to the fact that the group's Article 9 right to manifest (or hold) that belief was infringed. It seems likely that in future cases, a prohibition on practices of a well defined belief group – even if they are not practices followed by an 'identifiable

26 App No. 48420/10; [2013] IRLR 231.

section of the workforce' – will be held to place claimants at a 'particular disadvantage'. If, however the belief in question does not reach the required levels of cogency etc, it will be difficult to prove particular disadvantage to that group.

3.30   The Employment Code suggests that in some situations, the link between the protected characteristic and the disadvantage might be obvious. For example, dress codes create a disadvantage for some workers with particular religious beliefs.

3.31   In cases where it is not obvious that other individuals with the protected characteristic will share the disadvantage relied upon, it may be necessary to adduce statistical or other evidence (such as expert evidence[27]) to demonstrate that a 'group' disadvantage exists.[28]

Comparing like with like

3.32   Section 19(2)(b) of the EqA 2010 requires B to show that the relevant PCP puts or would put people who share B's protected characteristic at a particular disadvantage when compared with others. In undertaking that comparative exercise, the ET must ensure that it is comparing like with like.

3.33   EqA 2010 s23 provides: '(1) On a comparison of cases for the purposes of section 13, 14 or 19 there must be no material difference between the circumstances relating to each case'.

3.34   Under precursor legislation it was necessary for B to show that the 'requirement or condition' was (taking the SDA as an example) 'such that the proportion of women who can comply with it is considerably smaller than the proportion of men who can comply with it'. This led the courts to require claimants to identify an appropriate 'pool' of people to whom the requirement or condition would be applied (in order to compare like with like), and then produce statistical evidence of the proportions of those with and without the protected characteristic within the pool who could, and who could not, comply with the requirement or condition.

3.35   The identification of the appropriate 'pool' for comparison proved particularly difficult in the precursor legislation. Cox J commented when giving the judgment of the EAT in *Ministry of Defence*

---

27 Care is needed to ensure the expert is knowledgeable, independent. See paras 18.112–18.114.

28 Employment Code of Practice paras 4.11–4.14.

v DeBique[29]: 'pool selection in cases of indirect discrimination has troubled the Courts and tribunals for years'.

3.36   Under the EqA 2010 it may not always be necessary to create a formal pool and adduce statistics or other evidence of particular disadvantage.[30] The new approach is still very much in its infancy, and in practice, the old-style 'pool' analysis will remain relevant in many cases.

Obvious particular disadvantage and 'intrinsically liable' PCPs

3.37   Where the particular disadvantage to those possessing their protected characteristic is very clear the ET should be asked to take judicial notice of the point, and move directly on to the next stage of the claim without the need to create a formal pool and adduce statistics. One way of encouraging the ET to do so is to point to the Employment Code. This states that in some situations the link with the protected characteristic is obvious.[31] By contrast in cases in which it is less obvious how people sharing a protected characteristic are put (or would be put) at a disadvantage, statistics or personal testimony may help to demonstrate that a disadvantage exists.

3.38   Where a fact is 'obvious' a court may take 'judicial notice' of it. Some ETs have been willing to accept or assume, without the production of statistics, for example that:

- a significantly larger proportion of women take responsibility for childcare than do men, and therefore that a requirement to work full-time places women at a particular disadvantage when compared with men (*Funge v Ravensbourne College of Design and Communication*[32]);
- women are more likely to be single parents, have primary responsibility for child care, and work part-time (*Brookes v Manchester City Council*[33]);
- a PCP that a worker change their part-time working hours places women at a particular disadvantage, because more women have childcare responsibilities than do men (*McMullen v PS Photay & Associates*[34]);

29 [2010] IRLR 471.
30 See paras 3.37–3.45 and also 3.84.
31 Employment Code para 4.11.
32 Case Nos 1101233/07 and 1101597/07, Ashford ET, 23 July 2008.
33 Case No 2409542/07, Manchester ET, 9 March 2009, at para 46.
34 Case No 2329283/2008, London South ET, 12 June 2009.

- a PCP requiring workers to work in the office, rather than at home, places women at a particular disadvantage when compared with men (*McKinnon v Automated Control Services Ltd*[35]).

3.39 In *London Underground Ltd v Edwards (No 2)*,[36] the court held that, in addition to the statistical evidence about the claimant's own workplace, the ET was entitled to take into account common knowledge as to the 'high preponderance of single mothers having care for a child' in determining whether a new shift system impacted disproportionately on women. That case was decided under the Sex Discrimination Act (SDA) 1975 test, framed in terms of proportions. Under the more flexible test, ETs will be more willing to accept instances of obvious disadvantage without statistics.

3.40 However, in *Ramsden v MacMillan*[37] the Scottish EAT refused (under precursor legislation) to accept, without some concrete evidence, that a requirement of full-time working impacted disproportionately upon women within the Royal Navy. Similarly, in *Hacking and Paterson v Wilson*,[38] decided under the newer SDA 1975 test which was very similar to that in the EqA 2010, the EAT refused to assume that women would inevitably be disproportionately adversely affected by a refusal to grant a flexible working request.[39]

3.41 Claimants cannot presume that any ET will be willing to accept, without more, that a PCP of this type will place women at a disadvantage in every workforce. However, the Act gives the mere possibility (as opposed to the necessity[40]) of using statistical evidence even in gender cases.

'Intrinsically liable' PCPs

3.42 The new concept of indirect discrimination arises from EU law and in particular from free movement law. The EU Commission promoting the new model referred to *O'Flynn v Adjudication Officer*,[41] where the ECJ held that a legislative requirement that a funeral must take place in the United Kingdom before a payment can be made to meet

---

35 Case No 3104607/08, Southampton ET, 14 July 2009.
36 [1998] 1 ICR 494.
37 EATS/0003/04, 22 September 2004.
38 UKEATS/0054/09, 27 May 2010; [2011] EqLR 19.
39 See para 28.
40 The difference was specifically noted by Colomer A-G in his opinion in Case C-55/07 *Othmar Michaeler* [2008] ECR I-3135 see fn 52 of the opinion where it was made clear that this non-statistical approach is available in gender cases.
41 [1998] 1 ICR 608.

funeral expenses would be indirectly discriminatory if it was 'intrinsically liable to affect migrant workers more than national workers, and if there is a consequent risk that it will place the former at a particular disadvantage'.[42] There was no need for the claimant to produce evidence to show that the provision actually affected a substantially higher proportion of migrant workers.[43]

3.43   There are already examples of cases involving protected characteristics other than sex in which courts and ETs have accepted particular disadvantage without the need for concrete evidence. In *Noah v Desrosiers t/a Wedge*,[44] where the owner of a hair salon made it clear that she would not be willing to employ a Muslim woman who wore a headscarf as an assistant, counsel for the respondent conceded that a PCP of requiring an employee to display their hair when at work would put Muslims at a particular disadvantage when compared to others not of their faith. While this example confuses being Muslim with being a Muslim who believes that it is necessary to cover the hair, plainly the PCP is intrinsically liable to disadvantage those who do have that (religious) belief.

3.44   So, whilst previous authorities can be used to identify trends, there are no hard and fast rules as to when courts or tribunals will be willing to proceed in the absence of statistical or other concrete evidence. Even in cases that seem obvious, claimants will be best advised to produce such evidence as they can of particular disadvantage to their protected group. The kind of evidence that may be of assistance is discussed at para 3.84 below.

3.45   The Employment Code points out that the statistical analysis may not always be appropriate or practicable, especially when there is inadequate or unreliable information, or the numbers of people are too small to allow for a statistically significant comparison. In this situation, the ET may find it helpful for an expert to provide evidence as to whether there is any disadvantage and, if so, the nature of it.[45]

The 'pool' approach to showing particular disadvantage

3.46   If the disadvantage is not obvious, claimants may have to rely in practice on constructing a 'pool' for comparison, and then producing some evidence about the proportions within that pool. However, even in less obvious cases, the pool approach will not be the only way

---

42 See para 20.
43 See para 21.
44 Case No 2201/1867/07, London Central ET, 13 June 2008.
45 Employment Code para 4.13.

of showing particular disadvantage. It may be supplemented or even replaced by other forms of evidence, which are discussed further at para 3.84 below.

3.47   The Supreme Court in *Homer*[46] noted that the new formulation was,

> not intended to make it more difficult to establish indirect discrimination: quite the reverse (see the helpful account of Sir Bob Hepple in *Equality: the New Legal Framework*, Hart 2011, pp 64 to 68). It was intended to do away with the need for statistical comparisons where no statistics might exist. It was intended to do away with the complexities involved in identifying those who could comply and those who could not and how great the disparity had to be. Now all that is needed is a particular disadvantage when compared with other people who do not share the characteristic in question. It was not intended to lead us to ignore the fact that certain protected characteristics are more likely to be associated with particular disadvantages.

This point should be remembered when trying to understand the apparent complexities of the 'pool' approach, which is simply one way among others of revealing the relevant disadvantage.

The appropriate pool

3.48   Under the precursor legislation there were many cases on the identification of the pool. However, the appropriate pool should generally, as Sedley LJ commented in *Allonby v Accrington & Rossendale College*,[47] 'fall into place' once the PCP is identified.

3.49   The choice of a pool is not simply a matter of fact and it can be challenged on appeal. In *Allonby*, Sedley LJ described the process as one of 'logic', although he did accept that a logical process could produce more than one pool in some cases.[48]

3.50   Unfortunately, the higher courts have never set out any 'universal formula' on how to conduct this logical process.[49] The difficulties can be illustrated by considering two high-level cases: *Rutherford v Secretary of State for Trade and Industry (No 2)*[50] and *British Medical Association v Chaudhary*.[51]

---

46   *Homer v Chief Constable of West Yorkshire Police* [2012] UKSC 15, [2012] IRLR 601, [2012] Eq LR 594, [2012] ICR 704 at para 14.
47   [2001] EWCA Civ 529, [2001] IRLR 364.
48   See para 18.
49   Per Sedley LJ in *Grundy v British Airways* [2007] EWCA Civ 1020, [2008] IRLR 74 at para 29.
50   [2006] UKHL 19, [2006] ICR 785.
51   [2007] EWCA Civ 788, [2007] IRLR 800.

3.51   In *Rutherford*, the male claimant argued that the upper age limit for unfair dismissal claims (at the time, 65 years of age) was indirectly discriminatory against men. The majority of the House of Lords considered that the correct pool to test this proposition was the workforce aged over 65 as younger employees had no interest in continuing protection for those over 65. As the statutory bar applied to everyone over 65, there could be no disparate impact on men. Lord Walker held that the appropriate pool was the entire workforce on whom rights were conferred by the Employment Rights Act 1996 (which would appear to be the workforce under the age of 65, although parts of his analysis suggest that he was considering the whole workforce, including those over 65). Lord Nicholls appeared to base his analysis on the entire workforce, whether over or under the age of 65.

3.52   In *Chaudhary*, the claimant contended that the BMA's refusal to support claims of race discrimination against the various medical regulatory bodies was indirectly discriminatory against members of Asian origin. The Court of Appeal held that the appropriate pool comprised all BMA members who wanted the advice and support of the BMA for race discrimination claims against the specific medical regulatory bodies. As no member of the pool could comply with the requirement imposed by the BMA (ie that, in order to receive support, race discrimination claims should not be against the regulatory bodies), there was no disparate impact on any racial group.

3.53   Both these decisions have been subject to criticism. In *Chaudhary* itself, Mummery LJ commented that it was difficult to establish the ratio of the majority in *Rutherford*; comments which were echoed by Sedley LJ in *Grundy v British Airways*.

3.54   Also in *Grundy*, Sedley LJ considered the pools identified in *Chaudhary*, and pointed out that the single proper pool was arguably neither of those discussed; instead, it was members seeking the benefit of support for legal claims. Within that pool, a refusal to support race discrimination claims might well have had a substantial adverse impact on ethnic minority members.[52]

3.55   In the authors' respectful view, Sedley LJ's analysis of *Chaudhary* is consistent with the useful guidance given by Baroness Hale in *Rutherford (No 2)*, to the effect that the people in the pool should be those who want a particular benefit, or not to suffer a particular disadvantage, and will be differentially affected by a criterion applicable to that benefit or disadvantage.[53] Further, it is convincing because, in

52 [2007] EWCA Civ 1020, [2008] IRLR 74 at para 30.
53 [2006] ICR 785 at para 82.

identifying the benefit sought as support for legal claims, rather than support only for race discrimination claims, it avoids the pitfall of defining the pool by reference to the very characteristic which gives rise to the disadvantage.

3.56   This pitfall is one into which ETs following Baroness Hale's guidance too narrowly can easily fall. In the authors' view, *Hacking & Paterson, Hacking & Paterson Management Services Ltd v Wilson*[54] is an example of such a case. The respondents operated a practice of refusing any request by property managers for flexible working. The Scottish EAT took the view that it was bound by *Rutherford (No 2)* to conclude that the appropriate pool to test the discriminatory impact of that practice was limited to those property managers who wanted the benefit of flexible working. In the authors' respectful view, this approach defines the concept of 'benefit' too narrowly. Arguably, the benefit sought by the claimant, along with all other property managers, was to be able to work as a property manager, and the practice of refusing requests for flexible working disadvantaged her in doing so. If the benefit is thus defined, the appropriate pool to test the discriminatory impact of the practice would be all property managers (as had been held by the employment judge below).

3.57   Correctly applied, Baroness Hale's approach is likely to work well in cases involving national provisions, or where there is an existing workforce all of which – or a section of which – is likely to be affected by the PCP.

- In *London Underground v Edwards*,[55] the claimant, a female single parent with childcare responsibilities, argued that a new rostering system, which required her to work longer hours during the day, indirectly discriminated against women. The ET held that the appropriate pool for comparison consisted of single-parent train operators. The EAT overturned that decision, holding that the correct pool consisted of all train operators subject to the new rostering arrangements. The pool must consist of all those affected by the PCP in question, not just an arbitrary sub-set of those individuals. *Edwards* was considered in *Hacking & Paterson* and distinguished, on the basis that it involved the imposition of an obligation rather than a request for a benefit, but in the authors' view the cases are on all fours. The refusal to permit flexible working in *Hacking & Paterson* applied to all property managers; hence

---

54   UKEATS/0054/09, 27 May 2010; [2011] EqLR 19.
55   [1995] 1 ICR 574.

the property managers were the appropriate pool within which to test the discriminatory impact of the policy.

- In *R v Secretary of State for Employment ex p Seymour Smith and Perez (No 2)*,[56] where the impugned requirement was that employees have more than two years' service at 16 hours or more per week in order to bring an unfair dismissal claim, the House of Lords held that the appropriate pool was the entire workforce. All employed persons have an interest in having a remedy available to them should they be unfairly dismissed, so all should be included in the pool.

- In *Pike v Somerset County Council*,[57] the claimant claimed that a rule under which part-time (but not full-time) teaching service ceased to be pensionable if the teacher was already in receipt of a teacher's pension, was indirectly discriminatory against women. The employer argued that the appropriate pool to test this requirement was the whole of the teaching profession. The EAT and the Court of Appeal held that the only logical pool would consist of retired teachers who had returned to teaching, whether on a full- or part-time basis. Those teachers who had not retired would not be interested in post-retirement rules.

3.58   However, Baroness Hale's approach works less well where there are unlikely to be any statistics about the group which has a direct interest in, or is directly affected by, the advantage or disadvantage in question. A good example would be where a particular criterion is set out in a job advertisement. The 'interested' group in that situation would be those who are interested in applying for the job and are otherwise qualified for it, but it would be impossible to obtain statistical information in relation to such a group.

3.59   In such circumstances, the authorities suggest that a wider view as to the appropriate pool may be taken.

- *Price v Civil Service Commission*:[58] the claimant challenged as indirectly discriminatory a rule under which candidates for appointment as an executive officer in the Civil Service had to be less than 28 years of age. The EAT held that the correct pool was likely to consist of all those otherwise qualified for the position, but for the age bar.

---

56 [2000] 1 ICR 244.
57 [2009] EWCA Civ 808, [2010] 1 ICR 46.
58 [1978] 1 ICR 27.

- In *University of Manchester v Jones*,[59] the post of careers adviser was advertised with a preference for applicants aged 27–35. The claimant, who was aged 46 and was otherwise qualified for the post, contended that this indirectly discriminated against women. She argued that the appropriate pool to test the alleged discrimination was graduates who had obtained their degree as mature students. The Court of Appeal disagreed, and held that the correct pool was all those persons, male and female, who satisfied the job criteria save for the age requirement – thus in this case all graduates who had the experience required.

- An example of a case in which an admittedly imperfect wider pool was accepted is provided by *Greater Manchester Police Authority v Lea*.[60] The claimant challenged as indirectly discriminatory on grounds of sex a policy under which Greater Manchester Police would not generally consider individuals in receipt of an occupational pension for appointment. He relied on statistics showing the proportion of men and women in receipt of an occupational pension in the economically active population. The employer challenged this pool on the basis that it would include people who would not be qualified for the relevant position. The EAT held that the pool in such a case does not have to be shown to be a statistically perfect match of the people who would be capable of and interested in filling the post in question. It would have been open to the employer to show that the claimant's statistics distorted the true picture, but no such evidence had been produced.

3.60   Claimants should therefore consider what the pool is seeking to test and devise it accordingly. Claimants can encourage the ET to focus on the reason why courts began to identify pools in the first place. Sedley LJ commented in *Grundy*, under SDA 1975 s5(3), as under EqA 2010 s23(1), it is necessary to compare like with like. When deciding whether a PCP is indirectly discriminatory, the relevant circumstances in relation to one group must be the same, or not materially different from those of the other. The pool must not be narrowed by qualifications or conditions which are not logically relevant to the statistical exercise in hand.[61] Nor must it be widened to such a degree that it no longer tests the discriminatory impact of the challenged PCP.

3.61   So in *Jones*, it would have been illogical to limit the pool to those who had obtained their degree as mature students, as all potential

59 [1993] 1 ICR 474.
60 [1990] IRLR 372.
61 *Rutherford (No 2)* [2006] ICR 785, per Lord Walker of Gestingthorpe at para 66.

applicants to the post would have been affected by the age limits. Similarly, in *Edwards*, all of the workforce, not just those who were single parents, were affected by the new shift pattern. Conversely, in *Pike*, it would have been illogical to extend the pool to encompass the whole teaching profession, when only those teachers in receipt of a teacher's pension were affected by the PCP.

3.62 This analysis accords with the example given in the Statutory Code of Practice on Employment at para 4.18.

Showing 'particular disadvantage' in a pool using statistics

3.63 Statistics are not the only means of showing 'particular disadvantage' under the Act. However, in certain types of case – in particular those involving national pools, or identifiable pools of employees within a particular workplace, statistics will be available and can be useful. There are a number of cases which provide guidance on how best to approach a statistical analysis. Whilst those decided under the old 'proportions' test might now be decided differently on the facts, because the 'particular disadvantage' test is less stringent, the cases are still helpful in showing how statistics can be used.

3.64 In many cases, a simple mathematical approach will be the best way to analyse the statistics. Say that an employer will only put his employees on a particular sort of work, paid at a higher hourly rate, if they can lift 10kg unaided. The employer has 250 employees, 180 of whom are male, and 70 of whom are female. 150 of the employees are able to lift 10kg unaided, of whom 130 are male and 20 are female. In order to determine whether those statistics demonstrate a 'particular disadvantage' to women, the following steps can be followed:

- **Step 1**: Ascertain the number of women in the pool: 70.
- **Step 2**: Ascertain the number of women in the pool who are able to comply with the criterion: 20.
- **Step 3**: Divide the number of women who are able to comply with the criterion by the number of women in the pool: 20/70. Expressed as a percentage, this is 20/70 x 100% = 28.5%
- **Step 4**: Ascertain the number of men in the pool: 180.
- **Step 5**: Ascertain the number of men in the pool who are able to comply with the criterion: 130.
- **Step 6**: Divide the number of men who are able to comply with the criterion by the number of men in the pool: 130/180. Expressed as a percentage, this is 130/180 x 100% = 72.2%

3.65   This approach enables us to calculate the proportions of women and men in the pool who can comply with the criterion. It also allows us to calculate the proportions of those who cannot comply, simply by flipping the percentages (so 71.5 per cent of women in the pool cannot comply with the requirement, as against 27.8 per cent of men). In this example, it is easy to see from either comparison that the requirement puts women at a particular disadvantage.

3.66   In more complicated cases, it may be helpful to use the approach explained in *Jones v Chief Adjudication Officer*.[62] In that case, the Court of Appeal adopted a step-by-step test intended to 'predict' the appropriate proportions of those with and those without the protected characteristic in the pool – figures which can then be used to assess the extent of any discriminatory impact of a PCP.

- Identify the criterion for selection.
- Identify the relevant population, comprising all those who satisfy the other criteria for selection.
- Divide the relevant population into groups representing those who satisfy the criterion and those who do not.
- Predict statistically what proportion of each group should consist of women.
- Ascertain what are the actual male/female balances in the two groups.
- Compare the actual with the predicted balances.
- If women are found to be under-represented in the first group and over-represented in the second, it is proved that the criterion is discriminatory.

3.67   This is what happens if the *Jones* test is applied to the simple example discussed above:

- **Step 1**: The criterion for selection for the higher hourly rate is the ability to lift 10kg unaided.
- **Step 2**: The relevant pool (population) is 250 people, comprising 180 men and 70 women.
- **Step 3**: The group within that pool which does satisfy the criterion comprises 150 people. The remaining 100 people do not satisfy the criterion.
- **Step 4**: If the requirement is non-discriminatory, it should impact equally on men and women. Thus the proportion of women within the pool who are able to comply with the criterion should be equal to the proportion of men able to comply. The following formula

can be used to predict the number of men and the number of women who should be able to comply with the criterion.

(1) Calculate the percentage of men and women in the pool:
  180/250 x 100% = 72% men; 70/250 x 100% = 28% women.

(2) Assuming that the number who can comply (150) is distributed between males and females in the same proportions as males and females are distributed in the workforce, calculate what the number of men and women should be within the group who can comply.
  150 x 72% = 108 men; 150 x 28% = 42 women

- **Step 5**: The actual numbers who can comply are 130 men and 20 women.

- **Step 6**: The predicted numbers who can comply are 108 men and 42 women. This means that there are 22 too many men and 22 too few women in the complying group.

- **Step 7**: The calculations show that women are under-represented in the group of people who can comply with the requirement and over-represented in the group who cannot comply with it. 'Particular disadvantage' to women is established.

3.68   Where the proportions are less obvious than those in the example used, it may be helpful to combine all of the above approaches. Then the full range of figures can be considered: the proportions of (for example) men and women who are advantaged and disadvantaged by the criterion, as well as the actual numbers able to comply with it, which can then be compared with the 'predicted' numbers who would be able to comply with a non-discriminatory criterion.

3.69   A good example of such a case is *R v Secretary of State for Employment ex p Seymour-Smith and Perez (No 2)*.[63] This was a challenge to the requirement that employees had to have worked for two years, for 16 or more hours per week, before they could bring an unfair dismissal claim. The ECJ commented that the available statistics from 1985 (which showed that 77.4 per cent of men and 68.9 per cent of women were able to satisfy the extended qualifying period) did not seem to show that a significantly smaller percentage of women than men were able to satisfy the requirement. When the case returned to the House of Lords, however, analysis of the proportions over a six-year period showed that, the ratio of men to women who qualified was constant at approximately 10:9. The majority of the House of Lords considered that these statistics were sufficient to show that the qualifying requirements had a considerably greater adverse impact on women than on men.

3.70 　　As *Seymour-Smith* was a case brought under Article 119 EC, the test was whether the claimants could show that a 'considerably smaller percentage of women than men' were able to comply with the qualifying criterion. This is similar to the approach taken under the old test in the SDA 1975, which focused on comparing the proportions of men and women within the pool who could comply with the PCP. These individuals were described in the case-law as the 'advantaged' group. However, sometimes this focus on the proportions of people who can comply with the PCP will suggest that there is only a small disparity, whereas if the proportions of those who cannot comply (the 'disadvantaged' groups) are the primary focus, the disparity appears considerably greater.

3.71 　　This point is illustrated by the figures in *Seymour-Smith* itself. If instead of looking at the 68.9 per cent of women and 77.4 per cent of men who could comply with the unfair dismissal qualifying requirements in 1985, we consider that 31.1 per cent of women did not qualify, as compared with 22.6 per cent of men, the disparity appears much greater.

3.72 　　There has been much debate about whether it is legitimate for a court to look at the proportions of 'disadvantaged' as well as 'advantaged' groups within the pool in this way. There were indications that this approach could be legitimate in *Seymour-Smith* itself[64] and in the speeches of the minority[65] in *Rutherford (No 2)*. More recently, in *Grundy*[66] (which was an equal pay case), the Court of Appeal has held that there is no principle of law requiring the fact-finding ET always to base its test of disparity on the advantaged cohort. The ET was entitled to look at the proportions of both the advantaged and disadvantaged groups, and to focus on the latter.[67] In *Pike*, another equal pay case, no issue was raised in the Court of Appeal about the EAT's decision to look both at the proportions of the group that could, and of the group that could not, comply with the PCP.[68]

3.73 　　The adoption of the 'particular disadvantage' test will lead to fewer arguments about whether particular methodology (such as looking at the disadvantaged as well as the advantaged group) is valid in the

64　[2000] 1 WLR 435, per Lord Slynn of Hadley at para 20.

65　[2006] ICR 785, per Lord Nicholls at paras 4 and 5 and Lord Walker of Gestingthorpe at paras 65 and 67.

66　*Grundy v British Airways* [2007] EWCA Civ 1020, [2008] IRLR 74.

67　[2007] EWCA Civ 1020, [2008] IRLR 74, at paras 35 and 43.

68　[2009] EWCA Civ 808, [2010] 1 ICR 46, at paras 8 and 9.

context of an indirect discrimination claim. Instead, ETs and courts will probably show a greater willingness to look at available, reliable statistics from all angles, and to examine the position in terms of actual numbers affected (as per the *Jones* approach) rather than concentrating only on proportions.

3.74 In cases where the disparity in percentage terms is small, it may be worth obtaining evidence as to the significance of the percentage point difference from a statistician. Advisers and ETs are often unfamiliar with the mathematical concept of statistical significance and, if such evidence can be obtained, it could help to tip the balance in a borderline case.

Alternative approaches to showing 'particular disadvantage'

3.75 If statistics alone are to be relied upon to demonstrate 'particular disadvantage', they will need to be valid and reliable, and must not demonstrate only a fortuitous or transitory picture of disparate impact.[69] Frequently, no such statistics will be available. In such circumstances, claimants will need to bolster any statistics they have about their own workplace with other information. This could include national statistics, information about the general state of the labour market, or expert evidence.

What if the 'pool' is too small to produce valid statistics?

3.76 Perhaps the best example of a pool being too small to produce valid statistics is *London Underground Ltd v Edwards (No 2)*.[70] Of the train operators to whom the employer's new rostering system applied, all 2,023 (100 per cent) of the male train operators could comply with the new system, whereas one of the 21 women could not comply (95.2 per cent could comply). The employer argued that such a small percentage difference did not demonstrate disparate impact under the old SDA test. The Court of Appeal held that the ET was entitled to have regard to matters outside the statistical make-up of the pool, including:

- 'common knowledge' as to the high preponderance of single mothers who have care of a child; and
- the large discrepancy in the numbers of male and female train operators, which indicated that the job was difficult or unattractive for women,

69 See eg the comments of the ECJ referred to in *Seymour-Smith (No 2)* [2000] 1 WLR 435 at para 14.
70 [1999] 1 ICR 494.

- when deciding the question of disparate impact. It therefore upheld the ET's decision that a considerably smaller proportion of women than men could comply with the new roster
  arrangements.

3.77   A similar approach was adopted by the EAT in *Chief Constable of
Avon & Somerset Constabulary v Chew*.[71] The female claimant challenged a policy requiring individuals who wanted to work part-time to
comply with the normal shift pattern adopted by their district/depart-
ment. The EAT held that it was entitled to take a flexible approach to
assessing disparate impact, including consideration of whether the
policy was intrinsically likely to have a disparate effect as between
men and women, the make-up and overall numbers of the relevant
workforce, the question of whether any men were actually disadvantaged by the policy, and the history of the particular workforce.[72]

3.78   This type of approach fits far better with the 'particular disadvantage' test than it did with the old 'considerably smaller proportion'
test and is thus likely to be acceptable to ETs and courts where valid
and reliable statistical information is limited.

3.79   By way of contrast, the opposite result was reached in *Nelson v
Carillion Services Ltd*,[73] an equal pay claim where the female claimant
was paid less than comparators who had been transferred to Carillion from another employer under more favourable terms and conditions. In Ms Nelson's hospital wing, there were four male and two
female transferred stewards and one male and one female steward
who were on the less favourable Carillion terms. On the basis that
the appropriate pool consisted of those stewards who worked on
her wing, the claimant argued that women were disproportionately
adversely affected, because 80 per cent of the men were on the transferred terms, as opposed to only 66.67 per cent of women. The Court
of Appeal disagreed, holding that the pool adopted was 'artificial'
(there were in fact 300 workers who were transferred to Carillion)
and it was not clear that, within this very small pool, the statistics
showed a significant rather than fortuitous or short-term result.

3.80   Thus if a very small pool is selected, it must be a pool that is
appropriate to test the discrimination complained of, and it will generally be wise to obtain further statistics or evidence showing that
the disproportionate impact in the small group is reflected across the
organisation, and/or nationally.

---

71   EAT/503/00, 28 September 2001.
72   Paragraph 36(12) and (13).
73   [2003] EWCA Civ 544, [2003] ICR 1256.

3.81   A slightly different point arose in *Coker and Osamor v Lord Chancellor and Lord Chancellor's Department*,[74] where the two female claimants (one of whom was of Nigerian ethnic origin) challenged as indirectly discriminatory on grounds of sex and/or race the Lord Chancellor's decision to select a special adviser only from those people personally known to him. The ET held that the appropriate pool consisted of people who satisfied the requirements for the post apart from the personal knowledge requirement. There were no statistics as to the make-up of this pool, but the ET found that, because the Lord Chancellor had stated that women and those of the relevant ethnic origin represented only a very small minority of his acquaintances, disparate impact was made out. The Court of Appeal disagreed, holding that a requirement can only have a disproportionate adverse effect on members of a protected group if a significant proportion of the pool for comparison can satisfy the requirement. On the facts, the personal knowledge requirement excluded almost the entirety of the pool, which meant that its use could not lead to a finding of indirect discrimination.

3.82   The Court of Appeal went on to say that, as a result, making an appointment from within a circle of family, friends and personal acquaintances is seldom likely to constitute indirect discrimination.

3.83   The decision in *Coker* was widely criticised at the time,[75] and should a similar claim arise now it could well have a different outcome. The Court of Appeal was able to take the approach it did in *Coker* because the old 'considerably smaller proportion' test applied. Where only a tiny proportion of the relevant pool can meet the requirement, regardless of gender or ethnicity, that test is very difficult to apply. Using the 'particular disadvantage' test, however, there would now be a reasonable argument that, on the evidence available from the Lord Chancellor himself (who was no doubt an expert on his own social circle), potential female applicants, and those of the relevant ethnic origin were placed at a particular disadvantage by the requirement that they be personally known to him.

---

74 [2001] EWCA 1756, [2002] ICR 321.
75 See Highlights: January 2002 IRLR by Michael Rubenstein for a cogent criticism.

What non-pool-based evidence might be used to establish 'particular disadvantage'?

3.84　There is as yet little case-law dealing with the question of what type of evidence might assist in establishing 'particular disadvantage'. Much will depend on the facts of each individual case, but the following sources might be helpful:

- where the pool is not a national pool, national or international statistics relating to the same, or a similar PCP;
- published research into the effect of a particular type of PCP on persons possessing a protected characteristic (this could be academic research, or research contained in a journal, magazine or newspaper article);
- general statistics or written research evidencing the normal behaviour of groups possessing a particular protected characteristic;
- written or live expert evidence which establishes the general effect of a PCP on persons possessing the same protected characteristic as the claimant;
- lay witness evidence eg as to the effect of a particular PCP on those possessing a protected characteristic within a specific workplace.

Is the claimant placed at a 'particular disadvantage'?

3.85　Section 19(2) of the EqA 2010 requires the claimant to show both that the challenged PCP places persons within their protected group at 'a particular disadvantage', and also that it puts or would put him/her personally at that disadvantage.

3.86　The EAT in *Eweida v British Airways Plc*[76] provided some useful guidance on the circumstances in which a person will be able to show that they are personally placed at a particular disadvantage by a PCP. It took the view that Ms Eweida suffered a particular disadvantage as a result of the application of a PCP forbidding employees to wear jewellery, because she was refused the opportunity to work and earn money once she insisted on her right visibly to wear the cross. This was so despite the fact that there was no evidence to the effect that her religion imposed any requirement to wear the cross. The High Court took a similar view in the *Watkins-Singh* case, where the claimant wished to wear the Sikh kara at school.[77]

76 [2009] ICR 303.
77 See the detailed discussion at para 3.28.

3.87   The EAT in *Eweida* also commented that a person might be able to show a particular disadvantage even where the complaint was about a provision with which they had (reluctantly) complied – for example, where a woman with childcare responsibilities accedes to a requirement to work full time because her employer will not consider the possibility of part-time work and she cannot afford to lose her job. The EAT considered this followed from the change in wording from 'cannot comply' (under the old SDA 1975 and RRA 1976 provisions) to putting the claimant at a 'particular disadvantage'.

3.88   The use of the words 'it puts, or would put, B' at a particular disadvantage in EqA 2010 s19(2)(c) confirms that an individual may make an indirect discrimination claim even where they have not yet been placed at a particular disadvantage by the PCP complained of.

Must there be a 'causal link' between the protected characteristic relied upon and the 'particular disadvantage'?

3.89   A further complication relating to 'particular disadvantage' has arisen in some cases, where the courts have suggested that there is a need for a 'causal link' between the protected characteristic and the particular disadvantage complained of.

3.90   For example, in *Eweida*, the EAT held:[78]

> ... in order to fall within the terms of the legislation, it is still necessary that the particular disadvantage relied upon should stem from the religious beliefs held by the claimant. It is not enough that persons of the same religion and belief are fortuitously affected by the provision. It must be something connected with the religion or belief that causes the adverse effect.

3.91   The impact of this passage depends on what precisely is meant by it. If it is simply being said that there must be reliable evidence (in the forms of statistics or otherwise) to show that the PCP places persons possessing the relevant protected characteristic at a particular disadvantage, the comment is uncontroversial. If, however, it is being suggested that there must be some separately established causal link between the protected characteristic and the particular disadvantage, the authors respectfully take the view that this position is not supported either by the wording of section 19 or its predecessors, or by the European legislation.

---

78 [2009] ICR 303 at para 46.

3.92   Take the example of a claim for indirect discrimination based on statistics showing that women generally do less well in a particular psychometric test than men. The existing case-law does not suggest that, in order for the claimant to succeed, the claimant would have to prove that this was (for example) because women have poorer spatial awareness than men.

3.93   In *Gibson v Sheffield City Council*,[79] an equal pay case, Smith LJ raised the possibility of a 'causal link' requirement in a slightly different way. She commented that even where the claimant has produced evidence showing that a PCP places women at a particular disadvantage, a respondent should still be given the opportunity to demonstrate that what might appear to be a disadvantage to women arises from factors wholly unrelated to gender.[80] Smith LJ took the view that this analysis applied both in equal pay cases involving indirect discrimination, and in ordinary indirect discrimination claims. While there has been a long-running debate on this issue in the equal pay context,[81] this was the first time such a suggestion had been made in connection with the SDA 1975. The other members of the court did not adopt Smith LJ's comments (which were, in any event, obiter) and it might have been thought that her approach was not, therefore, generally accepted.

3.94   The decisions of the EAT and the Court of Appeal in *Chief Constable of West Yorkshire Police v Homer*[82] appeared to suggest that the causal link approach may be gaining support amongst the judiciary. However, the Supreme Court's judgment established that such a requirement does not exist.

3.95   Mr Homer was employed as a legal adviser with the Police National Database. He did not have a law degree. His employer offered him the opportunity and funding to take a law degree, but Mr Homer refused, as he would be retiring at age 65 and would not complete his degree until after that date. The employer then introduced a new career structure under which employees were required to have a law degree in order to reach the highest pay threshold, which also commanded the highest status. Mr Homer alleged that this amounted to indirect age discrimination. The ET agreed, and found that he and others in his age group of 60–65 had suffered particular disadvantage in comparison with those aged 30–59 because they were prevented

79   [2010] EWCA Civ 63, [2010] ICR 708.
80   At para 63.
81   See para 14.101.
82   [2009] ICR 223 (EAT), [2010] EWCA Civ 449, [2010] ICR 987 (CA).

from achieving the qualification for the highest pay threshold prior to retirement age.

3.96   The EAT allowed the employer's appeal,[83] and the Court of Appeal upheld that decision, albeit on somewhat different grounds.[84] The Court of Appeal held that the disadvantage caused to Mr Homer arose not out of his age, but out of his impending retirement at age 65. Mummery LJ said that the disadvantage was caused by his plan to stop work before he would be able to obtain his law degree. The same disadvantage would follow for younger employees who also stopped working before qualifying.[85]

3.97   However, the Court of Appeal also held that the age discrimination provisions should be interpreted in the same way as the other, longer standing discrimination legislation. Dismissing the claim on the basis that Mr Homer's disadvantage arose not from his age but his impending retirement is similar to dismissing a woman's claim that a requirement to work full time is indirectly discriminatory on the basis that her disadvantage arises not because of her sex, but because of the fact that she needs to care for her child. The argument that younger workers who choose to stop work early would also be disadvantaged is akin to an argument that men who choose to care for their children would also be disadvantaged.

3.98   When *Homer* was heard by the Supreme Court it held that the EAT and Court of Appeal were wrong to hold that what put Mr Homer at a disadvantage was not his age but his impending retirement.

3.99   The argument focusses on the words 'puts at' in section 19 requiring identification of what it is that puts him at – or causes – the disadvantage complained of. The respondent's approach required Mr Homer to be compared with anyone else who is nearing the end of his employment for whatever reason. The argument requires taking the particular disadvantage that is suffered by a particular age group for a reason which is related to their age and equating it with a similar disadvantage which is suffered by others but for a completely different reason unrelated to their age.

3.100   Baroness Hale[86] noted that such an argument, 'if it were translated into other contexts it would have alarming consequences for the law of discrimination generally. Take, for example, a requirement that employees in a particular job must have a beard. This puts women at

83 [2009] ICR 223.
84 [2010] EWCA Civ 449, [2010] ICR 987.
85 [2010] EWCA Civ 449, [2010] ICR 987 at para 48.
86 [2012] UKSC 15, [2012] IRLR 601 at para 13.

a particular disadvantage because very few of them are able to grow a beard. But the argument leaves sex out of account and says that it is the inability to grow a beard which puts women at a particular disadvantage and so they must be compared with other people who for whatever reason, whether it be illness or immaturity, are unable to grow a beard'.

3.101   Ascertaining disadvantage turned on making the correct comparison of persons in materially the same circumstances. Thus leaving work because of impending retirement is materially different from leaving for family reasons or taking early retirement. These involve choice. A person who is coming up against a mandatory retirement age does not have the same choice.

3.102   In rejecting the idea that there must be a causal link, Baroness Hale pointed out at para 17:

> The law of indirect discrimination is an attempt to level the playing field by subjecting to scrutiny requirements which look neutral on their face but in reality work to the comparative disadvantage of people with a particular protected characteristic. A requirement which works to the comparative disadvantage of a person approaching compulsory retirement age is indirectly discriminatory on grounds of age. There is, as Lord Justice Maurice Kay acknowledged, 'unreality in differentiating between age and retirement' [34]. Put simply, the reason for the disadvantage was that people in this age group did not have time to acquire a law degree. And the reason why they did not have time to acquire a law degree was that they were soon to reach the age of retirement.

3.103   Just before *Homer*, the Court of Appeal in *R (Bailey (Margaret)) v London Borough of Brent Council*,[87] concluded, following a review of the authorities, that a causal relationship or intrinsic link between the protected characteristic and the particular disadvantage will not be required in all cases.[88] It is suggested that *Homer* now makes it clear that the comparative disadvantage test does not involve a step of showing that the protected characteristic causes the disadvantage.

87   [2011] EWCA Civ 1586; [2012] EqLR 168.
88   See in particular the useful discussion at paras 45–50 and 100.

Justification: Is the PCP 'a proportionate means of achieving a legitimate aim'?

3.104 Under the old SDA 1975 and RRA 1976 tests, if a requirement or condition had disparate impact on a protected group, the employer had to provide objective justification for it in order to avoid a finding of indirect discrimination. Now, the employer has to show the PCP is a proportionate means of achieving a legitimate aim. The language of proportionality comes from European Directives.

3.105 The language used in the Directives[89] is different from, and imposes a more stringent test, than section 19(2)(d). The Directives require the means of achieving the legitimate aim relied upon by the employer to be 'appropriate and necessary' (emphasis added), as opposed to being 'proportionate'. The Supreme Court recognised, in *Homer*, the significance of and difference in the test derived from the Directives.

What may amount to a 'legitimate aim'?

3.106 There is no definition of 'legitimate aim' either in the Directives or in the EqA 2010.

3.107 The Employment Code, while making the point that the concept of 'legitimate aim' is nowhere defined, states:[90]

> The aim of the provision, criterion or practice should be legal, should not be discriminatory in itself, and must represent a real, objective consideration. The health, welfare and safety of individuals may qualify as legitimate aims, provided that risks are clearly specified and supported by evidence.

The Code goes on to say that reasonable business needs and economic efficiency may also be legitimate aims.[91]

3.108 There is case-law on whether saving costs can amount to a legitimate aim capable of justifying a discriminatory PCP. The domestic courts have taken a clear position that individual employers may not rely solely on cost considerations for justification, but that cost saving can be part of a group of legitimate aims being pursued by the employer (see *Cross v British Airways plc*[92]).

---

89 Eg Directives 2000/43 and 2000/78.
90 Employment Code para 4.28.
91 Employment Code para 4.29.
92 [2005] IRLR 423 at para 72.

3.109   The EAT in *Woodcock v Cumbria Primary Care Trust*[93] suggested that the 'costs plus' approach, adopted in *Cross* and endorsed in *Red-car and Cleveland Borough Council v Bainbridge*,[94] tended to involve parties and ETs in 'artificial game-playing' to try to find an additional factor, and went on to say:[95]

> If the matter were free from authority it would seem to us that an employer should be entitled to seek to justify a measure, or a state of affairs, producing a discriminatory impact ... on the basis that the cost of avoiding that impact, or rectifying it, would be disproportionately high.

3.110   However, the EAT's approach in *Woodcock* has not been followed by the higher courts. The Court of Appeal in the same case[96] re-endorsed the approach that cost saving alone cannot constitute a legitimate aim. Most recently, in *O'Brien v Ministry of Justice*,[97] the Supreme Court ruled that, whilst a state may decide for itself how much to spend on any area of social policy, any discriminatory rule or practice within that area must be justified by reference to a legitimate aim other than the simple saving of cost.[98] The decision makes it clear that the same approach will apply to private employers. Lord Hope and Baroness Hale, giving the judgment of the court, said:

> [T]he fundamental principles of equal treatment cannot depend upon how much money happens to be available in the public coffers at any one particular time or upon how the State chooses to allocate the funds available between the various responsibilities it undertakes. That argument would not avail a private employer and it should not avail the State in its capacity as an employer.[99]

Identifying the 'legitimate aim' being pursued by the employer.

3.111   It is important to identify the true, underlying legitimate aim pursued by the employer. In some cases, employers have defined the 'legitimate aim' so narrowly that only the PCP applied will suffice to achieve the aim, frequently including means within the definition of the aim being pursued. If an employer is able to do this, there is a

---

93 UKEAT/489/09, [2011] ICR 143.
94 [2008] ICR 249.
95 [2011] ICR 143 at para 32.
96 [2012] EWCA Civ 330 at para 66.
97 [2013] UKSC 6.
98 See para 69.
99 See para 74.

high risk that the claimant will lose even before the 'proportionality' stage is reached.[100]

3.112   Two examples can be used to illustrate such a situation:

- In *Blackburn v Chief Constable of West Midlands Police*,[101] the female claimant challenged as indirectly discriminatory a policy under which individuals working a 24/7 rotating shift received a special priority payment. The ET found that the employer's 'wish to reward night-time working' was a legitimate aim. In circumstances where that conclusion had not been challenged on appeal, the Court of Appeal found that it was not open to the claimant to argue that alternative schemes (such as using a scoring matrix which did not give special recognition to 24/7 working, or providing special priority payments to those who were excused from 24/7 working for childcare reasons) would have been effective to achieve different but related aims. No alternative schemes were put forward by the claimant that achieved the aim of rewarding night-time working.

- In *Ladele v London Borough of Islington and Liberty*,[102] the claimant, a Christian employed as a registrar of births, deaths and marriages, sought to challenge a requirement that she conduct civil partnership registrations. The legitimate aim relied upon by Islington was the provision of a service to its clients which was effective in terms of practicality and efficiency, and complied with its overarching policy of being 'an employer and public authority wholly committed to the promotion of equal opportunities and to requiring all its employees to act in a way which does not discriminate against others'. The EAT and Court of Appeal found that this was indeed Islington's aim, and that it was legitimate. Exempting the claimant from performing civil partnerships would not have achieved that aim.[103]

3.113   In both of these cases, the identification of the legitimate aim determined the outcome. Had the ET found that the chief constable's true aim in *Blackburn* was to ensure effective 24/7 coverage, the outcome might well have been different. Similarly, had Ms Ladele's

---

100 See, for a more detailed discussion of this tactic, Aaron Baker 'Proportionality and Employment Discrimination in the UK' (2008) 37(4) *ILJ* 305.

101 [2008] EWCA Civ 1208, [2009] IRLR 135.

102 [2009] EWCA Civ 1357, [2010] ICR 532.

103 This finding was upheld by the ECtHR in *Ladele* Application no 51671/10, 15 January 2013.

submission that Islington's aim was to 'provide effective civil partnership arrangements' been accepted, she might have won her case.

3.114   It is therefore very important that claimants pin down an employer's case on legitimate aim at an early stage. If that aim is so narrowly
defined as to constitute a potential knock-out blow, claimants will
need to consider whether any evidence can be obtained to show that
the true aim pursued is broader in scope. This could include internal
policy documents, or evidence from witnesses.

3.115   There are statements in some recent cases that suggest the courts
will be receptive to arguments to the effect that the concept of 'legitimate aim' is being unfairly manipulated in such a way as to narrow
the reach of the discrimination legislation.

3.116   In the *JFS* case,[104] Lord Hope (who held, with the minority, that the
school's policy did not amount to direct discrimination), considered
the means that could be adopted to achieve the school's legitimate
aim of 'educating those who, in the eyes of the Office of the Chief
Rabbi, are Jewish, irrespective of their religious beliefs, practices and
observances, in a school whose culture and ethos is that of Orthodox
Judaism'. Munby J had concluded at first instance that an alternative
admissions policy based on such factors as adherence or commitment to Judaism would not be a means of achieving the legitimate
aim. Lord Hope held that this missed the point; the question was
whether putting the claimant at a disadvantage was a proportionate
means of achieving the aim of the policy. He took the view that the
governing body had not given thought to the question of whether a
less discriminatory policy – such as admitting children recognised
as Jewish by other branches of Judaism, or trying to achieved a balanced composition of pupils committed to the Jewish religion – could
have been adopted without undermining the religious ethos of the
school.[105]

3.117   It is certainly arguable that the alternative means suggested by
Lord Hope do not achieve the very narrow objective set out by the
school. Lord Rodger and Lord Brown made exactly this point in their
minority judgments. However, his comments may be of assistance
to claimants in seeking to persuade ETs to avoid the narrow *Blackburn* approach.

3.118   A slightly different point was made by the Court of Appeal in
Allen v GMB,[106] the facts of which are set out at para 3.13 above. The

104 [2009] UKSC 15, [2010] 2 AC 728.
105 [2009] UKSC 15, [2010] 2 AC 728 at para 212.
106 [2008] EWCA Civ 810, [2008] ICR 1407.

ET had found that the union's policy of prioritising pay protection for (mainly male) 'losers' under the new pay scheme over obtaining back pay for historically underpaid women was intended to achieve the legitimate aims of: avoiding privatisations, job losses and cuts in hours, avoiding or minimising 'losers' and, if 'losers' were inevitable, getting the best possible pay protection for them. However, it concluded that the policy was not a proportionate means of achieving those aims.

3.119 The EAT overturned this decision on the basis that the only way of achieving those aims was to apply the policy in fact applied by the union. However, the Court of Appeal held that, in reaching this conclusion, the EAT had given too narrow a definition to the 'means' used to achieve the union's legitimate aim. The Court of Appeal found that the ET had been entitled to find that the steps taken to secure the historically underpaid members' agreement to the prioritising of protection of 'losers' formed part of the 'means' of achieving the aims. These steps had included 'manipulating' those members into accepting the deal 'by a marked economy of truth' in what the union said and wrote to them, and had not been proportionate.

3.120 Importantly, the Court of Appeal also confirmed that if a legitimate objective is achievable only by disproportionate means, it will not be susceptible to justification. Ultimately, it will always be open to Claimants to say that the discriminatory impact of the policy is so great that it cannot be considered proportionate, even if the aim is legitimate.[107]

Proportionality

What is the test of proportionality?

3.121 If an employer is able to show that the PCP relied upon is in pursuit of a 'legitimate aim', he must go on to prove that it is 'a proportionate means' of achieving that aim.

3.122 The Employment Code suggests that 'proportionate' must be defined by reference to the European jurisprudence:[108]

> Although not defined by the Act, the term 'proportionate' is taken from EU Directives and its meaning has been clarified by decisions of the CJEU (formerly the ECJ). EU law views treatment as proportionate if it is an 'appropriate and necessary' means of achieving a legiti-

107 This may in fact have been the basis for Lord Hope's comments in the *JFS* case; see para 211.
108 Employment Code para 4.31.

mate aim. But 'necessary' does not mean that the provision, criterion or practice is the only possible way of achieving the legitimate aim; it is sufficient that the same aim could not be achieved by less discriminatory means.

3.123   This approach has subsequently been elaborated in *Homer*, where it was stated that the approach of the ET and the IDS Handbook on age discrimination, which regarded the terms 'appropriate', 'necessary' and 'proportionate' as 'equally interchangeable' was not correct. The Act has to be read in the light of Directive 2000/78: to be proportionate, a measure has to be both an appropriate means of achieving the legitimate aim and (reasonably) necessary in order to do so. Baroness Hale explained:[109]

> Some measures may simply be inappropriate to the aim in question: thus, for example, the aim of rewarding experience is not achieved by age related pay scales which apply irrespective of experience (*Hennigs v Eisenbahn-Bundesamt; Land Berlin v Mai*, Joined Cases C-297/10 and C-298/10 [2012] 1 CMLR 18); the aim of making it easier to recruit young people is not achieved by a measure which applies long after the employees have ceased to be young (*Kücükdeveci v Swedex GmbH & Co KG*, Case C-555/07, [2010] 2 CMLR 33). So it has to be asked whether requiring existing employees to have a law degree before they can achieve the highest grade is appropriate to the aims of recruiting and retaining new staff or retaining existing staff within the organisation. The EAT expressed some scepticism about this [45, 46].

> 'A measure may be appropriate to achieving the aim but go further than is (reasonably) necessary in order to do so and thus be disproportionate. ... both the Directive and the Regulations require that the criterion itself be justified rather than that its discriminatory effect be justified ...

3.124   The Supreme Court went on to point out that part of the assessment of whether the criterion can be justified entails a comparison of the impact of that criterion upon the affected group as against the importance of the aim to the employer. It has to be asked whether it is reasonably necessary in order to achieve the legitimate aims of the employer to disadvantage the claimant in the way in which the claimant was disadvantaged.

3.125   The Supreme Court explained that to some extent the answer depends upon whether there were non-discriminatory alternatives available to the means adopted by the employer. If there is a more proportionate means of achieving the legitimate aims of the employer then the employer may fail to justify the use of the PCP.

109 [2012] UKSC 15, [2012] ICR 704, [2012] IRLR 601 at para 22.

3.126   'Proportionality' is to be understood as a means of implementing the Directive test of justification stemming from *Bilka-Kaufhaus GmbH v Weber von Hartz*.[110] This was a case brought under
Article 119 EC, by women who worked part time and were as a result
excluded from the employer's occupational pension scheme. The
ECJ held that the measures adopted by the employer could only be
objectively justified if they corresponded to a real need on the part of
the undertaking, were appropriate with a view to achieving the objectives pursued and were necessary to that end.

3.127   *Bilka* was considered in *Hampson v Department of Education and
Science*,[111] an indirect discrimination case in the case brought under
the RRA 1976 when the old objective justification test still applied.
The requirement was that, in order to be regarded as a qualified
teacher in the United Kingdom, individuals must have completed
an approved UK course or a course approved as comparable. This
required 'an objective balance between the discriminatory effect of
the condition and the reasonable needs of the party who applies
the condition'.[112] Thus the domestic courts did not wholeheartedly
endorse the *Bilka* test, referring to 'reasonable needs' rather than
'necessity' on the part of the employer.

3.128   In *Barry v Midland Bank*,[113] Lord Nicholls held that the UK test
required a balancing exercise. The more serious the disparate impact
on women, or on men, as the case may be, the more cogent must be
the objective justification.

3.129   In *Allonby v Accrington & Rossendale College*,[114] the claimant challenged as indirectly discriminatory on the ground of sex a decision by
her employer to terminate the contracts of all part-time lecturers and
invite them to reapply as sub-contractors. Sedley LJ emphasised the
importance of weighing the justification against the discriminatory
effect of the condition, and concluded:

> Once a finding of a condition having a disparate and adverse impact
> on women had been made, what was required was at the minimum
> a critical evaluation of whether the college's reasons demonstrated a
> real need to dismiss the applicant; if there was such a need, consid-
> eration of the seriousness of the disparate impact of the dismissal
> on women including the applicant; and an evaluation of whether the
> former were sufficient to outweigh the latter.

110 [1987] 1 ICR 110.
111 [1989] ICR 179.
112 At p 191 (Balcombe LJ).
113 [1999] ICR 859 at p870.
114 [2001] EWCA Civ 529, [2001] 1 ICR 1189.

3.130   All of the previous authorities were considered and analysed in *Hardys & Hansons v Lax*,[115] a case where the claimant's request to job-share her role was rejected. The Court of Appeal held:

> Section 1(2)(b)(ii) [SDA 1975] requires the employer to show that the proposal is justifiable irrespective of the sex of the person to whom it is applied. It must be objectively justifiable (*Barry*) and I accept that the word 'necessary' used in *Bilka* is to be qualified by the word 'reasonably'. That qualification does not, however, permit the margin of discretion or range of reasonable responses for which the appellants contend. The presence of the word 'reasonably' reflects the presence and applicability of the principle of proportionality. The employer does not have to demonstrate that no other proposal is possible. The employer has to show that the proposal, in this case for a full-time appointment, is justified objectively notwithstanding its discriminatory effect. The principle of proportionality requires the tribunal to take into account the reasonable needs of the business. But it has to make its own judgment, upon a fair and detailed analysis of the working practices and business considerations involved, as to whether the proposal is reasonably necessary.

3.131   *Bilka* excepted, the cases discussed above were all decided under the old 'objective justification' test. In *Homer* however the Supreme Court stressed the differences between the tests and the importance of considering justification by reference to whether the means adopted are:

- an appropriate means of pursuing that aim;
- reasonably necessary for the pursuit of that aim.[116]

3.132   So, under the new test used in the Act, ETs and the courts will be more willing to place emphasis on the European definition of proportionality. In *Homer* the Supreme Court referred to the judgment of Mummery LJ in *R (Elias) v Secretary of State for Defence*[117] (in fact decided under the old law), where he held that the standard of justification in indirect race discrimination cases was the *Bilka* test, and went on to set out a three-stage test: 'First, is the objective sufficiently important to justify limiting a fundamental right? Secondly, is the measure rationally connected to the objective? Thirdly, are the means chosen no more than is necessary to accomplish the objective?'

---

115 [2005] EWCA Civ 846, [2005] ICR 1565.
116 *Homer v Chief Constable of West Yorkshire Police* [2012] UKSC 15, [2012] IRLR 601, [2012] ICR 704 at paras 22–25.
117 [2006] EWCA 1293, [2006] 1 WLR 3213.

3.133   Mummery LJ's analysis was approved by Lord Mance[118] in the *JFS* case, and referred to by the EAT in *Azmi v Kirklees Metropolitan Borough Council*.[119]

3.134   In several employment cases decided before *Homer* the 'balancing reasonable needs' position had prevailed. A good example is *MacCulloch v Imperial Chemical Industries Plc*,[120] where the EAT held that ETs must weigh the reasonable needs of the undertaking against the discriminatory effect of the employer's measure, and make its own assessment of whether the former outweighs the latter. This approach was followed by subsequent divisions of the EAT in *Loxley v BAE Systems (Munitions and Ordnance) Ltd*;[121] *Seldon v Clarkson Wright & Jakes*;[122] *Pulham v London Borough of Barking and Dagenham*[123] and *HM Land Registry v Benson*.[124]

3.135   In the light of *Homer* it is clear now that ETs should adopt the European approach to proportionality An ET may be persuaded to do this by the following:[125]

- Claimants can rely on *Homer* and the comprehensive analysis of the proportionality exercise provided by the Court of Appeal in *Elias*, as endorsed by Lord Mance in the *JFS* case.
- If the legitimate aim relied upon by the employer can practically be achieved by a policy which has a less discriminatory impact than the one in fact adopted, then the more discriminatory policy will not be proportionate.[126] If the claimant can make plausible suggestions of less discriminatory policies that should defeat an employer's proportionality arguments. Claimants should therefore

118 Albeit obiter, as he held that the entry criteria adopted by JFS were directly discriminatory.

119 [2007] IRLR 484.

120 UKEAT/119/08, [2008] 1 ICR 1334 at para 10.

121 UKEAT/156/08, [2008] 1 ICR 1348 at para 22.

122 [2009] IRLR 267 at para 62 (the EAT judgment was upheld and endorsed by the Court of Appeal, [2010] EWCA Civ 899, [2011] ICR 60, although this point was not specifically addressed).

123 UKEAT/516/08, [2010] ICR 333 at paras 15 and 40.

124 UKEAT/0197/11, [2012] ICR 627, 10 February 2012 at paras 36–37.

125 Aaron Baker suggests, in his article 'Proportionality and Employment Discrimination in the UK' (2008) 37(4) *ILJ* 305–28 that it is also legitimate to put forward evidence demonstrating the degree to which other persons possessing the same characteristic as the claimant are likely to be disadvantaged. He writes that this could include evidence of the economic and psychological impacts of discrimination – for example, stress-related health problems, and reduced economic participation and social inclusion. This research may be found in sociological literature.

126 See *Homer* at para 25 and eg *Seldon* [2009] IRLR 267 at para 62.

ensure that they provide as much information as possible about alternative ways to achieve their employer's aim in their witness statements.

- Claimants can rely on the Court of Appeal judgment in *Allonby*. This stresses the importance of the extent of the disadvantage to the protected group. Claimants will normally be able to provide compelling evidence of the significant impact the discriminatory provision has had on their life.

3.136 The CJEU has also made it clear that reliance by employers on matters that are 'simply generalisations concerning certain categories of employees' will not be sufficient to constitute objective justification.[127]

3.137 Examples of justification analyses emphasising some of these aspects include:

- *Osborne Clarke Services v Purohit*:[128] The EAT held that the employer could not justify a rule under which non-EEA nationals would not be considered for training contracts simply by saying that they did not believe they would be able to obtain a work permit for such candidates. In the absence of any evidence of dialogue with the authorities, or any attempts to apply for a permit, the employer 'could not begin to establish the level of evidence that is required to prove a justification on an objective basis'.
- *MoD v DeBique*:[129] The PCP relied upon by the claimant as being discriminatory under the RRA 1976 was that she could not have a member of her extended family (her half-sister) to stay with her in the Service Families Accommodation because she was a foreign national only entitled to stay in the United Kingdom for a short period. The EAT upheld the ET's decision that the MoD should have sought a relaxation of the immigration policy, or a concession, in the claimant's case.
- *Pulham*:[130] The EAT held that in order properly to weigh the discriminatory impact of a PCP against the cost of eliminating that impact, the ET must be given sufficient information both about the discriminatory impact on the claimants, and about the alleged costs and the financial background against which the affordability of those costs falls to be judged.

---

127 See eg *Nimz v Freie und Hansestadt Hamburg* C-184/89, [1991] ECR I-297.
128 UKEAT/0305/08/ZT, [2009] IRLR 341.
129 [2010] IRLR 471.
130 [2010] ICR 333 at para 46.

3.138　The greater the discriminatory impact, the more likely it is that, even if an aim can be said to be legitimate, the price of achieving it is so disproportionate that it cannot be justified. Such impact needs to be evidenced before the ET will find against the respondent.

3.139　Because the test is objective, it is possible for an employer to show that a particular PCP is a 'proportionate means of achieving a legitimate aim' even if the particular aim relied upon at trial was not in the employer's mind at the time. However, in certain circumstances, it may be more difficult for employers to justify a PCP by reference to an aim not considered when the PCP was applied.[131] It is easy to see why this might be so: if an employer gave no thought to a particular aim at the time of imposing a PCP, he/she may well have very little evidence that can be used to show the importance of that aim at the time. It is particularly the case for a public authority which has not met its obligations under the Public Sector Equality Duties.[132]

Examples of 'proportionate means of achieving a legitimate aim'

3.140　There is some guidance on the factors ETs take into account in considering whether a particular PCP is a proportionate means of achieving a legitimate aim from case-law. Many of the following cases were decided under the old law, and each will depend very much on its own facts. The evidence of 'necessity' and 'particular disadvantage' produced to the ET by the parties will have been crucial in each case.

3.141　**Length of service:** Questions originally arose about the justifiability of using length of service as a criterion for higher pay in an equal pay context.[133] The point now frequently arises in age discrimination cases, particularly those involving redundancy schemes. In *Rolls Royce Plc v Unite the Union*,[134] the Court of Appeal held that a redundancy selection scheme which awarded one point for each year of service was a proportionate means of achieving the legitimate aim of 'the reward of loyalty and the overall desirability of achieving a stable workforce in the context of a fair process of redundancy selection'. In

---

131　See *Elias* [2006] EWCA 1293, [2006] 1 WLR 3213 at para 129 and *Starmer* [2005] IRLR 862 at para 43 and *O'Brien v Ministry of Justice* [2013] UKSC 6 at para 48.

132　See para 14.110.

133　See para 16.47.

134　[2009] EWCA Civ 387, [2010] 1 WLR 318.

so holding, the court took into account the fact that the length of service criterion was only one of many, and was not determinative.[135]

3.142   **Health and safety requirements**: Complying with health and safety requirements clearly has the potential to amount to a legitimate aim. However, in order to show that a discriminatory PCP is a proportionate means of achieving a legitimate aim, employers will need to produce clear and cogent evidence to that effect. Contrast *British Airways plc v Starmer*,[136] where the EAT held that BA had failed to prove that the claimant's request to fly at 50 per cent of full-time hours would result in any reduction in its safety standards, with *Panesar v Nestle Co Ltd*,[137] where the EAT held that the employer was justified in refusing to give Mr Panesar an interview for a job producing coffee and chocolate because he refused to shave off his beard. The employer in *Panesar* relied on the need to ensure food hygiene, but produced no evidence of a real threat to hygiene caused by beards. That case was heard in 1979: under the law as it now stands, such evidence would have to be produced (as would evidence to the effect that less discriminatory policies, eg covering the beard, would not be effective).

3.143   **Effective education of children**: In *Azmi v Kirklees Metropolitan Borough Council*,[138] the EAT held that the need to raise the educational achievements of school pupils, particularly those from minority ethnic backgrounds, many of whom had English as a second language, was a legitimate aim. The EAT also found that a policy banning face coverings (which prevented the claimant, who was a Muslim teaching assistant, from wearing her particular veil in classes taught by men, which she wished to do) was a proportionate means of achieving that aim, on the basis of evidence from the school that the claimant's communication with the children was less effective when she was wearing her veil.

3.144   **Cost considerations**: As has already been discussed above, the current state of the law is that that the simple saving of cost will not be sufficient to justify indirect discrimination.[139]

3.145   **Union negotiations**: The courts have stated in various age discrimination cases that the fact that an agreement is made with the trade unions is potentially a relevant consideration when determin-

135 See para 100.
136 [2005] IRLR 862.
137 [1980] IRLR 60.
138 [2007] 1 ICR 1154.
139 See *O'Brien v Ministry of Justice* [2013] UKSC 6 at paras 69 and 74.

ing whether treatment under that agreement is proportionate, but it cannot be determinative of the issue.[140]

3.146 **Practical points**

- Careful consideration should be given to the question of whether the PCP relied upon is so closely linked to a protected characteristic as to be indissociable or inseparable from it. This may mean that the conduct complained of amounts to direct rather than indirect discrimination. If there is any doubt, claimants should set out both forms of discrimination in their ET1 form.
- Claimants can demonstrate that the PCP puts or would put persons sharing their protected characteristic at a 'particular disadvantage' in a number of ways.
  - it may be obvious as a matter of fact;
  - the risk of disadvantage may be something that can be deduced from the PCP itself ("intrinsically liable to disadvantage");
  - statistics from the claimant's workplace may demonstrate a particular disadvantage;
  - if there are no such statistics, other evidence such as national statistics, academic or other research, expert or witness evidence may help.
- If the 'particular disadvantage' to the relevant group is likely to be disputed, claimants should try to obtain supportive evidence from as many of these different sources as possible.
- Respondents may seek to justify a potentially discriminatory PCP by reference to a very narrowly defined 'legitimate aim', which can only be achieved using that PCP. In such circumstances it may be open to claimants to argue:
  - that this is not the true aim pursued by the respondent; or alternatively
  - that the aim is only achievable by disproportionate means, and therefore cannot be justified.
- Respondents can not justify an indirectly discriminatory PCP solely because it will make cost savings.
- Respondents may try to argue that what looks like a budgetary justification for a PCP is in fact something else (for example, that the PCP is to prevent undeserved windfalls, or to ensure fairness

within the workforce as a whole). Claimants should encourage tribunals to give very careful scrutiny to such arguments, which may be an attempt to evade the prohibition on 'cost' justifications.

- In considering whether the means used to achieve the Respondent's aim are proportionate, close scrutiny of the following aspects is necessary:
  - Are the adopted means appropriate to achieve the aim?
  - Are they reasonably necessary to achieve that aim?
- An argument that a particular PCP is not a proportionate means of achieving a legitimate aim is more likely to be successful if claimants can:
  - provide examples of less discriminatory ways of achieving the same aim;
  - produce convincing evidence that the PCP will have a serious impact on them and others with their protected characteristic, which is out of proportion to any benefit to their employer.
  -

CHAPTER 4

Disability discrimination

continued

> ## Key points
> - A claimant does not have to have a disability to bring a claim of direct discrimination because of disability or harassment because of disability
> - Indirect discrimination now extends to the protected characteristic of disability
> - Discrimination arising from disability and the duty to make reasonable adjustments can be claimed only by disabled people
> - There is an overarching duty to make reasonable adjustments contained in section 20 of the Act and the detail of the duty is contained in Schedule 8

4.1   This chapter considers two types of discrimination that are specific to disability – discrimination arising from disability and the duty to make reasonable adjustments. Before considering these in detail, however, the chapter explains the concepts of direct and indirect discrimination in the context of disability.

Background

4.2   The precursor legislation, the Disability Discrimination Act (DDA) 1995 did not initially contain a concept of direct discrimination.[1] It was recognised that disability was in many ways 'different' and that a different approach was required to tackle some of the most common forms of discrimination based on disability. What was then known as 'disability related discrimination'[2] was capable of covering direct discrimination, but it could be justified.

4.3   The DDA 1995 was amended in 2004 so as to provide for direct discrimination that was not subject to justification.[3] Such little case-law as there was is clearly relevant for the purposes of direct disability discrimination under the EqA 2010. The provisions are essentially the same.

---

1   Unlike eg the Race Relations Act 1976 and the Sex Discrimination Act 1975.
2   DDA 1995 s3(1).
3   To ensure compliance with Employment Framework Directive 2000/78.

The legislative provisions

4.4   The definition of direct discrimination is contained in section 13 of the EqA 2010.[4] A person, A, discriminates against another if, because of disability, A treats B less favourably than A treats or would treat others. The phrase 'because of' covers treatment based on, for example, an association with a disabled person.[5] It also applies where an individual is treated less favourably because an employer perceives them to have a disability. The courts will, in due course, have to address the argument that such a person would not have to show that they are a disabled person under the section 6 test of the EqA 2010. It was raised in *J v DLA Piper*[6] where the EAT allowed the appeal on other grounds, offering little support for this argument. However, given the general position that 'because of' in section 13 does include perceived characteristics, the courts will have to give greater consideration to the argument in cases under the Act.

4.5   Section 23 of the EqA 2010 contains the comparator provisions for direct discrimination, stating that there must be no material difference between the circumstances relating to each case. Thus the treatment of the claimant must be compared with that of an actual or hypothetical comparator who does not share the same protected characteristic as the claimant but who is or is assumed to be in not materially different circumstances from the claimant. However, note that where the claimant is a disabled person, those circumstances include their respective abilities. This mirrors the provision in the DDA 1995 and cases under the DDA provisions, such as *Aylott v Stockton on Tees Borough Council*[7] and *High Quality Lifestyles v Watts*[8] will remain pertinent to any questions arising in relation to direct disability discrimination.

4.6   Although this has not been examined in great detail in the case-law, it seems likely that the specific reference to 'abilities' is intended to make clear that where the abilities themselves are directly referable to the disability, they must nevertheless be present in the comparator for the purposes of this type of discrimination. So that where the disability is the cause of an inability to do a particular job, that

---

4 See chapter 2.
5 *Coleman v Attridge Law* UKEAT/0071/09/JOJ.
6 [2010] IRLR 936.
7 [2010] IRLR 994.
8 [2006] IRLR 850.

inability, though directly related to the protected characteristic, must necessarily be present in the comparator.[9]

4.7   This does mean that direct discrimination in relation to disability is a relatively narrow type of discrimination. Anything outside of this would fall within the sphere of discrimination arising from disability – meaning that it will be open to justification.

4.8   EqA 2010 s6, which deals with the protected characteristic of disability, makes it clear that the protected characteristic is a particular disability. Section 13(3) makes it clear that non-disabled people cannot bring a claim based on more favourable treatment of a disabled person. Together these clarify that a person with a particular disability may bring a claim based on less favourable treatment as compared to someone with a different disability. Thus someone with a mental illness, who experiences stigma attached to their impairment that people with other impairments may not experience, may compare themselves to those other persons with different disabilities.

4.9   Direct discrimination arises most commonly in cases of obvious prejudice, or, more often, where assumptions are made about abilities without an individual consideration of the person. In the case of disability, those assumptions may prove to be correct[10] – but that does not affect whether or not there has been disability discrimination. For example, an employer receives an application from an individual with epilepsy to do a job that involves climbing up telegraph poles. On seeing that the applicant has epilepsy, the employer refuses to even consider interviewing him, even though he appears to be appropriately qualified and meets the shortlisting criteria. This would clearly be a case of direct discrimination. Even if it turned out, on examination, that he could not do a fundamental part of the job, that would be relevant only to damages.

4.10   If there is any doubt it is sensible to set out a claim for direct disability discrimination and for discrimination arising from disability.

---

9   The Employment Code at para 3.29 makes clear that an appropriate comparator will be a person who does not have the person with a disability's impairment but who has the same abilities or skills as that person (regardless of whether those abilities or skills arise from the disability itself). It gives the example (at para 3.30) of a man with arthritis, who types at 30 wpm and is rejected for a typing job. The comparator is a person without arthritis but with the same wpm and accuracy. If the person with the disability in that case was unable to lift heavy weights (not a requirement of the typing job) it would not be necessary to find a comparator who also could not lift heavy weights.

10   See on the issue of assumptions, validity and direct discrimination the case of *European Roman Rights Centre v Immigration Officer at Prague Airport* [2004] UKHL 55: a stereotype remains a stereotype even if true of some of the group.

Following disclosure, or replies to requests for further information, it may be advisable to discontinue the direct discrimination claim and focus instead on defeating any justification argument on discrimination arising from disability.

Indirect discrimination

4.11   The DDA contained no concept of indirect discrimination as the Government felt that discrimination arising from disability and the application of the duty to make reasonable adjustments combined to cover this form of discrimination. However, Directive 2000/78 applied indirect discrimination to disability.[11]

4.12   As one of the stated Government aims of the Act , however, was harmonisation of the legislation so far as possible indirect discrimination was applied to disability.[12]

The legislative provisions

4.13   Section 19 of the EqA 2010 contains the definition of indirect discrimination. For the purposes of disability discrimination, the section states:

(1) A person (A) discriminates against another (B) if A applies to B a provision, criterion or practice which is discriminatory in relation to a relevant protected characteristic of B's.

(2) For the purpose of subsection (1), a provision, criterion or practice is discriminatory in relation to a relevant protected characteristic of B's if –

(a) A applies, or would apply, it to persons with whom B does not share the characteristic;

(b) it puts, or would put, persons with whom B shares the characteristic at a particular disadvantage when compared with persons with whom B does not share it;

(c) it puts, or would put, B at that disadvantage, and

(d) A cannot show it to be a proportionate means of achieving a legitimate aim.

4.14   EqA 2010 s19(2)(b) requires a claimant to show that the relevant PCP 'puts or would put persons with whom [he/she] shares the [protected characteristic] at a particular disadvantage when compared with persons with whom [he/she] does not share it'. In undertaking that com-

11   See Directive 2000/78, Art 2(2)(b)(ii).
12   See chapter 3 for indirect discrimination.

parative exercise, an ET must ensure that it is comparing like with like.[13]

4.15   EqA 2010 s23 – the provision regarding comparators – also applies to indirect discrimination . As set out above, it provides: 'On a comparison of cases for the purposes of section 13, 14 or 19 there must be no material difference between the circumstances relating to each case ...'.

4.16   The application of a pool-based comparator requirement in relation to disability has the potential to create difficulties. For example, in considering a 'no dogs' requirement that prevents disabled people with assistance dogs from entering a building, is the pool of people who can comply with the condition exclusive or inclusive of those who have dogs but who are not disabled? If the comparison is to be like with like, is it then with people who have dogs, but who are not disabled?

4.17   The new approach to indirect discrimination overcomes this difficulty if it can be shown that the PCP is intrinsically liable to disadvantage a group of people due, for example, to the normal behaviour of that group. Thus a person with a disability who requires the help of an assistance dog is intrinsically liable to be disadvantaged by a ban on dogs. It is not necessary to reach the stage of considering a pool-based comparison.[14]

4.18   Also given, however, that there is no requirement, as in the direct discrimination provisions, for the comparison to include the abilities of the disabled person it is arguable that any abilities, or similarly disabilities, of the disabled person must be disregarded, and thus the comparison must be with people who do not have a dog for disability-related reasons.

4.19   Indirect discrimination and the duty to make reasonable adjustments can frequently overlap. However, note there is a knowledge requirement for the duty to make reasonable adjustments to apply that does not apply in relation to indirect discrimination cases. This is likely to be particularly useful in recruitment cases, where there is often no knowledge of disability (particularly given the provisions of section 60 prohibiting disability enquiries pre-employment).[15]

4.20   Where for example, an employer in a recruitment context applies a provision criterion or practice of full attendance in order for an application to be shortlisted, it could be argued that the PCP of having full

13 See chapter 3.
14 See paras 3.18–3.30.
15 See paras 9.62–9.67

attendance places disabled people at a particular disadvantage and thus that there is potential indirect discrimination, dependent upon any justification advanced. Knowledge of disability is irrelevant for the purposes of indirect discrimination. In contrast, knowledge is relevant to reasonable adjustments. Even though it may be possible to argue that once absence had been identified an employer ought reasonably to have made enquiries and so been expected to know of the disability, triggering the duty, there would undoubtedly be legal argument over this. An indirect discrimination claim, however, would avoid this.

4.21   So far as justification is concerned, the same principles will apply in relation to disability as are outlined below under discrimination arising from disability, given that the same justification applies.

Discrimination arising from disability

Background

4.22   The DDA contained three types of discrimination direct, disability-related and failure to make reasonable adjustments.

4.23   Disability-related discrimination was initially interpreted broadly. In *Clark v Novacold Ltd*[16] the ET and, subsequently, the EAT held that the comparator for the purposes of less favourable treatment, in an ill-health dismissal case, would be someone with the same amount of time off but who did not have a disability. The Court of Appeal overturned the decision of the EAT, holding that the correct comparator is someone to whom the 'reason' for less favourable treatment does not apply'. If a disabled employee is dismissed because of being unable to do a particular job, the treatment should be compared with treatment afforded to a person who does not have the disability and therefore can do the job rather than a person who cannot do the job but does not have a disability.

4.24   *Clark* was disapproved in the case of *Lewisham London Borough v Malcolm*[17] when the House of Lords held that the comparator for the purposes of disability-related discrimination was in essence the same as that for direct discrimination.

---

16   [1999] ICR 951.
17   [2008] UKHL 43, [2008] 1 AC 1399, [2008] IRLR 700.

4.25   The Government then issued a consultation paper[18] in which it examined options to in effect reinstate the pre-*Malcolm* approach to disability-related discrimination. This led to a completely new provision in the Act, which is detailed below.

The legislative provisions

4.26   EqA 2010 s15 only applies to a 'disabled person'. Discrimination arising from disability in section 15 requires the ET to consider the following:

> (1) A person (A) discriminates against a disabled person (B) if –
>   (a) A treats B unfavourably because of something arising in consequence of B's disability, and
>   (b) A cannot show that the treatment is a proportionate means of achieving a legitimate aim.
> (2) Subsection (1) does not apply if A shows that A did not know, and could not reasonably expected to know, that B had the disability.

4.27   Section 15 makes it clear that the provision is intended to (a) have no comparator and (b) capture treatment which was in essence 'related to' as opposed to based directly upon, the disability.[19]

Unfavourably

4.28   The case-law under the DDA 1995 prior to *Malcolm* is likely to be illustrative in relation to some of the concepts contained in discrimination arising from disability.

4.29   Firstly, a claimant will need to show that they have been treated 'unfavourably'. The language deliberately does not state 'less favourable' as this would automatically invite a comparison. It is likely to be relatively easy to show this part of the definition.

4.30   The Employment Code states at para 5.7 of the term 'unfavourably':

> For discrimination arising from disability to occur, a disabled person must have been treated 'unfavourably'. This means that he or she must have been put at a disadvantage. Often, the disadvantage will be obvious and it will be clear that the treatment has been

---

18 *Improving Protection from Disability Discrimination* (Office of Disability Issues, November 2008).

19 The wording of the Act was changed to ensure these effects: see House of Commons Public Bill Committee on the Equality Bill Session 2008–09, col 275 (17 June 2009) Solicitor-General, which may be cited if an ET or court is satisfied that the legislation is ambiguous and the statement satisfies the criteria in *Pepper v Hart* [1993] AC 593 at p 640C.

unfavourable; for example, a person may have been refused a job, denied a work opportunity or dismissed from their employment. But sometimes unfavourable treatment may be less obvious. Even if an employer thinks that they are acting in the best interests of a disabled person, they may still treat that person unfavourably.

In consequence of

4.31   Secondly, a claimant will need to show that this treatment is because of something arising in consequence of their disability. 'In consequence of their disability' has the potential to be very broad, and it is likely that some of the case-law on disability-related discrimination will be useful in this regard. Perhaps the broadest interpretation of disability-related discrimination appeared in the case of *Murphy v (1) Slough Borough Council and (2) Governing Body of Langley Wood School*.[20] Ms Murphy had been advised not to have children because of her disability and had a child by a surrogate mother. She asked for paid leave following the birth of the child. The EAT overturned an ET's decision that the refusal of paid leave was not less favourable treatment for a reason related to disability, but concluded the treatment was justified because of the financial position of the school. The main feature in the case was whether the school or the LEA was the proper respondent, as this would impact on the question of justification. The EAT concluded it was the school.

4.32   The most common scenarios will be sickness absence as a consequence of disability; reduced earning capacity; and performance-related issues.

4.33   The Employment Code of Practice says:[21]

> The consequences of a disability include anything which is the result, effect or outcome of a disabled person's disability. The consequences will be varied, and will depend on the individual effect upon a disabled person of their disability. Some consequences may be obvious, such as an inability to walk unaided or inability to use certain work equipment. Others may not be obvious, for example, having to follow a restricted diet.

4.34   The example given in the Code is as follows:

> **Example:** A woman is disciplined for losing her temper at work. However, this behaviour was out of character and is a result of severe pain caused by cancer, of which her employer is aware. The disciplinary action is unfavourable treatment. This treatment is because

20   EAT/1157/02, 26 May 2004.
21   At para 5.9.

of something which arises in consequence of the worker's disability, namely her loss of temper. There is a connection between the 'something' (that is, the loss of temper) that led to the treatment and her disability. It will be discrimination arising from disability if the employer cannot objectively justify the decision to discipline the worker.

Justification

4.35   The respondent must show that the treatment of the person with the disability is a proportionate means of achieving a legitimate aim. This means that it must be an appropriate and reasonably necessary means of achieving that aim. The case-law on justification of disability-related discrimination, which had a low threshold for justification ('material and substantial reason'[22]), shed no light on justification under the Act and should not be relied upon as the trigger concepts are entirely different.

4.36   The new test is the same test as applies in relation to indirect discrimination.[23] The principles do not need to be repeated here, but note that the treatment must be justified against a background of interference with fundamental rights including the rights set out in the UN Convention on the Rights of Persons with Disabilities.[24]

4.37   Paragraph 5.21 of the Employment Code states that if an employer has failed to make a reasonable adjustment that would have prevented or minimised the unfavourable treatment, it will be very difficult for them to show that the treatment was objectively justified. Similarly if the employer is a public authority and subject to the public sector equality duty in EqA 2010 s149, it will be very difficult for it to justify treatment where it has not satisfied the requirement to have due regard to the equality objectives set out in that section in the exercise of its functions as an employer.[25]

Knowledge

4.38   There will be no discrimination arising from disability if the employer shows that he did not know or could not reasonably be expected to know of the disabled person's disability.[26] The introduction of this

---

22 See eg *Jones v Post Office* [2001] ICR 805.
23 For which see paras 3.104–3.145.
24 See chapter 19.
25 See chapter 16 and para 3.18.
26 EqA 2010 s15(2).

requirement settles the debate in cases such as *Heinz v Kenrick*,[27] *Taylor v OCS Group Ltd*[28] and *Malcolm*,[29] where their Lordships made varying comments about knowledge of disability: all agreed that some knowledge was required, but the degree of knowledge, and knowledge of precisely what, was not agreed upon.

4.39   The burden of proving the section 15(2) defence is on the employer. The employer must show therefore both that it did not know that the disabled person had the disability in question and that it could not reasonably have been expected to know that the disabled person had the disability. However, it seems unlikely that the employer would have to show that they did not know that the person satisfied the definition under the EqA 2010 (ie that a particular impairment amounts to a disability).The defence will not be available if the employer knows that an individual has an impairment, or ought reasonably to be expected to know. In practice the employer should make enquiries where it is possible that a disability may be a factor in particular behaviour – for example in a disciplinary situation.

4.40   The employer has no defence if it has knowledge of the disability. The defence is therefore much narrower than that an employer may rely upon in relation to the duty to make reasonable adjustments. There the employer can rely on proving a lack of knowledge of the consequences of the disability, or any adverse impact to which the disabled person may be put as a consequence of the disability. However, those factors are irrelevant under section 15. So long as an employer knows of the disability, or ought reasonably to know about it, it will have no defence under section 15(2) of the EqA 2010.

4.41   The Employment Code makes the point very clear:[30]

> An employer must do all they can reasonably be expected to do to find out if a worker has a disability. What is reasonable will depend on the circumstances. This is an objective assessment. When making enquiries about disability, employers should consider issues of dignity and privacy and ensure that personal information is dealt with confidentially.

4.42   Where an employer's agent or employee (such as an occupational health adviser or an HR officer) knows, in that capacity, of a worker's or applicant's or potential applicant's disability, the employer will not usually be able to claim that they do not know of the disability, and

27 [2000] IRLR 144.
28 [2006] IRLR 613.
29 [2008] UKHL 43, [2008] 1 AC 1399, [2008] IRLR 700.
30 At para 5.15.

that they cannot therefore have subjected a disabled person to discrimination arising from disability.[31]

4.43   Discrimination arising from disability will overlap with the duty to make reasonable adjustments – and to some extent with indirect discrimination. So it is sensible to set out all these types of discrimination in the claim form to the ET. This is particularly the case where knowledge is likely to be an issue. Care must be taken to review on a regular basis whether it is appropriate to continue with a claim for a number of different types of discrimination (if they involve producing very different evidence), or whether in fact the same result will be obtained whatever type is claimed.

The duty to make reasonable adjustments

4.44   The duty to make reasonable adjustments remains the key to disability equality in the EqA 2010 as it was in the DDA 1995. Only a person with a disability may require reasonable adjustments to be made. The law has been made consistent across all the fields of operation of the Act. Those familiar with reasonable adjustments in employment cases will find that the changes to the duty are relatively minor in that context. They are unlikely to result in a different outcome from that which would have been achieved under the DDA.

The legislative provisions

4.45   Section 20 of the EqA 2010 sets out the overarching duty to make reasonable adjustments. It takes the form of a set of three requirements.

20 Duty to make adjustments
> (1) Where this Act imposes a duty to make reasonable adjustments on a person, this section, sections 21 and 22 and the applicable Schedule apply; and for those purposes, a person on whom the duty is imposed is referred to as A.
> (2) The duty comprises the following three requirements.
> (3) The first requirement is a requirement, where a provision, criterion or practice of A's puts a disabled person at a substantial disadvantage in relation to a relevant matter in comparison with persons who are not disabled, to take such steps as it is reasonable to have to take to avoid the disadvantage.

---

31 Employment Code para 5.17.

(4) The second requirement is a requirement, where a physical feature puts a disabled person at a substantial disadvantage in relation to a relevant matter in comparison with persons who are not disabled, to take such steps as it is reasonable to have to take to avoid the disadvantage.

(5) The third requirement is a requirement, where a disabled person would, but for the provision of an auxiliary aid, be put at a substantial disadvantage in relation to a relevant matter in comparison with persons who are not disabled, to take such steps as it is reasonable to have to take to provide the auxiliary aid.

(6) Where the first or third requirement relates to the provision of information, the steps which it is reasonable for A to have to take include steps for ensuring that in the circumstances concerned the information is provided in an accessible format.

(7) A person (A) who is subject to a duty to make reasonable adjustments is not (subject to express provision to the contrary) entitled to require a disabled person, in relation to whom A is required to comply with the duty, to pay to any extent A's costs of complying with the duty.

(8) A reference in section 21 or 22 or an applicable Schedule to the first, second or third requirement is to be construed in accordance with this section.

(9) In relation to the second requirement, a reference in this section or an applicable Schedule to avoiding a substantial disadvantage includes a reference to –

(a) removing the physical feature in question,

(b) altering it, or

(c) providing a reasonable means of avoiding it.

(10) A reference in this section, section 21 or 22 or an applicable Schedule (apart from paragraphs 2 to 4 of Schedule 4) to a physical feature is a reference to –

(a) a feature arising from the design or construction of a building,

(b) a feature of an approach to, exit from or access to a building,

(c) a fixture or fitting, or furniture, furnishings, materials, equipment or other chattels, in or on premises, or

(d) any other physical element or quality.

(11) A reference in this section, section 21 or 22 or an applicable Schedule to an auxiliary aid includes a reference to an auxiliary service.

(12) A reference in this section or an applicable Schedule to chattels is to be read, in relation to Scotland, as a reference to moveable property.

(13) The applicable Schedule is, in relation to the Part of this Act specified in the first column of the Table, the Schedule specified in the second column.

21 Failure to comply with duty

(1) A failure to comply with the first, second or third requirement is a failure to comply with a duty to make reasonable adjustments.

(2) A discriminates against a disabled person if A fails to comply with that duty in relation to that person.

4.46   The detail of the application of the duty in relation to work is contained in Schedule 8 to the EqA 2010. Employers must comply with the first (PCP adjustment) second (physical feature adjustment) and third requirement (provision of auxiliary aid) contained in section 20.[32]

4.47   Note that the PCP must be applied by or on behalf of the employer.[33] It is only in respect of physical premises occupied by the employer that the duty to make reasonable adjustments to physical features applies.

4.48   In relation to deciding to whom to offer employment the adjustments to be considered are to PCPs for determining to whom employment should be offered, as well as auxiliary aids and services. Adjustments to physical features are not relevant here as a prospective employer will not be obliged to alter a physical feature for an interview: they may, however, need to adjust a practice of holding interviews in inaccessible premises.[34]

4.49   At first sight it may appear that there is an argument that 'employment by A' includes recruitment because duties are owed to applicants for that employment. However, 'employment by A' is what is to be adjusted ('a relevant matter') and applicants for employment by A can ask for adjustments to be made to the employment itself, rather than the interview process for determining to whom that employment is offered.

4.50   The full range of adjustments is applicable to employees.

Trigger for the duty

4.51   We consider the concepts of 'provision criterion or practice', 'physical feature' and 'auxiliary aid' below[35] In relation to those matters there is a common trigger. The trigger for the duty is that there

---

32   EqA 2010 Sch 8 para 2(1).

33   EqA 2010 Sch 8 para 2(2). It is likely that the concept of PCP will cover all arrangements made by or on behalf of the employer. However, it will not extend to matters relating to personal needs: *Kenny v Hampshire Constabulary* [1999] ICR 27, [1999] IRLR 76, unless it can be argued that an auxiliary aid is reasonably needed (an argument not open to Mr Kenny).

34   This is the effect of EqA 2010 Sch 8 para 2(3) and (4).

35   See paras 4.73–4.78.

must be 'substantial disadvantage' in comparison with persons who are not disabled (and it must be in relation to a relevant matter[36]). 'Substantial' means more than minor or trivial.[37] The threshold that must be met in order for the duty to be triggered is accordingly low and accords with the reasonable accommodation provision in Directive 2000/78,[38] which refers to reasonable accommodation where required in a particular case.

Comparison

4.52   The comparison for the purposes of the reasonable adjustment duty is not the same as that required in direct or indirect discrimination. EqA 2010 s23, which sets out the requirements for comparative circumstances in relation to direct and indirect discrimination, does not apply to the duty to make reasonable adjustments.[39]

4.53   There does have to be some comparison made, though, given the wording of the provisions. The comparison should be made between the disabled person and those who are in not materially different circumstances to the claimant. The proper comparator can only be identified with regard to the disadvantage caused by, for example, the PCP in issue. In *Archibald v Fife Council*[40] the House of Lords asked what is the substantial disadvantage that the disabled person suffers by comparison with persons who are not disabled? The requirement cannot be to perform the essential functions of the job, because that is placed on everyone who holds the job. However, the terms of a disabled person's contract of employment do not mean that, once the disabled person becomes disabled, she is forced to perform the essential functions of her job despite being unfit to do so. If an employee becomes so disabled that she cannot perform the essential functions of her job under her contract of employment, she is liable to be dismissed. This is what the House identified as the substantial disadvantage suffered in *Archibald*'s case. They identified the arrangement (PCP) as the contractual term, whether express or implied, which provides for her dismissal in these circumstances. That arrangement places the disabled person at a substantial disadvantage by comparison with persons who are not disabled, because

36   Ie deciding to whom to offer employment and employment (EqA 2010 Sch 8 para 5(1), table).
37   EqA 2010 s212(5).
38   Article 5.
39   EqA 2010 s23(1).
40   [2004] UKHL 32, [2004] IRLR 65, [2004] ICR 954.

she is liable to be dismissed on the ground of disability whereas they are not.

4.54   The appropriate comparators in *Archibald* were therefore other employees of the employer who are not disabled, can therefore carry out the essential functions of their jobs and are, accordingly, not liable to be dismissed on the ground of disability.

4.55   On the basis of this reasoning, the Court of Appeal in *Smith v Churchills Stairlifts plc*[41] held that the proper comparator is readily identified by reference to the disadvantage caused by the relevant arrangements.[42] This means that the proper comparator in a reasonable adjustment case will be the non-disabled persons who are subject to the PCP but not disadvantaged thereby because they do not suffer the disadvantage suffered by the disabled person as a result of the application of the PCP.

4.56   *Walters v Fareham College Corporation*[43] illustrates the application of the principles most helpfully.

4.57   Ms Walters, a lecturer, became unwell and was absent because of sickness in February 2006. At an absence meeting, in July, she said she wanted to return to work on a phased basis. Her employer said a further report would be obtained, and there would be another meeting. The occupational health report produced for the second meeting suggested that she might be able to consider a phased return to work in September, but that it was unlikely that she would be fit to return to her full role/hours before the beginning of 2007.

4.58   W was informed that dismissal was one of the options to be considered at a further meeting in September at which the employer learned she had been diagnosed with fibromyalgia. They discussed the possibility of her returning to work in January 2007 on a part-time basis, but the decision was then taken to dismiss W. She brought a complaint before the ET of disability discrimination on the grounds of failure to make reasonable adjustments and disability-related discrimination.

4.59   The employer, on appeal alleged that the ET erred in finding failure to make reasonable adjustments, as it had failed properly to consider the correct comparative exercise.

4.60   The EAT held that when considering a breach of the duty to make adjustments, there were circumstances in which it would not be

41 [2005] EWCA Civ 1220, [2006] ICR 524, [2006] IRLR 41.
42 At para 40.
43 [2009] IRLR 991.

necessary for the ET to identify the non-disabled comparators. The EAT said:[44]

> In many cases the facts would speak for themselves and the identity of the non-disabled comparators would be clearly discernible from the provision, criterion or practice found to be in play. The more general comparative exercise required in a reasonable adjustments claim, involving a class or group of non-disabled comparators, differed from that which was understood and applied in the individual, like for like comparison required in cases of direct sex or race discrimination or in disability-related discrimination claims.

4.61 It had not been necessary for the employee to satisfy the ET that someone who did not have a disability but whose circumstances were otherwise the same as hers would have been treated differently. To hold otherwise would defeat the purpose of the disability discrimination legislation.[45]

4.62 It is important to ensure that the factors relating to the comparators are properly identified, because it is a question of fact for the ET.[46] This means that it is difficult to overturn an adverse finding by appealing to the EAT.

4.63 Whether there is a substantial disadvantage can be tested by reference to PCPs, physical features and (under the Act) auxiliary aids.[47] Thus in deciding which part of EqA 2010 s20 applies, careful analysis of the impact of each of these aspects is required. However, in identifying the disadvantage, the ET (and therefore the claimant) needs to be precise. It must be a disadvantage that is identifiable and substantial and must be in comparison with persons who are not disabled. It is not enough for the ET to identify a disadvantage in general non-comparative terms.[48]

Knowledge – the respondent's defence

4.64 There is a defence for the employer (A) in the following terms, all of which must be established by the employer (A):[49]

> (1) A is not subject to a duty to make reasonable adjustments if A does not know, and could not reasonably be expected to know –

44 [2005] EWCA Civ 1220, [2006] ICR 524, [2006] IRLR 41 at paras 56–57.
45 At paras 58–59.
46 *Cave v Goodwin* [2001] EWCA Civ 391.
47 See *Environment Agency v Rowan* [2008] ICR 218.
48 *RBS v Ashton* [2011] ICR 632.
49 See EqA 2010 Sch 8 Part 3 para 20.

(a) in the case of an applicant or potential applicant, that an interested disabled person is or may be an applicant for the work in question;

(b) [in any case referred to in Part 2 of this Schedule], that an interested disabled person has a disability and is likely to be placed at the disadvantage referred to in the first, second or third requirement.

4.65   In the case of (b) logically this defence appears to operate as follows:

- If the employer can show that it did not know either
  - that the claimant was a disabled person, or
  - that the claimant would be substantially disadvantaged compared to non-disabled persons then
- the employer must go on to show that it could not not reasonably be expected to know
  - that the claimant was a disabled person, or
  - that the employer would be substantially disadvantaged compared to non-disabled persons.

The case-law interpreting the same provision under the DDA 1995[50] applies to paragraph 20 of Schedule 8.

4.66   The EAT held in *Eastern & Coastal Kent PCT v Grey*[51] that the employer must prove each of the following component parts of the defence:

- A did not know that the disabled person has a disability;
- A did not know that the disabled person is likely to be at a substantial disadvantage compared with persons who are not disabled;
- A could not reasonably be expected to know that the disabled person had a disability; and
- A could not reasonably be expected to know that the disabled person is likely to be placed at a substantial disadvantage in comparison with persons who are not disabled.

4.67   This appeared to mean that once an employer had knowledge – or imputed knowledge – of a disability, they could be liable for a failure to make reasonable adjustments, even if they had no idea of the individual effect that it might have.

4.68   The EAT in *Secretary of State for Work and Pensions v Alam*[52] disagreed with *Eastern and Coastal Kent PCT*. It cannot be taken to be

50   DDA 1995 s4A(3).

51   [2009] IRLR 429.

52   [2010] ICR 655, [2010] IRLR 283.

authority for the proposition that an employer cannot benefit from the defence unless it proves all of the points in para 4.66 above.

4.69   The EAT analysed the test in the following questions:

- The actual knowledge question: Did the employer know both that the employee was disabled and that his disability was liable to place the employee at a substantial disadvantage compared to non-disabled persons? If the answer to that question is: 'no' then there is a second question, namely,
- The deemed knowledge question: Ought the employer to have known both that the employee was disabled and that his disability was liable to place the employee at a substantial disadvantage compared to non-disabled persons?

4.70   If the answer to that second question is 'no', then the defence is established and there is no duty to make reasonable adjustments. If the answer is yes to either, then the defence fails and the employer must show that the adjustments would not have been reasonable in all the circumstances of the case.

4.71   It is suggested that *Alam* is plainly the better decision, and is in keeping with the aim and language of both Acts.

Nature of the duty

4.72   The breadth of the duty to make adjustments was set out authoritatively in the House of Lords case of *Archibald v Fife Council*.[53] These are set out most clearly in Baroness Hale's judgment.[54] In essence:

- Consider what the employer's arrangements (PCPs) are.
- Do they place the disabled person at a substantial disadvantage compared to non-disabled persons?
- The steps should be aimed at preventing the substantial disadvantaged identified.
- The duty is to take such steps as it is reasonable in all the circumstances of the case for the employer to have to take. To the extent that the duty to make reasonable adjustments requires it, the employer is not only permitted, but obliged to treat a disabled person more favourably than others.

We will now discuss these elements. It is important always to analyse the case in accordance with these steps. Much of the danger for an ET in reasonable adjustment cases lies in failing to analyse precisely

53   [2004] ICR 954.
54   At paras 62–68.

what the substantial disadvantage to the particular disabled person may be and in failing to think of the adjustments relative to that disadvantage[55] rather than considering disadvantage in more generalised terms.

'Provision criterion or practice'

4.73 The words 'provision criterion or practice' (PCP) cover the way in which a workplace or work is organised. The Employment Code says that the phrase 'provision, criterion or practice' should be construed widely so as to include, for example, any formal or informal policies, rules, practices, arrangements or qualifications including one-off decisions and actions.[56]

4.74   Examples of PCPs include requirements to:

- work certain hours;
- carry out a particular type of work;
- work in a particular way, using a particular piece of machinery or software (for example a requirement to read standard print);
- work at a particular location.

In *Newcastle Upon Tyne Hospitals NHS Foundation Trust v Bagley*[57] the EAT suggested that the mishandling of a disabled person's application for an allowance from the NHS Pensions Agency, delaying it by several months, did not amount to a PCP but simply a recitation of what happened. So even if the concept of PCP is very broad it will not apply to everything done by the employer. It suggests that there must be something more to it. It must be capable of being described as a 'practice' at the least, it is suggested.

Auxiliary aids and services

4.75 It is worth considering, in any case, whether what is being sought by way of a reasonable adjustment should in fact be sought by way of an auxiliary aid. Employers' (and advisers') thinking tends to be less well developed on this aspect of reasonable adjustments because they were not specifically referred to in the DDA 1995 in relation to employment. However, in practice they are often the appropriate means of overcoming a disadvantage caused by a PCP.

---

55 See *Newcastle upon Tyne Hospitals NHS Foundation Trust v Bagley* UKEAT/0417/11 and *Royal Bank of Scotland v Ashton* [2011] ICR 632.

56 Employment Code para 6.10. See also para 4.5.

57 UKEAT/0417/11.

4.76 The Employment Code defines an auxiliary aid as something that provides support or assistance to a disabled person. It can include provision of a specialist piece of equipment such as an adapted keyboard or text-to-speech software. Auxiliary aids include auxiliary services;[58] for example provision of a sign language interpreter or a support worker for a disabled worker.[59]

4.77 In addition to the examples given in the Code, it may also require the provision of information in alternative formats,[60] extra training and support – including disability equality training. These examples illustrate the breadth of the concept and are not intended to place any limitation on it. What is important is the aim of the aid or service. Does it provide support or assistance to the disabled person and, but for the provision of that auxiliary aid, would the disabled person be put at a substantial disadvantage in comparison with persons who are not disabled?

Physical features

4.78 Physical features are defined for the purposes of the duty to make reasonable adjustments:[61]

- a feature arising from the design or construction of a building;
- a feature of an approach to, exit from or access to a building;
- a fixture or fitting, or furniture, furnishings, materials, equipment or other chattels, in or on premises; or
- any other physical element or quality.

They will include include steps, stairways, kerbs, exterior surfaces and paving, parking areas, building entrances and exits (including emergency escape routes), internal and external doors, gates, toilet and washing facilities, lighting and ventilation, lifts and escalators, floor coverings, signs, furniture and temporary or moveable items.[62] Thus the Employment Code gives the example of clear glass doors in a workplace presenting a substantial disadvantage to a worker with a visual impairment. Note that the feature must be one of premises occupied by the employer before the duty arises.[63] An approach to a building occupied exclusively by the landlord over which the

---

58 EqA 2010 s20(11).
59 Employment Code para 6.13.
60 EqA 2010 s20(6).
61 EqA 2010 s20(10).
62 Employment Code para 6.12.
63 EqA 2010 Sch 8 para 2.

employer simply has a right of entry would not give rise to a duty in the employer to make adjustments to that approach.

What steps might have to be taken?

4.79   The EqA 2010 does not set out a list of examples of the sorts of steps that may need to be taken under the provisions. It is clear, however, that the examples in DDA 1995 s18(1)(b) remain pertinent as the Employment Code repeats them in the main. It gives examples of potential adjustments, and illustrates these with factual examples. The point of the examples is to give a sense of how the duty operates in practice, so that the employer should not be able to rely on the fact that some adjustments does not explicitly appear in the Code. It is enough if the suggested adjustment is similar to them, in the sense of being capable of achieving the objectives of reasonable adjustments. The Code sets out the following:

- making adjustments to premises;
- providing information in accessible formats;
- allocating some of the disabled person's duties to another worker;
- transferring the disabled worker to fill an existing vacancy;[64]
- altering the disabled worker's hours of work or training;
- assigning the disabled worker to a different place of work or training or arranging home working[65];
- allowing the disabled worker to be absent during working or training hours for rehabilitation, assessment or treatment;
- giving, or arranging for, training or mentoring (whether for the disabled person or any other worker);
- acquiring or modifying equipment;
- modifying procedures for testing or assessment;[66]
- providing a reader or interpreter;

64 The case-law, however, goes further than this requiring, in appropriate circumstances, the creation of a post. See *Southampton City College v Randall* [2006] IRLR 18 and *Chief Constable of South Yorkshire Police v Jelic* [2010] IRLR 744, which permits swapping jobs (even where the non-disabled worker is content in the existing job).

65 This may involve the employer using a mobility clause in the contract to move an existing employee to create a vacancy (see *Garret v Lidl Ltd* UKEAT 0541/09).

66 In *Lowe v Cabinet Office* ET/2203187/10 the ET did not allow a claim to have the standards of the assessment of the essential competences of the job to be modified on the facts of the case. In *Lowe* standards of assessment of communication skills caused a substantial disadvantage to an applicant with Asperger's Syndrome.

- providing supervision or other support;
- allowing a disabled worker to take a period of disability leave;
- participating in supported employment schemes, such as Workstep;
- employing a support worker to assist a disabled worker;
- modifying disciplinary or grievance procedures for a disabled worker;[67]
- adjusting redundancy selection criteria for a disabled worker;
- modifying performance-related pay arrangements for a disabled worker.[68]

4.80   The duty is extremely broad. In *Chief Constable of South Yorkshire Police v Jelic*[69] a serving police officer with chronic anxiety syndrome claimed a failure to make reasonable adjustments. In the particular circumstances of the case it would have been reasonable (1) to swap the jobs being undertaken by the claimant and another police constable in the circumstances; or alternatively (2) to medically retire the claimant on a police pension and immediately re-employ him in a civilian support staff role in the force.

4.81   The chief constable's appeal alleging that the ET could not, in law, decide that either of these could be reasonable adjustments under the EqA 2010 was rejected by the EAT.

4.82   The EAT has also held that the duty applies in certain situations where the employment relationship has ended.[70] Thus it would apply to an employer whose employee resigns as a result of their disability. It might be reasonable to reinstate the person.

4.83   The employer's sick pay arrangements will frequently be the subject of challenge. Where an employee is absent from work as a result of the employer's failure to make a reasonable adjustment for them, a failure to extend the provision of sick pay beyond the contractual entitlement may also constitute a failure to make a reasonable

---

67   See eg *OCS Group Ltd v Mr AJ Taylor* UKEAT/0803/04, later [2006] IRLR 613, CA.
68   These are at para 6.33 and occupy four pages of the Employment Code. Paragraph 6.34 goes on to emphasise that they (or others) may need to be combined. Again the real question is the potential to achieve the effect of removing the comparative disadvantage to the worker with disabilities.
69   [2010] IRLR 744.
70   *Hinsley v Chief Constable of West Mercia* UKEAT/0200/10 (a case concerning resignation due to depression).

adjustment.[71] However, where all adjustments have been made which would encourage a return to work, and the original absence is not the result of a failure by the employer to make adjustments, it is very unlikely that a refusal to make an adjustment to the contractual sick pay arrangements will be a failure to make a reasonable adjustment.[72]

'Reasonable steps'

4.84   The test of 'reasonableness' is an objective one, and reasonableness is to be determined by the ET.[73] This means that a claimant must ensure that all the known factors showing the reasonableness of the adjustment are put before the ET. It is difficult to appeal against a question of fact, which is for the ET to determine.[74]

4.85   The Act does not set out what factors must be taken into account in determining whether or not an adjustments is a 'reasonable' one for an employer or prospective employer to have to take. A factor may be present to a greater or lesser extent. Having regard to that degree of presence the ET will ask whether the step sought is reasonable to take to remove the disadvantage of the claimant.[75] The Employment Code repeats the factors that were mentioned explicitly in the DDA 1995 as follows:

- whether taking any particular steps would be effective in preventing the substantial disadvantage;[76]
- the practicability of the step;
- the financial and other costs of making the adjustment and the extent of any disruption caused;
- the extent of the employer's financial or other resources;

71 CA in *Nottinghamshire County Council v Meikle* [2004] IRLR 703 and see the example of sick pay adjustment in the Employment Code para 7.22 to the same effect.

72 *O'Hanlon v Comrs for HM Revenue & Customs* [2007] ICR 1359: such cases would be exceptional according to the EAT in *Royal Bank of Scotland v Ashton* [2011] ICR 632.

73 *Smith v Churchill's Stairlifts plc* [2006] IRLR 41.

74 As the Employment Code puts it 'ultimately the test of the "reasonableness" of any step an employer may have to take is an objective one and will depend on the circumstances of the case' (para 6.29).

75 See eg *Romec Ltd v Rudham* UKEAT/0069/07.

76 The claimant does not have to show that it would remove the disadvantage, nor that it has a good or real prospect of doing so. It is enough if there is a prospect that it will succeed (*Leeds Teaching Hospital v Foster* UKEAT /0552/10, [2011] EQLR 1075).

- the availability to the employer of financial or other assistance to help make an adjustment (such as advice through Access to Work[77]); and
- the type and size of the employer.

4.86   In constructing questions for a respondent the claimant should consider addressing these factors and those mentioned below. They will also provide a framework for obtaining documentation from the respondent at the disclosure phase of a case.

4.87   In *Cordell v FCO*,[78] the EAT considered that the following factors should also be taken into account:

- the size of any budget dedicated to reasonable adjustments;
- what the employer has chosen to spend in what might be thought to be comparable situations;
- what other employers are prepared to spend; and
- any collective agreement or other indication of what level of expenditure is regarded as appropriate by representative organisations.

4.88   The EAT upheld ET decision that the cost of providing lip speakers required so that the claimant could take up a diplomatic posting (around £300,000) was too great to be 'reasonable' steps for the purpose of the duty.

4.89   In *Leeds Teaching Hospital NHS Trust v Foster*,[79] the EAT held that when considering whether an adjustment is reasonable, it is sufficient for an ET to find that there would be a prospect of the adjustment removing the disabled person's disadvantage; it does not have to be satisfied that there is a 'good' or 'real' prospect of that occurring. The ET was therefore entitled to conclude that the respondent had failed to make a reasonable adjustment when it failed to place the claimant on its redeployment register. The ET was entitled to conclude on the evidence that had the claimant been placed on the redeployment register, there was a good prospect, let alone a prospect, that a suitable post for him would have become available.

4.90   In practical terms *Environment Agency v Rowan*[80] emphasises the need for an analytic approach to the duty to make adjustments. The EAT found that an ET could not properly make a finding that

---

77   This is a scheme whereby funding is provided for adjustments required by a disabled person, either in relation to a new post, or where an existing employee has become disabled.

78   [2012] ICR 280.

79   UKEAT/0552/10, [2011] EqLR 1075.

80   [2008] IRLR 20.

an employer failed to make reasonable adjustments without first addressing what, if any, duty to make adjustments has arisen. The ET should approach the duty by identifying:

- the PCP applied by or on behalf of the employer; or
- the physical feature of premises occupied by the employer (it should be borne in mind that identification of the substantial disadvantage suffered by the claimant may involve a consideration of the cumulative effect of both the 'provision, criterion or practice applied by or on behalf of an employer' and the 'physical feature of the premises' so it would be necessary to look at the overall picture);
- the identity of the non-disabled comparators (where appropriate); and
- the nature and extent of the substantial disadvantage suffered by the claimant

4.91 When setting out a claim for reasonable adjustment it is important to identify the comparative substantial disadvantage of the claimant; and what steps could be taken to alleviate this disadvantage. If not done at the pleading stage, this will need to be done either in correspondence (asking for permission to amend the claim if necessary) or at a case management discussion.

4.92 Once potential reasonable steps have been identified by the claimant, it is for the respondent to prove that they would not be reasonable steps for it to have to take.[81]

4.93 The questions procedure (or information obtained if the procedure is not available) can be used to establish the resources of the respondent. The respondent will have to make disclosure in respect of these resources and in respect of other adjustments it has made etc. A trade union may be able to provide information about what similar organisations spend on reasonable adjustments. However, it is important to remember that as the duty to make reasonable adjustments is an objective one, it will be open to the ET to look beyond a specific budget for reasonable adjustments where the respondent clearly has sufficient resources for that budget to be larger.

4.94 It may be necessary to obtain expert evidence on adjustments and their feasibility. This may be obtained from a disability specific organisation (for example the Royal National Institute of Blind People); or it may be in the form of a report from Access to Work.

---

81 See *Project Management Institute v Latif* [2007] IRLR 579 para 53.

4.95   Other organisations can provide technical evidence: for example an organisation called Remap specialises in adapting equipment for disabled people (such as a forklift truck which has been adapted for someone with only one arm to use).

4.96   ## Practical points

- Consider at the earliest stage the full range of potential disability claims
- If in doubt about whether a claim is direct or discrimination arising from disability, plead both in the alternative and review the claim regularly to see if disclosure makes one or other claim no longer worth pursuing
- When pleading reasonable adjustments identify the PCP, the substantial disadvantage, the comparator if appropriate and the reasonable step to be taken. If the precise nature of the adjustment needed is not clear, obtain as much further information as possible but ensure that you are in a position to at least identify the PCP and the substantial disadvantage at the time of issuing the claim.

CHAPTER 5

Harassment

Key points

- Section 26 of the EqA 2010 unifies existing legislation and clarifies harassment. Section 26 defines harassment, which now includes three specific types:
  - harassment that involves unwanted conduct that is related to a relevant characteristic and has the purpose or effect of creating an intimidating, hostile, degrading, humiliating or offensive environment for the complainant or violating the complainant's dignity;[1]
  - sexual harassment that is unwanted conduct of a sexual nature where this has the same purpose or effect as the first type of harassment;[2]
  - treating someone less favourably because they have either submitted to or rejected sexual harassment, or harassment related to sex or gender reassignment.[3]
- A person with a protected characteristic (say being female) may harass another person with that same characteristic.
- Harassment is only unlawful under section 26 where it is related to a relevant protected characteristic. These are:[4]
  - age;
  - disability;
  - gender reassignment;
  - religion or belief;
  - sex;
  - sexual orientation.
- The definition of the protected characteristic may be important in each case.[5]
- Pregnancy and maternity and marriage and civil partnership are not covered by section 26.
- Associative harassment is prohibited.
- The EHRC has published guidance on employees' rights and employers' responsibilities in relation to harassment, which may assist in the workplace and to indicate best practice.[6]

1 EqA 2010 s26(1).
2 EqA 2010 s26(2).
3 EqA 2010 s26(3).
4 EqA 2010 s26(5).
5 See chapter 1.
6 *Your rights to equality at work: working hours, flexible working and time off. Equality Act 2010 Guidance for Employees*, Vol 2 of 6 (July 2011), p35 ff.

The relevance of the pre-Equality Act 2010 case-law and other legislation

5.1   Only some of the old case-law is relevant to the interpretation of the Act. We consider those cases that assist below.

5.2   Protection from Harassment Act (PHA)1997 case-law has little relevance for harassment claims under section 26 of the EqA 2010.[7] In *Dhaliwal*[8] the EAT made clear that assistance is not to be sought from those 'entirely separate provisions'. Claimants should be aware of when it is appropriate to use the PHA 1997 (which requires separate county court proceedings).

5.3   A person who is being bullied at work may not know why this is happening. It is prudent to consider other remedies, outside the Act, that may be available. Thus a case involving 'harassment' in the non-technical sense may involve:

- unlawful discrimination;
- harassment contrary to the PHA 1997;
- issues relating to health and safety at work (Health and Safety at Work Act 1974 and other legislation);
- whistleblowing detriment;
- breach of contractual duties (for example breach of the implied term of trust and confidence; provision of reasonable support, provision of a safe place of work; and the duty to investigate complaints);
- personal injuries claims (stress and mental health consequences of bullying).

The statutory provisions

5.4   Under section 26 of the EqA 2010 a person (A) harasses another (B) if:

A engages in unwanted conduct related to a relevant protected characteristic, and the conduct [has the prohibited purpose or effect].[9]

The conduct is prohibited if it has either the purpose or the effect of –

- violating B's dignity, or
- creating an intimidating, hostile, degrading, humiliating or offensive environment for B.[10]

7   *Richmond Pharmacology v Dhaliwal* [2009] ICR 724, [2009] IRLR 336.
8   [2009] ICR 724, [2009] IRLR 336.
9   Under previous legislation there was no uniform definition of the first type of harassment.
10 EqA 2010 s26(1) ('the prohibited purpose or effect').

5.5   A also harasses B if:

- A engages in unwanted conduct of a sexual nature; and
- the conduct has the prohibited purpose or effect.[11]

5.6   A also harasses B if:

- A or another person engages in unwanted conduct of a sexual nature (or that is related to gender reassignment or sex);
- the conduct has the prohibited purpose or effect; and
- because of B's rejection of (or submission to) the conduct, A treats B less favourably than A would treat B if B had not rejected or submitted to the conduct.[12]

5.7   Each of the following must be taken into account in deciding whether conduct has the prohibited purpose or effect under the EqA 2010:

- the perception of B;
- the other circumstances of the case;
- whether it is reasonable for the conduct to have that effect.[13]

Protected characteristics

5.8   Section 26(5) of the EqA 2010 states that the harassment provisions cover the protected characteristics of age, disability, gender reassignment, religion or belief, sex and sexual orientation. Pregnancy and maternity and marriage and civil partnership are not (at least explicitly) covered.

5.9   The omission of the protected characteristic of pregnancy and maternity from EqA 2010 s26(5) has led to suggestions that the Act does not prohibit harassment on these grounds.[14]

---

11 EqA 2010 s26(2).
12 EqA 2010 s26(3).
13 EqA 2010 s26(4).
14 See Sean Jones 'Equality Act 2010: The Pregnancy Discrimination Mystery' at www.employmentcasesupdate.co.uk/site.aspx?i=ed6083. The argument continues that harassment on the grounds of pregnancy or maternity could be the subject of a direct discrimination claim under EqA 2010 s13, subject to the question of whether section 13 covers direct pregnancy and maternity discrimination. Whilst EqA 2010 s212 defines detriment such as to exclude harassment, section 212(5) provides that, where the Act disapplies a prohibition on harassment in relation to a specified protected characteristic, conduct relating to that characteristic may nevertheless amount to a detriment within section 13.

5.10 It is arguable that the omission was not intended to lead to this result. It appears likely that the reason why there is a separate section (section 18) prohibiting direct pregnancy/maternity discrimination is that discrimination of this kind does not require a comparator, and does not, therefore, fit easily into the direct discrimination provisions of section 13. This argument does not apply in relation to harassment, as section 26 requires only that the unwanted conduct be 'related to' sex. This wording quite naturally covers harassment arising from pregnancy and maternity (as all such harassment must be 'related to' sex). There is no need for any separate prohibition of harassment 'related to' the protected characteristic of pregnancy or maternity and there is no express exclusion of unwanted conduct relating to pregnancy as a form of sexual harassment. Moreover the prohibition on harassment relating to sex in the Directives would be apt to include harassment relating to pregnancy.[15]

5.11 Moreover harassment related to pregnancy and maternity was caught by the pre-EqA 2010 legislation. In *Nixon v Ross Coates Solicitors*,[16] gossip about the paternity of the claimant's child was held to be harassment related to sex.

5.12 Claimants should plead any conduct that could amount to pregnancy or maternity-related harassment as harassment under section 26, pregnancy discrimination under section 18 (if applicable) and direct pregnancy/maternity and sex discrimination under section 13.

What is harassment?

5.13 The Explanatory Notes give the following examples of harassment:

- A white worker who sees a black colleague being subjected to racially abusive language could bring a claim for harassment if the language also causes offence to the white worker.
- An employer who displays any material of a sexual nature, such as a calendar featuring pictures of topless women, may be harassing

15 On analogous arguments to those deployed in relation to pregnancy dismissals in Case C-177/88 *Dekker v Stichting Vormingscentrum voor Jong Volwassenen (VJV-Centrum) Plus* [1990] ECR I–3941, [1992] ICR 325, CJEU; Case 179/88 *Handels-og Kontorfunktionaerernes Forbund I Danmark v Dansk Arbejdsgiverforening* [1992] ICR 332, [1991] IRLR 31, CJEU and Case C-32/93 *Webb v EMO Air Cargo (UK) Ltd* [1994] QB 718, [1994] 4 All ER 115, CJEU.
16 UKEAT/0108/10, [2010] EqLR 284, 6 August 2010.

employees (whether male or female) where this makes the work-place an offensive place to work.

- A shopkeeper propositions one of his shop assistants. She rejects his advances and is then turned down for a promotion that she would have got if she had not turned down the sexual advances. The shop assistant would have a claim for harassment.

5.14   To this could be added that 'outing' someone without their permission may constitute harassment[17] as could calling a worker with a same-sex partner by names appropriate to the opposite sex.[18] Clearly the section covers a very wide range of activity.[19] The guidance for employers produced by the Equality and Human Rights Commission gives the following example, together with those set out at para 5.13 above:

> During a training session attended by male and female workers, a male trainer directs a number of remarks of a sexual nature to the group as a whole. A female worker finds the comments offensive and humiliating to her as a woman. She can claim harassment even though the remarks were not specifically directed at her.[20]

5.15   Despite having three separate definitions of harassment there is much similarity in the terms used. For example the terms 'unwanted conduct', 'conduct has the purpose or effect', 'violating B's dignity', and 'creating an intimidating, hostile, degrading, humiliating or offensive environment for B' are common to all three definitions.

5.16   Further, the factors that must be taken into account in deciding whether there has been harassment ('the perception of B'; 'the other circumstances of the case'; and 'whether it is reasonable for the conduct to have that effect') are common across all three definitions.

5.17   In *Richmond Pharmacology v Dhaliwal*[21] the EAT gave guidance on the approach that should be adopted in relation to the common core

---

17   See *HM Land Registry v Grant* UKEAT/232/09, [2010] IRLR 583 and [2011] EWCA Civ 769, [2011] ICR 1390 for arguments to this effect. The claimant's harassment claim was not upheld on the facts of the case, at least in part because he had already come out as gay, albeit to colleagues in a different office.

18   Acas *Sexual orientation and the workplace*, produced under the previous legislation.

19   The EHRC guidance, p36 gives the example of constant criticism of a worker with a learning disability.

20   See 'What equality law means for you as an employer: managing workers' *Equality Act 2010 Guidance for employers* Vol 5 of 5 (EHRC, July 2011).

21   UKEAT/458/05, [2009] ICR 724, [2009] IRLR 336.

of harassment and this can be adapted for the new definition without violence:

- Did the alleged perpetrator engage in 'unwanted conduct'?
- Did the conduct identified have (a) the prohibited purpose or (b) the prohibited effect?
- Was the conduct 'related to' the protected characteristic?

5.18   It is important to set out the case for the ET according to this framework even if there are overlaps between them.

Unwanted conduct related to a relevant protected characteristic[22]

Unwanted conduct

5.19   The conduct must be unwanted.[23] The ET will look at the following factors:

- the objective nature of what was said or done. Was it so offensive that it would obviously be unwanted?[24] if not,
- did the context of what was said or done render it offensive of itself so as to be obviously unwanted? if not,
- has it been made clear to the alleged perpetrator that the conduct is unwanted?

5.20   It is not necessary for the alleged perpetrator to know that the conduct is unwanted save in the final example. Lack of intent is not a

---

22 EqA 2010 s26(1)(a).
23 The Employment Code at para 5.8 makes clear that 'The word "unwanted" means essentially the same as "unwelcome" or "uninvited". "Unwanted" does not mean that express objection must be made to the conduct before it is deemed to be unwanted. A serious one-off incident can also amount to harassment.'
24 The Employment Code example at para 5.8 is one which is obviously offensive in this sense, but could be viewed as a product of context: 'In front of her male colleagues, a female electrician is told by her supervisor that her work is below standard and that, as a woman, she will never be competent to carry it out. The supervisor goes on to suggest that she should instead stay at home to cook and clean for her husband. This could amount to harassment related to sex as such a statement would be self-evidently unwanted and the electrician would not have to object to it before it was deemed to be unlawful harassment.'

defence.[25] In *Reed*[26] the EAT gave guidance about 'unwanted' behaviour. The context was allegations of sexual harassment:[27]

> as to whether the conduct is unwelcome, there may well be difficult factual issues to resolve. In general terms, some conduct, if not expressly invited, could properly be described as unwelcome. A woman does not, for example, have to make it clear in advance that she does not want to be touched in a sexual manner. At the lower end of the scale, a woman may appear, objectively, to be unduly sensitive to what might otherwise be regarded as unexceptional behaviour. But because it is for each person to define their own levels of acceptance, the question would then be whether by words or conduct she had made it clear that she found such conduct unwelcome. It is not necessary for a woman to make a public fuss to indicate her disapproval; walking out of the room might be sufficient. Tribunals will be sensitive to the problems that victims may face in dealing with a man, perhaps in a senior position to herself, who will be likely to deny that he was doing anything untoward and whose defence may often be that the victim was being over-sensitive. Provided that any reasonable person would understand her to be rejecting the conduct of which she was complaining, continuation of the conduct would' be unwanted.

5.21   The vulnerability of the claimant may also be a factor in determining whether participation in 'banter' indicates that the conduct was not 'unwanted'. Thus, in *Munchkins Restaurant Ltd v Kamarzyn*,[28] it was open to an ET to find that employees had been harassed despite many years of putting up with sexually explicit inquiry, banter, and bullying from an employer which, on occasion, they initiated in order to deflect the employer from inquiring about their sex lives. The EAT made an important and useful observation on the nature of harassment (and sexual harassment in particular):

> [The ET] made the point that in its view the waitresses were migrant workers with no certainty of continued employment, save at Munchkins, that there were considerations of convenience for one, that they were constrained by financial and in some cases parental pressure; that they had the fear that they might not obtain other work; that they had the comfort of Miss Guillery acting as a cushion until she left; and that they managed, therefore, to find a balance between conduct which was unwelcome and unlawful, as the Tribunal went on to find, and the advantages which their job gave them. The members of the workforce got on well with each other amongst themselves. *One*

25 See *Reed and Bull Information Systems Ltd v Stedman* [1999] IRLR 299, EAT.
26 [1999] IRLR 299.
27 [1999] IRLR 299 at para 30.
28 UKEAT 0359/09, 28 January 2010.

of the lay members of this Tribunal has observed that there are many situations in life where people will put up with unwanted or even criminal conduct which violates their personal dignity because they are constrained by social circumstances to do so. A classic example, she points out, is that of the battered wife who for the sake of the children may remain at home permitting herself to be subject to violence, none of which she wishes, but all of which she endures because there is a greater benefit in what takes place. But it does not make the violence right. Putting up with it does not make it welcome, or less criminal. It is therefore not completely beyond the scope of reason to think that women in this particular situation should behave as they did. As to initiating conversation it is explained in the passages we have cited by the Tribunal as being a defensive move on behalf of the Claimants, enabling them to divert much of the intentions of Mr Moss from the intrusive personal questioning which otherwise would have taken place as to their own sexual preferences, habits and contacts. Accordingly, taken as a general point we see nothing in the perversity appeal. [Emphasis added]

5.22   In situations in which the nature of the behaviour and the context is such that the unwanted nature of the conduct is not clear what is B required to do? It has been said[29] that:

> the words or conduct must be unwelcome to the victim and it is for her to decide what is acceptable or offensive. The question is not what (objectively) the Tribunal would or would not find offensive ... in deciding whether something is unwelcome, there can be difficult factual questions for a Tribunal; some conduct may be so clearly unwanted that the woman does not have to object to it expressly in advance. At the other end of the scale is conduct which normally a person would be unduly sensitive to object to, but because it is for the individual to set the parameters, the question becomes whether that individual has made it clear that she finds that conduct unacceptable.

5.23   It is not necessary for B to express discomfort with a particular course of conduct in words, nor would it be necessary for B to air views publicly. It follows therefore that, in certain circumstances, it may be sufficient for B simply to walk out of a room, provided that any reasonable person would understand B to be denouncing the conduct.[30]

5.24   Similarly, where B rejects A's invitation for dinner, it would be unlikely that this would amount to unwanted conduct unless A persists with it. Here the ET will look at the series of events as a whole. The ET will not carve up a course of alleged unwanted conduct into

29 Per Lindsay J in *Whitley v Thompson* UKEAT/1167/97, 14 May 1998.
30 *Reed and Bull Information Systems Ltd v Stedman* [1999] IRLR 299, EAT.

individual incidents. Once unwelcome conduct has been displayed, the victim may be bothered by further incidents, which, in a different context, would appear unobjectionable.

'Related to'

5.25   The term 'related to' is not further defined.[31] However, there must be a connection of some sort between the act complained of and the protected characteristic. A conscious intention to cause embarrassment to another person because of their physical characteristics related to gender would be caught.[32] It would also be harassment where, for example, an individual is required to undertake certain menial tasks due to his race.

5.26   In *Equal Opportunities Commission v Secretary of State for Trade and Industry*[33] the High Court held that that an earlier definition of sexual harassment containing the phrase 'on the ground of' did not implement this definition and hence did not properly implement the European legislation. It imported a requirement of causation or ratiocination. The European law makes harassment dependent simply on a connection or association with sex.

5.27   Clearly therefore 'related to' is intended to be wider than 'on the grounds of' and will capture all conduct that previously was captured by the 'on the ground of' test. Thus racist name-calling directed at one ethnic minority employee and overheard by the claimant, who was also an ethnic minority employee[34] and viewing pornographic images in the presence of a woman,[35] will be conduct related to a protected characteristic.

5.28   This view is consistent with the Employment Code,[36] which defines the term 'related to' as follows: 'Unwanted conduct "related to" a protected characteristic has a broad meaning in that the conduct does not have to be because of the protected characteristic.'

---

31 The Employment Code at para 5.9 points out that it is intended to have a broad meaning. The conduct does not have to be 'because of' the protected characteristic. The Code gives examples.
32 See eg *Insitu Cleaning Co Ltd v Heads* [1995] IRLR 4, EAT.
33 [2007] EWHC 483 (Admin), [2007] ICR 1234, [2007] IRLR 327.
34 *Chin v Post Office*, EAT, 24 February 1998; and see *Moxam v Visible Changes Ltd* UKEAT/2067/11, [2012] EqLR 202.
35 *Moonsar v Fiveways Express Transport Ltd* [2005] IRLR 9, EAT.
36 See the Employment Code at paras 5.9–5.10 where a number of examples are given.

5.29   The wording is broad enough to capture harassment based on a third person's protected characteristics[37] or mistaken attribution of the characteristic.[38] The Employment Code makes clear that there may be harassment where a person is generally abusive to other workers but, in relation to a particular worker, the form of the unwanted conduct is determined by that worker's protected characteristic. It suggests that where there is any connection with a protected characteristic this will be sufficient for the unwanted conduct to be related to that characteristic.[39]

Unwanted conduct of a sexual nature (EqA 2010 s26(3)(b))

5.30   The second definition under EqA 2010 s26 provides that A also harasses B if A engages in unwanted conduct of a sexual nature. In addition the conduct must have the prohibited purpose or effect.[40]

5.31   Generally the dispute in this type of case will centre on whether conduct that has occurred is unwanted or whether it was of a sexual nature. It is suggested that the test to be applied is an objective test in both cases.

5.32   The type of conduct covered is not specifically defined in the EqA 2010, in contrast to the definition of sexual harassment under the Sex Discrimination Act 1975, which included the phrase 'any form of unwanted verbal, non-verbal or physical conduct'. However, in keeping with the style in which the Act is drafted, it is suggested that the reference to 'unwanted conduct of a sexual nature' is intended to be perfectly general language aimed at capturing any form of such conduct. It will therefore include such conduct.

5.33   The Employment Code refers to conduct of a sexual nature using the same words and covering 'verbal, non-verbal or physical conduct including unwelcome sexual advances, touching, forms of sexual assault, sexual jokes, displaying pornographic photographs or drawings or sending emails with material of a sexual nature.'[41]

5.34   Thus it is suggested that the ET will be able to determine whether conduct is sexual conduct by reference to:

37 *Saini v All Saints Haque Centre* UKEAT/227/08, [2009] IRLR 74 (religion).
38 *English v Thomas Sanderson Blinds Ltd* [2008] EWCA Civ 1421, [2009] ICR 543, [2009] IRLR 206 (sexual orientation).
39 Giving the example that a white worker might claim harassment as a result of the racial abuse of his black co-worker: para 5.10.
40 See para 5.4 above.
41 Employment Code para 5.13.

- the nature of the conduct itself. Certain conduct is unequivocally sexual. Reference to sexual activities, or attributes[42] would fall into this category as would overtly sexual physical contact;
- the context[43] (in which behaviour which would not, of itself, be thought of as sexual conduct ordinarily takes on a sexual nature).

5.35   The conduct does not have to be directed at B. Sexual conduct towards a third party that has the required effect on B will be sufficient (provided it has the harassing effect).[44]

5.36   Also, provided the conduct is of a 'sexual nature' and the victim is affected in the required way, it is irrelevant whether or not the act of harassment was undertaken because the victim was female (or male). The section does not require any particular protected characteristic to be invoked by B and appears to establish 'sexual nature' harassment as a free-standing prohibition. It would thus cover 'horseplay' taking the form of some indecent act[45] or bullying that has a sexual element to it.

5.37   The types of conduct which would now fall under this heading of sexual harassment could include:

- a coarse remark especially if associated with unwanted touching;[46]
- unwelcome sexual advances;
- forms of sexual assault;
- sexual jokes;
- displaying pornographic photographs[47] or drawings or sending emails with material of a sexual nature.

---

42   Eg *Insitu Cleaning Co Ltd v Heads* [1995] IRLR 4, EAT.

43   Thus certain double entendres may constitute conduct of a sexual nature depending on the context it is suggested. See also *Chief Constable of the Lincolnshire Police v Stubbs* [1999] IRLR 81, [1999] ICR 547, EAT and *Reed and Bull Information Systems Ltd v Stedman* [1999] IRLR 299, EAT.

44   The Employment Code at para 5.10 gives an example illustrating that this is the breadth of the concept.

45   Eg *Jones v ICS Cleaning Services Ltd* (EAT/811/99) (men grabbing each others' genitals as a form of greeting; staff being held down, tickled and trousers removed; arm wrestling; mock fighting).

46   *Chief Constable of the Lincolnshire Police v Stubbs* [1999] IRLR 81. [1999] ICR 547, EAT.

47   *Moonsar v Fiveways Express Transport Ltd* [2005] IRLR 9, EAT.

Rejecting or submitting to certain conduct (EqA 2010 s26(3))

5.38 The third definition under EqA 2010 s26 states that A also harasses B if the following conditions are satisfied:

- A or another person engages in unwanted conduct of a sexual nature or that is related to gender reassignment or sex.
- The conduct must have the prohibited purpose or effect.
- Finally, because of B's rejection of or submission to the conduct, A treats B less favourably than A would treat B if B had not rejected or submitted to the conduct.

5.39 Section 26(3)(c) would apply to a scenario where, for example, an employer or manager sexually propositions an employee. She rejects his advances and is subsequently turned down for a promotion opportunity that she believes she would have got had she accepted the sexual advances.[48]

5.40 This provision makes explicit that it is A's conduct or another person's conduct that triggers the protection. Thus where B alleges that they were subjected to a sexual assault outside work, A may not treat B less favourably because B rejected or submitted to that conduct.[49]

5.41 The provision also applies to situations where there is unwanted conduct related to gender reassignment and the recipient (B) is treated less favourably than B would have been had B not rejected (or submitted to) that conduct. So if B is transsexual and is insulted by A's customers; reacts negatively to these insults and as a result of doing so is not sent to those customers B might be able to claim that harassment has occurred, if it has the requisite purpose or effect.

5.42 The initial unwanted conduct must be sufficiently serious to satisfy the 'prohibited purpose or effect' test.[50]

5.43 Finally, it is important to note that section 26(3) explicitly contains a comparative test. It must be shown that A has treated B less favourably than a comparator (real or hypothetical) who has not submitted to or rejected (as the case may be) the relevant conduct.

48 See Explanatory Notes to Act p 28, paras 98–102. This is also the example given in the Employment Code para 5.15.
49 Employment Code para 5.15.
50 See paras 5.44–5.65.

Prohibited 'purpose or effect'

5.44   In all cases of harassment the claimant must show that the perpetrator engaged in the unwanted conduct with the prohibited purpose or effect, namely of violating B's dignity, or creating for B an intimidating, hostile, degrading, humiliating or offensive environment.

Purpose

5.45   In considering whether particular conduct had the prohibited purpose, the ET must investigate the alleged harasser's motive or intention. It will have to draw inferences from the evidence in order to ascertain whether the harasser had the prohibited purpose. Claimants will therefore need to ensure that the case includes examples of incidents that would suggest that the respondent had the prohibited purpose. Inferences may be drawn from relevant displays of hostility towards a characteristic; the perpetrator may ridicule the characteristic in other contexts, for example.

5.46   If conduct has the prohibited purpose, it does not matter whether it has that effect on B.[51] In particular it is not necessary to consider B's perception of the unwanted conduct. It is only when considering whether unwanted conduct has the prohibited effect that the Act requires an ET to consider the factors set out in section 26(4).

5.47   It may also be more advantageous for a claimant to allege that conduct had the prohibited purpose, rather than relying solely on its effect, because if a particular comment or act was unintentional, ETs may be less willing to find that it had the prohibited effect.[52]

Effect

5.48   Most cases will be concerned with the effects of unwanted conduct. Even if conduct is not intended to cause harassment, a claim may nonetheless be brought if it has the effect of violating B's dignity or of creating for B an intimidating, hostile, degrading, humiliating or offensive environment.

5.49   In *Dhaliwal* the EAT suggested boundaries to the concept of harassment:[53]

---

51 *Richmond Pharmacology v Dhaliwal* UKEAT/458/08, [2009] ICR 724, [2009] IRLR 336 at para 14 and Employment Code para 5.17.

52 See eg *Dhaliwal* at para 22, and further para 5.49 below.

53 [2009] ICR 724, [2009] IRLR 336 at para 22. The particular remark complained of in *Dhaliwal*, and held to constitute harassment, albeit close to the borderline,

We accept that not every racially slanted adverse comment or conduct may constitute the violation of a person's dignity. Dignity is not necessarily violated by things said or done which are trivial or transitory, particularly if it should have been clear that any offence was unintended. While it is very important that employers, and tribunals, are sensitive to the hurt that can be caused by racially offensive comments or conduct (or indeed comments or conduct on other grounds covered by the cognate legislation to which we have referred), it is also important not to encourage a culture of hypersensitivity or the imposition of legal liability in respect of every unfortunate phrase. We accept that the facts here may have been close to the borderline, as the Tribunal indeed indicated by the size of its award.

5.50 There is some suggestion from the case-law that harassment will not be found to have taken place where the conduct is 'de minimis'. The concept of 'de minimis non curat lex' (the law does not pay attention to trivial disadvantage) (a) is a creature of its time and what may be regarded in one era as trivial disadvantage may be regarded as a substantial disadvantage in another; (b) sits very ill alongside the Directives, which suggest that the principle of equal treatment is incompatible with any discrimination whatsoever.

5.51 However, in *Whitley v Thompson*[54] the EAT refused to find that an employer's act of giving a 'light peck or kiss' to a young female member of his staff was necessarily a 'detriment' for the purposes of the Sex Discrimination Act 1975, even though the attention was unwanted. It would certainly be open to an ET to find that this was harassment. However, on the facts of that case the EAT found that there was no error of law by the ET, which found there was no harassment. It is not clear that such a conclusion would be reached today.

5.52 In the context of considering whether unwanted conduct has the prohibited effect, it is necessary to deal with the requirements of section 26(4) of the EqA 2010.

Assessing whether conduct has the prohibited effect

5.53 The ET must have regard to the following:[55]

- the perception of the recipient of the conduct;
- the other circumstances of the case;
- whether it is reasonable for the conduct to have that effect.

was 'We will probably bump into each other in future, unless you are married off in India.'
54 EAT/1167/97, 14 May 1998.
55 EqA 2010 s26(4).

5.54   ETs will therefore have to consider both a subjective and an objective test, while also weighing up all other relevant factors in any given case. Weight will be attached to the claimant's perception but this will not be the overriding factor in an ET's assessment of the effect on an individual.

The perception of the recipient of the conduct

5.55   When looking at the perception of the recipient of the conduct (B), the question to ask is whether they regarded the conduct as having the requisite effect. This element of the test is subjective, although an objective element is introduced by the later requirements. It depends on how B regards the treatment.

5.56   In attempting to evidence this aspect of the test, care must be taken in writing the witness statement for B. It should include the factual circumstances of the case and make clear exactly what B's perception of the treatment was. In relation to evidence dealing with perception, the ET will not necessarily have anyone on it who shares a similar life experience to B. Therefore the passages of evidence dealing with perception should ensure that the ET has an appropriate understanding of why B feels as they do about the conduct. The more trivial the conduct might appear to an outside observer, the more the evidence should place it in the context of B's perception.

The other circumstances of the case

5.57   Examples of factors that an ET may take into account as 'the other circumstances' can include the circumstances of the person experiencing the conduct. This will include the following factors among others:

- the individual's health, mental health or mental capacity;
- cultural norms;
- previous experience of harassment;
- differences in age and/or status;
- fluency in English or other relevant language.[56]

5.58   The ET must consider any factors that can reasonably be perceived as having a bearing on the proceedings. Furthermore, an important consideration for the ET as part of their examination of the facts ought to be the perpetrator's Article 10 right to freedom of expression

---

56 See Employment Code para 5.18(b); it also includes the environment in which the conduct takes place.

afforded to him by the European Convention of Human Rights, in relation to which, see further paras 5.66–5.74 below.

Whether it is reasonable for the conduct to have that effect

5.59   The precursor legislation provisions on harassment provided that conduct should only be regarded as having the prohibited effect if, having regard to all the circumstances including in particular the perception of the claimant, it should reasonably be considered as having that effect.

5.60   The position under the EqA 2010 is subtly different. The reasonableness of the claimant's perception is only one of the factors to be taken into account by the ET.

5.61   The EAT in *Dhaliwal*, dealing with the old law, said this about the 'reasonableness' factor:[57]

> '... the victim must have felt, or perceived, her dignity to have been violated or an adverse environment to have been created. That can, if you like, be described as introducing a 'subjective' element; but overall the criterion is objective because what the tribunal is required to consider is whether, if the claimant has experienced those feelings or perceptions, it was reasonable for her to do so. Thus if, for example, the tribunal believes that the claimant was unreasonably prone to take offence, then, even if she did genuinely feel her dignity to have been violated, there will have been no harassment within the meaning of the section. Whether it was reasonable for a claimant to have felt her dignity to have been violated is quintessentially a matter for the factual assessment of the tribunal. It will be important for it to have regard to all the relevant circumstances, including the context of the conduct in question'.

5.62   While the EqA 2010 does not exclude liability for harassment in circumstances where it is not reasonable that the conduct should have had the prohibited effect, this will undoubtedly be an important factor to take into account. It is likely that an unreasonable reaction to relatively benign conduct will not be covered by section 26.

5.63   It is therefore particularly important that, as discussed at para 5.56 above, advisers provide details of any personal circumstances of the claimant – whether that be experience of previous harassment, illness or difficult life events – which explain why it is reasonable for this particular claimant to have perceived the conduct as having the prohibited effect. As stated by the EAT in *Dhaliwal*, the ET will want to avoid a construction of the Act which fosters a culture of hyper-

---

57   UKEAT/458/08, [2009] ICR 724, [2009] IRLR 336 at para 15.

sensitivity, and it is therefore extremely important to emphasise any sensitising context.[58]

5.64   ETs will also consider the implications of various rights such as that of academic freedom and freedom of expression (as set out in Article 10 of the European Convention on Human Rights); see further at paras 5.66–5.74 below

5.65   Where a victim of alleged harassment has participated in offensive conduct similar to that which forms the basis of his or her complaint, it is unlikely that it will be reasonable for such conduct to have a harassing effect. This was the case in *Thomas Sanderson Blinds v English (No 2)*.[59] The ET had found that the claimant had himself engaged in extremely offensive behaviour and therefore he could not reasonably have considered that the conduct of which he now complained violated his dignity or created an intimidating, hostile, degrading, humiliating or offensive environment.

Human rights and harassment

5.66   ETs are required to balance human rights of the alleged perpetrator, for example the rights to freedom of expression[60] and of academic freedom against the right not to be offended. However, it is important to emphasise in any case in which such a defence is raised as a factor that Article 10 ECHR only protects the responsible expression of free speech.[61] It does not protect hate speech or speech that harasses a person.[62] Similarly the claimant will have a right to respect for their private and family life. This will include the ability to form relationships, such as friendships, at work.

5.67   Article 10 ECHR protects not only,

the information or ideas that are favourably received or regarded as inoffensive or as a matter of indifference, but also those that offend,

---

58   Employment Code para 5.18(c) states: 'A tribunal is unlikely to find unwanted conduct has the effect, for example, of offending a worker if the tribunal considers the worker to be hypersensitive and that another person subjected to the same conduct would not have been offended'. See also *Heafield v Times Newspaper Ltd* UKEAT/PA/1305/12/BA.

59   UKEAT/0316/10; UKEAT/0317/10, 21 February 2011, [2011] EqLR 688.

60   Article 10 of the European Convention on Human Rights.

61   See eg *Jersild v Denmark* (A/298) (1995) 19 EHRR 1, (1994) *Times* 20 October.

62   See *X v FRG* No 9235/81, 29 DR 194: complaint that suppression of Nazi pamphlets infringed freedom of speech provision declared manifestly ill-founded by the Commission.

shock or disturb; such are the demands of that pluralism, tolerance and broad-mindedness without which there is no democratic society.[63]

5.68   It has long been a limitation on free speech that it must not incite racial hatred. In part the ECHR jurisprudence has seen any attempt to use the ECHR as a means of protecting a person's own race hate speech or racism as an attempt to use the Convention to undermine the values which underpin it and therefore contrary to Article 17 of the Convention.

5.69   Article 17 aims to prevent individuals or groups with totalitarian aims from exploiting the principles of the Convention to further their own interests. Convention rights, particularly that of freedom of expression, should not be invoked in a manner that is contrary to Article 15.

5.70   Thus in *Gündüz v Turkey*[64] the court stated that expressions seeking to spread, incite or justify hatred based on intolerance, including religious intolerance, do not enjoy the protection as freedom of expression afforded by Article 10 ECHR. To qualify as race hate speech a particular level of violence would need to be advocated.

5.71   In *Gay News Ltd v United Kingdom*[65] the applicants were publisher and editor of a journal for homosexuals and were found guilty of the common law offence of blasphemous libel in connection with the publication of a certain poem. The applicants complained that this conviction amounted to an unjustified interference with their freedom of expression under Article 10 ECHR. Their complaints were considered inadmissible by the ECtHR because they were considered manifestly ill-founded. The ECtHR observed that the offence of blasphemy did not as such raise any doubts as to its necessity for the protection of rights of others, including protection of religious feelings, in a democratic society.

5.72   Issues will arise in connection with the display of items that others in the workplace find offensive. Thus although expression is permitted to shock as set out above, the ECHR will permit rules limiting the freedom of expression to avoid, as far as possible, expressions that are 'gratuitously offensive to others' and that as a result do not contribute to any form of public debate capable of furthering progress in

63 Judgments of the ECtHR in *Handyside v United Kingdom* (1979–80) 1 EHRR 737; *Sunday Times v United Kingdom* (1979–80) 2 EHRR 245; *Lingens v Austria* (1986) 8 EHRR 407; *Oberschlick v Austria* (1995) 19 EHRR 389; *Jersild v Denmark* (1995) 19 EHRR 1, App No 29271/95 and *Dichand v Austria*, 26 February 2002, unreported.
64 (2005) 41 EHRR 5.
65 (1983) 5 EHRR 123.

human affairs.[66] Thus a gratuitously offensive poster may constitute harassment because the Article 10 rights of the person who put it there are not engaged. Similarly an item said to have artistic content does not, automatically as a result of that status, constitute responsible free speech.[67] Whether an expression is responsible expression of free speech will depend as much on the manner (tone style and spirit) of presentation as on the content of what is presented.[68]

5.73   In the context of religion or belief, those professing a religion or belief need to remember that that pluralism, tolerance and broad-mindedness are hallmarks of a 'democratic society' and that those who choose to exercise the freedom to manifest their religion cannot reasonably expect to be exempt from all criticism. They must tolerate and accept the denial by others of their religious beliefs and even the propagation by others of doctrines hostile to their faith.[69] None of these will constitute harassment, unless the manner of delivery renders them harassment.

5.74   Moreover the context of what is alleged to be harassment will be all important. Thus in *Gündüz v Turkey*[70] the court took account of the fact that the leader of an Islamic sect made certain statements during a pluralistic television debate. The mere strength of feeling of the person perpetrating harassment, or the fact that they consider the harassment to be a direct result of a belief or religion that they hold will not form part of the context.[71]

Third party liability (EqA 2010 s40)

5.75   The EqA 2010 provides in section 40 for protection against harassment of employees by a person other than their employer.[72] This protection is restricted to the employer – employee relationship as defined in the Act. So it is not available to office holders and others who do not work under a contract of service or personally to execute

---

66 *Otto-Preminger Institute v Austria* (1995) 19 EHRR 35.

67 See *Wingrove v UK* (1997) 24 EHRR 1.

68 See also *R v Lemon* [1979] 1 QB 10.

69 See *IA v Turkey* (2007) 45 EHRR 30 at paras 23–28.

70 (2005) 41 EHRR 5.

71 For an explanation of how the United States has dealt with these matters see *Peterson v Hewlett-Packard*, 358 F3d 599 (2004), where US Court of Appeals upheld the dismissal of a worker for refusing to remove a poster with various biblical passages condemning homosexuality.

72 This is dealt with in the Employment Code at paras 10.19–10.24.

any work. The Coalition Government has tabled legislation revoking the third party harassment provisions in section 40, which will leave employees harassed by someone other than their employer reliant on the general provisions of the Act.[73] For a discussion of liability for third party harassment other than under section 40, see below.

5.76   Section 40(2) provides that A (an employer) will be treated as harassing B where, in the course of B's employment, a third party harasses B and A 'failed to take such steps as would have been reasonably practicable to prevent the third party' from harassing B.

5.77   Even if that condition is satisfied, A will not be liable unless 'A knows that B has been harassed in the course of B's employment on at least two other occasions by a third party; and it does not matter whether the third party is the same or a different person on each occasion'.[74] Section 40(4) provides that a third party is a person other than A, or an employee of A's.

5.78   The Employment Code gives the following example:[75]

> An employer is aware that a female employee working in her bar has been sexually harassed on two separate occasions by different customers. The employer fails to take any action and the employee experiences further harassment by yet another customer. The employer is likely to be liable for the further act of harassment.

5.79   An employer is required to take reasonably practicable steps to prevent a third party from harassing an employee. The use of the phrase 'reasonably practicable' indicates a difficult test for the employer to satisfy. The ET in considering whether the employer has failed to take such steps as were reasonably practicable will consider

- what steps were taken?
- were there any further steps that were reasonably practicable that should have been taken and could have been taken by the employer?

5.80   In that context it will ask whether any such further steps would have been of any consequence or have had any realistic chance of success. But even if the step identified had no realistic chance of success, if in fact it was reasonably practicable for it to be done, it should have been

---

73   See the Enterprise and Regulatory Reform Bill. The provisions are to be revoked by what is currently clause 58.-
74   EqA 2010 s40(3).
75   At para 10.20.

done,[76] and the employer will have failed to take such steps as were reasonably practicable to take to prevent such harassment.

5.81   The Employment Code suggests the following are reasonably practicable steps that an employer could take to prevent such harassment, depending on the size and resources of the employer[77]:

- having a policy on harassment;
- notifying third parties that harassment of employees is unlawful and will not be tolerated, for example by the display of a public notice;
- inclusion of a term in all contracts with third parties notifying them of the employer's policy on harassment and requiring them to adhere to it;
- encouraging employees to report any acts of harassment by third parties to enable the employer to support the employee and take appropriate action;
- taking action on every complaint of harassment by a third party

5.82   The decision of the EAT in *Sheffield City Council v Norouzi*,[78] albeit decided under the Race Relations Act 1976, is illustrative of how an employer could fall foul of section 40 and will inform the approach of ETs following the expected revocation of section 40(2)–(4). In *Norouzi*, the Council was found liable for acts of racial harassment carried out by a child living in a residential care home against the claimant social worker, who was employed by the council. The child had behavioural difficulties and regularly made racially offensive comments against the claimant. The ET had found that the council had been notified of the abuse against the claimant, yet had failed to act to stop the abusive behaviour.

5.83   The decision in *Norouzi* is noteworthy for another reason. The EAT took the view, albeit without deciding the matter, as the point had not been in issue before the ET, that the decision in *R (Equal Opportunities Commission) v Secretary of State for Trade and Industry*[79] applied equally to 'race' harassment as to 'sex' harassment. Thus it stated that European law, in the form of Directive 2000/43, which covered all relevant conduct 'related to race', meant that:

---

76 *Canniffe v East Riding of Yorkshire Council* [2000] IRLR 555, EAT (under RRA 1976 s41).

77 Employment Code para 10.24.

78 UKEAT/497/10, [2011] IRLR 897.

79 [2007] EWHC 483 (Admin), [2007] ICR 1234, [2007] IRLR 327.

... [A]n employer could be held liable on appropriate facts for the conduct of, for example, a supplier or customer ... It might be the case that an employer could be held liable for failing to take action where there is a continuing course of offensive conduct, which the employer knows of but does nothing to safeguard against. The employer could be responsible for failing to act, albeit not responsible for the third party actions in themselves ...[80]

5.84 This was important in *Norouzi* itself because a line of authority under the old Sex Discrimination Act (which was thought also to apply to the Race Relations Act 1976) suggested that there could be no liability on an employer for third-party harassment. It will be similarly important once section 40(2)–(4) is revoked by the Enterprise and Regulatory Reform Bill. The significance of the point in connection with the 2010 Act, which currently provides protection against third-party harassment in certain circumstances, is that there may be an argument that the limitations placed on that protection (eg the requirement for harassment on at least two other occasions before the employer can be held liable) contravene European law.

5.85 All three of the relevant Directives (2000/43, 2000/78 and 2006/54) prohibit, under the heading of harassment, 'unwanted conduct related to' any of the protected characteristics, and this wording is, as the court held in the *EOC* case, broad enough to cover a failure to deal with offensive actions by third parties. However, the court in the *EOC* case was careful to say that a knowing failure to deal with such conduct is required. The courts in the future may be asked to settle whether such a knowing failure can arise in the absence of two previous incidents of harassing conduct.

Protection from Harassment Act 1997

5.86 Section 1(1) of the PHA 1997 provides that a person must not pursue a course of conduct that amounts to harassment of another and that he knows or ought to know amounts to harassment of the other.

---

80 This explanation is in fact taken from the skeleton produced by Mr Pannick, counsel for the Secretary of State; see para 37 of the *EOC* case. What the court itself held was that 'if, by reference to the disapproved authority of *De Vere Hotels*, it could have been shown that the employers knew of continuing and/or regular objectionable conduct by Mr Manning, and failed to take any steps to prevent it, it could be said that they were thereby themselves indulging in unwanted conduct (including omission) in relation to sex, with the consequent upsetting effect on the claimant waitress.'

The prohibition is enforceable by the creation of a criminal offence[81] and a civil remedy.[82] 'Harassment' is not exhaustively defined by the Act but section 7(2) provides that it includes 'alarming the person or causing the person distress'.

5.87   In *Rayment v Ministry of Defence*[83] the High Court considered what kind of conduct would amount to a breach. It considered the cases of *Hammond v International Network Services*[84] and *Green v DB Group Services*[85] both of which indicate the kind of behaviour that will constitute PHA harassment. It concluded that the conduct must be of the following nature:

- it occurs on at least two occasions;
- it is targeted at the claimant;
- it is 'calculated' (in an objective sense of being likely) to cause alarm or distress;
- it is objectively judged to be oppressive and unreasonable.

5.88   The Court of Appeal in *Veakins v Keir Islington*,[86] referring back to the decision of the same court in *Ferguson v British Gas Trading Ltd*[87] referred to an additional requirement, namely that the harassment has to be of an order to sustain criminal liability. However, the court made it clear that the important question is whether the conduct is 'oppressive and unacceptable' as opposed to merely unattractive, unreasonable or regrettable. If this is the case, then (given that the requirements under the statute are the same for the criminal and civil offences), the breach should be made out.

5.89   However, in *Rayment* the High Court, although quoting from *Veakins*, did not focus on the requirement of sustaining criminal liability. It proceeded to identify, from a long list of incidents of harassment alleged by a female army driver, three acts that it decided satisfied the test of harassment. The incidents are not of the type envisaged by the Court of Appeal in *Veakins*, namely, being told to repay a month's salary, the issue of a final warning and a sacking. The High Court held these incidents were 'unwarranted, unfair and wrong'.

---

81   PHA 1997 s2.
82   PHA 1997 s3.
83   [2010] EWHC 218, [2010] IRLR 768 and see *SKA v CRH* [2012] EWHC 2236 (QB) most recently.
84   [2007] EWHC 2604.
85   [2006] EWHC 1899, [2006] IRLR 764.
86   [2009] EWCA Civ 1288, [2010] IRLR 132.
87   [2009] EWCA Civ 46, [2010] 1 WLR 785.

5.90   Many acts that could be raised by an employee where harassment is being alleged would probably fall within the same category of being unwarranted, unfair and wrong.

5.91   The second lesson from this case is that while it suggests it may be easier to establish harassment under the Act, the claims will not necessarily trigger significant compensation. Here, despite there being evidence of psychiatric injury, the compensation awarded amounted to £7,000

5.92   Since *Rayment* and *Veakins*, the Court of Appeal has considered the Act in *Iqbal v Dean Manson Solicitors*,[88] and held that the sending of three letters questioning a solicitor's integrity and accusing him of conduct unbefitting to the legal profession in the course of litigation could arguably amount to a course of harassing conduct within the meaning of the PHA 1997 even if the letters did not individually meet the standard of harassment established in the case-law. The course of conduct should be looked at as a whole, as acts that individually appear innocuous can, when examined together with other acts, contribute to a course of conduct amounting to harassment.

5.93   It is useful to be aware of the existence of this remedy which in appropriate cases should be used in conjunction with claims for any personal injuries arising out of the harassment in question. Finally it is possible to obtain an injunction to restrain PHA harassment.

5.94 ## Practical points

- Support for persons experiencing harassment can be obtained from the Directgov website under the heading 'Bullying in the workplace'. This gives general practical advice.
- A person who believes that they may be the subject of a course of harassment should keep a diary of the events cataloguing the course of conduct, which may be relied upon both internally in a grievance and for the purposes of any ET proceedings, should the internal procedure fail to resolve the problem.
- The witness statement of a person bringing a claim for unlawful harassment needs to cover:
  - the protected characteristic or triggering act of unwanted sexual conduct;

---

88 [2011] EWCA Civ 123, [2011] IRLR 428; see also *Marinello v City of Edinburgh Council* [2011] IRLR 669, Ct Sess.

- the unwanted conduct, giving the factors which rendered the conduct unwanted. This will include any explicit indication given to the perpetrator, or simply an explanation as to why the conduct was so offensive;
- the perceptions of the recipient of the conduct (again making clear why it was offensive etc). This part of the witness statement should have regard to the factors in EqA 2010 s26(4) and the Employment Code.
- the evidence of the intention of the perpetrator or, if there is none, the evidence of the effect of the unwanted conduct in terms of the prohibited conduct or effect.

• Very often it will be difficult for a person who has experienced harassment to have to repeat their experience many times so it is a good idea for an adviser to try to obtain the detailed account at the start if possible.

• Often harassment cases involve a great deal of detailed factual information. A good way to structure the witness statement (and the claim form) is as follows:

Facts	Reaction	Reasonableness of reaction
Incident 1 Eg 'During a monthly meeting, around my birthday, the manager said that I was in my second childhood now that I have reached 60, and he needs someone with get up and go. My co-workers started to call me "Granddad" and laugh at me.'	'I felt insulted, but also since that time I have felt worried about my future at work, as the manager may carry on laughing along with the rest of the staff. It makes it difficult for me to talk to people about the jobs we are working on without this kind of "banter" being flung at me. I now feel uncomfortable going to work when I used not to feel that way.'	'No one else has to put up with this kind of insult and "banter". I feel particularly aggrieved because my father has Alzheimer's and the reference to a "second childhood" felt cruel. I don't engage in this kind of banter. I have tried to discourage similar behaviour when I have come across it. I am working long hours for the company and my health was not good at the time of the incidents.'
Incident 2 Etc		

Victimisation

Key points

- Section 27 of the EqA 2010 defines victimisation. Employees and workers are protected by section 39(3) and (4) in Part 5 of the Act. A victimises B if A subjects B to a detriment because B has done a protected act or A believes B has done so or may do so.
- There is no need to rely on or identify a comparator (hypothetical or real).
- 'Protected act' means:
  - bringing proceedings under the EqA 2010 (s27(2)(a));
  - giving evidence or information in connection with proceedings under the EqA 2010 (s27(2)(b));
  - doing any other thing for the purposes of or in connection with the EqA 2010 (s27(2)(c));
  - making an allegation (whether express or not) that anyone has contravened the EqA 2010 (s27(2)(d)). This includes references to breach of an equality clause or rule (s27(5)); and
  - being involved in a 'relevant pay disclosure' (within the meaning of s77(3)–(4)).
- The burden of proof provision applies to victimisation claims (s136).

Background and statutory provisions

6.1   Under the EqA 2010 it remains the case that 'the primary object of the victimisation provisions ... is to ensure that persons are not penalised or prejudiced because they have taken steps to exercise their statutory rights or are intending to do so'.[1]

6.2   Victimisation claims often succeed where the primary discrimination claim does not. The aim of the provision is to permit in good faith allegations of discrimination to be made and investigated without those bringing them or assisting in bringing them being deterred from doing so for fear of retribution by the employer. 'The victims of long-standing and deep-seated injustice should not be made to feel guilty if they pursue their claims for justice.'[2] Without the provision, protection against discrimination would be nominal.

---

1 Lord Nicholls in *Chief Constable of the West Yorkshire Police v Khan* [2001] UKHL 48, [2001] 1 WLR 1947, [2001] IRLR 830 at para 16.
2 See *St Helens Metropolitan Borough Council v Derbyshire* [2007] UKHL 16, [2007] ICR 841 at para 30, per Baroness Hale.

6.3   Victimisation is a form of 'other prohibited conduct' under the EqA 2010 and is not a form of discrimination.[3]

6.4   The EqA 2010 focuses on protecting against retribution for what an individual has done, so the claimant in a victimisation claim need not have the relevant protected characteristic.[4] A consequence of this is pointed out in the Employment Code: It applies to former employees[5] if they have the relevant causal connection to a protected act.

6.5   Section 27 provides that:

- A person (A) victimises another person (B) if A subjects B to a detriment because:
  - B does a protected act, or
  - A believes that B has done, or may do, a protected act.
- Each of the following is a protected act:
  - bringing proceedings under the EqA 2010;
  - giving evidence or information in connection with proceedings under the EqA 2010;
  - doing any other thing for the purposes of or in connection with the EqA 2010;
  - making an allegation (whether or not express) that A or another person has contravened the EqA 2010.
- Giving false evidence or information, or making a false allegation, is not a protected act if the evidence or information is given, or the allegation is made, in bad faith.
- The section applies only where the person subjected to a detriment is an individual.
- The reference to contravening the EqA 2010 includes a reference to committing a breach of an equality clause or rule.

Elements of victimisation

6.6   In order to succeed in a claim for victimisation, claimants will need to prove that:

- they did, or intended to do, or the employer believed that they had done or were about to do a protected act; and

---

3   It used to be a form of discrimination requiring proof of less favourable treatment and was prohibited under precursor legislation: SDA 1975 s4(1), RRA 1976 s2(1), DDA 1995 s55(1), RBR 2003 reg 4, SOR 2003 reg 4 and AR 2006 reg 4.

4   See Employment Code para 9.3 and eg *Veitch v Red Sky Group Ltd* [2010] NICA 39.

5   Employment Code para 9.4.

- they were subjected to a detriment; and
- the reason for the detriment was the protected act.

'Protected act'

6.7 EqA 2010 s27(2) covers a broad range of actions that will amount to a 'protected act'. When bringing a claim for victimisation, it is important for the claimant to identify what the protected act is and what category it falls into (ie which subsection of section 27 they rely on). More than one form of protected act can be put forward in the alternative as the reason for the detrimental treatment.

'Bringing proceedings under the Act'

6.8 EqA 2010 s27(2)(a) is self-explanatory: it will protect anyone who has brought proceedings under the Act or anyone who the employer believes may bring such proceedings.[6]

'Giving evidence or information in connection with proceedings under the Act'

6.9 EqA 2010 s27(2)(b) applies where a person gives evidence or information whether in a court or ET or in any other process (such as an internal investigatory or grievance process). However, it must be in connection with proceedings brought under the Act.[7] The section characterises the 'act'. Victimisation protection extends to retribution where the employer believes that the recipient of the detriment may give evidence or information in connection with such proceedings and therefore punishes the informant before the proceedings have started.

6.10 If the act falls outside the scope of EqA 2010 s27(2)(b), it may constitute a protected act under section 27(2)(c), which is broader.

---

6 Examples under precursor legislation would be *Chief Constable of West Yorkshire v Khan* [2001] UKHL 48, [2001] IRLR 830 and *St Helens Metropolitan Borough Council v Derbyshire* [2007] UKHL 16, [2007] ICR 841 discussed below at paras 6.35–6.39.

7 Proceedings may be brought in the county courts (for goods and services discrimination) or in the administrative courts (eg for judicial review of a public body's failure to have due regard to the equality objectives in EqA 2010 s149) as well as in criminal courts for various regulatory offences under the Act.

'Doing any other thing for the purposes of or in connection with the Act'

6.11   EqA 2010 s27(2)(c) is a catch-all provision. A case that illustrates its breadth is *National Probation Service for England and Wales (Cumbria Area) v Kirby*.[8] An employee of Asian origin complained to her manager that there was racial tension between herself and a white female colleague. Miss Kirby worked with both women in a bail hostel. She was interviewed about the alleged racial tension and stated she was not aware of any such problems. Miss Kirby was subsequently involved in an altercation with a resident in the hostel and none of her colleagues assisted her. She successfully claimed victimisation under the Race Relation Act (RRA) 1976. The EAT held that her involvement in the interview amounted to a protected act and that the reason her colleagues had not assisted her was because of such involvement.

'Making an allegation (whether or not express) that A or some other person has contravened the Act'

6.12   Where a person alleges treatment that could amount to a contravention of the EqA 2010 (even though they do not put it in such terms) they do a protected act. There is no requirement for the complainant to make any express reference to the Act or even use the words 'discrimination' or 'harassment' etc.[9] However, it must be plain that it is a complaint about a protected characteristic, as the purpose of the legislation is not to protect all complaints about anything. In making an allegation therefore it is important to try to set out what protected characteristics are involved. This may aid early and internal resolution of the discrimination issue, but it will also ensure that there can be no doubt whether there is an issue of victimisation should there be retribution.

6.13   The precursor legislation was interpreted to mean that there had to be an allegation which if proven would have amounted to a contravention of the relevant act. In *Waters v Metropolitan Police Comr*,[10] the protected act relied on was an allegation, made by the claimant to her employer, about sexual harassment she had suffered from one of her male colleagues. The harassment had occurred outside the

8   [2006] IRLR 508, EAT, decided under precursor legislation.
9   It (or possibly the context) must indicate that there is a protected characteristic at issue in the complaint: *Beneviste v Kingston University* UKEAT/0393/05, 17 March 2006, para 29 ff.
10   [1997] ICR 1073, [1997] IRLR 589.

course of the male colleague's employment, but while the claimant was at work. She was then subjected to a detriment by reason of having made the allegation.

6.14   The Court of Appeal held that the claim for victimisation could not succeed because, even if the claimant were able to prove sexual harassment against the male colleague, no liability could have passed to the employer because it occurred outside the scope of the male employee's employment. Accordingly, the facts alleged could never amount to unlawful discrimination by the employer and therefore there was no protected act in the first instance. In such circumstances, any mistreatment to which the claimant was subjected could not, logically, have been by reason of the protected act.

6.15   The Act is phrased differently. Rather than requiring allegations that 'would amount to a contravention' of the relevant Act (if proven) all that now seems to be required is an allegation (in good faith) that any person has contravened the Act. Accordingly, it would seem that even if the facts alleged could not (as a matter of law) amount to a breach of the Act, but the complainant alleges breach there will be a protected act and, subject to the requirement of good faith, the person alleging that breach may be protected against retribution for having made it or it being suspected that they may make such an allegation.

6.16   Thus the allegation must make clear that it relates to a protected characteristic, but the section appears broad enough that allegations that could not in law amount to a contravention of the Act nonetheless are protected acts. This should not be surprising however. The social purpose of the provision is to protect even mistaken allegations made in good faith.

6.17   The Act makes clear that there will be a protected act if the recipient of the treatment alleges that someone other than the employer has contravened the Act.[11]

'Being involved in a relevant pay disclosure'

6.18   A relevant pay disclosure is a protected act that falls within the scope of section 27, by reason of EqA 2010 s77(4), which states:

> (4) The following are to be treated as protected acts for the purposes of the relevant victimisation provision-
> (a) seeking a disclosure that would be a relevant pay disclosure;
> (b) making or seeking to make a relevant pay disclosure;
> (c) receiving information disclosed in a relevant pay disclosure.

---

11   However, there must be a contravention expressly or otherwise alleged: see *British Airways Engine Overhaul Ltd v Francis* [1981] IRLR 9, [1981] ICR 278.

6.19 The definition of the term 'relevant pay disclosure' is set out in EqA 2010 s77(3), which states:

> (3) A disclosure is a relevant pay disclosure if made for the purpose of enabling the person who makes it, or the person to whom it is made, to find out whether or to what extent there is, in relation to the work in question, a connection between pay and having (or not having) a particular protected characteristic.

6.20 The questions that will arise on this definition will include whether a disclosure was made/received with a particular purpose or not and if so whether that purpose is simply the subjective motivation of the person making the disclosure or the person receiving it or whether the test is an objective test relating to the type of information which is disclosed or the form of disclosure. Does the provision protect a person who is seeking to establish whether the respondent has a genuine material factor defence, for example? As a relevant pay disclosure can be made where the person receiving the information is seeking to establish the extent (including whether it is to no extent) that there is a connection between pay and gender, it is suggested that the answer is clearly affirmative.

Bad faith and incorrect allegations

6.21 A person will not be protected against a detriment for making a disclosure if they make allegations or provide information/evidence which is both false and done in bad faith.[12] It is necessary for the employer to prove both elements. If the allegation or information is factually incorrect but the person making it believes it to be true, they will be protected. If the allegation or information is factually true, but the motivation for making the allegation/giving the information is improper they will still be protected.[13]

6.22 The Employment Code states:[14] 'A worker cannot claim victimisation where they have acted in bad faith, such as maliciously giving false evidence or information or making a false allegation of discrimination. Any such action would not be a protected act.'

6.23 Proving bad faith is notoriously difficult because it is rare for a respondent employer to be able to show that the claimant employee neither believed the content of their allegation nor made such allegation in good faith. As such, it is only in cases where there is good

---

12 EqA 2010 s27(3).
13 Employment Code para 9.14.
14 Employment Code para 9.13.

evidence as to both issues that such an argument should be run. It is not enough to merely assert bad faith.[15] The manner of making the false allegation may indicate bad faith.[16] If a respondent makes an allegation of bad faith it is sensible at an early stage to ensure that proper details are given of the bad faith relied upon, in order to prevent opportunistic use of information that arises in the course of the hearing.

'Detriment'

6.24   The victimisation provisions do not require less favourable treatment but protect persons from suffering unfavourable treatment in the form of a 'detriment' because they have done a protected act.

6.25   The victimisation provisions of the precursor legislation required proof of 'less favourable treatment'. Now it is not necessary to identify a real or hypothetical comparator who has been and/or would have been treated more favourably or carry out any form of comparative exercise at all to establish victimisation.

6.26   It is no longer open to an employer to defend ill-treatment of a person who has done a protected act by arguing that a comparison cannot be made because they treat all persons equally badly, irrespective of whether they have done a protected act or not. However, it can be argued that the cause of the detriment was poor management not the protected act.

6.27   The Explanatory Notes to the Act identify various examples of how the victimisation provisions will apply, including the following:[17]

- A woman makes a complaint of sex discrimination against her employer. As a result, she is denied promotion. The denial of promotion is victimisation.
- An employer threatens to dismiss a staff member because he thinks she intends to support a colleague's sexual harassment claim. This threat could amount to victimisation.

---

15 For a recent case where allegations of falsity and bad faith were found to have been made out, see *Bhardwaj v FDA*, UKEAT/0157/11 and UKEAT/0158/11, 4 October 2011.

16 *HM Prison Service v Ibimidun* [2008] IRLR 940. Note that this case also deals with causation by some other factor than the protected act (namely the manner of the delivery of the disclosure).

17 See para 103 of the Equality Act 2010 Explanatory Notes, revised edition (August 2010), which can be found at: www.legislation.gov.uk/ukpga/2010/15/pdfs/ukpgaen_20100015_en.pdf.

- A man with a grudge against his employer knowingly gives false evidence in a colleague's discrimination claim against the employer. He is subsequently dismissed for supporting the claim. His dismissal would not amount to victimisation because of his untrue and malicious evidence.

6.28   Evidence of less favourable treatment will sometimes be valuable when seeking to prove that the reason for the treatment was because of the protected act. If the claimant can point to another person in materially similar circumstances (save for the fact that that other person has not done a protected act) who has not been subjected to a detriment, the ET may infer that the reason for the detriment was the protected act. Claimants can consider putting forward such evidence where available.

What is a 'detriment' under the Act?

6.29   'Detriment' is not defined in the EqA 2010. It is commonly used in discrimination and whistleblowing law. It covers a wide range of acts, from seemingly trivial ones to far more serious matters. The Employment Code gives guidance on the concept:[18]

> Generally, a detriment is anything which the individual concerned might reasonably consider changed their position for the worse or put them at a disadvantage. This could include being rejected for promotion, denied an opportunity to represent the organisation at external events, excluded from opportunities to train, or overlooked in the allocation of discretionary bonuses or performance-related awards.

It will include a threat made to the worker which the worker takes seriously (when it is reasonable for them to take it seriously).[19]

6.30   This approach mirrors that in the pre-existing case-law.[20] An unjustified sense of grievance will not amount to a detriment.[21]

6.31   There is no need for there to be financial disadvantage (such as reductions in pay, withholding bonuses etc) or for there to be a change in terms and conditions. Anything from more trivial matters, such as being ostracised at work, to more serious matters, such

---

18   Employment Code para 9.8.
19   Employment Code para 9.9.
20   *Shamoon v Chief Constable of the Royal Ulster Constabulary* [2003] UKHL 11, [2003] ICR 337, [2003] IRLR 285 at paras 31–37.
21   *Barclays Bank plc v Kapur (No 2)* [1995] IRLR 87, CA and *Shamoon v Chief Constable of the Royal Ulster Constabulary* [2003] UKHL 11, [2003] ICR 337, [2003] IRLR 285 at paras 35 and 105.

as physical/verbal abuse etc, could potentially amount to detriments under the Act.

6.32   Examples which are given in paras 9.8–9.9 of the Employment-Code are as follows:

- A senior manager hears a worker's grievance about harassment. He finds that the worker has been harassed and offers a formal apology and directs that the perpetrators of the harassment be disciplined and required to undertake diversity training. As a result, the senior manager is not put forward by his director to attend an important conference on behalf of the company. This is likely to amount to detriment.

- An employer threatens to dismiss a staff member because he thinks she intends to support a colleague's sexual harassment claim. This threat could amount to victimisation, even though the employer has not actually taken any action to dismiss the staff member and may not really intend to do so.

Dismissal

6.33   EqA 2010 s27 itself does not make reference to dismissal. However, section 39(4)(c) of the Act prohibits an employer from dismissing an employee/worker because they have done or were about to do (or were believed to have done or be about to do) a protected act. In *Credit Agricole Corporate and Investment Bank v Wardle*[22] an employee complained that the reason he had not been promoted was due to his race. He was subsequently dismissed and the ET found that his dismissal was because of the protected act.

6.34   'Dismissal' under the EqA 2010 includes: non-renewal of a fixed-term contract, direct dismissal and constructive dismissal as they are defined in the ERA 1996.

Causation: 'because'

6.35   There must be a causal connection between the protected act (or belief concerning the doing of a protected act) and the detriment. There is liability only if the detriment is because of the doing of a protected act or because the perpetrator believes that the worker has done, or may do, a protected act. The Employment Code makes it clear that if the protected act is one of the reasons for the detrimental treatment, but not the only reason, the treatment will amount to victimisation.

22   [2011] EWCA Civ 770, [2011] IRLR 604.

It does not need to be the only reason for the treatment.[23] It does not have to be the principal reason for the treatment.

6.36   However, the protected act must have had a 'significant influence' and/or have been an 'important' causative factor.[24] Accordingly, where the alleged victimiser subjects the complainant to a detriment solely for another reason, there will be no victimisation.

6.37   ETs must therefore investigate the reason for the detriment, whether conscious or subconscious. It is not sufficient to show that 'but for' the protected act, the complainant would not have been subjected to the detriment.

6.38   This can be seen from the case of *Chief Constable of West Yorkshire v Khan*,[25] which was decided under the victimisation provisions of the RRA 1976. Mr Khan claimed race discrimination and before the final hearing asked for a reference to another prospective employer. His employer refused to provide the reference because it might prejudice its defence to the claim. The House of Lords held that the reason for not providing the reference was not because Mr Khan had done a protected act, but because of the employer's need to protect its position in the litigation. A reference would have been provided if there had been no outstanding proceedings and one would be provided in the future, following conclusion of the proceedings. Accordingly, it could not logically be said that the protected act was the reason for withholding the reference, and the claim failed. In *Khan* if a simple 'but for' test had been applied, the claimant's claim would have succeeded.

6.39   In *St Helens Metropolitan Borough Council v Derbyshire*[26] the House of Lords stated that acts by an employer during proceedings would either be: (a) legitimate steps to protect its position (albeit that such acts may have unfavourable consequences for the complainant); or (b) detriments within the meaning of the legislation. In deciding which the proper starting point is the reasonable employee's perception of whether the conduct amounts to victimisation or is simply a reasonable and fair step in proceedings. Letters sent to multiple complainants in an equal pay claim, warning them of the implications on all staff if they continued their claims and inviting them to withdraw the claims, were detriments.

---

23 Employment Code para 9.10.
24 See *Nagarajan v London Regional Transport* [2000] 1 AC 501 at 513A and 519D–E, [1999] IRLR 572 at paras 19 and 35, HL.
25 [2001] UKHL 48, [2001] IRLR 830.
26 [2007] UKHL 16, [2007] ICR 841. See also *South London & Maudsley NHS Trust v Dathi* [2008] IRLR 350 on the issue of absolute immunity, not argued in this case or in *Khan*.

6.40   It is likely that the principles will still apply under the new Act. Accordingly, if the complainant seeks to rely on an alleged detriment that is nothing more than the other party taking a reasonable and genuine step in the legal proceedings, this is unlikely to amount to victimisation. It is not possible to rely on statements made in the course of judicial proceedings themselves due to a protective principle known as 'judicial immunity' from claims.[27]

6.41   There is no need to prove any motivation or intent on the part of the alleged victimiser in order to establish liability. A person can apply a detriment to another without deliberately, intentionally and/ or maliciously doing so. Indeed, the victimiser could be unaware that the explanation for why they subjected the person to the detriment is because of the protected act. Yet, if the reason is the protected act, that person will be liable for victimisation. In *Nagarajan v London Regional Transport*[28] Lord Nicholls stated: 'Although victimisation has a ring of conscious targeting, this is an insufficient basis for excluding cases of unrecognised prejudice from the scope of [section 27].'

6.42   The concept of 'significant influence' in this context can also be attributed to Lord Nicholls:[29]

> Decisions are frequently reached for more than one reason. Discrimination may be on racial grounds even though it is not the sole ground for the decision. A variety of phrases, with different shades of meaning, have been used to explain how the legislation applies in such cases: discrimination requires that racial grounds were a cause, the activating cause, a substantial and effective cause, a substantial reason, an important factor. No one phrase is obviously preferable to all others, although in the application of this legislation legalistic phrases, as well as subtle distinctions, are better avoided so far as possible. If racial grounds or protected acts had a significant influence on the outcome, discrimination is made out.

6.43   This approach can also be seen as requiring that the claimant need only prove that the discriminatory reason was 'of sufficient weight'

---

27 *Singh v Reading Borough Council* UKEAT 0540/12, 12 February 2013, which concerns reliance on such statements for constructive dismissal. At the time of writing permission to appeal to the Court of Appeal has been granted. See also *South London Maudsley NHS Trust v Dathi* [2008] IRLR 350 and *Parmar v East Leicester Medical Practice* [2011] IRLR 641, where the claimant tried to bring victimisation proceedings based on statements in witness statements served in a previous discrimination claim (dismissed on jurisdictional grounds). The EAT upheld the ET's order striking out the victimisation claim on the basis that the statements attracted judicial proceedings immunity.

28 [2000] 1 AC 501, [1999] IRLR 572.

29 [2000] 1 AC 501 at 513A, [1999] IRLR 572 at para 19.

in the decision-maker's mind in order to succeed in their claim.[30] In practice, this is a fairly low threshold.

6.44 The reason for the treatment is a question of fact for the ET to determine in each case. This means that the loser will generally have difficulty appealing against the decision of the ET on those facts. Of course, where the alleged victimiser has no knowledge of the complainant's protected act, it is logically impossible for any treatment to be consciously and/or subconsciously because of such act. Knowledge of the protected act is a precondition for a finding of victimisation.[31]

6.45 Specific caution must be taken with cases where the manner in which a person goes about doing the protected act could be said to be the sole cause of the detriment. For example, an employee who alleges discrimination against a manager but does so loudly and aggressively in public, in front of customers/clients. The employer may well wish to discipline the employee for their outburst, not because of its content, but because of the manner of its delivery. Clearly, being called to a disciplinary meeting is likely to amount to a detriment and the employee could allege that the reason for the detriment is because of the outburst. The ET would need to consider whether the content of the complaint was an effective cause of the disciplinary, or whether it was genuinely because of the employee's inappropriate conduct, ie their manner.[32]

6.46 A good illustration of this point is to be found in *Martin v Devonshires Solicitors*.[33] The claimant made serious allegations of harassment against the employer's senior partners. The grievance investigation concluded that not only were the allegations false, but further that the claimant had made them because she had a mental illness, which made her delusional. The claimant was subsequently dismissed because the employer felt it was too risky to continue to employ her in circumstances where she was convinced she had been harassed and might bring more allegations, which would make working relations impossible. Her claims for victimisation failed both in the ET and on appeal to the EAT. The EAT held that the reason for the dismissal constituted 'a series of features and/or consequences

30 *Owen & Briggs v James* [1982] ICR 618, [1982] IRLR 502, CA and *O'Donoghue v Redcar and Cleveland Borough Council*) [2001] EWCA Civ 701, [2001] IRLR 615 at para 26.
31 See *Scott v London Borough of Hillingdon* [2001] EWCA Civ 2005.
32 See *HM Prison Service v Ibimidun* [2008] IRLR 940, EAT.
33 [2011] ICR 352, EAT.

of the complaint which were properly and genuinely separable from the making of the complaint itself'.[34]

6.47   The word 'because' in the EqA 2010 signals the need for a causal connection. Previously a claimant had to prove that the treatment was 'by reason that' or 'on the grounds that' he/she had done a protected act. The reason for the change in wording is simply to make the concepts more accessible.

Temporal connection between protected act and detriment

6.48   There is no limit on the time that may elapse between the doing of the protected act and the detriment suffered as a result. Victimisation can occur at any time after an individual has done a protected act. In para 9.12 of the Employment Code, the following example is given:

> In 2006, a trade union staff representative acted on behalf of a colleague in a claim of age discrimination. In 2009, he applies for a promotion but is rejected. He asks for his interview notes which makes a reference to his loyalty to the company and in brackets was written the words 'tribunal case'. This could amount to victimisation despite the three-year gap.

6.49   The example given involves very clear evidence of the causal connection between the protected act and the detriment. However, in most cases, there is no such evidence available and the ET is likely to have to make its decision based on inferences.[35]

6.50   In cases where the evidence is less clear, a large time gap between the act and the detriment can render it more difficult to prove the causal connection. Conversely, where a detriment is imposed shortly after the protected act, it is usually more suspect and hence it may be easier to prove causation.

6.51   Note that if a person did a protected act within the meaning of any of the precursor legislation prior to the date the EqA 2010 came into force (1 October 2010) but is subjected to a detriment after that date, they are protected under the Act.[36] So if an employee complained that he was being discriminated against on grounds of his race in September 2010 and in January 2011 he was refused a pay rise because he had made such complaint, his claim would fall under the EqA 2010, not the race relations legislation.

---

34   [2011] ICR 352 at para 23.

35   See chapter 2.

36   In accordance with Article 8(2) of the Equality Act 2010 (Commencement No 4, Savings, Consequential, Transitional, Transitory and Incidental Provisions and Revocation) Order 2010 SI No 2317.

Victimisation after the employment relationship has ended

6.52   Pursuant to EqA 2010 s108, former employees are protected from acts of discrimination and harassment that occur after the end of the employment relationship (if the act(s) arise out of and are closely connected to the previous relationship). However, section 108 does not extend this protection to those who face acts of victimisation after cessation of the employment relationship. Indeed, section 108(7) expressly excludes such protection. The Employment Code at para 10.62 incorrectly states that post-termination victimisation is dealt with under the victimisation provisions. On the face of the Act that is not the case.

6.53   The omission in EqA 2010 s108(7) is not due to a deliberate decision not to protect former employees from post-termination victimisation. Under the precursor legislation acts of post-termination victimisation were covered. Such protection is required moreover by ECJ authority,[37] on the interpretation of the Equal Treatment Directive (Directive 76/207).[38]

6.54   The EqA 2010 must therefore be regarded as impermissibly lessening the protections guaranteed by the Directives, or it must be subjected to interpolation of words so as to render it compliant with the Directives.[39] Claimants who are subjected to detriment after the termination of their employment because they have done a protected act may, in the alternative, be able to rely on the whistleblowing provisions contained in the Employment Rights Act 1996. A complaint about a breach of the EqA 2010 may qualify for protection under s43B(1)(b) of the 1996 Act (as it could show that the employer is failing to comply with a legal obligation to which it is subject). If the employee or worker is subjected to a detriment as a result, this will be unlawful under s47B(1) of the 1996 Act even if the detriment is imposed after the end of their employment (see *Woodward v Abbey National Plc (No 1)*.[40]

---

37 See *Coote v Granada Hospitality Ltd* C-185/97 [1998] ECR I-5199, [1998] All ER (EC) 865, [1998] 3 CMLR 958.
38 The House of Lords subsequently adopted this approach: *Relaxion Group plc v Rhys-Harper* [2003] UKHL 33, [2003] 2 CMLR 1329, [2003] ICR 867.
39 See chapter 19.
40 [2006] EWCA Civ 822, [2006] ICR 1436]. See further on this point paras 8.9–8.15 below.

Burden of proof

6.55   EqA 2010 s136 applies the same burden of proof to 'any proceedings relating to a contravention of this Act'. Accordingly, the burden of proof applicable in discrimination claims also applies to victimisation claims.[41]

---

41   See chapter 17, paras 17.83–17.89.

Maternity and parental rights

continued

Key points

- The relevant UK equality law is based on EU law both under the EqA 2010 and under the family leave provisions. Regular reference to these sources is needed.
- Scope: Pregnancy and anything related to the pregnancy, including maternity leave.
- It is unlawful under the EqA 2010 to treat a pregnant woman unfavourably because of anything within that scope.
- There is no need to compare the woman's position with anyone else's.
- The 'protected period': is from conception to the end of additional maternity leave (AML) (this is the maximum period).
- It ends two weeks after any miscarriage occurring before 24 weeks of pregnancy.
- The unfavourable treatment is pregnancy discrimination only if it either (a) happens during the protected period, or (b) is decided upon during the protected period save that discrimination because a woman wishes to exercise, or has exercised her right to maternity leave can occur at any time.
- If treatment is found to be pregnancy or maternity discrimination and occurs during the protected period, it cannot also be found to be sex discrimination.
- There are rights relating to taking statutory maternity leave for which the employee must give proper notice, available from the start of employment, but those with 26 weeks' service at the expected week of childbirth (EWC) or at the date of being told of the matching for adoption may be entitled to paternity or adoption leave.
- The contract is protected during statutory maternity leave, statutory adoption leave and additional paternity leave, and if redundant during these periods the employee must be offered any suitable vacant alternative employment. More generally remuneration terms are protected via the sex equality clause and rule and the maternity equality clause and rule.
- Refusal to allow an employee to return to the same job after maternity or adoption leave or additional paternity leave may be discrimination.

Introduction[1]

7.1 This chapter summarises the main maternity, paternity and adoption rights. Details of rights to time off to care for dependents and the right to request flexible working are found in the LAG publication *Maternity and Parental Rights*.[2]

7.2   It focuses on discrimination on grounds of pregnancy and maternity leave under the EqA 2010. Before the Act protection against such discrimination was in the Sex Discrimination Act (SDA) 1975 and, in relation to pay, the Equal Pay Act (EqPA) 1970.

7.3   The main maternity and family provisions are found in employment rights legislation.[3] However, discrimination law may provide greater protection than these specific statutory provisions.

The main statutory provisions

7.4 The main relevant UK statutory provisions are:

- the EqA 2010, which covers pregnancy and maternity discrimination in work and in non-work cases, contractual and non-contractual employment terms, recruitment, promotion, training and dismissal.
- the ERA 1996:
  - section 47C: the right not to be subjected to detriment for a reason relating to leave for family and domestic reasons;[4]
  - section 47E: the right not to be subjected to detriment relating to flexible working;[5]

---

1 The Department for Business Innovation and Skills produces helpful guidance that can be downloaded from www.bis.gov.uk. Go to 'publications' and type 'maternity' in the 'contains' box. *Pregnancy at work: what you need to know as an employee / employer – babies due on or after 3 April 2011* can be downloaded as two documents. BIS also produce *Rights for Dads at work*. The HSE produces *A guide for new and expectant mothers who work,* leaflet INDG373, which can be downloaded from its website (www.hse.gov.uk).

2 C Palmer, J Wade, A Heron, K Wood *Maternity and Parental Rights: a guide to parents' legal rights at work* (3rd edn, Legal Action Group, 2006).

3 Employment Rights Act (ERA) 1996 and associated regulations.

4 ERA 1996 s47C is not a standalone right but depends on regulations prescribed under section 47C. See the Maternity and Parental Leave etc Regulations 1999, the Paternity and Adoption Leave Regulations 2002 and the Paternity and Adoption Leave (Adoption from Overseas) Regulations 2003. However, a complaint to an ET is brought under ERA 1996 s48(1).

5 ERA 1996 s48(1).

- – sections 55–56: the right to time off, with pay, for ante-natal care;[6]
- – section 57A: the right to reasonable time off to take action which is necessary to deal with certain dependants;[7]
- – sections 66–69: the right to pay if suspended from work on maternity grounds;[8]
- – sections 71–75: maternity leave;
- – sections 75A–75D. adoption leave;
- – sections 76–79: parental leave;[9]
- – sections 80A–80E: paternity leave;
- – sections 80F–80I: flexible working;[10]
- the Social Security Act (SSA) 1989, which implemented Directive 86/378/EEC on equal treatment in occupational social security schemes and covers employment-related benefit schemes, including pensions;[11]
- the Maternity and Parental Leave Regulations (MAPLE) 1999;
- the Paternity and Adoption Leave Regulations (PAL) 2002;
- the Additional Paternity Leave Regulations (APL) 2010;
- the Flexible Working (Eligibility, Complaints and Remedies) Regulations (FWE) 2002;
- the Flexible Working (Procedural Requirements) Regulations (FWP) 2002;
- the Part time Workers (Prevention of Less Favourable Treatment) Regulations (PTW) 2000;
- the Agency Workers Regulations 2010;[12]
- the Management of Health and Safety at Work Regulations (MHSW) 1999.[13]

---

6 ERA 1996 s57.
7 ERA 1996 s57B.
8 ERA 1996 s70.
9 ERA 1996 s80.
10 ERA 1996 s80H.
11 Oddly, only SSA 1989 Sch 5 para 5 has been repealed (unfair maternity provisions). Paragraph 5A (unfair paternity leave provisions), para 5B (unfair adoption leave provisions) and para 6 (unfair family leave provisions) remain. The relevant provisions are now found in Directive 2006/54/EC. Note that Directive 86/378/EEC has been repealed.
12 In force from 1 October 2011, shortly before the deadline for the implementation of the Temporary Agency Work Directive.
13 The HSE website (see fn 1 above) provides links to these regulations and other legislation found at www.legislation.gov.uk.

EU law

7.5   The main provisions of EU law relating to maternity and family rights are:

- Article 157 of the Treaty on the Functioning of the European Union (TFEU) (on equal pay in contractual and non-contractual terms);[14]
- Council directive 2006/54/EC (the Equal Treatment Directive (ETD)) on the implementation of the principle of equal opportunities and equal treatment of men and women in matters of employment and occupation, which recast and repealed the four major directives on gender equality.[15] From 15 August 2009, references to any repealed gender Directive in other EC legislation are to be read as referring to the corresponding provisions in this Directive;
- Council Directive 92/85/EEC, the Pregnant Workers Directive (PWD);
- Council Directive 96/34/EC, the Parental Leave Directive (PLD), as extended to the UK by Council Directive 97/75/EC;
- Council Directive 97/81/EC, the Part time Workers Directive (PTWD);
- Council Directive 2000/78/EC, the Framework Employment Directive (FED) combating discrimination on the grounds of religion or belief, disability, age or sexual orientation;
- Council Directive 2008/104/EC, the Temporary Agency Work Directive (TAWD).

Rights to leave and time off work for family reasons under the Employment Rights Act 1996

7.6   The rights to leave and time off for family reasons, set out in the ERA 1996 and associated regulations are summarised below.

---

14   Article 157 was initially Article 119 of the Treaty of Rome which later became Article 141 of the consolidated version of the EC Treaty.

15   Directives 75/117/EEC (equal pay), 76/207/EEC (equal treatment), 86/378/EEC (occupational social security) and 97/80/EC (burden of proof).

Paid time off for ante-natal care

7.7   Pregnant employees are entitled to reasonable paid time off during working hours for ante-natal care, which may include relaxation and parent craft classes.[16] BIS produce a good practice guide for employers on fathers-to-be and ante-natal appointments.[17]

Health and safety protection

7.8   Pregnant women, new and breastfeeding mothers are entitled to protection for their health and that of their baby. This includes an obligation on the employer:

a) to carry out a risk assessment where there are women of child-bearing age in the workplace[18] – this must cover any risk which might affect the health and safety of a pregnant or breastfeeding woman or a woman who has given birth in the previous six months[19] or their child;

b) once the employer has notice of a worker's pregnancy, or that she has given birth in the previous six months, or is breastfeeding, to assess health and safety risks to her and her child;[20]

c) to take any necessary preventive action to remove any risk, such as adjusting the worker's working conditions;

d) if the risk cannot be removed, to redeploy the employee to suitable alternative work on no less favourable terms and conditions;[21]

e) if redeployment is not possible, to suspend the employee on full pay for as long as is necessary.[22]

7.9   The employer's duty under (b)–(d) is triggered by written notice. If the employer cannot establish that the worker still counts as a 'new or expectant mother' the duty may be avoided.[23] However, a simple letter should be sufficient proof but in any event the employer can

---

16   ERA 1996 ss55–56.

17   See fn 1 for website address of BIS.

18   MHSW 1999 regs 3(1) and 16(1).

19   This includes a woman who had a stillborn child after 24 weeks of pregnancy.

20   The PWD does not limit the protection against risk only to a 'baby' who is being breastfed. MHSW reg 16(1)(b) does so, although the definition of 'new and expectant mother' in reg 1(2) does not. 'Baby' should be given an extended meaning. Nor does the PWD limit protection to employees.

21   ERA 1996 s67.

22   ERA 1996 ss66 and 68–69.

23   MHSW 1999 reg 18(2)(c).

require a certificate from a doctor or midwife as proof of pregnancy.[24] An agency worker should give notice to both the employment agency and the end user.[25]

7.10   The Health and Safety Executive (HSE) has issued guidance on the known risks associated with pregnancy or maternity and how employers can comply with their legal obligations.[26] The HSE may prosecute an employer for failure to carry out its obligations. Such failures, including failure to carry out an individual risk assessment where the duty has been triggered, may be pregnancy or maternity discrimination.[27]

Maternity leave

7.11   All employees are entitled to 26 weeks' ordinary maternity leave (OML) and a further 26 weeks' additional maternity leave (AML).[28] Since 1 April 2007, there is no qualifying period for AML. The only requirement is to give proper notice. No later than the end of the 15th week before the expected week of childbirth (EWC), an employee must give her employer notice of her pregnancy, the EWC and the date on which she intends OML to start. If it is not reasonably practicable to give timely notice, it should be given as soon as reasonably practicable. Notice only needs to be in writing if the employer so requests. An employee may change the start date for OML if she gives 28 days' notice, or, if that was not reasonably practicable, as soon as it was so practicable. The employer must inform the employee of the date leave ends.[29]

7.12   Leave cannot start earlier than the start of the 11th week before the EWC. It must start on the earliest of:

- the day after the day on which childbirth occurs;[30] or
- during the four weeks before the EWC, the day after the first day

---

24 MHSW 1999 reg 18(2)(a)(ii).
25 How the duty should be implemented and by whom may be at issue. For general guidance, go to www.gov.uk/agency-workers-your-rights/.
26 For details, see fn 1.
27 *Hardman v Mallon* [2002] IRLR 516, EAT, *O'Neill v Buckinghamshire County Council* [2010] IRLR 384, EAT.
28 MAPLE 1999 regs 4–7.
29 MAPLE 1999 reg 7(6).
30 Even if that is earlier than the 11th week before the EWC. Note that MAPLE 1999 reg 2(1) defines 'childbirth' as including 'the birth of a child whether living or dead after 24 weeks of pregnancy'. For statutory maternity pay (SMP) purposes, the Social Security Contributions and Benefits Act (SSCBA) 1992 s171(1) defines 'confinement' to similar effect. For the equivalent provisions in paternity leave, see PAL 2002 reg 4(5).

of any pregnancy-related absence, although the employer can ignore the odd day of absence.[31]

7.13 Since 1 April 2007, a woman may take up to 10 'keeping in touch' days during which she can do some work for her employer without ending SMP, OML or AML.[32] She and the employer should agree pay and hours. There must be no compulsion on the employee to agree to work.[33] This is separate from keeping in reasonable contact during leave, for example informing the employee about any changes at work, including job vacancies.

7.14 A woman has the right to return to exactly the same job after OML. There is similar entitlement on a return to work after AML, although if it is not reasonably practicable for the employer to permit her to return from AML to her old job, she must be given another job that is both suitable for her and appropriate for her to do in the circumstances.[34] If a woman is given a different job, or if her responsibilities have been changed, and this is for a reason related to her absence on maternity leave, this is likely to be maternity discrimination.[35]

Ordinary and additional adoption leave

7.15 Employees with 26 weeks' service at the date of notification of matching for adoption are entitled to 26 weeks' ordinary adoption leave (OAL) and 26 weeks' additional adoption leave (AAL). They must give proper notice (similar to that required for maternity leave) and the employer must inform the employee of the date leave entitlement ends.

31 MAPLE 1999 reg 6. This trigger rule was unsuccessfully challenged in Case C-411/96 *Boyle v EOC* [1998] ECR 1-6401, [1998] IRLR 717. Note that for SMP purposes, one day of pregnancy-related absence during this four-week trigger period is sufficient to commence the maternity pay period on the following day: see Statutory Maternity Pay (General) Regulations (SMP) 1986 reg 2(4).

32 SMP 1986 reg 9A and MAPLE 1999 reg 12A. 'Work' includes training or any activity undertaken so as to keep in touch with the workplace. Note that regulation 12A(5) prevents any such work during the compulsory leave period, ie the two weeks after childbirth; see also regulation 8.

33 MAPLE 1999 reg 12A(6) and PAL 2002 reg 21A(5). An employee is protected against detriment and unfair dismissal for working, considering to work, or refusing to work during 'keeping in touch' days for maternity, paternity and adoption leave: MAPLE 1999 reg 20(3)(eee) and PAL 2002 reg 28(1)(bb).

34 MAPLE 1999 reg 18(2).

35 But see *Blundell v Governing Body of St Andrew's Roman Catholic Primary School* [2007] ICR 1451, [2007] IRLR 652, EAT, on the issues to address when considering whether the job is the 'same' or not.

7.16   OAL is like OML and AAL like AML, with the benefit of the same terms during leave, the 'keeping in touch' days, and the same right to return after leave.[36] However, if adoption leave has begun but the placement is then cancelled, or the child dies or is returned to the adoption agency, leave and statutory adoption pay will continue for eight weeks.[37]

Paternity leave

7.17   An employee who is the father of the child, or the partner of the child's mother or of the child's adopter, is entitled to paternity leave if they have been employed for at least 26 weeks ending in the 15th week before the EWC or in the week in which notification of matching for adoption was given.[38] If someone is not married or in a civil partnership, they must be living with the mother or adopter and child in an 'enduring family relationship'.[39] Leave must be taken within 56 days after the birth or adoption. An employee can choose to take leave for either one or two weeks, but the two weeks must be consecutive.[40]

7.18   Additional paternity leave (APL) is available where the EWC or, in adoption cases, the date of notification of matching, is on or after 3 April 2011. The full conditions are in the APL Regulations 2010, which provide a similar package of rights in anticipation of, during and after leave to OML and AML. Those who satisfy the detailed substantive, evidential and notice conditions may take from two to 26 weeks' APL during the period from 20 to 52 weeks after the birth or placement for adoption. If the mother dies within 12 months of the child's birth or adoption, the conditions are modified and may permit APL to last until the end of the year from the child's birth or adoption. If the child dies, or the adoption is disrupted, APL continues for eight weeks.

Parental leave

7.19   Since 8 March 2013, all employees with one year's service who have responsibility for a child under five are entitled to 18 weeks' unpaid

---

36   PAL 2002 Part 3.
37   PAL 2002 reg 22 and Statutory Paternity Pay and Statutory Adoption Pay Regulations (SPAP) 2002 reg 22.
38   PAL 2002 regs 4 and 8.
39   PAL 2002 reg 2(1), with reg 2(2) listing the relatives who cannot count as a 'partner'.
40   PAL 2002 regs 5 and 9.

leave where the leave is to care for the child. If the employer does not have its own scheme, a default scheme applies. This provides that no more than four weeks' leave a year may be taken in respect of any individual child. Unless that child is entitled to disability living allowance, leave must be taken in whole weeks.[41]

Rights during leave

7.20   An employee on OML, OAL, AML or AAL (and for EWCs or adoptions falling on or after 3 April 2011, an employee on APL) is entitled to the benefit of all the terms and conditions of employment that would have applied had she not been absent[42] – except for terms about remuneration.[43] Only sums payable to an employee as wages or salary are treated as 'remuneration'.[44] This means that an ordinary pregnancy and maternity discrimination claim may be made about benefits in kind, such as use of a mobile or company car, or holiday entitlement.

7.21   Pay is dealt with under the EqA 2010 ss72–76. Such employees will be entitled to statutory maternity/adoption pay and to all contractual rights except full pay. The maternity equality clause[45] ensures that any pay increase is taken into account when calculating maternity-related pay and will be implemented in full on the return to work. A bonus does not accrue during maternity leave except where it relates to the two weeks' compulsory maternity leave.[46] However, an employee should receive pay, including any bonus earned outside the maternity leave period, at the time she would have received it had she not been on maternity leave.[47]

7.22   Occupational pension rights continue to accrue as if the employee was not absent. If she is paid when on maternity leave, she will accrue pension rights as though she were paid her usual salary even though her contributions will be based on actual pay (see chapter 15).

---

41 MAPLE 1999 reg 16 and Sch 2. Parental leave is extended to 18 weeks by the Parental Leave (EU Directive) Regulations 2013 SI No 283.

42 Following Case C-284/02 *Land Brandenburg v Sass* [2004] ECR I-11,143, [2005] IRLR 147, ECJ and *EOC v Secretary of State for Trade and Industry* [2007] EWHC 483 (Admin), [2007] ICR 1234. See MAPLE 1999 reg 9 and PAL 2002 reg 12.

43 ERA 1996 ss71(5)(b), 73(5)(b), 75A(4)(b) and 75B(5)(b).

44 MAPLE 1999 reg 9(3) and PAL reg 19(3).

45 EqA 2010 ss73 and 74.

46 EqA 2010 s74(7)(b) and see *Hoyland v Asda Stores Ltd* [2006] CSIH 21, [2006] IRLR 468.

47 EqA 2010 s74(7)(a) and (c).

7.23   Contractual and statutory holiday entitlement accrues during OML, OAL, AML AAL and APL alike. A worker is able to take accrued holiday entitlement, whether contractual or statutory during a period other than her maternity leave.[48] Employees are bound by their own contractual obligations. Working on up to 10 'keep in touch' days will not affect leave or statutory pay.[49]

7.24   Parental leave is treated differently. An employee taking parental leave is entitled to return to work: usually to the same job, but if certain conditions apply the return may be to another job that is suitable and appropriate in the circumstances.[50] Otherwise an employee on parental leave is only entitled to:

- the benefit of the employer's implied obligation of trust and confidence;
- notice of the employer's termination of the contract of employment;
- compensation in the event of redundancy;
- disciplinary or grievance procedures;[51]
- membership of a pension scheme;[52]
- accrued statutory holiday entitlement.[53]

7.25   If a woman is treated unfavourably because she is pregnant or on maternity leave that will be pregnancy and maternity discrimination. For example, it is likely to be such discrimination if a woman on maternity leave is missed out in a consultation exercise on a reorganisation or when allocating future job tasks; or if she is not informed about promotion opportunities.[54]

Time off for dependants

7.26   Employees are entitled to unpaid 'reasonable' time off to deal with unexpected or sudden events affecting their dependants, for example

---

48   Case C-342/01 *Merino Gomez v Continental Industrias del Caucho SA* [2004] ECR I-2605, [2005] ICR 1040, [2004] IRLR 407; and in the analogous context of accruing the right to annual leave during sick leave see Case C-520/06 *Stringer v HMRC* [2009] ECR I-179, [2009] ICR 932, [2009] IRLR 214.
49   See para 7.15.
50   MAPLE 1999 reg 18; note that the right to return varies where there is a combination of different types of leave.
51   MAPLE 1999 reg 17.
52   SSA 1989 Sch 5.
53   Under the Working Time Regulations 1998.
54   See, eg *Paul v Visa International Service Association* [2004] IRLR 42, EAT; *Secretary of State for Justice v Slee* UKEAT/349/06, 20 July 2007 and *NUT v Watson* UKEAT/204/06, 13 June 2006.

to deal with the illness of the dependant or of the usual carer; unexpectedly having to make alternative care arrangements; or being called in to deal with a school incident.[55]

Flexible working

7.27 Employees of at least 26 weeks' standing are entitled to request flexible working to care for children under 17; under 18 if the child is disabled; or to care for certain adults, including those living at the same address.[56] This is additional to the existing protection against indirect sex discrimination.[57]

7.28 The employer must go through a prescribed procedure but if it does so properly and considers that one or more specified grounds applies, for example an inability to recruit additional staff, it can lawfully refuse the request. Even if the employer does breach procedure, the maximum award is eight weeks' pay.[58] Although ERA 1996 s80G(1)(b) provides for a subjective test based on the employer's view of the situation, the objective reality may help found an indirect sex discrimination claim.

7.29 The details of these rights, including the prescribed notice requirements, are outside the scope of this book but are set out in detail in *Maternity and Parental Rights.*[59]

Categories of employees entitled to maternity and family leave

7.30 Only employees, ie those with a contract of employment, are entitled to maternity, adoption, paternity and parental leave, time off for dependants and to make flexible working applications. 'Workers' are not entitled to maternity or other leave under domestic law although the PWD does apply to 'workers'. To the extent that the UK rights taken as a whole fail to provide the same protection to all workers in this respect, UK law fails properly to implement the EU Directive against which it must be measured (the PWD).

55 ERA 1996 s57A. See *Qua v John Ford Morrison Solicitors* [2003] ICR 482, [2003] IRLR 184, EAT and *Truelove v Safeway Stores* [2005] ICR 589, EAT.
56 ERA 1996 s80F and FWE 2002 regs 3, 3A and 3B.
57 See chapter 3.
58 FWE 2002 reg 7, with a week's pay limited by ERA 1996 s227(1)(za) to the maximum amount.
59 3rd edn, Legal Action Group, 2006.

7.31   'Workers' are protected by the PTW Regulations 2000. Employees, contract workers and those holding a personal or public office are protected by the Act. The distinction between an 'employee' and a 'worker' is often not easy to draw and those with a stable employment relationship may be 'employees' as a matter of law, even if they are classified explicitly as 'workers'.

Special cases

7.32   There are special provisions relating to leave and other maternity, paternity and parental rights for various individuals in relationships akin to employment.

- Members of the armed forces are treated in the same way as employees in relation to all relevant rights, save for the right to request flexible working.[60] Protection under the PTW Regulations 2000 is partial only (there is no protection relating to training obligations or dismissal[61]). In some cases they may be required to make a service complaint about a matter before being able to complain to an ET.[62]
- Police officers have similar rights to those of employees by virtue of the Police Regulations. They are also protected under the PTW Regulations 2000.
- Those employed in share fishing are excluded from the various family rights. Their position is analogous to self-employment.[63]
- Members of the clergy of the Church of England have been entitled to paid maternity, paternity, parental and adoption leave on the same terms as employees since 1 January 2011,[64] subject to some additional obligations relating to cover for their leave.[65] Clergy of other denominations and faiths are not covered by the 2010 Directions, but the case-law suggests that it is possible that they may fall within the definition of 'employee' in some circumstances.[66]

---

60   ERA 1996 ss191–192.
61   PTW 2000 reg 13.
62   EqA 2010 ss120–121; see further para 17.35.
63   ERA 1996 s199(2).
64   Ecclesiastical Offices (Terms of Service) Directions 2010 No 1923 para 2.
65   2010 Directions para 2(2).
66   See eg *New Testament Church of God v Stewart* [2007] EWCA Civ 1004, [2008] ICR 282 and *President of the Methodist Conference v Preston (formerly Moore)* [2011] EWCA Civ 1581, [2012] IRLR 229.

Protection against detriment and dismissal

7.33   The ERA 1996 also provides some protection against dismissal[67] and detriment[68] where the principal reason for the treatment relates to, or is, a prescribed one, that is by reason of:

- the employee's pregnancy;
- the fact that she has given birth to a child and the detriment or dismissal takes place during OML or AML;[69]
- the application of a relevant health and safety requirement or recommendation;
- the fact that the employee took, sought to take or availed herself of the benefits of OML, AML, parental leave or time off for dependants;[70]
- the fact that the employee took or sought to take OAL or AAL, paternity leave or APL, or that the employer believed taking such leave was likely;[71]
- the fact that the employee undertook, considered undertaking or refused to undertake work on 'keeping in touch' days;[72]
- a failure to return after AML, AAL or APL where the employer had failed to notify the employee of the date the additional leave should end, or had given less than 28 days notice and it was not reasonably practicable to return on that day;[73]
- the fact that the employee 'declined' to sign a workforce agreement relating to MAPLE 1999, or did, or proposed to do, anything as a workforce representative or candidate for a MAPLE 1999 agreement;[74]
- a redundancy during maternity, adoption or APL where the employee was not offered vacant suitable alternative employment[75]);
- an application for or exercise of a right to flexible working or having brought proceedings about flexible working.[76]

---

67 ERA 1996 s99 with MAPLE 1999 reg 20, or for APL with APL 2010 reg 34.
68 ERA 1996 ss47C and 47E; MAPLE 1999 reg 19 and APL 2010 reg 33.
69 MAPLE 1999 regs 19(2)(b), (5) and 20(3)(b), (4).
70 MAPLE 1999 regs 19(2)(d), (e) and 20(3)(d), (e).
71 PAL 2002 regs 28(1)(a), (b) and 29(3)(a), (b) and APL 2010 regs 33 and 34(3)(a), (b). APL 2010 regs 33 and 34 came into force on 6 April 2010.
72 MAPLE 1999 regs 19(2)(eee) and 20(3)(ee); PAL 2002 regs 28(1)(bb) and 29(3)(bb) and APL 2010 reg 33(1)(d).
73 MAPLE 1999 regs 19(2)(ee) and 20(3)(ee); PAL 2002 regs 28(1(c) and 29(3)(c) and APL 2010 regs 33(1)(c) and 34(3)(c).
74 MAPLE 1999 regs 19(2)(f), (g) and 20(3)(f), (g).
75 See paras 7.39–7.42.
76 ERA 1996 ss47E and 104C.

7.34 These protections are not subject to any qualifying period of service (apart from the period required to qualify for adoption or APL in the first place). Thus an employee who is subjected to a disadvantage, or is dismissed for a reason set out above, or for a related reason (for example if the dismissal is because of pregnancy-related sickness[77]) can claim:

- detriment under the ERA 1996. Detriment and dismissal are mutually exclusive[78] but can be claimed in the alternative;
- automatically unfair dismissal, where there has been an actual or constructive dismissal;[79]
- ordinary unfair dismissal if the employee has one year's service; and/or
- pregnancy and maternity discrimination for acts, including dismissal,[80] done, decided upon, or not done, during and because of pregnancy, OML or AML (known as the 'protected period');[81]
- sex discrimination for acts, including dismissal, done or not done outside the protected period (for example if the reason for the treatment is because the employee is, or is believed to be trying to get, pregnant) and for treatment within the protected period that is because of sex rather than something to do with pregnancy, OML or AML.[82]

Redundancy during maternity leave

7.35 Where an employee is made redundant during her maternity or adoption leave she is entitled, in preference to other redundant employees, to be offered any suitable alternative vacancy with her employer, its successor or an associated employer.[83] The new contract must take effect immediately after the previous contract and the work must be suitable in relation to the employee and appropriate for

---

77 Note that for purposes of pregnancy and maternity discrimination, EqA 2010 s18(2)(b) puts this point beyond doubt.
78 MAPLE 1999 reg 19(4) and PAL 2002 reg 28(2).
79 ERA 1996 s99; MAPLE 1999 reg 20(1) or (2) and PAL 2002 reg 29(1) or (2).
80 Constructive dismissal is defined as dismissal for all types of discrimination; see EqA 2010 s39(7)(b).
81 EqA 2010 s18. Note that with a miscarriage or still birth prior to 24 weeks, the 'protected period' ends two weeks from the end of the pregnancy: s18(6)(b).
82 Sex discrimination and pregnancy and maternity discrimination are mutually exclusive, with the EqA 2010 intended to achieve a seamless result; see EqA 2010 s18(7).
83 MAPLE 1999 regs 10 and 20(2) and PAL 2002 regs 23 and 29(2).

her to do in the circumstances. The terms and conditions must not be substantially less favourable. The issues of suitability and equivalence of terms and conditions are to be determined objectively, taking into account the claimant's personal circumstances and work experience.[84]

7.36 Failure to offer such a vacancy, where it exists, makes the dismissal automatically unfair under the ERA 1996 s99 if the reason or principal reason for the dismissal is redundancy.[85]

7.37 For those entitled to APL, the APL Regulations 2010 provide for an equivalent package of rights.

7.38 If the employer fails to consult a woman on maternity leave about possible redundancy it could be either pregnancy and maternity discrimination or sex discrimination. There is no extra protection for those on adoption or additional paternity leave.

Remedies

7.39 The specific remedies available for breach of these statutory maternity and parental rights are outside the scope of this book but are set out in *Maternity and Parental Rights*.[86] Remedies for discrimination are set out in chapter 18.

Pregnancy and maternity discrimination

General principles

7.40 Pregnancy and maternity are treated differently from other types of protected characteristics under the EqA 2010. A woman claiming discrimination because of pregnancy or maternity is not required to compare her treatment with that of an actual or hypothetical male or female comparator.[87] It is important not to underestimate the strength of this protection. It requires substantive equality, not just formal equality. As the ECJ put the point in *Sarkatzis Herrero*

---

84 *Simpson v Endsleigh Insurance Services Ltd* [2011] ICR 75, EAT at para 31.
85 MAPLE 1999 reg 20(1)(b) and PAL 2002 reg 29(1)(b).
86 3rd edn, Legal Action Group, 2006.
87 Although it is not an error when addressing why a woman was treated in the way she was to consider how a comparator would be treated: *Madarassy v Nomura International plc* [2007] EWCA Civ 33, [2007] ICR 867 at paras 118–19 and *Fletcher v Blackpool and Fylde & Wyre Hospitals NHS Trust* [2005] ICR 1458, [2005] IRLR 689, EAT at para 106.

v Instituto Madrileno de la Salud,[88] this precludes any unfavourable treatment of a female worker on account of maternity leave or in connection with such leave, without regard to whether such treatment affects an existing employment relationship or a new employment relationship. Mrs Herrero was required to defer the start of a new job, thus losing seniority, because of being on maternity leave. The fact that other people, in particular men, may, on other grounds, have been treated in the same way had no bearing on an assessment of her position, since the deferment of the date on which her new career was deemed to have started stemmed exclusively from the maternity leave to which she was entitled.

7.41   *Herrero* is in a line of EU authority dealing with pregnancy-related discrimination, which includes *Webb v EMO Air Cargo (UK) Ltd,*[89] *Tele Danmark A/S v Handels-og Kontorfunktionaerernes Forbund I Danmark,*[90] *Busch v Klinikum Neustadt GmbH & Co Betriebs-KG,*[91] *Dekker v Stichting Vormingscentrum voor Jonge Volwassenen Plus,*[92] *Brown v Rentokil*[93] and *CNAVTS v Thibault.*[94] Each of these cases makes it clear that, where a woman is treated unfavourably by reason of her pregnancy or maternity leave, a finding of sex discrimination cannot be avoided by arguing that a man in similar circumstances would have been treated in the same way. Nor can unfavourable treatment of a woman by reason of pregnancy or maternity leave be justified by reference to the economic loss that will be suffered as a result of her pregnancy or absence.

7.42   The ECJ's treatment of pregnancy and maternity requires the ET to ask what the factual criterion is in order to determine the reason for the impugned treatment. Establish what the criterion was, first. If it has anything to do with the pregnancy or maternity leave it is likely to be explicitly discriminatory and an exploration for the reasons for the treatment may be unnecessary.[95]

7.43   For example, if pregnancy sickness causes absence that disrupts work, the reason for the treatment is the pregnancy: a problem with

88   Case C-294/04 [2006] ECR I-1513, [2006] IRLR 296 at paras 41 and 46 of the ECJ judgment.
89   [1994] QB 718, [1994] ICR 770, ECJ.
90   Case C-109/00 [2001] ECR I-6993, [2004] ICR 610.
91   Case C-320/01 [2003] ECR I-2041, [2003] IRLR 625.
92   Case 177/88 [1990] ECR I-3941, [1992] ICR 790.
93   [1998] ECR I-4185, [1998] ICR 790.
94   Case C-136/95 [1998] ECR I-2011, [1999] ICR 160.
95   This is similar to the approach in *R (E) v Governing Body of JFS* [2009] UKSC 15, [2010] 2 AC 728: see the discussion of direct discrimination in chapter 2.

disruption is the reason for the reason. Once the core reason has been identified, it is not necessary to go further and ask 'why' a second time.[96]

7.44　It is only if there is any doubt over what were the criteria for the treatment that the mental processes of the alleged discriminator should be considered.

7.45　The approach in JFS means that a number of cases need to be re-examined.[97]

7.46　The pre-EqA 2010 case of *Fletcher v Blackpool and Fylde & Wyre Hospitals NHS Trust*[98] helpfully summarises the key principles relating to pregnancy and maternity discrimination, including key ECJ decisions. Its emphasis that discrimination involves the application of different rules to comparable situations or the application of the same rule to different situations remains a valuable guide to the correct approach:[99]

> As applied to pregnancy and maternity cases, the second limb of this definition means that treating pregnant women workers or women on maternity leave in the same way as other employees during the 'protected period' (that is the start of pregnancy through to the end of maternity leave), in circumstances in which they are disadvantaged because of their pregnancy or maternity, is applying the same treatment to different situations and is therefore discrimination. In this way, the law aims to ensure substantive equality for working women, who would otherwise be disadvantaged by their pregnancy.

7.47　Thus in the case of pregnancy-related sickness given above, pointing to the disruption caused by intermittent and unpredictable incapacity does not prevent the reason for the treatment being the characteristic.[100] Once the criterion upon which the treatment is based has

---

96　In the context of race discrimination, see *Amnesty International v Ahmed* [2009] ICR 1450, [2009] IRLR 884, EAT. This uses the phrase 'inherent in the act itself', rather than the *JFS* use of 'criterion'. Although the two are similar, the *JFS* approach is arguably wider.

97　Eg *Blundell v Governing Body of St Andrew's Catholic Primary School* [2007] ICR 1451, [2007] IRLR 652. On the *JFS* approach, it is difficult to see why there should not be a finding of discrimination if the same facts arose today. The criterion or reason for the treatment was the pregnancy. The motive of tackling any disruption, however benign, is secondary as the additional disruption would be caused by the maternity leave.

98　[2005] ICR 1458, [2005] IRLR 689, EAT and note the discussion about the 'reason why' and the discussion of the context of *Fletcher* in *Chief Constable of Hampshire Constabulary v Haque* UKEAT/483/10, [2012] EqLR 113.

99　*Fletcher* [2005] ICR 1458, [2005] IRLR 689, EAT at para 64.

100　See the discussions of reasons in *Amnesty International v Ahmed* [2009] ICR 1450, [2009] IRLR 884, EAT.

been identified, it is not permissible to go further to consider motive. Thus if the core reason, or criterion, for the unfavourable treatment is a pregnancy-related illness, that is pregnancy discrimination.[101] The question is ultimately one of the causes of the treatment. If they include pregnancy the claim will be established.

The Equality Act 2010

7.48   The claimant must show the following to establish discrimination on the basis of pregnancy and maternity:[102]

- the treatment:
  - was unfavourable, and
  - was because of pregnancy or maternity and
- (for pregnancy discrimination) the treatment was decided upon, done, or not done, during the protected period, or
- (for maternity discrimination) the treatment was because she had taken or sought to take OML or AML.

7.49   EqA 2010 s18(1) refers to pregnancy and maternity as a protected characteristic for the purposes of Part 5 of the Act, which deals with work.[103] They are not listed separately as protected characteristics in the Act. Where a claim involves these as part of multiple characteristics, claimants will have to set them out as alternatives.[104]

7.50   If the treatment is pregnancy or maternity discrimination a finding of sex discrimination cannot be made in relation to it.[105] They can be set out as alternatives in making a claim. The EqA 2010 also does not prevent a finding of discrimination based on any of the other protected characteristics.

7.51   Pregnancy and maternity are not listed as protected characteristics for the purposes of indirect discrimination.[106] However, any woman who was indirectly discriminated against because she was pregnant or a new mother would 'by definition, be able to make a claim of indirect sex discrimination, since any provision or practice which disadvantages pregnant women or new mothers is disadvantageous to

---

101 See EqA 2010 s18(2)(b).
102 EqA 2010 s18.
103 EqA 2010 s17(1) has the same effect for non-work cases.
104 EqA 2010 s14 is not being brought into force under the Coalition Government; see para 2.77.
105 See EqA 2010 s18(7).
106 EqA 2010 s19(3).

women'.[107] Harassment under the EqA 2010 does not include pregnancy and maternity as protected characteristics.[108] Harassment does not require a comparator. Conduct because of pregnancy or maternity would clearly be 'related to' the protected characteristic of sex.[109]

Discrimination in work cases[110]

7.52 EqA 2010 s18 defines pregnancy and maternity discrimination separately. It is pregnancy discrimination where:

A person (A) discriminates against a woman if, in the protected period in relation to a pregnancy of hers, A treats her unfavourably –
(a) because of the pregnancy, or
(b) because of illness suffered by her as a result of it.

7.53 It is maternity discrimination if a person treats a woman unfavourably because she is on compulsory maternity leave.[111]

7.54 It is also maternity discrimination if a person treats a woman unfavourably because she is exercising, or seeking to exercise, or has exercised or sought to exercise the right to OML or to AML.[112]

7.55 What comes within the scope of EqA 2010 s18 should be interpreted broadly to be consistent with UK and EU jurisprudence. Thus in *Brown v Stockton-on-Tees Borough Council*[113] Mrs Brown was selected for redundancy because she needed maternity leave. That was manifestly a reason connected with her pregnancy. It was not a remote cause of her dismissal (as the Court of Appeal had held). It was the reason why she was selected rather than one of the other employees. Therefore it would have been an abuse of language to say that the reason for her dismissal was not directly and intimately connected to her pregnancy.[114] Therefore if the pregnancy plays a role in the decision the decision will be within the scope of section 18.

---

107 Solicitor General, Committee Stage, 8th Sitting 16 June 2009.
108 EqA 2010 s26.
109 For a fuller discussion see paras 1.102–1.106.
110 Provisions relating to protection of pregnancy and maternity in non-work situations, which fall outside the scope of this book, are to be found at EqA 2010 s17.
111 EqA 2010 s18(3).
112 EqA 2010 s18(4).
113 [1989] 1 AC 20.
114 *Brown v Stockton-on-Tees Borough Council* [1989] 1 AC 20, per Lord Griffiths at 25F–G, [1988] IRLR 263 at para 12. At that stage there was no separate unfair dismissal protection for maternity leave.

7.56   There must first be a pregnancy for other effects to be related to it so that in the CJEU case *Mayr v Bäckerei und Konditorei Gerhard Flöckner OHG* IVF treatment does not give rise to pregnancy for the purposes of PWD until a fertilised embryo has been implanted into the uterus. The CJEU also pointed out that where implantation would be immediate, dismissal during that short and important stage of IVF constitutes direct sex discrimination.[115]

The 'protected period'

7.57   The protected period starts when the woman becomes pregnant. If she has the right to OML and AML, it ends at the end of AML. If she returns to work earlier, the protected period ends with her return to work. However, it cannot end during compulsory maternity leave. For a standard workplace, this is the two weeks starting with the birth but for a workplace that counts as a factory the exclusion period is four weeks. During the compulsory maternity leave period it is a criminal offence to allow a woman to work for an employer.[116]

7.58   If the woman does not have the right to statutory maternity leave, for example if she is not an employee, or if the pregnancy ends before the 24th week before the EWC, the protected period ends two weeks from the end of the pregnancy.[117] If the pregnancy ended on a Monday, the last day of the protected period would be the second Sunday following. If, say, after a miscarriage there were further complications occurring after the end of that two-week period, any adverse treatment would be outside the protected period so would have to be considered as sex discrimination.

7.59   If, however, the pregnancy ends after 24 weeks, whether with a stillbirth or a live birth, that entitles the woman to full OML and AML and therefore to the maximum protected period if she wishes to take her full statutory maternity leave.[118] Pressure from the employer for her to return is likely to be pregnancy discrimination under EqA 2010

---

115   Case C-506/06 [2008] ECR I-1017, [2008] IRLR 387, and see the obiter discussion in *Sahota v Home Office* [2010] ICR 772.

116   EqA 2010 s213(3) and ERA 1996 s72(1). The Public Health Act 1936 s205 provides for the criminal offence, albeit the fine on conviction is a maximum of £200. A 'factory' is defined by the Factories Act 1961 s175. The definition is broad. It includes, for example, abattoirs and dry docks.

117   EqA 2010 s18(6)(b).

118   EqA 2010 s213 defines references to maternity leave by reference to rights conferred by the ERA 1996. MAPLE 1999 reg 2(1) defines 'childbirth' as including 'the birth of a child whether living or dead after 24 weeks of pregnancy'.

s18(2) because she is still in the protected period, and/or maternity discrimination under section 18(4) because she is seeking to exercise her right to statutory maternity leave.

7.60   How long the protected period continues depends on whether the woman takes all of her SML. Employees are now all entitled to 26 weeks' OML and to 26 weeks' AML. The only requirement is to give proper notice.

7.61   Determining the protected period is important because, as mentioned above:

- unfavourable treatment during the protected period can be unlawful pregnancy discrimination;
- if a decision is taken during the protected period and only implemented afterwards, the implementation is treated as having occurred in the protected period.[119]

7.62   However, if the unfavourable treatment is decided upon and happens outside the protected period entirely and is because of pregnancy or maternity, it should be considered as sex discrimination. So if a woman is unfavourably treated because she is trying to get pregnant, that will not be pregnancy discrimination, but it might be maternity discrimination.

7.63   Maternity discrimination under EqA 2010 s18(4) is treated differently from pregnancy discrimination under section 18(2). It is not restricted to treatment during or decided upon in the protected period. The only role of the protected period in relation to maternity discrimination is that section 18(7) excludes unfavourable treatment within the protected period that is found to be either pregnancy or maternity discrimination from also being found to be sex discrimination.

'Pregnancy of hers'

7.64   The pregnancy must be that of the worker and it must be a current rather than prospective one.

7.65   There is no pregnancy and maternity discrimination by association. However, if a man is treated less favourably because of his partner's pregnancy, that could be sex discrimination.[120]

---

119 EqA 2010 s18(5) putting into domestic law the effect of the ECJ's decision in Case C-460/06 *Paquay v Societe d'Architectes Hoet & Minne SPRL* [2007] ECR I-8511, [2008] ICR 420.
120 The Scottish EAT has held in *Kulikaoskas v Macduff Shellfish* [2011] ICR 48 that the SDA 1975, even when read with the broader wording of the PWD, did not

'Because of'

7.66   For treatment to be 'because of' the pregnancy, the employer must believe or suspect that the woman is pregnant; also she must actually be pregnant. However, if the woman is treated unfavourably because of a pregnancy-related illness, all the employer need know is the fact of the illness. If the treatment is unfavourable and is because of the illness and the illness in fact is a result of pregnancy, discrimination under EqA 2010 s18(2)(b) is made out.[121]

7.67   Once the employer knows of the pregnancy, whether from the woman or through the grapevine, then it is possible to establish discrimination under EqA 2010 s18(2)(a).

7.68   If the woman was not actually pregnant, then any less favourable treatment because of the pregnancy would be sex discrimination. In this situation, case-law establishes that there is no need for a comparator,[122] although use of a comparator is not prohibited and may assist to show less favourable treatment or to identify the reason for the unfavourable treatment.[123]

7.69   The Employment Code gives an example of an employer exhibiting at a trade fair. If a pregnant member of the sales team had expected to attend but was not invited, it would help her to show that this unfavourable treatment was because of her pregnancy if she could show that she had been invited in previous years, or that other non-pregnant members of the sales team, whether male or female, were invited. If, however, there was evidence of a long-standing practice of rotating the participants, that might help the employer show that the treatment was because of the practice and that the pregnancy was only a coincidence.[124]

---

prohibit associative discrimination. The Court of Session has referred this issue to the CJEU.

121   This is based on the ordinary statutory interpretation of EqA 2010 s18(2)(b), which provides a different context to the knowledge of illness than that considered in *Del Monte Foods Ltd v Mundon* [1980] ICR 694, [1980] IRLR 224, EAT, although note that the Employment Statutory Code of Practice suggests, at para 8.18, that knowledge of pregnancy continues to be required in all circumstances.

122   See *Fletcher* [2005] ICR 1458, [2005] IRLR 689. However, as such a claim would have to be brought under EqA 2010 s13, which specifically refers to 'treating [the claimant] less favourably than others', as opposed to section 18, which does not, there may be an argument that the wording of the statute requires a comparator in such cases. This point requires judicial clarification.

123   See *Madarassy* [2007] EWCA Civ 33, [2007] ICR 867.

124   Employment Code para 8.19.

7.70   The same approach would apply, for example, to an employer deciding that the employee providing maternity cover was a better performer than the one on maternity leave.[125] If there was no pre-pregnancy history of managing performance issues, dismissing the employee on maternity leave is likely to be because her absence on leave enabled the identification of someone the employer preferred. The core reason for, or the criterion for, the treatment is the absence on maternity leave. The identification of 'performance' issues here is the reason for the reason; it is the motive, or a secondary reason to explain why the criterion underpinning the decision was selected.[126]

Examples of unfavourable treatment

7.71   The Employment Code gives a number of examples of the types of treatment that would amount to unlawful discrimination:[127]

- where the reason for the unfavourable treatment is:
  - that because of the woman's pregnancy she will be temporarily unable to do the job she is employed to do, including cases where for her to perform that work would be a breach of health and safety regulations;
  - the costs to the business of covering her work;
  - any absence due to a pregnancy-related illness;
  - performance issues, or her inability to attend a disciplinary hearing due to morning sickness or other pregnancy-related conditions;
- failure to consult a woman on maternity leave about changes to her work or about possible redundancy;
- disciplining a woman for refusing to carry out tasks due to pregnancy-related risks;
- assuming that a woman's work will become less important to her after childbirth and giving her less responsible or less interesting work as a result;
- depriving a woman of her right to an annual assessment of her performance because she was on maternity leave;
- excluding a pregnant woman from business trips.

---

125 Employment Code para 8.20.
126 See further the discussion at paras 7.44–7.55 above.
127 See Employment Code paras 8.22 and 8.23.

7.72   Other examples include:

- if pregnancy absence or pregnancy-related performance or time keeping issues prevent a fair assessment of her work during a probationary period, deciding to dismiss her rather than to postpone the assessment;
- the costs of carrying out or of implementing a risk assessment;
- transferring part of her work to another worker because she would not be able to complete that work during maternity leave;
- demoting or dismissing an employee, or giving her inferior work because she is pregnant, absent with pregnancy sickness or on maternity leave or has just returned from leave, or because any of those reasons cause disruption or difficulty in the way the business operates;
- failing to notify or consult a woman on maternity leave about a reorganisation or work plans for the year ahead;
- failing to notify a woman on maternity leave of training opportunities or job vacancies;
- forcing a woman to resign, having told the employer about the pregnancy, because of the general hazards she knows about in the workplace and her employer's failure to carry out a risk assessment.

7.73   This list is not exhaustive. Unfavourable treatment because of similar reasons is likely to be pregnancy and maternity discrimination if it occurs during the protected period. It is important not to underestimate the strength of the protected status afforded to pregnancy and maternity.

7.74   The converse is that an employer also has to avoid being disproportionately helpful. This protection requires only that which is reasonably necessary to compensate for the disadvantages occasioned by pregnancy or maternity. Providing treatment that is disproportionately favourable may expose an employer to a sex discrimination claim by a disadvantaged colleague.[128]

Complying with other laws

7.75   If the unfavourable treatment is required to comply with laws protecting women who are pregnant or have recently given birth it is excluded from being discrimination by the EqA 2010 Sch 22 para 2. This could be, for example, if the employer medically suspends a

128 *Eversheds Legal Services Ltd v De Belin* [2011] IRLR 448, EAT.

pregnant night-shift worker whose doctor has certified that she cannot work nights. Dismissal is not permitted.[129]

The 'occupational requirement' defence

7.76 In some cases, the occupational requirement defence may apply.[130] However, EqA 2010 Sch 9, para 1(2)(a) does not apply this defence to cases where a person is subjected to any other detriment (EqA 2010 s39(2)(d)). For example, if a heavily pregnant catwalk model was excluded from a show she would normally have done, but not dismissed, the occupational requirement defence would not apply.

7.77 **Practical points**

- If there is evidence that other pregnant workers have been treated in a discriminatory way in that, for example, they have not been allowed to return to the same job and work, this may give rise to an inference that the complainant, who has been treated in a similar way, has been treated unfavourably because of her pregnancy or maternity leave.
- The opposite is also true, so an employer should lead evidence of past reasonable treatment of pregnant women or those on maternity leave to help negative an inference that the reason for unfavourable treatment is the pregnancy, a pregnancy-related illness or maternity leave. However, past reasonable treatment is not conclusive. For example, a changed and adverse financial climate may cause pressure to discriminate.
- The burden of proof provisions apply in relation to maternity and pregnancy discrimination and to other contraventions of the Act.

129 For medical suspension, see para 7.8 above.
130 See chapter 13.

Other unlawful acts

Key points

- Section 111 of the EqA 2010 prohibits A from instructing B to do anything in relation to C which contravenes the Act;
- A is prohibited from causing B to do such acts to C.
- A is prohibited from directly or indirectly inducing B to do such acts to C.
- B (the person instructed etc) can bring proceedings in addition to C (the recipient of the unlawful act).
- It is unlawful for A to instruct (etc) B1 to help A or B2 to do an unlawful act to C.

Instructing, causing or inducing contraventions

8.1   Section 111 of the EqA 2010 makes it unlawful for a person to instruct, cause or induce someone to discriminate against, harass or victimise another person or to attempt to do so.[1] However, for the section to apply, the relationship between the person giving the instruction or causing or inducing the act of discrimination/harassment/victimisation and the person whom they instruct or cause or induce to commit the act must be one in which discrimination/harassment or victimisation is prohibited. This will include all the relationships set out in Part 5 of the Act. The relationships are:

- employer – employee;
- employer – job applicant;
- principal – contract worker;
- chief officer – police officer;
- partnership/LLP – partner, partnership applicant;
- barrister/advocate – pupils/devils (and applicants) and tenants/member of stable;
- office giver[2] – office holder/applicant;
- qualifications body – person requiring qualification;
- employment service provider – recipient of employment service;
- trade organisation – member/applicant for membership;
- local authority – member.

---

1 See the Employment Code para 9.16, which gives the example of a GP instructing the receptionist not to register anyone with an Asian name.
2 This shorthand is expanded at paras 11.44–11.63.

8.2   EqA 2010 s111 extends the scope of protection available under the precursor legislation: such protection differed according to which protected characteristic was in issue. Under the Act the person targeted for discrimination etc and the recipient of the instruction etc are both able to bring proceedings. Irrespective of whether an individual has suffered a detriment, the EHRC can bring proceedings.[3]

8.3   The recipient of the instruction or inducement will have a claim (or cause of action) against the instructor. The instructor does not actually have to cause or induce the recipient to do an act that is unlawful under the EqA 2010. It is simply the act of instructing, causing or inducing (or attempting to do so) that is in itself unlawful.

8.4   In the case of an individual, however, the person instructed etc (B) will only have a claim against the instructor (A) if

- as a result of
- A's conduct
- B is subjected to a detriment.[4]

8.5   Thus if a GP were to instruct the receptionist not to register anyone with an Asian name and subjected the receptionist to a detriment for not following the instruction, the receptionist would have a claim in the ET without more. The potential patient's claim would be brought in the county court as it relates to the provision of services under Part 3 of the EqA 2010.

8.6   'Instruction' is a clear concept. Where the instructor gives an instruction in the form of a general instruction not to provide a benefit for a class of persons, that will, it is suggested, obviously be an instruction to commit a series of unlawful acts. 'Instruction' will be given its ordinary meaning. As it is the act of instructing that is unlawful it does not matter if the instruction is obeyed or implemented.[5]

8.7   'Causing' and 'inducing' require a little more clarification. The concept of causing in this context will need to be clarified in the case-law. However, it is capable of capturing the situation in which A causes B, without B knowing that it is an unlawful act, to do something to C which is unlawful under the EqA 2010. The term 'person' in the Act includes a company. However, the section does not permit a company to make a claim against a managing director of the company who causes the company to commit an act of unlawful discrimination. This is because the relationship between the managing

3   EqA 2010 s111(5)(c) and Employment Code para 9.24.
4   EqA 2010 s111(5).
5   Employment Code para 9.16.

director (A) and the company (B) is not such that an act by A against B could be unlawful under the relevant parts of the Act.

8.8   An inducement may be direct or indirect[6] and may amount to no more than persuasion. It does not have to involve a benefit or loss to the recipient. For example, there would be an inducement in the following situation: in a despatch company where the employees are all male and there is a lot of sexual banter the HR assistant receives a job application from a woman. The manager comments that it would be easier if such applications were 'lost'. Even though the manager had not made any direct threat or promise, this is likely to amount to unlawful inducement. The manager has encouraged the HR assistant to commit an act of discrimination because of sex. The Employment Code[7] gives the example of a partner in an accountancy firm suggesting that hiring a physically disabled senior receptionist would reflect poorly on the decision-maker's judgment. Hinting that such a decision might affect the decision-maker's future would be likely to amount to causing or attempting to cause the decision-maker to act unlawfully by discriminating against the person with the disability.

Relationships that have ended

8.9   EqA 2010 s108 makes it unlawful to discriminate against or harass someone after a relationship covered by the Act has ended. The section states that a person A must not discriminate against another B in certain circumstances. Section 218 gives effect to Schedule 28, which lists where 'discrimination' is defined or otherwise explained. It states in the index of defined expressions that discrimination is explained in sections 13–19,[8] 21 (failing to comply with the duty to make reasonable adjustments) and 108 (post-termination).

8.10   Therefore, EqA 2010 s108 does not apply specifically to acts of victimisation. Section 120 confers powers on the ET in respect of Part 5, sections 108, 111 or 112 as they relate to Part 5 of the Act. However, the victimisation provisions arise in Part 2 of the Act and acts of victimisation in Part 5 are rendered unlawful only in respect of employees. Section 83 defines 'employment' in current terms only. Thus a person who is no longer an employee, and who is the subject

6 EqA 2010 s111(4).

7 Employment Code para 9.18.

8 These cover discrimination which is direct (s13), combined (s14), arising from disability (s15), pregnancy and maternity based (s18) and indirect (s19).

of victimisation will not be able, on the face of it, to bring a claim before the ET in respect of that victimisation by the former employer. This means that a person who is given an unfair reference and cannot get a job as a result of doing a protected act appears to be without redress.

8.11　However, in order to comply with the requirements of the Directives 2000/78, Directive 2000/43 and the gender recast Directive the provisions of the EqA 2010 relating to victimisation of an employee[9] must be read expansively[10] so as to extend to ex-employees. Read in this way the ET will continue to have jurisdiction to hear post-termination victimisation claims and there will be no regression from previous protection.

8.12　An early case will need to establish the solution set out above.[11] Claimants who are subjected to detriment after the termination of their employment because they have done a protected act may, in the alternative, be able to rely on the whistleblowing provisions contained in the Employment Rights Act 1996. A complaint about a breach of the EqA 2010 may qualify for protection under s43B(1)(b) of the 1996 Act (as it could show that the employer is failing to comply with a legal obligation to which it is subject). If the employee or worker is subjected to a detriment as a result, this will be unlawful under s47B(1) of the 1996 Act even if the detriment is imposed after the end of their employment (see *Woodward v Abbey National Plc (No 1)*.[12]

8.13　EqA 2010 s108(3) makes it clear that the protection against discrimination and harassment will apply even if the relationship in question came to an end before section 108 came into force.

8.14　In order for EqA 2010 s108 to apply, the discrimination or harassment must arise out of and be closely connected to a relationship that used to exist between the victim and the alleged perpetrator. In addition the protection will only apply if a person could have enforced protection against discrimination and/or harassment if they were still in the relationship that has ended. The Act says that the conduct of the respondent must be of such a description that would have contravened the Act if it had occurred during the relationship. It is

9　EqA 2010 s39(4) in particular.

10　See, by direct analogy *Coote v Granada Hospitality Ltd* [1999] IRLR 452 (after the preliminary ruling in the ECJ in C/185/97, at [1998] IRLR 656) and the reasoning in *Rhys-Harper v Relaxion Group plc* [2003] IRLR 484 in the House of Lords.

11　Permission to appeal to the Court of Appeal was given on this point in *Rowstock Ltd and another v Jessemey (EHRC intervening)* [2012] UKEAT/0112/12.

12　[2006] EWCA Civ 822, [2006] ICR 1436].

clear that this is a threshold requirement only and means that the conduct must be of a type that would constitute a contravention in the employment relationship.

8.15   Post-termination harassment does not extend to marriage and civil partnership or pregnancy/maternity as the harassment provisions do not apply to those protected characteristics.[13] These must therefore be analysed in terms of discrimination in relation to post-termination treatment. Equally, there is no protection against post-termination discrimination by association based on marriage/civil partnership or pregnancy/maternity because the discrimination by association protection does not apply to these protected characteristics.[14] Post-termination discrimination (whether direct or indirect) will only apply in the context of work to the protected characteristic of marriage and civil partnership as the provisions in the EqA 2010 only apply to marriage and civil partnership in the work context.

Close connection

8.16   The requirement for the discrimination or harassment to be closely connected to the previous relationship between the victim and the alleged perpetrator is not elucidated in the EqA 2010 or in the Explanatory Notes. The Employment Code does not provide any further clarity, stating that 'closely connected to' is a matter of degree to be judged on a case-by-case basis.[15] The purpose of the provision is to protect against discrimination arising out of the relationship. Thus, for example, if an employer regularly invites employees (and ex-employees if they are 'good leavers') to functions, this is a benefit in relation to which discrimination would have a close connection to the previous employment. Other benefits that are directly linked to the employment relationship would include (a) provision of tax information (b) co-operation with the benefits agency by providing information concerning previous employment and (c) references whether oral or written.

8.17   An obvious example of direct discrimination post-termination would be that of an employee who receives an inaccurate and negative job reference from her former employer because she is a lesbian.[16]

---

13   EqA 2010 s26(5) does not list these characteristics as protected against harassment.
14   EqA 2010 s18 has this effect, see paras 1.64, 2.67 and 7.65.
15   Employment Code para 10.58.
16   Employment Code, example at para 10.58.

8.18   Case-law has held that the refusal to provide an employment reference to an ex-employee would be conduct sufficiently connected to the prior employment relationship.[17]

8.19   Remarks made outside an ET hearing during the course of ET proceedings can constitute discrimination that arises out of and is closely connected to the relationship of employment, which has ended.[18] A failure to settle a judgment debt owed by an employer to a former employee arising out of an earlier award by an ET in respect of a discrimination claim made by the employee came within the post-termination jurisdiction and may constitute victimisation.[19] In the earlier case of *D'Souza v Lambeth Borough Council*,[20] the House of Lords held that a discriminatory failure by an employer to comply with a reinstatement order did not arise from the employment relationship.

8.20   The Court of Appeal in the *Coutinho v Rank Nemo* case noted that there were difficulties in setting up a single test to decide what protection the law extended to an ex-employee against acts of discrimination and victimisation by a former employer after the termination of their employment relationship. The court observed that Parliament needed to enact one reasonably workable test for determining discrimination liability in the area of expired employment and concluded that, unless that was done, courts and ETs would regularly face difficulties.[21] The test that has been produced in EqA 2010 s108 essentially leaves the question of close connection to be decided on the facts.

Reasonable adjustments

8.21   EqA 2010 s108(4) requires reasonable adjustments to be made for disabled people even after a relationship has ended, but only if they continue to be at a substantial disadvantage as compared with people without a disability. Section 108 stipulates that the sections dealing with disability are to be read as if the relationship had not ended.[22]

17 *Coote v Granada Hospitality Ltd* C-185/97 [1985] ECR I-5199.
18 *Nicholls v Corin Tech* (2008) UKEAT/0290/07/LA (conduct that was intended or calculated to deter a former employee from continuing ET proceedings to vindicate his rights).
19 *Coutinho v Rank Nemo* [2009] ICR 1296.
20 [2003] ICR 867.
21 See eg as demonstrated in *Woodward v Abbey National Plc (No 1)* [2006] ICR 1436, a whistleblower case involving post-termination detriment.
22 EqA 2010 s108(5) in relation to sections 20, 21 and 22 and their schedules; and see Employment Code para 10.60.

Liability of employers and principals

8.22   By virtue of EqA 2010 s109, employers will be liable for acts of discrimination, harassment or victimisation committed by their employees in the course of employment.[23] Principals (including employers) are liable for such acts committed by their agents while acting under the principal's authority.[24] The liability of employers and principals is in addition to any liability on the part of the actual discriminator. It makes no difference whether the employer or principal knew or approved of what was done.[25]

In the course of employment or within the authority of a principal

Employees

8.23   Employers are liable for unlawful acts committed by their employees in the course of their employment.[26] The phrase 'in the course of employment' should be interpreted as it would be understood in everyday speech. It is a much wider concept than vicarious liability under non-statutory 'torts'.[27]

8.24   'In the course of employment' includes acts in the workplace and may also extend to situations such as work-related social functions or business trips abroad.[28] In some cases it may be difficult to tell whether an act is 'in the course of employment' and the circumstances of the particular case will be determinative. In *Waters v Metropolitan Police Comr*,[29] a sexual assault by one off-duty police officer on another in a police section house was not 'in the course of employment'. However, in *Chief Constable of the Lincolnshire Police v Stubbs*,[30] the EAT held that an ET was entitled to find that sexual harassment by a police colleague in a pub, where the officer had gone for a leaving

---

23   EqA 2010 s109(1).
24   EqA 2010 s109(2).
25   EqA 2010 s109(3) and see the Employment Code paras 10.45–10.52.
26   EqA 2010 s109(1) and Employment Code para 10.45. This is the case whether or not the employer knows about the act of the employee.
27   Ie non-contractual wrongs; there is an authoritative discussion in the Court of Appeal in *Jones v Tower Boot Co Ltd* [1997] ICR 254.
28   Employment Code para 10.46 and the examples given there.
29   [1997] IRLR 589.
30   [1999] IRLR 81, [1999] ICR 547.

party after her duty had ended, was 'in the course of employment'.[31] In *Sidhu v Aerospace Composite Technology Ltd*,[32] the employer was held not to be liable for a racist attack committed during the course of a 'family day' organised by an employer and held at an amusement park. It may have been relevant to the decision that the majority of those attending the event were family and friends, rather than employees. Factors that are likely to assist an ET to decide whether the act is carried out in the course of the perpetrator's employment or not include the following:[33]

- location: did the incident take place on the employer's premises (or a place over which the employer had sufficient control)? Thus the employer is unlikely to be liable for sexual advances at a co-worker's house outside office hours;[34]
- was either the complainant or the alleged perpetrator on duty at the time of the act?
- timing of the event at which the act took place: was it during working hours, just after or at a wholly different time?
- who was there? Did the event permit partners of employees, customers or wholly unrelated people?

8.25 The more 'remote' from work the less likely that the act will be in the course of employment. Thus a chance meeting in the supermarket is unlikely to result in an act in the course of employment. Claimants should therefore ensure that the evidence of close proximity to the workplace or work done is presented to the ET.

Agents

8.26 Any unlawful act committed with the express or implied authority of the principal will be treated as having been done by the principal.[35] It is no defence for the principal to allege that he did not give the agent authority to discriminate so long as the agent has authority to do an act that may be carried out in a lawful or a discriminatory manner.[36] However, a principal will not be liable for unlawful discrimination carried out by its agent where the agent acted in contravention of

31 This is the example in the Employment Code para 10.46.
32 [2001] ICR 167.
33 See the discussion in *Chief Constable of Lincolnshire v Stubbs* [1999] IRLR 81.
34 *HM Prison Service v Davis* EAT/1294/98.
35 EqA 2010 s109(2) and Employment Code para 10.48.
36 *Lana v Positive Action Training in Housing (London) Ltd* [2001] IRLR 501.

the principal's express instructions not to discriminate because the agent will not have acted with the 'authority' of the principal.

8.27   The Employment Code makes clear that it 'does not matter whether the principal knows about or approves of the acts of their agents. An agent would be considered to be acting with the principal's authority if the principal consents (whether this consent is expressed or implied) to the agent acting on their behalf. Examples of agents include occupational health advisers engaged but not employed by the employer or recruitment agencies'.[37]

Reasonable steps defence for employers

8.28   There is a 'reasonable steps' defence open to employers (but not to principals) in EqA 2010 s 109(4) that allows an employer to avoid liability if it can show that it took all reasonable steps to prevent its employees from acting unlawfully. The steps that an employer must have taken will be in respect of the period of time prior to the alleged discrimination and not in response to the discriminatory conduct. The steps taken by an employer are likely to be reasonable if there are no further reasonably practicable steps that the employer could have taken. The difference in the wording of the Act from the precursor legislation ('from doing in the course of his employment acts of that description'[38]) suggests that the employer must take all reasonable steps to prevent the employee from acting unlawfully. The intention however of the legislation is the same.

8.29   In practice if the employer seeks to assert this defence the claimant should look at the steps recommended in the Employment Code as action that employers can take to ensure that they comply with the Act.[39]

8.30   The test of 'reasonable steps' is likely to be approached by the ET establishing:

- what preventative steps the employer did take and then ask;
- what further steps could have been taken.[40]

8.31   Reasonable steps will include:

- implementing and reviewing an equality policy;[41]

---

37 Employment Code para 10.48.
38 See for example section 41 of the repealed Sex Discrimination Act 1975.
39 See Employment Code para 10.47 and Part 2 of that Code, chapters 16–19.
40 *Canniffe v East Riding of Yorkshire Council* [2000] IRLR 555.
41 See *Caspersz v Ministry of Defence* UKEAT/0599/05/LA.

- ensuring employees are aware of the policy and its implications for them through induction and refresher training;
- training managers (and particularly supervisors) in harassment and discrimination issues;
- dealing effectively with employee complaints and grievances.

8.32   The size and resources available to an employer will be relevant in determining what is reasonable.

8.33   The employer or principal cannot be held liable for any criminal offences under the EqA 2010 committed by their employee or agent.[42]

8.34   However, if the employee or agent reasonably rely upon a statement by the employer or principal that an act is not unlawful, then the employee or agent will not be liable for the unlawful act.[43] EqA 2010 s110(4) and (5) make it an offence, punishable by a fine of (currently) up to £5,000, if an employer or principal knowingly or recklessly makes a false statement about the lawfulness of doing something under the Act.

8.35   Contrary to case-law and the position under the previous legislation, there is now no requirement in EqA 2010 s110 for the employee or agent to know that they are acting unlawfully in order to be held liable. This is because the liability of employees and agents is now dealt with separately from the provisions relating to aiding a contravention (which are contained in section 112). The Explanatory Notes to the Act make the point that section 110 takes a more direct approach to employee and agent liability than the previous law and state specifically that it is not necessary to show that the employee or agent knew that the act was unlawful.[44]

8.36   EqA 2010 s110(7) excludes liability of employees and agents in respect of disability discrimination in the field of education in schools (ie education claims) as such claims cannot be enforced against individuals. However, disability discrimination in the context of employment within schools is not excluded.

---

42 EqA 2010 s109(5) except for those in the provisions on transport services for disabled people in Part 12 of the Act.

43 EqA 2010 s110(3).

44 See para 370, p82.

Aiding contraventions

8.37   EqA 2010 s112 makes it unlawful knowingly to help someone to discriminate against, harass or victimise another person. It is also unlawful to help with an instruction to discriminate or to help with causing or inducing these unlawful acts, or to help with these acts after a relationship has ended.[45]

8.38   However, it will not be unlawful if the person who is knowingly aiding the perpetrator of discrimination/harassment/victimisation has been told that the act is lawful and they reasonably believe this to be true. 'Reasonable belief' here means the belief of the helper but having regard to the nature of the act and how obviously discriminatory it is, the authority of the person making the statement as to its lawfulness and the knowledge that the helper has or ought to have. EqA 2010 s112(3) and (4) make it an offence, punishable by a fine of (currently) up to £5,000, if the actual perpetrator knowingly or recklessly makes a false statement about the lawfulness of doing something under the Act.

8.39   A person who knowingly aids an act of discrimination/harassment/victimisation will be treated as having done the act themselves. This will mean that the individual will be jointly and severally liable for any compensation found to be payable to the complainant.[46]

8.40   EqA 2010 s112(6) excludes liability in respect of disability discrimination in the field of education in schools as such claims cannot be enforced in respect of individuals.

Help

8.41   'Help' does not have a technical meaning and should not be interpreted as 'procure, induce or cause'.[47] An unlawful act will be committed even where the degree of help is 'not substantial or productive, so long as it is not negligible'.[48] The Employment Code gives the example of a manager asking a worker to look in the HR files and let him know the sex of each candidate, explaining that he wants to filter out the male candidates. The worker may commit an unlawful act in

---

45   Employment Code para 9.25.
46   *Hackney LBC v Sivanandan* UKEAT/75/10, [2011] ICR 1374 and [2013] EWCA Civ 22, where it was confirmed that an ET has no power to apportion the compensation payable to the claimant between individual respondents, contrary to the earlier decision of the EAT in *Way v Crouch* [2005] ICR 1362.
47   See Employment Code para 9.27.
48   Employment Code para 9.27.

giving the manager this help, even if the manager is unsuccessful in excluding the male candidates.

8.42 Two elements are required under EqA 2010 s112 – the mental element inherent in 'knowingly' and the fact of helping. Simply letting a discriminatory act go unchallenged is not sufficient.[49] Nor is it sufficient for a person merely to tolerate an environment in which discrimination is able to occur.[50] In *Anyanwu and Ebuzoeme v South Bank Students' Union and South Bank University*,[51] the House of Lords concluded that the help provided need not be productive or even substantive so long as it was more than negligible. However, in another judgment of the House of Lords, under precursor legislation[52] *Hallam v Avery*,[53] the House of Lords concluded that the fact that police officers had been 'helpful' in a general sense (by sharing information) to the council in imposing extra conditions on a wedding of a gypsy couple was not enough. On the former principles if the potential 'aider' merely suspects that a discriminatory act will occur, without actually wanting it to come about, that was insufficient to trigger liability. However, the new legislation may need to be interpreted in a different way. The Employment Code makes clear that the helper does not have to intend that that unlawful discrimination should result from the help. It is necessary that the helper knows at the time of giving the help that discrimination etc is a probable outcome.[54] 'Help' under EqA 2010 s112 cannot be unconscious or even reckless.

8.43 Thus where legal advisers give objective legal advice in good faith as to the protection of their clients' interests and act strictly upon their clients' instructions, they will generally not be held liable for knowingly helping any discrimination carried out by the client. Thus in *Bird v Sylvester*[55] the legal advisers were not helping their client to discriminate in making an application for costs against an unsuccessful litigant in a discrimination claim.

---

49 *Shepherd v North Yorkshire County Council* [2006] IRLR 190.
50 *Gilbank v Miles* [2006] ICR 1297.
51 [2001] ICR 391.
52 RRA 1976.
53 [2001] ICR 408.
54 Employment Code para 9.28.
55 [2008] ICR 208.

Void and unenforceable terms in contracts, agreements and rules

8.44   A term of a contract, the rules of an undertaking or a collective agreement may constitute an act of discrimination. The EqA 2010 deals with such rules and contract terms by rendering them unenforceable. Any term of a collective agreement is void in so far as it:

- constitutes
- promotes or
- provides for

treatment that is of a description prohibited under the EqA 2010.[56] 'Collective agreement' is defined in the Trade Union and Labour Relations (Consolidation) Act 1992 as meaning any agreement or arrangement made by or on behalf of one or more trade unions and one or more employers or employers' associations.[57] Under TULRCA 1992 the agreement must relate to one or more of the following matters:

- terms and conditions of employment, or the physical conditions in which any workers are required to work;
- engagement or non-engagement, or termination or suspension of employment or the duties of employment, of one or more workers;
- allocation of work or the duties of employment between workers or groups of workers;
- matters of discipline;
- a worker's membership or non-membership of a trade union;
- facilities for officials of trade unions; and
- machinery for negotiation or consultation, and other procedures, relating to any of the above matters, including the recognition[58] by employers or employers' associations of the right of a trade union to represent workers in such negotiation or consultation or in the carrying out of such procedures.

8.45   A term of such an agreement is void in so far as it has any of the characteristics above. The Employment Code states that a collective

---

56   EqA 2010 s145(1).
57   TULRCA 1992 s178.
58   'Recognition' in this context, in relation to a trade union, means the recognition of the union by an employer, or two or more associated employers, to any extent, for the purpose of collective bargaining; and 'recognised' and other related expressions shall be construed accordingly (TULRCA 1992 s178(3)).

agreement will be void in so far as it leads to conduct prohibited by the EqA 2010.[59] However, this does not appear to be an accurate summary of the law. If the collective agreement 'promotes' unlawful conduct, then it is voided so far as it does that in addition to where it 'provides' for or 'constitutes' an unlawful act.

8.46   The term is void rather than unenforceable so that the term has no effect whatsoever. Thus an agreement containing such a term could not be incorporated into the individual's contract. For example a collective agreement that required jobs in a particular part of a factory to be given only to men would be void, so that a woman who applied could not be refused on those grounds.[60]

8.47   Where the claimant needs the agreement to be amended rather than simply declared to have been void an argument could perhaps be constructed that where a collective agreement is in breach of a provision of EU law the underlying Directives[61] require that sanctions should be effective, dissuasive and proportionate so that the agreement should be delared amended.[62] In *Unison v Brennan*[63] the EAT (Elias P) held, deploying the same arguments that the United Kingdom was bound to give effect to its Community law obligations by providing an effective remedy to persons seeking a declaration that provisions in a collective agreement were contrary to the principle of equal treatment. That remedy was to be no less favourable to that given to similar domestic claims.[64]

8.48   The provisions are aimed at ensuring that there is a full range of remedies for claimants. Article 16 of Directive 2000/78, for example, provides:

> Member states shall take the necessary measures to ensure that: (a) any laws, regulations and administrative provisions contrary to the principle of equal treatment are abolished; (b) any provisions contrary to the principle of equal treatment which are included in contracts or collective agreements, internal rules of undertakings or rules governing the independent occupations and professions and workers' and employers' organisations are, or may be, declared null and void or are amended.

---

59 Employment Code para 10.68.
60 Explanatory Notes para 478, p 102.
61 See chapter 19.
62 See for example C-33/89 *Kowalska v Freie und Hanestadt Hamburg* [1990] IRLR 447 and C-184/89, *Nimz v Freie und Handesstadt Hamburg* [1991] IRLR 222.
63 [2008] ICR 955.
64 See [2008] ICR 955 at paras 47–71.

8.49   Thus in a case of indirect discrimination a provision of a collective
agreement can be challenged if it would place persons with a shared
protected characteristic at a disadvantage even if the disadvantage
has not yet accrued to any one person.[65] Thus collective agreements
may be challenged (sometimes from unexpected quarters) using the
voiding provisions.[66]

Discriminatory rules of undertakings

8.50   EqA 2010 s145 (2) renders unenforceable any rule of an undertaking that discriminates against a person or would otherwise lead to
conduct prohibited by the Act. A rule of an undertaking is defined
in section 148 as a rule by a qualifications body or trade organisation
in relation to membership or conferral of a qualification, or a rule
made by an employer for application to employees and prospective
employees.[67] For example, an indirectly discriminatory rule of a qualifications body that required that applicants must have two years' previous experience with a British firm would be unenforceable against
a person who had the equivalent experience with a foreign firm. It
would remain enforceable against a person who did not have the
required experience at all (provided it could be justified).[68]

Declarations

8.51   EqA 2010 s146 enables an ET to declare void or unenforceable a term
of a collective agreement or a rule of an undertaking that contravenes
section 145, as applicable, when a person thinks it may have the effect
of discriminating against them in the future.

8.52   However, there is no power for an ET to modify or amend the
offending term or rule; it is able only to declare the term void (or
unenforceable in the case of a rule). The parties to the collective agreement are then left in a position where they will need to renegotiate.

8.53   EqA 2010 s142 makes clear that a person who would have been
disadvantaged by an unenforceable terms of a contract can continue
to rely on it so as to obtain any benefit to which the term entitles that

65 EqA 2010 s19.
66 *Rolls-Royce plc v Unite the Union* [2009] EWCA Civ 387, [2010] ICR 1; the
employer took the unusual step of seeking Part 8 CPR declaratory relief: see
paras 121–128 for implications of the existence of the provisions now forming
section 145.
67 Employment Code paras 10.68–10.69.
68 Taken from the Explanatory Notes.

person.[69] However, if the term was never incorporated into the individual's contract (save in the case of disability[70]) the individual may not rely on the unenforceable rule. Certain non-contractual terms[71] that have been declared unenforceable due to disability may nonetheless be relied upon. The person may rely on the non-contractual terms.

8.54   EqA 2010 s146 contains a table setting out who can make a complaint in each instance. The first table applies to a person seeking to make a complaint about a term of a collective agreement:

Description of person who made collective agreement	Qualifying person
Employer	A person who is, or is seeking to be, an employee of that employer
Organisation of employers	A person who is, or is seeking to be, an employee of an employer who is a member of that organisation
Association of organisations of employers	A person who is, or is seeking to be, an employee of an employer who is a member of an organisation in that association

The following table applies to a person seeking to make a complaint about a rule of an undertaking:

Description of person who made rule of an undertaking	Qualifying person
Employer	A person who is, or is seeking to be, an employee of that employer
Trade organisation[70] or qualifications body	A person who is, or is seeking to be, a member of the organisation or body A person on whom the body has conferred a relevant qualification A person seeking conferment by the body of a relevant qualification

---

69 EqA 2010 s142(1): 'unenforceable against a person'.
70 EqA 2010 s142(2).
71 Within the meaning of EqA 2010 s142(2). These are non-contractual terms of an agreement relating to the provision of an employment service or provision under a group insurance arrangement of facilities by way of insurance.

The Explanatory notes to the EqA 2010 give the example of a person who is studying for an engineering qualification who is told he will only be eligible for it if he passes a test of his ability to write English. He can ask an ET to declare that the rule requiring the test is indirectly discriminatory and therefore, if unjustified, is unenforceable.

Discriminatory terms of a contract

8.55   Pursuant to EqA 2010 s142(1), a term of a contract will be unenforceable insofar as it 'constitutes, promotes or provides for treatment ... that is of a description prohibited by this Act [EqA]'. The term is only unenforceable if complying with it/applying it has the effect of discriminating against a person or otherwise leading to conduct prohibited by the Act. However, a person who would have been disadvantaged by any such term will still be able to rely on it so as to obtain any benefit to which it entitles him/her. This is why the provision only renders such terms unenforceable, rather than void. A good example is given in the Explanatory Note,[73] at paragraph 460:

> A term in a franchise agreement which included a requirement that the franchisee should only employ Asian people (which would be unlawful direct discrimination because of race unless an exception applied) could not be enforced by the franchisor. But the franchisee could still obtain any benefit he is due under the term, for example he could continue operating the franchise. However, if the franchisee complied with the discriminatory term, a person discriminated against under it could make a claim against the franchisee for unlawful discrimination under other provisions in the Act.

8.56   By reason of EqA 2010 s142(4), the phrase 'treatment of a description prohibited' by the Act excludes a contractual term that should be modified as a result of an implied gender equality or maternity equality clause. This appears to be an odd exception, however, the ethos behind it must be that in respect of such clauses, there are discrete mechanisms for remedying the discriminatory effect (ie EqA 2010 ss66 and 73). In the Explanatory Notes to the Act, it states that: 'This section does not apply to a term of contract modified by an equality clause under Part 5, Chapter 3, because once the term is modified it is no longer discriminatory'.[74]

---

72 For the meaning of 'trade organisation' see para 11.113; for the meaning of 'qualifying body' see para 11.65.

73 www.legislation.gov.uk/ukpga/2010/15/pdfs/ukpgaen_20100015_en.pdf .

74 See paragraph 459 of the Explanatory Notes to the Act.

8.57 EqA s142 will also not apply in respect to contractual terms which may breach the public sector equality duty or the public sector duty regarding socio-economic inequalities. Again, the reason for this exclusion is that different enforcement mechanisms apply.[75]

8.58 In respect to the protected characteristic of disability only, EqA 2010 s142(2) renders unenforceable any non-contractual terms of agreements relating to the provision of employment services (within EqA s56(2)(a) to (e)) or group insurance arrangements for employees. These terms are referred to in EqA s142(3) as 'relevant non-contractual terms'. Therefore, a term in a group private health insurance scheme that is discriminatory in respect to disabled persons would be unenforceable. Similarly, any terms of policies which regulate the provision of an employment service (such as vocational training, work placements, career advice, etc.) which discriminate against disabled persons would also be unenforceable.

8.59 Under EqA 2010 s143, a county court or the Sheriff can make an order that a contractual term which offends EqA 2010 s142 be removed or modified. However, there is a requirement to give notice on every person who would be affected by such an order and each such person has to be afforded an opportunity to make representations as to the order. Paragraph 463 of the Explanatory Note gives the following example:

> A person renting an office in a serviced office block could ask for a term in the rental contract to be amended if the term discriminated indirectly, for example by including an unjustified requirement that people entering the premises remove any facial covering (thus discriminating against Muslim women). The term could be adjusted by the court or sheriff to allow special arrangements to be made to satisfy both genuine security needs of other users and the religious needs of Muslim women visiting the Claimant.

75 See EqA 2010 s148.

Avoiding discrimination in recruitment

Key points

- Discrimination, harassment and victimisation are unlawful at all stages of the recruitment process. That includes:
  - the content of the job description and person specification;
  - the manner and place in which the job is advertised;
  - the selection procedure deployed to select and narrow the field of candidates;
  - the job offer itself.
- It is unlawful to ask employees questions about their health before making a job offer, save in specified circumstances and then only for a small number of specified purposes.
- Positive discrimination is never required, but it is permissible when and only when certain conditions are met (which is likely to be very rarely).
- Recruitment cases are notoriously difficult to win. Asking questions of a prospective employer prior to issuing proceedings will be extremely important so that advisers can elicit as much information as possible about any potential claims in advance

Introduction

9.1   The EqA 2010 makes it unlawful for employers to discriminate against, victimise or harass prospective employees at the recruitment stage. It also introduces some innovations, particularly a (qualified) prohibition on asking applicants questions about health and disability before making a job offer; as well as positive action specific to the recruitment stage.

9.2   This chapter considers how discrimination can be identified at the different stages of recruitment:

- the job requirements (often captured in a job description and person specification);
- the process of finding candidates;
- the process of selecting candidates;
- the content of job offers.

The main statutory provisions

9.3   Under the EqA 2010 there are three types of unlawful acts of discrimination and victimisation:[1]

39 Employees and applicants

(1) An employer (A) must not discriminate against a person (B) –

(a) in the arrangements A makes for deciding to whom to offer employment;

(b) as to the terms on which A offers B employment;

(c) by not offering B employment.

Arrangements

9.4   These are the arrangements that the employer makes for deciding to whom to offer employment, ie the procedure used to decide who to appoint. It includes procedure in a general sense (eg the use of an interview) but also the manner in which the procedure was applied (eg the way the interviewer behaved and the decision-making criteria). The Employment Code points out that 'arrangements' refer to the policies criteria and practices used in the recruitment process including the decision-making process. 'Arrangements' are not confined to those which an employer makes in deciding who should be offered a specific job. They apply to arrangements for deciding who should be offered employment more generally. They will include adverts, the application process and the interview stage.[2]

9.5   *Brennan v J H Dewhurst Ltd*[3] is a good example of unlawful arrangements. When interviewed for a job in a butcher's shop the shop manager made it quite clear to Ms Brennan that he did not want to appoint a woman. The district manager then decided for financial reasons that nobody should be appointed. Miss Brennan therefore would not have got the job even if she had been a man. The tribunal dismissed her claim. However, the EAT held that the interview was part of the arrangements made for deciding to whom to offer employment. The arrangement was applied in a discriminatory manner (by the shop manager) and was therefore unlawful. It did not matter that the district manager had no intention of discriminating

---

1   EqA 2010 s39(3) is in like terms to s39(1), save that the word 'discriminate' is replaced by the word 'victimise'

2   Employment Code para 10.8.

3   [1983] IRLR 357, [1984] ICR 52, EAT. Approved in *Nagarajan v London Regional Transport* [1999] UKHL 36, [1999] IRLR 572, [1999] ICR 877. See also *Roadburg v Lothian Regional Council* [1976] IRLR 283, IT.

on grounds of sex when he had decided that an interview would be used to determine selection, nor any knowledge when he delegated the task of interviewing to the shop manager that the shop manager had discriminatory views.

9.6   The Employment Code is admissible as evidence and must be taken into account by ETs where relevant.[4] It notes in relation to recruitment arrangements:

- the practice of recruitment on recommendation by staff can lead to discrimination.[5] Advertising widely is likely to create a wider and more diverse pool; advertising internally only may not result in diversity in the workforce.[6] Those absent from work (including those on maternity leave) should be included in the internal advertisement of a job.[7]
- Adverts should reflect the job description and person specification and avoid discriminatory wording or words that suggest that reasonable adjustments will not be provided.[8]
- A standardised selection process (allowing for reasonable adjustments) may assist in ensuring equality and objectivity in the application process.[9] Likely reasonable adjustments include provision on request of application forms and information in accessible formats.[10] The Employment Code makes detailed recommendations on how an employer can avoid discrimination in the selection assessment and interview process.[11]

Terms on which employment is offered[12]

9.7   Direct discrimination in such terms is prohibited: it is unlawful to offer to pay a black job applicant less than a white job applicant because of race. Indirect discrimination and all other acts prohibited by EqA 2010 are impermissible. Thus if, for example, a job is offered only on a full-time basis, this is capable of constituting indirect

---

4   Equality Act 2006 s15(4).
5   Employment Code para 16.20.
6   Employment Code para 16.21.
7   Employment Code para 16.22.
8   Employment Code paras 16.23–16.26.
9   Employment Code para 16.32. The Employment Code recommends that personal information be detachable from the application form (paras 16.39–16.42), and the employer can be asked why this was not done.
10 Employment Code paras 16.34–16.38.
11 Employment Code paras 16.43–16.68.
12 EqA 2010 s39(1)(b).

discrimination against a female applicant with child-caring responsibilities.[13] Another example would be including a mobility clause in an offer of employment, which requires the prospective employee, if employed, to travel long distances. This too would be capable of being indirectly discriminatory against female applicants with child-caring responsibilities.[14] The Employment Code makes clear that 'terms' covers things such as pay and bonuses or other benefits. In respect of sex/pregnancy/maternity discrimination a term of an offer of employment relating to pay is unlawful where, if it were accepted by the employee, it would give rise to a breach of an equality clause or rule.[15]

Not offering employment

9.8   An obvious example of an unlawful act of this kind is refusing to appoint an applicant because of a protected characteristic. *Osborne Clarke Services v Purohit*[16] gives a less obvious example. Mr Purohit was refused employment because he required but did not have a work permit allowing him to work in the United Kingdom. He was of Indian origin. The ET found, and the EAT agreed, that the requirement to have a work permit was indirectly discriminatory and had not been, on the facts, justified since it may well have been possible for Mr Purohit to obtain a work permit if offered the job.

9.9   There are, however, important limits to the scope of protection to job-seekers. In *Padgett v Serota and the Board of Trustees of the Tate Gallery*,[17] a case decided under the similar provisions of the Employment Equality (Religion and Belief) Regulations (EERBR) 2003, but which is likely to apply equally to the EqA 2010, the EAT gave guidance as to the breadth of the scope of protection.

9.10   Mr Padgett was a performance artist who submitted a tender to the Tate Gallery to produce a piece of artwork. The Tate Gallery did not have a particular job on offer at the time. It had a rolling open tender programme, which, the ET found, was particularly open ended. It was little more than an indication of the general policy adopted by the Tate in respect of acquiring art and setting up exhibitions. Mr

---

13 Employment Code para 16.9.
14 See eg *Meade-Hill & National Union of Civil and Public Servants v British Council* [1996] 1 All ER 79, [1995] ICR 847, [1995] IRLR 478, CA.
15 Employment Code para 10.9.
16 [2009] IRLR 341, EAT.
17 17 December 2007, unreported, UKEAT/0097/07/LA and UKEAT/0099/07, [2007] All ER (D) 239 (Dec).

Padgett's tender was unsuccessful. He presented a discrimination claim alleging that he had been unsuccessful because of his Unitarian beliefs.

9.11   The EAT held that the scope of regulation 6 of the EERBR 2003 (the equivalent provision to EqA 2010 s39) was not unlimited. In general terms, it applied where an employer was recruiting employees. The EAT drew a distinction between having employment to offer, on the one hand, and being prepared on the other hand to listen to a proposal that, if accepted, might mature into an offer of employment. It held that EERBR reg 6(1) applied where an employer had employment to offer. It did not apply merely because an employer was prepared to entertain a proposal for some new piece of work which (if accepted) might then lead to an offer of employment. The EAT gave the following example of the distinction it drew:[18]

> If a theatre production company decides to put on a specific musical, and for that purpose carries out auditions for the parts, it has employment to offer and is making arrangements for deciding to whom it will offer the employment. But if a theatre production company is open to new ideas, and is approached by an actor or group of actors with a proposed musical or play, the mere fact that it is prepared to consider the proposal, or may even have encouraged such proposals, does not mean it has employment to offer or is making arrangements for offering the employment.

9.12   It is also unlawful for an employer to harass a job applicant in relation to employment with the employer.[19] This might occur if, for example, an applicant was subjected to humiliating personal questioning at an interview and the reason for the conduct related to a protected characteristic.

Selection in practice

9.13   This chapter now goes on to consider the ways in which unlawful discrimination can arise at the various different stages of recruitment and the practical steps recommended by the Employment Code that it would be sensible for an employer to take to avoid discrimination.

18   *Padgett* at para 37.
19   EqA 2010 s40(1)(b).

Stage 1: Job requirements

9.14 These are the things that the employer will require the applicant to be willing and able to do and the things which the employer requires the applicant to have. For example, the employer might require the applicant to be willing and able to fulfil the duties of the post and also to do so on a full-time basis. The employer might also require or prefer the applicant to have certain qualifications, experience, skills and so on. These requirements and preferences are often stipulated in writing in job descriptions and person specifications.

Direct discrimination in job requirements

9.15 Direct discrimination can be built into the job requirements. For instance it might be a requirement of the job that the post-holder is white. Unless there is a genuine occupational requirement (GOR)[20] for the post-holder to be white, an unsuccessful job applicant who was declined on grounds of their race, could bring a claim pursuant to s39(1)(c) Act.[21]

Indirect discrimination

9.16 Job requirements can also be indirectly discriminatory. The discrimination can take a wide variety of different forms. For example, consider a job that requires the post-holder to work full-time. A female applicant, who is unsuccessful because she can only work part-time because of child-caring responsibilities, might bring an indirect discrimination claim and in most cases it would probably fall to the employer to justify the full-time requirement. Likewise a requirement to work in different parts of the country (a mobility clause) could be indirectly discriminatory for similar reasons.[22]

9.17 Age restrictions may be directly discriminatory in relation to the characteristic of age but they are also capable of amounting to indirect discrimination in respect of other characteristics such as sex. For example, in *Price v Civil Service Commission*[23] a requirement for applicants to be between the ages of 17½ and 28 was found to be

---

20 See chapter 13.
21 See the recommendations in the Employment Code paras 16.4–16.9.
22 *Meade-Hill & National Union of Civil and Public Servants v British Council* [1996] 1 All ER 79, [1995] ICR 847, [1995] IRLR 478, CA.
23 [1977] 1 WLR 1417, [1978] ICR 27, [1977] IRLR 291, EAT and [1978] IRLR 3 (No 2), IT. See also *Perera v Civil Service Commission (No 2)* [1983] IRLR 166, [1983] ICR 428.

indirect sex discrimination. Fewer women could comply with that
requirement than men, given that many women take career breaks
to have children. Now this would be attacked in respect of both
characteristics.

9.18   Requirements as to experience often give rise to indirect discrimination. In *Falkirk Council v Whyte*,[24] a requirement for candidates
to have management training and supervisory experience was held
to be indirectly discriminatory against a female applicant. The applicants consisted mainly of women in low grade posts and men in
management posts. The requirement had a disparate impact on men
and women, but was not justified on the facts.

9.19   Similarly, in the context of qualifications, a requirement to have
a particular UK qualification may be indirect race discrimination if
equivalent qualifications from abroad are not accepted.[25] Similarly a
requirement to speak good English could be indirectly racially discriminatory if basic English would in fact suffice.[26] The Employment
Code makes the more general point that tasks and duties set out in
a job description should be objectively justifiable as necessary to the
post and the job description should not overstate duties that are only
occasional or marginal.[27]

Disability discrimination

9.20   Often disability discrimination in relation to job requirements arises
from a failure to make reasonable adjustments and/or discrimination arising from disability.[28] The Employment Code points out that
where there are different ways of performing a task, the job description should not specify how the task should be done, but should simply state what outcome needs to be achieved.[29]

9.21   For example, the person specification of a particular job requires
applicants to have five years of experience doing a particular task.
This could easily place disabled people at a substantial disadvantage.
If a disabled applicant had only four years' experience, but would have
had five had it not been for a long period of disability-related absence

24 [1997] IRLR 560, EAT. See also *McCausland v Dungannon DC* [1993] IRLR 583, NICA.
25 See eg *Bohon-Mitchell v Common Professional Examination Board and Council of Legal Education* [1978] IRLR 525, IT. See also *J H Walker Ltd v Hussain* [1996] IRLR 11, [1996] ICR 291, EAT.
26 See also *Osborne Clarke Services v Purohit* [2009] IRLR 341, at para 14.8 above.
27 Employment Code para 16.7.
28 See chapter 4.
29 Employment Code para 16.8.

it might well, in the circumstances, be necessary for the employer to adjust the requirement in the case of the disabled applicant so as to accept four years' experience (a failure otherwise to make reasonable adjustments).[30] If the requirement was not capable of objective justification it would also amount to indirect discrimination, and hence itself be unlawful. This would result in the withdrawal generally of the requirement rather than simply a requirement to adjust it in the individual case.

9.22   The duty to make adjustments also applies to the substantive requirements of the job, such as those that might be found in the job description. For example the job description may involve the post-holder travelling extensively by car. If a disabled applicant were unable to do so, it might be a reasonable adjustment to adjust the requirements of the job for the disabled employee such that she could work from a single location, or travel less frequently, or travel by train, or some combination thereof.

9.23   Reasonableness of the adjustment places a limit on the duty to make adjustments to the job requirements. Thus in *Hart v Chief Constable of Derbyshire Constabulary*[31] a probationary police constable was, as a result of her disability, unable to demonstrate an ability to carry out certain tasks where there was a real risk of confrontation. This was a requirement for successful completion of her probation period. The EAT found that the chief constable was not obliged to make adjustments to this requirement under the DDA 1995. The chief constable was under a duty, by reason of regulation 12 of the Police Regulations (which provides that constables must be able to transfer to another police force without a further period of probation), to ensure that constables had satisfactorily completed the probationary requirements. In such circumstances, it was reasonable for the chief constable to refuse to lower the standard normally expected of a probationer and the adjustment sought was not reasonable in all the circumstances of the case. The EAT drew an analogy with the provisions relating to competence standards applied by qualifying bodies.[32]

---

30 See also *Paul v National Probation Service* [2004] IRLR 190, EAT and *Hammersmith and Fulham LBC v Farnsworth* [2000] IRLR 691, EAT.

31 [2007] All ER (D) 78 (Dec), 6 December 2007, UKEAT/0403/07.

32 See paras 11.81–11.85 and for a similar approach in a case involving qualifying bodies *Burke v College of Law* [2012] EWCA Civ 87.

The Code

9.24   The Code makes a number of specific recommendations in relation to job descriptions and person specifications. It is worth setting out some of the key recommendations, the logic of which should be apparent from the discussion above:

- The job description should be in writing, so as to focus attention on the requirements of the job and provide a clear benchmark against which to measure candidates. Merely reproducing the job description of the previous incumbent may lead to discrimination occurring.[33]
- Include a job title and job aim without indicating any predisposition to candidates with a particular protected characteristic (for example, 'matron' might suggest a predisposition to recruit a woman; 'office junior' a predisposition to recruit a young candidate), unless any of the exceptions apply.[34]
- Concisely and accurately set out the job duties and responsibilities, including only duties and responsibilities that are necessary parts of the job.
- Exclude unnecessary requirements, criteria and conditions.
- Avoid working conditions and patterns that might be indirectly discriminatory.
- Clearly the job description should be produced in accessible form if so requested by a disabled person.

9.25   The Code recommends that there be a person specification document to accompany the job description and set out the blend of skills, qualifications and experience that is considered necessary to fulfil the job description. The Code offers similar advice in respect of the person specification as it does in respect of the job description. It also recommends the following:[35]

- Avoid unnecessarily restrictive criteria relating to skills or knowledge: the employer should make clear, where appropriate, that qualifications equivalent to those specified are acceptable.
- Criteria should be capable of objective measurement. For example, concepts such as 'leadership' should be defined in terms of measurable skills and qualities that contribute to it.

---

33 See Employment Code paras 16.4–16.9.
34 See *Equal Opportunities Commission v Robertson* [1980] IRLR 44, IT for some judicial discussion of this.
35 See Employment Code paras 16.10–16.18.

- Requirements relating to health or disability may be discriminatory unless they are GORs or could not be removed by making reasonable adjustments. Where health requirements are specified this should be done carefully and with particularity.

9.26 The extent of the employer's compliance with this guidance in the Code can be used in cross-examination and/or questions asked prior to issuing proceedings.

Stage 2: Finding candidates

9.27 The techniques used by employers to bring vacancies to the attention of potential job applicants form part of the arrangements for determining to whom to offer employment. A general rule of thumb is that the larger and the more diverse the group of people to whose attention the employer brings the vacancies, the better.

9.28 The more closed the recruitment process, the greater the risk of existing inequalities being replicated and perpetuated, for example by indirect discrimination.

9.29 EqA 2010 ss157–158 make provision for positive action. Section 158, which applies uniquely to recruitment and promotion, is considered in some detail at Stage 3 of this chapter below. Section 157 applies at the recruitment stage but is not unique to it. It is considered in detail in chapter 12.

Advertisements

9.30 One of the most common ways of bringing a vacancy to prospective candidates' attention is by advertising the vacancy in one way or another.

9.31 The EqA 2010, however, does not contain any provisions specifically relating to job advertisements and repeals the EHRC's former power to apply for a court order restraining unlawful advertising.[36]

9.32 However, it is plain that advertisements form part of the arrangements for determining to whom to offer employment and therefore that, if a prospective job applicant is deterred from applying for a job because the advert shows an intention to discriminate, that applicant can bring a claim against the person advertising (and potentially the company placing the advert or otherwise aiding the unlawful arrangement).

---

36 EqA 2010 Sch 26 para 14.

9.33   In *Cardiff Women's Aid v Hartup*,[37] the employer specifically indicated in a job advertisement that a 'black or Asian woman' was required. Ms Hartup did not apply for the job but presented a complaint under the RRA 1976 in the ET. The ET held that the advert was part of the arrangements for determining to whom to offer employment and Ms Hartup's discrimination claim therefore succeeded. The EAT disagreed and in allowing the employer's appeal held that in causing the advert to be published the employer was merely indicating an intention to discriminate not in fact discriminating. The EAT therefore concluded that the applicant had no cause of action and that only the Commission for Racial Equality could bring proceedings in respect of the advert pursuant to the powers it then had to restrain adverts that indicated an intention to discriminate.

9.34   It is doubtful that the reasoning in Hartup remains good law for reasons that will shortly become clear. But first it is worth considering *NTL v Difolco*,[38] a case brought under the DDA 1995, which arrived by a different route at a similar conclusion to Hartup.

9.35   In *Difolco*, the Court of Appeal doubted whether the fact of advertising a full-time job could constitute an arrangement for the purpose of a reasonable adjustments claim, because if so the advertisement 'would potentially discriminate against the whole innominate class of possible disabled applicants for the job', which was thought to be absurd. The analysis does not hold true under the EqA 2010. The duty to make adjustments for a particular job applicant or potential applicant only applies if the employer knows that 'an interested' disabled person is or may be an applicant for the work in question.[39] It simply does not apply to the whole innominate class of possible disabled applicants. There is therefore no absurdity in holding that the advertisement is part of the arrangements for determining to whom to offer employment.[40]

9.36   *Hartup* is incompatible with the decision of the ECJ in *Centrum voor Gelijkheid van Kansen en voor Racismebestrijding v Firma Feryn*.[41]

---

37 [1994] IRLR 390, EAT.

38 [2006] EWCA Civ 1508, 12 October 2006.

39 EqA 2010 Sch 8 paras 5(1) and 20(1)(a).

40 The absurdity argument may be more convincing in relation to indirect discrimination, which, under the Act, is unlawful and knowledge of disability does not appear to be a necessary element of that cause of action. However, only people actually interested a particular job can bring a discrimination complaint in respect of a discriminatory advert under EqA 2010 s39(1)(a) so liability is not open ended.

41 Case C-54/07, [2008] ECR I-5187, [2008] All ER (EC) 1127, [2008] ICR 1390, [2008] IRLR 732.

A Belgian employer made public statements to the effect that it would not employ Moroccans because its customers would not want to give them access to their premises. A complaint was brought in the Belgian national courts by the Belgian equivalent of the EHRC. On a reference for a preliminary ruling the ECJ held that the employer's act was an act of direct discrimination since it would strongly dissuade candidates from certain ethnic backgrounds from applying.[42] Indeed, this was so despite the fact that there was no identifiable 'victim'. Plainly in that case the employer's public statement was held to be an act of direct discrimination, not merely an intention to discriminate.[43] Such reasoning is the inevitable logic of the Directives on which the discrimination legislation is based. *Hartup*, therefore, should not be followed in future.

9.37 Along similar lines, in *Padgett v Serota and the Board of Trustees of the Tate Gallery*[44] the EAT ruled that there did not need to be a job application before EERBR 2003 reg 6(1), the equivalent of EqA 2010 s39(1)(a), would apply. Otherwise an employer who made it impossible for a particular employee to apply for a job on grounds of a protected characteristic would avoid liability altogether.

9.38 *Firma Feryn* is not authority for the proposition that anybody who sees a discriminatory advert can sue in respect of it, and neither is *Padgett*. In *Keane v Investigo*, the EAT considered *Firma Feryn*, and held that in order for an individual to sue in respect of a discriminatory job advertisement, it was necessary that they in fact had an interest in the job and in applying for it.[45]

9.39 If a job advertisement shows an intention to discriminate and it dissuades a genuine prospective applicant from applying, then that individual is likely to have a sound claim by reference to EqA 2010 s39(1)(a).

9.40 A discriminatory advert is likely to be good evidence of discrimination later on in the recruitment process. An employee who responds to a discriminatory advert and is unsuccessful in their application

---

42 Contrary to Article 2(2)(a) of Directive 2000/43. EqA 2010 s13 is now the domestic legislation implementing the Directive and essentially reflects its wording.

43 The reasoning of the ECJ also receives support from domestic law. See *Brindley v Tayside Health Board* [1976] IRLR 364, a case that the EAT in *Hartup* considered but departed from for reasons that are, in the author's view, unconvincing.

44 UKEAT/0097/07, 17 December 2007 and UKEAT/0099/07, [2007] All ER (D) 239 (Dec); see para 9.9 above.

45 UKEAT/0389/09, 11 December 2009. See also to like effect *Berry v Recruitment Revolution* UKEAT/0190/10, 6 October 2010.

could rely on the advert if they suspected that the decision to decline their application was discriminatory.

9.41   Directly discriminatory content will be easier to identify (eg 'homosexuals need not apply' or 'waitress wanted'). Indirectly discriminatory content is more difficult to identify. Initially the claimant will need to identify whether the advert places a group at a particular disadvantage; thus 'full-time' could easily dissuade potential applicants with primary child-caring responsibilities from applying, the preponderance of whom are likely to be women. However, if it is clear from either the advert or other material that the job could easily be job-shared, the full-time requirement would not be justified and would therefore be discriminatory.

9.42   Some adverts might evidence both direct and indirect discrimination. For example, those that use terms like 'recent graduate' or 'energetic'. These could easily suggest that applications from older candidates are not welcome. Even if the terms are not being used as a proxy for 'young' they may nonetheless be indirectly discriminatory. Requiring an applicant to have graduated recently is likely disproportionately to rule out older applicants and in many cases the criterion will not be justified. There are few jobs in which it would actually make a material difference when the applicant graduated.

9.43   In construing advertisements, the words used should be given their ordinary meaning as they would be understood by ordinary reasonable people.[46] It is not a question of the intention of the writer.

9.44   Where the positive action conditions in EqA 2010 s157 are satisfied, not all apparently discriminatory adverts will in fact be unlawful. Thus in some circumstances it would not be unlawful to state, for example, that applications from trans-gender candidates are particularly welcome.

Internal and informal recruitment

9.45   The Code discourages recruiting exclusively from existing staff since this will perpetuate any existing lack of diversity in the workforce and may result in discrimination. If the employer's workforce under-represents members of a particular group defined by reference to a protected characteristic, then prospective employees belonging to that group who are excluded from applying for vacancies because of

---

46   See *Race Relations Board v Associated Newspapers Group Ltd* [1978] 1 WLR 905, [1978] 3 All ER 419.

the policy of recruiting from internal candidates may well have legitimate discrimination claims.[47]

9.46   If recruitment is restricted to internal candidates the Code recommends that the vacancy reaches the attention of all of the workforce. Employers should ensure that employees who are away from work (eg on maternity leave or disability-related sick leave) are informed of vacancies.[48]

9.47   Informal recruitment occurs when employers secure applications by informal means such as through personal contacts, the contacts of their employees or recruit from a small number of places (such as particular schools, colleges, universities, trade unions etc).

9.48   The problem with recruitment practices of this kind is that they too have a tendency to be discriminatory for similar reasons as those explained above in respect of recruitment from among existing staff. For example, indirect discrimination could arise if an employer recruited exclusively or almost exclusively through the careers service of a particular Christian faith school. This method of recruitment would be likely to put, for example, Muslim would-be applicants at a particular disadvantage if Muslims are, as may well be the case, underrepresented at that school. It may be hard for employers to justify such recruitment practices.[49]

9.49   There are, however, some instances in which an employer will be more likely to be able to justify restricting vacancies to internal candidates. These would include redundancy situations in which vacancies are restricted to employees at risk of redundancy in order to avoid dismissals. This is particularly true if any of the staff at risk of redundancy are women on maternity leave.[50]

9.50   In the case of *Coker v Lord Chancellor*[51] the Court of Appeal drew a distinction between recruiting by informal methods, such as personal recommendations from employees and word of mouth on the one hand, and on the other recruiting from a circle of family, friends and acquaintances. It warned that the former could constitute discrimination, but held that the latter seldom would. The reasoning

47 Employment Code para 16.20.
48 Employment Code para 16.22–16.23.
49 See eg *The Record Production Chapel, Daily Record and Sunday Mail Ltd, West Branch of the Scottish Graphical Division of SOGAT v Turnbull* UKEAT/955/83, 16 April 1984.
50 See Maternity and Parental Leave etc Regulations 1999 SI No 3312 reg 10(1) and (2) .
51 *Coker and Osamor v Lord Chancellor and Lord Chancellor's Department* [2001] EWCA 1756, [2002] ICR 321, [2002] IRLR 80.

does not convince and it is doubtful in any event following a change in the wording of the definition of indirect discrimination that *Coker* continues to represent the law.[52]

Employment service-providers

9.51   More commonly known as employment agencies, employment service-providers are persons (natural and legal) who, among other things, are in the business of finding employment for people or supplying employers with people to do work.[53] The protection conferred by the EqA 2010 cannot be avoided simply by delegating the task of identifying and/or selecting candidates to an employment agency. A number of points can be made about using them:

- It is unlawful for an employer to instruct, cause or induce an employment service-provider to discriminate.[54] Thus it would be unlawful for an employer to instruct the employment service-provider to produce a heterosexual-only shortlist.
- It would be unlawful for the employment service-provider to comply with such instructions. If it did so it would plainly be aiding the employer to discriminate and aiding discrimination is unlawful.[55]
- Under the EqA 2010 it is unlawful for employment service-providers, who have essentially the same duties as employers, to discriminate.[56]
- Even if the employer does not instruct, cause or induce the employment service-provider to discriminate, if that is what the employment service-provider does, then the employer may thereby discriminate against potential job applicants by recruiting through that employment service-provider.

9.52   The use of employment service-providers to 'headhunt' individuals to fill senior 'white collar' jobs is also capable of being discriminatory. Clearly, if viable candidates are excluded on grounds of a protected characteristic, that will amount to direct discrimination. But the practice can also be indirectly discriminatory. For example, if the only potential applicants targeted are those already in a senior position in a particular area of work, that might indirectly discriminate against

52 See also paras 3.81–3.83.
53 EqA 2010 s56(2).
54 EqA 2010 s110.
55 EqA 2010 s111.
56 EqA 2010 s55.

women if women are underrepresented in that cohort because of historical 'glass ceilings'. This is precisely the type of recruitment practice that can simply replicate and thereby perpetuate existing inequalities.

Recruitment from particular geographical areas

9.53   Employers who recruit only from particular geographical areas may, depending on the demographics of the area in question, indirectly discriminate. The discrimination is most likely to be against members of particular racial or religious groups.

9.54   In *Hussein v Saint Complete Housing Furnishers*[57] a black prospective employee was refused employment because of the area he came from. Two features of that area were material. Firstly, that it had high unemployment. Secondly, that it had a large black community compared to other surrounding areas. An ET held that Mr Hussein had been indirectly discriminated against.

The Employment Code

9.55   The Employment Code gives detailed guidance on advertising job opportunities.[58] It supports the view that where the advertisement is placed forms part of the arrangements for determining to whom to offer employment.

9.56   If the advertisement is placed in such a way that it will not, or will be substantially less likely to, come to the attention of people who share a protected characteristic and who would want to apply for the position, the arrangements may well be indirectly discriminatory. For this reason the Code advises that advertisements are placed in such a way that they reach a diverse audience, for example by using a variety of publications and media.

9.57   The employer that does not follow the recommendations made in the Code increases the risk of a finding of discrimination being made against it. The Code recommends that employers should not advertise jobs internally only as this will not help to diversify the workforce. If a job is advertised internally only it should be accessible to the entire workforce. The content should be screened and in particular content that depicts or perpetuates stereotypes should be avoided (eg an advert for a nursing vacancy which pictures only female nurses).

---

57 [1979] IRLR 337, IT.
58 Employment Code paras 16.19–16.29.

9.58   The Employment Code advises that when delegating recruitment to third parties, such as employment agencies, employers should give the third party a copy of their equality policy, and the job description and person specification for the posts the employer is hoping to fill.[59]

Stage 3: Choosing candidates

9.59   Whatever process employers adopt to bring vacancies to potential candidates' attention, they must also avoid discrimination in the process of identifying the candidates to whom they actually offer jobs. The process adopted varies greatly, but common features include the use of application forms, interviews, tests and the like.

9.60   The Employment Code gives some detailed best practice guidance. While it is not unlawful in and of itself to fail to comply with the guidance given in the Code, ETs may consider whether the employer's failure to comply with the recommendations is a matter from which inferences can be drawn. For claimants therefore the Employment Code is a very useful source of ideas for areas of cross-examination. Employers who do not adopt best practice in recruitment will be more vulnerable to discrimination claims.

9.61   The EqA 2010 contains some important innovations new to discrimination law which apply at the selection stage, most notably in respect of asking candidates questions related to health and taking positive action.

Enquiries about disability and health

9.62   The EqA 2010 prohibits employers from asking job applicants questions about their health before making a job offer, save in certain narrowly defined circumstances.[60]

9.63   It is unlawful for employers to ask about an applicant's health until such time as they have been offered a job or, if the employer is not able to offer the applicant a job, until such time that the applicant has been included in a pool of people from whom the employer intends to select someone to offer a job when the employer is in a

---

59 Employment Code para 16.31.
60 EqA 2010 s60.

position to do so.[61] A breach of the prohibition is an unlawful act; but enforcement action can only be brought by the EHRC.[62]

9.64 The effect for the individual of EqA 2010 s60 is as follows. While a breach of section 60 does not amount to unlawful disability discrimination in itself, if the employer relies on information given in response to a question unlawfully asked, that reliance may amount to unlawful disability discrimination.[63]

9.65 Thus for example, before offering an employee a job the employer asks the employee whether they have had any mental health problems. The applicant confesses that they previously suffered from severe depression but that they are no longer symptomatic. The employer for that reason declines to offer the employee a job. Assuming that the applicant's depression was serious enough to constitute a disability within the meaning of the EqA 2010, then the employer's act may well be an unlawful act of disability discrimination contrary to section 39(1)(c).

9.66 If the employer relies on an answer given to a prohibited question in making the employment decision, the burden of proof shifts to the employer. Making use of the answer is deemed to be a matter from which an ET could conclude that the employer has contravened the EqA 2010.[64]

When may the employer rely on and ask questions concerning health?

9.67 The exceptions to the general rule require careful consideration. If a question related to the health of an applicant is 'necessary'[65] for one of a number of purposes then it not unlawful. The permitted purposes are:

- for the purpose of establishing whether the applicant will be able to undergo an assessment, or whether there will be a duty to make reasonable adjustments in order to enable the applicant to do so.[66] Assessment in this context means interview or other process designed to give an indication of a person's suitability for

61 EqA 2010 s60(1).
62 Pursuant to its powers under Part I of the Equality Act 2006. See EqA 2010 s60(2).
63 EqA 2010 s60(3) and (11).
64 EqA 2010 ss60(5) and 135(2).
65 EqA 2010 s60(6).
66 EqA 2010 s60(6)(a).

the work concerned.[67] Thus, for example, if an employer whose offices are accessible only by stairs invites an applicant to an interview it would be permissible to ask the employee whether they are a wheelchair user, or whether they are able to climb stairs, so long as the purpose of the question is to determine whether the applicant will be able to attend the offices for interview and/or to determine what adjustments might need to be made to enable the applicant to be interviewed (eg holding the interview elsewhere or installing ramps).

• to establish whether the applicant will be able to carry out a function that is intrinsic to the work concerned.[68] An example might be asking an applicant for a job in a factory processing peanuts whether they are allergic to peanuts and if so how severely. However, EqA 2010 s60(7) provides that if the employer has a reasonable belief that there may be a duty to make reasonable adjustments for the applicant in connection with the work the applicant is interested in, then the employer is only permitted to ask a question about the applicant's health if the question remains necessary once the duty to make adjustments has been complied with. Given the general prohibition on asking health questions at the recruitment stage, this state of affairs is most likely to occur in circumstances in which the employer has prior knowledge of the applicant (for example because they are an existing employee) or if the applicant has volunteered health or disability-related information.

To take an example of how EqA 2010 s60(6)(b) and (7) might work together: an employer advertises a job for a porter. The job involves moving heavy boxes. If necessary, the boxes could easily be moved with the assistance of mechanical aids that remove the requirement for heavy manual lifting. Further one of the employer's existing employees applies for the job. That employee has had back problems in the past caused by heavy lifting. The employer may well in those circumstances have a reasonable belief that if the employee were given the porter job, there would be a duty to adjust the job removing any requirement for the employee to do heavy lifting and that this could reasonably be achieved by providing mechanical aides. In those circumstances the employer could not rely on section 60(6)(b) to ask questions about that employee's health/disability.

67 EqA 2010 s60(12).
68 EqA 2010 s60(6)(b).

- for the purpose of monitoring diversity in the range of persons applying for work.[69] Thus employers will continue to be able to undertake equal opportunities monitoring.
- for the purpose of taking positive action in accordance with EqA 2010 s157.[70]
- if it is a GOR of the work the applicant applies for, that the applicant has a particular disability, then the employer may ask the applicant whether they have that disability.[71]

Positive action in selection

9.68   EqA 2010 157 Act applies generally, including at the recruitment stage and is discussed in detail in chapter 12. A good example of positive action at the selection stage that might potentially fall within section 157 is the provision of training to persons who share a particular protected characteristic to assist them to fulfil the job requirements and then compete with other candidates.

9.69   EqA 2010 s158 sets out provisions that apply specifically to recruitment and promotion. The positive action provisions are engaged if an employer reasonably thinks that persons who share a protected characteristic suffer a disadvantage connected to the characteristic, or participation in an activity by persons who share a protected characteristic is disproportionately low.[72] The Act does not prohibit employers from treating people who share the protected characteristic more favourably in the context of recruitment[73] and promotion if the aim of doing so enables or encourages persons who share the protected characteristic to either overcome or minimise the disadvantage, or participate in the activity.

9.70   However, more favourable treatment is only permitted if:[74]

- there is a tie-break between candidates; and
- the employer does not have a policy of treating persons who share the characteristic more favourably than others;
- the more favourable treatment is a proportionate means of achieving the aim of overcoming or minimising the disadvantage people who share the protected characteristic face, or enabling

---

69 EqA 2010 s60(6)(c).
70 EqA 2010 s60(6)(d).
71 EqA 2010 s60(6)(e) and (8). See also para 13.107 for references to the Employment Code.
72 EqA 2010 s158(1).
73 Recruitment is defined at EqA 2010 s158(5).
74 EA 2010 s158(4).

people who share the protected characteristic to participate in the activity.

Eligibility to work in the United Kingdom

9.71   There are good reasons why employers might want to check whether a job applicant can lawfully work in the United Kingdom before offering employment. This forms part of the selection process and raises discrimination issues.

9.72   The Immigration, Asylum and Nationality Act 2006 sets out a system of civil penalties for employers who employ illegal migrant workers and a criminal offence in respect of those who do so knowingly. A statutory defence is available to employers who employ illegal migrant workers if they do so unknowingly and have carried out certain pre-employment checks. The checks include the employer inspecting original copies of certain documents and retaining copies in one of a number of prescribed formats.

9.73   Unless carefully managed, the process of checks is capable of being discriminatory. The main risk is in respect of race discrimination. The UK Border Agency has published guidance to assist employers to make checks in a way that avoids racial discrimination.[75] In essence, the guidance is that all applicants should be treated the same. In other words the same checks should be made of all applicants regardless of their appearance. It should not be assumed that since one applicant is white he has the right to work in the United Kingdom, but since another is black or speaks with an accent he does not. The UK Border Agency also advises that the employer adopts a written policy dealing with the checks that are made, how and by whom.

9.74   It is for the individual employer to determine at what stage checks are made. The essential thing is that the checks are made pre-employment. It is likely to be most convenient for this to be late on in the application process since this will reduce the number of people in respect of whom checks need to be made. Thus it might be convenient for the employer to ask all employees at the application stage whether they have the right to work in the United Kingdom, but only to check documents of, for instance, shortlisted candidates, or candidates offered work.

---

75 *Border and Immigration Agency Code of Practice: Guidance for Employers on the Avoidance of Unlawful Discrimination in Employment Practice While Seeking to Prevent Illegal Working.*

Selection tests and assessment centres

9.75 Some employers require applicants to undertake formal tests whether at an assessment centre or otherwise as part of the selection process. This method of recruitment is only as good as the design and accessibility of the test and assessment centre. Such arrangements can be discriminatory.

9.76 A good example is provided by the facts of *Project Management Institute v Latif*.[76] Ms Latif was registered blind and disabled within the meaning of the DDA 1995. She sought to become an accredited member of the Project Management Institute. In order to do so it was necessary for her to take certain exams on a computer at a test centre. Certain adjustments were made, such as allowing Ms Latif a reader/recorder and she was given twice the amount of time allotted to other candidates. However, Ms Latif remained dissatisfied about the extent of the adjustments made because they did not remove the substantial disadvantage at which she was placed. She presented a disability discrimination claim. The ET found that the Institute had breached the duty to make reasonable adjustments by failing to allow Ms Latif to take the examination on a stand-alone computer at the test centre, onto which computer certain specialist software designed for blind people could have been installed. The EAT dismissed the Institute's appeal.

Interview

9.77 Interviews are a key part of the 'arrangements' for determining to whom to offer employment.

9.78 If an interviewer makes it clear that he does not want to appoint a candidate because they have a protected characteristic, that is capable of amounting to direct discrimination.[77] Similarly, words of discouragement spoken by interviewers on protected grounds can also amount to discrimination.[78] Interviewers should guard against being influenced by irrelevant, but potentially discriminatory factors. For example, in *Staffordshire CC v Bennett*[79] an African-Caribbean woman was unsuccessful following her interview on the basis that she did

---

76 [2007] IRLR 579, EAT.

77 See *Brennan* [1983] IRLR 357, [1984] ICR 52, EAT, para 14.6 above.

78 *Simon v Brimham Associates* [1987] ICR 596, [1987] IRLR 307, EAT. Compare *Saunders v Richmond Upon Thames Borough Council* [1978] ICR 75, [1977] IRLR 362, EAT.

79 UKEAT/67/94, 3 July 1995. However, contrast *Martins v Marks & Spencer plc* [1998] ICR 1005, [1998] IRLR 326, CA.

not have the right personality for the job. The interviewers were put off by poor eye contact during the course of the interview. The ET found that in fact she was not offered the job because her 'face did not fit' because she was from a different racial background from the interviewers. The EAT dismissed the employer's appeal and referred to the Judicial Studies Board training, which records that African-Caribbean people often avoid eye contact with those in authority as it is regarded as polite to do so.

The Employment Code

9.79   The Employment Code gives detailed guidance about best practice during the selection process. The selection process itself can take any number of different guises. Typically it will start with an application form and then move to some form, or forms, of assessment(s), such as an interview or other type of formal test. The Code gives detailed guidance on all these matters. Some key recommendations are set out below.

9.80   The Employment Code offers some valuable general advice, which should help employers to avoid discrimination and also assist the ET in determining an allegation of discrimination:[80]

- keep records of each stage of the selection processes and record in writing the decisions taken at each stage and why. This includes, for example, keeping copies of advertisements, application forms and interview notes. Deciding how long to retain records should balance the need to keep them to evidence and explain recruitment decisions against an applicant's rights under the Data Protection Act 1998;
- staff involved in selection should receive training on the employer's equality policy and its application to recruitment;
- if possible, the same staff should be responsible for selection at all stages to ensure consistency.

9.81   Application forms are part of the arrangements for determining to whom to offer employment. The key recommendations made by the Employment Code in respect of application forms are that:[81]

- personal and sensitive information relating to protected characteristics is detachable so that it can be used for monitoring without forming part of the decision-making process;

---

80   See Employment Code paras 16.43–16.49.
81   See Employment Code paras 16.32–16.42.

- questions about protected characteristics, if asked, should be given context that clearly explains what they are needed for. They should only be asked if they are necessary for the purpose of GORs or positive action or are permitted health or disability questions;
- the form should not ask for photos unless they are essential for selection purposes;
- the form should be provided in accessible format on request by a disabled person (for example, by email, Braille, Easy Read, large print, audio tape or computer disc);
- the employer should normally accept applications from disabled candidates in an accessible format.

9.82 The Employment Code makes a number of recommendations in respect of tests and assessments during the recruitment process. Key ones are as follows:[82]

- the test should correspond to the job in question and measure as closely as possible the appropriate levels of the skills and abilities included in the person specification;
- it may be reasonable to adjust the test for disabled candidates to avoid breaching the duty to make reasonable adjustments (see *Latif* above at para 9.76, but note also *Hart* at para 9.23 above);
- all candidates should be given the same tests except in certain very limited cases.

9.83 Many employers adopt recruitment processes that have multiple stages. Typically, for example, the process begins with an application form. The applications are marked, and a shortlist compiled of people progressing to the next stage. Some key recommendations in the Employment Code in respect of shortlisting are as follows:[83]

- it is better for more than one person to be involved in shortlisting to help reduce the chance of bias;
- the marking system should be agreed before applications are assessed (including the cut-off point);
- where more than one person is involved in selection, applications should be marked separately before a final mark is agreed between the markers;
- selection should be based only on the information provided in the application form, CV or, in the case of internal applicants, any formal performance assessment reports;

82 See Employment Code paras 16.52–16.53.
83 See Employment Code para 16.50.

- the weight given to each criterion in the person specification should not be changed during shortlisting.

9.84 The Employment Code makes a number of recommendations in respect of best interview practice:[84]

- the employer should be flexible about times to avoid indirect discrimination. For example, women are more likely to have difficulties attending an interview held at a time that coincides with the 'school run';
- questions at the interview should be limited to those relating to the application form, job description and person specification form;
- irrelevant personal questions, especially those related to protected characteristics should be avoided;
- interviewers should have equality training and training about interviews to help them avoid taking into account discriminatory and irrelevant factors.

9.85 The Employment Code recommends that employers should avoid making references part of the initial selection process.[85] It states that 'references should only be obtained, and circulated to members of the selection panel, after a selection decision has been reached'. The rationale is that the initial selection decision should so far as possible be based on objective factors that measure an applicant's suitability for a job, rather than on possibly subjective, unfair, or even discriminatory, views of past employers.

Stage 4: Job offers

9.86 The final stage of the recruitment process is the job offer (and the employee's reaction to it). As noted above, by EqA 2010 s39(1)(b), it is unlawful to discriminate as to the terms on which employment is offered.[86] It seems that this provision will only apply where employment has actually been offered.[87]

9.87 The full spectrum of discrimination might occur at the job offer stage. This would include, for example, making less favourable offers to some candidates on grounds of protected characteristics. It would

---

84 See Employment Code paras 16.57–16.64.
85 See Employment Code para 16.65.
86 See para 9.7 above.
87 See *Ogilvie v Harehills Conservative Club Ltd & Parry* UKEAT/449/92, 26 April 1993.

also include making an offer that incorporated discriminatory job requirements (on which see the discussion above). There is a significant overlap, then, between discrimination at this stage of recruitment and the other stages discussed above.

9.88   A good example of discrimination particular to the job offer stage is given by the facts of *Peninsula Business Services v Malik.*[88] The job required the post-holder to carry out certain work on a computer. The claimant could do that work if a particular form of software was installed on a computer at the employer's workplace, which she could use. The claimant was offered the job on the understanding that the software would be installed. Unfortunately, there followed a long delay and still the relevant software was not installed. The claimant therefore could not commence work. When she could wait no longer she presented a disability discrimination claim (she was not being paid). Plainly it would be arguable that the respondent discriminated in the terms of the job offer. The offer was (on one analysis at least) conditional on the claimant being able to do the computer work. That condition placed the claimant at a substantial disadvantage compared to non-disabled job applicants because she, unlike them, was unable to do the computer work without specialist software. An adjustment to the offer would have been promptly to install the required software. On the assumption that such an adjustment would have been reasonable, the terms of the job offer were discriminatory in that they failed to make reasonable adjustments.

The Employment Code

9.89   The Employment Code advises that it is good practice for employers to offer feedback to unsuccessful shortlisted candidates if this is requested. It suggests that by demonstrating objective reasons for the applicant's lack of success, based on the requirements of the job, an employer can reduce the risk of facing allegations of discrimination.[89] However, it is suggested that no inference can be drawn from an employer's general policy of not providing feedback. Manifestly if it is done selectively, that may give rise to discrimination.

---

88 UKEAT/0340/08, 26 January 2010. The case is mentioned for its facts rather than its outcome.
89 See Employment Code para 16.72.

CHAPTER 10

Discrimination in employment

continued

Key points
- EqA 2010 s39 prohibits discrimination by employers (and prospective employers) against both existing and prospective employees (job applicants).
- EqA 2010 s83 of the Act defines 'employment' and includes self employed persons, provided they carry out the work personally.
- There is no qualifying period for these rights.
- Illegality of the contract may not prevent a claim being made.
- The Employment Code provides material for cross-examination on all aspects of the employment relationship. Practical steps are given in chapters 17 and 18 of the Employment Code.

The scope of the employment provisions

10.1 EqA 2010 s83 sets out the definition of 'employment' that applies throughout the Act[1] (bar minor exceptions[2]):

(2) 'Employment' means –
(a) employment under a contract of employment, a contract of apprenticeship or a contract personally to do work;
(b) Crown employment;
(c) employment as a relevant member of the House of Commons staff;
(d) employment as a relevant member of the House of Lords staff.

10.2 This chapter focuses on the definition of 'employment' (and the associated words 'employer' and 'employee') within the context of the Equality Act 2010.[3]

'Employment'

10.3 Under the precursor legislation, the definitions of 'employment' varied slightly across the instruments, but were identical in their practical application. The definition in EqA 2010 s83 appears, but

1 EqA 2010 s212.
2 Within the context of occupational pensions schemes, the definition in section 124 of the Pensions Act 1995 is preserved (due to EqA 2010 s212(11)).
3 See chapter 11 for treatment of discrimination in occupations and non-employment bodies.

is not, broader in scope, since it refers to Crown employment etc. Cases decided under the precursor legislation are likely to remain instructive.

10.4   The definition of 'employment' in EqA 2010 s83 is wider than the definition in the Employment Rights Act (ERA) 1996 s230(5), which includes only those working under a contract of employment (ie those working under a contract of service, not those working under a contract for services). In *Quinnen v Hovells*[4] (decided under the SDA 1975) the EAT stated that:[5]

> The concept of a contract for the engagement of personal work or labour lying outside the scope of a master-servant relationship is a wide and flexible one, intended by Parliament in our judgment to be interpreted as such. Its application to particular circumstances will depend very much upon the facts of each case as and when they arise. One comment can however safely be made. This case confirms that those who engage, even cursorily, the talents, skill or labour of the self-employed are wise to ensure that the terms are equal as between men and women and do not discriminate between them.

10.5   In the context of discrimination 'employment' requires a claimant to prove, since *Mirror Group Newspapers v Gunning*[6] three irreducible minimum requirements in order to meet the definition:

- that there is a contract between the parties;
- that the contract requires the worker to perform work personally; and
- in cases where the contract imposes various obligations, it must be shown that the dominant purpose of the contract is for the personal service.

Requirement 1: Contract between the parties

10.6   A contract is an agreement between the parties for 'consideration' (work for money, for example). Ordinary principles of general contract law determine whether one exists. There is no requirement for there to be a document setting out any or all of the terms of the agreement as it can be oral and/or in writing and its terms can be express or implied. If there are no express written terms, it is for the ET to determine the terms of the contract relying on available and

4 [1984] IRLR 227.
5 At para 24.
6 [1986] IRLR 27 and see also *Patterson v Legal Services Commission* [2004] IRLR 153 at para 21, where this test is affirmed.

relevant evidence (eg emails, course of conduct, oral testimony etc). The contract must be between the person who is actually carrying out the work and the person/company for whom the work is carried out.[7]

10.7   There must be mutuality of obligation (the worker obliged to work, the employer obliged to give consideration), or there is no contract of any sort.[8]

Agency workers

10.8   The position of agency workers is now dealt with under EqA 2010 s41. In agency situations there is a so-called 'tripartite' relationship between the three actors: the worker contracts with the agency; the agency then contracts (separately) with the end user. As such, there is not usually a contract between the worker and the end user (although in some cases the ET may imply such a contract). The Act protects agency workers separately from discrimination by the person engaging their services (the end user).[9]

10.9   There are no practical situations in which an agency worker would need to rely on the definition of 'employee' under the EqA 2010 as a result of the existence of s41. However, if there is doubt about whether the relationship is in fact between an end user and contract worker or between employer and employee, the claims should be set out as alternatives in the claim form.

10.10   In some agency cases a contract may be *implied* between the worker and the end user, such that they can fall within 'employment' under the EqA 2010 also. For example, if the agency is doing little more than recruiting the individual at the outset and/or processing payroll for the end user and/or if the agency has little or no contact with the worker and no control over the work undertaken. For all practical purposes, the worker's relationship with the end user cannot be distinguished from one of employment.

10.11   Most of the cases where a contract has been implied between end user and worker were decided under the ERA 1996 using the definition of employment contained in ERA 1996 s230 but the same principles apply under the EqA 2010 for the purpose of establishing whether a contract exists between the parties.

---

7 See *Muschett v HM Prison Service* [2010] IRLR 451 and *X v Mid Sussex CAB* [2013] IRLR 146.

8 *Stephenson v Delphi Diesel Systems Ltd* [2003] ICR 471.

9 See EqA 2010 s41 and chapter 11.

10.12   If it is necessary to prove that the claimant is entitled to the protection against discrimination under EqA 2010 s39 against the end user (as opposed to relying on EqA 2010 s41) the burden falls on the claimant to prove that matter.[10]

10.13   A finding of an employment contract with the end user can result from the end user's high degree of control over the claimant.[11] In *Franks v Reuters Ltd*,[12] the worker had been working for the end user on a full-time basis for more than five years. The Court of Appeal stated that it is not correct for an ET or court hearing such a case:

> ... to conclude that an individual is not an employee without first determining as a fact whether, on a consideration of all the relevant evidence (including what was said and done, as well as any relevant documents), there was an implied contract of service ...

10.14   Where an agency worker has worked for a long period of time for the end user, an ET should consider the possibility of an implied contract.[13] A restrictive test is used: whether it is *necessary* to imply a contract between the worker and the end user in order to explain the relationship between them.[14] So if the arrangements between the worker, agency and end user are genuine and adequately explain the interaction between the three parties, it is unlikely that a direct contract between the worker and end user will be implied.[15]

Illegal contracts

10.15   It used to be the case that because the terms of a contract tainted by illegality could not be enforced, any statutory rights that depended upon the existence of a contract between the parties would not apply. In *Leighton v Michael and Charalambous*,[16] the claimant was paid gross, without deductions for income tax and national insurance. She complained, was subsequently dismissed, and issued claims under the SDA 1975. At first instance, the ET stated that in order to fall within the employment provisions of the SDA 1975: 'it is essen-

---

10 See *Modahl v British Athletic Federation* [2001] EWCA Civ 1447, [2002] 1 WLR 1192.

11 See *Motorola Ltd v Davidson and Melville Craig Group Ltd* [2001] IRLR 4.

12 [2003] IRLR 423.

13 See the (obiter) remarks of the CA in *Brook Street Bureau (UK) Ltd v Dacas* [2004] IRLR 358.

14 *Cable & Wireless plc v Muscat* [2006] IRLR 354 and *James v Greenwich Council* [2007] IRLR 168.

15 *James v Greenwich LBC* [2008] IRLR 302 and *National Grid v Wood* [2007] UKEAT/432/07. See also *Tilson v Alstom Transport* [2011] IRLR 169.

16 [1996] IRLR 67.

tial that the worker be able to rely upon a contract of employment'. It went on: 'In the present case, in our view, she is not entitled to rely upon the contract because of the illegality to which she was an undoubted party.' However, on appeal, the EAT reversed this decision, holding that an ET's jurisdiction to hear a discrimination claim does not depend upon the existence of an enforceable contract of employment. A claim under the pay provisions of the Act, however, may be so reliant. Put another way, the illegality in a contract in a pay claim may be inextricably linked to the contract as the contract must be valid for pay to be claimed.

10.16   Notwithstanding that a contract that is tainted by illegality cannot normally be enforced, a discrimination claim is not founded in contract and does not seek to enforce contractual obligations. Therefore, in contrast to claims for unfair dismissal and redundancy (which will usually fail if the contract is tainted with illegality[17]), the ET could well have jurisdiction to hear a discrimination claim in such circumstances.

10.17   In *Hall v Woolston Hall Leisure Ltd*,[18] the Court of Appeal stated that illegality should only bar a claimant from being eligible to bring a claim for discrimination in employment where the acts of discrimination are so inextricably linked to the illegality that to allow the claimant to pursue the claim amounts to condoning the illegal conduct.[19] In that case, the court found that the employee's discriminatory dismissal was not inextricably bound up with the illegality (notwithstanding that she was aware of and had acquiesced to the employer's non-deduction of tax and National Insurance). Accordingly, the claimant was not precluded from pursuing her claim.

10.18   The principles in Hall give different results depending on the degree to which the acts of discrimination are linked to the illegality.[20] Thus in *Vakante v Addey and Stanhope School*,[21] the Court of Appeal upheld the EAT decision that an employee could not pursue discrimination claims due to illegality. In that case, the claimant was a Croatian national who had commenced work without a work permit and had falsely and knowingly indicated to the respondent that

17 See the Court of Appeal discussion in *Colen v Cebrian (UK) Ltd* [2004] IRLR 210 for determining when a contract tainted by illegality can still be enforceable in claims for unfair dismissal/wrongful dismissal.
18 [2000] IRLR 578.
19 See the discussion at para 46 of the judgment.
20 See *Hounga v Allen* [2012] EWCA Civ 609, [2012] IRLR 685, which also discusses *Vakante*.
21 [2005] ICR 231.

he did not need such a permit. He was later dismissed and brought claims against the respondent, including claims for race discrimination. The Court of Appeal distinguished Hall and stated:[22]

> As for the illegal conduct here (a) it was that of the applicant; (b) it was criminal; (c) it went far beyond the manner in which one party performed what was otherwise a lawful employment contract; (d) it went to the basic content of an employment situation – work; (e) the duty not to discriminate arises from an employment situation which, without a permit, was unlawful from top to bottom and from beginning to end. It was not a case of innocent oversight or an acceptable misunderstanding. Mr V had been clearly informed in writing of the true position. Instead of making an application for a work permit, he obtained work with the respondent by making a false statement. Mr V was solely responsible for his illegal conduct in working for the respondent and creating an unlawful situation, on which he had to rely in order to establish that there was a duty not to discriminate against him ... the complaints by Mr V of his discriminatory treatment in employment are so inextricably bound with the illegality of conduct in obtaining and continuing that employment with the respondent that, if it were to permit him to recover compensation for discrimination, the tribunal would appear to condone his illegal conduct.

10.19   However, *Hounga v Allen*[23] stresses that the correct approach is that in *Hall*, explaining *Vakante* as an application of those principles.

10.20   The Code of Practice gives an example:[24]

> An employee is aware that her employer is not deducting income tax or National Insurance contributions from her wages which, in this particular situation, is illegal. She queries this but her employer tells her: 'It's the way we do business.' Subsequently, she is dismissed after her employer becomes aware that she is pregnant. She alleges that the reason for her dismissal was her pregnancy and claims discrimination because of her pregnancy. While she knew that her employer was not paying tax on her wages, she did not actively participate in her employer's illegal conduct. The illegal performance of the contract was in no way linked to her discrimination claim. In the circumstances, she may be able to pursue her claim, despite her knowledge of her employer's illegal conduct.

22 See paras 34–36.
23 [2012] IRLR 685, endorsing the test in *Hall* while reversing the outcome in the EAT.
24 Employment Code para 10.5.

Requirement 2: Obligation to perform work personally

10.21   The contract between the parties must oblige the worker to perform the work personally, rather than simply to complete a task irrespective of who carries it out. In *Gunning v Mirror Group Newspapers Ltd*[25] the claimant was the daughter of an independent wholesale newspaper distributor who purchased papers from the appellants and resold them to newsagents. His contract with the appellant did not expressly require him to distribute the newspapers personally. As he was nearing retirement, he requested that the appellants continue the contract with his daughter when he retired (because she had been helping him to run the business for several years). The appellants did not give the contract to the claimant (the daughter) and she issued a claim under the employment provisions of the SDA 1975. On appeal, the Court of Appeal held that because the principal purpose of the contract with the father was to distribute the newspapers, and there was no requirement that he be involved personally in distribution, his contract was not a 'contract personally to execute any work or labour' and therefore the daughter would not be employed under such a contract. Accordingly, if there had been any discrimination against her, it was not in relation to 'employment', such that the ET did not have jurisdiction to hear her complaint.

10.22   In *Hugh-Jones v St John's College, Cambridge*,[26] the EAT held that a research fellow fell within the employment provisions of the SDA 1975. More recently, in *Mingeley v Pennock & Ivory*,[27] the Court of Appeal had to determine whether an independent taxi driver who paid a taxi company a weekly sum in return for using their radios services could complain of racial discrimination under the employment provisions of the RRA 1976. He had a contract that entitled him to use the radio equipment itself and to receive bookings from the company. He was free to attend work as and when he wished, at which time he would log onto the radio system and the company would allocate bookings to him. He did not need to inform the company when he was or was not working. The Court of Appeal held that due to the absence of any obligation on his part to do work for the respondent, less still to do work personally, he could not bring such a claim.

25 [1986] 1 WLR 546, [1986] 1 All ER 385.
26 [1979] ICR 848.
27 [2004] IRLR 373.

10.23   In *Loughran and Kelly v Northern Ireland Housing Executive*,[28] the House of Lords gave a very broad interpretation to the term 'personal service'. In this case, two solicitors' firms (one comprising solely of two partners and one being a sole practitioner) applied for contracts with Northern Ireland Housing Executive. As part of the application, the firms were required to designate a particular partner to take responsibility for the work and designate a solicitor to carry it out. Both firms designated partners of the firm not only to oversee the work, but also to carry it out personally. Both firms were denied contracts and issued claims alleging that the reason was because of their Catholic beliefs. The House of Lords held that the partners of the firms were entitled to claim. It stated that because a firm of solicitors has no legal existence independent of the partners, when each firm sought to contract with the respondent, the individual claimants were simultaneously seeking to enter into a contract personally to execute work. It was noted that if the firms had designated an assistant solicitor to carry out the work personally (rather than a partner of the firm) no claim could lie under these provisions. This principle would not apply in situations where a company applied for such a contract, because in such cases, the company is regarded as a separate legal 'person'. (Note that under EqA 2010 ss 44–46, special provisions apply to protect partners from unlawful discrimination: see chapter 1).

10.24   In contrast to *Loughran and Kelly*, in *Patterson v Legal Services Commission*,[29] it was held that the claimant (who had applied to be a franchisee of legal services, but had been rejected) was not entitled to bring a claim under the employment provisions of the RRA 1976 because there was nothing in the contract that would have required her to perform work personally.

10.25   When seeking to prove that a person was under a personal obligation to perform the work, it is useful to show that the worker could not have delegated the work to another and/or that if they were allowed to do so, they had to get permission from the contractor before doing so. Where the contractor states that the worker could have sent anyone to do the work (without prior approval) provided that the work was done, it will be difficult to assert that the contract required personal service.

---

28 [1998] IRLR 593.
29 [2004] IRLR 153, [2003] EWCA Civ 1558, [2004] ICR 312.

Requirement 3: Dominant purpose

10.26 Even if a claimant can show there was a contract and that it placed them under an obligation to perform work personally, they must also prove that the *dominant purpose* of the contract was for the provision of such personal services. In *Mingeley v Pennock & Ivory* (discussed above) the Court of Appeal stated that because the dominant purpose of the contract was the provision of the radio services (and bookings) rather than the performance of work or labour, the claimant was not 'employed' by the taxi company within the meaning of the RRA 1976.

10.27 Similarly, in *Gunning v Mirror Group Newspapers Ltd* (discussed above) the Court of Appeal stated that the dominant purpose of the contract 'was simply the regular and efficient distribution of newspapers' not one of personal service.

Volunteers

10.28 There is a *question* whether volunteers are protected against discrimination under the Act. The Court of Appeal in *X v Mid Sussex CAB*,[30] ruled that unpaid volunteer workers were not protected by the DDA provisions relating to employment. It held that such unpaid activities fall outside the scope of the terms: 'occupation', 'employment' and/or 'vocational training' which are set out in Article 3 of Council Directive 2000/78. Such exclusion would apply equally to all protected characteristics.

10.29 The Supreme Court rejected the appellant's appeal. The appeal was rejected for eight main reasons:

1) Directive 2000/78 does not cover all activities. On considering the equality Directives, the court concluded that the EU Commission clearly did not have voluntary activities in mind as falling within the scope of the reformulations of the personal scope articles such as Article 3. Thus the scope of the Directive was carefully defined, differing according to context.

2) Although the concept of 'occupation' must be understood as operating alongside 'employment' and 'self-employment' in Article 3 of the Directive, the context indicates that it was aimed at access to sector of the work market. That phrase is concerned with preventing discrimination from qualifying or setting up as s solicitor, plumber, greengrocer or arbitrator.[31]

---

30 [2011] IRLR 335, CA.
31 See *Hashwani v Jivraj* [2011] UKSC 40, [2011] 1 WLR 1872 at para 49.

3) If the Directive was intended to apply to voluntary activity, 'occupation' would have been carried through expressly into the context of 'employment and working conditions, including dismissals and pay' in Article 3. The omission of any reference to voluntary workers, if they were intended to be protected against 'dismissal' on discriminatory grounds, was significant.

4) The phrase 'employment and occupation' was carried through into article 1 of the Framework Directive from the title to the Directive and then from various recitals, starting with recital 4 which refers to Convention No 111 of the International Labour Organisation prohibiting discrimination in that context. The legislative history of that convention spoke against inclusion of voluntary activity.

5) The EU Commission's original proposal and the annexed impact assessment (COM(1999) 565 final) which led ultimately to the Framework Directive were focused exclusively on situations of employment or self-employment, and did not consider or address voluntary activity in any shape or form.

6) The European Parliament did, during the consultation process which preceded the making of the Directive, propose amendments to include unpaid and voluntary work. However the Council did not accept the addition of 'unpaid or voluntary work'.

7) The EU Commission kept the implementation in national legal systems of the Framework Directive under review, but never suggested that the United Kingdom or any member state has failed properly to implement the Directive by failing to include voluntary activity.

8) The appellant had argued that voluntary work which was closely analogous to employment did fall within the intended scope. The appellant and the EHRC proposed a multi-factorial test for such unpaid work. However the Court held that this would lead to uncertainty and disputes, and, had some but not all voluntary activity been intended to be covered, the Directive would have given some indication as to where the line should be drawn.

10.30   The Court concluded that, in the absence of a contract, discrimination against unpaid workers fell outside the scope of the Directive.

10.31   Volunteers are not wholly left without a remedy in this area. It may be necessary to start proceedings for discrimination in the County Court under the goods and services provisions of the Equality Act 2010.

10.32   The volunteer will need to argue that the organisation for which voluntary work is done is a provider of services to the public or a section of the public. If the organisation is selective in terms of its volunteer membership, it may be an 'association' for the purposes of the Equality Act 2010.[32] It will only be in cases where the discrimination is marked that this is likely to be a proportionate course to take. Of course in the County Court, the claimant may be able to obtain an injunction to prevent the continuation of discrimination. At the time of writing no cases attempting this approach have been started.[33]

10.33   As the law now stands, whether a volunteer is regarded as working in 'employment' depends on whether there is a contract under which the provision of personal services is the dominant purpose.

10.34   Cases that pre-dated *X* went either way. In *De Lourdes Armitage v Relate*,[34] an ET-level decision, a volunteer was held to be in 'employment' within the meaning of the RRA 1976 due to the fact that the contract between the parties entitled the volunteer to training for which she was obliged to undertake a minimum number of hours' work per week. In *South East Sheffield CAB v Grayson*,[35] the EAT stated that because there was no obligation on the volunteer to render personal service, it was immaterial that the respondent CAB provided her with training and reimbursed her expenses – no employment relationship could exist under the DDA 1995 in the absence of personal service.

Who is an 'employer' under the Equality Act 2010?

10.35   It is important to note that persons/companies can be liable for discrimination under the employment provisions of the EqA 2010 even if they do not yet engage the services of a worker/employee. A good example is given in the Code of Practice:[36]

> A man sets up a new gardening business and advertises for men to work as gardeners. A woman gardener applies for a job but is rejected because of her sex. She would be able to make a claim for direct discrimination even though the businessman is not yet an employer as he does not yet have any employees.

32 See 'Volunteers' status under anti-discrimination law: where to now?' www.cloisters.com/news-pdf-downloads/2012-december-olivia-faith-dobbie-x-v-cab.pdf for details.

33 It is also worth noting that during the passage of the EqA 2010, the government was asked about volunteers being covered under the employment provisions. Baroness Thornton stated (Hansard, 04/03/2009, col 725), that volunteers are already covered by the current prohibition of discrimination in the provision of facilities, in the same way as anyone else, in existing anti-discrimination legislation, which will be retained within the Equality Bill.

34 IT Case No 43438/94 (11 October 1994), [1994] DCLD 26.

35 [2004] IRLR 353.

36 Employment Code para 10.6.

Territorial scope of the Equality Act 2010

10.36   The EqA 2010 is silent on its territorial scope. It has adopted the approach in the ERA 1996, which is to leave it to ETs to determine whether they have jurisdiction or not.[37] To determine this, the ET will use the test established in *Lawson v Serco*.[38] A claim may be brought in the civil courts[39] or ET.[40]

10.37   Previously workers in an employment relationship with a foreign element were only able to bring discrimination claims in the domestic ET if they worked 'wholly or partly in Great Britain'.[41] This requirement no longer applies.

10.38   The Explanatory Notes to the EqA 2010 specifically refer to the ERA approach by saying:

> As far as territorial application is concerned, in relation to Part 5 (work) and following the precedent of the *Employment Rights Act 1996*, the Act leaves it to tribunals to determine whether the law applies, depending for example on the connection between the employment relationship and Great Britain.

10.39   It is clearly the intention of the Act that the principles developed in respect of unfair dismissal should be applied to employment discrimination claims. The case-law on the test for territorial jurisdiction can no longer be relied upon in so far as it relies on a test to determine whether the employee was working wholly or partly in Great Britain.[42]

10.40   Even under the precursor legislation in cases where the employee worked solely outside of Great Britain where the rights sought to be enforced stemmed from directly enforceable rights of equal treatment under the Treaty or Directives, the legislation was to be read so as to afford jurisdiction to hear the complaint. The territorial limitations had to be set aside or a compatible construction of those restrictions had to be found.[43]

---

37 See the Explanatory Notes to the Act.
38 [2006] UKHL 3, [2006] ICR 250.
39 EqA 2010 s114.
40 EqA 2010 s120.
41 Former provisions: SDA 1975 ss6 and 10; RRA 1976 ss4 and 8; DDA 1995 ss4 and 68; RBR 2003 regs 6 and 9; SOR 2003 regs 6 and 9 and AR 2006 regs 7 and 10.
42 Cases such as *Saggar v Ministry of Defence* [2005] EWCA Civ 413, in *British Airways Plc v Mak* [2011] EWCA Civ 184.
43 *Ministry of Defence v Wallis & Grocott* [2011] EWCA Civ 231.

10.41   In *Duncombe v Department for Education & Skills*[44] the Supreme Court recognised that two people doing the same work in two different countries within the European Union should be afforded the same protections under Directive 1999/70/EC. They were not required to determine how that principle might be achieved. It was not necessary to determine whether the approach arising from *Wallis* or *Bleuse* was correct. In all but the clearest of cases, care must be taken to review up-to-date authority when considering territorial scope.

Principles established in Lawson

10.42   The EqA 2010 is likely to be treated in the same way as the ERA 1996. In *Lawson v Serco Ltd, Botham v MOD* and *Crofts v Veta Ltd*[45] the House of Lords set out the general principles by which jurisdiction should be determined in the ERA 1996. Lord Hoffmann divided workers into three categories and gave guidance as to whether or not the ET had jurisdiction to hear the case in each.

The standard case

10.43   When the employee is working in Great Britain at the time of the alleged prohibited conduct then there will be no question as to territorial scope and the complaint will be within the jurisdiction of the ET.

10.44   Even when the employer is not British, if the prohibited conduct about which the employee complains took place while the employee was working in Great Britain then the ET will have jurisdiction to hear the complaint.

Peripatetic employees

10.45   The situation becomes more complex when the employee works outside Great Britain either on a short-term business trip or intermittently, such as airline pilots or international salespersons.

10.46   The decisive feature, according to *Lawson v Serco*, was the place where the employee was based. This was a question for the ET having considered the place at which the employee started and ended assignments.

---

44 [2011] 2 All ER 417, concerning the framework agreement on fixed term work concluded by ETUC, UNICE and CEEP.

45 [2006] ICR 250.

Expatriate employees

10.47   For those who live and work abroad, following the principles of *Lawson v Serco*, they will not be able to bring their claim under the EqA 2010 in the ET unless there are 'exceptional circumstances'.

10.48   The House of Lords gave two examples that may constitute exceptional circumstances: first, an employee who works abroad but with the purpose of furthering the business objectives of a company based in Great Britain, such as a journalist based in the country from which they report; secondly, an employee based in a political or social enclave, for example on a military base.

General rule – fact and degree

10.49   The three categories from Lawson provide examples only and are not hard and fast rules. Not all cases will easily fall into one of the three categories. In each case, the ET must consider how strong the connection is between the claimant and Great Britain and British employment law.

10.50   In *Duncombe v Secretary of State for Children, Schools and Families (No 2)*,[46] the Supreme Court considered whether teachers employed by the Secretary of State for Children, Schools and Families to work in European Schools were protected against unfair dismissal under the ERA 1996. It was accepted that the employment relationship did not fall within any of the classic categories of Lawson. Ultimately it was decided that the employees had an overwhelmingly closer connection with Britain and British employment law than with any other system of law such that it was right for them to enjoy protection against unfair dismissal.

10.51   In *Ravat v Halliburton Manufacturing and Services Ltd*[47] the employee was working on a rotational basis working for 28 consecutive days in Libya followed by 28 consecutive days at his home in Preston, England. He reported to an operations manager based in Libya on a daily basis but to an African region finance manager based in Cairo but employed by a UK subsidiary of Halliburton in respect of policy and compliance issues. The work in Libya was being carried out by a Halliburton associated company based in Germany. He contacted Halliburton human resources in both Aberdeen and Libya if he had any human resources queries. He was paid in sterling into a UK bank

46   [2011] ICR 1312.
47   [2012] UKSC 1, [2012] IRLR 315.

account. He was in Libya when his employment was terminated. It was held that the British ET did have jurisdiction to hear the claim.

10.52 Territorial jurisdiction cannot be determined by an agreement between the parties as to jurisdiction, contractual or otherwise.[48] ETs must weigh up all the facts and, as Lord Hope said in *Ravat*, consider[49] 'whether the connection between the circumstances of the employment and Great Britain and with British employment law was sufficiently strong to enable it to be said that it would be appropriate for the employee to have a claim for unfair dismissal in Great Britain'.

10.53 This approach to territoriality in cases brought under the Equality Act 2010 was approved by the Court of Appeal in *Clyde and Co LLP v Van Winkelhof*,[50] a case concerning a solicitor who worked in both Tanzania and the United Kingdom.

10.54 Taken together it is arguable that *Ravat* and *Duncombe* propound a test that jurisdiction is conferred on the country with the closer connection, rather than the connection having to achieve a particular level of proximity, and Lord Hope's comment in the text must be seen in the light of his statement at paragraph 27 in *Ravat*: 'I agree that the starting point needs to be more precisely identified. It is that the employment relationship must have a stronger connection with Great Britain than with the foreign country where the employee works'.[51]

10.55 In *Simpson v Intralinks*[52] Langstaff P considered questions of jurisdiction relating to equality legislation. The company's registered office was in London, but the claimant lived and worked in Frankfurt. Her contract provided that the German law would prevail in cases of disputes, giving the place of jurisdiction as Frankfurt. She could be transferred within Germany for operational reasons and could be required to travel within and outside Germany from time to time. She spent some time working in London.

10.56 Langstaff P held that Article 19 of the Brussels Regulation[53] permitted the claims to be brought in the UK and applied Article 6(2)

48 *Bleuse v MBT Transport Ltd* [2008] IRLR 264, EAT, per Mr Justice Elias (President) at para 43.
49 At para 29.
50 [2012] EWCA Civ 1207, [2012] IRLR 992 at paras 88–100.
51 See Jacques Algazy QC, 'Is Ravat Old Hat?' available on www.cloisters.com.
52 [2012] UKEAT 0593/11, [2012] ICR 1343.
53 Council Regulation (EC) No 44/2001 of 22 December 2000 on jurisdiction and the recognition and enforcement of judgments in civil and commercial matters applies (in force since 1 March 2002).

of the Rome Convention. Although the applicable law of the contract was German law, Article 7(2) of the Rome Convention[54] meant that, notwithstanding this, as the Sex Discrimination Act 1975 and Equal Pay Act 1970 were mandatory laws of the UK (which apply regardless of the jurisdiction of the contract). There was no limit on their territorial scope or applicability. The case gives a detailed analysis of the principles to be applied under the Brussels Regulation and the Rome Convention.

Discrimination in employment and occupation

10.57   For all those persons falling within the scope of the work provisions of the EqA 2010, discrimination protection applies:

- in recruitment (see chapter 9);
- to terms and conditions of employment;
- to opportunities for promotion and training;
- to benefits, facilities and services;
- to any other detriments; and
- to the termination of the employment relationship.

Probation periods

10.58   Employees are often recruited for a probationary period at the start of their employment. The existence of a designated probation period does not affect the individual's rights under the EqA 2010 (and/or other employment legislation).

10.59   However, where such a scheme is imposed, employers must ensure that any monitoring, training and/or appraisal programmes do not discriminate because of any of the protected characteristics. For example, it would be discriminatory to prevent a woman who became pregnant during her probation from completing/passing her probation period because of her pregnancy.

---

54 80/934/EEC: Convention on the law applicable to contractual obligations opened for signature in Rome on 19 June 1980. The Rome Convention was replaced on 17 December 2009 by Regulation (EC) No 593/2008 on the law applicable to contractual obligations. For torts (arguably including those under the Equality Act 2010) see Regulation (EC) No. 864/2007 on the Law Applicable to Non-Contractual Obligations (Rome II), which came into force on 11 January 2009, and which sets standard rules for deciding the governing law for many non-contractual civil and commercial disputes (mainly tort cases) in EU member states.

10.60   The following section on assessment of capability should be read in conjunction with this one when considering potential discrimination in respect of appraisal programmes implemented during probation.

10.61   The following example is given in the Employment Code to illustrate discriminatory behaviour during a probation period:[55]

> An employer decides not to confirm a transsexual employee's employment at the end of a six months probationary period because of his poor performance. The employee is consequently dismissed. Yet, at the same time, the employer extends by three months the probationary period of a non-transsexual employee who has also not been performing to standard. This could amount to direct discrimination because of gender reassignment, entitling the dismissed employee to bring a claim to the Employment Tribunal.

Assessment of capability

10.62   Work performance is monitored in a variety of ways across large and small organisations. A large employer may have a formal structure of bi-annual 360 degree appraisals with specific objectives set and monitored whereas a smaller employer may require each manager to meet with each employee for an informal work review each month. Whatever structure is adopted, the principles of transparency, consistency and non-discrimination must apply to all. Performance management systems taking the form of an ongoing dialogue with employees can prevent problems arising and may also remove the need for a mandatory retirement age in the workplace.

10.63   To avoid discrimination in the appraisal process, the Employment Code recommends the following:

- Make sure that performance is measured by transparent, objective and justifiable criteria using procedures that are consistently applied.
- Check that, for all workers, performance is assessed against standards that are relevant to their role.
- Ensure that line managers carrying out appraisals receive training and guidance on objective performance assessment and positive management styles.
- Monitor performance assessment results to ensure that any significant disparities in scores apparently linked to a protected characteristic are investigated, and steps taken to deal with possible causes.[56]

---

55 Employment Code para 10.14.
56 Employment Code para 17.81.

Promotion and training

10.64 Under EqA 2010 s39, employers must ensure that opportunities for promotion, training and development are open equally to all.[57] When advertising a role or training opportunity internally, this will usually require universal advertising of the opportunities across the entire workforce. If an employee is absent from work because of something arising in consequence of their disability or for parental or adoption leave the employer should inform the absentee of any opportunities.[58] If an employer fails to inform such employees, this could amount to discrimination.

10.65 If the employer assumes that such employees would not be interested in any such opportunities (for whatever reason, such as childcare etc) this too could amount to direct discrimination if the same assumption would not be made in respect of the comparator.

10.66 In *Horsey v Dyfed CC*,[59] an applicant was refused secondment for a two-year training course that was based close to her husband's place of work. As part of the reason for refusing her the training, the respondent was influenced by its belief that she would not return to work for the council and would opt to stay near her husband. The assumption that women will follow their husbands was held to be directly discriminatory.

Practical arrangements

10.67 The arrangements for delivering training and/or assessing ability must be considered and monitored to ensure they do not discriminate against persons indirectly.[60] For example, conducting training over a residential weekend may place those with childcare commitments at a disadvantage. This could amount to indirect discrimination on grounds of sex and/or age (since generally, more women than men have child care commitments and young employees tend to have fewer such commitments). Further, if there are, for example, blind employees, the employer may be expected to provide training materials in Braille etc.[61] Possible discriminatory factors include:

---

57 Employment Code para 16.20.
58 Employment Code para 16.22.
59 [1982] IRLR 395.
60 Employment Code para 17.71.
61 Employment Code para 17.72.

- dates set for training, including whether any religious festivals or holidays coincide with such dates;
- the hours during which training is organised: consider offering flexible hours to ensure a greater number of employees are able to take up the opportunity;
- training activities/exercises that may involve the use of language/contact and/or sharing of personal information that employees with certain protected characteristics may find inappropriate (for example, a gay/lesbian employee who does not wish to disclose their sexual orientation may not wish to reveal the name of their partner).

As can be seen from the above examples, discrimination within the context of promotion and development can take the form of direct discrimination (such as an assumption that female employees are less career-minded than male employees) or indirect discrimination (such as requiring a minimum length of service for applying for a role) or a failure to make reasonable adjustments.

Equality and diversity training and monitoring

10.68   The Employment Code recommends a systematic approach to developing and maintaining good practice as the best way of showing an organisation is taking its legal responsibilities seriously.[62] Employers should ensure that all managers are fully trained in equality and diversity matters relevant to promotion and training,[63] such that managers:

- understand their legal responsibilities under the EqA 2010 and how the employer's equality policy applies to training, promotion and development and other workplace policies, practices and decisions;
- recognise the employees' individual needs in the workplace, irrespective of protected characteristics. This will require managers to be able to identify and make provision for discharging any positive obligations (such as those owed under the duty to make reasonable adjustments for disabled workers);
- encourage all employees to apply for training and development opportunities equally, including those absent from the workplace so as to ensure that no employee is overlooked due to a protected characteristic;

62 Employment Code para 18.1.
63 Employment Code paras 18.18–18.22.

- monitor the take-up of training and development opportunities in respect of persons sharing protected characteristics to see if there is a trend/pattern in terms of the effect on a certain characteristic;[64]
- where such trends demonstrate that a particular group sharing a protected characteristic appears to be under-represented in any form of development opportunity, steps should be taken to minimise disparities and identify and remove any barriers faced by such groups.[65]

Secondary liability and the statutory defence

10.69   Under EqA 2010 s109(1) and (3), employers can be liable for the unlawful acts/omissions of their employees acting in the course of their employment. As such, employers are well-advised to maintain records of all equality and diversity training, since this may allow an employer to run a defence (that all reasonably practicable steps have been taken to prevent the discriminator from doing acts of the description done) under section 109(4).[66]

10.70   Where an employer has not provided any equality and diversity training or has not kept managers up to date in their training, this can be valuable evidence for a claimant seeking to establish discrimination. Questions about managers' training and the thoroughness/currency of training can be asked in written questions procedures (or correspondence) and can provide good material for cross-examination.

Benefits

10.71   The rules or requirements governing an employee's access to benefits, such as private health care, health insurance, bonuses, pension arrangements, gym memberships, company cars, mobile phones etc must not discriminate unlawfully. The protection against discrimination in relation to benefits applies irrespective of whether the benefits are contractual and/or discretionary.

10.72   For example, if an employer provided a benefit only to those working full-time, this could amount to indirect discrimination against female workers. Equally, an employer that provides free gym memberships to all employees under the age of 50 years (on the assumption

---

64   Employment Code paras 18.23–18.31.
65   Employment Code paras 18.31–18.34.
66   See para 8.28 for details.

that those aged more than 50 years would not use such a benefit) will be directly discriminating on grounds of age.

10.73 Of course, where there is direct age discrimination and/or indirect discrimination in relation to any other protected characteristic, there may be scope for justifying the discriminatory effect by demonstrating that the treatment is a proportionate means of achieving a legitimate aim. There are also some discrete automatic exceptions under the Act that allow an employer to provide certain benefits in certain specific circumstances without being liable for discrimination, even though the effect of the benefit schemes could otherwise be said to be discriminatory.

Any other detriment

10.74 Under EqA 2010 s39, employees are protected from being subjected to any other 'detriment'. In order to demonstrate 'detriment', there is no need to show a physical or economic loss. The principle in *Ministry of Defence v Jeremiah*[67] that 'a detriment exists if a reasonable worker would or might take the view that the [treatment] was in all the circumstances to his detriment' was approved in later cases (see *Shamoon v Chief Constable of Royal Ulster Constabulary*[68] and *Chief Constable of West Yorkshire Police v Khan*[69]). An unjustified sense of grievance about an act that is allegedly discriminatory will not suffice. According to the Code of Practice:[70]

> Generally, a detriment is anything which the individual concerned might reasonably consider changed their position for the worse or put them at a disadvantage. This could include being rejected for promotion, denied an opportunity to represent the organisation at external events, excluded from opportunities to train, or overlooked in the allocation of discretionary bonuses or performance-related awards.

10.75 The Code of Practice gives the following example:[71]

> An employer does not allow a black male employee an opportunity to act up in a management post, even though he has demonstrated

---

67 [1979] IRLR 436.

68 [2003] ICR 337, [2003] All ER 26.

69 [2001] IRLR 830.

70 Employment Code para 9.8 deals with the concept of a 'detriment' under the victimisation provision of the Act, however the concept is identical for the purposes of all unlawful acts under the Act (discrimination, harassment, victimisation etc). Indeed, para 10.17 refers back to para 9.8 when discussing the concept of 'detriment' in this context.

71 Employment Code para 10.17.

enthusiasm by attending relevant training courses and taking on additional work. He has also expressed an interest in progressing within
the business. Instead the employer offers the acting up opportunity
to an Asian woman because he perceives Asian people as more hard-
working than black people. If the black worker were able to demonstrate that he was better qualified for the acting up position compared
to his Asian colleague, he could claim discrimination because of race
on the basis that he was subjected to a detriment.

10.76   In early authorities on precursor legislation, certain acts were held
not to amount to detriments on the basis that they were so trivial
or minor as to fall outside the scope of the anti-discrimination provisions. The language of the day described them as 'de minimis'
acts.[72] However, such an approach is incompatible with the Directives on which the EqA 2010 is based, and is unnecessary, given the
definition of 'detriment' that is now current. A de minimis detriment
would be a 'detriment' that a reasonable worker would not see as a
detriment. However, if there is a detriment that a reasonable worker
would view as such then the requirement in the Directives that there
should be no discrimination whatsoever precludes an interpretation
that permits application of a de minimis rule.[73]

Types of detriments

10.77   Examples of detriments under the precursor legislation provide guidance on the types of detriment to be prohibited:

- offensive remarks – even if the comments are insufficient to
  create a claim for constructive unfair dismissal and even if the
  employee is prepared to tolerate them: see *De Souza v Automobile
  Association*[74] (but see also *Smith v Vodafone UK Ltd*[75] where comments were held not to be detriments under the SDA 1975);
- allegations by the employer against the employee that they have
  harassed another person – even if no further action is taken in
  respect to the allegation (see *Olasehinde v Panther Securities*[76]);
- disciplinary action against an employee;
- failing to resolve a grievance timeously or at all;

---

72 See eg *Peake v Automotive Products Ltd* [1997] IRLR 365.
73 See eg Directive 2000/78 Article 2.1.
74 [1986] IRLR 103.
75 UKEAT/0052/01.
76 UKEAT/0554/07, 30 July 2008.

- instructing an employee to discriminate against another person (see *Showboat Entertainment Ltd v Owens*[77] and *BL Cars Ltd v Brown*[78]);
- removal of certain duties/responsibilities from an employee's role and/or demotion to a different role – even if there is no impact upon pay (see *Shamoon*);
- relocation or transfers and/or requirement to work at a specific site (see *Deson v BL Cars*[79]) even if there is no reduction in pay or other effects on terms and conditions;
- changes to working hours; shift pattern; allocation of shifts etc that are less attractive to the employee (see *Williams-Drabble v Pathway Care Solutions Ltd*[80]);
- social exclusion in the workplace;
- providing too much work and/or insufficient work;
- refusal to provide a reference or providing an unfavourable reference.

Terms and conditions

10.78 Employers are forbidden from offering or setting terms that discriminate against a prospective or actual employee because of any protected characteristic. Such terms are voided by EqA 2010 s142.

10.79 Terms and conditions include, but are not limited to, pay, job descriptions and duties, benefits including pension and car allowance, working hours, overtime, bonuses, dress codes, holiday entitlement, sickness leave, maternity, paternity and adoption leave, disciplinary rules and grievance procedures.

10.80 The terms under which the employee operates can be express or implied, they can be agreed in writing in contractual and policy documents or orally through on-the-job training or agreements as to working arrangements. While it is common for some terms to be agreed orally it is good practice to ensure that any agreements, and the reasons for them, are recorded.

10.81 A sex equality clause is implied into every contract of employment.[81] By virtue of this clause, any term that is less favourable to one person when compared to a corresponding term of a comparator of

77 [1984] IRLR 7.
78 [1983] IRLR 193.
79 UKEAT/173/80.
80 ET Case No 2601718/04.
81 EqA 2010 s66.

the opposite sex who is employed on equal work will be modified so as to eliminate the difference.

10.82   The effect of the sex equality clause on equal pay is dealt with in full in chapter 14. The effect of the Act on contract terms, collective agreements and rules of undertakings is set out in chapter 8.

The Employment Code

10.83   Chapter 17 of the Employment Code gives the EHRC's recommendations on how employers can avoid discrimination in employment. It covers:

- working hours (para 17.6 and following) including flexible working[82] (para 17.8), rest breaks, (para 17.13);
- sickness absence (para 17.16 and following), including: disability-related sickness absence (para 17.20 and following), pregnancy-related absences (para 17.25 and following), absences related to gender reassignment (para 17.27), absences in relation to in vitro fertilisation (para 17.28), maternity, paternity adoption and parental leave (para 17.30 and following), emergency leave (para 17.32) and annual leave (para 17.33 and following);
- accommodating workers' needs including: dress codes (para 17.39), language in the workplace (para 17.44), understanding needs (para 17.52), quiet rooms (para 17.57), food and fasting (para 17.60), washing and changing facilities (para 17.62), breast-feeding (para 17.64);
- acceptable behaviour outside the workplace (para 17.65);
- induction (para 17.67) training and development (para 17.69), appraisals (para 17.78);
- promotion and transfer (para 17.82);
- disciplinary and grievance matters including: dealing with grievances (para 17.94 and following), disciplinary procedures (para 17.98), avoiding disputes and conflict (para 17.100).

Equality policies in the workplace

10.84   The Employment Code also provides useful material for assessing the equality policies of employers and thus for cross-examination on the employer's commitment to ensuring equality in the workplace. The following points can be relied on usefully:

---

82   See also chapter 7.

- planning an equality policy (18.5 and following), which emphasises the need to make clear that the policy will be applied; the common content of equality policies (para 18.8);
- implementation: whether there are plans for implementation of the policy (para 18.11), whether anything was done to promote and communicate the policy (para 18.13). These paragraphs discuss the means available for wide dissemination, and emphasise that it should not be a one-off event (para 18.16);
- backing of senior people: is there explicit backing and if so how is this manifested? (para 18.17). What training has there been? (para 18.18 and following);
- review of the policy and other policies (para 18.32 and following).

10.85 The Code also deals with monitoring of equality policies.[83] Claimants will be able to ask about the product of monitoring by means of written questions or by asking for documentation containing them. Failure to comply with the recommendations of the Employment Code may be taken into account where considered relevant by the ET in the process of drawing inferences in a discrimination claim.

Dismissal and post-termination discrimination

The meaning of 'dismissal'

10.86 The concept of dismissal is not explicitly defined in the EqA 2010. The concept covers the same situations as the ERA 1996 s95 by section 39(7) including

- express dismissal by the employer; and
- expiration of a fixed-term contract without renewal.[84] This includes expiry upon a certain date (prescribed in advance) and/ or upon the happening of a specified event (agreed in advance). If the employer renews the contract on the same terms before the specified expiry date and/or event, this will not amount to a dismissal; and
- the employee resigns in circumstances in which he/she is entitled to terminate the contract without notice due to their employer's conduct, namely a constructive dismissal.[85]

---

83 Employment Code para 18.25.
84 EqA 2010 s39(7)(a).
85 EqA 2010 s39(7)(b).

10.87   An employee seeking to bring a dismissal claim carries the burden of proving that he/she was dismissed, whether directly or constructively. In many cases the facts giving rise to a claim for unfair dismissal may also give rise to a claim for discrimination by dismissal.

Constructive dismissal

10.88   A constructive dismissal arises where an employee resigns in response to a breach of contract by the employer of a term of the contract that is fundamental enough to entitle the employee to terminate the agreement without notice. There must be something done by the employer that is of such a nature that the employee is entitled to resign and treat him/herself as having been dismissed.

10.89   If the employee proves resignation in response to an act of discrimination or victimisation by the employer,[86] that dismissal is likely also to amount to a constructive unfair dismissal under the ERA 1996.[87]

10.90   Not every breach of a statutory right, such as the prohibition on discrimination, will necessarily amount to a breach of the contractual implied term of trust and confidence (see *Doherty v British Midland Airways Ltd*,[88] *Shaw v CCL Ltd*[89] and see *Greenhof v Barnsley MBC*[90]).

10.91   Claimants should consider setting out in the claim form details of unfair (constructive) dismissal in all cases where they have resigned due to the employer's behaviour that involves discrimination provided they satisfy the definition of 'employee' under the ERA 1996 and have the requisite service for unfair dismissal.

10.92   In *Williams v J Walter Thompson Group Ltd*,[91] the claimant, who was blind, resigned because her employer did not provide suitable training and equipment. She claimed disability-related discrimination and a breach of the duty to make reasonable adjustments. The Court of Appeal held that, on the facts found by the ET, it ought to have concluded that the treatment suffered by the claimant was the effective cause of her resignation, and thus that her constructive dismissal was itself discriminatory.

---

86   EqA 2010 s39(2)(c) and/or s39(4)(c).
87   See *Nottinghamshire County Council v Meikle* [2004] IRLR 703, CA.
88   [2006] IRLR 90, EAT.
89   [2008] IRLR 284, EAT.
90   [2006] IRLR 98, EAT.
91   [2005] EWCA Civ 133, [2005] IRLR 376.

10.93   In *Bower v Schroder Securities Ltd*,[92] a woman was paid a far lower bonus than male colleagues. She relied on this, along with other incidents, to resign and claim constructive and discrimination by dismissal. Her claims were upheld, with the ET finding that her resignation was partly caused by the discrimination she suffered.[93]

10.94   An employee is not required to give notice when they resign in response to a repudiatory breach of contract by the employer, but if they do choose to give notice, this does not prevent the resignation amounting to a constructive dismissal. Employees would be sensible to set out the reasons, including the discriminatory factors, for the decision to resign. The ET can then properly focus on those reasons.

10.95   Where an employee works out a period of notice, this may in some cases undermine their case for either constructive unfair dismissal or discriminatory constructive dismissal:

- the ET may doubt whether the treatment to which the employee has been subjected was really as serious as they contend, which could undermine the case for alleging fundamental breach and/ or establishing discrimination;
- the ET may question whether the resignation was genuinely in response to the employer's conduct;
- working out the notice period could undermine any injury to feelings award. This is because, when assessing damages for injury to feelings, the ET will look for evidence of the degree of upset or distress suffered by the employee. If the employee continued to work after giving notice of termination, this could suggest that the working environment and/or the treatment suffered at work did not cause them severe upset.

10.96   Claimants should ensure that any reasons why they worked out the notice period, such as financial pressure, are set out fully in the witness statements prepared for the ET. Moreover if a grievance was being pursued in order to try to resolve matters during the notice period, the ET will want to be informed of this.

10.97   If the employee continues to work after a fundamental breach of the contract, it is sensible for them to ensure that the employer is

---

92 [2001] ET/3203104/99.

93 Note that discrimination need not be the sole or even the principal cause for the dismissal (whether direct or constructive); as long as the protected characteristic had a significant influence on the outcome, the dismissal will amount to discrimination (see eg *Nagarajan v London Regional Transport* [2000] 1 AC 501 per Lord Nicholls at 513).

aware that they are working 'under protest' in the sense that they do not accept what the employer has done.

10.98   A breach of the implied term of trust and confidence is always repudiatory.[94] However, there is no breach if the employer had reasonable or proper cause for its action or inaction. The test is objective and does not depend on the employee actually having lost trust and confidence. So long as the breach plays 'at least a part' in the decision to resign, causation is made out.[95]

Relationship between unfair dismissal and discrimination by dismissal

10.99   The prohibition on unfair dismissal under the ERA 1996 and the prohibition on discriminating against a worker by dismissing them are clearly different prohibitions. In *Mid-Suffolk District Council v Edwards*[96] the EAT pointed out that:[97]

> ... the test of unfair dismissal, under the Employment Rights Act (ERA) 1996, and the test of a non-discrimination by dismissal under the Disability Discrimination Act (DDA) 1995 are different and ... the latter is a higher test than the former. It may be that an applicant is fairly dismissed under the ERA but it does not necessarily follow that the dismissal is non-discriminatory under the DDA.

10.100   However, it will be rare for discrimination by dismissal to be reasonable.[98] Indeed, the Employment Code states:[99]

> Provided that the employee had one year or more continuous employment at the date of termination, a dismissal that amounts to a breach of the Act [the Act] will almost inevitably be an unfair dismissal as well. In such cases, a person can make a claim for unfair dismissal at the same time as a discrimination claim.

---

94 *Morrow v Safeway Stores* [2002] IRLR 9.

95 See *Nottinghamshire County Council v Meikle* [2004] IRLR 703 at para 33. For a summary of the basic principles, see *London Borough of Waltham Forest v Omilaju* [2005] IRLR 35 at para 14. However, note that if the claimant has not employed the grievance procedure, compensation may be subject to a reduction. See paras 17.4–17.8.

96 [2001] ICR 616, [2001] IRLR 190.

97 [2001] ICR 616, [2001] IRLR 190 at para 42.

98 See eg *Shaw v CCL Ltd* [2008] IRLR 284; *Nottinghamshire County Council v Meikle* [2004] IRLR 703 and *Greenhof v Barnsley Metropolitan Borough Council* [2006] IRLR 98.

99 Employment Code para 10.16. Note that for employment commencing on or after 6 April 2012, the qualifying period for ordinary unfair dismissal is two years.

10.101 Although rare, an act of discrimination may fail to give rise to a right to terminate the contract without notice and hence to a constructive dismissal.[100]

10.102 The key differences between claims for unfair dismissal and discrimination by dismissal are:

- Discrimination by dismissal applies both to those working under a contract of service (to whom rights under ERA 1996 definition of employment are given) and, in addition, those working under a contract for services. These are people who are under a contract personally to execute work.
- There is no qualifying period for eligibility to claim discrimination. To bring a claim for unfair dismissal, an employee must have the requisite minimum service.[101]
- No basic award is recoverable in claims for discrimination by dismissal.[102]
- Similarly, compensation for loss of statutory rights (usually in the region of £250–350) which is available in claims for ordinary unfair dismissal, is not available for discrimination by dismissal.
- Compensation for ordinary unfair dismissal is capped[103] whereas there is no such cap on financial losses resulting from discrimination by dismissal.
- Upon a finding of discrimination by dismissal, the employee will be entitled to a declaration of discrimination and recommendations. This is not available/applicable in cases of unfair dismissal.
- If the unfair dismissal claim succeeds, the employee can seek reinstatement or re-engagement, which are not remedies available for discrimination by dismissal.
- Damages for injury to feelings and aggravated damages are only available in claims for discrimination by dismissal. Similarly, damages can be recovered for personal injuries caused by unlawful acts of discrimination, harassment or victimisation. There is no scope for claiming these heads of damages in an unfair dismissal claim.

100 For an example see *Amnesty International v Ahmed* [2009] ICR 1450, [2009] IRLR 884.
101 For employees who were employed prior to 6 April 2012, and dismissed at any time thereafter, the qualifying period is one year. Employees who were/are engaged on or after 6 April 2012, will need two years' service with the employer before qualifying for protection against unfair dismissal.
102 See ERA 1996 ss118–122 for an explanation of the basic award recoverable in unfair dismissal claims.
103 At the time of writing, the cap for a compensatory award is £74,200 (this is in addition to a basic award); see ERA 1996 s124.

- The right to serve a statutory questionnaire is only available in discrimination claims.

Unfair dismissal

10.103 The test for ordinary unfair dismissal is set out in ERA 1996 s98 and comprises two stages:

- Firstly, the sole or principal reason for the dismissal must fall within one of the potentially fair reasons for dismissal set out in ERA 1996 s98(2) and (1)(b), namely: capability and qualifications; conduct; redundancy; contravention of a statutory duty or restriction; or some other substantial reason of a kind such as to justify the dismissal.[104]
- Secondly, in all the circumstances of the case (including the size and administrative resources of the employer) it must be reasonable for the employer to treat that reason as a sufficient reason to dismiss the employee (ERA 1996 s8(4)).

10.104 As the assessment of reasonableness at the second stage must be made in the light of all the circumstances of the case, it is necessary to have regard to the manner in which the dismissal was carried out and the context of the profession/business.

10.105   Further, the ET is bound to apply the so-called 'range of reasonable responses' test.[105] This requires the ET to make its decision by considering whether a hypothetical reasonable employer might have dismissed in the same way and in the same circumstances as the actual respondent did in the case. If it takes the view that a reasonable employer could have done so, it should find that the dismissal was fair, even if the ET feels it would have acted differently. It is not for the ET to impose its own personal subjective judgment as to what is and is not fair.[106]

---

104 Under ERA 1996 s98(2)(ba), there used to be a further potentially fair reason for dismissal, namely retirement. This was inserted by the Employment Equality (Age) Regulations 2006 and repealed from 1 October 2011 by way of the Employment Equality (Repeal of Retirement Age Provisions) Regulations 2011. There was a special regime (procedure) for 'retirement dismissals' which, if followed, would protect employers against a finding of unfair dismissal. The relevant provisions were ERA 1996 ss98ZA–98ZF.

105 See *Sainsbury's Supermarkets Ltd v Hitt* [2003] IRLR 23, CA and *Iceland Frozen Foods Ltd v Jones* [1983] ICR 17, EAT.

106 See *Foley v Post Office and HSBC Bank (Formerly Midland Bank) v Madden* [2000] ICR 1283, [2000] IRLR 827, CA. A detailed exposition of unfair dismissal is outside the scope of this book. See Tamara Lewis *Employment law: an adviser's handbook* (9th edn, Legal Action Group, 2011).

Discrimination by dismissal

10.106 Dismissal because of a protected characteristic will generally be unlawful under the EqA 2010. The discussion that follows is limited to some of the more commonly-occurring instances grouped by reference to the potentially fair reasons for dismissal under the ERA 1996. However, the Employment Code gives recommendations to employers on how they may avoid discrimination. Failing to follow these recommendations may be taken by an ET to be evidence from which an inference that discrimination has taken place can be made.

10.107 The Employment Code makes the following recommendations:

- decision-makers should be trained in their obligations under the EqA 2010;[107]
- having written procedures for dismissal assists consistency and fairness;
- avoid dismissing a worker with a protected characteristic for performance or behaviour that would be overlooked or condoned in others who do not share the characteristic;[108]
- reasonable adjustments to the dismissal process should be considered for persons with disabilities, in addition to whether the dismissal is for a reason arising from disability.[109] In capability procedures reasonable adjustments[110] ought also to be considered;[111] (whilst the Code does not recommend it, it should be noted that reasonable adjustments should also be considered to an actual dismissal);
- there should be procedures for capability and conduct issues;[112] employers should observe the following:[113]
  - apply procedures for managing capability or conduct fairly and consistently (or use Acas's Guide on Discipline and Grievances at Work, if the employer does not have their own procedure);

---

107 Employment Code para 19.3.
108 Employment Code para 19.4.
109 Employment Code para 19.5.
110 The limits to the duty to make adjustments to performance standards are well-illustrated by the case of *Hart v Chief Constable of Derbyshire Constabulary*, UKEAT/0403/07, 6 December 2007, where the EAT held that the respondent was not obliged to lower the standard required to be confirmed in employment as a police constable following the probationary period.
111 Employment Code para 19.9.
112 Employment Code para 19.8.
113 Employment Code para 19.10.

- ensure that any decision to dismiss is made by more than one individual, and on the advice of the HR department (if the employer has one);
- keep written records of decisions and reasons to dismiss;
- monitor all dismissals by reference to protected characteristics; and
- encourage leavers to give feedback about their employment; this information could contribute to the monitoring process.

Redundancy

10.108 The most commonly occurring problems[114] are where:

- the pool of employees from which selection will be made is determined in a discriminatory way;
- a selection process is instituted, but the selection criteria allow for subjective bias (ie considerations such as the 'ability to fit in' with the business), which could lead to discriminatory decisions. Good evidence in support of a claim for discrimination in a redundancy exercise could include the marking sheets used by assessors. Sometimes markers annotate the basis of their decision during the interviews and such notes could evidence a discriminatory bias;
- the selection criteria are themselves discriminatory (eg if higher marks are awarded to employees who are able to commit to full-time hours, this could amount to indirect sex discrimination against women);
- even where the selection criteria appear to be sufficiently objective, the assessors may mark candidates in a discriminatory way against those criteria. Again, under-scoring or over-scoring could be conscious or subconscious; and
- the method of assessment could itself give rise to indirect discrimination.

10.109 A suggested approach to redundancy selection criteria to determine whether they discriminate is as follows:

- Analyse what criteria are being used.
- Do any involve explicit reference to a protected characteristic? If the characteristic is age, ask whether its use can be justified.[115]

---

114 See eg *Chagger v Abbey National Plc* [2010] IRLR 47 (race discrimination selection); *Whiffen v Milham Ford Girls' School and Oxfordshire County Council* [2001] EWCA Civ 385 (indirect sex discrimination); *Eversheds Legal Services Ltd v De Belin* [2011] IRLR 448 (EAT) (sex discrimination) and *Rolls-Royce Plc v Unite the Union* [2009] EWCA Civ 387 (justified age discrimination).
115 See chapter 2.

- Are any of the criteria so subjective that there is a danger of stereotypes being applied by the decision-maker? If so consider whether there is evidence that this may have been occurring. (Consider whether direct discrimination.)
- If there is no explicit reference to protected characteristics, are any criteria likely to place persons with a particular protected characteristic at a particular disadvantage? If so do they place the claimant at that particular disadvantage?
- If there are such disadvantaging criteria, is there any evidence that the employer can justify the use of them? What is the evidence for the aim being pursued? Are the criteria appropriate and necessary as ways of achieving that aim?[116]

10.110 Useful sources of evidence could include a comparison between employees' CVs, or marks in the selection exercise to see if the claimant's lower marks call for an explanation. Where there are two employees with similar credentials, qualifications and achievements, yet one is given a demonstrably lower score, this could give rise to inferences of discrimination.[117]

10.111 In *British Sugar Plc v Kirker*,[118] the claimant was dismissed for redundancy after 17 years. He had a visual impairment that amounted to a disability. In a competitive assessment for redundancy, he scored 0 out of 10 for 'performance and competence' even though he had never been criticised in either aspect. He also scored 0 out of 5 for 'potential'. The ET stated that it was:

> left with a clear inference that he was viewed by the respondents' managers as somehow different from his colleagues. The origin of that view ... lay in his disability. It coloured the judgments which those managers made in the selection process.

10.112 The decision was upheld by the EAT. Accordingly, where there is good evidence (such as past performance appraisals) which indicates an employee's strengths/abilities, yet the employee receives low scores for those competencies in a redundancy exercise (or in any competitive assessment or capability exercise), this can provide useful evidence to support an inference that the low marks were awarded because of the protected characteristic.

---

116 See chapter 3.
117 *Network Rail Infrastructure v Griffiths-Henry* [2006] IRLR 865, EAT para 17 is a good example of balancing evidence of this sort in order to prove discrimination within a particular context.
118 [1998] IRLR 624, EAT.

10.113   Further evidence in support of discriminatory marking can be found in statistical data. If the data demonstrates that those sharing a protected characteristic generally obtained lower scores, this could support an inference that the marking was discriminatory, and/or that the method of assessment indirectly discriminated against those with the particular characteristic.

10.114   Indirect discrimination in redundancy selection can take many forms. One of the less obvious circumstances where the assessment itself could be said to be indirectly discriminatory was uncovered by the Commission for Racial Equality (now EHRC) in its publication *A Fair Test? Selecting Train Drivers at British Rail*. The CRE found that aptitude tests used by British Rail to select train drivers had an indirectly discriminatory effect on persons of Asian origin, who were seen to approach the questions more cautiously (and slowly) than white comparators. As marks were awarded where the candidate had attempted a greater number of questions, white candidates tended to score more highly. When considering whether methods of selection/assessment in a redundancy exercise are discriminatory, cases about selection for recruitment, bonuses or promotion can be useful.

10.115   It is also possible to define the pool for redundancy selection in a discriminatory way. For example, take an employer with 20 employees who do exactly the same tasks, but half of them work full-time and half work part-time. The employer decides to reorganise the business so that it has just ten full-time and five part-time employees. The employer decides that only the ten part-time employees need to be placed at risk and enter a competitive process for the five part-time roles that will remain. This could amount to indirect discrimination on grounds of sex (if there is a greater proportion of female than male part-time workers). It would be more acceptable to place all of the employees at risk and invite them to put themselves forward for: part-time work, or full-time work, or both. Employees could then be assessed against objective criteria in groups according to their preferred work patterns.

10.116   In *Whiffen v Milham Ford Girls School*,[119] the employer decided not to include fixed-term staff in the pool for redundancy (where they would be considered for the remaining roles and/or alternative roles), choosing to simply dismiss them instead. This was held to be indirectly discriminatory against women by the Court of Appeal, on the basis that a greater proportion of women than men worked under the fixed-term contracts.

119 [2001] EWCA Civ 385, [2001] ICR 1023, [2001] IRLR 468.

10.117 Similarly, in *Clarke v Eley (IMI) Kynoch Ltd*,[120] the EAT held that selection criteria that required the dismissal of part-time workers before considering the position of full-time staff were indirectly discriminatory on grounds of sex.

10.118 Where absence or attendance records are considered as part of the redundancy process, employees who have taken time off for medical appointments in connection with a disability may be placed at a substantial disadvantage in that process. This could give rise to disability discrimination. There is no absolute requirement for an employer to discount all disability-related absences (see *Royal Liverpool Children's NHS Trust v Dunsby*[121]), so the question of whether some or all disability-related absences should be discounted under the employer's duty to make reasonable adjustments will depend on the particular circumstances of the case.

10.119 Applying a redundancy policy of 'last-in first-out' is likely to amount to age discrimination, since the newest employees (the ones 'last-in') are likely to be younger. However, it has been suggested that the use of 'last-in first-out' may be justifiable as a proportionate means of achieving a legitimate aim if it is just one of many criteria utilised in the redundancy process (see *Rolls Royce plc v UNITE*[122]). It may also amount to indirect sex discrimination.[123]

10.120 The Employment Code makes the following recommendations in relation to redundancy dismissal:

- Adopt a selection matrix containing a number of separate selection criteria rather than just one selection criterion, to reduce the risk of any possible discriminatory impact.[124]
- Ensure that the selection criteria are objective.[125]
- 'Flexibility' – for example, willingness to relocate or to work unsocial hours, or ability to carry out a wide variety of tasks – may amount to discrimination because of (or arising from) disability or because of sex.[126]

---

120 [1983] ICR 165, [1982] IRLR 482, EAT.
121 [2006] IRLR 351, EAT.
122 [2009] EWCA Civ 387, [2010] 1 WLR 318, [2010] ICR 1.
123 Employment Code para 19.14.
124 Employment Code para 19.12.
125 Employment Code para 19.13.
126 Employment Code para 19.16. The suggestion appears to be that this would be direct sex discrimination. It is more likely to be indirect sex discrimination and the Code should not be read as suggesting otherwise. To the extent that it does, it is an incorrect statement of the law.

- The disadvantaging impact on persons with disabilities of redundancy criteria should be met by reasonable adjustments.[127]
- Alternative vacancies should be allocated on non-discriminatory bases;[128] subject to the rules relating to women on OML or AML in a redundancy.[129]

Capability

10.121 ERA 1996 s98(3) states that:

'capability', in relation to an employee, means his capability assessed by reference to skill, aptitude, health or any other physical or mental quality, and 'qualifications', in relation to an employee, means any degree, diploma or other academic, technical or professional qualification relevant to the position which he held.

10.122 This is the commonly accepted approach to the concept of capability as a reason for dismissal. A capability procedure within a work place will be aimed at meeting the issues that might lead to dismissal for such reasons. However, more recently HR managers have started to concentrate on performance management at an earlier stage than capability problems that might result in dismissal. One area in which performance management procedures are important is in relation to whether it is necessary for the business to have a retirement age.[130]

10.123 When considering dismissing an employee for capability, the employer should have regard to whether the employee is or might be disabled and, if so, whether the disability, or something arising in consequence of the disability, is causally connected to their performance.

10.124 If the employee is disabled, the employer may be under a duty to make reasonable adjustments to assist the employee in reaching an acceptable standard of performance and/or might be expected to make an adjustment to any performance targets, provided that such an adjustment is reasonable.

10.125 Sometimes the employee with a disability will have been absent from work sick repeatedly or for a sustained period, such that they are not physically at work sufficiently regularly to cover the tasks required. In such circumstances there may be various reasonable

127 Employment Code para 19.17.
128 Employment Code para 19.18.
129 Employment Code para 19.19 and chapter 7.
130 See *Seldon v Clarkson Jakes Wright (Age UK intervening)* [2012] UKSC 16, [2012] ICR 716, [2012] IRLR 590.

adjustments that could allow the employee to remain at work, including redeployment into a less demanding role, a job-share or part-time working.

10.126 In *Fareham College Corporation v Walters,*[131] the claimant had been absent on sick leave continuously for over six months due to fibromyalgia when she was dismissed on grounds of capability. In dismissing the claimant, the college had ignored the advice of the medical expert who had suggested a phased return to work as a reasonable adjustment. The ET found that the college had failed to make various reasonable adjustments and also that the dismissal was an act of disability-related discrimination. The EAT agreed, holding that it was 'impossible' to disentangle the failure to make reasonable adjustments from the decision to dismiss. As the ET had found, the claimant was dismissed because the alternatives to dismissal involved making adjustments which the employer considered unacceptable.[132]

10.127 Under the EqA 2010, a dismissal of a disabled person for capability could amount to a breach of sections 15 or 20 depending on the facts of the case. As stated above, an employer would be well advised to consider discounting a proportion of any disability-related absences as a reasonable adjustment and/or loosening their absence triggers when applying them to a disabled employee, but this is not an absolute requirement (see *Dunsby* above).[133]

10.128 Capability dismissals could also give rise to race (nationality/national origin) discrimination in circumstances where someone is dismissed for being unable to speak, write or read a language sufficiently well. The employer would then be expected to show that the requirement to speak the language to that standard is objectively justified as being necessary to the role.[134]

10.129 In a rather more obvious case of discrimination, *Mallidi v The Post Office,*[135] the employer decided to introduce aptitude tests as a requirement for workers seeking to progress from casual to permanent status. The claimant failed the test and was dismissed. However, it transpired that there were white employees who had not been required to undergo the aptitude test and were confirmed rather than being dismissed. The ET inferred that the reason why the claimant

---

131 [2009] IRLR 991, EAT.
132 [2009] IRLR 991 at para 68.
133 See para 10.115 and chapter 4.
134 See, in relation to language requirements, Employment Code para 17.44.
135 [2000] ET/2403719/98, [2001] DCLD 47.

was dismissed was her race. Where a group of persons sharing a pro-tected characteristic is singled out for less favourable treatment, this is likely to provide strong evidence supporting an inference that the reason for the treatment was the protected characteristic.

Conduct

10.130   Where the conduct of a disabled employee is related to their disabil-ity, the employer should consider whether reasonable adjustments can be made to assist the employee to minimise or manage the con-duct issue and/or transfer them to a role where the conduct will not be problematic.

10.131   Dismissals for absence or lateness could also be said to be dis-criminatory if, for example, the cause of the absence or lateness is the employee's childcare commitments.

10.132   Dismissing an employee for refusing to comply with a uniform policy could be discriminatory because of religion or belief. How-ever, in the context of sex discrimination a line of cases suggests that as long as the standards set are equivalent between the sexes, the treatment will not be considered to be less favourable.[136] Religion or belief discrimination might arise if the breach of the uniform policy involves wearing an item that the employee regards as being part of their religious or philosophical belief system.[137] Similarly, dismiss-ing an employee who objects to particular duties on religious or philosophical grounds could give rise to a claim for discrimination by dismissal.[138]

10.133   Another commonly occurring issue is where an employee is dis-missed for misconduct due to having taken unauthorised leave and/or having taken more than their authorised leave, in circumstances

---

136 *Smith v Safeway plc* [1996] IRLR 456; *Department for Work and Pensions v Thompson* [2004] IRLR 348 and *Dansie v Comr of Police for The Metropolis* UKEAT/0234/09.

137 See contrasting decisions on the facts in this context in *R (Watkins-Singh) v Aberdare Girls' High School Governors* [2008] EWHC 1865 (Admin), [2008] 3 FCR 203, [2008] ELR 561 and *Eweida v British Airways plc* [2010] EWCA Civ 80, [2010] ICR 890, subsequently *Eweida v United Kingdom* [2013] IRLR 231, concerning protection of Article 9 ECHR rights.

138 See *McFarlane v Relate Avon Ltd*, [2010] ICR 507, [2010] IRLR 196 (EAT) and [2010] EWCA Civ 880, [2010] IRLR 872 and *London Borough of Islington v Ladele* [2009] ICR 387, [2009] IRLR 154 (EAT) and [2009] EWCA Civ 1357, [2010] 1 WLR 955, [2010] ICR 532 for discussion of this point. The decisions in both cases ultimately went against the employee and their Article 9 ECHR claims failed: *Eweida v United Kingdom*, above.

where the leave was for religious reasons and/or to visit family abroad.

10.134 In *Khan v NIC Hygiene Ltd*[139] an employee departed for a pilgrimage to Mecca for five weeks, having requested to take his annual holiday entitlement alongside an additional week of unpaid leave to cover the period. He had not received formal authority before he left and he was dismissed upon his return. The ET held that the dismissal was discriminatory (under the then applicable Religion and Belief Regulations 2003). In most cases of this sort, it will be relatively straightforward for an employer successfully to argue that the effective cause of the dismissal was the absence itself and/or the breach of policy (in leaving without prior authority), but employers should be aware of the risk of claims of this nature.

Retirement

10.135 Dismissal for retirement is dismissal because of age. Following the decision in *Heyday*[140] consultations and the eventual abolition of the default retirement age, all retirement dismissals occurring after 1 October 2011[141] have to be objectively justified as amounting to less favourable treatment because of age.[142]

Automatically unfair dismissals

10.136 ERA 1996 ss98B–104 set out various circumstances in which a dismissal will be regarded as automatically unfair. In such cases, there is no need for the employee to have satisfied the qualifying period and the normal two-stage unfair dismissal test under section 98 will not apply. Some of these automatic unfair dismissals may also amount to discrimination, while others are wholly unrelated to discriminatory treatment. The circumstances include:

- taking leave for family reasons;[143]
- in connection with pregnancy, maternity or childbirth;[144]

---

139 ET/1803250/04 (unreported) but discussed in Emp LJ 2005, 61(Jun) Supp (Employment & Human Resources 2005), 20–21.

140 *R (Age UK) v Secretary of State for Business, Innovation and Skills* [2009] EWHC 2336 (Admin), [2010] ICR 260, [2009] IRLR 1017.

141 Pursuant to the Employment Equality (Repeal of Retirement Age Provisions) Regulations 2011 SI No 1069, which repealed and amended EqA 2010 Sch 9.

142 See para 2.81.

143 ERA 1996 s99.

144 ERA 1996 s99.

- performing certain health and safety activities;[145]
- refusal of Sunday working by shop and betting employees;[146]
- the making of a protected disclosure;[147]
- asserting a right to flexible working.[148]

10.137 Dismissal for asserting a statutory right[149] is not itself a form of discrimination. However, if the right which the employee seeks to assert is, say, the right to maternity leave, and the employee is dismissed because of that assertion, then the dismissal is likely to be discriminatory as well as automatically unfair. Dismissal for making a protected disclosure or asserting a statutory right may also amount to victimisation where the rights asserted are protected by the EqA 2010.

Relationships that have ended

10.138 EqA 2010 s108 makes it unlawful to discriminate against and/or harass an employee/worker after termination of the working relationship ('post-termination discrimination').[150]

10.139   Conduct that would not be unlawful under the EqA 2010 if the employment relationship was subsisting will not be unlawful if it occurs after that relationship has ended. As an example, protection against post-termination harassment will not extend to marriage and civil partnership or pregnancy/maternity, because the harassment provisions do not apply to those protected characteristics.[151] Equally, there is no protection against post-termination discrimination by association based on marriage/civil partnership because discrimination by association protection does not apply to this protected characteristic.

10.140   The requirement for the unlawful treatment to be closely connected to the previous relationship between the complainant and the discriminator is not elucidated in the EqA 2010 or in the Explanatory Notes. The Employment Code, states:[152] 'The expression "closely connected to" is not defined in the Act but will be a matter of degree

145 ERA 1996 s100.
146 ERA 1996 s101.
147 ERA 1996 s103A.
148 ERA 1996 s104C.
149 Prohibited under ERA 1996 s104.
150 See chapter 8.
151 See further on the ambit of the harassment provisions para 5.8.
152 Employment Code para 10.57.

to be judged on a case-by-case basis.' It gives the example: 'A worker who receives an inaccurate and negative job reference from her former employer because she is a lesbian could have a claim against her former employer for direct discrimination because of sexual orientation.'

10.141   It would also apply to an ex-employee with a disability required to attend a meeting after the end of the employment relationship. It could be a grievance meeting or an appeal against dismissal. If the ex-employee requires reasonable adjustments to be made to assist them in participating in the meeting, and such adjustments are not made, they are likely to be eligible to claim post-termination breach of the duty to make reasonable adjustments.

10.142   The following example is given in the Employment Code:[153] 'A former worker has lifetime membership of a works social club but cannot access it due to a physical impairment. Once the former employer is made aware of the situation, they will need to consider making reasonable adjustments.'

10.143   Examples from previous cases include:

- refusal to provide a reference to an ex-employee and/or provision of a reference that is unfavourable (see *Coote v Granada Hospitality Ltd*,[154] *Relaxion Group plc v Rhys-Harper*[155] and *Chief Constable of the West Yorkshire Police v Khan*[156]);
- negative remarks made outside the hearing room during the course of ET proceedings (see *Nicholls v Corin Tech*[157]);
- failure to pay a judgment debt owed by an employer to a former employee in respect of an award for compensation for a previous discrimination claim (see *Coutinho v Rank Nemo (DMS) Ltd*[158]).

10.144   *D'Souza v Lambeth Borough Council*,[159] where it was held that a discriminatory failure by an employer to comply with a reinstatement order was not sufficiently connected is a puzzling counter-instance.

---

153 Employment Code para 10.60.
154 C-185/97, [1998] ECR I-5199, [1999] ICR 100, ECJ.
155 [2003] UKHL 33, [2003] ICR 867. The discussion within the speeches in that case is useful in indicating what may amount to a sufficient connection. See in particular para 139 ff.
156 [2001] UKHL 48, [2001] 1 WLR 1947, [2001] ICR 1065.
157 UKEAT/0290/07/LA, 4 March 2008.
158 [2009] EWCA Civ 454, [2009] ICR 1296.
159 [2003] UKHL 33, [2003] ICR 867.

Post-termination victimisation

10.145   Despite the breadth of protection provided by EqA 2010 s108, it can be seen that there now appears to be no provision for post-termination victimisation at all. Indeed, protection against post-termination victimisation is expressly excluded from the scope of section 108 by way of subsection (7).[160] Note that para 10.62 of the Employment Code states that post-termination victimisation is covered by the victimisation provisions themselves.

10.146   ## Practical points

- A contract can be found if there is any consideration: something given by the 'employer' to the worker for the work. This may be something other than pay.
- To show that the contract is one 'personally to do work', focus on providing evidence that the work is to be done by the claimant, and cannot be delegated to someone chosen by him/her.
- Writing the witness statement for cases establishing the territorial jurisdiction of the ET requires the claimant to provide details demonstrating a sufficient connection to the UK, including time spent in the UK, the nature of the work etc. Evidence establishing that the connection with the UK is closer than to another country will render this conclusion more likely.
- In all employment cases close attention should be paid in the witness statement to establishing the less favourable (or unfavourable or unwanted) treatment and the known details of any actual comparators. It is likely that there will be documentation that may assist which can be sought on disclosure from the employer.
- In dealing with the employer's evidence, in questioning witnesses for example, attention should be given to the level of compliance with the Employment Code's advice to employers on how to avoid discrimination. The ET should be invited to infer discrimination by the employer from any relevant non- compliance.
- In preparing an argument for the ET in an unfair dismissal and discrimination case, take care to address the issues separately, as

---

160 For a discussion of a potential solution to this anomaly short of new legislation, see chapter 6. Also see *Coote v Granada Hospitality Ltd* C-185/97, [1998] ECR I-5199, [1999] ICR 100, ECJ and *Relaxion Group plc v Rhys-Harper* [2003] UKHL 33, [2003] ICR 867.

unreasonable conduct by the employer does not automatically result in a finding of less favourable treatment.

- Ensure that if possible the discrimination issues have been raised under the employer's internal grievance or equal opportunities procedure to avoid a reduction in any compensation for discrimination.

CHAPTER 11

Discrimination in occupations and non-employment bodies

Key points

- The EqA 2010 has provisions prohibiting discrimination in occupations or by bodies that have connections with or facilitate employment, and in some relationships akin to employment.
- The provisions deal with:
  - contract workers and principals;
  - police officers;
  - partnerships and LLPs;
  - barristers and advocates;
  - appointments to personal and public offices;
  - qualifications bodies;
  - employment service-providers, including employment agencies and providers of vocational training;
  - trade organisations;
  - local authority members.
- Generally provision is similar or even identical to that covering employment. But there are a number of differences. It is important to look at the precise wording of the relevant provision as the protection may differ from that provided by EqA 2010 s39.
- The exceptions to prohibitions on discrimination vary according to the particular type of body or relationship covered. Exceptions can be difficult to locate in the Act.

Introduction

11.1   The EqA 2010 prohibits discrimination in employment and occupation as well as by certain bodies that have connections with or facilitate employment. If a trade union were to refuse to admit someone as a member for being gay, that would amount to direct discrimination by a trade organisation. A company, which obtained the services of a woman through an agency, ceasing to require her services because she is pregnant would amount to pregnancy discrimination in a contract worker relationship.

11.2   In the precursor legislation the provisions about employment-related discrimination by other bodies varied slightly between the legislation. All now are contained within Part 5 of the EqA 2010. This chapter deals with:

- EqA 2010 s41: contract workers and principals;
- EqA 2010 s42: police officers;

- EqA 2010 ss44 and 45: partnerships and limited liability partnerships;
- EqA 2010 ss47 and 48: barristers and advocates;
- EqA 2010 ss49–51: appointments to personal and public offices;
- EqA 2010 s53: qualifications bodies;
- EqA 2010 s55: employment service-providers, including employment agencies and providers of vocational training;
- EqA 2010 s57: trade organisations;
- EqA 2010 s58: local authority members carrying out official business.

11.3 In general, these provisions prohibit discrimination, harassment and victimisation and impose a duty to make reasonable adjustments in the same way as the employment provisions under EqA 2010 s39, and are subject to the same exceptions. However, there are certain exemptions specific to some of these categories, which are detailed in the relevant sections below.

Contract workers and principals

The relationship of contract worker and principal

11.4 The EqA 2010 allows contract workers to bring claims for discrimination, harassment, victimisation and a failure to make reasonable adjustments against a 'principal'.[1]

11.5 The Explanatory Notes point out[2] that contract workers are protected from discrimination both by their employer (which may be, for example, the agency that supplies a temporary office worker to a particular company) under EqA 2010 s39, and by the 'principal' to whom they are supplied, under section 41. In an agency-type situation, consideration should always be given to the question of whether there is in fact an employment relationship between the worker and the end-user, such that section 39 may be relied upon as between them (see *Cable & Wireless v Muscat*,[3] *James v Greenwich LBC*[4] and *Muschett v HM Prison Service*,[5] which applies the *James* analysis in the context of the broader definition of 'employee' contained in the RRA 1976).

1 EqA 2010 s41.
2 At para 147.
3 [2006] EWCA Civ 220, [2006] ICR 975.
4 [2008] EWCA Civ 35, [2008] ICR 545.
5 [2010] EWCA Civ 25, [2010] IRLR 451.

11.6   *What needs to be established for the relationship*: EqA 2010 s41(5) provides that a 'principal' is a person (X) who makes work available for an individual (Y) who is:

- employed by another person[6] (Z); and
- supplied by Z in furtherance of a contract to which the principal X is a party (whether or not Z is a party to it).

11.7   An individual (Y) supplied under such an arrangement is a contract worker as defined by EqA 2010 s41(7), and work made available in this way is contract work as defined by section 41(6).

11.8   The Employment Code[7] clarifies the meaning of this provision. It makes the point that a 'principal' is often known as an 'end-user'. It also points out that the contract does not have to be in writing. It uses the example of a nurse working at an NHS trust who is employed and supplied to the NHS trust by a private healthcare company. It makes clear that the worker must work wholly or partly for the principal, even if they also work for their employer, but they do not need to be under the managerial power or control of the principal. Contract workers can include employees who are seconded to work for another company or organisation and employees of companies who have a contract for services with an employment business.[8]

11.9   The EqA 2010 is intended to codify the case-law, which gave a broad construction to the equivalent provisions of the precursor legislation. The relationships that were covered under the previous case-law will remain covered and the principles from these cases will remain effective.

- In *Harrods Ltd v Remick*,[9] Harrods granted licences for departments of its stores, where the licensee's goods would be sold. The claimants, who were the licensee's employees, had to be approved by Harrods, observe Harrods' rules regarding dress, behaviour and deportment, and wear a Harrods uniform. Under the licence arrangement, the goods on sale in the department would be sold to Harrods immediately before their sale to the public. The Court of Appeal held that the claimants were doing work for Harrods, which was therefore their principal for the purposes of the RRA 1976. It was not necessary for the principal to have managerial

6 Employment is defined by EqA 2010 s83 as meaning employment under a contract of employment, a contract of apprenticeship or a contract personally to do work.
7 Employment Code para 11.5.
8 Employment Code para 11.6.
9 [1998] ICR 156, [1998] 1 All ER 52.

power over the contract workers, and the claim could be made against Harrods even though the work was in fact made available to the claimants by the licensee, their employer. The Employment Code states:[10]

> There is usually a contract directly between the end-user and supplier, but this is not always the case. Provided there is an unbroken chain of contracts between the individual and the end-user of their services, that end user is a principal for the purposes of the Act and the individual is therefore a contract worker.

- In *MHC Consulting Services v Tansell*,[11] the claimant was employed by, and offered his services as a computer consultant through, his own company. He entered into a contract with an employment agency, MHC, to provide computer consultancy services for MHC to MHC's client Abbey Life. The Court of Appeal held that in those circumstances, Abbey Life was a principal in relation to the claimant even though there was no direct contract between the principal and the claimant's employer. This result is now made explicit in EqA 2010 s41(5).
- In *Jones v Friends Provident Life Office*,[12] the claimant's husband, who ran an estate agency trading as Wynchester Investments (WI), became an authorised representative of Friends Provident, and also an introducer, allowing him to introduce clients to a company representative of Friends Provident. Only the company representative could sell Friends Provident's products. The claimant, who worked for her husband, became a company representative. It was found that a contract worker/principal relationship existed between Friends Provident and the claimant even though there was no contract between WI and Friends Provident to the effect that WI would supply the claimant to do the sales work. It was enough that Friends Provident would have contemplated that WI would need to employ someone to sell its products, would have a large say in how the work was carried out, and could terminate the claimant's appointment as a company representative.
- In *Leeds City Council v Woodhouse*,[13] the claimant was employed by WN, an arm's length management organisation that carried out the management functions of the council in respect of a number of residential properties, under a management agreement. WN

---

10 Employment Code para 11.8.
11 [2000] ICR 789, [2000] IRLR 387, CA.
12 [2003] NICA 36, [2004] IRLR 783.
13 [2010] EWCA Civ 410, [2010] IRLR 625.

had to manage the properties within the confines of a business plan agreed with the council, and the management agreement set out an extensive performance management framework. Most of WN's finance came from the council. In such circumstances the Court of Appeal upheld the ET's finding that the claimant's work was being done for the council, and that the council was a principal within the meaning of the RRA 1976. The Court of Appeal observed that it would not always be necessary for a claimant to show that a principal was able to control and influence his work in order to fall within the provisions.

11.10   Whether a particular set of facts gives rise to a contract worker/principal relationship within the meaning of what is now EqA 2010 s41 should not be determined as a preliminary issue,[14] as this issue will, save in very straightforward cases, require extensive findings of fact, better made following a full hearing.

The prohibited acts

11.11   The acts or omissions precluded by the EqA 2010 in the contract worker/principal relationship are similar to those precluded in the employment relationship, albeit a little narrower.

11.12   The principal must not discriminate against the contract worker:

- as to the terms on which the principal allows the worker to do the work;
- by not allowing the worker to do or continue to do the work;
- in the way the principal affords the worker access, or by not affording the worker access, to opportunities for receiving a benefit, facility or service;
- by subjecting the worker to any other detriment.[15]

11.13   The principal must not, in relation to contract work, harass the contract worker.[16] This wording is broad enough to cover harassment in the process of selection for such work, the work itself, and potentially harassment after the work is finished.

11.14   The principal must not victimise the contract worker in relation to the matters set out at para 11.12 above.[17]

---

14 See *Leeds City Council v Woodhouse* [2010] EWCA Civ 410, [2010] IRLR 625.
15 EqA 2010 s41(1).
16 EqA 2010 s41(2).
17 EqA 2010 s41(3).

11.15 The principal owes the contract worker a duty to make reasonable adjustments, regardless of any similar duty the contract worker's employer may have towards him.[18] This recognises the fact that the location of the work or the responsibility for the systems of work and the arrangements surrounding the work are likely to be with the principal, rather than the employer. The employer may have no control at all over the physical environment in which the contract worker has to work, although he will also owe a separate, albeit perhaps overlapping, duty to make reasonable adjustments for the contract worker as his employee. The Employment Code makes clear that it would be reasonable for a principal and the employer of a contract worker to co-operate with each other with regard to any steps taken by the other to assist the contract worker.[19]

11.16 The Employment Code[20] notes that, in deciding whether any, and if so, what, adjustments would be reasonable for a principal to make, it will be relevant to consider the period for which the disabled contract worker may be appointed. Adjustments that would be reasonable where the appointment is for six months may well not be reasonable if the appointment is only for two weeks.

Police officers

11.17 EqA 2010 s42 deems a constable for the purposes of the work provisions of the Act to be employed:

- by the chief officer[21] in respect of any act done by the chief officer in relation to a constable or appointment to the office of constable;

---

18 EqA 2010 s41(4).
19 Employment Code para 11.14. It points out that it is good practice for the principal and the employer to discuss what adjustments should be made and who should make them.
20 Employment Code para 11.13.
21 By EqA 2010 s43(2), 'Chief Officer' means (a) in relation to an appointment under a relevant Act [defined at s43(8)], the chief officer of police for the police force to which the appointment relates; (b) in relation to any other appointment, the person under whose direction and control the body of constables or other persons to which the appointment relates is; (c) in relation to a constable or other person under the direction and control of a chief officer of police, that chief officer of police; (d) in relation to any other constable or any other person, the person under whose direction and control the constable or other person is.

- by the responsible authority[22] in respect of any act done by the authority in relation to a constable or appointment to the office of constable.[23]

11.18   As this category of person is deemed to be an employee under these provisions, no further special provision needs to be made in the EqA 2010. The Employment Code deals with discrimination against police officers.[24]

11.19   Claimants should first determine who has performed the act or omission constituting prohibited conduct under the EqA 2010. It may sometimes be difficult to determine whether the act is one of the chief officer, or the responsible police authority. In such circumstances it is likely to be sensible to plead the claim against both the chief officer and the responsible authority.

11.20   Holding an appointment as a police cadet[25] is treated as employment by the chief officer or the responsible authority in the same way.[26]

11.21   Constables serving with the Civil Nuclear Constabulary are treated as employees of the Civil Nuclear Police Authority.[27]

11.22   Constables seconded to serve at the Serious Organised Crime Agency (SOCA) or the Scottish Police Services Authority (SPSA) are to be treated as employed by those organisations in respect of any act done by them in relation to the constable.[28]

11.23   Constables at the Scottish Crime and Drugs Enforcement Agency (SCDEA) are treated as employed by the Director General of SCDEA

---

22   By EqA 2010 s43(3), 'responsible authority' means (a) in relation to an appointment under a relevant Act, the police authority that maintains the police force to which the appointment relates; (b) in relation to any other appointment, the person by whom a person would (if appointed) be paid; (c) in relation to a constable or other person under the direction and control of a chief officer of police, the police authority that maintains the police force for which that chief officer is the chief officer of police; (d) in relation to any other constable or any other person, the person by whom the constable or other person is paid.

23   EqA 2010 s42(1).

24   Employment Code para 11.15 ff. This points out that the chief constable will be vicariously liable under EqA 2010 s109 for the unlawful acts of one officer against another.

25   Defined at EqA 2010 s43(4) as a person appointed to undergo training with a view to becoming a constable.

26   See EqA 2010 s42(2).

27   EqA 2010 s42(3) and Energy Act 2004 s55(2).

28   EqA 2010 ss42(4), (5) and 43(5), (6).

in respect of any act done by the Director General in relation to the constable.[29]

Partnerships

11.24 This is not a book about partnership law, but it is useful to be aware of the definition of a partnership, which is not set out in the EqA 2010 itself, but in various other Acts to which reference is made in sections 44–46, which prohibit discrimination by different types of partnership.[30]

11.25 The Act covers three types of partnership:

- EqA 2010 s44 covers general partnerships. A general partnership is 'the relation which subsists between persons carrying on a business in common with a view of profit'.[31] All three elements must be satisfied. The nature of the relationship in a formal partnership is likely to be contained in the partnership agreement, which may, for example, contain the provisions relating to appointment, retention and retirement of partners. Persons who have entered into partnership with one another are collectively known as a 'firm'.[32]
- EqA 2010 s44 also extends to cover limited partnerships. A limited partnership consists of one or more persons called general partners, who are liable for all debts and obligations of the firm, and one or more persons called limited partners, who, at the time of entering into the partnership, contribute a stated sum, but are not liable for the debts or obligations of the firm beyond the amount contributed.[33] The prohibitions in the Act apply only in relation to general partners, who will be the partners involved with the operation of the firm.[34]
- EqA 2010 s45 covers limited liability partnerships (LLPs). An LLP is a body corporate, with legal personality separate from that of its members, which is formed by being incorporated under the Limited Liability Partnerships Act 2000.[35]

---

29 EqA 2010 ss42(4), (6) and 43(7).
30 Partnerships are dealt with in the Employment Code paras 11.18–11.23.
31 Partnership Act 1890 s1(1) and EqA 2010 s46(2).
32 Partnership Act 1890 s4(1) and EqA 2010 s46(2).
33 Limited Partnerships Act 1907 s4(2) and EqA 2010 s44(8).
34 EqA 2010 s44(8).
35 Limited Liability Partnerships Act 2000 s1(2) and EqA 2010 s46(4).

11.26 The term 'partner' is often loosely used to apply, for example, to a 'salaried' partner in an accountancy firm, who will not be a partner for the purposes of the discrimination legislation, but will be regarded as an employee with a title, whose employment rights are determined by EqA 2010 s39. If there is any doubt as to whether section 39 or one of sections 44 or 45 applies in a particular case, it would be sensible to plead the claim under both potentially applicable sections.[36]

11.27 There was previously some disparity between the partnership provisions in the RRA 1976 and those in the other discrimination legislation, but the prohibitions contained in the EqA 2010 are the same for all protected characteristics. In particular, there is no longer any lower limit on the size of the partnership before the provisions will apply, so even where there are only two partners in a partnership, one may sue the other for an act of discrimination.[37]

11.28 The provisions of EqA 2010 ss44 and 45 prohibit firms and LLPs, and proposed firms and LLPs, from discriminating against a person:

- in the arrangements they make for deciding to whom to offer a position as a partner/member;[38]
- in the terms on which they offer the person a position as a partner/ member;[39] and
- by not offering the person a position as a partner/member.[40]

11.29 The sections also prohibit discrimination against a partner or member (B) as to the terms on which B is a partner;[41] in the way B is afforded access, or by not affording B access to opportunities for promotion, transfer or training or for receiving any other benefit, facility or service;[42] by expelling B;[43] or by subjecting B to any other detriment.[44]

---

36 See for a full discussion of this point in the context of an argument that a fixed share partner in a solicitor's firm was an employee *Tiffin v Lester Aldridge LLP* [2012] EWCA Civ 35, [2012] 1 WLR 1887 at paras 57–68 and further *Bates van Winkelhof v Clyde & Co LLP* [2012] EWCA Civ 1207, [2012] IRLR 992 at paras 51–67.

37 See eg *Dave v Robinska* [2003] ICR 1248, EAT.

38 EqA 2010 ss44(1)(a) and 45(1)(a).

39 EqA 2010 ss44(1)(b) and 45(1)(b).

40 EqA 2010 ss44(1)(c) and 45(1)(c).

41 EqA 2010 ss44(2)(a) and 45(2)(a).

42 EqA 2010 ss44(2)(b) and 45(2)(b). Benefits could include access to a company car or to a child care scheme: see para 164 of the Explanatory Notes.

43 EqA 2010 ss44(2)(c) and 45(2)(c).

44 EqA 2010 ss44(2)(d) and 45(2)(d).

11.30   'Expelling' a partner or member of an LLP is defined as including reference to the termination of the person's position:

- by the expiry of a period (including a period expiring by reference to an event or circumstance);
- by an act of the partner or member, including giving notice, in such circumstances that the partner or member is entitled, because of the conduct of other partners or members, to terminate the position without notice;
- (in the case only of a partner of a firm) as a result of the dissolution of the partnership.[45]

11.31   Therefore, as an example in the Explanatory Notes explains, a gay partner who, because of constant homophobic banter, feels compelled to leave his position as a partner can claim to have been expelled from the partnership because of his sexual orientation.[46] Such a claim would be determined in a way similar to a constructive dismissal claim made by an employee under EqA 2010 s39.

11.32   Firms and LLPs must not harass partners or members,[47] and existing and proposed firms and LLPs must not harass a person who has applied for the position of partner or member.[48]

11.33   The prohibitions in relation to victimisation are the same as those for discrimination, as set out at paras 11.28–11.31 above.[49]

11.34   Firms and proposed firms, and LLPs and proposed LLPs, are under a duty to make reasonable adjustments.[50] Where such a body is required to make a reasonable adjustment under the EqA 2010, the costs of making that adjustment are to be treated as an expense of the firm or LLP, and the extent to which the partner or member (or proposed partner or member) should bear the cost must not exceed such amount as is reasonable, having regard to their entitlement to share in the profits of the firm or LLP.[51] So, for example, if a disabled partner in a firm receives 15 per cent of the firm's profits, it is likely to be reasonable to ask them to contribute 15 per cent of the cost of an adjustment (such as a specially modified chair), but it may not be reasonable to require a higher contribution.[52]

---

45 EqA 2010 ss46(6).
46 Explanatory Notes para 161.
47 EqA 2010 ss44(3)(a) and 45(3)(a).
48 EqA 2010 ss44(3)(b), 44(4), 45(3)(b) and 45(4).
49 EqA 2010 ss44(5), (6) and 45(5), (6).
50 EqA 2010 ss44(7) and 45(7).
51 EqA 2010 Sch 8 paras 7(2) and 8(2).
52 Employment Code para 11.23.

11.35   Dealing briefly with the procedural aspects of all claims against firms, proceedings may be brought against the firm itself but will also be properly constituted if they are brought against named partners. In general, any action will be brought against all partners save for the recipient of the discrimination.[53]

11.36   Partnerships and justification: A rule of a partnership agreement may need to be justified due to unfavourable treatment arising from disability, less favourable treatment because of age, or because it places the claimant and the claimant's protected characteristic group at a particular disadvantage. A significant feature of the partnership agreement is that it is assumed to be a bargain between people of equal bargaining power. This will be taken to be an important feature in any discussion of justification.[54]

Barristers and advocates

11.37   Under EqA 2010 s47, it is unlawful for a barrister or a barrister's clerk to discriminate against or victimise a person in the arrangements made for deciding to whom to offer a pupillage or tenancy, as to the terms on which pupillage or tenancy is offered, or by not offering pupillage or tenancy.[55] Employed barristers are of course employees and are dealt with under the Act as such (and not separately). The same is likely to be true of those engaged in 'alternative business structures'.

11.38   Once an individual has become a pupil or tenant, the EqA 2010 prohibits a barrister or barrister's clerk from discriminating against or victimising them:

- as to the terms on which they are a pupil or tenant;
- in the way they are afforded access, or not afforded access, to opportunities for training or gaining experience or receiving any other benefit, facility or service;
- by terminating the pupillage;
- by subjecting them to pressure to leave chambers;
- by subjecting them to any other detriment.[56]

---

53 *Dave v Robinska* [2003] ICR 1248, EAT at paras 23 and 24.
54 See *Seldon v Clarkson Jakes Wright* [2012] UKSC 16, [2012] ICR 716, [2012] IRLR 590 at para 65 and in the EAT (with more emphasis) [2009] 3 All ER 435, [2008] UKEAT/0063/08 paras 51–54.
55 EqA 2010 s47(1) and (4). The Employment Code deals with advocates and barristers at paras 11.24–11.30.
56 EqA 2010 s47(2) and (5).

11.39 A reference to a tenant includes a barrister who is permitted to work in chambers, such as a squatter or a door-tenant.[57]

11.40 A barrister or barrister's clerk is also prohibited from harassing a pupil, tenant or an applicant for pupillage or tenancy,[58] and is subject to the duty to make reasonable adjustments.[59]

11.41 The EqA 2010 also prohibits individuals from discriminating against, harassing or victimising a barrister in relation to instructing that barrister.[60] As explained in the Explanatory Notes, perhaps the most common type of situation intended to be covered by this provision is where a barrister is not instructed because of, or owing to mistaken assumptions about, a protected characteristic they possess. One example might be where instructions are given to a Christian barrister in chambers in preference to a Hindu barrister, because the solicitor feels that the Hindu barrister would not properly be able to represent his Christian client.[61]

11.42 Similar provisions apply in relation to advocates and devils in Scotland.[62]

11.43 The Explanatory Notes state, in relation to both of the above sections, that, unlike the previous legislation, they no longer protect clients and clerks from discrimination by barristers or advocates.[63] This is because such individuals can respectively seek redress under the 'goods and services' provisions,[64] and the other work provisions of the EqA 2010.[65]

Personal and public office-holders

11.44 EqA 2010 ss49–52 prohibit discrimination against individuals who are, or wish to become, personal or public office-holders. These sections are designed to be fall-back provisions, which will not apply unless the claimant is not covered by one of the other provisions of the Act, and, in particular, by the employment provisions at section 39.[66]

57 EqA 2010 s47(9).
58 EqA 2010 s47(3).
59 EqA 2010 s47(7) and Employment Code para 11.30.
60 EqA 2010 s47(6).
61 Explanatory Notes para 164.
62 EqA 2010 s48.
63 Explanatory Notes paras 164 and 167.
64 See Part III.
65 In particular, EqA 2010 ss39–41.
66 EqA 2010 Sch 6 paras 1 and 2, and the Explanatory Notes at paras 172 and 177.

11.45   The provisions in relation to personal and public office in EqA 2010 ss49–50 are essentially the same, save that the two sections deal with two different types of office.[67]

- A 'personal office' is defined as an office or post to which a person is appointed to discharge a function personally under the direction of another person, and in respect of which an appointed person is entitled to remuneration.[68] 'Remuneration' does not include expenses, or amounts paid in compensation for loss of income or benefits that the person would have received had they not been performing this office or post.[69]
- A 'public office' is an office or post:
  - appointment to which is made by a member of the executive;
  - appointment to which is made on the recommendation of, or subject to the approval of, a member of the executive; or
  - appointment to which is made on the recommendation of, or subject to the approval of, the House of Commons, the House of Lords, the National Assembly for Wales or the Scottish Parliament.[70]

11.46   Where an office is a personal and a public office at the same time, it is to be treated as a public office.[71]

11.47   Appointment to a post does not include election to it, so elected officers will not be covered by the provisions.[72] EqA 2010 Sch 6 provides that political offices are excluded from the provisions, and sets out an exclusive list of such offices (which includes offices within political parties). Life peerages and honours and dignities conferred by the Crown do not amount to personal or public offices.[73]

11.48   The 'personal office-holder' provisions are likely to cover, for example, company directors who have no contract of employment.[74] The 'public office-holder' sections will probably cover members of non-departmental public bodies,[75] and judges and members of tribunals such as the Employment Tribunal, the VAT Tribunal and the

---

67 See Employment Code paras 11.31–11.35.
68 EqA 2010 s49(2).
69 EqA 2010 s49(11).
70 EqA 2010 s50(2).
71 EqA 2010 s52(4).
72 EqA 2010 s52(5).
73 EqA 2010 Sch 6 para 3.
74 Employment Code para 11.33.
75 Examples given in the Employment Code include statutory commissions and the BBC Trust; see para 11.48.

Immigration and Asylum Chamber. Such statutory officials have only relatively recently come within the ambit of discrimination legislation following amendments to the RRA in 2003, and the SDA in 2005 to include protection for office-holders.

11.49　The provisions do not, however, apply to police officers or officers within the armed forces.[76]

11.50　A person (A) who has the power to appoint individuals to a personal or public office must not discriminate against, or victimise, a person (B):

- in the arrangements A makes for deciding to whom to offer the appointment;
- in the terms on which A offers B the appointment;
- by not offering B the appointment.[77]

11.51　Similarly, A must not, in relation to the office, harass a person seeking or being considered for the appointment, and the duty to make reasonable adjustments will apply to A.

11.52　The provisions also deal with discrimination against individuals already appointed to an office. In these sections, the individual prohibited from doing discriminatory acts is the 'relevant person'.[78] Broadly speaking, the 'relevant person' will generally be the individual who has control over, or responsibility for, the particular act of which the claimant complains. Thus where the complaint is about a term of appointment, the relevant person will be the person who has power to set the term. This may be a different person from, for example, the person who has the power to afford access to a particular opportunity which is denied to a claimant.

11.53　The 'relevant person' cannot be the House of Commons, the House of Lords, the Scottish Parliament or the National Assembly of Wales.[79]

11.54　A 'relevant person' (A) must not discriminate against or victimise a person (B) appointed to personal or public office:[80]

- as to B's terms of appointment;
- in the way A affords B access, or by not affording B access, to

---

76　Separate provision is made for these groups, at EqA 2010 ss42–43 (see paras 17.18–17.24) and s121 respectively.
77　EqA 2010 ss49(3), (5) and 50(3), (5).
78　Defined in EqA 2010 s52(6).
79　EqA 2010 s52(6).
80　Where the public office is one which falls within EqA 2010 s50(2)(a) or (b), namely an office or post to which appointment is made by a member of the executive, or appointment to which is made on the recommendation of, or subject to the approval of, a member of the executive.

opportunities for promotion, transfer or training, or for receiving any other benefit, facility or service;
- by terminating the appointment;
- by subjecting B to any other detriment.[81]

11.55   Where the public office falls within EqA 2010 s50(2)(c), which covers situations where appointment to the office/post is made on the recommendation of, or subject to the approval of, the House of Commons, House of Lords, Scottish Parliament or National Assembly of Wales, termination of the appointment is not covered by the legislation.[82]

11.56   'Terminating the appointment' includes termination by expiry of a period, including expiry on a particular event or circumstance. However, termination on the expiry of a period will not be covered if the appointment is renewed on the same terms immediately after the termination.[83] The phrase also covers termination by the claimant in circumstances where they are entitled, because of the relevant person's conduct, to terminate the appointment without notice (ie a constructive dismissal-type situation).[84]

11.57   A relevant person must not harass a person who has been appointed to a personal or public office in relation to that office[85] and is also under a duty to make reasonable adjustments.[86]

11.58   In respect of sex or pregnancy and maternity discrimination, a term of an offer of an appointment to office that relates to pay will only be treated as discriminatory where, if accepted, it would give rise to an equality clause (such that the equal pay provisions of the EqA 2010 would apply), or where the offer of the term constitutes direct or dual discrimination.[87] This provision means that office-holders are subject to the same limitations as employees in claims for pay-related sex discrimination.

11.59   The types of situation likely to be covered by these provisions include:
- a refusal by a company board to appoint a candidate as a director because they are black.

81   EqA 2010 ss49(6), (8) and 50(6), (9).
82   EqA 2010 s50(7) and (10).
83   EqA 2010 s52(8).
84   EqA 2010 s52(7)(b).
85   EqA 2010 ss49(7) and 50(8).
86   EqA 2010 ss49(9) and 50(11).
87   EqA 2010 ss49(12) and 50(12). The Coalition Government has said that it will not bring the dual discrimination provisions into force.

- a decision by a company to terminate the appointment of a director because she is pregnant.[88]
- a decision by a government minister, who has power to appoint the non-executive board members of a non-departmental public body, not to appoint a particular candidate because he is gay.[89]

11.60 In addition to the protection for those interested in, or holding, public office provided by EqA 2010 s50, section 51 prohibits a person (A) with the power to make recommendations about, or approve, appointments to public offices from discriminating against or victimising a person (B):

- in the arrangements made for deciding who to recommend for appointment or to whose appointment to give approval;
- by not recommending B for appointment to the office;
- by making a negative recommendation of B for appointment to the office;
- by not giving approval to the appointment of B to the office.[90]

11.61 A is also prohibited from harassing any person seeking or being considered for such a recommendation or approval.[91]

11.62 Persons with the power to make a recommendation for or give approval to an appointment to a public office are also under a duty to make reasonable adjustments.[92]

11.63 EqA 2010 s51 applies only where the public office in question is one to which appointments are made by a member of the executive (section 50(2)(a)), or on the recommendation of, or subject to the approval of, a member of the executive (section 50(2)(b)). In section 50(2)(a) cases, section 51 will apply only if a relevant body (ie a body established by or in pursuance to an enactment, or by a member of the executive[93]) has the power to make recommendations for, or approve, appointments. This would cover, for example, a situation

---

88 These are both examples of direct discrimination in respect of a personal office given in the Explanatory Notes at para 172. Should the directors in these examples have contracts of employment, they would fall within EqA 2010 s39, and would not need to rely on section 49.

89 An example of a potential claim under EqA 2010 s50, from para 177 of the Explanatory Notes.

90 EqA 2010 s51(1) and (3).

91 EqA 2010 s51(2).

92 EqA 2010 s51(4).

93 EqA 2010 s51(5).

where recommendations are made, or approval given, by a non-departmental public body.[94]

Qualifications bodies

11.64 Certain trades and professions require or prefer individuals to obtain a particular qualification or authorisation before they will be allowed to start working. EqA 2010 s53, which prohibits discrimination by qualifications bodies, is intended to prevent discrimination in conferring this kind of crucial qualification.

Which qualifications and bodies are covered?

11.65 The types of qualifications and bodies that are covered by the section are defined in EqA 2010 s54. A 'qualifications body' for the purposes of section 53 is an authority or body that can confer a relevant qualification,[95] which is in turn defined as: 'an authorisation, qualification, recognition, registration, enrolment, approval or certification which is needed for or facilitates engagement in a particular trade or profession'.

11.66 The provisions do not cover general 'educational' qualifications conferred by schools or local education authorities, such as GCSEs, A-levels and university degrees, or providers of vocational training.[96]

11.67 It is apparent from the definition in EqA 2010 s54 that, as qualifications that 'facilitate engagement' in a trade or profession are covered, the qualification need not necessarily be a requirement of entry into the trade or profession.

11.68 There is no clear explanation of the necessary elements of a 'qualification' in the EqA 2010, or in the case-law that arose out of the pre-existing legislation, but some helpful comments appear in the few decisions on the point.

- In *Loughran and Kelly v Northern Ireland Housing Executive*,[97] Lord Slynn referred to the decision in *Department of the Environment for Northern Ireland v Bone*, where the court held that the concept of a 'qualification' entailed:

---

94 See para 179 of the Explanatory Notes. An example of 'relevant bodies' given in the Employment Code is a statutory commission; see para 11.48.
95 Or renew, or extend the conferment of a particular qualification: EqA 2010 s54(5).
96 EqA 2010 s54(4).
97 [1999] 1 AC 428, [1998] IRLR 593.

- some sort of status conferred on an employee or self-employed person in relation to his work, or the work which he proposes to do;
- a status that relates only to a person carrying on that work or trade, profession or calling; and
- is either necessary for the lawful carrying on thereof or making that carrying on more advantageous.[98]

In his judgment (which in any event dealt with the slightly different provisions of the Fair Employment (Northern Ireland) Act 1976), Lord Slynn did not fully endorse this statement of the law, querying in particular the word 'status'.

- In *Patterson v Legal Services Commission*,[99] the Court of Appeal held that the concept of 'facilitating engagement' in a profession meant making it easier or less difficult to, among other things, carry on the profession.
- In *Ahsan v Watt*,[100] Lord Hoffmann (who gave the only judgment) held that the notion of an authorisation or qualification suggests some kind of objective standard that the qualifying body applies; an even-handed and 'transparent' test that people may pass or fail. The qualifying body vouches to the public for the qualifications of the candidate, and the public relies on the qualification in offering employment or professional engagements.

11.69 Some examples of qualifications and bodies held to be covered by the similar provisions in the pre-existing legislation are:

- the Common Professional Examination Board and the Council of Legal Education (in conferring a certificate of eligibility to complete the academic stage of training for the Bar);[101]
- the College of Law and the Solicitors' Regulation Body, in assessing the Legal Practice Course;[102]
- the Department of Education and Science (as it then was), in granting qualified teacher status;[103]

---

98 [1999] 1 AC 428 at 439F, [1998] IRLR 593 at para 30.
99 [2003] EWCA Civ 1558, [2004] ICR 312, [2004] IRLR 153.
100 [2007] UKHL 51, [2008] IRLR 243.
101 *Bohon-Mitchell v Common Professional Examination Board and Council of Legal Education* [1978] IRLR 525.
102 *Burke v College of Law*, UKEAT/0301/10, 8 March 2011, [2011] EqLR 454 and [2012] EWCA Civ 87.
103 *Hampson v Department of Education and Science* [1989] IRLR 69.

- the GMC in conferring medical qualifications, although see paras 11.73–11.76 below;[104]
- the Legal Services Commission, in granting a franchise to do legal aid work.[105]

11.70   By contrast, in *Tattari v Private Patients Plan Ltd*,[106] the Court of Appeal held that the respondent (PPP), a provider of medical and healthcare insurance cover, was not covered by the equivalent of EqA 2010 s53 in the RRA 1976 when it refused to include the claimant on a list of specialists. The section referred to an authority or body that conferred recognition or approval needed to enable an individual to practise a profession, exercise a calling or take part in some other activity. It did not cover a body that was not authorised to confer such qualification or permission, but that demanded a particular qualification for the purpose of its commercial agreements.[107]

11.71   A similar approach was taken by the House of Lords in *Loughran and Kelly v Northern Ireland Housing Executive*.[108] The claimants' firms were not shortlisted for the panel maintained by the respondent for conducting litigation arising out of particular types of public liability claims. The House of Lords held that 'qualification' could not cover the appointment of a duly qualified professional person to carry out remunerated work on behalf of a client, however prestigious the client.[109] This decision can be contrasted with that in *Patterson*, where *Loughran* was distinguished on the basis that, in granting a legal aid franchise, the LSC was not simply selecting a solicitor to perform services that they were already qualified to perform; it was also satisfying itself that the applicant met the LAFQAS standards.[110]

11.72   In two long-running cases against the Labour Party arising out of a failure to select particular individuals as prospective councillors,

---

104 See for example *Tariquez-Zaman v The General Medical Council,* UKEAT/0292/06/, UKEAT/0517/06, 20 December 2006.
105 *Patterson v Legal Services Commission* [2003] EWCA Civ 1558, [2004] ICR 312, [2004] IRLR 153.
106 [1998] ICR 106, [1997] IRLR 586, CA.
107 [1998] ICR 106 at 111F–G, [1997] IRLR 586 at para 23.
108 [1999] 1 AC 428, [1998] IRLR 593.
109 [1999] 1 AC 428 at 440F–G, [1998] IRLR 593 at para 34. Although this case concerned the Fair Employment (Northern Ireland) Act 1976 s23, Lord Slynn expressed the view that the definition of qualification in that Act was wider than in the RRA 1976.
110 [2003] EWCA Civ 1558, [2004] ICR 312, [2004] IRLR 153 at para 77.

Triesman v Ali[111] and *Ahsan v Watt*[112] (both cases have had various names over the years), the Court of Appeal and the House of Lords respectively have held that the Labour Party does not act as a 'qualifications body' conferring a relevant qualification in these circumstances. In *Ali*, the Court of Appeal held that the Labour Party was not the type of qualifying body to which the section was intended to apply, as its activities were for its own political purposes, in the same way as PPP's activities in the *Tattari* case were for its own commercial purposes. In *Ahsan*, the House of Lords held that the notion of an authorisation or qualification was far removed from the basis on which a political party chooses its candidates. The main criterion for such a selection is likely to be the popularity of the candidate with the voters, which is not akin to the type of objective criteria used to confer a qualification or authorisation.[113]

General exception: The statutory appeal

11.73　There is a significant general exception to the right to bring a claim against a qualifications body in an ET. Under EqA 2010 s120(7), no such claim may be brought where the act complained of may, by virtue of an enactment, be subject to an appeal or proceedings in the nature of an appeal.

11.74　This exception, which was also contained within the precursor legislation, has been interpreted fairly broadly by the courts. Thus in *Khan v General Medical Council*,[114] the Court of Appeal held that the exception covered a procedure under which an individual applying for registration as a medical practitioner could apply to the Review Board for Overseas Qualified Practitioners for a review of the GMC's refusal. This was despite the fact that the Review Board's only power was to state its opinion as to whether or not the decision should stand to the president of the GMC, who did not have to follow the recommendation. The Court of Appeal took the view that the process had to be considered as a whole (including the roles of the Review Board and the president) and so regarded, there was clearly a power to reverse the GMC's decision. The court also held that this amounted to an

111 [2002] EWCA Civ 93, [2002] IRLR 489.
112 [2007] UKHL 51, [2008] IRLR 243.
113 It should be noted that Mr Ahsan in fact won his case under what was then RRA 1976 s12 because the Labour Party had failed to appeal the EAT's decision that section 12 applied. The Labour Party was therefore estopped from challenging the EAT's ruling based on the later judgment in *Triesman v Ali*.
114 [1996] ICR 1032, [1994] IRLR 646, CA.

effective judicial remedy, in that Parliament had decided to favour the additional specialisation of a statutory tribunal in this field over the more general expertise of the ET.

11.75   In *Chaudhary v Specialist Training Authority Appeal Panel*,[115] the Court of Appeal confirmed that claimants cannot circumvent *Khan* by bringing a claim not in respect of the original decision of the relevant body, but in respect of the decision of the appeal panel. A procedure such as that contemplated in what is now EqA 2010 s120(7) could not work if it could be defeated by reference to the absence of a further appeal from the appeal tribunal.[116]

11.76   In *Tariquez-Zaman v General Medical Council*,[117] the EAT considered, obiter, whether the ability to bring judicial review proceedings against a determination of the GMC could oust the jurisdiction of the ET. The EAT held that judicial review could aptly be described as proceedings in the nature of an appeal, as its essence is the conduct of the case by someone different from the person against whom a complaint has been made, or who has decided it at first instance, with the opportunity of a reversal of the judgment.[118] However, in *Uddin v GMC*,[119] Slade J did not regard judicial review as being adequate where the acts complained of were unlikely to be susceptible to judicial review.

The forms of conduct covered

11.77   In general, EqA 2010 s53 prevents qualifications bodies from discriminating against or victimising applicants for a qualification in the arrangements made for deciding upon whom to confer the qualification; as to the terms upon which the qualification is offered, or by not conferring the qualification on the applicant.[120]

11.78   Similarly, once a qualification has been conferred, the qualifications body must not discriminate against or victimise the recipient by withdrawing the qualification, by varying the terms on which the recipient holds the qualification, or by subjecting the recipient to any other detriment.[121]

115 [2005] EWCA Civ 282, [2005] ICR 1086.
116 [2005] EWCA Civ 282, [2005] ICR 1086 at para 30.
117 UKEAT/0292/06, UKEAT/0517/06, 20 December 2006.
118 See paras 30–31.
119 [2012] UKEAT/0078/12 paras 32–36.
120 EqA 2010 s53(1) and (4).
121 EqA 2010 s53(2) and (5).

11.79   The qualifications body must not, in relation to conferment by it of a relevant qualification, harass a person who holds the qualification, or an applicant for the qualification.[122]

11.80   Qualification bodies are also under a duty to make reasonable adjustments,[123] subject to the important exception discussed below.

Specific exception – competence standards and qualification bodies

11.81   The most important exception to EqA 2010 s53 relates to disability discrimination. Where a qualifications body applies a competence standard to a disabled person, this will not amount to disability discrimination unless it is discrimination by virtue of section 19 of the Act (the indirect discrimination provision). There is therefore no duty to make reasonable adjustments to a competence standard.

11.82   A competence standard is defined as 'an academic, medical or other standard applied for the purpose of determining whether or not a person has a particular level of competence or ability'.[124]

11.83   The Employment Code does not cover qualifications bodies, and a separate code is due to be published at some point in the future. Until this code appears, some useful guidance as to the ambit of the competence standard exception can be found in the Revised Code of Practice: Trade Organisations, Qualifications Bodies and General Qualifications Bodies (2008)[125] made under the DDA 1995. The following points will be particularly relevant to claimants.

- A requirement or condition is likely to amount to a competence standard if, for example, it is a requirement that a person has a particular level of knowledge of a subject, or has the strength or ability to carry out a particular task or activity. If, however, the condition is that a person has a certain length of experience of doing something, that will not be a competence standard if it does not determine a particular level of competence or ability.[126]
- There will often be a difference between a competence standard and the process by which attainment of the standard is measured.[127] Thus while a qualifications body might be able to insist on maintaining a particular pass mark in an examination,

122 EqA 2010 s53(3).
123 EqA 2010 s53(6).
124 EqA 2010 s54(6).
125 The *Revised Code of Practice* can be found on the EHRC website: www.equalityhumanrights.com.
126 *Revised Code of Practice* paras 8.28–8.29.
127 *Revised Code of Practice* para 8.30.

for example, it would generally remain under a duty to make reasonable adjustments in relation to the arrangements for sitting that examination (which might include allowing dyslexic candidates additional time, or providing special equipment for blind candidates[128]).

- In some cases, however, the process of assessing whether a competence standard has been achieved will be inextricably linked to the standard itself. For example, where a qualification is conditional on having a practical skill or ability that must be demonstrated by completing a practical test, the ability to take the test may itself amount to a competence standard.[129]

11.84   An example of this last point can be found in the decision of the EAT in *Burke v College of Law*.[130] The claimant, who had multiple sclerosis, requested various adjustments in relation to the Legal Practice Course examinations, one of which was that he be given additional time (beyond the 60 per cent extension already granted to him) to complete the examinations. The EAT held that the requirement to complete the paper within a limited time was a competence standard. This was because the purpose of the examination was to assess the ability of the candidate to demonstrate their competence and capability in the subject-matter under time pressure, replicating the transaction aspects of work as a solicitor. In the circumstances, the College of Law was under no duty to make reasonable adjustments to the time-limited nature of the examinations, even though it had in fact agreed to make some such adjustments.

11.85   It is important to remember that, where a competence standard is indirectly discriminatory, a claim may still be brought. Thus if, for example, a fitness standard or a medical requirement disproportionately disadvantages persons with a disability, or with a particular disability, that standard or requirement will have to be shown to be a proportionate means of achieving a legitimate aim. The new indirect disability discrimination provisions contained within the EqA 2010 are likely to make it easier for claimants to circumvent the 'competence standard' exemption.

11.86   The other exceptions to the duty on qualifications bodies not to discriminate are similar to the exceptions to EqA 2010 s39. The

---

128 See eg *Project Management Institute v Latif* [2007] IRLR 579, EAT.

129 *Revised Code of Practice* para 8.31.

130 UKEAT/0301/10, 8 March 2011, [2011] EqLR 454. The case was subsequently appealed to the Court of Appeal [2012] EWCA Civ 37, but the competence standard point was not considered further.

exception permitting the imposition of requirements relating to sex, marriage and sexual orientation applies to qualifications bodies where the employment or public office for which the qualification is required itself qualifies for the 'religious requirements' exception.[131]

Employment service-providers

11.87 EqA 2010 s55 is a wide-ranging provision that prohibits discrimination by employment service-providers.[132] The section does not, as the wording might suggest, cover only employment agencies, but a variety of activities as set out at section 56(2) of the Act:

- the provision of vocational training;
- the provision of vocational guidance;
- making arrangements for the provision of vocational training or vocational guidance;
- the provision of a service for finding employment for persons;
- the provision of a service for supplying employers with persons to do work;
- the provision of a service in pursuance of arrangements made under section 2 of the Employment and Training Act (ETA) 1973 (functions of the Secretary of State relating to employment);
- the provision of a service in pursuance of arrangements made or a direction given under ETA 1973 s10 (careers services);
- the exercise of a function in pursuance of arrangements made under section 2(3) of the Enterprise and New Towns (Scotland) Act 1990 (functions of Scottish Enterprise etc. relating to employment);
- an assessment related to the conferment of a relevant qualification within the meaning of EqA 2010 s53 (except in so far as the assessment is by the qualifications body which confers the qualification).

11.88 Under the precursor legislation, vocational training and employment service-providers were dealt with in separate sections. EqA 2010 s55 brings all these bodies together in one provision.

What is 'vocational training' and 'vocational guidance'?

11.89 The references to vocational training and guidance in EqA 2010 s56(2) do not include training or guidance covered by another provision in

---

131 EqA 2010 Sch 9 para 2(3)–(6), and see further para 13.36.
132 Employment Code para 11.53 ff.

Part II, so if an employer provides its own employees with vocational training, that will be covered by section 39, not section 55.[133]

11.90   EqA 2010 ss55–56 also do not cover training or guidance for pupils of a school to which section 85 of the Act applies (ie most schools in the United Kingdom), as long as it is training or guidance to which the responsible body of the school has power to afford access.[134] Similarly, training or guidance for students of universities, other institutions of higher education and institutions of further education is excluded, as long as the governing body of the institution has power to afford access to the training or guidance.[135]

11.91   EqA 2010 s56(6) defines vocational training as meaning:

- training for employment; or
- work experience (including work experience the duration of which is not agreed until after it begins).

11.92   Examples of training covered by this section given in the Explanatory Notes are providing CV-writing classes, English or maths classes to help adults into work, training in IT skills or providing work placements.[136]

Other employment service-providers

11.93   As explained above, EqA 2010 s55 also extends to cover organisations in the nature of employment agencies (in so far as the claimant is not in an employment relationship, as defined by section 39, with the employment agency), recruitment consultancies, or careers services.[137]

What conduct is prohibited?

11.94   Bodies concerned with the provision of an employment service must not discriminate against or victimise any person:

- in the arrangements made for selecting persons to whom to provide or to whom to offer to provide the service;
- as to the terms on which the service-provider offers to provide the service to the person; or
- by not offering to provide the service to the person.[138]

133 EqA 2010 s56(3).
134 EqA 2010 s56(4).
135 EqA 2010 s56(5).
136 Explanatory Notes at para 190.
137 See the example in the Employment Code para 11.54.
138 EqA 2010 s55(1) and (4).

11.95 There are also provisions applying to an existing relationship between an employment service-provider (A) and a service user (B), to the effect that A must not, in relation to the provision of an employment service, discriminate against or victimise B:

- as to the terms on which A provides the service to B;
- by not providing the service to B;
- by terminating the provision of the service to B;
- by subjecting B to any other detriment.[139]

11.96 The employment service-provider must not, in relation to the provision of an employment service, harass a person who asks the service-provider to provide the service, or a person for whom the service-provider provides the service.[140]

11.97 An employment service-provider is also under a duty to make reasonable adjustments.[141]

11.98 The provisions in relation to reasonable adjustments differ according to whether or not the employment service provided consists of a vocational service, which is defined, under EqA 2010 s56(7), as referring to:

- the provision of an employment service within the meaning of EqA 2010 s56(2)(a)–(d), namely:
  - provision of vocational training;
  - provision of vocational guidance;
  - making arrangements for the provision of vocational training or guidance; and
  - the provision of a service for finding employment for persons (this definition presumably covers an employment agency), including a service for assisting people to retain employment;[142] and
- the provision of an employment service within the meaning of EqA 2010 s56(2)(f) or (g) in so far as such a service also falls within section 56(2)(a)–(d); but not
- the provision of work experience, which is excluded under EqA 2010 s56(7)(a).

11.99 Under EqA 2010 s55(7), the duty imposed on vocational service-providers to make reasonable adjustments is the same as that imposed on service-providers under EqA 2010 s29(7). Schedule 2 of

139 EqA 2010 s55(2) and (5).
140 EqA 2010 s55(3).
141 EqA 2010 s55(6).
142 EqA 2010 s56(7) and (7)(b).

the Act[143] makes it clear that the duty on service-providers to make reasonable adjustments is an anticipatory duty. This means that, in the context of vocational service provision, the duty is owed not just to a particular disabled service user of whom the service-provider is aware, but to disabled people at large who might need to use the service.

11.100   The vocational service-provider must therefore think about what disabled people with a range of impairments might reasonably need. This could include adjustments such as installation of a disabled toilet, or provision of a hearing loop for those with hearing impairments.

11.101   In respect of employment service-providers who do not provide a 'vocational service' as defined, the normal 'employment' (non-anticipatory) duty applies. It goes on to say that the enforcement mechanism in relation to vocational services is the same as for any other provision contained in Part 5 (section 55(7)). Thus claims about a vocational service-provider's failure to make reasonable adjustments should be brought in an employment tribunal, not the county court.

11.102   Both the Explanatory Notes[144] and the Employment Code[145] can be interpreted as stating that the anticipatory duty is placed on employment service-providers other than those offering a vocational service, but not on those offering a vocational service. However, this does not appear to reflect the drafting of the EqA 2010, which appears to suggest the opposite. It is unlikely to make a great difference, however, in practice.

11.103   The Employment Code provides some examples of what might amount to discrimination contrary to EqA 2010 s55.

- An employment agency only offers its services to people with EEA passports or identity cards. This could be indirect race discrimination as it would put at a particular disadvantage non-European nationals who do not hold a European passport, but who have the right to live and work in the United Kingdom without immigration restrictions.[146]
- A headhunting company fails to put forward women for chief executive positions because it believes that women are less likely

---

143 Which has effect in relation to EqA 2010 s29(7) by virtue of s31(9).
144 At para 188.
145 Employment Code paras 11.57 and 11.58.
146 Employment Code para 11.54. This is a good example of the type of 'general' arrangement prohibited by EqA 2010 s55(1)(a).

to succeed in these positions as they will leave to get married and start a family. This could amount to sex discrimination.[147]

- An adviser for a careers guidance service is overheard by a transsexual client making offensive and humiliating comments to a colleague about her looks and how she is dressed. This could amount to harassment related to gender reassignment.[148]

11.104 A useful practical point relating to the enforcement of the provisions of EqA 2010 s55 can be found in *Lana v Positive Action Training In Housing (London) Ltd*.[149] A trainee quantity surveyor, L, had a contract with Positive Action (PA) under which they were to provide her with vocational training, and they in turn had a contract with Walker Management (WM), under which the latter would provide L with a placement on which to carry out her training. WM terminated L's placement. L argued that this had been done because she was pregnant, and therefore amounted to sex discrimination. She brought a claim against PA on the basis that, in terminating her placement, WM had been acting as their agent. The EAT agreed that, under the terms of the contract between PA and WM, WM had authority to terminate the agreement, and PA was therefore liable for its actions in doing so under the equivalent of EqA 2010 s109(2).

11.105 This decision confirms that trainees should be able to bring a claim directly against an organisation (A) that has agreed to provide them with training, and which then places them with another body (B) to do the training, even if the discriminatory conduct itself was that of B, as long as B has authority under its legal relationship with A to do the act of which complaint is made.

Exceptions

11.106 The exceptions to EqA 2010 s55 are similar in nature to the exceptions for employers and other bodies covered by Part 5. Thus an employment service-provider will not contravene section 55(1) or (2) if it can show that:

- its treatment of the complainant relates only to work that the complainant could lawfully be denied under the occupational requirements provisions set out in EqA 2010 Sch 9 paras 1–4;[150] or

147 Employment Code para 11.55.
148 Employment Code para 11.56.
149 [2001] IRLR 501, EAT.
150 EqA 2010 Sch 9 para 5(1).

- its treatment of the complainant relates only to training for work of that description.[151]

11.107 This means that if, for example, a particular church is able to refuse to offer a woman an appointment as a priest under EqA 2010 Sch 9 para 2, no claim can be brought against an employment service-provider for refusing to provide that woman with vocational training for the priesthood within that church.[152]

11.108   An additional type of exception for employment service-providers is set out in EqA 2010 Sch 9 para 5(3). This paragraph states that an employment service-provider will not contravene section 55(1) or (2) if it can show that:

- it relied on a statement made to it by a person with the power to offer a particular kind of work to the effect that having (or not having) the particular protected characteristic was an occupational requirement for that work; and
- it was reasonable for the employment service-provider to rely on the statement.

11.109 Thus if a church erroneously made a statement to a provider of vocational training for the priesthood that it could refuse, under EqA 2010 Sch 9 para 2, to accept women as priests, the vocational training provider might be able to rely on that statement as absolving it from liability under section 55(1) or (2), as long as its reliance on the statement was reasonable.

11.110   Under EqA 2010 Sch 9 para 5(4), there are criminal penalties for knowingly or recklessly making a false or misleading statement of this kind.

11.111   It is also worth noting that, under the Employment Act 1989 s8, the Secretary of State has the power to provide for discrimination in favour of lone parents in connection with payment for certain types of training (which would otherwise contravene provisions prohibiting discrimination against married people). Provision for such positive action has been made under the Sex Discrimination Act 1975 (Exemption of Special Treatment for Lone Parents) Order 1989, and a statutory instrument of the same name dating from 1991. These provisions have survived the advent of the EqA 2010.

---

151 EqA 2010 Sch 9 para 5(2).
152 See further para 13.36. The provision may not be compatible with Directive 2006/54, which contains no eqivalent of the GOR exception in Article 4 of Directive 2000/78.

Trade organisations

11.112 EqA 2010 s57 prohibits discrimination by trade organisations.

11.113 A trade organisation is defined, in EqA 2010 s57(7), as:

- an organisation of workers;
- an organisation of employers, or
- any other organisation whose members carry on a particular trade or profession for the purposes of which the organisation exists.

11.114 This definition is in the same terms as that in the pre-existing anti-discrimination legislation.

11.115 It was held under the old provisions of the SDA 1975 that it was not necessary for an organisation to have a membership comprising exclusively of eg employers in order for it to fall within the definition of a trade organisation. In *National Federation of Self-Employed and Small Businesses Ltd v Philpott*,[153] the EAT held that a federation that comprised mainly employers but also included a minority of self-employed members with no employees was a trade organisation.

11.116 A similarly broad approach was taken in *Sadek v Medical Protection Society*.[154] It was argued on behalf of the Society that it could not be an organisation of workers because the majority of its members were not properly described as 'workers', but practised professions. The Court of Appeal rejected this argument, holding that it was an attempt to imbue the concept of a profession with an aura and exclusivity which was inconsistent with the language of the RRA 1976 (under which the claim was brought), which defined 'profession' as including 'any vocation or occupation'. The Society was therefore 'an organisation of workers'. Had this not been the case, the Court of Appeal would have held that the Society was an organisation 'whose members carry on a particular trade or profession for the purposes of which the organisation exists', in the sense that it enabled or assisted its members to carry on their profession. This was so even though its members practised a number of different medical/healthcare professions.

11.117 It appears likely that a similarly broad definition of trade organisation will persist under the EqA 2010.

11.118 The definition cannot, however, be pushed too far. In *General Medical Council v Cox*,[155] the EAT held that the GMC was not a trade organisation because its functions, as defined by statute, were pri-

---

153 [1997] ICR 518, EAT.
154 [2004] EWCA Civ 865, [2004] ICR 1263.
155 EAT/76/01, 22 March 2002, (2003) 70 BMLR 31.

marily directly or indirectly concerned with setting and attaining the professional standards that serve to protect the public. The predominant purpose was not, therefore, to benefit its members. The claim was brought against the GMC as a trade organisation because, at that time, the DDA 1995 contained no prohibition on discrimination by a qualifications body, an anomaly that has now been rectified.

11.119   Examples of bodies covered by EqA 2010 s57 given in the Explanatory Notes include trade unions, the Chambers of Commerce, the British Medical Association, the Institute of Civil Engineers and the Law Society.[156]

11.120   A trade organisation may not discriminate against or victimise persons who wish to become members:

- in the arrangements it makes for deciding to whom to offer membership;
- as to the terms on which it is prepared to admit such persons as members;
- by not accepting a person's application for membership.[157]

11.121   A trade organisation is also prohibited from discriminating against or victimising a person who is already a member:

- in the way it affords the member access, or by not affording the member access, to opportunities for receiving a benefit, facility or service;
- by depriving the member of membership;
- by varying the terms on which the member is a member;
- by subjecting the member to any other detriment.[158]

11.122   A trade organisation may not, in relation to membership of it, harass a member or an applicant for membership.[159]

11.123   The duty to make reasonable adjustments applies to trade organisations.[160]

11.124   It will generally be obvious who is a 'member' of a trade organisation, and thus entitled to bring a claim under EqA 2010 s52(2) and (5). Where an individual's membership status is not obvious, the Court of Appeal in *1 Pump Court Chambers v Horton*[161] has held that

---

156 Explanatory Notes para 192.
157 EqA 2010 s57(1) and (4).
158 EqA 2010 s57(2) and (5).
159 EqA 2010 s57(3).
160 EqA 2010 s57(6).
161 [2004] EWCA Civ 941, [2005] ICR 292.

the ET must consider the rights and duties of the person in relation to the organisation.

11.125 In *Horton*, the claimant had successfully obtained a pupillage with the respondent chambers, but a month before he was due to start, asked to defer the pupillage for one year owing to ill health arising from a disability. The chambers refused, and the claimant brought a claim under the DDA 1995, on the basis that the chambers was a trade organisation. He succeeded on that point, but the Court of Appeal held that he was not, as a pupil, a member of the chambers, taking into account the fact that pupils had different obligations from tenants (eg in relation to rent) and were not permitted to partake in a number of activities of the chambers.

11.126 Laddie J commented that being a member of a trade organisation:[162]

> must involve becoming, in a real sense, part of the team, bound by at least some significant parts of the rules of the organisation and benefiting in at least some significant ways from the privileges and benefits enjoyed by close association with others in the organisation.

11.127 While the immediate problem demonstrated by *Horton* has now been resolved, in that pupils and applicants for pupillage have the right not to be discriminated against under EqA 2010 s47,[163] the comments made by the Court of Appeal are still likely to be of use in determining who will qualify as a 'member' of a trade organisation more generally.

11.128 Trade organisations are not currently covered by the Employment Code of Practice. A separate code dealing with qualifications bodies and trade organisations was due to be published at some point in the future.[164]

Local authority members

11.129 EqA 2010 s58 prevents local authorities from discriminating against members of the authority (eg councillors) who are carrying out their official business.

---

162 [2005] ICR 292 at para 42, the minority judgment.
163 See paras 11.37–11.43 above. The precursor legislation had already been amended in order to allow such claims.
164 As at the time of writing there is some doubt as to whether there will be further codes issued in the foreseeable future. It is more likely that guidance will be produced by the EHRC.

11.130   Protection for members of local authorities only previously existed under the DDA 1995. The Act extends this protection to cover all protected characteristics.

11.131   For these purposes, a local authority is defined by EqA 2010 s59(2) It covers, for example, county councils, district councils, London borough councils, the Greater London Authority and similar bodies in Wales, Scotland and the Isles of Scilly.

11.132   'Official business' is defined as doing anything:

- as a member of the authority;
- as a member of a body to which the person is appointed by, or following nomination by, the authority or a group of bodies including the authority; or
- as a member of any other public body.[165]

11.133   'Member' is defined only in relation to the Greater London Authority, and means the Mayor of London or a member of the London Assembly.[166]

11.134   Local authorities are prohibited from discriminating against or victimising a member of the authority in relation to that member's carrying out official business:

- in the way the authority affords the member access, or by not affording the member access, to opportunities for training or for receiving any other facility;
- by subjecting the member to any other detriment.[167]

11.135   Under EqA 2010 s58(4), a member will not be held to have been subjected to a detriment for the purposes of section 58(1)(b) or (3)(b) if the complaint is that they:

- were not appointed or elected to an office of the authority;
- were not appointed to or elected to an office of, a committee or sub-committee of the authority;
- were not appointed or nominated in exercise of an appointment power[168] of the authority.

---

165 EqA 2010 s59(4).
166 EqA 2010 s59(5).
167 EqA 2010 s58(1) and (3).
168 This refers to a power of the authority, or of a group of bodies including the authority, to make appointments to a body or nominations for appointment to a body; EqA 2010 s58(5).

11.136 Essentially, this means that the anti-discrimination provisions in EqA 2010 s58 do not apply to election or appointments to posts within the local authority.[169]

11.137 EqA 2010 s58(3) contains a prohibition on harassing members of the authority in relation to carrying out their official business, and section 58(5) provides that local authorities are under a duty to make reasonable adjustments.

11.138 Examples of conduct contravening EqA 2010 s58 given in the Explanatory Notes and the Code are as follows:

- A local authority fails to equip meeting rooms with a hearing loop for a member who has a hearing impairment, in order to enable her to take full part in the business for which she has been elected. This could potentially amount to a failure to make reasonable adjustments.[170]
- A councillor of Chinese origin sits on a local council's policy scrutiny committee. Officers of the council often send him papers for meetings late or not at all, which means he is often unprepared for meetings and unable to make useful contributions. His colleagues, none of whom are Chinese, do not experience this problem. This could amount to direct discrimination against the councillor by the authority.[171]

---

169 Explanatory Notes para 194.

170 Explanatory Notes para 195. A similar example in relation to a blind councillor who is not provided with documents in Braille is provided in the Employment Code at para 11.67.

171 Employment Code para 11.64.

CHAPTER 12

Positive action

> ## Key points
> - Positive Action is voluntary not compulsory
> - It enables employers and others to take positive steps to address disadvantage which has arisen historically based on protected characteristics
> - It may provide a defence to a claim of discrimination

Introduction

12.1   The EqA 2010 allows

- employers;
- principals;
- partnerships, LLPs;
- barristers and advocates;
- those who make appointments to personal and public offices; and
- employment service-providers

to take positive action measures to improve equality for people who share a protected characteristic.[1] The Employment Code devotes considerable space to the forms of positive action because they were politically controversial. They appear to go to the heart of the debate concerning whether equality is compatible with merits-based selection. However, as the Employment Code immediately points out, the aim of the positive action provisions is to help improve equality. Thus the need for positive action policies, which are recognised in every relevant international agreement concerning equality, stems from the concept of equality, which enjoins treating like cases in a like manner and unlike cases in an unlike manner.

12.2   The Employment Code stresses that these are 'optional measures' and describes the circumstances when positive action could be appropriate, with examples of approaches that employers might consider taking.[2]

12.3   There have been a series of cases decided by the CJEU, which have addressed positive action steps – see for example *Serge Briheche v Minstre de l'Intererieur, Ministre de l'Education Nationale and Ministre de la Justice*,[3] which provides a good review of the prior case-law.

1 EqA 2010 s158.
2 Employment Code para 12.2.
3 Case C-319/2003, [2004] ECR I-8807.

Positive action v 'positive discrimination'

12.4   Positive action is not the same as positive discrimination, which is unlawful in most cases.[4]

12.5   Clearly employers etc may take action that benefits those from a particular group if it does not amount to or involve less favourable treatment of others. Equally action to eradicate discriminatory policies or practices will normally be lawful. The Employment Code gives the example[5] of placing a job advertisement in a magazine with a largely lesbian and gay readership as well as placing it in a national newspaper.

12.6   A worker whose ability to see job adverts in the national newspaper is not impeded by the existence of the advert cannot reasonably complain of a detriment. The existence of the advertisement in the magazine simply serves to ensure that those with the sexual orientations gay or lesbian are encouraged to make applications.

12.7   The Employment Code also gives the example of an employer reviewing recruitment processes to ensure that they do not contain criteria that discriminate because of any protected characteristic.

12.8   Neither of these examples from the Employment Code would be classed as 'positive action'.

12.9   However, there are actions such as reserving places on a training course for a group sharing a protected characteristic that can only be lawful if they meet

- the statutory conditions for positive action measures and
- do not exceed the limitations set out in the EqA 2010.

12.10   The EqA 2010 provides the following conditions. A person (P) must reasonably think that persons who share a protected characteristic:

- suffer a disadvantage connected to the characteristic;
- have needs that are different from the needs of persons who do not share that protected characteristic;
- participate in an activity to a disproportionately low level.[6]

12.11   The Act does not, if any of those criteria are satisfied, prohibit P from taking any action if it is:

---

4 The Employment Code does not make this qualification but positive discrimination could be lawful in direct age discrimination cases and in cases of a non-disabled worker being treated less favourably than a disabled worker.

5 Employment Code para 12.5.

6 EqA 2010 s158(1).

- a proportionate means (ie an appropriate and necessary means) of
- achieving the aim of either
  - enabling persons who share the protected characteristic to overcome that disadvantage connected to the characteristic; or
  - encouraging persons who share the protected characteristic to overcome that disadvantage connected to the characteristic;
  - enabling persons who share the protected characteristic to minimise that disadvantage connected to the characteristic;
  - encouraging persons who share the protected characteristic to minimise that disadvantage connected to the characteristic;
  - meeting the needs identified that are different from the needs of persons who do not share that protected characteristic;
  - enabling persons who share the protected characteristic to participate in the identified activity in which participation by persons who share a protected characteristic is disproportionately low;
  - encouraging persons who share the protected characteristic to participate in the identified activity in which participation by persons who share a protected characteristic is disproportionately low.

12.12   On the face of the EqA 2010 the provision covers a very wide range of activities. The scope of the powers rests on the distinction between 'enabling' and 'encouraging'. Enabling would appear to permit an employer etc to apply lower standards in assessments to members of a protected characteristic group, provided this was a proportionate means of achieving the legitimate aim of enabling the members of the group to participate etc and the disadvantage this action overcame was connected to the protected characteristic of the group members.

12.13   However, there are restrictions on the use of EqA 2010 s158. It does not apply to treating a person (A) more favourably in connection with recruitment or promotion than another person (B) because A has the protected characteristic but B does not.[7] Also a political party has specific positive action powers in respect of selections arrangements for Parliamentary, Welsh Assembly and local government elections. Where these apply, the positive action provisions under section 158 do not in addition apply.[8]

---

7   EqA 2010 s159(3).
8   See EqA 2010 s104 for the selection of candidates by registered political parties.

12.14   The Employment Code points out that action can be taken when any one of the conditions exist, even if they overlap.[9]

12.15   The Code makes clear the type of conduct which can be justified in practice. It is worth looking closely at one of the examples that shows how the recommendations the Code makes elsewhere for avoiding discrimination can be used to ensure positive action:[10]

> **Example**: A large public sector employer monitors the composition of their workforce and identifies that there are large numbers of visible ethnic minority staff in junior grades and low numbers in management grades. In line with their equality policy, the employer considers the following action to address the low numbers of ethnic minority staff in senior grades:
> - Reviewing their policies and practices to establish whether there might be discriminatory criteria which inhibit the progression of visible ethnic minorities;
> - Discussing with representatives of the trade union and the black staff support group how the employer can improve opportunities for progression for the under-represented group;
> - Devising a positive action programme for addressing under-representation of the target group, which is shared with all staff;
> - Including within the programme shadowing and mentoring sessions with members of management for interested members of the target group. The programme also encourages the target group to take advantage of training opportunities such as training in management, which would improve their chances for promotion.

12.16   Note that the actions mentioned in the example amount to less favourable treatment of those who are not in the target group. However, plainly, if the employer is correct in ascertaining under-representation, the means adopted are proportionate means of achieving the aim of participation etc. Note also that the employer is not identifying a specific disadvantage suffered by members of the group, but is looking at the end result of the way in which current approaches are operated. If the employer became aware of a specific disadvantage suffered by members of the group having the protected characteristic in common then action could be taken to overcome that specific disadvantage.

12.17   The example illustrates the difference between the various bases for positive action. One strand identifies either specific disadvantages or specific needs experienced by the members of the group. The response to such identification is to minimise or enable members of

---

9 Employment Code para 12.13.
10 Employment Code para 12.6.

the group to overcome that factor or to meet those needs. However, the other strand looks at the outcome (participation in an activity), and seeks to remedy the lack of participation.

12.18   The Code refers to 'positive discrimination' as involving preferential treatment to benefit members of a disadvantaged or underrepresented group who share a protected characteristic, in order to address inequality. The Code states, generalising, that these actions do not meet the statutory requirements for positive action, and will be unlawful unless a statutory exception applies.[11] However, positive discrimination can be lawful in relation to age and, as the Code points out,[12] it can be lawful in relation to more favourable treatment of persons with disabilities. The Code's example makes clear the type of treatment which is prohibited:[13]

> **Example:** An LLP seeks to address the low participation of women partners by interviewing all women regardless of whether they meet the criteria for partnership. This would be positive discrimination and is unlawful.

Voluntary nature of positive action

12.19   The Code points out that positive action is optional.[14] However, it is worth pointing out that it is also lawful, so that it will form a defence to a claim of less favourable treatment as nothing in the EqA 2010 prohibits it.

12.20   The rationality of some of the restrictions which an employer may seek to place on recruitment can, perhaps, be challenged by reference to the factors set out for the business case for positive action in the Code:

- a wider pool of talented, skilled and experienced people from which to recruit;
- a dynamic and challenging workforce able to respond to changes;
- a better understanding of foreign/global markets;
- a better understanding of the needs of a more diverse range of customers – both nationally and internationally.

---

11 Employment Code para 12.7.
12 Employment Code para 12.8.
13 Employment Code para 12.7.
14 Employment Code paras 12.9 and 12.10 also spell out the business advantages that positive action could bring.

What does 'reasonably think' mean?

12.21   Under EqA 2010 s158 the employer etc must reasonably think that one of the conditions applies. They will need to have some evidence to show that one of the conditions applies. The Code makes clear that it does not need to be sophisticated statistical data or research:[15]

> It may simply involve an employer looking at the profiles of their workforce and/or making enquiries of other comparable employers in the area or sector. Additionally, it could involve looking at national data such as labour force surveys for a national or local picture of the work situation for particular groups who share a protected characteristic. A decision could be based on qualitative evidence, such as consultation with workers and trade unions.

'Disadvantage'

12.22   'Disadvantage' is not defined in the EqA 2010. It is suggested, however, that, as when it appears in the context of indirect discrimination under section 19, it has the same meaning as detriment, so that it must be something that a reasonable worker would regard as such, and not simply trivial disadvantages that would not reasonably be viewed as such.

12.23   The Code's approach is consonant with this suggestion. It states that:[16]

> 'disadvantage' may include 'exclusion, rejection, lack of opportunity, lack of choice and barriers to accessing employment opportunities. Disadvantage may be obvious in relation to some issues such as legal, social or economic barriers or obstacles which make it difficult for people of a particular protected group to enter into or make progress in an occupation, a trade, a sector or workplace.

12.24   The Code explains that the EqA 2010 does not limit the action that could be taken to overcome (or minimise) disadvantage.[17] However, the action must satisfy the statutory conditions and be a proportionate way of achieving the aim of overcoming a 'genuine disadvantage'. The Code gives examples of the type of action that might achieve this aim:

- targeting advertising at specific disadvantaged groups, for example advertising jobs in media outlets that are likely to be accessed by the target group;

15 Employment Code para 12.14.
16 Employment Code para 12.16.
17 Employment Code para 12.17.

- making a statement in recruitment advertisements that the employer welcomes applications from the target group, for example 'older people are welcome to apply';
- providing opportunities exclusively to the target group to learn more about particular types of work opportunities with the employer, for example internships or open days;
- providing training opportunities in work areas or sectors for the target group, for example work placements.

'Needs'

12.25   The Code presents an interpretive restriction on the concept of needs. While the EqA 2010 itself does not link the need to the protected characteristic causally, but states that the needs of those in the group must be different from those not in the group, the Code makes clear that there must be a link between past discrimination or disadvantage or due to factors that apply especially to people who share their characteristic they have different needs.

12.26   The Code states:[18]

> A group of people who share a particular protected characteristic have 'different needs' if, due to past or present discrimination or disadvantage or due to factors that especially apply to people who share that characteristic, they have needs that are different to those of other groups. This does not mean that the needs of a group have to be entirely unique from the needs of other groups to be considered 'different'. Needs may also be different because, disproportionately, compared to the needs of other groups, they are not being met or the need is of particular importance to that group.

It is clear however that the link can be indirect and can be remote. This is made clear by the example that follows the text in the Code:[19]

> **Example:** An employer's monitoring data on training shows that their workers over the age of 60 are more likely to request training in advanced IT skills compared to workers outside this age group. The employer could provide training sessions primarily targeted at this group of workers.

12.27   Once again there is no limit on the action that can be taken, save proportionality, and the requirement to meet one of the conditions. The Code points to a requirement that the action should be aimed

18   Employment Code para 12.18.
19   Employment Code para 12.18.

at meeting genuinely different needs. This suggests that the test has two aspects:

- Does the employer etc reasonably believe that the needs exist?
- Are the needs genuinely different?

The alternative is that the test is wholly objective and the ET must determine whether the conditions are satisfied. It is suggested that neither a wholly objective test nor a mixed objective subjective test was the intention of the legislation. The Code's reference to 'genuinely different needs' must be interpreted in the context of the contrast between EqA 2010 s158(1) and (2). When dealing with what the Act does not prohibit, a purely objective test is employed (the action must be proportionate to the aims). In dealing with the precursor conditions in section 158(1) what the person reasonably thinks is used as the test. Therefore it is suggested that the intention behind the legislation was to permit positive action where the employer etc had a reasonable belief that the conditions are satisfied even if they are not. The reference to 'genuinely different' needs in the Code should be seen as referring to the requirement that the person using positive action should be acting in good faith.

12.28   The Code suggests that action under EqA 2010 s158(2)(b) could include:

- providing exclusive training to the target group specifically aimed at meeting particular needs, for example English language classes for staff for whom English is a second language;
- the provision of support and mentoring, for example to a member of staff who has undergone gender reassignment;
- the creation of a work-based support group for members of staff who share a protected characteristic who may have workplace experiences or needs that are different from those of staff who do not share that characteristic. (The Act's provisions on members associations might be relevant here: see the Code on services and public functions.)

'Encourage participation'

12.29   For the purposes of EqA 2010 s158(1)(c) the person must reasonably believe that participation in the activity by those who share a protected characteristic is disproportionately low. The Code again makes the point that the employer will need to have some reliable indication or evidence that participation is low compared with that of other groups or compared with the level of participation that could reasonably be expected for people from that protected group.[20] The Code gives a good example of what would and would not constitute 'disproportionately low':[21]

> **Example:** An employer has two factories, one in Cornwall and one in London. Each factory employs 150 workers. The Cornish factory employs two workers from an ethnic minority background and the London factory employs 20 workers also from an ethnic minority background.
>
> The ethnic minority population is 1% in Cornwall and 25% in London. In the Cornish factory the employer would not be able to meet the test of 'disproportionately low', since the number of its ethnic minority workers is not low in comparison to the size of the ethnic minority population in Cornwall. However, the London factory, despite employing significantly more ethnic minority workers, could show that that the number of ethnic minority workers employed there was still disproportionately low in comparison with their proportion in the population of London overall.

12.30 Thus the comparison may be, for example, with:[22]

- the proportion of people with that protected characteristic nationally;
- the proportion of people with that protected characteristic locally;
- the proportion of people with that protected characteristic in the workforce.

12.31 The Code gives examples of the type of action that can be taken at para 12.24. The limitation on action is its purpose of encouraging or enabling participation in the activity.

'Proportionate'

12.32 In this context the Code suggests that 'proportionate' refers to the balancing of competing relevant factors. However, as the concept of proportionality has now been interpreted for the purposes of the EqA 2010 (and precursor legislation) as meaning appropriate and necessary, the Code goes on to set out that these issues must be addressed. The employer etc will have to address the aim relied upon as the basis for the positive action. The Code also states other relevant factors:

---

20 Employment Code paras 12.21 and 12.23.
21 Employment Code para 12.21.
22 See the examples at Employment Code para 12.22.

- the objective of the action taken, or to be taken, including the cost of the action.[23]
- the seriousness of the relevant disadvantage, the degree to which the need is different or the extent of low participation;
- the impact of the action on other protected characteristic groups;
- relative disadvantage/need/participation of these other protected characteristic groups;[24]
- whether the action is an appropriate way to achieve the aim identified?
- whether the action is reasonably necessary to achieve the aim, or (in all the circumstances) would it be possible to achieve the aim as effectively by other actions which are less likely to result in less favourable treatment of others?[25]

12.33   Lawful positive action may become unlawful because it outlives its purpose or becomes disproportionate, for example if it continues indefinitely without reviews that justify its continuation within the tests set out in EqA 2010 s158. For example the action taken may have already remedied the situation that had been a precondition for positive action.[26] Employers etc should indicate that action will be taken while the conditions apply, and should monitor the impact of the action and progress to the aim.[27]

Positive action and disability

12.34   EqA 2010 s13 does not permit a direct discrimination claim to be brought by a person because of disability where the complaint is that a disabled person has been treated more favourably than a non-disabled person. Further in order to claim indirect disability discrimination it is necessary to be a person with a particular disability.[28] The consequence of this is that employers can without unlawful discrimination restrict recruitment training and promotion to persons with disabilities.[29] A person with a particular disability could, however, bring a claim of discrimination against an employer if employment were restricted to those with a different impairment, unless the positive

23 Employment Code para 12.26.
24 Employment Code para 12.27.
25 Employment Code para 12.28.
26 Employment Code para 12.30.
27 Employment Code para 12.31.
28 EqA 2010 s19.
29 Employment Code para 12.32 and the example given there.

action provisions were met. The employer etc may also use the positive action provisions lawfully to achieve the aims in EqA 2010 s158. In particular positive action can be used to meet the needs of persons with disabilities which are different to the needs of others. Positive action is capable of dealing with a category of needs of a whole group. The duty to make reasonable adjustments in the employment context is by contrast an individual duty owed to the particular person with a disability.

12.35   The Act also provides[30] for positive action in the form of a 'tie-break' provision. Where a person (P) reasonably thinks that:

a) people who share a protected characteristic suffer a disadvantage connected to the characteristic, or
b) participation in an activity by people who share a protected characteristic is disproportionately low[31]

an employer etc will be able to treat A more favourably in connection with recruitment or promotion than another person B, because A has the protected characteristic, when B does not, in order to enable or encourage people sharing that protected characteristic to overcome or minimise that disadvantage or participate in that activity.[32]

12.36   This can only be done, however, where:

a) A is as qualified as B to be recruited or promoted;
b) P does not have a policy of treating people who share the protected characteristic more favourably in connection with recruitment or promotions than people who do not share it; and
c) taking the action in question is a proportionate means of overcoming or minimising disadvantage/encouraging participation in activity where it is disproportionately low.[33]

12.37 Recruitment is defined as follows:[34]

A process for deciding whether to:
(a) Offer employment to a person
(b) Make contract work available to a contract worker
(c) Offer a person a position as a partner in a fir or a proposed firm
(d) Offer a person a position as a member of an LLP or a proposed LLP
(e) Offer a person a pupillage or tenancy in a barristers' chambers

---

30 EqA 2010 s159.
31 EqA 2010 s159(1).
32 EqA 2010 s159(2) and (3).
33 EqA 2010 s159(4).
34 EqA 2010 s159(5).

(f) Take a person as a an advocate's devil or offer a person membership of an advocate's stable
(g) Offer a person an appointment to a personal office
(h) Offer a person an appointment to a public office recommend a person for such an appointment or approve a person's appointment to a public office or
(i) Offer a person a service for finding employment

12.38   This provision was not brought into force at the time of the rest of the EqA 2010's implementation and so was not addressed in the Employment Code – rather it was implemented in April 2011.[35] Guidance since brought out by the Equality and Human Rights Commission[36] says of these provisions as follows:

> The other positive action step an employer can take is to decide to appoint an applicant from a group sharing a protected characteristic if they reasonably believe this group to be disadvantaged or underrepresented in the workforce or if their participation in an activity is disproportionately low.
>
> The employer can only use these 'tie-break' provisions when faced with a choice between two candidates who are as qualified as each other. It is also possible, though it would be unusual, that a tie-break situation could arise where more than two candidates were equally qualified for the post.
>
> Although it is most likely that an employer would use the tie-break provisions at the end of the recruitment process, they can also treat an applicant more favourably at any earlier stage of the process. But they can only choose to use these provisions if it is a proportionate way of enabling or encouraging people from the disadvantaged or underrepresented group to overcome or minimise the disadvantage of that group.
>
> **For example:**
> A housing advice service has no Muslim employees, even though it is located in an area where there is a high Muslim population. When a vacancy arises, there are two candidates of equal merit. One candidate is Muslim and the other is not. The advice service could choose to offer the job to the Muslim candidate under the positive action provisions, so that the non-Muslim candidate could not claim religious discrimination.
>
> An employer must not have a general policy of treating people with the relevant protected characteristic more favourably in connection with recruitment.

35 Equality Act 2010 (Commencement No 5) Order 2011 SI No 96.
36 www.equalityhumanrights.com/advice-and-guidance/guidance-for-workers/recruitment/positive-action-and-recruitment/.

Positive action and the public sector equality duties

12.39   Public authorities are obliged to have due regard to the equality objectives set out in EqA 2010 s149 in the exercise of all their functions,
including their function as employer. First, as the Employment Code
points out,[37] such authorities may wish to consider using positive
action to help them comply with those duties. Second a failure to use
positive action may amount to a failure to comply with the public sector equality duty.[38]

Implementing positive action lawfully

12.40   Those advising employees may be interested in the use of positive
action in two different contexts:

- as a means of achieving greater equality for employees from
groups defined by a protected characteristic;
- challenging the use of positive action as a defence to action that
has been taken by the employer.

12.41   The Code gives steps which an employer should follow to establish
the defence in practical terms at para 12.35 and following. This recommends that the employer draws up an action plan providing evidence
and outcomes aimed at – potential means of achieving those aims.

12.42   Practical points

- It is most likely that advisers will come across the positive action
provisions in an ET3
- If it is raised as a defence by an employer to a claim of discrimination, further information will need to be sought of the disadvantage that it is alleged that is connected to a protected characteristic;
the alleged needs that a different; or the low level of participation alleged; and on what basis it is believed that the criteria are
satisfied.
- The information will also need to identify on what basis it is considered that the action is proportionate

---

37 Employment Code para 12.34.
38 See chapter 16.

CHAPTER 13

Occupational requirements and other exceptions related to work

continued

Key points

- It is only in very limited circumstances that a genuine and determining occupational requirement (GOR) can be relied upon.
- The burden of showing that it is a GOR is on the employer.
- The GOR must be for a particular post, not a blanket exception for a generic type of post.
- The requirement related to the protected characteristic must be necessary.
- The necessity must be in order to achieve a legitimate aim.
- And it must be a proportionate means of achieving that aim.
- The test for proportionality is the same as in other justification contexts.

Introduction

13.1   This chapter examines two categories of important limitations on the principle of equality in employment and occupation. First, genuine determining occupational requirements and, secondly, the general and specific exceptions created by the EqA 2010.

Occupational requirements

13.2   The starting point for an understanding of 'occupational requirements' is the European law on which they are based, taking the Framework Directive as the model. Where the employer seeks to rely on an occupational requirement it is important to ensure that the use being made of the occupational requirement (or 'genuine occupational requirement' (GOR)) is consistent with the purposes for which GORs were introduced.

13.3   Recitals to Directive 2000/78 state that in very limited circumstances, a difference of treatment may be justified where a characteristic related to one of the protected characteristics constitutes a genuine and determining occupational requirement, when the objective is legitimate and the requirement is proportionate.[1]

13.4   Article 4 then provides that a difference of treatment that is based on a characteristic related to one of the protected characteristics will not constitute discrimination where, by reason of (a) the nature of

---

1 Preamble para 23 .

the particular occupational activities concerned or (b) the context in which they are carried out, such a characteristic constitutes a genuine and determining occupational requirement. However, the objective must be legitimate and the requirement must be proportionate.[2]

13.5   In *Wolf v Stadt Frankfurt am Main*[3] the CJEU held that a rule limiting recruitment to intermediate career posts in the professional fire service to persons of not more than 30 years of age should be regarded as laying down rules relating to recruitment conditions within the meaning of Article 3(1)(a) of Directive 2000/78. The CJEU considered Article 4 and stated that to examine whether the difference of treatment based on age in the national legislation at issue was justified, it was necessary to establish whether physical fitness was a characteristic related to age and, if so, whether it constituted a genuine and determining occupational requirement for the activities in question or for carrying them out, provided that the objective pursued by the legislation was legitimate and the requirement was proportionate. Thus the starting point for GORs is to check whether the characteristic demanded is a characteristic linked to the protected characteristic.

13.6   There is a further GOR available in Article 4(2) of Directive 2000/78 whereby member states can keep existing national legislation or provide for future legislation incorporating national practices existing at the date of adoption of the Directive. The laws or practices must relate to occupational activities within churches and other public or private organisations the ethos of which is based on religion or belief. The laws or practices must provide that a difference of treatment based on a person's religion or belief will not constitute discrimination where, by reason of the nature of these activities or of the context in which they are carried out, a person's religion or belief constitutes a genuine, legitimate and justified occupational requirement, having regard to the organisation's ethos. The difference of treatment on the basis of religion or ethos must be implemented taking account

2 Directive 2000/78 Article 4(1), Directive 2000/43 Article 4 and see also Directive 2006/54 Article 14(2) which provides: 'Member States may provide, as regards access to employment including the training leading thereto, that a difference of treatment which is based on a characteristic related to sex shall not constitute discrimination where, by reason of the nature of the particular occupational activities concerned or of the context in which they are carried out, such a characteristic constitutes a genuine and determining occupational requirement, provided that its objective is legitimate and the requirement is proportionate.' Note that neither this Directive nor 2000/43 contain an equivalent of Article 4(2).

3 Case C-229 08, [2010] 2 CMLR 32, [2010] All ER (EC) 939, [2010] IRLR 244.

of member states' constitutional provisions and principles, as well as the general principles of Community law, and should not justify discrimination on another ground. Therefore it is not possible to use a religion and belief GOR to justify, for example, age discrimination.

13.7   In *R (Amicus) v Secretary of State for Trade and Industry*,[4] certain trade unions applied for the annulment of certain provisions of the Employment Equality (Sexual Orientation) Regulations 2003, which implemented the sexual orientation aspects of the Directive. The relevant provisions permitted exceptions to the general prohibition of discrimination on the grounds of sexual orientation on the basis of GOR, including occupation for the purposes of an organised religion and benefits dependent on marital status. The implementation survived this challenge. However, during the course of the challenge clarification was provided as to the scope of the exceptions.

13.8   GORs are lawful only so far as they are consistent with the provisions of the Directive underpinning the law on the protected characteristic in question. Article 4 of the Framework Directive[5] sets out the circumstances in which a GOR may be applied and the criteria for a valid GOR in respect of age, disability sexual orientation and religion or belief. Occupational requirements were a feature of the precursor legislation, though framed slightly differently depending upon the ground with which they were concerned.

13.9   The GOR exception[6] applies to all protected characteristics and is a generic exception. Paragraph 1 provides:

(1) A person (A) does not contravene a provision mentioned in sub-paragraph (2)[7] by applying in relation to work a requirement to have a particular protected characteristic, if A shows that, having regard to the nature or context of that work –
(a) it is an occupational requirement,
(b) the application of the requirement is a proportionate means of achieving a legitimate aim, and
(c) the person to whom A applies the requirement does not meet it (or A has reasonable grounds for not being satisfied that the person meets it).

---

4 [2004] EWHC 860, [2007] ICR 1176, [2004] IRLR 430.
5 See eg Directive 2000/43 (Race Directive) Art 4, Directive 2000/78 (Framework Directive) Art 4 and Directive 2006/54 Art 14(2).
6 EqA 2010 Sch 9 para 1.
7 Ie EqA 2010 s39(1)(a) or (c) or (2)(b) or (c) (applicants and employees); s41(1)(b) (contract workers); s44(1)(a) or (c) or (2)(b) or (c) (partnerships); s45(1)(a) or (c) or (2)(b) or (c) (LLPs); s49(3)(a) or (c) or (6)(b) or (c) (personal offices); s50(3)(a) or (c) or (6)(b) or (c) (public offices) or s51(1) (recommendations for appointments to public office).

13.10   The burden of proving that the exception applies is on the employer. They are exceptions from the principle of non-discrimination, so the exceptions must be construed narrowly.[8]

Application of the exception

13.11   The following approach can usefully be adopted to determine whether a GOR applies:

- What is the particular protected characteristic relied upon by the employee?
- What is the protected characteristic relied upon by the employer for the GOR?
- Is the characteristic relied upon by the employer related to the protected characteristic?
- Is the characteristic relied on by the employer an 'occupational requirement' Is it necessary as opposed to being desirable to do the occupation?
- What is/are the aim(s) that the application of the occupational requirement is seeking to achieve and is/are those aim(s) legitimate?
- Is the application of the occupational requirement a 'proportionate means' of achieving that/those legitimate aim(s)?
- Does the person to whom it applies not meet the occupational requirement? Or does the employer have reasonable grounds for not being satisfied that they do?

Particular protected characteristic

13.12   Note that the requirement has to be the possession, in most cases, of the protected characteristic. The Framework Directive refers to a characteristic related to the protected characteristic.[9] However, a member state may implement a Directive by provisions that are more favourable to the protection of the principle of equal treatment than those set out in the Directive.[10] For the purposes of the Act, however the protected characteristic must be possessed by the job occupant.

---

8 Observance of the principle of proportionality requires every derogation from an individual right to reconcile, so far as is possible, the requirements of the principle of equal treatment with those of the aim pursued (see Case C-476/99 *Lommers* [2002] ECR I-2891, para 39)

9 See C-229/08 *Wolf v Stadt Frankfurt am Main* [2010] 2 CMLR 32, [2010] All ER (EC) 939, [2010] IRLR 244.

10 See eg Framework Directive 2000/78 Art 8.

13.13   Generally it is obvious what the particular protected characteristic is. It is the sex of an individual, or their race, or religion or belief. Certain characteristics can be defined by reference to a negative. Thus a racial group can be defined by reference to a negative definition (eg non-EU nationals). In this context, however, there are two important differences.

13.14   First, for gender reassignment, the occupational requirement must be 'not to be a transsexual person'.[11] Second the protected characteristic in the case of marriage and civil partnership is of not being married or a civil partner, as opposed to being married or a civil partner.[12] This leads to the conclusion that it is not possible to construct a GOR of being married or a civil partner, and that it is not possible to require that a post-holder be transsexual.

13.15   Further the EqA 2010 refers to the possession of a 'particular protected characteristic'. When the Act uses this phrase when referring to a person, it has the following meanings:

- age:[13] refers to a person of a particular age group (which may be defined by reference to age, whether by reference to a particular age or to a range of ages). It is therefore possible to define a group by negative reference, eg anyone who is not 50;
- disability:[14] refers to a person who has a particular disability, and a reference to persons who share a protected characteristic is a reference to persons who have the same disability;
- race:[15] is a reference to a person of a particular racial group, which again can be defined by negative reference to a group;[16]
- religion or belief:[17] refers to a person of a particular religion or belief.[18] However, a reference to persons who share a protected characteristic is a reference to persons who are of the same religion or belief (or lack thereof);
- sex:[19] refers to a man or to a woman;

11 EqA 2010 Sch 9 para 1(4)(a). The definition in section 7(3) defines the protected characteristic as being a transsexual person.
12 EqA 2010 Sch 9 para 1(4)(b).
13 EqA 2010 s5(1)(a).
14 EqA 2010 s6(3).
15 EqA 2010 s9(2).
16 See EqA 2010 s9(3) and *Orphanos v Queen Mary College* [1985] AC 761, [1985] IRLR 349, HL.
17 EqA 2010 s10(3).
18 Which includes a lack of either.
19 EqA 2010 s11.

- sexual orientation:[20] refers to a person who has a particular sexual orientation. A reference to persons who share a protected characteristic is a reference to persons who are of the same sexual orientation.

13.16   The use of the phrase therefore throws up the following problem. In the case of race and age it is possible to define an age by reference to a group and hence use a negative to define the protected characteristic that the person must have in order to satisfy the GOR. However, in relation to sexual orientation and particularly disability this is not possible. In the case of sex, where there are two genders only this may not matter. Similarly in practical terms sexual orientation raises no particular difficulties. However, in relation to disability it means that it is not possible to define a GOR by reference to a negative (not having schizophrenia), and neither is it possible to have a determining occupational requirement that can be satisfied by persons having different disabilities. It would not be possible to have a GOR covering visual impairments (unless they are viewed as a unitary disability).

Meaning of 'occupational requirement'

13.17   Having a particular protected characteristic must be a requirement for the work that is to be done. It must be a genuine and determining occupational requirement.[21] EqA 2010 Sch 9 para 1 makes it clear that an occupational requirement can only be applied to 'work' having regard to 'the nature or context of that work'. Therefore an ET will have to consider the actual work undertaken within a particular post. They must not consider the post-holder or the organisation as a whole. The focus must be on the specific duties and work undertaken within a post.

13.18   The Employment Code gives the example of a local council setting up a health project to encourage older people from the Somali community to make more use of health services. The example posits that the post would involve visiting elderly people in their homes so the post-holder would need to have good knowledge of the culture and language of potential clients. The Code suggests that the council

---

20 EqA 2010 s12(2).
21 See eg Directive 2000/43 (Race Directive) Art 4, Directive 2000/78 (Framework Directive) Art 4 and Directive 2006/54 (Recast Directive) Art 14(2).

could rely on the occupational requirement exception to recruit a health worker of Somali origin.[22]

13.19 An employer cannot simply say that all employees within their organisation must have a particular protected characteristic. They must be able to justify the occupational requirement for each and every post. The Employment Code recommends that employers should not have a blanket policy of applying an occupational requirement exception; 'they should also reassess the job whenever it becomes vacant to ensure that the statutory conditions for applying the occupational requirement exception still apply'.[23]

13.20 The ET will not merely accept an assertion from an employer that there is an occupational requirement but will apply an objective test, taking into account the employer's perspective. The ET will look beyond this to the particular requirements of the post and the nature of the work.

13.21 The explanatory notes to the EqA 2010 state that 'the requirement must be crucial to the post, and not merely one of several important factors'.[24] Consequently the burden on an employer is heavy. In this way the requirement must be a determining requirement in accordance with the underlying Directives.

13.22 An employer will need to give careful consideration as to whether there is anything about the particular context within which the work is being undertaken that highlights the importance of particular protected characteristics. Claimants should seek early and detailed disclosure of any such evidence, by means of written questions in open correspondence or the questionnaire procedure (if available).

Identifying the legitimate aim

13.23 Once the particular work, its nature and context has been carefully identified it should be fairly obvious whether there is a legitimate aim that is being sought. However, it will be for the employer to identify the legitimate aim in this context, as it is for the employer to establish that the facts fall within the exception. Therefore it is important to identify the real aim. For example the aim may itself be a description

---

22 Employment Code para 13.9. The difficulty with this example is that the requirement is to have good knowledge of the culture and language of the potential clients. Having such knowledge is plainly not the protected characteristic. The example appears to have been drafted in accordance with the Directive, but not in accordance with the EqA 2010.

23 Employment Code para 13.20.

24 Explanatory notes para 791.

of the means of achieving a further aim. Thus the aim of achieving a particular pattern of working will probably be explained by the aim of that pattern of work, rather than standing as an aim in itself.

13.24   In this context examples of legitimate aims would include preserving the privacy and decency of a person so that someone of a particular sex would be required to undertake a care role. Similarly it would be a legitimate aim to require authenticity or realism in acting roles. Where a service is specifically aimed at a group who is vulnerable or who has specific needs, it may give rise to a requirement that someone with a particular characteristic provide that service. The legitimate aim would be to overcome disadvantage suffered by that group and to encourage them to access the service. Note that the aim effectively identifies the protected characteristic as a means of achieving that aim in this context. Arguments based on this type of consonance between post-holder and protected characteristic group require particular scrutiny. An obvious example, however, is given in the Explanatory Notes. A rape counsellor may be required to be a woman, and not a transsexual person even if she has a gender recognition certificate, to avoid causing the service-users distress.[25] However, it should be noted that this example is based on an objective analysis of the vulnerable state of the women using the service (as a rule). In another context, clearly, a simple appeal to customer preference would be likely to fail. Thus the (alleged) demands of a young clientele for a fashion shop to have young employees serving them would be unlikely to form the basis of a GOR.

Proportionality

13.25   The requirement to have a particular protected characteristic must be an appropriate and necessary (ie a proportionate) means of achieving the legitimate aim. The ET will consider whether imposing the occupational requirement is a proportionate means of achieving that particular (identified) legitimate aim. The ET should ask whether there are other ways of achieving the aim that are less restrictive. If a claimant can point to other such means, it will be difficult for an employer to show that the requirement was a proportionate means of achieving the aim.

13.26   The question of proportionality will inevitably be considered alongside the question of the particular work to be undertaken and the aim that is being pursued.

25 Explanatory notes para 789.

13.27   The test for proportionality is the same in this context as the one used in other justification contexts.[26] Use of the requirement that the person occupying the post possess the protected characteristic must reconcile, so far as it is possible to do so, the principle of equal treatment and the exception thus made to it. So the use of the requirement to have the particular protected characteristic would have to be the least discriminatory means of achieving the stated aim.

Not meeting the requirement

13.28   Either the person does or does not meet the requirement to have a particular protected characteristic. The claimant will either have the protected characteristic or not.

13.29   It does not matter what the perception of the employer may be. Thus if the claimant does not have the protected characteristic and all other parts of the test are satisfied, the employer will succeed in establishing the GOR. Certain characteristics, such as non-visible disabilities, belief or religion, or sexual orientation do not readily lend themselves to immediate verification. As Richards J noted[27] in a case dealing with the precursor legislation on religion and belief:[28]

> it cannot be right that an employer, having asked the plainly permissible initial question whether a person meets that requirement, is bound in all circumstances to accept at face value the answer given or is precluded from forming his own assessment if no answer is given.

So if the person does in fact have the protected characteristic, but the employer does not believe that they do, the EqA 2010 permits the employer to establish a GOR by reference to the employer's reasonable beliefs about the claimant, save in the case of sex.

13.30   EqA 2010 Sch 9 para 1(1)(c) requires the employer in this respect to show that the employer has reasonable grounds for not being satisfied that the person meets the requirement that they have the protected characteristic. If the employer can do this, they may still rely on the exception.

13.31   The test for whether the employer had 'reasonable grounds' for their belief is not a wholly subjective test. Simple suspicion is not

---

26 See paras 3.121–3.145.

27 *R (Amicus) v Secretary of State for Trade and Industry* [2004] EWHC 860 (Admin), [2007] ICR 1176, [2004] IRLR 430.

28 Employment Equality (Religion or Belief) Regulations (RRB Regs) 2003 SI No 1660.

enough. Specific evidence and examples will be required to demonstrate reasonable belief. Mere stereotyping would not be permitted, because the grounds must be 'reasonable'.

13.32 Where the requirement is to be of a particular sex then the exception only applies where the person is not of a particular sex. Here the employer's belief is irrelevant.[29]

Circumstances in which the exceptions may apply – personal scope

13.33 The exceptions apply to employers, principals, contract work, partners, members of Limited Liability Partnerships and those with the power to appoint or remove or recommend appointment of office-holders.[30]

13.34 The exception does not apply to offering discriminatory terms for a position. It applies to the offer of or refusal to offer the position itself, and dismissal or expulsion from that position. However, it does not allow for discriminatory terms to be applied.[31]

13.35 Moreover the exception does not apply to a situation in which a person had been subjected to 'any other detriment'.[32] This retains the limitation under the precursor legislation.

'Organised religion' exceptions

13.36 Directive 2000/78 (age, disability, religion and belief, sexual orientation) and 2000/43 (race) contain a further type of genuine and determining occupational requirement. Directive 2006/54 (gender) contains no such further provision.[33] The exception applying to organised religion is at Article 4 of Directive 2000/78. Article 4(2) provides that states may maintain national legislation or provide future legislation. However, the legislation can only incorporate national practices existing at the time of the adoption of the Directive. This fixes the social policy of the states, so that a state could not introduce a new national practice in this regard. The practices must be ones pursuant

29 EqA 2010 Sch 9 para 1(4) in claims of sex discrimination.
30 EqA 2010 Sch 9 para 1(2).
31 See EqA 2010 Sch 9 para 1(2). Note that eg section 39(1)(b) is not included within the scope of the exception.
32 See EqA 2010 s39(2)(d).
33 It has solely Article 14.

to which, in the case of occupational activities within churches and other public or private organisations the ethos of which is based on religion or belief, a difference of treatment based on a person's religion or belief does not constitute discrimination. The preconditions for such a practice to be lawful are that, by reason of the nature of the activities or of the context in which they are carried out, a person's religion or belief constitute a genuine, legitimate and justified occupational requirement, having regard to the organisation's ethos. The article states that if the Directive's provisions are otherwise complied with, including the requirement that use of the GOR should not justify discrimination on a ground other than religion or belief, it does not prejudice the right of churches and other public or private organisations, the ethos of which is based on religion or belief, acting in conformity with national laws, to require those working for them to act in good faith and with loyalty to the organisation's ethos. Note, however, that these are not free-standing exceptions. The provisions of the Directive are not to prejudice that right, provided that the GOR does not discriminate otherwise than as a difference in treatment based on religion or belief.

13.37   Thus if the requirement discriminates on race or sexual orientation Article 4(2) cannot provide the basis for justification. Article 4(1) must be used.

UK law

13.38   The EqA 2010 follows the approach in the precursor legislation to the religion exception. On 20 November 2009, the European Commission had sent reasoned opinions to the UK government stating, inter alia, that the Government had failed to transpose the Employment Framework Directive correctly as the exceptions allowed to the principle of non-discrimination on the basis of sexual orientation for religious employers are broader than those permitted by the Directive. As a reasoned opinion is preceded by a formal letter, the government would have already been aware of the issues raised by the Commission.

13.39   The original text of the Equality Bill set out the 'organised religion' exception in more restrictive terms in two respects than is found in the final EqA 2010. First, it required the application of the relevant requirement to be a proportionate means of achieving either the compliance or the non-conflict principle (see paras 13.59–13.70 below). Second, it gave a narrow definition to 'employment for the purposes of an organised religion'.

13.40   This version would presumably have met the requirements of the Directive, Article 4(2). However, those more restrictive elements of the exceptions did not survive the passage of the Bill.

13.41   It is difficult to see how UK law now is consistent with the requirements of the Directive in this respect.

13.42   The religion exceptions can be divided into two parts in domestic law, namely:

- those in which the employment is for the purposes of an organised religion[34]; and
- those in which the organisation has an ethos based on religion or belief.[35]

Organised religion

13.43   To fall within this exception, the employer must satisfy four conditions:

1) one of the following requirements is applied;[36]
   (a) to be of a particular sex;
   (b) not to be a transsexual person;
   (c) not to be married or a civil partner;
   (d) not to be married to, or the civil partner of, a person who has a living former spouse or civil partner;
   (e) relating to circumstances in which a marriage or civil partnership came to an end;
   (f) related to sexual orientation.
2) the employment is for the purposes of an organised religion;
3) the requirement:
   (a) engages the compliance principle; or
   (b) engages the non-conflict principle;
4) the person does not meet the requirement or the employer has reasonable grounds to believe that they do not.[37]

Requirement to be applied

13.44   At first sight it appears that the scope of the exception is much narrower than the general GORs noted above because the requirement

---

34   EqA 2010 Sch 9 para 2(1).
35   EqA 2010 Sch 9 para 3.
36   EqA 2010 Sch 9 para 2(4)
37   This does not apply where the requirement is to be of a particular sex by EqA 2010 Sch 9 para 2(4).

must be one of those listed in EqA 2010 Sch 9 para 2(4). In relation to gender, and marital and civil partnership status, this is true. In particular UK law must, in the case of gender, be interpreted so that it applies only in situations in which a GOR would under EU law be justified in any employment.

13.45   The scope of the exception concerning the circumstances in which a marriage or civil partnership came to an end and in relation to sexual orientation, however, appears to be potentially much broader. The requirement is not to have any particular sexual orientation. The requirement may be 'related to' sexual orientation.

13.46   If it is intended to cover matters such as whether a person is celibate or not or engages in particular sexual practices, it immediately raises the question of whether such matters are related to sexual orientation at all. The exception must be construed narrowly. The concept of a matter being related to sexual orientation (and nothing else) is difficult to fathom. For example a prohibition on having sexual intercourse outside marriage is a prohibition on sexual conduct rather than conduct that is specifically related to sexual orientation. Similarly a prohibition on a particular type of sexual intercourse appears to be a prohibition on sexual conduct rather than anything related to sexual orientation.

13.47   In any event the provision is either incompatible with Article 4 of the Framework Directive or must be construed so as to avoid providing a basis for discrimination on the grounds of sexual orientation. This is because the Directive states that the 'difference in treatment ... should not justify discrimination on another ground'. Hence the implementing legislation cannot be construed so as to give rise to discrimination on the grounds of sexual orientation. It can only justify less favourable treatment on the ground of religion and belief. Given that it cannot justify discrimination on any other ground, it is suggested that the GOR will only be available where it would in any event satisfy the requirements of Article 4(1) of the Directive 2000/78.

13.48   We suggest that ultimately the organised religion exception cannot be rendered compatible with the requirements of the Directive and hence must be disapplied even in cases between individuals,[38] as it is 'for the national court, hearing a dispute involving the principle of non-discrimination ... as given expression in Directive 2000/78, to provide, within the limits of its jurisdiction, the legal protection which individuals derive from European Union law and to ensure

---

38   C-555/07 *Seda Kücükdeveci v Swedex GmbH & Co KG* [2010] ECR-I-365, [2010] IRLR 3346 paras 51–56.

the full effectiveness of that law, disapplying if need be any provision of national legislation contrary to that principle'.[39]

Employment for the purposes of organised religion

13.49   The Act contains no specific definition of what is meant by 'employment for the purposes of organised religion' or of 'organised religion'. The legislature chose not to use the wording of the Framework Directive, which would have included any public or private organisation the ethos of which is based on religion or belief. 'Organised religion' has a clearly more limited scope. In any event in order to give effect to the rights of belief organisations under the ECHR to manifest their beliefs on a non-discriminatory footing, the exception would have to be construed so as to include any organised belief organisation (consistently with the Directive). Note however that the concept of 'organised religion' must, by virtue of section 10 of the EqA 2010, be taken to include organisations lacking religion. Thus the GOR would appear to apply to any organisation that has a religion or belief ethos.

13.50   The Explanatory Notes state that this exception 'is intended to cover a very narrow range of employment: ministers of religion and a small number of law posts, including those that exist to promote and represent religion'.[40] In dealing with the question of proportionality the Employment Code states:[41] 'The occupational requirement exception should only be used for a limited number of posts, such as ministers of religion and a small number of posts outside the clergy including those which exist to promote or represent the religion.'

13.51   In particular the Notes suggest that 'a church youth worker who primarily organises sporting activities' is unlikely to be within the provision but a 'youth worker who mainly teaches Bible classes' may be.[42] The Code provides a similar example, namely:[43]

> The trustees of a Mosque want to employ two youth workers, one who will provide guidance on the teachings of the Koran and the other purely to organise sporting activities not involving promoting or representing the religion. The trustees apply an occupational requirement for both workers to be heterosexual. It might be lawful to apply the occupational requirement exception to the first post but not the

---

39 See C-144/04 *Mangold* [2005] ECR I-9981 para 77.
40 Explanatory Notes para 790.
41 Employment Code para 13.13.
42 Explanatory Notes para 790.
43 Employment Code para 13.15.

second post because the second post does not engage the 'compliance' or the 'non-conflict' principle.

13.52   The question of which roles are 'for the purposes of organised religion' has no clear answer. In reality it will affect only a small number of posts. It is likely that the post would have to be within a specific religious body, such as a place of worship or a training college for a religious body. Furthermore particular consideration would have to be given to the requirements of the post, as opposed to the organisation, to determine whether that employment is for the purposes of organised religion.

13.53   Matters that are likely to be relevant include whether the post includes teaching religious doctrine, promoting the religion and assisting in the observance of religious practices. The exception is a derogation from the principle of equal treatment, and must therefore be construed narrowly. So construed it is only the essential purposes of a religion that may engage any exception that this provision may create.

13.54   Under the precursor legislation, an ET considered this exception in *Reaney v Hereford Diocesan Board of Finance*.[44] Mr Reaney, a gay man, applied for the job of diocesan youth worker. He said on his application form that he had been in a same-sex relationship until a few weeks before he applied. An interview panel decided that he was the best candidate for the post. The Bishop, however, took the view that he needed assurances about Mr Reaney's future lifestyle. Mr Reaney said he would remain celibate during his employment, which was in accordance with the pastoral position of the Church of England to the effect that any kind of sexual behaviour outside of marriage does not accord with the Christian faith. The Bishop decided not to appoint Mr Reaney on the basis, he said, of his 'practice and lifestyle', rather than his sexual orientation.

13.55   The ET upheld Mr Reaney's claim, and in doing so considered the GOR in regulation 7(3) of the Employment Equality (Sexual Orientation) Regulations, in relation to employment for the purposes of an organised religion. They accepted that Mr Reaney's employment was for such a purpose, and also that the requirement (which, importantly, they defined as a requirement not to enter into a sexual relationship with another person), was applied so as to avoid conflicting with the strongly held religious convictions against homosexuality of a significant number of the religion's followers. However, the ET did not accept that Mr Reaney failed to meet that requirement, or that

44 ET/1602844/06, 17 July 2007.

his potential employer was reasonably not satisfied that he met it. Mr Reaney was, the ET held, committed to fully complying with the respondent's requirement. As to the respondent's perception of his fulfilment of the requirement, the Regulations were phrased in the present, rather than the future, tense, so the Bishop's concerns about the future were not relevant. In any event, there was no good reason for the Bishop to disbelieve Mr Reaney's assurances about his future conduct.

The compliance principle

13.59   The compliance principle is defined in EqA 2010 Sch 9 para 2(5) as where 'the requirement is applied so as to comply with the doctrines of the religion'.

13.60   The reference to the doctrines of the religion may point to the fact that the purposes of organised religion giving rise to the possibility of an exceptional requirement are those which are necessarily tied to the propagation of doctrine rather than those purposes which the persons organising the religion currently believe to be desirable.

13.61   It is a very narrow exception. It may require the ET to decide for itself the doctrines of a religion. If a particular doctrine is not shared by the organised religion, but merely by a belief group within that religion, the latter cannot rely on the exception. This is because the group is defined by reference to a belief rather than a religion.

13.62   The courts have always stated that it is not for them to resolve matters of religious doctrine.[45] However, the ET will have to identify the relevant doctrines of the religion. In certain faiths this will be straightforward. It will be a matter of the faith's own legal structure (for example Canon law). Other religions do not have such structures and the question of whether or not some belief is a doctrine of the religion will not be easily settled.

13.63   In many religions there is not unanimity on certain aspects of the outworking of the religion, particularly in relation to gender, sexuality and marriage. The requirements set out in EqA 2010 Sch 9 para 2(4) go to the heart of many organised religions' difficult doctrinal debates. Further difficulties may arise as to whether a matter is a doctrine of a religion or simply a preferred practice of a religion. The ET will also have to tackle the problem of a religion that teaches two doctrines that appear to be mutually contradictory. Thus a religion

---

45   See for example Lord Hope in *R (E) v JFS* [2009] UKSC 15, [2010] 2 WLR 153 at para 157.

may have a prohibition on homosexual acts, but at the same time hold a doctrine that all persons are created equal. It is suggested that if the requirement cannot be applied in practice without contravening another doctrine of the organised religion, the exception cannot apply as the requirement cannot be applied 'so as to comply with the doctrines of the religion'. The use of the plural in this context is, it is submitted, intentional. It is only if the requirement can be applied so as to be consistent with all of the doctrines that the exception can apply. Had the intention been otherwise the legislature could have used the much simpler formula that the requirement is applied to comply with 'a doctrine' of the religion. In those circumstances all that would have been necessary would be the identification of a doctrine requiring the prohibition in question.

13.64   For parties to litigation, where the doctrine cannot be agreed upon, it is likely that expert evidence will be required to establish what is or is not a doctrine of the religion. Undoubtedly however the question will have to be objectively assessed and it will be insufficient for a religious organisation simply to assert that a belief is a matter of doctrine of the relevant organised religion.

13.65   It is submitted that the compliance principle will be impossible to apply in most religious contexts. The Employment Code seeks to deal with this exception at paras 13.12–13.13.

The non-conflict principle

13.66   Given that the compliance principle is likely to be ineffective, reliance is more likely to be placed on the 'non-conflict' principle. This principle is where 'because of the nature or context of the employment, the requirement is applied so as to avoid conflicting with the strongly held religious convictions of a significant number of the religion's followers'.[46]

13.67   The wording of the principle is significant. It is necessary that the requirement is imposed to avoid conflicting with the strongly held religious convictions of a significant number of the religion's followers. Contrary to the apparent suggestion in the Employment Code, this cannot be satisfied where there is objection from members of a congregation. The example at para 13.12 in the Code must be seen as referring to the followers of an evangelical religion rather than simply a church. The requirement appears to be

---

46 EqA 2010 Sch 9 para 2(6).

- the aim of the application of the requirement is to avoid conflicting with strongly held religious convictions;
- there must be a significant number of the religion's followers whose views are (a) strongly held and (b) there is a risk of conflict with those views.

13.68 The distinction between a denomination or sect of a religion and the religion itself is, it is suggested, clear. It would not be open for an evangelical church to rely on this exception unless it could show that a significant number of Christians held strongly a view with which the employment of the person would conflict.

13.69 Although, therefore, the principle appears to avoid the doctrinal debates of the first route, it is plain that in most cases it will be impossible to apply. Establishing whether there are a significant number of the religion's followers with a strongly held view would seem to be a remote possibility. It will be necessary for the employer to establish that a significant number of the religion's followers strongly hold the particular religious conviction.

13.70 In some religions the particular issue may be well-known and well-understood. In other contexts, more focused evidence may be required, again perhaps from an expert, to establish what the religious conviction is and whether a significant number of followers hold that belief.

Not meeting the requirement

13.71 This provision mirrors that of EqA 2010 Sch 9 para 1(1)(c) regarding GORs.[47]

Applicable provisions

13.72 The 'organised religion' exception applies to employment and to personal and public office-holders. It applies to the offer or refusal to offer employment, dismissal and to access to promotion, transfer or any other benefit.[48] In other words it does not permit harassment and it does not permit subjecting a person to any other detriment, such as disciplinary sanctions. Thus if a person is suspended prior to being dismissed the organisation can rely on the exception only in respect of the dismissal but not the suspension (itself potentially an act of less favourable treatment).

47 See paras 13.28–13.32.
48 EqA 2010 Sch 9 para 2(2) and 2(7).

Ethos based on religion or belief

13.73　EqA 2010 Sch 9 para 3 provides:

> A person (A) with an ethos based on religion or belief does not contravene a provision mentioned in paragraph 1(2) by applying in relation to work a requirement to be of a particular religion or belief if A shows that, having regard to that ethos and to the nature or context of that work –
>
> (a) it is an occupational requirement,
>
> (b) the application of the requirement is a proportionate means of achieving a legitimate aim, and
>
> (c) the person to whom A applies the requirement does not meet it (or A has reasonable grounds for not being satisfied that the person meets it).

13.74　This provision largely mirrors the GOR exception. It applies to the same sections in relation to, for example, employers and contract work.[49] It also requires that the requirement is an occupational requirement and its application is a proportionate means of achieving a legitimate aim.[50] It enables the exception to apply where the person does not meet the requirement and where there are reasonable grounds for believing that they do not meet it.[51] At first sight it appears that the only requirement that can be applied is that the person be of a particular religion or belief. EqA 2010 s10 defines 'religion or belief' as including a reference to a lack of religion or belief. A reference to a person with an ethos based on religion or belief therefore includes a person with an ethos based on a lack of religion or belief.

13.75　The key point in this provision is whether an organisation has 'an ethos based on' the protected characteristic 'religion or belief'. This ties into whether the requirement to be of a particular religion or belief (or lack of it) is an occupational requirement.

13.76　It will be for the organisation to show that it has an ethos based on religion or belief (or its lack). The Employment Code[52] defines an 'ethos' as 'the important character or spirit of the religion or belief. It may also be the underlying sentiment, conviction or outlook that informs the behaviours, customs, practices or attitudes of followers of the religion or belief'. The Code and the Explanatory Notes suggest that evidence of this might include the organisation's founding

---

49　On which see para 13.33.

50　On which see paras 13.17–13.27.

51　On which see paras 13.28–13.32.

52　Employment Code para 13.17.

constitution.[53] One may also look to documents such as internal policies, vision statements and the objectives of the organisation but only in so far as they point to the aims of the religion or belief system. It is not possible for an ad hoc ethos to be created by a policy statement that applies only to the organisation but not to the religion or belief as a necessary and fundamental part of its purpose.

13.77   Once the ethos has been established, it may be taken into account when considering whether the requirement to be of a particular religion or belief is an occupational requirement. When determining whether something is an occupational requirement, consideration can be had to the nature or context of the work, as well as the ethos. As noted above in relation to the general occupational requirement exception, careful consideration will have to be given to the particular work to be done within the specific post.

General exceptions

13.78   The EqA 2010 removes certain activity generally from its scope. Thus an employer does not commit an unlawful act under the Act only by doing something for the purpose of safeguarding national security where the action is proportionate for that purpose.[54] Schedule 6 excludes certain offices. The Welsh Language Act 1993 allows public employers to require workers who can speak, write and read Welsh sufficiently well for a range of posts. In some cases, Welsh-language skills may be an essential requirement for appointment; in others, the worker may need to agree to learn the language to the required level within a reasonable period of time after appointment.

Acts authorised by statute or the executive

13.79   There will be no contravention of the work provisions of the EqA 2010 where:

- in pursuance of a piece of primary legislation;
- in pursuance of a piece of secondary legislation;
- to comply with a requirement imposed by a member of the executive by virtue of an enactment;
- in pursuance of arrangements made by or with the approval of, or for the time being approve by, a Minister of the Crown;

---

53   Explanatory Notes para 795 and Employment Code para 13.17.
54   EqA 2010 s192 and Employment Code para 13.56.

- to comply with a condition imposed (whether before or after the passing of the EqA 2010) by a Minister of the Crown,

A discriminates against B because of B's nationality, or A applies a PCP which relates to B's place of ordinary residence, or the length of time B has been present or resident in or outside the UK or an area within it.[55]

13.80   Essentially, this exception permits direct nationality discrimination and indirect race discrimination on the basis of residency requirements where the discrimination is required by law, ministerial arrangements or ministerial conditions (eg the Immigration Rules).[56] It does not permit harassment or victimisation related to nationality. As an exception to the principle of non-discrimination, the provision is to be interpreted narrowly: if there is any discretion as to how the legislation etc is to be pursued or complied with, or if what is imposed is not a requirement or condition, then the exception will not apply.[57]

13.81   More generally the employer does not contravene the provisions of the EqA 2010 relating to work in respect of something that it must do pursuant to the requirements of an enactment[58] so far as it relates to:

- age;
- disability;
- religion or belief.[59]

13.82   A second type of action is also exempt in relation to a slightly different group of protected characteristics. Thus the employer does not contravene the EqA 2010 in relation to work where the act is something the employer is obliged to do pursuant to a requirement or condition imposed by virtue of an enactment by a Minister of the Crown, or one of various members or officials of the Welsh or Scottish devolved government.[60] The protected characteristics that this rule affects are:

- disability; and
- religion or belief.

55   EqA 2010 Sch 23 para 1.
56   Explanatory Notes para 988 and Employment Code para 13.54.
57   See by analogy *Hampson v Department of Education and Science* [1989] ICR 179, [1989] IRLR 69, CA.
58   Including measures of the General Synod of the Church of England and acts of the devolved executives.
59   EqA 2010 Sch 22 paras 1–3 and Employment Code para 13.49.
60   EqA 2010 Sch 22 paras 1–3 and Employment Code para 13.49.

Other exceptions specific to work

13.83 There are a very limited number of further exceptions specific to work:

- relating to age;[61]
- specific exceptions for the armed forces;[62]
- employment services;[63]
- provision of services to the public and claims by employees in respect of such services;[64]
- supported employment for persons with disabilities;[65]
- educational appointments for religious institutions;[66]
- restrictions on Crown employment;[67]
- training for non-EEA nationals;[68]
- communal accommodation (sex and gender reassignment).[69]

Exceptions relating to age

13.84 In addition to the general justification defence for direct age discrimination in EqA 2010 s13(2), Schedule 9 also provides for specific age exceptions. Following a review of the default retiring age,[70] it was announced on 13 January 2011 that it would be phased out.[71] From 6 April 2011 employers could no longer issue notifications of retirement. Between 6 April and 1 October 2011 only those who had been notified of retirement prior to 6 April and whose retirement date was before 1 October 2011 could be compulsorily retired. From 1 October 2011 employers are not entitled to retire people at 65 without consent unless they can justify the dismissal as an act of potential direct age discrimination.[72] Individual employers may have a default retirement age; however, they will need to be able to objectively justify it. Thus

---

61 EqA 2010 Sch 9 paras 7–16.
62 EqA 2010 Sch 9 para 4 and Employment Code paras 13.21–13.23.
63 EqA 2010 Sch 9 para 5 and Employment Code paras 13.24–13.25.
64 EqA 2010 Sch 9 para 19 and Employment Code para 13.46.
65 EqA 2010 s193(3) and Employment Code para 13.48.
66 EqA 2010 Sch 22 para 3 and Employment Code para 13.50.
67 EqA 2010 Sch 22 para 5 and Employment Code para 13.53.
68 EqA 2010 Sch 23 para 4 and Employment Code para 13.55.
69 EqA 2010 Sch 23 para 3 and Employment Code para 13.57.
70 See strategy report *Building a Society for All Ages*, TSO, July 2009.
71 After *R (Age UK) v Secretary of State for Business, Innovation and Skills* [2009] EWHC 2336 (Admin), [2010] ICR 260 especially at para 130.
72 Using the test set from *Seldon v Clarkson Jakes Wright* [2012] UKSC 16, [2012] ICR 716; see paras 2.81–2.99 above.

the EqA 2010 was amended by the Employment Equality (Repeal of Retirement Age Provisions) Regulations 2011[73] to remove the Byzantine retirement procedures, the retirement exception and the exception permitting employers to refuse to employ a person when they were within six months of the employer's default retirement age. All such decisions now need to be justified if the reason for the treatment is the person's age.

Enhanced redundancy benefits

13.85 Where non-statutory redundancy payments are calculated using the same formula irrespective of age, it is not discriminatory to give one person a greater payment than another.[74] However, one of the following methods must be employed:

- removing the statutory scheme's maximum ceiling on a week's pay so that an employee's actual weekly pay is used in the calculation; or
- raising the statutory ceiling on a week's pay so that a higher amount of pay is used on the calculation; and/or
- multiplying the appropriate amount for each year of employment set out in the statutory formula by a figure of more than one.

13.86 In other words where a formula is used that is in the same form as ERA 1996 s162, then this will not be discriminatory even though it may result in older people receiving more than younger people. The formula in the ERA 1996 uses a week's pay multiplied by a number according to the age of the person multiplied by their length of service. Outside this exception the employer will have to justify such redundancy payments that otherwise may amount to indirect age discrimination.

13.87 Clearly for an enhanced redundancy payment the relevant week's pay and/or factor for their age and/or the calculation of length of service will be more generous than that provided by ERA 1996 s162. However, the point is that an exception has been created so that a standard formula may be applied to all employees where age, and indirectly age through length of service, will discriminate against certain age groups.

13.88 Employers may only give enhanced redundancy payments to:[75]

a) those entitled to a payment under ERA 1996 s135;

73 SI No 1069.
74 EqA 2010 Sch 9 para 13(1)–(6) and see Employment Code para 14.26.
75 See EqA 2010 Sch 9 para 13(2) and Employment Code para 14.27.

b) a person who agrees to termination of employment but would otherwise be entitled to a payment under (a) above;

c) a person who would have been entitled to a payment under (a) above but for the two years' continuous service requirement;

d) a person who agrees to termination of employment but would otherwise be entitled to a payment under (c) above.

Benefits

13.89   There are several aspects of the benefits exception:

- benefits based on length of service;
- life assurance;[76]
- child care;[77]
- national minimum wage;[78]
- marital status;[79]
- group insurance schemes;[80]
- occupational pension schemes.[81]

13.90   **Benefits based on length of service**: Where a person has less than five years' service, it does not amount to discrimination to put them at a disadvantage in relation to 'the provision of a benefit, facility or service' in so far as the disadvantage is because they have a shorter period of service than their comparator.[82]

13.91   The Explanatory Notes state that this provision 'ensures that an employer does not have to justify paying or providing fewer benefits to a worker with less service than a comparator, should such a practice constitute indirect discrimination because of age. [It is] as an absolute defence' where it is awarded in relation to service of five years or less.[83] It is open to a member state to introduce an absolute exception of this nature under Article 6(1) of Directive 2000/78. What the state cannot do is to water down the test for justification of indirect discrimination, not in relation to a difference of treatment, but a whole category of difference in treatment.

---

76 EqA 2010 Sch 9 para 14 and Employment Code para 14.30.
77 EqA 2010 Sch 9 para 15.
78 EqA 2010 Sch 9 paras 11–12.
79 EqA 2010 Sch 9 para 18(2) and Employment Code para 14.34.
80 EqA 2010 Sch 9 para 20 and Employment Code para 14.36.
81 EqA 2010 Sch 9 para 16 and s61 and Employment Code para 14.38. See para 15.63.
82 EqA 2010 Sch 9 para 10(1).
83 Explanatory Notes para 819.

13.92   Where a person has more than five years' service, any such disadvantage is only permissible where the employer 'reasonably believes that doing so fulfils a business need'.[84] This may be for example encouraging loyalty or motivation, or rewarding experience.[85]

13.93   The length of service of the relevant employee may be calculated according to the number of weeks they have worked for the employer at a particular level or any level. Where the requirement is for service at a particular level, the employer must 'reasonably regard [this] as appropriate'.[86] This will be an objective test and is likely to be tied into the particular benefit that is being given. Periods of absence, or periods reasonably regarded as related to periods of absence may be discounted 'so far as it reasonable'.[87] However, where previous service is taken into account by virtue of ERA 1996 s218, or similar, then EqA 2010 Sch 9 para 10(6) provides that it must be taken into account for the purposes of this exception.

13.94   The proper interpretation of this part of the exception remains contentious. An ET in *Harrison v MOD*[88] considered the proper interpretation of the precursor legislation. The ET had regard to the remarks of the Court of Appeal in *Rolls Royce v UNITE*[89] concluding that the test was partly subjective and partly objective. However, the test is not the same as a band of reasonable views test. The *Harrison* ET also held that

- the employer bears the burden of proof in relation to each component of the test;
- the employer is entitled to rely on any assumption that use of length of service in determining pay is proportionate and necessary to achieve a legitimate aim (for the purposes of justification under EqA 2010 s19) or any assumption that the use of length of service appears to the employer to fulfil a business need. However, the test to rebut the presumption requires the claimant only shows that there is evidence which if established at trial may rebut the general rule that length of service may be used;[90]

---

84   EqA 2010 Sch 9 para 10(2).
85   Explanatory Notes para 820.
86   EqA 2010 Sch 9 para 10(3) and (4).
87   EqA 2010 Sch 9 para 10(5).
88   Case No 240365/2008.
89   *Rolls Royce v Unite* [2009] EWCA Civ 387, [2009] IRLR 576 at paras 101–103, 136–139 and 167–170.
90   The test is set out in *Wilson v HSE* [2009] EWCA Civ 1074, [2010] ICR 302, [2010] IRLR 59.

- the employer must prove the exception for each award of a benefit which places the claimant at a disadvantage due to length of
service.[91]

13.95   **Life assurance:** Where an employer provides life assurance cover to
workers who have had to take early retirement because of ill health
they are entitled to make that provision from when the person retires
up to the normal retirement age of the age of 65.[92] The aim of the
exception is to ensure that employers continue to provide such benefits to everyone. As the Explanatory Notes state 'if employers were
no longer able to impose – or had to objectively justify – a "cut off"
for the provision ... there is a real risk they would simply 'level down'
in other words, they would cease to offer it to anyone'.[93] Thus the
exception appears to be consistent with the requirement of Directive
2000/78 that there should be an employment policy objective justifying its use.[94]

13.96   **Child care:** Employers may offer certain benefits to parents, both
birth/adoptive parents and those with parental responsibility, in
relation to children up to and including the age of 16, without other
employees making a complaint that such treatment constitutes less
favourable treatment of them on the grounds of the child's age.[95]
Specifically an employer may facilitate paying for some or all of the
cost of provision of child care; helping a parent to find a suitable
person to provide care; enabling a parent to spend more time providing care or otherwise assisting them regarding the care the parent
provides.[96]

13.97   **National minimum wage:** Employers may base their pay structures, in respect of young persons employed or working as apprentices on the national minimum wage legislation and continue to use
the development bands it provides.[97]

13.98   To qualify for this exception the employer is not limited to paying
the amounts in the bands, as long as pay is structured in the same
way.

---

91 And see Aitkens LJ in *Rolls Royce v UNITE* [2009] EWCA Civ 387, [2009] IRLR
576 at paras 137–138 and *Harrison* Case No 240365/2008 at para 118.
92 EqA 2010 Sch 9 para 14.
93 Explanatory Notes para 837.
94 See eg C-447/09, *Prigge v Deutsche Lufthansa AG* [2011] IRLR 1052, CJEU, at
paras 77–82.
95 EqA 2010 Sch 9 para 15.
96 EqA 2010 Sch 9 para 15(3).
97 EqA 2010 Sch 9 paras 11–12.

Specific other exceptions

13.99   The final part of EqA 2010 Sch 9 deals with various 'other exceptions' that have no particular link between them.

Non-contractual payments during maternity leave

13.100 An employer is permitted not to provide any benefit relating to pay to a woman while on maternity leave.[98] This does not include maternity related pay, pay when she is not on maternity leave and bonus payments when she is on compulsory maternity leave.[99] As the explanatory notes state, this provision 'does for non-contractual terms and conditions of employment relating to pay what is done for contractual terms in section 74'.[100]

13.101   Note that, as the Employment Code points out,[101] the scope of this exception is limited to non-contractual payments. Moreover it does not apply to maternity related pay which arises from a pay increase the woman would have received had she not been on leave. Thus if there is a 2 per cent pay increase during her maternity leave, her maternity pay must be based on the increased amount from the point the increase takes effect for all.[102]

Benefits dependent on marital status

13.102 Employers may provide a benefit exclusively for married workers, provided the benefit accrued before 5 December 2005,[103] or where payment is in respect of periods of service before that date.[104] The maintenance of 5 December 2005 as the date from which benefits to married workers cannot preclude those in a civil partnership could be challenged following the CJEU decision in Case C-267/06 *Maruko v Versorgungsanstalt der deutschen Buhnen.*[105] In that case, the CJEU, in applying the Framework Directive, refused to limit the period from

---

98 EqA 2010 Sch 9 para 17.

99 EqA 2010 Sch 9 para 17(2).

100 Explanatory Notes para 845.

101 Employment Code paras 8.39 and 8.40.

102 Practitioners should also look at the Equal Pay Code for more details of lawful and unlawful terms and conditions for women who are pregnant or on maternity leave (see also EqA 2010 s72–76 and paras 7.21–7.22).

103 Ie before the Civil Partnership Act 2004 came into force.

104 EqA 2010 Sch 9 para 18(1)and Employment Code para 14.35.

105 [2008] ECR-I-1757, [2010] IRLR 450, CJEU.

which a registered life partner had become entitled to survivor's benefits under a pension. This could lead to a challenge to this exception
in EqA 2010 Sch 9 and the continuation of 5 December 2005 as a key
date.

13.103   In addition EqA 2010 Sch 9 para 18 allows benefits, facilities or
services to only be provided to married persons and civil partners.
The example in the Explanatory Notes is of an occupational pension
scheme that pays out only to surviving married and civil partners,
which could be indirectly discriminatory because it might disadvantage gay couples.[106] Such a scheme would be permitted by this
exception.

Provision of services to the public

13.104 Where an employer provides services to the public and an employee
complains that they are discriminated against in the provision of
those services, EqA 2010 Sch 9 para 19 provides that they cannot
bring that claim under Part 5 of the EqA 2010. In other words they
cannot claim in their capacity as an employee, and instead they would
have to bring the claim in the county court under Part 3.

13.105   However, where the complaint is that the service differs from that
provided to other employees, is provided under the terms of their
contract or relates to training, then the claim can be brought under
EqA 2010 Part 5.[107]

Insurance contracts

13.106 EqA 2010 Sch 9 para 20 provides an exception in the employment
context, where premiums are paid or benefits are provided under
annuities, life insurance policies, accident insurance policies or similar. In other words where risk assessment is a key factor in determining the premium or benefit.

13.107   By virtue of this paragraph employers are allowed to pay premiums or benefits to employees that differ on the grounds of gender
reassignment, marriage, civil partnership, pregnancy, maternity or
sex. However, it must be reasonable to pay a different premium/ben-
efit and the difference must be determined by reference to actuarial
or other data, on which it is reasonable to rely.

---

106 See Explanatory Notes para 847.
107 EqA 2010 Sch 9 para 19(3).

13.108   Following the ECJ's decision in Case C-236/09 *Test-Achats v Conseil des ministres*,[108] the extent to which gender can be taken into account when setting insurance premiums is doubtful. The ECJ held that from 21 December 2012, EU insurers will not be permitted to take gender into account as a risk factor in calculating premiums or benefits payable under insurance products. This is based on EU equality law applicable to the provision of services. The relevant provision is not repeated in any of the employment-related Directives.

13.109   It is the employer, not the insurer, who is responsible for making sure that provision of benefits under such group insurance schemes comply with the above exception.[109]

Disability health questions

13.110   There are six situations in which it will be lawful for the employer to ask questions related to disability or health:[110]

- reasonable adjustment needed for the recruitment process;[111]
- monitoring purposes;[112]
- implementing positive action measures;[113]
- occupational requirements;[114]
- national security;[115]
- function intrinsic to the job.[116]

For further details of these exceptions, see para 9.67 above.

13.111 Practical points

Whenever one advises a claimant and the employer raises an exception to what would otherwise be unlawful discrimination, the following should be considered:

- Because these are exceptions to the principle of non-discrimination, the burden of proof is on the employer.

108 [2011] ECR-I-773, [2012] 1 WLR 1933, [2012] All ER (EC) 441.
109 Employment Code para 14.37.
110 See EqA 2010 s60(6) and (14).
111 Employment Code para 10.29.
112 Employment Code para 10.32.
113 Employment Code para 10.33.
114 Employment Code para 10.34.
115 Employment Code para 10.35.
116 Employment Code paras 10.36–10.38.

- Exceptions are to be narrowly construed.
- Make good use of correspondence with the respondent, or the written questions procedure in the ET rules of procedure (if available) or the questionnaire procedure especially in relation to:
  - what work the post actually requires;
  - what the aim of the exception is; and
  - whether that aim is legitimate.
- Think about whether the means to achieve the aim are really appropriate and necessary. Is there any other way that the same aim could be achieved? Where a religious exception is relied upon, consider whether expert evidence may assist.
- Consider whether the exception relied upon is compatible with the requirements of the underlying EU law.

Equality of terms

continued

Key points

- All claims that pay differentiates between protected characteristics must be dealt with either under EqA 2010 s39 (or equivalent) or in the case of sex discrimination under EqA 2010 ss64–71. Maternity and pregnancy pay discrimination must be dealt with under sections 72–76. This chapter deals with sex-related pay discrimination, referred to hereafter as 'pay discrimination'.
- From October 2010 the EqA 2010, the Treaty on the Functioning of the European Union (TFEU) Article 157 and the recast Equal Treatment Directive govern discrimination claims.
- The Equality and Human Rights Commission (EHRC) has issued the Equal Pay Code (EPC) to which regard must be had.
- Claims made before the relevant commencement date come under the Equal Pay Act 1970. For straddling claims there are transitional provisions.
- A pay discrimination claim arises where an employer has acted in breach of a sex equality clause (SEC) implied into the claimant's contract of employment.
- A SEC is implied into a woman's contract of employment where she has less favourable contractual terms than an actual man ('the comparator'), who works or has worked in the 'same employment' as her and she performs or has performed 'equal work' to him. However, an employer may successfully defend a breach of the SEC where there is a valid 'material factor' defence.
- In a direct sex discrimination pay claim a hypothetical comparator may be relied upon if no actual comparator can be found.
- Claims can be brought in the ET or civil courts.
- The circumstances of the case will dictate the applicable time-limit. The claimant can claim compensation for the losses that flow from the breach of the SEC for up to six years before the date of claim.
- Employees are protected against retribution for giving or receiving disclosures about workplace pay.
- Equal pay audits are encouraged.

Introduction

14.1   This chapter considers each stage of a pay discrimination claim pursuant to the EqA 2010. Flowchart 1 at the end of this chapter has also
been produced in order to guide claimants through the complex process. In 2008, the EHRC warned that women's hourly pay, excluding
overtime, was 17.1 per cent less than men's pay. For part-time workers the pay difference is 35.6 per cent.[1] We assume that the claimant
is a woman in this chapter. A man can bring a pay discrimination
claim or 'piggy-back' off a successful claim by a woman. Piggy-back
claims by men can be made on a contingent basis: they do not have
to wait for a woman's claim to succeed.[2]

The law: an overview

14.2   Prior to October 2010, pay discrimination claims were governed by
the Equal Pay Act (EqPA) 1970. The EqA 2010 closely follows the
structure of the Equal Pay Act 1970 although the concept of 'equal
pay' has been relabelled as 'equality in terms'.

14.3   Article 157[3] of the TFEU (and the recast Equal Treatment Directive 2006/54) also enshrines the principle of equal pay and comple-
ments the EqA 2010:

• Each member state shall ensure that the principle of equal pay for
male and female workers for equal work or work of equal value
is applied.

• For the purposes of this Article, 'pay' means the ordinary basic or
minimum wage or salary and any other consideration, whether in
cash or in kind, which the worker receives directly or indirectly, in
respect of his employment, from his employer.

14.4   Using Article 157 a woman can bring a claim within a wider range of
circumstances than contained in the EqA 2010. So a woman should
always include a claim under this provision in her claim in case any
element of her complaint cannot succeed under the Act alone. A key
difference is that Article 157 requires only a 'single source' for the

---

1   Equality and Human Rights Commission, *Equal Pay Position Paper* (March
2009).

2   *Hartlepool Borough Council v Llewellyn* [2009] IRLR 796, EAT.

3   Formerly Article 141 of the consolidated EC Treaty; originally Article 119 of the
Treaty of Rome.

inequality and putting it right and this does not apply to claims under the Act.[4]

14.5   The EHRC has issued a statutory code (the EPC).[5] The EPC does not itself impose legal obligations. However, it helps explain the legal obligations under the EqA 2010 and it is admissible as evidence. ETs and courts considering an equal pay claim are obliged to take into account any part of the code that appears relevant to the proceedings.[6] If employers and others who have obligations under the EqA 2010's equal pay provisions follow the guidance in the EPC, it may help to avoid an adverse decision by an ET or court in such proceedings. Guidance, which may be issued by any department or organisation, does not have to be taken into account by the ET, and is not authoritative, unlike the EPC, which, as set out above, has statutory force.

14.6   Finally, explanatory notes were published alongside the EqA 2010; these assist when trying to understand the new legislation.

The key questions in an equal pay claim

Question 1: Can the claimant bring a pay discrimination claim?

14.7   The following people can bring claims for pay discrimination: employees, apprentices, contract workers or self-employed persons (if their contracts require personal performance of work), Crown employees, House of Commons and House of Lords staff.[7]

14.8   There is no period of qualifying service before a woman can bring a claim.

Question 2: Can the claimant identify an actual male comparator with more favourable contractual terms than her?

14.9   There must be an actual comparator undertaking 'equal work' who is in receipt of better contractual pay.

---

4 *North Cumbria Acute Hospitals NHS Trust v Potter* [2009] IRLR 176, EAT.
5 Under Equality Act 2006 s14. It was approved by the Secretary of State and laid before Parliament on 27 July 2010.
6 Equality Act 2006 s15(4).
7 EqA 2010 s83.

14.10   If the identity of any potential comparator is uncertain, use pre-action correspondence or the questionnaire procedure,[8] ideally before starting proceedings although the written answers procedure may be used after proceedings have started.[9] Otherwise if enough detail can be provided to identify a named comparator, the employer can be ordered to do so.[10]

Hypothetical comparators

14.11   The EqA 2010 does not permit a hypothetical comparator in pay discrimination claims; instead there must a 'flesh and blood' comparator.[11] However, it is possible to rely on a hypothetical comparator in a sex discrimination (as opposed to pay discrimination) claim. The relationship between sex and pay discrimination is addressed below.[12]

Opposite sex

14.12   A comparator must be of the opposite sex to the claimant.[13]

Contractual benefits

14.13   A comparator must be receiving (or have received in the past) better contractual terms than the claimant. This is plain from the EqA 2010 s66, which describes the SEC as applying to the 'terms' of the claimant's 'work', thus referring to her contract of employment.

66 Sex equality clause

    (1) If the terms of A's work do not (by whatever means) include a sex equality clause, they are to be treated as including one.

    (2) A sex equality clause is a provision that has the following effect –

        (a) if a term of A's is less favourable to A than a corresponding term of B's is to B, A's term is modified so as not to be less favourable;

        (b) if A does not have a term which corresponds to a term of B's that benefits B, A's terms are modified so as to include such a term.

---

8   See *North Tyneside Primary Care Trust v Aynsley* EAT/489/08 at paras 3–4.
9   See paras 14.147–14.152.
10 Employment Tribunals (Constitution & Rules etc) Regulations 2004 SI No 1861 Sch 6 and Employment Tribunals (Equal Value) Rules of Procedure r5(b)(i).
11 EqA 2010 s79 defines 'comparators', with section 64(2) intended to maintain the effect of pre-existing case-law.
12 See paras 14.22–14.26.
13 EqA 2010 s64(1).

(3) Subsection (2)(a) applies to a term of A's relating to membership of or rights under an occupational pension scheme only in so far as a sex equality rule would have effect in relation to the term.

(4) In the case of work within section 65(1)(b), a reference in subsection (2) above to a term includes a reference to such terms (if any) as have not been determined by the rating of the work (as well as those that have).

14.14   The equal pay provisions in the EqA 2010 apply only to contractual terms and conditions.[14] As with the Equal Pay Act 1970,[15] the EqA 2010 applies to a wide range of terms and conditions: basic salary, overtime pay, commission payments, on-call and stand-by payments, bonuses and allowances, travel concessions, sick pay and ill-health benefits, severance and redundancy payments, training and skills development allowances, and occupational pensions.

14.15   It is not always easy to draw the distinction between contractual and non-contractual terms and conditions. The EqA 2010 contains no guidance on this distinction.

14.16   The lack of a clear distinction between contractual and non-contractual terms is particularly evident in respect of bonuses where employers often provide discretionary bonuses. The fact that a benefit is described as 'discretionary' does not mean that it is non-contractual. Evidential factors that tend to indicate that a benefit, such as a bonus, is contractual as opposed to non-contractual may include the following:

• it is paid in connection with employment, arises or is derived from the employment relationship;[16]
• it has not been withheld from anyone;[17]
• it is paid regularly eg year on year; and
• it is a progression-based pay increase or regrading, but on the facts occurs virtually automatically.[18]

14.17   An example would be an allocation of share options under the terms of an employer's discretionary share option scheme. The employer can legitimately choose to award no shares whatsoever. This will not fall within the equal pay provisions of the EqA 2010 and any claim in respect of such a scheme must be brought as a direct sex

---

14 EPC paras 28–31.
15 *Garland v British Rail Engineering Ltd* [1982] ICR 420, HL.
16 *Davies v Neath Port Talbot County Borough Council* [1999] ICR 1132, EAT.
17 *Hoyland v Asda Stores Ltd* [2006] CSIH 21, [2006] IRLR 468.
18 *Nimz v Freie und Hansestadt Hamburg* [1991] IRLR 222, CJEU and *Hall v Revenue Comrs* [1998] IRLR 466, CJEU.

discrimination claim. There must be a term in the woman's contract that can be modified or inserted to bring it into line with an equivalent term in her male comparator's contract for the equal pay provisions to apply. This will not be the case if the terms of the scheme that permits a discretionary allocation are the same for the man and the woman.[19] In short, advisers should be careful to analyse whether discretionary benefits are in practice a part of an employee's contract of employment and hence fall under the pay discrimination provisions. The claim for sex discrimination should be put in the claim form as an alternative argument available to the claimant if there is any doubt.

Non-contractual benefits

14.18   Where a claimant wishes to complain that she has been subjected to sex discrimination in relation to a non-contractual benefit, she cannot bring a claim under the pay discrimination provisions contained in the EqA 2010 but may have a claim for sex discrimination under the Act's other provisions.[20]

Term by term analysis

14.19   The exercise of comparing the contractual terms of the claimant and her comparator must be undertaken on a term-by-term basis.[21] There is no prohibition on the claimant identifying and relying on terms in the comparator's contract that are the most beneficial to her.[22]

14.20   Also the classification of terms can be a complicated exercise and one where there is scope for considerable disagreement. For example, a comparator may receive a payment that is described as being a 'productivity bonus' yet in reality it is paid automatically, which means that it is properly described as being part of the comparator's basic pay. In those circumstances, a claimant should bring a pay discrimination claim alleging that she is entitled to receive the

---

19   *Hosso v European Credit Management Ltd* [2011] EWCA Civ 1589, [2012] IRLR 235.

20   See paras 14.22–14.26.

21   *Hayward v Cammell Laird Shipbuilders Ltd* [1988] IRLR 257, HL and *Brownbill v St Helens and Knowsley Hospital NHS Trust* [2011] EWCA Civ 903, [2012] ICR 68.

22   Unless the terms are not separate but relate to the same subject matter: see *Degnan v Redcar and Cleveland Borough Council* [2005] IRLR 615, CA, approving the EAT's judgment at [2005] IRLR 179.

difference between her basic pay and the comparator's basic pay plus the incorrectly described 'productivity bonus'.[23]

14.21   By contrast, where contracts provide for higher rates of pay for unsocial hours than for hours within the normal working day, and those rates in turn differ as between the claimants and their comparators, the terms that fall to be compared are those in each contract relating to pay for unsocial hours. This is so even if the claimant's combined basic and unsocial hours pay is higher than that of her comparator. In such circumstances, the comparator might have a pay discrimination claim in connection with the term as to basic pay.[24]

Sex discrimination

14.22   The sex discrimination and pay discrimination provisions in the EqA 2010 are entirely separate and mutually exclusive; a remedy cannot be given under both regimes simultaneously.[25] They may be put in the claim form as alternatives between which the claimant must eventually make a choice.

14.23   A claimant should utilise the sex discrimination regime in the following circumstances:

- she wishes to bring a claim based on a non-contractual benefit; or
- she wishes to bring a claim based on a contractual benefit that relates to pay, her claim is for direct discrimination but her claim would fail under the pay discrimination provisions because a SEC or rule has no effect.[26]

14.24   This second category did not exist under the Equal Pay Act 1970. The Explanatory Notes suggest that this category will come into play where a claimant cannot point to an actual comparator but there is evidence that a hypothetical man would have been treated more

23   See, eg, *Degnan v Redcar and Cleveland BC* [2005] IRLR 615, CA.
24   See, eg, *Brownbill v St Helens and Knowsley Hospital NHS Trust* [2011] EWCA Civ 903, [2012] ICR 68.
25   EqA 2010 s70 provides that the relevant sex discrimination provision has no effect in relation to a term that is or would be included or modified by a sex equality clause, or (for occupational pensions only) a rule. Section 61(10) prevents any overlap between a non-discrimination rule and a sex equality rule in occupational pensions schemes. Section 71 preserves the right to bring a direct sex discrimination claim if a sex equality clause or rule would have no effect, eg, if there is no actual comparator.
26   EqA 2010 s71.

favourably, for example where an employer has said words to the effect that, 'I would pay you more if you were a man.'[27]

14.25   Claimants may also be able to use this category to bring pay discrimination claims relying upon a comparator who is a successor. The position under the pay discrimination regime is that a claimant may rely only on a comparator who is her predecessor or contemporary.[28] The new provision opens up the possibility of relying on a successor but using the sex discrimination provisions.

14.26   It is important to remember that, where a claimant brings a complaint under the sex discrimination provisions, as opposed to the pay discrimination regime, she will not be able to take advantage of some of the more generous features of the pay discrimination scheme such as the longer time-limits.[29]

Multiple comparators

14.27   There is nothing expressly preventing the claimant from choosing several comparators. It will often be advisable for her to rely on a range of different comparators when commencing a claim because:

- she will probably have little or no information about her colleagues' pay packages so choosing the most 'advantageous' comparator may be influenced partly by luck;
- the validity of a comparator might not be established until late in the litigation, for example until after equal value has been determined; and
- it may be possible for a claimant to 'cherry pick' the most advantageous male comparator in respect of each of his contractual terms.

14.28   The claimant who names more than one comparator increases her chances of a successful outcome. Claimants should avoid a 'scatter gun' or incautious approach. Reliance on an excessive number of comparators or highly speculative comparators may amount to an abuse of process.[30] Further, the less typical a chosen comparator, the more likely that a material factor defence will be successful.

14.29   To keep claims manageable, the ET may order the claimant to select the most obviously relevant representative comparators from within a class of employees named by the respondent.

---

27   Explanatory Notes paras 246 and see EPC para 63.
28   See paras 10.55–10.58.
29   See paras 14.115–14.128.
30   See Lord Bridge in *Leverton v Clwyd CC* [1989] AC 706.

Question 3: Was the comparator performing 'equal work' to the claimant at the relevant time?

14.30   A comparator must have performed 'equal work' to the claimant at the time that his terms were more favourable than the claimant's terms and conditions. There are three forms of 'equal work' as between a claimant and her comparator which are recognised by the EqA 2010:

- her work is like his work ('like work');[31]
- her work is rated as equivalent to his work under a job evaluation scheme ('rated as equivalent');[32] or
- her work is of equal value to his work ('equal value').[33]

14.31   Like work and work rated as equivalent cases use the standard tribunal rules of procedure.[34] Equal value claims use the modified rules of procedure.[35]

Like work

14.32   A claimant (A) is performing 'like work' to her comparator (B) where they are both doing the same work or, if not the same work, then work of a broadly similar nature without differences of practical importance. This definition is outlined in the EqA 2010 s65(2) and (3) as follows:

> (2) A's work is like B's work if –
>   (a) A's work and B's work are the same or broadly similar, and
>   (b) such differences as there are between their work are not of practical importance in relation to the terms of their work.
> (3) So on a comparison of one person's work with another's for the purposes of subsection (2), it is necessary to have regard to –
>   (a) the frequency with which differences between their work occur in practice, and
>   (b) the nature and extent of the differences.

14.33   This formulation is almost identical to the language used in the Equal Pay Act 1970. It is very likely that the case-law on 'like work' under the Equal Pay Act 1970 will continue to apply.

---

31   EqA 2010 s65(1)(a).
32   EqA 2010 s65(1)(b).
33   EqA 2010 s65(1)(c).
34   Employment Tribunals (Constitution & Rules) Regulations 2004 SI No 1861 Sch 1.
35   Employment Tribunals (Constitution & Rules) Regulations 2004 Sch 1 modified by Sch 6. Sch 6 prevails if there is any conflict.

14.34   The EqA 2010 contains essentially a two-stage test:[36]

- Are the claimant and her comparator actually performing work that is the same or of a broadly similar nature?
- If so, are there any differences between the work undertaken by the claimant and her comparator and do they have any practical importance in relation to their contractual terms?

14.35   The claimant must prove that she can satisfy the first limb of the test. For example, a woman and man will be performing work that is the 'same' where they are both bank cashiers at the same counter or both serving meals in the same restaurant.

14.36   In contrast a woman and man will be performing work that is 'broadly similar' where they are both shop assistants in different sections of the same department store or where a female cook prepares lunch for the directors whereas a male chef cooks breakfast and lunch for the employees in the canteen.[37]

14.37   It is for the employer to prove that any differences between the work of the claimant and the comparator are sufficiently significant so as to lead to the conclusion that there is no 'like work'.[38] Thus a female primary school administrator and a male secondary school administrator will not be performing work that is 'broadly similar' where the size of the relevant schools leads to a difference in the tasks undertaken by each individual so that he has a greater strategic and managerial role.[39]

Work rated as equivalent

14.38   A claimant (A) is performing 'worked rated as equivalent' to her comparator (B) if a job evaluation study (JES) gives an equal value to their jobs in terms of the demands made on the employees, or would have given them an equal value if the evaluation had not used a gender-specific system. This definition is contained in EqA 2010 s65(4), (5) and s80(5) as follows:

Section 65

(4) A's work is rated as equivalent to B's work if a job evaluation study –

---

36 *Shields v E Coomes (Holdings) Ltd* [1978] ICR 1559.

37 *Shields v E Coomes (Holdings) Ltd* [1978] ICR 1559. Additional examples are outlined at paras 36–37 of the EPC.

38 *Shields v E Coomes (Holdings) Ltd* [1978] ICR 1559.

39 *Morgan v Middlesbrough Borough Council* [2005] EWCA Civ 1432.

(a) gives an equal value to A's job and B's job in terms of the demands made on a worker, or

(b) would give an equal value to A's job and B's job in those terms were the evaluation not made on a sex-specific system.

(5) A system is sex-specific if, for the purposes of one or more demands made on a worker, it sets values for men different from those it sets for women.

Section 80

(6) A job evaluation study is a study undertaken with a view to evaluating, in terms of the demands made on a person by reference to factors such as effort, skill and decision-making, the jobs to be done –

(a) by some or all of the workers in an undertaking or group of undertakings ...

14.39 The EqA 2010 provides very little practical guidance in relation to identifying valid job evaluation studies. However, principles established in Equal Pay Act 1970 cases will remain good law.

14.40 Essentially, a JES will ordinarily be valid for the purposes of a pay discrimination claim where:

- it is analytical;[40]
- it is capable of impartial application;[41]
- it is primarily based on objective criteria (although some subjective measures are acceptable);[42]
- it focuses on criteria that are gender balanced rather than place over emphasis on attributes that only one sex is likely to possess;[43] and
- it has been completed and implemented.[44]

14.41 The burden of proof in demonstrating that the JES is valid rests on the party who is seeking to rely on it.[45] If the claimant is arguing that she has been rated as equivalent to her comparator she will have to prove the validity. The employer will have the burden of proving that it is valid where the employer is pursuing a defence under EqA 2010 s131(6)–(7).

---

40 *Eaton Ltd v Nutall* [1977] ICR 272, EAT and *Bromley v Quick Ltd* [1988] ICR 623, CA.
41 *Eaton Ltd v Nutall* [1977] ICR 272, EAT.
42 *Bromley v Quick Ltd* [1988] ICR 623, CA.
43 *Rummler v Dato-Druck GmbH* [1987] ICR 774.
44 *Arnold v Beecham Group Ltd* [1982] ICR 744, CJEU and *O'Brien v Sim-Chem Ltd* [1980] ICR 573, CJEU.
45 *Bromley v Quick Ltd* [1988] ICR 623, CA.

14.42   A claimant is rated as equivalent to her comparator where she receives the same or a higher score than him under a JES.[46]

Equal value

14.43 A claimant (A) is performing work which is of equal value to her comparator (B) where she is performing a different job to him but an assessment of the demands imposed on A and B in terms of factors such as effort, skill and decision-making reveal that A's work should be weighed as being the same or of greater value than B's work.

14.44   A claimant may only bring an equal value claim where she is not able to rely on the 'like work' or 'rated as equivalent' provisions outlined above.[47]

14.45   The definition of 'equal value' is contained in EqA 2010 s65(6) as follows:

> (6) A's work is of equal value to B's work if it is –
>> (a) neither like B's work nor rated as equivalent to B's work, but
>> (b) nevertheless equal to B's work in terms of the demands made on A by reference to factors such as effort, skill and decision-making.

14.46 The EPC also suggests that it would be appropriate to examine additional factors such as the nature of the work performed, the training or skills necessary to do the job, the conditions of work and/or the decision-making that is part of the role.[48] Usefully, the EHRC and the British Chambers of Commerce have also produced joint guidance to help small and medium-sized businesses to estimate whether different jobs are of equal value.[49]

14.47   If there is a JES in relation to the work involved already in existence, and the study finds that the claimant's work is not of equal value to the work of the comparator, the ET is required to come to the same decision unless it has a good reason to suspect that the study is discriminatory or unreliable.[50] If the study is not discriminatory or unreliable, the ET must strike out the equal value claim at the stage 1 equal value hearing.[51]

---

46 *Redcar and Cleveland Borough Council v Bainbridge* [2007] EWCA Civ 929, [2008] ICR 238.
47 EqA 2010 s65(6)
48 See EPC para 47.
49 Available at www.equalityhumanrights.com.
50 EqA 2010 s131(6)–(7).
51 EqA 2010 s131(6)–(7) and Employment Tribunals (Constitution & Rules) Regulations 2004 Sch 6 r4(3)(a).

Assessment of equal value

14.48   In assessing whether work is of equal value, the EqA 2010 describes the task to be undertaken by the ET.

14.49   There are very detailed procedural rules that are intended to assist the parties establish whether the claimant and her comparator are performing work of equal value. ETs are given specific powers to make orders in equal value cases in order to enable robust case management and to try and get the claims heard within a reasonable time.[52] Schedule 6 to the ET rules includes an indicative timetable for equal value proceedings.[53] The second flowchart[54] is based on that timetable and on the standard directions. ETs can depart from the standard directions.

Use of expert evidence

14.50   The EqA 2010 gives the ET the power to require an independent expert, designated by the ACAS, to prepare a report on the question of whether the demands, work tasks, skills of the claimant and comparator are of equal value. Unless the ET withdraws its request for a report it must wait for the expert's report before deciding whether the work is of equal value.[55]

14.51   Parties do still continue to instruct their own experts in order to challenge the findings made by the independent expert. It is not an open-ended right and the party expert's evidence must be based on the facts (as agreed or as found by the ET) relating to the question of whether the claimant's work is of equal value to that of the comparator.[56]

14.52   In *Middlesbrough Borough Council v Surtees (No 2)*[57] the EAT held that a party expert may challenge the independent expert's methodology or arithmetic if there is no challenge made to the facts found by the ET or as agreed by the parties. Significantly, the EAT acknowledged the fact that there are a variety of methodologies that may be

---

52 See Employment Tribunals (Constitution & Rules) Regulations 2004 SI No 1861 Sch 6. These rules also applied to the Equal Pay Act 1970.

53 Rule 5 gives the standard orders that may be made at a stage 1 equal value hearing; rule 4 deals with its conduct. Rule 8 gives the standard orders that may be made at a stage 2 equal value hearing; rule 7 deals with its conduct.

54 Flowchart 2 in 'Practical points' below.

55 EqA 2010 s131(1)–(5); and see Explanatory Notes paras 428–31.

56 Employment Tribunals (Constitution & Rules) Regulations 2004 Sch 6 r11(4).

57 [2008] ICR 349, [2007] IRLR 981.

applied by experts to evaluate jobs. In other words, there is always ground for disagreement.

14.53   In some cases, it may be possible to argue that there is no need to go through the time-consuming process of appointing an independent expert at all. A particular example is where a claim is brought in respect of a period prior to a JES, where the claimant and comparator jobs have subsequently been assessed as equal under the study. If it is agreed that the jobs have remained unchanged since before the study, this may be sufficient evidence of equal value prior to the evaluation.

14.54   However, caution is needed because most large JESs give each job a points score that will then fall within one of a number of broad bands. In such cases, the mere fact that a claimant's job has been placed in the same band as her comparator's will not in itself show that the jobs are of equal value. Even where there is only a small difference in the points awarded to the two roles, that will not necessarily be sufficient to demonstrate equal value. If, however, the claimant's job received a higher points score than her comparator's, that may well be a good indication of prior equal value, assuming that there are no factors particular to the evaluation that undermine such a conclusion.[58]

Question 4: Was the comparator employed contemporaneously to the claimant or prior to her employment at the relevant time?

14.55   At the time that the comparator was in receipt of more favourable terms and conditions than the claimant, he must have performed 'equal work' either:

- contemporaneously to the claimant;[59] or
- prior to the start of the claimant doing the work in respect of which she claims[60]

14.56   The EqA 2010 does not contain any additional detail concerning the practical implications of relying on a comparator who is a predeces-

---

58 See for guidance on this point *Hovell v Ashford and St Peter's Hospitals NHS Trust* [2009] EWCA Civ 670, [2009] ICR 1545 at paras 31–41.
59 EqA 2010 s64(1).
60 EqA 2010 s64(2). This provision did not appear in the Equal Pay Act 1970 and its inclusion in EqA 2010 reflects and is inspired by the position established by the ECJ in *Macarthys v Smith* [1980] ICR 672.

sor to the claimant. However, the case-law under the Equal Pay Act 1970 remains good law and assists:

- There is no limit on how far into the past a claimant may go to identify her chosen comparator. There is a time-limit on the amount of back pay that may be awarded but no limit on the period over which comparison may be made.[61]
- The comparison of the comparator's terms must be limited to those terms that he enjoyed at the termination of his doing the relevant work. There is no scope for attempting to ascertain the likely pay rises which he would have received subsequent to the date of his departure.[62]

14.57 There may be practical difficulties in relation to the ability to compare a claimant's terms with the terms enjoyed by her comparator if he was employed on that work a long time ago. For example the quality of available pay information may be poor, and inflationary or other increases are likely to have diminished any pay differential. So it is always advisable to select comparators who have been contemporaneously employed with the claimant for as long as possible.

14.58 There is nothing in the EqA 2010 which suggests that claimants may not rely on a successor as a comparator. The position under the Equal Pay Act 1970 was explained in *Walton Centre for Neurology and Neuro Surgery NHS Trust v Bewley*.[63] The EAT held that it was invalid for a claimant to rely on a comparator who was her successor under the Equal Pay Act 1970 or Article 157. If this remains the position under the EqA 2010 in respect of pay discrimination EqA 2010 s71 may give scope for a sex discrimination claim.[64]

Question 5: Were the claimant and comparator engaged in the 'same employment' at the relevant time?

14.59 Under the Equal Pay Act 1970, a claimant could only rely on a comparator if they were engaged in the 'same employment'. The phrase 'same employment' does not appear in the EqA 2010. However, the

61 *Kells v Pilkington* [2002] IRLR 693, EAT.
62 *Walton Centre for Neurology and Neuro Surgery NHS Trust v Bewley* [2008] ICR 1047, EAT.
63 [2008] ICR 1047, EAT.
64 See para 14.25. We take the view that s64(2) does not allow a successor comparator due to the prior case-law. However, the wording suggests it is possible to rely on a successor comparator. This would represent a step beyond the current understanding of EU law but is arguable.

definition of a valid comparator in section 79(2)–(4) mirrors the definition of 'same employment' contained in the Equal Pay Act 1970 as interpreted in *Lawson v Britfish Ltd*.[65]

14.60   The requirements of EqA 2010 s79 are as follows:

(2) If A is employed, B is a comparator if subsection (3) or (4) applies.

(3) This subsection applies if –

(a) B is employed by A's employer or by an associate of A's employer,

(b) A and B work at the same establishment.

(4) This subsection applies if –

(a) B is employed by A's employer or by an associate of A's employer,

(b) B works at an establishment other than the one at which A works, and

(c) common terms apply at the establishments (either generally or as between A and B).

14.61   So, at the time that the claimant and comparator were engaged in 'equal work' and he was receiving more favourable contractual pay, the following conditions must be satisfied:

• the claimant and comparator are employed by the same employer or by associated employers; and

• the claimant and comparator both work at the same establishment; or

• they work at different establishments but where common terms and conditions are observed.

Identical employer

14.62   'Employer' is not defined under the EqA 2010 for the purposes of establishing whether a claimant and her comparator have the identical employer. Similarly, no definition was contained in the Equal Pay Act 1970. However, in practice, it is unlikely to cause any significant practical problems.

Associated employers

14.63   The EqA 2010 stipulates that two employers, X and Y, will be associated where either X or Y has direct or indirect control of the other or both X and Y are directly or indirectly controlled by a third party.[66]

---

65 [1987] ICR 726, [1988] IRLR 53, EAT.
66 EqA 2010 s79(9) and EPC para 51.

Same establishment

14.64   The EqA 2010 does not contain a definition of 'same establishment'. Similarly, no definition was contained in the Equal Pay Act 1970 and it is a point that had been tested very little by the courts until the recent case of *City of Edinburgh Council v Wilkinson*.[67]

14.65   The EAT decision in that case, which advocated a broad approach towards the definition of 'same establishment' so as to ensure that pay discrimination claims were not made excessively difficult to pursue,[68] has now been overruled in Scotland by the Court of Session.[69] The Court of Session rejected the EAT's statement that there is a presumption that a single undertaking, such as a local council, is a single establishment unless there is evidence that rebuts this presumption and leads to the conclusion that the undertaking should be conceptually divided into separate constituent parts such as departments. The court held instead that the term 'establishment' is largely directed to the place of work, by which it did not mean an individual place of work such as a room or even necessarily a building, but the broader notion of a complex or group of buildings considered as a whole. Examples would include a university campus, or a school.

14.66   *Wilkinson* was decided under the Equal Pay Act 1970, but it seems likely that this approach will continue to apply under the EqA 2010.

14.67   The EqA 2010 does recognise the difficulties that the notion of 'same establishment' may pose for mobile workers. Accordingly, at section 80(3) it is stated that, 'If work is not done at an establishment, it is to be treated as done at the establishment with which it has the closest connection'. No definition of the term 'closest connection' is provided within the EqA 2010 and the matter is not addressed in the EPC. Moreover, there is no equivalent provision in the Equal Pay Act 1970 to assist with the interpretation of the new section.

14.68   It is suggested that in practice the ET is likely to focus on the following factors when determining which 'establishment' should be relied upon for the purposes of EqA 2010 s79(3) and (4):

- time spent at the alleged establishment and other work bases;
- location of direct management;
- location of any resources or support provided to the claimant or comparator eg secretarial services, storage for materials/tools;
- location of payroll services.

67 [2010] IRLR 756, [2011] CSIH 70, [2012] IRLR 202.
68 EATS/0002/09, [2010] IRLR 756 at paras 61–63 and 68–69.
69 [2011] CSIH 70, [2012] IRLR 202.

14.69   So for example, it is likely that a human resources manager will be employed at an office in Birmingham where she spends the majority of the week visiting her employer's branches all over the United Kingdom, but her line manager and secretarial support is based in Birmingham.

Common terms and conditions

14.70   The EqA 2010 does not contain a definition of 'common terms and conditions' but the concept was explored extensively under the Equal Pay Act 1970. This contains similar language to the EqA 2010. There it was held that there are 'common terms and conditions' in each of the following scenarios:

- terms and conditions governed by the same collective agreement and applied generally at the establishments of the claimant and her comparator or specifically to the claimant and her comparator.[70]
- broad similarity between the terms and conditions of the claimant and her comparator or those applied generally at their establishments.[71]

14.71   Two Scottish judgments of Lady Smith in *Dumfries and Galloway v North*[72] and *City of Edinburgh Council v Wilkinson*[73] have proved controversial on this issue. In *North*, she held that the 'common terms and conditions' test required there to be a 'real possibility' that the comparator could be employed in his job at the claimant's establishment. However, she subsequently accepted in *Wilkinson* that her analysis in *North* was wrong, holding that it would be sufficient to show that members of the comparator group are always employed on the same terms and conditions, wherever they work. The Court of Session in *North* agreed with this analysis.[74]

14.72   In Scotland a further layer of complexity has been added to the test by the decisions of the Court of Session in *North* and in *Wilkinson*.[75] In *Wilkinson*, Lord Eassie held that it is not appropriate to consider, in determining the 'common terms and conditions' issue, whether a comparator hypothetically transferred to the claimant's

---

70   *Leverton v Clwyd CC* [1989] AC 706, HL.
71   *British Coal Corporation v Smith* [1996] ICR 515, HL.
72   [2009] ICR 1352, EAT.
73   [2010] IRLR 756, EAT at para 75.
74   [2011] CSIH 2, [2011] SC 372, [2011] IRLR 239 at para 39.
75   [2011] CSIH 70, [2012] IRLR 202.

establishment might undergo adjustments in his terms and conditions in accordance with the practices at that establishment. By contrast, both Lady Paton and Lord Hardie took the view that this question should form part of the practical circumstances to be considered by the ET. Their approach would mean that an ET might need to analyse whether, for example, a gardener transferred to work at a school would be employed on different terms eg hours or holidays. This point remains unresolved as, on the facts, it did not have to be determined to reach a decision in *Wilkinson*.

14.73   There is no support for the view[76] that the slightly different wording contained in the Act, which refers to 'common terms and conditions ... either generally or as between A and B', may be narrower than that under Equal Pay Act 1970 s1(6), which requires 'common terms and conditions' to be observed 'either generally or for employees of the relevant classes'. Neither the Explanatory Notes, nor the EPC[77] support this view, suggesting that the Equal Pay Act 1970 analysis will continue to apply.

14.74   Where a claimant is able to satisfy the conditions of 'same employment', the claim will proceed to Question 7 below.

14.75   However, if the above conditions are not satisfied, the claimant cannot bring a claim under the pay discrimination provisions in the EqA 2010 alone and should try to bring a claim under the Act as interpreted in light of Article 157. The conditions that must be satisfied for this type of claim are considered at Question 6 below.

Question 6: Is there a 'single source' for the terms and conditions of the claimant and her comparator?

14.76   There will be a category of claimants who are not able to satisfy the test of 'same employment' explored in Question 5 above with respect to their preferred comparator:

- a claimant who wants to rely on a comparator who is employed by her employer, but at a different establishment and on very different terms and conditions; or
- a claimant who wants to rely on a comparator who is employed by a different employer.

14.77   These may still bring a claim under the EqA 2010 but only by relying on the wider ambit of Article 157. To do this, the claimant must

---

76 For example, Michael Rubenstein; see IRLR Highlights [2012] IRLR 177.
77 EPC para 55.

show that there is a single source for the terms and conditions of the comparator and her. This 'single source' test applies only to claims reliant on Article 157. Claims brought solely under the EqA 2010 do not need to satisfy this requirement.

14.78   Such a 'single source' will exist where there is a common 'body' that is responsible for the inequality in their pay.[78]

14.79   In most cases, the 'single source' will be the employer of both the claimant and comparator although it may be possible to bring claims as between separate employing bodies. In respect of this second category, the following guidance is provided by the EPC[79] which is based on the facts in *South Ayrshire Council v Morton*:[80]

> A woman teacher can compare herself to a man employed by a different education authority where the difference in their pay is due to terms and conditions set by a national scheme and can be remedied by a national negotiating body.

14.80   In reality, the situations in which a 'single source' will exist as between different employers will be rare.

14.81   If a 'single source' does exist, the claimant's claim will proceed to Question 7. Otherwise, the claim will fail.

Question 7: Breach of the sex equality clause

14.82   Once a claimant has satisfied Questions 1–4 and either 5 or 6 in a pay discrimination claim, she will have established that there has been a breach of the SEC.

14.83   The SEC is the cornerstone provision by which the terms of the claimant's contract will be modified so as to ensure that her terms are no less favourable than the terms enjoyed by her comparator.[81] Where the comparator benefits from a term that is not available to the claimant, the effect of the SEC is to include such a term in the claimant's contract of employment. The pay discrimination provisions in the EqA 2010 provide a contractual remedy to a claimant by altering her contract of employment on a permanent basis.

---

78 *Lawrence v Regent Office Care Ltd* [1999] ICR 654; *South Ayrshire Council v Morton* [2002] ICR 956; *Robertson v DEFRA* [2005] ICR 750; *Allonby v Accrington and Rossendale College* [2004] ICR 1328; *Armstrong v Newcastle Upon Tyne NHS Hospital Trust* [2006] IRLR 124; *Potter v North Cumbria Acute NHS Trust* [2009] IRLR 176; *City of Edinburgh Council v Wilkinson* UKEAT/0002/09 and *Beddoes and others v Birmingham City Council* UKEAT/0037/43.

79 EPC para 57.

80 [2002] ICR 956, CS.

81 EqA 2010 s66.

14.84 Notwithstanding a breach of the SEC, an employer may still defeat a pay discrimination claim if there is a valid 'material factor' defence (Question 8).

Question 8: Is there a valid 'material factor' defence?

14.85 An employer will defeat a pay discrimination claim based on a breach of a SEC where there is a valid 'material factor' defence.[82]

14.86 Although the language is very different to the Equal Pay Act 1970's 'genuine material factor' defence, the new section 69 is intended to codify and clarify the old 'genuine material factor' defence.[83] On that basis the case-law developed under the Equal Pay Act 1970 will apply.

14.87 EqA 2010 s69 states:

(1) The sex equality clause in A's terms has no effect in relation to a difference between A's terms and B's terms if the responsible person shows that the difference is because of a material factor reliance on which –
  (a) does not involve treating A less favourably because of A's sex than the responsible person treats B, and
  (b) if the factor is within subsection (2), is a proportionate means of achieving a legitimate aim.
(2) A factor is within this subsection if A shows that, as a result of the factor, A and persons of the same sex doing equal work to A's are put at a particular disadvantage when compared with persons of the opposite sex doing work equal to A's.
(3) For the purposes of subsection (1), the long-term objective of reducing inequality between men's and women's terms of work is always to be regarded as a legitimate aim.
  ...
(6) For the purposes of this section, a factor is not material unless it is a material difference between A's case and B's case.

14.88 'Responsible person' is not spelt out explicitly in the EqA 2010 for section 69. However, in keeping with the Equal Pay Act 1970, it is suggested that it is intended to be a reference to A's employer.[84]

14.89 The 'material factor' defence set out in the EqA 2010 can be reduced to the issues raised in the analysis outlined below.

---

82 Set out in EA 2010 s69.
83 Explanatory Notes paras 236–40. This also explains that the adverb 'genuine' has been abandoned as it added no meaning to the nature of the defence.
84 The EPC appears to assume this: EPC paras 75–90.

Question 8A: Can the claimant's employer demonstrate that there is a material reason or 'factor' that explains the difference between the terms enjoyed by the claimant and her comparator?

14.90   The employer must prove that there is a 'factor' or explanation which accounts for the differential in pay.[85] This must be the actual reason or cause for the differential and it must be sufficient to explain the difference between the terms applied to the comparator as opposed to the claimant.[86] Moreover, it must provide an explanation for the entire time period under consideration.[87]

14.91   The EPC stresses that employers will be required to provide cogent evidence of the 'factor' relied upon and the extent to which it contributed to the difference between the claimant and her comparator.[88]

14.92   If the employer cannot prove that there is an explanation for the difference in the terms applied to the claimant and her comparator, it will not be able to rely on the 'material factor' defence and the claim will succeed.

14.93   The claimant's employer must also prove that the factor relied upon is 'material'.[89] That is, it must be significant and relevant.[90] If the employer cannot prove that the factor is material, it will not be able to rely on the 'material factor' defence and the claim will succeed.

14.94   The EPC stresses that whether the defence is established depends on the circumstances of the particular case,[91] but it gives examples of the type of explanation that may be material factors:

- personal differences between workers such as experience and qualifications;
- geographical differences, such as a location weighting;
- unsocial hours, rotating shifts, and night working.[92]

85 EqA 2010 s69(1)
86 *Glasgow City Council v Marshall* [2000] ICR 196, HL.
87 *Benveniste v University of Southampton* [1989] ICR 617, CA.
88 EPC para 76.
89 EqA 2010 s69(6).
90 *Glasgow City Council v Marshall* [2000] ICR 196 and EPC para 76.
91 EPC para 78.
92 EPC para 77.

Question 8B: Can the claimant's employer demonstrate that the factor is not tainted by direct sex discrimination?

14.95   The employer must show that the factor is not tainted by direct sex discrimination.[93] So the reason for the difference in the terms of the claimant and her comparator must not be because she is a woman and he is a man. If the factor is directly discriminatory on the grounds of sex then the 'material factor' defence must fail and the claim will succeed. The EPC gives the example of a tainted factor: a bank pays maintenance men more than administrators because men are perceived to be the breadwinners.[94]

Question 8C: Can the claimant demonstrate that the factor creates a disparate impact on her and similarly placed women?

14.96   At this stage, the burden of proof shifts back to the claimant to demonstrate that, while the factor is not directly discriminatory, it does place her (and other women doing 'equal work' to her) at a particular disadvantage when compared with men doing 'equal work' to her.[95] In other words, the claimant is given the opportunity to show that the factor creates a disparate impact along the lines of gender.

14.97   There are a number of different ways in which a factor will be shown to have a disparate impact on the claimant and similarly placed women:

- The employer has implemented a provision, criterion or practice (PCP) which applies to men and women but which places women at a particular disadvantage. For example, an employer provides a higher hourly rate for full-time employees in circumstances where most part-time employees are female.[96]
- There is valid statistical evidence that demonstrates that two groups of employees undertaking equal work receive different terms and conditions and there is a sufficiently substantial disparity in the gender breakdown of the two groups to indicate that the difference in pay is tainted by sex.[97]

93   EqA 2010 s69(1)(a).
94   EPC para 82.
95   EqA 2010 s69(2) and *Nelson v Carillion Services Ltd* [2003] ICR 1256.
96   This type of discrimination is discussed extensively in chapter 3.
97   *Enderby v Frenchay Health Authority* [1994] ICR 112, CJEU; *Bailey v Home Office* [2005] EWCA Civ 327, [2005] ICR 1057 and *Grundy v British Airways (No 1)* [2008] EWCA Civ 875, [2008] IRLR 74.

- The employer has implemented a pay system that lacks transparency but that leads, on average, to women earning less than men in respect of a relatively large number of employees.[98]
- The explanation for the pay differential is attributable to historical sex discrimination. For example, the employer has implemented pay protection or 'red circling' in order to compensate individuals for the loss of discriminatory pay.[99]

14.98   If the claimant can demonstrate that there is disparate impact in relation to the factor that explains the pay differential, the burden of proof shifts back to the employer to answer Questions 8D and 8E below.

14.99   However, if the claimant cannot prove disparate impact then there will be no evidence that the pay differential is tainted by discrimination and the employer will have a valid 'material factor' defence and there is no need to consider Questions 8D and 8E. The claim is defeated by the defence in these circumstances.

Question 8D: Can the claimant's employer demonstrate that the factor is gender-neutral notwithstanding the evidence of disparate impact?

14.100 At this point, the employer has the opportunity to prove that even if there is disparate impact on the claimant and similarly placed women (Question 8C above), the factor is actually wholly free from any sex discrimination.

14.101 This part of the defence is derived from the judgments of the Court of Appeal in *Gibson v Sheffield City Council*[100] and *Armstrong v Newcastle upon Tyne NHS Trust*[101] and not from the EqA 2010. Moreover these cases do not speak with one voice and do not sit comfortably with all of the case-law in this area, such as *Brunnhofer v Bank Der Osterrichischen Postparkasse AG*,[102] *Glasgow City Council v Marshall*[103] and *Enderby v Frenchay Health Authority and Secretary of*

---

98 *Handels-og Kontorfunktionaerernes Forbund I Danmark v Dansk Arbejdsgiverforening* ('Danfoss') [1989] ECR 3199, CJEU.

99 *Redcar & Cleveland Borough Council v Bainbridge* [2008] EWCA Civ 885, [2009] ICR 133, [2008] IRLR 776.

100 [2010] EWCA Civ 63, [2010] ICR 708, [2010] IRLR 311.

101 [2005] EWCA Civ 1608, [2006] IRLR 124.

102 [2001] ECR I-4961, [2001] IRLR 571, CJEU.

103 [2000] ICR 196, HL.

State for Health.[104] However, in practice the ET is, we suggest, likely
to adopt the approach proposed here.[105]

14.102   Where there is evidence that demonstrates that there is disparate
impact on one gender it will be rare for an employer to be able to
demonstrate that a factor is wholly unrelated to gender.[106] This is particularly so if the disparate impact has continued for a long period.[107]
However, if the employer can prove a wholly non-discriminatory
explanation for the disparate impact, it will have a valid 'material factor' defence and the claim will be defeated.

14.103   If the employer cannot prove that there is a wholly non-discriminatory explanation for the disparate impact which the factor has on
women, the analysis moves to consider Question 8E.

Question 8E: Can the claimant's employer demonstrate that the factor is a proportionate means of achieving a legitimate aim?

14.104   The employer must prove that the factor is a proportionate (ie appropriate and necessary) means of achieving a legitimate aim.[108] In other
words, the employer will be obliged to show that it can objectively
justify the pay differential notwithstanding the disparate adverse
impact on the claimant and similarly placed women.

Legitimate aim

14.105   The employer must demonstrate that there was a legitimate aim that
led to the implementation of the pay practice at the heart of the pay
discrimination claim. The employer cannot rely on aims that are discriminatory[109] and the validity of a legitimate aim will be dependent
upon the surrounding circumstances. Thus if an employer can show
that the only way to ensure adequate staffing of unsocial hours shifts

104 [1994] ICR 112, CJEU.
105 It is consistent with the thrust of *Gibson* (CA), and with EAT discussion in its
postscript in *Newcastle upon Tyne Hospitals NHS Foundation Trust v Armstrong*
UKEAT/69/09, [2010] ICR 674 at paras 66–73.
106 *Redcar & Cleveland Borough Council v Bainbridge* [2008] EWCA Civ 885, [2009]
ICR 133, [2008] IRLR 776; *Coventry CC v Nicholls* [2009] IRLR 345, EAT and
Gibson v Sheffield City Council [2010] IRLR 311 and see also, in cases where
claimants can point to a PCP, *Cooksey v Trafford BC* UKEAT/0255/11, [2012]
EqLR 744 at para 97.
107 *Gibson v Sheffield City Council* [2010] ICR 708 para 71 per Smith LJ.
108 EqA 2010 s69(1)(b).
109 *R v Secretary of State for Employment ex p EOC* [1995] 1 AC 1, [1994] ICR 317, HL.

is to pay a shift premium, then even if there is evidence that more men than women work those shifts and receive the extra payments, the material factor defence may succeed.[110]

14.106   In contrast, suppose a firm of accountants structures employees' pay on the basis of success in building client relationships. It uses as one of the key indicators of that success the number of functions attended out of hours. Due to childcare responsibilities, fewer women than men can participate in these functions and women's pay is much lower. The firm cannot show that attendance at these functions produces better client relationships or other business outcomes that warrant the pay premium, taking into account the disadvantage to women. It is unlikely in these circumstances to be able to justify the payment.[111]

14.107   Section 69(3) of the Act explicitly states that the long-term objective of reducing inequality between men's and women's terms of work is always to be regarded as a legitimate aim. This provision will apply where employers introduce pay protection or 'red circling' in order to 'soften the blow' of introducing new pay schemes which lead to a decrease in the pay of male-dominated jobs so as to ensure equality in pay going forward. A similar scheme was considered in *Redcar & Cleveland BC v Bainbridge*[112] and more recently in *Bury Metropolitan BC v Hamilton; Council of the City of Sunderland v Brennan*.[113]

Proportionate means

14.108   The employer must also demonstrate that the pay practice is a proportionate means of achieving the legitimate aim. In order to satisfy this test, the employer must show that all of the following conditions apply:[114]

- the pay practice corresponds to a real need on the part of the employer;
- it is appropriate with a view to achieving the objective pursued; and
- it is reasonably necessary to achieve that objective.

---

110 EPC para 87.
111 EPC para 87.
112 [2008] EWCA Civ 885, [2009] ICR 133, [2008] IRLR 776.
113 [2011] ICR 655 upheld in [2012] EWCA Civ 413, [2012] ICR 1216.
114 *Bilka-Kaufhaus GmbH v Weber von Hartz* [1987] ICR 110, CJEU as interpreted in *Hardys and Hanson plc v Lax* [2005] EWCA Civ 846, [2005] ICR 1565 and *Homer v Chief Constable of West Yorkshire Police* [2012] UKSC 15, [2012] ICR 704, [2012] IRLR 601.

14.109   The strong emphasis on the European definition of proportionality in the speeches in *Homer* should result in greater scrutiny of employers' actions than may have been the case under the old 'objective justification' test; see further paras 3.121–3.145 above.

14.110   Some examples where employers previously have been successful in the former test of objective justification are as follows:[115]

- **Market forces**: An employer may be able to show that in order to attract or maintain employees, it is necessary to pay them a premium provided that the market itself is not sex tainted.[116]

- **Separate collective bargaining process**: An employer may be able to demonstrate that the difference in terms and conditions arises due to different negotiating processes for separate jobs. However, this defence will be unlikely to succeed where the negotiating structure is divided along gender lines and has the effect of prolonging differences between men and women.[117]

- **Length of service**: An employer may successfully argue that a difference in terms and conditions arises from a need to reward length of service.[118]

- **Shift payments**: An employer may be able to show that payments made on account of special shifts and shifts worked at unsocial hours will be a valid defence to a pay discrimination claim.[119]

- **Pay protection**: A carefully constructed pay protection scheme may constitute a valid defence.[120]

115 Cases decided under the former test should be regarded with some care. The more stringent approach now required by the EqA 2010 and *Homer* could lead to a different outcome.

116 *Rainey v Greater Glasgow Health Board* [1987] IRLR 26, HL. Two examples of cases where the market forces defence was unsuccessful because the market relied upon was found to be sex-tainted are: *Ratcliffe v North Yorkshire* [1995] ICR 833, HL and *Newcastle NHS Hospital Trust v Armstrong* [2010] ICR 674, EAT. The most recent analysis in *Armstrong* is to the effect that the employer must have known that the work in question was 'women's work', and have been willing to take advantage of that fact if an otherwise valid market forces defence is to be defeated on grounds of sex taint. This position is controversial and is likely to be tested again in the near future.

117 *Redcar & Cleveland Borough Council v Bainbridge* [2008] EWCA Civ 885, [2009] ICR 133 and *British Airways v Grundy (No 2)* [2008] EWCA Civ 875, [2008] IRLR 815.

118 *Cadman v HSE* [2004] EWCA Civ 137, [2005] ICR 1546, [2006] ICR 1623 and *Wilson v HSE* [2009] EWCA Civ 1074, [2010] ICR 302.

119 *Blackburn v Chief Constable of West Midlands Police* [2008] EWCA Civ 1208, [2009] IRLR 135.

120 *Redcar & Cleveland Borough Council v Bainbridge* [2008] EWCA Civ 885, [2009] ICR 133 and see *Haq v Audit Commission* [2012] EWCA Civ 1621, [2013] EqLR 130.

- **TUPE transfer**: A pay differential arising out of the obligatory protection of the comparator's terms and conditions following a transfer to which the Transfer of Undertakings (Protection of Employment) Regulations 2006 is likely to be defensible.[121]
- **Productivity**: A properly monitored genuine productivity bonus scheme will probably be a valid defence.[122]

14.111   If the employer is able to demonstrate that the sex-tainted pay differential can be objectively justified, it will have a valid 'material factor' defence. Otherwise, the claimant's pay discrimination claim will succeed.

Exclusions

14.112   There are exceptions to the applicability of the pay discrimination regime.[123] These can be summarised as follows:

- A SEC will not operate on any terms of employment that are governed by law regulating the employment of women.[124] This exclusion also existed in the Equal Pay Act 1970 and was designed to prevent men from asserting the equality clause in order to claim the same protection as was afforded to women under special legislation such as health and safety provisions.[125]
- A SEC will not have effect on terms giving special treatment to women in connection with pregnancy or childbirth.[126]

Jurisdiction of the courts

14.113   A pay discrimination complaint can be determined in either the ET or the civil courts.[127] The ET may also make a declaration as to the

---

121   SI No 246, see *Skills Development Scotland Co Ltd v Buchanan* UKEATS/0042/10, [2011] EqLR 955, 25 May 2011.
122   *Redcar & Cleveland Borough Council v Bainbridge and Others* [2008] EWCA Civ 929, [2008] ICR 249.
123   EqA 2010 Sch 7 Part 1.
124   This is also the case with the maternity equality clause discussed at paras 7.20–7.21 above.
125   Explanatory Notes para 785 and EqA 2010 Sch 7 Part 1.
126   Discussed at paras 7.20–7.23 above.
127   EqA 2010 s127(1)–(2) and (9).

rights and obligations of an employee and her employer.[128] In practice, it will usually be preferable to commence proceedings in the ET for the following reasons:

- Employment judges have extensive experience in the employment field, which makes them best suited to adjudicate upon complex equal pay claims.
- The costs regime is far more onerous in the civil courts.
- The civil courts may strike out a complaint relating to a breach of the SEC if it is considered that it could more conveniently have been addressed by the ET.[129]
- The civil courts may refer (or ask a party to refer) any question that arises in relation to an equality clause to the ET for it to determine and stay the main proceedings in the meantime.[130]

14.114   It may be advisable to launch proceedings in the civil courts in order to pursue a complaint that would otherwise be time-barred in an ET as the stringent time-limits[131] do not apply to civil claims, which are governed by the generous time-imits applicable to breach of contract claims. The Supreme Court has recently held that in such circumstances, a claim brought in the civil court should not generally be struck out on the basis that it could more conveniently have been addressed by the ET.[132]

Time-limits

14.115   A pay discrimination complaint may not be presented to an ET 'after the end of the qualifying period'.[133] The EqA 2010 contains a series of different qualifying periods depending on the circumstances surrounding each complaint.[134]

---

128 EqA 2010 s127(3); the civil court can declare the terms of the contract in any event.
129 EqA 2010 s128(1).
130 EqA 2010 s128(2).
131 Outlined below at paras 14.115–14.128.
132 *Abdulla v Birmingham City Council* [2012] UKSC 47, [2013] 1 All ER 649, [2012] ICR 1419.
133 EqA 2010 s129(2).
134 EqA 2010 s129(3).

Standard cases (six months from last day of employment)

14.116   A standard case is a case which is not one of the following:[135]
- a stable work case,[136]
- a concealment case,[137]
- an incapacity case[138] or
- a combined concealment and incapacity case.[139]

In practice, the vast majority of pay discrimination cases will fall into the standard category.

14.117   A complaint must be lodged before six months beginning with the last day of the claimant's employment; that is, employment under the contract of employment that contains the SEC that is relied on as part of the pay discrimination claim. It follows that time starts to run from the termination of the contract and not simply the ending of a particular 'job'.[140]

14.118   Claimants need to know about the possibility that significant changes in the terms of a contract could amount to the rescission/termination of the contract, which could have the effect of triggering the time-limits.[141] In this context it is also important to remember that, where a claimant's employment is transferred under TUPE, time will begin to run from the date of the transfer in respect of any equal pay claim relating to the pre-transfer period (although the claim should be brought against the transferee).[142]

Stable work cases (six months from end of stable working relationship)

14.119   A stable work case will exist where the pay discrimination claim relates to a period when the claimant was in a stable working relationship with her employer.[143] The EqA 2010 does not contain a definition of a 'stable working relationship'. However, based on the cases

---

135   EqA 2010 s130(2).
136   See paras 14.119–14.121.
137   See paras 14.122–14.123.
138   See paras 14.124–14.126.
139   See paras 14.127–14.128.
140   *National Power plc v Young* [2001] ICR 328, [2001] IRLR 32, CA and *Preston v Wolverhampton Healthcare NHS Trust* [2001] UKHL 5, [2001] ICR 217.
141   *Slack v Cumbria CC* [2009] EWCA Civ 293, [2009] IRLR 463.
142   *Sodexo Ltd v Gutridge* [2009] EWCA Civ 729, [2009] ICR 1486.
143   EqA 2010 s130(3).

that considered a similar provision in the Equal Pay Act 1970, it is likely to refer to a situation where an employee is employed by the same employer on a succession of contracts due to the nature of the work, the employer's requirements or a minor change in terms and conditions that leads to the issuing of a new contract. Breaks between the contracts, say, for school vacations,[144] and no breaks at all[145] are unlikely to disturb the stability of the working relationship. A complaint must be lodged before six months beginning with the day on which the stable working relationship ended.

14.120   The EPC explains that whether it is a stable work case will depend on the facts.[146] It gives examples of facts that would or would not mark the end of a stable working relationship. Thus, for example, where a woman is on a series of contracts in what is essentially the same job (for example a teaching assistant on a series of annual contracts) or a progression within the same job (for example an administrative assistant who progresses to administrative officer), time will not start to run with the issue of a new contract.

14.121   Likewise, where a woman reduces her hours following a period of maternity leave and is issued with a new contract, this will not trigger the time-limit as it is a stable employment relationship.

Concealment cases (six months from the date of discovery, with reasonable diligence)

14.122 A concealment case will exist where the claimant's employer has:[147]

- concealed a fact (called a 'qualifying fact') that is relevant to the pay discrimination claim;
- without knowledge of which the claimant could not reasonably have been expected to bring proceedings; and
- the claimant did not discover or could not with reasonable diligence have discovered the fact until after the last day of her employment or after a stable working relationship.

14.123 A complaint must be lodged before six months beginning with the day on which the claimant discovered (or could with reasonable diligence) have discovered the qualifying fact.[148]

---

144 *Preston v Wolverhampton Healthcare NHS Trust* [2004] ICR 993.
145 *Slack v Cumbria CC and Others* [2009] EWCA Civ 293, [2009] ICR 1217, [2009] IRLR 463.
146 EPC para 137.
147 EqA 2010 s130(4), (6) and (10).
148 And see EPC para 141.

Incapacity cases (six months from cessation of incapacity)

14.124 An incapacity case will exist where the claimant had an incapacity during the six months beginning with the later of: [149]

- the last day of the claimant's employment; or
- the day on which the stable working relationship between the claimant and the employer came to an end.

14.125 A complaint must be lodged before six months beginning with the day on which the claimant ceased to have the incapacity.

14.126   'Has an incapacity' in England and Wales means the woman has not attained the age of 18 or lacks capacity within the meaning of the Mental Capacity Act 2005. In Scotland it means she has not attained the age of 16 or is incapable within the meaning of the Adults with Incapacity (Scotland) Act 2000. [150]

Concealment and incapacity cases

14.127 A concealment and incapacity case will arise where the claimant had an incapacity during the period of six months beginning with the later of either: [151]

- the last day of the claimant's employment or the day on which the stable working relationship between the claimant and the employer came to an end; or
- the day on which the claimant discovered or could with reasonable diligence have discovered a fact that is relevant to the pay discrimination claim and without the knowledge of which the claimant could not reasonably have been expected to bring the proceedings.

14.128 A complaint must be lodged before six months beginning with the later of the days on which the period would begin if the case was merely a concealment or incapacity case.

Compensation

14.129 In standard or stable working cases, the ET or a civil court may award the claimant arrears of pay or damages which flow from the breach

149 EqA 2010 s130(7) and (10)
150 EPC para 142.
151 EqA 2010 s130(6), (7) and (10).

of a SEC for six years before the day on which the proceedings were instituted. In all other cases, arrears of pay or damages are recoverable from the day on which the breach first occurred.[152] A slightly different regime applies in Scotland.[153]

Terms of work that prevent the disclosure of pay information

14.130 The following rights apply to all of the protected characteristics and not just sex. It is often difficult for claimants who suspect that they are being paid less than other employees to obtain concrete information about whether their suspicions are well founded.

14.131 The EqA 2010 introduces protection for discussions in relation to pay that is designed to ensure that there is greater transparency and dialogue within workplaces about pay.[154]

14.132 The protection is introduced in two ways:

- Any term of a person's work that purports to prevent or restrict a person from sharing information about the terms of that person's work or discussing their pay with others, is unenforceable under the EqA 2010, but only in so far as that person seeks to make a 'relevant disclosure'.[155]
- Protection from victimisation for:
  - seeking a disclosure that would be a relevant pay disclosure;
  - making or seeking to make a relevant pay disclosure;
  - receiving information disclosed in a relevant pay disclosure.[156]

14.133 The expression 'term of a person's work'[157] is unusual. It clearly means more than merely the contractual terms. Thus if there was a disciplinary rule that prohibited such sharing, it would be unenforceable. If a person were dismissed for having done so, the dismissal would be unfair as no reason could be shown for it. Moreover the EqA 2010 protects disclosure of information about 'the terms of P's

---

152 EqA 2010 ss132 and 135(1)–(5).
153 EqA 2010 ss132(5) and 135(6)–(10). In Scotland the arrears day is the first day of the period of five years ending with the day on which the proceedings were commenced. Alternatively if there is a relevant incapacity, fraud or error the period of 20 years ending with that day.
154 Explanatory Notes para 271.
155 EqA 2010 s77.
156 EqA 2010 s77(4)
157 In EqA 2010 s77(1).

work' which would include discussions of non-contractual pay elements.[158] A relevant disclosure is a disclosure made for the purpose
of finding out whether there is a connection between the difference
in pay and a protected characteristic.[159]

14.134   The disclosure must be made to a 'colleague'. This term is not
defined in the EqA 2010, and the EPC states that it is likely to have
similar scope to the definition of a comparator, as the intention is to
protect the seeking of pay information for the purpose of identifying
pay discrimination.[160] However, the EPC's analysis is perhaps flawed
because the colleague in question might be someone who is not able
to be a comparator, but who is supplying information about other
workers who could be comparators. The colleague might for example
be an agency worker with whom no comparison would properly be
made.

14.135   There is no general prohibition on clauses that hinder pay discussions, only clauses that hinder pay discussions aimed at establishing the existence of discrimination. However, the breadth of the
protected characteristics means that many discussions on pay differentials will consist of relevant disclosures. The requirement relating
to an aim would be satisfied by a disclosure aimed, at ascertaining,
among other things, whether discrimination was taking place.[161] The
EPC makes clear by an example, however, that two male colleagues
simply comparing their respective salaries are unlikely to be making
a relevant pay disclosure unless they are investigating pay disparities
that may be linked to a protected characteristic.[162]

14.136   Importantly however, the making of a relevant disclosure or
receiving information provided by such a disclosure is a protected
act and the victimisation provisions apply.[163] An employee making
such a disclosure therefore has a remedy if the employer imposes
sanctions as a result of the discussion of pay inequality.[164]

---

158 However, note that the EPC simply talks in terms of contractual obligations
and contractual terms. The example given at para 109 concerning bonus
payments may indicate the breadth intended. However, the EPC is, it is
respectfully suggested, wrong if it seeks to indicate a restrictive interpretation
of the EqA 2010.

159 EqA 2010 s77(3) and Explanatory Notes para 269.

160 EPC para 105.

161 There will be an issue about whether the primary purpose of the discussion
must be to investigate protected characteristic related pay differentials.

162 EPC para 107.

163 EqA 2010 s77(4) and (5).

164 See paras 6.15–6.20 above for further discussion.

14.137   A relevant disclosure can be made more widely than simply to colleagues. Trade union officials or indeed anyone else may be included so long as the disclosure is with a view to finding out pay differences connected with protected characteristics.[165]

14.138   The EPC suggests that protection will be afforded to pay discussions which include but are not limited to:[166]

- asking a colleague to provide information about their pay and/or benefits;
- providing information to a colleague about pay and benefits; and
- receiving information from a colleague about pay and benefits.

14.139   To benefit from the protection from victimisation, the disclosure conversation must have been intended to discover whether there was a connection between a protected characteristic and a difference in pay. Thus suppose a female employee thinks she is underpaid compared with a male colleague. She asks him what he is paid and he tells her. The employer takes disciplinary action against the man as a result. The man can bring a claim for victimisation against the employer for disciplining him.[167]

14.140   By contrast a female employee who discloses her pay to one of her employer's competitors with a view to getting a better offer could be in breach of a confidentiality clause in her contract. The employer could take legal action against her in relation to that breach.[168]

14.141   There will be an issue to be determined by the courts and ETs concerning the degree to which (a) the purpose of the disclosure must exclusively be to investigate protected characteristic related pay differentials or whether it can be one of the purposes of the conversation; (b) the disclosure or enquiry must be express to attract the protection on their face.

14.142   If it is to assist claimants. the provision requires cooperation from colleagues in providing details of their pay. Where they are unwilling to provide this information, claimants may still be able to obtain pay information about potential comparators by means of the questionnaire procedure or if this is absent by means of correspondence, disclosure and the written answers procedure during preparation for an ET hearing.

---

165 EqA 2010 s77(3) and (5).
166 EPC para 108.
167 Explanatory Notes para 271.
168 See EPC example at para 109.

14.143   In some sectors, pay transparency provisions contained in other Acts may be of assistance in obtaining pay information.[169]

Gender pay gap information

14.144   During the passage of the Equality Bill, the EHRC was commissioned by the Labour Government to develop metrics for reporting and publicly sharing gender pay gap information on a voluntary basis.[170] A range of voluntary measures were suggested including reporting on differences between:

- median hourly earnings between men and women;
- average basic pay and total average earnings of men and women by grade and job type; or
- men's and women's average starting salaries.

14.145   However, as a result, in addition to the introduction of protection in relation to discussions about pay as a means of providing greater transparency about pay, the EqA 2010 as enacted contained a power to make regulations requiring private and voluntary sector employers with 250 or more employees to publish information about the difference in pay between their male and female employees.[171] The regulations may not require the employer, after the first publication, to publish any more frequently than annually.[172] Penalties are also envisaged for failure to comply with the regulations.[173]

14.146   The Coalition Government's Government Equalities Office has now stated that the Government does not intend to take this provision forward. Instead, it has introduced a voluntary 'Think, Act, Report' framework, which it states 'aims to encourage and support organisations to take a simple step-by-step journey to improve gender equality in their organisations'.[174] In Scotland public authorities are required to publish information relating to equal pay.[175]

---

169   See eg Localism Act 2011 s38: this requires relevant authorities (which include local authorities and fire rescue services) to provide details of the remuneration of their chief officers.

170   EHRC Gender Pay Gap Reporting Proposals, 19 January 2010.

171   EqA 2010 s78.

172   EqA 2010 s78(4).

173   EqA 2010 s78(5).

174   See: www.homeoffice.gov.uk/publications/equalities/womens-equality/ gender-equality-reporting/think-act-report-framework?view=Binary.

175   See chapter 16 on the public sector equality duties and employment.

Questionnaires

14.147 At the moment, the EqA 2010 contains a mechanism for obtaining information so that a potential claimant can gather information from the person she suspects has acted unlawfully by means of a prescribed questionnaire procedure.[176] Questionnaires were originally introduced to permit claimants to formulate their claims as well as ascertaining whether they have a claim.

14.148 In essence, an employee can ask questions that will help her to establish whether or not she is in receipt of equal pay and, if not, the reasons for the pay difference.

14.149 A question or response is admissible as evidence in any ET proceedings, whether or not the question or the response is contained in the prescribed questionnaire or response form.[177]

14.150 The ET cannot order an employer to respond to a questionnaire, but if the employer fails to respond without reasonable excuse within eight weeks, or responds with an evasive or equivocal answer, the ET may draw an adverse inference at the hearing, save in circumstances where certain limited statutory exceptions would apply.[178]

14.151 The statutory questionnaire procedure cannot be used to require an employer to disclose an employee's personal details, unless the ET orders the employer so to do. There is helpful guidance on this topic provided by the Information Commissioner.[179]

14.152 The Coalition Government brought forward legislation to abolish the questionnaire procedure.[180] It suggested in its consultation document, incorrectly, that the aim of questionnaires was originally a pre-action mechanism to assist with filtering out weak cases. The consultation ignored the other purpose of the questionnaire, which is to assist with the formulation of cases. Thus it is likely that one of the most distinctive features of UK discrimination law, which is commented upon favourably in many other countries by representatives of claimants, will be lost on the bonfire of 'red tape'. Should this happen, claimants are advised to seek disclosure of documents

176 EqA 2010 s138 and see further the EPC paras 111–118; Explanatory Notes paras 447-50.

177 EqA 2010 s138(3).

178 EqA 2010 s138(4).

179 See further EPC paras 111–18 in relation to requests pursuant to the Data Protection Act and Freedom of Information Act requests. The appropriate guidance can be obtained from the Information Commissioner's website: www.ico.gov.uk.

180 The Enterprise and Regulatory Reform Bill, nearing the end of the parliamentary process at the time of writing.

which would reveal the information they previously sought under the questionnaire procedure. Recent CJEU case-law has stressed that an inference may be drawn from the employer's failure to provide the documentation that would be necessary to establish the primary facts in a case of discrimination.[181]

Equal pay audits

14.153   In addition to providing commentary on the EqA 2010, the EPC contains in Part Two a section referred to as 'Good equal pay practice'. The EHRC recommends that all employers carry out equal pay audits.[182] Particular pay practices that will allow gender inequality to persist are as follows:

- lack of transparency and unnecessary secrecy over grading and pay;
- discretionary pay systems (eg merit pay and performance-related pay);
- non-payment of bonuses or other incentive payments during maternity leave;
- different non-basic pay terms and conditions for different groups of employees (eg attendance allowances, overtime or unsocial hours payments);
- more than one grading and pay system within an organisation;
- long pay scales or ranges;
- overlapping pay scales or ranges, where the maximum of the lower pay scale is higher than the minimum of the next higher scale, including 'broad banded' structures where there are significant overlaps;
- managerial discretion over starting salaries;
- market-based pay systems or supplements not underpinned by job evaluation;
- JES that has been incorrectly implemented or not kept up to date; and
- indefinite or lengthy pay protection policies.

---

181   Case C-415/10 *Galina Meister v Speech Design Carrier Systems GmbH* [2012] 2 CMLR 39, [2012] ICR 1006, 19 April 2012 at para 47: 'it cannot be ruled out that a defendant's refusal to grant any access to information may be one of the factors to take into account in the context of establishing facts from which it may be presumed that there has been direct or indirect discrimination. It is for the referring court to determine ...'

182   A model can be found on the Commission website www.equalityhumanrights.com.

14.154 Most employers believe that they provide equal pay for equal work. The Equal Pay Code of Practice recommends that 'an equal pay audit is the most effective way of establishing whether an organisation is in fact providing equal pay'.[183]

Male 'piggy-back' claims

14.155 The beneficiaries of pay discrimination provisions will usually be women, but a successful claim on behalf of women can benefit men. A male claimant may make a claim using as his comparator the woman who has brought a successful claim. In such cases, commonly called 'contingent' or 'piggy-back' claims, the success of the woman in her primary claim will lead to an improvement in her terms of employment. A male claimant may then seek to rely on her as a comparator and her improved terms as the basis for his own claim. Significantly, the claim can be made before the resolution of the woman's claim, although the male claimant's 'right' will only crystallise once the woman succeeds in her claim. Importantly, his right to arrears is not limited to the date when the comparator woman presented her claim; he can recover arrears of pay to the same extent as the woman.[184]

Maternity equality clauses

14.156 The EqA 2010 introduces a new feature to equal pay. In employment or personal or public office cases,[185] if the terms of a woman's work do not include a maternity equality clause (MEC) they are treated as including one.[186] This is a provision of the contract having certain effects, set out below.

14.157 The MEC operates so as to modify a term of the woman's work that provides for maternity related pay.[187] Maternity related pay is non-SMP pay to which the woman is entitled as a result of being pregnant (or in respect of times when she is on maternity leave) to be calculated by reference to her pay at a particular time (T). However the following conditions must be satisfied:

---

183 EPC, Part Two, para 163.
184 *Hartlepool Borough Council v Llewellyn* [2009] ICR 1426, [2009] IRLR 796, EAT.
185 EqA 2010 s72.
186 EqA 2010 s73.
187 By EqA 2010 s74(9).

440 Discrimination in employment / chapter 14

a) after T but before the end of the protected period[188] her pay increases, or it would have increased if she had not been on maternity leave;

b) the maternity pay is not (i) what her pay would have been had she not been on maternity leave or (ii) does not make up the difference between SMP and what her pay would have been had she not been on maternity leave;

c) the terms of her work do not provide for maternity related pay to be subject to an increase (i) when her pay for the job increases or (ii) when her pay would have increased had she not been on maternity leave.[189]

If these three conditions are satisfied the MEC operates in the following ways:

a) it subjects the woman's pay to any pay increase occurring after T but before the end of the protected period; or

b) it subjects her pay to any increase that she would have received during that same period had she not been on maternity leave.[190]

14.158 The MEC also modifies terms of the woman's work relating to certain particular types of pay, which must be paid as they would normally be paid had she not been on maternity leave.[191] These provisions apply to:

a) any pay (including pay by way of bonus) in respect of times before the woman is on maternity leave (so, as would appear obvious, a woman's pay earned before she started her maternity leave must be paid in full);

b) pay by way of bonuses in respect of times when the woman is on compulsory maternity leave;

c) pay by way of bonus in respect of times after the end of the protected period.

14.159 The MEC may also modify any term of the woman's work which provides for pay after the end of the protected period. It does so where the term does not provide for that pay to be subject to any increase to which it would have been subject had she not been on maternity leave and it modifies it so that it has that effect.[192]

---

188 See EqA 2010 s18 and paras 7.57–7.63 for definition.
189 EqA 2010 s74(2)–(4).
190 EqA 2010 s74(5).
191 EqA 2010 s74(6)–(7).
192 EqA 2010 s74(8).

14.160 Where a term in a woman's contract relates to membership of or rights under an occupational pension scheme, the MEC's effect will be limited to the same scope as the maternity equality rule which applies in such schemes.[193]

14.161 The EqA 2010 makes it clear that other pregnancy or maternity discrimination provisions have no effect in relation to the terms of the woman's work which is modified by a MEC or maternity equality rule.[194] This provision makes it clear that women on maternity leave cannot use other provisions of the EqA 2010 (eg section 18 combined with ss39(2), 49(6) or 50(6)) to claim that they should be paid in full whilst on maternity leave.

14.162 Practical points

The two flowcharts on the following pages are intended to assist claimants and advisers in navigating through an equal pay claim. Flowchart 1 sets out a series of questions which correspond to the legal 'stages' of an equal pay claim, and will need to be answered in most cases in order to determine whether the claim is likely to succeed. Flowchart 2 sets out the procedure which will be followed by an ET in dealing with an equal value claim.

193 An OPS is deemed to have a maternity equality rule if it does not actually have one. This is dealt with in EqA 2010 s75 and see para 15.51 below.
194 EqA 2010 s76.

Flowchart 1

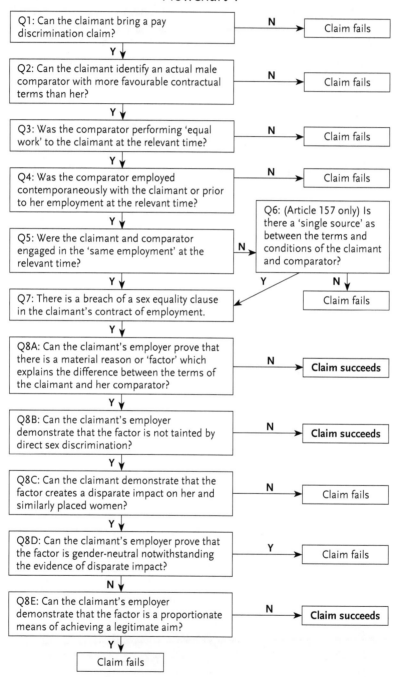

Flowchart 2

Claim

4 weeks

Response

3 weeks

Stage 1 equal value hearing

No independent expert appointed — next step, full hearing

OR

Independent expert appointed. If the tribunal consider it appropriate, eg, a party is not legally represented, it may at any time order that expert to assist in establishing the facts

---

Standard orders

Decide period within which R must grant access to C to interview comparators

Within 2 weeks

Disclose names of any comparators, or
Sufficient information to enable the employer to identify the comparators
Identify the period at issue for each comparison

Within 4 weeks

If given sufficient information to identify unnamed comparators, employer to name them
Parties to provide each other with written job descriptions for the claimant and any comparator
Each party lists the facts they consider relevant to the equal value question, sends to other

Within 8 weeks

Joint agreed statement on job descriptions, facts relevant to the question, and facts in dispute (as to facts or relevance) with a summary of reasons for disagreeing

Within 10 weeks

Stage 2 equal value hearing

The facts now found are final – subject to the IE applying to amend, add or omit any facts

---

8 weeks

Independent expert's report sent to parties and tribunal

4 weeks

Written questions put to expert
Disclosure to parties, experts and tribunal of written statements of any facts relied upon

4 weeks

Expert's written answers
Joint statement of facts and issues agreed and disagreed, with a summary of reasons for disagreement

4 weeks

Full hearing

CHAPTER 15

Pensions

continued

Key points

- The non-discrimination rule introduced by EqA 2010 s61 is inserted into all occupational pension schemes (OPSs) from 1 October 2010 and is not backdated.
- The non-discrimination rule prohibits discrimination in respect of any of the protected characteristics.
- Employees and office-holders can be in a work-related OPS (as opposed to a personal pension or a stakeholder pension). The Pensions Regulator keeps a register of all OPSs.
- An equality rule is a sex equality rule or a maternity equality rule. If an equality rule already has effect in relation to the scheme, or would have effect but for stated exceptions, the equality rule takes precedence and the non-discrimination rule does not have effect (in respect of those characteristics).
- In respect of the period before the commencement date, the previous legislation continues to apply.
- Payments under OPSs constitute 'pay' under Article 157 (ex 119 EC) of the Treaty on the Functioning of the EU (TFEU) and the EqA 2010.
- Article 157 applies to most aspects of OPSs including (but not limited to):
  - access to an OPS;
  - pensionable ages;
  - contributions made by the employer and employee;
  - transitional provisions;
  - survivors' benefits.
- Article 157 does not apply to:
  - the statutory social security scheme, including state retirement pension;
  - the use of actuarial factors in funded defined benefit schemes;
  - additional voluntary contributions.
- 17 May 1990 is the date the ECJ gave judgment in *Barber v Guardian Royal Exchange Assurance Group*[1] holding that an occupational pension was 'pay' within Article 119, now Article 157. The effects of Barber were limited to after the date of judgment of the ECJ.

---

1 C-262/88 [1990] IRLR 240.

Background

15.1   This chapter examines non-discrimination in pensions and the special provision relating to gender and maternity equality. Although much of the chapter is devoted to examining gender equality, this merely reflects the historical genesis of many of the equality provisions with which we have to deal. Occupational pensions comprise one part of the tripartite system of provision for pensions for those who have reached pensionable age, the other two parts being the state pension scheme and income-related pension credit. The history of state pensions reveals systemic gender discrimination against women from the 1940s, which is slowly being addressed.

15.2   Traditionally men and women retired at different ages with occupational schemes tending to follow the former state pensionable ages of 60 for women and 65 for men.

15.3   Different treatment for women was introduced in 1940.[2] Its continuance is explicitly permitted by Council Directive 79/7/EEC on equal treatment for men and women in social security. The Directive allows member states to exclude from its scope 'the determination of pensionable ages for the purposes of granting old-age and retirement pensions and the possible consequences for other benefits'.[3] However, although this was increasingly seen as anomalous it was not until the ECJ's decision in *Barber v Guardian Royal Exchange Assurance Group*,[4] which required equalisation in the private sector, that made introducing equalisation in the state pension scheme inevitable, despite the continuance of the right to derogate.

15.4   *Barber* held that an occupational pension was 'pay', coming within the scope of what is now Article 157 of the TFEU. As such, an age condition that varied according to sex was not permissible. Under the Article 157 principle of equal pay for equal work, Mr Barber, made compulsorily redundant at 52 years, was entitled to the same pension benefits under the Guardian scheme as a woman aged 52 years.

15.5   Equalisation in state retirement pensions is provided for by the Pensions Act 1995. This provides, as amended, for phasing in a common state pensionable age of 65 years over the period from 2010 to 2018. Women born before 6 April 1950 are not affected at all. Women born before 6 April 1953 are not affected by the acceleration. From 6 November 2018 there will be a common pensionable age of 65 years

---

2 Old Age and Widows' Pensions Act 1940.

3 Article 7(1)(a).

4 C-262/88 [1991] 1 QB 344, [1990] ICR 6116, [1990] IRLR 240.

for men and women. By April 2020 the common pensionable age will rise to 66 years, some six years earlier than originally planned. Under current law, state pensionable age is planned to increase to reach 68 years by 2046.[5]

Types of pension

15.6   The main types of pension are:

- basic state pension;
- additional state pension: SERPS, the state earnings-related pension scheme, in respect of earnings from 6 April 1978 to 5 April 2002 and S2P, state second pension, in respect of earnings from 6 April 2002;
- graduated retirement benefit, in respect of graduated national insurance contributions paid on earnings between 1961 and 5 April 1975;
- OPS;
- personal pension schemes;
- stakeholder pensions;
- pension credit: income-related provision for those whose capital and income falls below set limits.

Statutory social security pension scheme

15.7   Once a person reaches state pensionable age, whether or not retired, the basic state pension is paid at a flat rate, although extra pension (or a taxable lump sum payment) can be gained by deferring a claim. Maximum basic state pension depends on having paid, been treated as having paid, or been credited with sufficient national insurance contributions to make each year of the contributor's working life a 'qualifying year'.

15.8   State pension payments do not count as 'pay' for the purposes of Article 157.

15.9   Graduated retirement benefit was the first earnings-related supplement to the basic state pension. It is only since April 2010 that there has been equalisation in entitlement. The graduated scheme ended for new contributors in 1975. After a gap of three years, SERPS,

---

5 PA 1995 Sch 4 Part 1 sets out exhaustively the day pensionable age will be attained for people born within specific date ranges. Increases beyond 67 years are expected to be kept under review and may not be implemented.

a standalone earnings-related pension, was introduced. SERPS was repackaged in April 2002 to become the S2P, which currently is proposed to be subsumed in a new single-tier pension from about 2017.

15.10   Employees earning over a lower earnings limit and their employers must contribute to the national insurance scheme. Currently if the employer provides an OPS or an approved personal pension scheme providing benefits at least equivalent (or treated as equivalent) to those provided by S2P, there are lower contracted-out rates for employer and employee national insurance contributions. The additional pension is reduced by any occupational pension built up before 5 April 1997. Since that time a contracted-out scheme completely replaces the state additional pension. Further changes are expected from 2017.[6]

Personal pension schemes

15.11   These defined contribution schemes have no connection to the employment relationship. Traditionally taken out by self-employed people, they were extended to employees from 1988.[7] Employers may contribute to personal pensions, in a group personal pension scheme, in which case both the contributions and pensions would qualify as an 'employer-provided benefit'.

15.12   Since October 2001, employers, unless exempt, have been required to provide access to a registered stakeholder pension scheme.[8] Participation is voluntary and employers are not required to make contributions, although they must designate a scheme and provide a payroll facility for the deductions of contributions. Regulation of stakeholder schemes includes a cap on charges.

Auto-enrolment

15.13   Auto-enrolment to a private sector pension scheme, including an OPS, will be phased in over the period to 2016.[9] From 1 October 2012, starting first with the largest employers, an employer will be

---

6   For details of what is proposed, see the Explanatory Notes to the draft Pensions Bill: www.dwp.gov.uk/docs/draft-pensions-bill.pdf.

7   Social Security Act 1986.

8   Welfare Reform and Pensions Act 1999 s3 and Stakeholder Pension Schemes Regulations 2000 SI No 1403 regs 22 and 23.

9   For details, see the Pensions Regulator's website: www.thepensionsregulator.gov.uk.

required to enrol eligible employees into a qualifying workplace pension scheme and make contributions. Employers with fewer than 50 people in a PAYE scheme will not be covered until mid-2015 at the earliest. Once an employer's duties have been triggered, employees who decide to give notice to opt out and those aged under 22 years or over state pension age, or earning below the lower earnings limit are excluded. Employers must have a pension scheme in place or choose to enrol employees into the National Employer Savings Trust (NEST). Self-employed people may also enrol in NEST. Employees may continue making contributions to NEST after leaving, even if their current employer has chosen a different scheme.

Occupational pension schemes

15.14 OPSs are governed by the contract of employment, by legislative provisions, and by trust law. The pension is paid as a result of the employment relationship. Only employees and office-holders (such as directors) are eligible to join OPSs. There are two broad types of scheme.

- Salary-related or defined benefit schemes: These schemes must provide a minimum pension based on the scheme rules. The pension is based on the employee's salary at the time of retirement, or the average salary earned over all or just the final few years of employment. A fraction of that salary, usually between 1/60th and 1/80th of the final salary, is payable for each year of pensionable service. The employer's contributions are calculated to cover the costs of providing the pension. In defined benefit schemes employers take the risk of invested contributions falling in value. Given the increased cost of such schemes, many have closed to new and existing employees alike.
- Money purchase or defined contribution schemes: These schemes broadly require minimum contributions from the employer and safeguard protected rights. The resulting pension usually depends on the annuity that can be bought with the money contributed into the scheme given the value of that investment at the time of purchase. As such, the risk of investments falling in value is passed from the employer to the employee. Defined contributions schemes are becoming the norm.
- A combination of salary-related and money purchase schemes is sometimes adopted. As with the other schemes, these may be:
  - contributory, where the employee contributes a percentage of qualifying earnings; or

- non-contributory, where only the employer makes contributions.

Statutory public sector pension schemes

15.15 In *Bestuur van het Algemeen Burgerlijk Pensionfunds v Beune*[10] the ECJ held that pensions paid under a statutory civil service scheme were 'pay' within Article 141EC, (now Article 157 TFEU). The ECJ ruled that the only possible decisive criterion for whether a pension was 'pay' is whether it is paid to the worker as a result of the employment relationship between the employee and the former employer. If the pension paid by the public employer concerns only a particular category of workers, if it is directly related to the period of service, and if its amount is calculated by reference to the employee's salary, it is comparable to a private sector OPS.[11]

Part-time workers

15.16 Before 1994, part-time workers were generally excluded from OPS. The ECJ judgments in *Vroege v NCIV Instituut Voor Volkshuisvesting BV* and *Fisscher v Voorhuis Hengelo BV*[12] however held that an OPS that excluded part-time workers and married women contravened what is now Article 157. Those decisions generated a mass of claims and associated litigation. The history, with hyperlinks to key judicial decisions, is outlined in the 'part-time workers' section of the ET website.[13]

Miscellaneous aspects of OPS

15.17 **Retirement lump sums**: At retirement an individual will usually be able to choose to 'commute' pension rights to obtain a one-off tax free lump sum in return for a reduced rate pension.

15.18 **Actuarial factors**: These are linked to demographic assumptions, such as the relative life expectancies of men and women, which may require differential funding arrangements.

---

10 Case C-7/93 [1994] ECR I-4471, [1995] IRLR 103.
11 [1994] ECR I-4471, [1995] IRLR 103 at [45]. As such, the EAT's decision to opposite effect in *Griffin v London Pension Fund Authority* [1993] IRLR 248 must be regarded as wrongly decided.
12 C-57/93 *Vroege v NCIV Instituut voor Volkshuisvesting BV* [1994] IRLR 651 and C-128/93 *Fisscher v Voorhuis Hengelo BV* [1994] IRLR 662.
13 www.justice.gov.uk/tribunals/employment/part-time-workers/.

15.19   **Additional voluntary contributions (AVCs)**: These are voluntary payments made by employees to gain additional benefits. They are separately identified from the main pension fund.

15.20   **Bridging pensions**: For men who retire before reaching state pension age, these bridge the gap between the actual pension and the combined occupational pension and state pension to which a woman of the same age would be entitled if she had a full contributions record. A bridging pension ceases on the man reaching state pension age as that ends the unequal treatment that would have occurred but for the bridging pension. Note that a pension under a salary-related contracted out scheme may in practice result in different amounts for men and women of the same age. That difference is permitted if it is the effect of statutory adjustments to the additional state pension, including index linking any guaranteed minimum pension.[14]

The impact of European law

An overview

15.21   Article 157(1) TFEU, requires that: 'Each Member State shall ensure that the principle of equal pay for male and female workers for equal work or work of equal value is applied.'

15.22   Payments under OPSs count as pay within Article 157 and are subject to both the equality rule and the non-discrimination rule under EqA 2010. If a pension scheme trust deed contains provisions contrary to the principle of equal treatment, the trustees and employers must amend those provisions and are empowered to make non-discrimination and sex equality alterations to the scheme by resolution.[15] Such a resolution can bypass a scheme requirement to consult members.

The scope of Article 157

15.23   Article 157 applies to public and private sector employees, to contracts between private individuals and to all collective agreements that regulate paid employment. It applies to all types of payments and schemes arising out of the employer/employee relationship, including schemes provided for in legislation.

14   Equality Act 2010 (Sex Equality Rule) (Exceptions) Regulations 2010 SI No 2132 regs 2 and 3.
15   EqA 2010 ss62 and 68.

15.24   Article 157 overrides any conflicting provisions of national law. It has direct effect but is limited by time-limits and restrictions on backdating claims. For current employees EqA 2010 s79 requires an actual comparator. However, case-law under Article 157 goes wider than section 79, ensuring, for example, that comparison may also be made with a predecessor[16] or where a rule is indirectly discriminatory on grounds of sex, that there is no need for a comparator at all.[17] There is no specific provision for pensioner members, so it is arguable that a hypothetical comparator suffices in relation to the sex equality rule, as it does for the non-discrimination rule.

15.25   Article 157 prohibits sex discrimination, whether direct or indirect, in access to a pension scheme. The exclusion of women, or categories of women, such as married ones, breaches Article 157.[18] If part-time workers are treated less favourably, that is likely to be indirectly discriminatory. If such treatment cannot be objectively justified, it will also be unlawful.[19] CJEU case-law on objective justification, concerning the social security Directive 79/7/EEC, gives to states a wider margin for discretion in relation to their choice of social policy aims and the means chosen to achieve those aims than it does in relation to Article 157.[20] This is partly due to the way in which EU law views the operation of Directives and that of the treaty obligations.[21]

15.26   An OPS must deliver the same benefits to comparable men and women of the same age. That core principle applies whether the scheme is contracted out or not contracted out.[22]

15.27   The law in this area is complex and the following is a summary of the main points.

---

16   C-129/79 *Macarthys Ltd v Smith* [1980] IRLR 210. Note that EqA 2010 s64(2) provides that for the purposes of s66 to s70 alone, references to the work done by a comparator are not restricted to work done contemporaneously. That leaves the operation of section 65 (equal work) dependent on an actual current comparator unless helped by case-law under Article 157.

17   C-256/01 *Allonby v Accrington and Rossendale College* [1994] IRLR 224.

18   C-128/93 *Fisscher* [1994] IRLR 662.

19   See *Bilka Kaufhaus GmbH v Weber von Hartz* [1986] IRLR 586 and *Vroege v NCIV Instituut voor Volkshuisvesting BV* [1994] IRLR 651.

20   See, for example, C-317/93 *Nolte v Landesversicherungsanstalt Hanover* [1996] IRLR 225 and C-444/93 *Megner & Scheffel v Innungskrankenkasse Vorderpfalz* [1996] IRLR 236.

21   See chapter 19. Note that *O'Brien v Ministry of Justice* [2013] UKSC 6 holds that, although a state may decide on the total amount of its budget, it cannot use cost as a legitimate aim to justify discriminatory treatment in how the budget is allocated.

22   See *Barber* for contracted out schemes and C-110/91 *Moroni v Firma Collo GmbH* [1994] IRLR 130 for schemes that are not contracted out.

'Pay' under Article 157 TFEU

15.28 Article 157(2) provides that:

For the purpose of this article, 'pay' means the ordinary basic or minimum wage or salary and any other consideration, whether in cash or in kind, which the worker receives directly or indirectly, in respect of his employment, from his employer.

15.29 As such, 'pay' includes:

- pension schemes, whether they are contracted out or not contracted out of the statutory scheme, so long as they arise from the employment relationship;[23]
- schemes that are made compulsory by law, whether that is because of social policy or to considerations relating to competition in a particular economic sector, so long as they are part of the employment relationship;[24]
- schemes that supplement or complement the state scheme;[25]
- contributory and non-contributory schemes;[26]
- final salary and money purchase schemes;[27]
- access to OPSs;[28]
- pensionable ages applicable to such schemes;[29]
- employer contributions to pension schemes, which should be equal for men and women;[30]
- benefits paid under relevant pension schemes including those paid to survivors (so payment cannot be restricted to widows);[31]

---

23 C-262/88 *Barber v Guardian Royal Exchange Assurance Group* [1990] ICR 6116, [1990] IRLR 240.

24 C-435/93 *Dietz v Stichting Thuiszorg Rotterdam* [1996] IRLR 693. In the UK pension schemes are not compulsory, although from October 2012 the default position will be automatic enrolment, subject to the right of an individual employee to opt out.

25 C-262/88 *Barber v Guardian Royal Exchange Assurance Group* [1990] ICR 6116, [1990] IRLR 240 and C-110/91 *Moroni v Firma Collo GmbH* [1994] IRLR 240.

26 *Coloroll Pension Trustees Ltd v Russell* C-200/91 [1994] IRLR 586.

27 *Coloroll Pension Trustees Ltd v Russell* C-200/91 [1994] IRLR 586.

28 C-57/93 *Vroege v NCIV Instituut voor Volkshuisvesting BV* [1994] IRLR 651 and C-128/93 *Fisscher v Voorhuis Hengelo BV* [1994] IRLR 662.

29 C-262/88 *Barber v Guardian Royal Exchange Assurance Group* [1990] ICR 6116, [1990] IRLR 240.

30 C-69/80 *Worringham and Humphreys v Lloyds Bank* [1981] IRLR 178.

31 C-109/91 *Ten Oever v Stichting Bedrijfspensioenfonds voor het Glazenwassers-en Schoonmaakbedrijf* [1993] IRLR 601 and C-75 & 112/82 *Razzouk and Beydoun v European Commission* [1984] ECR 1509.

- transitional provisions aimed at reducing discrimination over a period (preventing the transitional preservation of existing rights if that would discriminate against the opposite sex);[32]
- indirect discrimination in pensions, such as the less favourable treatment of part-time workers, where that is not objectively justified.[33]

15.30 Article 157 applies to each element of remuneration. Achieving balance over the scheme as a whole is not a defence to direct discrimination, although it may provide justification for indirect discrimination (eg for applying different provisions to part-time than to full-time workers).

15.31 Transfer rights between pension schemes (eg on a change of employment) also fall within the scope of Article 157. If scheme 1 was discriminatory, scheme 2 must increase benefits in order to eliminate the effect of previous discrimination.[34] The core principle is that scheme members should receive a pension calculated in accordance with the principle of equal treatment. That may require treating transferees better than existing members. As with all other aspects of 'pay', this is also limited to service since 17 May 1990.[35]

15.32 Article 157 does not apply to:

- payments under a statutory social security scheme governed by legislation if the scheme involves no agreement within the trade or undertaking;
- the use of actuarial factors in final salary schemes;[36]
- where inequalities depend on the arrangements chosen for funding the scheme, differences are permitted in the amount of lump sums, transfer values and in early retirement reduced-rate pensions;[37]
- additional pension benefits flowing from AVCs, even though those contributions are an option within the scheme and are administered by the scheme;[38]
- bridging pensions.[39]

---

32 C-28/93 *Van Den Akker v Stichting Shell Pensoenfonds* [1994] IRLR 616 and C-408/92 *Smith v Avdel Systems Ltd* [1994] IRLR 602.
33 C-170/84 *Bilka Kaufhaus GmbH v Weber von Hartz* [1986] IRLR 586.
34 *Coloroll Pension Trustees Ltd v Russell* C-200/91 [1994] IRLR 586.
35 See para 15.40.
36 See paras 15.33–15.36.
37 C-152/91 *Neath v Hugh Steeper Ltd* [1994] IRLR 91.
38 C-200/91 *Coloroll Pension Trustees Ltd v Russell* [1994] IRLR 586.
39 See para 15.20 and see C-132/92 *Birds Eye Walls v Roberts* [1991] IRLR 29. Note that in *Beaune*, the ECJ did not accept that a difference in the state pension justified inequality in an occupational pension.

Actuarial factors

15.33   Actuarial factors are an exception to the requirement for equal treatment.[40] However, the gap in average life expectancy between men and women has been falling, weakening the legitimacy of this exception to equal treatment. The National Statistics Office, taking into account the continued improvements in mortality assumed in the 2008-based principal population projections, puts life expectancy for those aged 65 in 2008 at 21.0 years for males and 23.6 years for females.

15.34   Historically, however, women's pensions have been more expensive than those of men, usually requiring the employer to pay higher contributions. Where employer contributions are the same, men often receive higher pensions, simply because on average a woman will receive the lower pension for more years than would a man. Such differences in outcomes that depend on the arrangements for funding a pension scheme do not fall foul of Article 157.[41] Nor are they likely to fall foul of EqA 2010.[42]

15.35   Variation in pension pay between men and women is lawful if it is due to actuarial calculations in relation to:

- the calculation of employers' contributions; or
- the determination of benefits.

15.36   The object of taking actuarial factors into account is to provide equal periodical pension benefits for men and women. These are likely to affect:[43]

- lump sum payments, with a commuted periodical pension or part of such pension;
- periodical pensions granted in exchange for a lump sum payment;
- money purchase benefits within Pension Schemes Act (PSA) 1993 s181(1);
- transfer credits and any rights allowed to a member because of transferring from a personal pension scheme;

---

40   See the recast Equal Treatment Directive 2006/54/EC Art 9(1)(h), (j) and (k).

41   C-200/91 *Coloroll Pension Trustees Ltd v Russell* [1994] IRLR 586 at para 85.

42   See EqA 2010 Sch 7 Part 2 para 4 and regulations prescribed under para 5.

43   This list is derived from the Equality Act 2010 (Sex Equality Rule) (Exceptions) Regulations 2010 SI No 2132 reg 4. Note that C-152/91 *Neath v Hugh Steeper Ltd* [1994] IRLR 91 is limited to salary-related or defined benefit schemes as that was the context in which the questions had been put to the ECJ. However, these exceptions apply also to defined contribution schemes and arguably go wider than permitted.

- transfer payments, including a cash equivalent under PSA 1993 s94;
- periodical pensions payable on early deferred retirement;
- benefits payable to a pension credit member on statutory pension-sharing;
- benefits provided from additional voluntary contributions.

No need for a comparator

15.37   In *Coloroll*,[44] the ECJ had ruled that Article 157 did not generally apply to schemes that have at all times been single-sex schemes. However, in *Allonby v Accrington and Rossendale College*,[45] the ECJ dealt with the case of a self-employed agency worker who claimed access to the Teachers Superannuation Scheme, a statutory scheme that applied to all teachers. She had no comparator in the same employment as all the agency teachers employed by her agency were also self-employed and, like her, were excluded from the pension scheme. The ECJ decided that there would be sufficient proof of discrimination if it was shown that the rule requiring being employed under a contract of employment in order to join TSS was indirectly discriminatory, in that a significantly higher proportion of self-employed teachers than employed teachers were women.

Claims by men

15.38   Men and women can bring claims in appropriate circumstances. If a pension provision indirectly discriminates against women, for example in the former exclusion of part-time workers from pension schemes, and is found to be unlawful, that provision can no longer be applied to a man in a similar position. To do so would be direct discrimination. His comparators would be women who have succeeded in the indirect discrimination claim. He is entitled to claim arrears for the full period for which his female comparator is awarded arrears. He can also bring a claim contingent on his comparator's success and does not have to await an actual award.[46]

---

44   [1994] IRLR 586.
45   C-256/01 [1994] IRLR 224.
46   See the *Preston v Wolverhampton Healthcare NHS Trust* [1998] 1 WLR 280, [1998] IRLR 197, HL group of cases. Putting these points beyond doubt in the context of equal pay and bonus schemes not available to predominately female groups, see *Hartlepool Borough Council v Llewellyn* [2009] ICR 1426, [2009] IRLR 796, EAT.

Backdating

15.39 **Members and survivors:** CJEU case-law permits a degree of historical discrimination for essentially pragmatic reasons. The right to equal treatment for members and survivors in OPSs applies only to service from 17 May 1990, the date of the CJEU's judgment in *Barber*.[47] Prior to that date, member states and others involved in the provision of pensions had been entitled to consider that what is now Article 157 did not apply to occupational pensions. That assumption had been reasonable in light of the exceptions to the principle of equal treatment permitted by the social security and occupational social security Directives.[48] The CJEU accepted that the financial implications for pension schemes would cause serious difficulties if *Barber* was applied retrospectively. The position was put beyond doubt by annexing a protocol to that effect to what is now Article 157 TFEU.[49] However, where there will be no such serious difficulties the principle of equal treatment will be applied without temporal restriction.[50]

15.40 If length of service is not at issue, for example with a lump sum payment made in respect of death in service, Article 157 applies if the death occurred on or after 17 May 1990.

15.41 **The right to join:** The right to join an OPS is treated differently. A claim can be brought in respect of the period back to 8 April 1976, the date of the ECJ's judgment in *Defrenne*.[51] The history is outlined in *Preston v Wolverhampton Healthcare NHS Trust (No 2)*[52] where it was held that time-limit provisions cannot prevent an applicant from retroactively gaining membership of a scheme from 8 April 1976 or

---

47 *Barber v Guardian Royal Exchange Assurance Group* [1990] ICR 6116, [1990] IRLR 240 at paras 40–45.

48 Directive 79/7/EEC art 7(1) and Directive 86/378/EEC art 9(a).

49 The protocol to Article 157, whose predecessor came into force on 1 November 1993, now provides that: '[f]or the purposes of Article 157 of the Treaty on the Functioning of the European Union, benefits under occupational social security schemes shall not be considered as remuneration if and in so far as they are attributable to periods of employment prior to 17 May 1990, except in the case of workers or those claiming under them who have before that date initiated legal proceedings or introduced an equivalent claim under the applicable national law.'

50 C-267/06 *Maruko v Versorgungsanstalt der deutschen Bühnen* [2008] IRLR 450 at paras 77–78.

51 C-43/75 [1976] ICR 547. See also C-128/93 *Fisscher v Voorhuis Hengelo BV* [1994] IRLR 662; C-57/93 *Vroege v NCIV Instituut voor Volkshuisvesting BV* [1994] IRLR 651 and C-435/93 *Dietz v Stichting Thuiszorg Rotterdam* [1996] IRLR 693.

52 [2001] IRLR 237, HL.

from the date of commencement of employment, if later. The worker must pay the contributions relating to that period of membership.

'Levelling down'

15.42   EU law does not permit inequality to be eradicated by retrospective 'levelling down'.[53] Employees who have been disadvantaged must be given the same rights as other employees in relation to service before the discrimination was removed (though in cases to which the *Barber* restriction applies, only as from 17 May 1990). Treatment must be equalised upwards. However, once the discrimination has been removed, an employer may make cuts, if the cuts apply equally to men and women,[54] and if the contract permits unilateral disadvantageous variations. In addition, trust law and the terms of the trust deed in question may prevent trustees altering a scheme if it would reduce a member's future benefits. If that is the case, no such levelling down is permitted.[55]

15.43   It is, however, permitted to equalise (eg different pensionable ages) by levelling up to the higher age, even though that may reduce or remove the previously held discriminatory advantage of a lower pensionable age.[56]

Transfer of undertakings

15.44   OPSs are specifically excluded from the general rule that all the transferor's liabilities are transferred to the transferee where the Transfer of Undertakings (Protection of Employment) Regulations 2006 apply.[57] However, any provision of an OPS that does not relate to benefits for old age, invalidity or survivors is not treated as part of the scheme, so can transfer.[58] Article 3(4) of the Acquired Rights Directive 2001/23/EC disapplies Article 3(1) and (3) in relation to employees' rights to old age, invalidity or survivors' benefits under supplementary company or intercompany pension schemes outside the statutory social security schemes in member states.[59]

---

53 *Coloroll Pension Trustees Ltd v Russell* [1994] IRLR 586.
54 C-408/92 *Smith v Avdel Systems Ltd* [1994] IRLR 602.
55 *Lloyds Bank Pension Trust Corporation v Lloyds Bank plc* [1996] PLR 263, ChD.
56 C-28/93 *Van Den Akker v Stichting Shell Pensoenfonds* [1994] IRLR 616.
57 Transfer of Undertakings (Protection of Employment) Regulations 2006 (TUPE) SI No 246.
58 TUPE reg 10(2).
59 Acquired Rights Directive 2001/23/EC Article 3(4)(a).

15.45   In *Powerhouse Retail Ltd v Burroughs*,[60] part of the *Preston*[61] part-time pensions litigation, the House of Lords held that time under an equality clause ran from the end of employment with the transferor. Pension terms relating to benefits for old age, invalidity or survivors in effect dropped out of the contract and stayed with the transferor. Liability for breach of an equality clause in relation to those terms remained with the transferor. By parity of reasoning, liability for breach of an equality rule or of a non-discrimination rule that relates to benefits for old age, invalidity or survivors would remain with the transferor.

15.46   Redundancy provisions that are part of a pension scheme do transfer. In *Beckman v Dynamco Whicheloe Macfarlane Ltd*,[62] the CJEU held that the exceptions of old age, invalidity and survivors' benefits should be narrowly construed and restricted to benefits paid from the end of a person's normal working life. In Ms Beckman's case redundancy triggered the right to an early retirement benefit. Because that benefit was the consequence of an event occurring before normal pension age, it was subject to transfer and was enforceable against the transferee. That position was reinforced by the ECJ in *Martin v South Bank University*.[63]

The Equality Act 2010

Equality and non-discrimination rules

15.47   The EqA 2010 inserts an equality rule and a non-discrimination rule into all OPSs that do not include such a rule.[64] The Act says that a non-discrimination rule is a provision by virtue of which a 'responsible person'[65] must not discriminate against another person in carrying out any of the responsible person's functions in relation to the scheme. It also prohibits the responsible person from harassing or victimising the other person. It requires the responsible person to

60 [2006] UKHL 13, [2006] ICR 606, [2006] IRLR 381.
61 *Preston v Wolverhampton Healthcare NHS Trust* [1998] IRLR 197, HL at para 1.
62 C-164/00 [2002] IRLR 578.
63 C-4/01 [2004] IRLR 74.
64 EqA 2010 s61.
65 By EqA 2010 ss141 and 61(4) these are (a) the trustees or managers of a scheme, (b) an employer whose employees are, or may be, members of the scheme, or (c) a person exercising an appointing function in relation to an office (the holder of which is, or may be, a member of the scheme).

make reasonable adjustments. An ET has jurisdiction to determine an application by a responsible person for a declaration as to the rights of the responsible person and a worker in relation to a dispute about the effect of a non-discrimination rule.[66]

15.48   The rules are inserted (and effective) only from 1 October 2010. For the earlier period, individuals must turn to the precursor legislation.

15.49   The Act distinguishes between 'rules'[67] and 'clauses'.[68]

15.50   Within EqA 2010, 'rules' are inserted into occupational pension schemes. Each scheme receives one, and so may govern the pensions of many workers, regardless of the contract of employment under which they work. A rule works in a similar way to an equality clause. An equality clause is restricted in scope: to the terms of work under which a person is employed. This will cover contractual and non-contractual terms of work or occupation and would include the terms of appointment of an office-holder. It is those terms that the clause modifies.

15.51   An equality rule is defined as either a sex equality rule[69] or a maternity equality rule.[70]

- a sex equality rule requires that men and women are treated equally and modifies any less favourable term so as to achieve that equality. Where the term confers a discretion, that term is modified so as to prevent the exercise of discretion in a way that would be less favourable to one sex;[71]
- a maternity equality rule modifies any term relating to scheme membership, accrual of scheme rights and the determination of benefits, so as to ensure that any period when a woman is on maternity leave is treated as time when she is not. Where a term confers a discretion that is capable of affecting those matters, that term is modified so as to prevent discretion being exercised differently depending on whether she is on maternity leave or not.[72]

---

66 See EqA 2010 s120(2) and (3) (for trustees and managers of an OPS).
67 Defined via EqA 2010 s212(1) by s61 (non-discrimination rule), s67 (sex equality rule) and s75 (maternity equality rule).
68 Defined via EqA 2010 s212(1) by s66 (sex equality clause) or s73 (a maternity equality clause).
69 EqA 2010 s67.
70 EqA 2010 s212(1) via ss75 and 212(1).
71 EqA 2010 s67.
72 EqA 2010 s75. Note that section 75 applies to unpaid ordinary maternity leave only where the EWC began after 5 April 2003. Section 75 applies to unpaid additional maternity leave only where the EWC began after 4 October 2008 and in such cases does not apply to the accrual of scheme rights.

15.52   A precondition for the applicability of a sex equality rule is that the disadvantaged person and the comparator of the opposite sex do equal work. EqA 2010 s65 defines equal work as 'like work', work 'rated as equivalent' or work of 'equal value'.[73]

15.53   The material factor defence[74] applies to a sex equality rule. A sex equality rule does not apply if the trustees or managers of the OPS show that the difference in treatment between a man and a woman is 'because of a material factor which is not the difference of sex'.[75]

15.54   Where it operates in relation to an OPS, or in the case of a sex equality rule, would operate but for the fact that the different treatment is permitted because it is based on actuarial factors, or on different entitlements to the state pension, the equality rule takes precedence over the non-discrimination rule.[76] This means that the modifications made in respect of gender are not affected by the existence of a non-discrimination rule. This achieves the aim of ensuring that all characteristics under EqA 2010 are protected with appropriate modifications by a unified scheme of protection. The non-discrimination rule is only excluded in so far as an equality rule applies.[77]

15.55   Subject to the above, a non-discrimination rule must be read into every OPS.[78] The rule prohibits a responsible person from discriminating against, harassing or victimising a member or prospective[79] member in the carrying out any of the scheme functions. A responsible person is the employer of a scheme member, a scheme trustee or manager, and where an office-holder can become a scheme member, the person responsible for appointing them.[80]

15.56   The characteristics protected by the non-discrimination rule are age, disability, gender reassignment, marriage and civil partnership, race, religion or belief, sex, sexual orientation.[81]

15.57   For example, the non-discrimination rule prohibits any discrimination in relation to absences because of gender reassignment, or on adoption, paternity or parental leave in the same way that the maternity equality rule prohibits any discrimination in relation to maternity

73 See chapter 14.
74 See paras 14.85–14.111.
75 EqA 2010 s69(4).
76 EqA 2010 s61(10).
77 See Employment Code para 14.42.
78 EqA 2010 s61.
79 EqA 2010 s141(5).
80 EqA 2010 s61(4).
81 As defined in EqA 2010 ss4–12: see chapter 1. The prohibited conduct is defined in EqA 2010 ss13–17: see chapter 1.

leave. To avoid being treated less favourably requires being treated as if one was at work. EqA 2010 s75, which provides for the maternity equality rule, arguably illustrates what is required to prevent less favourable treatment in cases of absence. So, if a worker is to be treated as if they were at work, that in turn requires treating the worker as receiving full pay for pension purposes.[82] The employer must continue paying contributions. The absent employee, however, must pay contributions based only on any pay actually received. For any part of the absence that is unpaid, no contributions would be payable.[83]

Reasonable adjustments

15.58   There is a duty on a responsible person to make reasonable adjustments.[84] A responsible person must comply with the duty in relation to a person with a disability 'who is or may be a member of the scheme' when 'carrying out ... functions in relation to the scheme'.[85] The limitation on an employer's duty (lack of knowledge or constructive knowledge) does not apply to a responsible person. The schedule is drafted so as not to apply to OPSs. However, this makes no practical difference as asking for an adjustment is likely to give the responsible person knowledge or constructive knowledge in any event.

15.59   All members of a scheme are likely to share a common substantial disadvantage in understanding the complexities of the pension scheme. However, a person with a learning disability is likely to experience a greater disadvantage in understanding the scheme. Communicating the nature of the scheme to members and prospective members is arguably part of carrying out a responsible person's[86] 'functions in relation to the scheme'.[87] There may, for example, be an obligation to explain the scheme in user-friendly ways arising out of this duty to make reasonable adjustments.

15.60   The Employment Code gives, as an example of the duty to make adjustments, the example of a final salary scheme where disability means a worker has to reduce her hours in the last two years before

---

82   EqA 2010 s75(3) and (4).
83   EqA 2010 s75(7).
84   EqA 2010 s61(11). Thus sections 20 and 21 are applicable.
85   EqA 2010 Sch 8 para 19.
86   EqA 2010 s61(4).
87   EqA 2010 Sch 8 Part 2 para 19 and see section 20(6), which includes providing information in an accessible format as a reasonable adjustment; and section 63(2) which in the context of pension credit members includes the provision of information within the scope of 'communications'.

retirement resulting in a lower pension than if she had not been disabled.[88] The EHRC suggest that a reasonable adjustment would be to take her 20-year period of full-time work into account by converting her part-time salary to its full-time equivalent and balancing that with an equivalent cut in the pensionable period of her part-time work. A worker in this position would be likely to argue that making the corresponding cut in the period of her pensionable part-time work still puts her at a substantial disadvantage because of disability.

Exceptions

15.61   In shared pension cases on divorce or civil separation, a non-discrimination rule does not apply to the former spouse or civil partner. They are a pension credit member of the scheme, with rights deriving not from the scheme itself but from a court order.[89] However, in relation only to the functions of providing information or operating a dispute resolution procedure, a disabled pension credit member is treated as a deferred member or pensioner member of the scheme and is protected by the prohibition of discrimination, harassment and victimisation and by the duty to make reasonable adjustments.[90] A survivor is a beneficiary within the terms of the scheme. As such, a surviving dependent, spouse or civil partner has rights that derive from membership of the scheme, so they do not need the help of EqA 2010 s63.

15.62   Directive 2000/78 Article 6(2) permits member states to discriminate on grounds of age in the following limited ways:[91]

> Member states may provide that the fixing for occupational social security schemes of ages for admission or entitlement to retirement or invalidity benefits, including the fixing under those schemes of different ages for employees or groups or categories of employees, and the use, in the context of such schemes, of age criteria in actuarial calculations, does not constitute discrimination on the grounds of age, provided this does not result in discrimination on grounds of sex.

15.63   The EqA 2010 makes an exception to the prohibition of discrimination any practices, actions or decisions that relate to age and are specified in a ministerial order. Such exceptions must not go beyond the scope of the right to derogate found in Article 6(2). The exceptions

---

88 Employment Code para 14.44.
89 EqA 2010 s61(5) and Welfare Reform and Pensions Act 1999 s29.
90 EqA 2010 s63.
91 Employment Directive 2000/78 Art 6(2).

are set out in the Equality Act (Age Exceptions for Pension Schemes) Order (APO) 2010.[92] These include:

- minimum and maximum ages for admission to a scheme;
- minimum age for entitlement to or payment of an age-related benefit;
- minimum and maximum pensionable pay for admission to a scheme;
- the use of age criteria in actuarial calculations;
- differences in contribution level attributable to differences in pensionable pay;
- under money purchase schemes, contribution rates differing according to age where the object is to work towards equalising age related benefits for those otherwise in comparable situations;
- under defined benefit schemes, contribution rates differing according to age where the aim is to reflect the increasing cost of providing the defined benefits in respect of members as they get older;
- calculation of death benefit entitlement by reference to the lost years of prospective service;
- the 'early retirement pivot age' (earliest age at which benefit is payable without actuarial deduction) and 'late retirement pivot age' (earliest age at which benefit is payable with actuarial enhancement), including having different pivot ages for different groups of members.

15.64   This is not a complete list, just sufficient to give a flavour of the type of exceptions. In practice, it is essential to consider the exact terms of any exceptions provided for in the APO, as well as considering whether or not a particular exception is within the scope of Directive 2000/78 Article 6(2). For new exceptions that were not included in the equivalent provisions in 2006, there must be a consultation exercise.[93]

Enforcement and remedies

15.65   The civil courts can consider any claim that a pension scheme operates in a discriminatory manner whether due to breach of a non-discrimination rule or of an equality rule, or both.[94] However, ETs

---

92   SI No 2133.
93   EqA 2010 s61(9).
94   EqA 2010 s120(6) for non-discrimination rules and EqA 2010 s127(9) for equality rules.

also have jurisdiction.[95] As specialist tribunals, it is arguably more appropriate for ETs to consider such claims. The civil courts have power, of their own volition, or on application by a party, to refer any issue to an ET, staying or (in Scotland) sisting the proceedings until concluded. Alternatively, if more convenient, the civil court can simply strike out the claim or counterclaim.[96]

15.66　A responsible person, as defined[97], trustees or managers of an OPS may apply to an ET for a declaration as to their rights and those of a member in relation to a dispute about the effect of a non-discrimination rule or of an equality rule. Scheme members and pensioner members may also bring applications or complaints. An employer, who in any event is defined as a responsible person, is treated as a party and as such is entitled to appear and be heard.[98]

15.67　Beneficiaries, including survivors, are not dealt with clearly in EqA 2010. Section 212(11) defines the types of member listed by reference to Pensions Act (PA) 1995 s124. That in turn omits beneficiaries. However, the answer for any claim concerning an equality rule is found in EqA 2010 s135(11). This extends the definition of a pensioner member in that case to include a person entitled to the present payment of pension or other benefits derived through a member. An equivalent provision dealing with claims about a non-discrimination rule or a failure to make reasonable adjustments appears to have been omitted from EqA 2010. To avoid doubt about the basis of the right to bring a claim, claims should be made under both EqA 2010 and Article 157.

Time-limits

Non-discrimination rule

15.68　A complaint within EqA 2010 s120 must be brought within a period ending no later than three months starting from the date of the act complained about. If the act extends over a period, it is treated as done at the end of that period. Time can be extended if the ET considers it just and equitable to do so.

95　EqA 2010 s120 for non-discrimination rules and EqA 2010 s127 for equality rules.

96　EqA 2010 s122 for non-discrimination rules and EqA 2010 s128 for equality rules. This test raises practical considerations only, see *Birimingham City Council v Abdulla* [2012] UKSC 47, [2013] IRLR 38.

97　EqA 2010 s61(4).

98　EqA 2010 s120(5) for non-discrimination rules and EqA 2010 s127(8) for equality rules.

Equality rule

15.69 The time-limit for breach of an equality rule is different. This is a type of equal pay claim. As such, a claim must be brought during the period of six months beginning with the last day of the employment or appointment.[99] Except in the situations outlined below, no extension of time is possible.[100]

15.70 In a stable employment case, the six months starts to run on the day the stable employment relationship ended.[101]

15.71 Members of the armed forces have an additional three months to claim if the complaint or application relates to their terms of service. This is because they must first make a complaint under the service complaint procedures.[102]

15.72 Time is extended if the worker is incapable within the meaning of the Mental Capacity Act 2005, or in Scotland the Adults with Incapacity (Scotland) Act 2000. In this case time starts to run when the incapacity ends.[103]

15.73 Time is also extended in a concealment case. This is where a worker could not reasonably have been expected to have begun proceedings without knowledge of the fact that had been deliberately concealed. Here, the six months starts on the day they discovered, or could with reasonable diligence have discovered, the fact at issue.[104]

15.74 If a claim is both a concealment case and an incapacity case, the six months starts on the later of the two possible dates.[105]

Remedies

Non-discrimination rule

15.75 If a non-discrimination rule has been breached, an ET can make a declaration about the terms on which a person should be admitted to the pension scheme and the terms on which members are treated.[106] Additionally an ET may declare that the complainant has the right

---

99 EqA 2010 s129.
100 EqA 2010 s129(2).
101 EqA 2010 s129(3) and s130(3); for more about stable employment cases, see paras 14.119–14.121.
102 EqA 2010 s129(4).
103 EqA 2010 ss129(3), 130(8), (9) and 140(6), (7).
104 EqA 2010 ss129(3), (4) and 130(5), (6).
105 EqA 2010 s129(3) and (4).
106 EqA 2010 s126(1).

to be admitted to the scheme, or has the right to membership of the scheme without discrimination.[107]

15.76 An ET can award compensation only for injured feelings or for the failure to comply with a recommendation. It cannot compensate for any loss caused by the unlawful discrimination. In pension cases, that would not present difficulty unless the loss has already materialised. If loss has materialised, the claimant should ask for a recommendation that the respondent takes specified steps for the purpose of obviating or reducing the adverse effect of the breach of the non-discrimination rule.[108] An ET can award compensation for failure to comply with a recommendation and it is arguable that the effect of EqA 2010 s126(3)(b) is to bypass the section 126(3)(a) restriction of compensation to injury to feelings.

15.77 In the case of breach of the section 61(11) duty to make reasonable adjustments, an ET is not restricted by EqA 2010 s126 unless the contravention falls plainly within the literal terms of section 126(1). Remedies may be awarded under the general rules found in section 124 and an ET is free to order the respondent to pay compensation for consequential loss as well as for injury to feelings.

Equality rule

15.78 Where an equality rule or equality clause has been breached in relation to scheme membership or scheme rights, an ET cannot award compensation.[109] Instead, it may make a declaration that the employee is entitled to be admitted to the scheme from a date set by the ET (but not earlier than 8 April 1976) or is entitled to have any rights which would have accrued under the scheme from a date set by the ET (but not earlier than 17 May 1990).

15.79 As well as a declaration about the parties' respective rights, an ET can award arrears to a pensioner member of an OPS for breach of an equality clause or rule:

- in a standard case, no more than six years arrears are payable (five years in Scotland);[110]
- if the member is incapable within the meaning of the Mental Capacity Act 2005, or in Scotland the Adults with Incapacity (Scotland) Act 2000, time starts to run when the incapacity ends;[111]

107 EqA 2010 s126(2).
108 EqA 2010 s124(3) and (7).
109 EqA 2010 s133(2)(b).
110 EqA 2010 s134(5).
111 EqA 2010 ss134(5), 135(5) and 141(6), (7).

- in a concealment case, where a member could not reasonably have been expected to have begun proceedings without knowledge of the fact that had been deliberately concealed, arrears are payable from the day on which the breach first occurred (or for up to 20 years in Scotland).[112] Any period during which the member is incapable, as above, is ignored.

15.80   The time-limit for bringing a claim in the civil courts in respect of these provisions will be six years.[113]

The Pensions Ombudsman

15.81   The Pensions Ombudsman has power to investigate and determine complaints made by a member (or by their survivor) about maladministration by the trustees or managers of an occupational or personal pension.[114] Do note that miss-selling complaints are normally dealt with by the Financial Ombudsman Service.[115]

---

112 EqA 2010 s134(5).
113 By analogy with the Equal Pay Act 1970 cases, *Birmingham City Council v Abdulla* [2012] UKSC 47, [2013] IRLR 38.
114 www.pensions-ombudsman.org.uk.
115 www.financial-ombudsman.org.uk.

Public sector equality duty

Key points

- General duty: A single new public sector equality duty extends to cover race, sex, pregnancy and maternity, gender reassignment, disability, age, sexual orientation and religion or belief and replaces the three pre-existing general statutory duties on public authorities to promote race,[1] disability[2] and gender[3] equality.
- Specific duties: There is power to provide for specific duties and these powers have been exercised in relation to England, Wales and Scotland.
- The duties are enforceable by judicial review, and not by private law claims (for example before the ET).
- They can have an impact in ET claims, particularly in justification arguments and in relation to reasonable adjustments.
- The equality duty is under review

16.1   This chapter deals with the general equality duty contained in EqA 2010 s149 as it affects employment and occupation. It does not cover what is known as the socio-economic duty, contained in section 1 of the Act, as the Coalition Government announced on 17 November 2010[4] that it was not intending to implement this provision.

The public sector equality duty

16.2   EqA 2010 Part 11 is entitled 'Advancement of Equality'. Section 149(1) sets out a public sector equality duty (PSED).

16.3   A public authority must, in the exercise of its functions, have due regard to the need to:

- eliminate discrimination, harassment, victimisation and any other conduct that is prohibited by or under the EqA 2010;
- advance equality of opportunity between persons who share a relevant protected characteristic and persons who do not share it;
- foster good relations between persons who share a relevant protected characteristic and persons who do not share it.[5]

1   RRA 1976 in April 2001, ss71 and 71A–71E.
2   DDA 1995 in December 2006, ss49A–49F.
3   SDA 1975 in April 2007, ss76A–6E.
4   www.homeoffice.gov.uk/media-centre/news/socio-economic.
5   EqA 2010 s149(1).

16.4 The public sector equality duty replaces the three pre-existing statutory duties on public authorities to promote race,[6] disability[7] and gender[8] equality. Protection under the EqA 2010 was extended to cover race, sex, pregnancy and maternity, gender reassignment, disability, age, sexual orientation and religion or belief.[9]

16.5 In practice, the duty means that public authorities must factor into the exercise of all their functions such as their decision-making process, or reviewing and planning new or existing policies, programmes and services, the impact of their decisions on people with any of the protected characteristics. Public authorities will need to use evidence to inform their objectives, to be transparent on progress and to actively engage with the issues that result in discrimination and disadvantage. This could mean a local authority in considering its support of its employees discovers that there is no support for people undergoing gender reassignment while in their employment, and deciding to fund support for its transgender workers.

To whom does the general PSED apply?

16.6 The PSED applies to the public authorities specified in EqA 2010 Sch 19.[10] These include ministers, the armed forces, the NHS, local government, educational bodies and the police.[11]

16.7 The PSED also applies to persons who are not public authorities but who exercise public functions. It applies only in respect of the public functions that they carry out.[12] These are often known as 'hybrid' public authorities. A public function is a function of a public nature for the purposes of the Human Rights Act 1998. It is important to be aware of the parallel definitions and case-law under Human Rights Act 1998 s6. This definition has proven to be difficult and lacks clarity.[13] It also means that hybrid organisations will not be affected by the duty in the exercise of their private functions.

---

6 In force in April 2001, RRA 1976 ss71 and 71A–71E.

7 In force in December 2006, DDA 1995 ss49A–49F.

8 In force in April 2007, SDA 1975 ss76A–76E.

9 Until the coming into force of the EqA 2010, there were no equivalent PSEDs for age, religion or belief or sexual orientation.

10 A minister has the power to amend EqA 2010 Sch 19.

11 EqA 2010 Sch 19.

12 EqA 2010 s149(2) .

13 See, for example, Seventh report of Session 2003–04, *The Meaning of Public Authority under the Human Rights Act*, HL Paper 39, HC 382. See further, and

16.8   The EqA 2010 seeks to consolidate the different approaches taken in previous legislation to application of the statutory equality duties. Previously, the RRA 1976 used a lengthy list,[14] while the disability and gender equality duties were applied to those who had 'functions of a public nature'. The Act now uses both of those methods.

16.9   There are exceptions to the coverage of the PSED.[15] The EqA 2010 disapplies the PSED with respect to age in relation to the education of pupils in schools, and the provisions of services to pupils in school and in relation to children's homes. However, employment by the school is covered.

16.10   A minister of the Crown may make regulations imposing specific duties on public authorities listed in EqA 2010 Sch 19 Part 1 to enable them to carry out the PSED more effectively.[16]

16.11   The final scanty regulations were promulgated on 9 September 2011[17] and apply to England only. They require a public authority listed in the Schedules to the Regulations to publish information to demonstrate its compliance with the general duty; and to prepare and publish one or more objectives it thinks it should achieve to do any of the objectives mentioned EqA 2010 s149(a)–(c) ie the general duty.

16.12   Separate regulations were promulgated in Wales for the specific duties. They are far more detailed than those applicable to England.[18] They require the publication of equality objectives, the authority having first complied with engagement provisions; to collect information to make arrangements for impact assessments; and have due regard to addressing the causes of pay gaps amongst those with protected characteristics. Authorities must also prepare and publish a strategic equality plan; and report on compliance with the PSED (this obligation also applies to Welsh ministers). There are also provisions relating to public procurement contained in the regulations.

16.13   Separate regulations were also promulgated in Scotland.[19] These require listed authorities to report progress on mainstreaming the equality duties; publish equality outcomes and report progress; assess

---

for example, *Aston Cantlow and Wilmcote with Billesey Parochial Church Council* [2003] UKHL 37, [2004] 1 AC 546 or *YL v Birmingham City Council* [2007] UKHL 27, [2008] 1 AC 95.

14 EqA 2010 Sch 19 in fact uses as its starting point RRA 1976 Sch 1A.
15 EqA 2010 Sch 18.
16 EqA 2010 ss153–155.
17 Equality Act 2010 (Specific Duties) Regulations 2011 SI No 2260.
18 Equality Act 2010 (Statutory Duties) (Wales) Regulations 2011 SI No 1064.
19 Equality Act 2010 (Specific Duties) (Scotland) Regulations 2012 SI No 162.

and review policies and practices; gather and use employee information; publish gender pay gap information; publish statements on equal pay; consider award criteria and conditions in relation to public procurement; and impose a duty on Scottish ministers to publish proposals to enable better performance.

16.14   The specific duties are largely evidential in nature. They are supposed to assist the public authorities to comply with the general duty and demonstrate that fact. They are not conclusive of compliance. It does not follow that because information has been collated, and objective(s) set, the authority will have complied with the PSED. There remains an obligation to have due regard to the duty in all functions.

16.15   The specific duties cannot be enforced by an individual. The EHRC is able to bring judicial review proceedings if necessary; and to issue compliance notices where appropriate. However, compliance or otherwise with them can nevertheless have evidential value in any case brought on the basis of a breach of the PSED or otherwise.

16.16   The case-law so far has concerned mainly the previous equality duties. However, there is no reason why the same interpretation should not be given to the expansion of the previous duties to all protected characteristics. Further, the Joint Committee on Human Rights has stated that the authoritative interpretation of the existing race equality duty, which was provided by the High Court in *R (Kaur and Shah) v London Borough of Ealing*,[20] should be regarded as applicable to the new wider PSED. The Committee stated that:[21]

> its focus should be on protecting individuals against discrimination, promoting good relations between different groups and ensuring that the needs of individuals and groups who face disadvantage are taken into account, with a view to ensuring that all individuals enjoy the right to equality and human dignity and are afforded equality of opportunity as full members of society.

16.17   In *R (Williams) v Surrey County Council*[22]– one of the many cases brought under the EqA 2010 regarding library closures – the court summarised helpfully the approach to the duties under the precursor legislation, repeating the approach of Blake J in *R (Rahman) v Birmingham City Council*[23] as follows:

---

20   [2008] EWHC 2062 (Admin) (29 July 2008).
21   JCHR Report on the Equality Bill, 27 October 2009, para 267.
22   [2012] EWHC 867 (QB), [2012] EqLR 656.
23   [2011] EWHC 944 (Admin).

- Due regard requires more than simply giving consideration to the issue and councillors should be aware of the special duties a council owes to the disabled before they take a decision.[24]
- 'Due regard' is the regard that is appropriate, in all the particular circumstances in which the public authority concerned is carrying out its function as a public authority. The public authority must also pay regard to any countervailing factors. The weight to be given to the countervailing factors is a matter for the public authority concerned rather than the court, unless the assessment by the public authority is unreasonable or irrational.[25]
- No duty is imposed to take certain steps or to achieve certain results. The duty is only to have due regard to the need to take the relevant steps. The court will only interfere if the local authority has acted outwith the scope of any reasonable public authority in the circumstances. The public authority will need to take steps to gather all the relevant information.[26]
- The law does not impose a statutory duty on public authorities requiring them to carry out a formal disability equality impact assessment (EIA) when carrying out their functions. At the most it imposes a duty on a public authority to consider undertaking an EIA along with other means of gathering information.[27]
- The due regard duty must be fulfilled before and at the time that a particular policy, which will or might affect disabled people, is being considered by the public authority. It involves a conscious approach and state of mind. It must be exercised in substance, with rigour and with an open mind. It is not a question of ticking boxes.[28]
- The duty imposed on the public authority is non-delegable. It remains on the public authority charged with it.[29]
- The duty is a continuing one.[30]
- It is good practice for those exercising public functions in public authorities to keep an adequate record, showing they had actually considered their disability equality duties. If records are not kept

24 R (Chavda) v London Borough of Harrow [2007] EWHC 3064 (Admin).
25 Dyson LJ (as he then was) in R (Baker) v Secretary of State for Communities and Local Government [2008] LGR 239 and R (Brown) v Secretary of State for Work and Pensions [2008] EWHC 3158 (Admin).
26 [2008] EWHC 3158 (Admin).
27 [2008] EWHC 3158 (Admin).
28 [2008] EWHC 3158 (Admin).
29 [2008] EWHC 3158 (Admin).
30 [2008] EWHC 3158 (Admin).

it may make it more difficult evidentially for a public authority to persuade a court that it has fulfilled the duty imposed.[31]

- Some of these principles have been drawn together as follows. There is no statutory duty to carry out a formal EIA. The duty is to have due regard, not to achieve certain results. Due regard does not exclude having regard to countervailing factors but is 'the regard that is appropriate in all the circumstances'. The test of whether a decision-maker has had due regard is a test of substance and not of mere form or box-ticking. The duty must be performed with rigour and with an open mind and is non-delegable. Members are heavily reliant on officers for advice in taking these decisions. That makes it doubly important for officers not simply to tell members what they want to hear but to be rigorous in both enquiring and reporting to them.[32]
- The clear purpose of EqA 2010 s149 is to require public bodies to give advance consideration to the issue of (race) discrimination before making any policy decisions that may be affected by such an issue. This is a salutary requirement which must be seen as an integral part of the mechanisms for ensuring the fulfilment and aims of anti-discrimination legislation. It is not possible to take the view that non-compliance is not a very important matter. Section 149 has a significant role to play.[33]
- Due regard must be an essential preliminary to any important policy decision, not a rearguard action following a concluded decision.[34]
- Consideration of the duties must be an integral part of the proposed policy not justification for its adoption.[35]
- The section 149 duty must be kept in mind by decision-makers throughout the decision-making process. It should be embedded in the process but can have no fixed content bearing in mind the range of potential factors and situations. What observance of that duty requires of decision-makers is fact-sensitive and varies considerably from situation to situation and from time to time and from stage to stage.[36]

31 [2008] EWHC 3158 (Admin).
32 *R (Domb) v London Borough of Hammersmith and Fulham* [2009] EWCA Civ 941.
33 *R (Elias) v Secretary of State for Defence* [2006] EWCA Civ 1293.
34 *R (Bapio Action Ltd) v Secretary of State for the Home Department* [2007] EWCA Civ 1139.
35 *R (Kaur) v London Borough of Ealing* [2008] EWHC 2062 (Admin).
36 *R (Bailey) v London Borough of Brent* [2011] EWCA Civ 1586 para 83.

- The importance of complying with EqA 2010 s149 is not to be understated. Nevertheless, in a case where the council was fully appraised of its duty and had the benefit of a most careful report and EIA an air of unreality may descend. Councils cannot be expected to speculate, or to investigate, or to explore, such matters ad infinitum, nor can they be expected to apply – indeed they are to be discouraged from applying – the degree of forensic analysis for the purpose of an EIA and of consideration of their duties under section 149 that a QC might deploy in court. The outcome of such cases is ultimately of course fact-specific.[37]

16.18   In addition, a helpful and concise summary of many of the above statements on the appropriate approach for the courts in considering whether or not there has been due regard to EqA 2010 s149 is to be found in *R (JM) v Isle of Wight Council*.[38]

Due regard

16.19   The above, as can be seen, is a summary of the principles derived from previous cases. The interpretation of 'due regard' has been explored by the courts in the context of the pre-existing equality duties.

16.20   In *R (Baker) v (1) Secretary of State for Communities and Local Government and (2) Bromley LBC*,[39] Dyson LJ stated:

> What is due regard? it is the regard that is appropriate in all the circumstances. These include on the one hand the importance of the areas of life of the members of the disadvantaged racial group that are affected by the inequality of opportunity and the extent of the inequality; and on the other hand, such countervailing factors as are relevant to the function which the decision-maker is performing.

16.21   In *R (Meany) v Harlow District Council*,[40] Davis J considered the duty in the context of a decision by a local authority to advertise an invitation to tender for its welfare rights and advice services. He stated that:

> what is 'due' depends on what is proper and appropriate to the circumstances of the case ... how much weight is to be given to the countervailing factors is a matter for the decision maker. But that does not

---

37 *Bailey* para 102 per Davis LJ.
38 [2011] EWHC 2911 (Admin), Lang J at paras 95–108.
39 [2008] EWCA Civ 141.
40 [2009] EWHC 559 (Admin).

abrogate the obligation on the decision maker in substance first to have regard to the statutory criteria on discrimination.

It is important to remember that the duty is not a duty to achieve a particular result, ie to achieve equality of opportunity. It is a duty to have due regard to the desirability of achieving that outcome.[41] It is also particularly important to consult adequately on equality issues.[42] The claimant's evidence shoiuld focus on building a view of the circumstances that require wieght to be given to equality.

Equality impact assessments

16.22 One way in which authorities can demonstrate that they have had due regard to the equality duty will be to have carried out an equality impact assessment (EIA). Although there was debate about whether these were required by the specific or general equality duties, the courts do appear to agree that evidence of such an assessment will assist in demonstrating due regard.[43]

16.23 Once an adverse impact has been identified, what must a public authority do?

16.24 In *Kaur & Shah v London Borough of Ealing*, the court stated:[44]

Once the Borough of Ealing had identified a risk of adverse impact, it was incumbent upon the borough to consider the measures to avoid that impact before fixing on a particular solution. It erred: in having recognised the problem whilst merely hoping to assess its extent after it had settled on its criteria.

16.25 In *R (Rahman) v Birmingham City Council*, Blake J stated:[45]

I accept Mr Clayton's submission, not disputed by Ms Mountfield, that where the PSED has been properly complied with the weight to be attached to the countervailing factors for adopting the policy impugned is for the Council and can only be reviewed by this Court on a challenge to an appropriate demanding test of irrationality having regard to the subject matter.

16.26 Having identified an adverse impact, the relevant countervailing factors must be weighed properly before an authority can be said to

---

41 *R (Brown) v Secretary of State for Work and Pensions* [2008] EWHC 3158 (Admin) at para 31.

42 See eg *R (Hajrula) v London Councils* [2011] EWHC 448 (Admin), [2011] EqLR 612.

43 See for example *R (Brown) v Secretary of State for Work and Pensions* [2008] EWHC 3158 (Admin) at paras 89–96.

44 [2008] EWHC 2062 at 44.

45 [2011] EWHC 944 (Admin).

have had 'due regard'. Due regard will not be had merely because the authority avoids irrationality in weighing the factors. In *Williams*, Wilkie J stated that whether there has been 'due regard' is a matter for the court to determine. By way of contrast, once there has been due regard, the question whether the decision ultimately taken is lawful, having regard to the weight to be given to that factor as well as to any countervailing factors, is a matter which can only be determined by the court applying the *'Wednesbury'* principles.[46]

16.27   The EqA 2010 sets out what is to be taken into consideration in relation to equality of opportunity. It states, at section 149(3), that the requirement for public authorities to have due regard to the advancement of equality of opportunity involves having due regard, in particular, to the need to:[47]

- remove or minimise disadvantages suffered by persons who share a relevant protected characteristic that are connected to that characteristic;
- take steps to meet the needs of persons who share a relevant protected characteristic that are different from the needs of persons who do not share it; and
- encourage persons who share a relevant protected characteristic to participate in public life or in any other activity in which participation by such persons is disproportionately low.

An example from the Explanatory Notes illustrates how this might operate. The duty could lead a police authority to review its recruitment procedures to ensure they did not unintentionally deter applicants from ethnic minorities, with the aim of eliminating unlawful discrimination.[48]

16.28   The wording reflects the wording of the positive action provisions in EqA 2010 s158.

16.29   'Equality of opportunity' has not previously been defined. In the case of *Baker*, the court accepted[49] the contentions put forward by the intervener that:

> the promotion of equality of opportunity is concerned with issues of substantive equality and requires a more penetrating consideration than merely asking whether there has been a breach of the principle of non-discrimination' ... and ... 'the equality of opportunity is of

46 [2011] EWHC 944 (Admin) at para 20.
47 EqA 2010 s149(3).
48 Explanatory Notes para 484.
49 *R (Baker) v Secretary of State for Communities and Local Government* [2008] EWCA Civ 141, [2008] LGR 239 at para 30.

opportunity in all areas of life in which the person or persons under consideration are, or may not be, at a disadvantage by reason of membership of a particular racial group. In practice, this is likely to include disadvantage in the fields of education, housing, healthcare and other social needs.

16.30 This approach means that a deeper analysis of what will achieve substantive equality is permitted and sometimes required so that the public authority can have due regard to the equality objectives. The EqA 2010 specifically states that the steps involved in meeting the needs of disabled persons that are different from the needs of non-disabled persons include steps to take account of disabled persons' disabilities.[50] This preserves an aspect of the disability equality duty, under which public authorities were obliged to have due regard to the need to take steps to take account of disabled people's disabilities.[51] It is also important to remember that positive discrimination in favour of disabled people is not unlawful.[52]

16.31 In *Pieretti v London Borough of Enfield*, a housing allocations case, the Court of Appeal said of the DDA equality duty in relation to taking steps to take account of disability:[53]

> If steps are not taken in circumstances in which it would have been appropriate for them to be taken, ie in which they would have been due, I cannot see how the decision-maker can successfully claim to have had due regard to the need to take them.

The court also made clear that the PSED applies to one-off decisions. The function of the public authority does not have to be exercised in making or reviewing general policy. The public authority will exercise its functions by making an individual decision. Thus a decision whether or not to hire or dismiss an employee or to make an adjustment may be affected by whether that is the best way to have due regard to the equality objectives in EqA 2010 s149.

16.32 'Fostering good relations' means that public authorities must have due regard to the need to tackle prejudice and promote understanding.[54] The existence of this part of the duty will lead public authorities to take a more active role in dealing with harassment at work, for example. It may lead the authority to review its policies regarding

50 EqA 2010 s149(4).
51 DDA1995 s49A.
52 EqA 2010 s13(3): a non-disabled person cannot complain if treated less favourably than a disabled person.
53 [2010] EWCA Civ 1104 at para 34.
54 EqA 2010 s149(5).

bullying at work because of the impact the structure of those policies has on particular equality groups. If there are different belief groups in the work place, the public authority may need to take steps to promote understanding between the different groups.

How favourably can public authorities treat relevant persons or groups of persons?

16.33   Compliance with the PSED enables public authorities to treat some persons more favourably than others, but it does not go as far as to enable what is known generally as positive discrimination (other than in relation to disability and transgender).[55] The provision does not intend to confer additional benefits for protected groups. Rather, it intends, for example, to recognise that the needs of some protected groups will require different treatment (for example scheduling training sessions at different times for those with child care needs, or on different days to take account of days of religious observance).

16.34   Thus the PSED to have due regard might lead an authority to provide mentoring or support groups for its female workers to encourage them to consider leadership roles in the authority. This would have the aim of advancing equality of opportunity for women. If women from particular ethnic minorities within the workforce were seen to have specific requirements, such as language needs, it may be appropriate for the authority to provide language training to meet their needs that are different to the other women in the group, in order to achieve greater promotion participation.

16.35   Some concern has been expressed that the extension of the duty to include religion or belief in EqA 2010 s149(3) could become problematic in that it may lead to public authorities believing that they must make separate and specific provision based on religious requirement and faith-based concerns.[56] However, it is clear that the aim of the duty is to remove barriers to participation, broadly, for those of faith and non-faith, not about facilitating the worship itself.[57] Thus this type of separate provision is unlikely to achieve the aim of ensuring full participation in the workforce.

---

55   EqA 2010 s149(6).
56   Such concerns were noted, for example, in the JCHR Report, 27 October 2009 at p88.
57   JCHR Report on the Equality Bill, 27 October 2009, paras 264–72.

16.36   One particular area where the public authority may be required to treat a person more favourably than others is in respect of disabled persons.[58] This is specifically provided for within EqA 2010 s149(4) as set out above.

16.37   EqA 2010 Sch18 also disapplies the equality of opportunity limb of the equality duty in relation to race, religion or belief or age in relation to immigration functions. [59] However, employment in immigration is not an immigration function and is not removed. Judicial decision-making is also outside the scope of the section 149 duty[60].

Codes of practice

16.38   The codes of practice are a useful tool when interpreting how the duties are to be put into practice. The EHRC has stated on its website[61] that it had originally intended to produce codes of practice on, inter alia, the PSED, but that the government had decided not to lay Codes of Practice. As a result it has produced text of a code as technical guidance. This guidance can be found on the Commission's website. The Guidance sets out at 2.21 what it calls the *Brown* principles, derived from the case of *R (Brown) v Secretary of State for Work and Pensions*[62] at para 119 as follows:

> 2.21 There are many cases in which the courts have considered whether a body has complied with the equality duties on race, disability and gender which the public sector equality duty has replaced. The principles set out in those cases will be relevant to the duty under s149.
>
> In *R (Brown) v Secretary of State for Work and Pensions* [2008] EWHC 3158 (Admin) the court considered what a relevant body has to do to fulfil its obligations to have due regard to the aims set out in the general equality duty. The six 'Brown principles' it set out[63] have been accepted by courts in later cases.[64] Those principles are that:

58   See in particular EqA 2010 s149(2) and (3).
59   This replaces the exception for immigration functions from the race duty in RRA 1976 s71A It also replaces SDA 1975 ss76A(3) and (4) and DDA 1995 ss49C and 49D relating to excepted bodies and functions.
60   EqA 2010 Sch 18 and s3.
61   www.equalityhumanrights.com/legal-and-policy/equality-act/equality-act-codes-of-practice-and-technical-guidance.
62   [2008] EWHC 3158 (Admin).
63   *R (Brown) v Secretary of State for Work and Pensions* [2008] EWHC 3158 at paras 90–96. While the guidance refers to six there are in fact seven principles bulleted.
64   Including cases about the duty in s149 of the Act. See, for example, *R (Greenwich Community Law Centre) v Greenwich LBC* [2012] EWCA Civ 496.

• In order to have due regard, those in a body subject to the duty who have to take decisions that do or might affect people with different protected characteristics must be made aware of their duty to have 'due regard' to the aims of the duty.

• Due regard is fulfilled before and at the time a particular policy that will or might affect people with protected characteristics is under consideration as well as at the time a decision is taken. Due regard involves a conscious approach and state of mind.

• A body subject to the duty cannot satisfy the duty by justifying a decision after it has been taken. Attempts to justify a decision as being consistent with the exercise of the duty when it was not, in fact, considered before the decision are not enough to discharge the duty.

• The duty must be exercised in substance, with rigour and with an open mind in such a way that it influences the final decision. The duty has to be integrated within the discharge of the public functions of the body subject to the duty. It is not a question of 'ticking boxes'. However, the fact that a body subject to the duty has not specifically mentioned [s149][65] in carrying out the particular function where it is to have 'due regard' is not determinative of whether the duty has been performed. But it is good practice for the policy or decision maker to make reference to [s149] and any Code or other non-statutory guidance in all cases where [s149] is in play. 'In that way the decision maker is more likely to ensure that the relevant factors are taken into account and the scope for argument as to whether the duty has been performed will be reduced'.

• The duty is a non-delegable one. The duty will always remain the responsibility of the body subject to the duty. In practice another body may actually carry out the practical steps to fulfill a policy stated by a body subject to the duty. In those circumstances the duty to have 'due regard' to the needs identified will only be fulfilled by the body subject to the duty if (1) it appoints a third party that is capable of fulfilling the 'due regard' duty and is willing to do so (2) the body subject to the duty maintains a proper supervision over the third party to ensure it carries out its 'due regard' duty.

• The duty is a continuing one.

• It is good practice for those exercising public functions to keep an accurate record showing that they had actually considered [the general equality duty] and pondered relevant questions. Proper record keeping encourages transparency and will discipline those carrying out the relevant function to undertake the duty conscientiously. If records are not kept, it may make it more difficult, evidentially, for a public

65 The equality duty in *Brown* was the Disability Equality Duty in s49A of the Disability Discrimination Act 1995. Later cases have confirmed that the principles in *Brown* also apply to the duty in s149 of the Act.

authority to persuade a court that it has fulfilled the duty imposed by [s149].

16.39 So far as the status of any guidance/codes is concerned, in *Brown* the court set out some helpful propositions about how important it is to follow them:[66]

> First, a public authority must take the Code into account when considering disability equality issues. If it decides to depart from it, cogent reasons must be given and they must be convincing: see: *Khatun* at para 47 per Laws LJ. However, we also agree with the statement of Laws LJ in that case that there are no higher positive duties to comply with the Code, pace remarks of Dyson J in *R v North Derbyshire Health Authority ex p Fisher* (1997) 10 Admin LR 27.

> Secondly, if a breach of the general duty in section 49A(1) is alleged and it appears to a court that relevant guidance given by the Code has been ignored, departed from, misconstrued or misapplied without cogent reason, then that may be a powerful factor that leads the court to conclude that there was a breach of statutory duty by the public authority. Thirdly, it would be for the public authority to explain clearly and convincingly the reason for the lapse.

16.40 Blake J has stated:[67]

> In general terms I consider the advice recently issued in non-statutory guidance by the Equality and Human Rights Commission ('Using the equality duties to make fair financial decisions') to be of assistance to decision makers such as this defendant in the no doubt very difficult decisions that have to be taken in this field.

16.41 In addition, where an authority has its own guidance on, for example, the conducting of impact assessments, it should follow it. The existence of such guidance gives rise to a legitimate expectation that it will be followed.[68] Many authorities have detailed policies and guidance previously adopted, so it is worth asking them.

---

66 *R (Brown) v Secretary of State for Work and Pensions* [2008] EWHC 3158 (Admin) at para 119.

67 *R (Rahman) v Birmingham CC* [2011] EWHC 944 (Admin) at [46].

68 *R (Kaur and Shar) v London Borough of Ealing* [2008] EWHC 2062 where it was said (para 27) that 'Good administration and fairness demands that a local authority like Ealing is only entitled to depart from its own policy where to do so represents a proportionate response to the circumstances which led the authority to consider such a departure.'

Enforcement

16.42 Any failure by an organisation in the performance of its general equality duty can be challenged only by way of judicial review. It is not subject to challenge by way of private law action[69] and therefore individuals are not able to claim damages for breach of statutory duty for a breach of this duty.[70]

16.43   The Joint Committee on Human Rights considers that there is a role for courts in reviewing whether public authorities have given effect to their procedural obligations to have due regard to the desirability of reducing inequality, and that guidance should specifically require public authorities to explain what steps they have taken to comply with the duty.[71]

16.44   While initially courts appeared reluctant to quash a decision once a breach of the equality duties had been found, the Court of Appeal was clear about the impact of such a breach in *R (C) v Secretary of State for Justice*.[72] There it quashed regulations made in relation to secure training centres where there had been no race equality impact assessment.

16.45   The EHRC has various enforcement powers in relation to both the general and the specific duties. Claimants seeking the involvement of the EHRC should write directly to the EHRC setting out the facts of the case and why they consider that the PSED is being breached. The EHRC can then consider exercising its powers.

How can the equality duties be used for claimants?

16.46 Although there is no private law right conferred by the PSED, it still can be relied upon by individuals, or groups on their behalf by way of judicial review. Thus trades unions could issue proceedings for breach of the PSED – if an employment policy were being introduced by a public sector body without due regard having been paid to the PSED.

16.47   The PSED may also be useful in running an ET case, as follows:

---

69 EqA 2010 s3.
70 This is explicitly set out in the EqA 2010 at s150, but it reflects the previous position under the discrimination legislation.
71 At para 32 of its Report, 27 October 2009.
72 [2008] EWCA Civ 882.

- Information from monitoring, and impact assessments of policies which may be indirectly discriminatory[73] can be sought in pre-action correspondence, questionnaires or by means of discovery of documents (or the written questions procedure in ET cases).
- What is reasonable for a public authority in the context of an adjustment (in disability cases) will be different because one of the circumstances of the case is the obligation which the authority has to have due regard to the equality objectives in EqA 2010 s149.
- When seeking to justify indirect discrimination, direct age discrimination, and discrimination arising from disability, the public authority will have to be able to show that it has had due regard. If it cannot do this, it will be more difficult for it to justify as appropriate and necessary, the means it has adopted to achieve its aim.[74]

16.48   Information on a potential breach of the duty, as indicated above, can be sought in a variety of question forms. However, questions to ask, as to whether the duty is being properly exercised, might include:

- Does a policy, or its effects, have a disproportionate or adverse impact upon persons who have a protected characteristic, or disadvantaged groups?
- Does a policy, or the way in which a function is carried out, discourage or worsen relations between different groups of people, some of whom have a protected characteristic?
- Are there other ways in which a policy could be formulated that would advance equality of opportunity for minority or protected groups?
- Is it necessary or proportionate to commission further research or consultation on the issue?

16.49   Another area in which the PSED is likely to have impact is in respect of public procurement. This requires public authorities to consider equality when outsourcing work, which also has a knock-on effect on the private sector. Thus employers who have findings of

---

73   In *R (Elias) v Secretary of State for Defence* [2006] EWCA Civ 1293, [2006] 1 WLR 3213 the Court of Appeal said that a significant factor in determining whether a public authority is able to justify what appears to be indirect discrimination is the extent to which it has complied with the general duty to have due regard to the need to promote equality.

74   *R (Elias) v Secretary of State for Defence* [2006] EWCA Civ 1293, [2006] 1 WLR 3213, [2006] IRLR 934.

discrimination against them may find that they have to account for these when tendering and show that they have robust anti-discrimination systems in place.

16.50 **Practical points**

- If an adviser is dealing with an employee employed in the public sector, or by a private organisation exercising a public function, consider whether the public sector equality duty might be relevant.
- Likely to be of particular relevance when dealing with disability, sickness absence and reasonable adjustments; justification for age discrimination and justification of indirect discrimination.
- Obtain information about whether and if so how the equality impact of any policy relevant to a claim has been assessed – using questionnaire, information request and/or FOIA.
- In a challenge using PSED the pre-claim correspondence and the claimant's witness statement should show the facts which add weight to the importance of equality in the circumstances of the case. These include:
  - impact of the decision, etc on the group;
  - vulnerability of the group;
  - the particular needs of the group;

  as well as any other factor showing the importance of equal opportunities or good relations etc for the members of the group.

Practice and procedure

continued

Key points

This chapter deals with the stages in a claim, which can involve the following:

- Pre-claim:
  - the grievance process and any other attempts at resolving the dispute pre-claim;
  - letter before claim;
  - when asking written questions – relevance and proportionality are key to the construction of a good set of questions from which the ET may draw inferences if the respondent is evasive, equivocal or fails to answer.
- The claim – pleadings:
  - presenting a claim to the ET;
  - employer enters a response.
- The claim – intermediate stages:
  - case management discussion;
  - applications for further and better particulars;
  - applications for disclosure;
  - medical evidence for claims of disability discrimination or psychiatric injury.
- The hearing:
  - preparation for the hearing:
    - i bundles
    - ii witness statements
  - the hearing.

Introduction

17.1 This book is primarily aimed at the substantive law on discrimination in employment and occupation. However, it is important that claimants and their advisers have a reasonable understanding of ET procedure. Hence this chapter aims to give an overview of the essential aspects of ET procedure as they may affect discrimination claims. Some changes during 2013 are likely but had not been announced at the time of writing. The ET has exclusive jurisdiction over complaints relating to Part 5 of the EqA 2010 (work). It also has jurisdiction in any case where a court refers a claim relating to a non-discrimination rule on the grounds that it can be determined more conveniently by an ET.[1]

1 EqA 2010 ss122 and 127.

Territorial jurisdiction

17.2   The precursor legislation had various forms of territorial limitation built in. The EqA 2010 intentionally omits these. The Act is likely to be treated in the same way as the ERA 1996 was in respect of unfair dismissal claims. Regulation 19 of the Employment Tribunals (Constitution and Rules of Procedure) Regulations (ET Regs) 2004[2] states that an ET in England and Wales only has jurisdiction over discrimination claims where:

- the respondent (or one of the respondents resides or carries on business in England and Wales;[3] or
- the proceedings are to determine a question that has been referred to the ET by a court in England or Wales.

17.3   Chapter 10 deals in depth with the question of jurisdiction.[4]

Pre-action

Appeals and grievances

17.4   Complaints relating to any act occurring before 6 April 2009 will remain subject to the transitional provisions from the previous statutory appeals and grievance procedures.[5] We consider below the current dispute resolution scheme, which aims to be a mechanism for employees and employers to resolve disputes (or matters which may turn into disputes) without legal action, based on ACAS *Code of Practice on Disciplinary and Grievance Procedures*.[6]

17.5   An ET must take any relevant provisions of the ACAS Code into account in determining liability.[7] This may be relevant in dismissal[8] cases where a failure to follow the ACAS disciplinary procedures may make the dismissal unfair regardless of whether it is discriminatory.

---

2 SI No 1861
3 A company resides in England if it has registered office there (*Odeco (UK) Inc v Peacham* [1979] ICR 823). Conversely a company operating in England is carrying on business in England even if it is not registered there (*Knulty v Eloc Electro-Optiek and Communicatie BV* [1979] ICR 827).
4 See paras 10.36–10.53.
5 Employment Act 2008 (Commencement No 1, Transitional Provisions and Savings) Order 2008 SI No 3232.
6 April 2009, issued under TULRCA 1992 s199.
7 TULRCA 1992 s207.
8 The code only applies to employees and does not apply to workers.

However, in discrimination claims ETs may increase or decrease awards by up to 25 per cent for non-compliance.[9] The ACAS Code applies to all dismissals except those on the grounds of redundancy setting out basic requirements when considering the dismissal of an employee or a disciplinary sanction. It also applies to dismissals and lesser sanctions on grounds of poor performance even if not normally considered 'disciplinary' sanctions.

17.6   The ACAS Code should be read with the ACAS Guide.[10] It gives guidance on good industrial relations practice. Departure from these norms will generally only be significant in direct discrimination cases if comparators received the benefit of the steps and the claimant did not. In relation to a dismissal complaint these documents recommend:

- establishing the facts of the case;
- informing the employee of the problem;
- holding a meeting with the employee to discuss the problem;
- allowing the employee to be accompanied at the meeting;
- deciding on appropriate action;
- providing the employee with an opportunity to appeal.

Before presenting an ET claim an employee should normally submit an internal appeal against his dismissal. It should include a written statement setting out the grounds on which the decision is being challenged. If invited the employee should attend an appeal hearing. If the ACAS Code's appeal process is not followed an opportunity to resolve the dispute may be missed. If the failure to attend is judged by the ET to be unreasonable, it has the power to punish non-compliance. It can reduce any award 'if it considers it just and equitable in all the circumstances to do so' by up to 25 per cent.

Where the complaint relates to a constructive dismissal or something other than dismissal

17.7   If the complaint is about something other than an express dismissal, the grievance procedures should be followed. This applies to all types of complaint including most under the EqA 2010 and includes constructive dismissal. Under the ACAS Code:

- the employee should inform the employer in writing of the nature of the grievance;

9 As a result of TULRCA 1992 s207A.
10 *ACAS Guide: Discipline and Grievances at Work* (2011).

- the employer must arrange a formal meeting to discuss the grievance;
- the employee should attend the meeting and has the right to be accompanied by a colleague or trade union representative;
- the employer should decide what action to take following the meeting and should inform the employee of his decision;
- if the grievance is not resolved the employee may appeal against the decision;
- the employer should hold an appeal meeting that should be chaired by a manager not previously involved in the case;
- the outcome of the appeal should be communicated in writing.

17.8   If the procedure is not completely followed by the employee or employer the ET may reduce/increase any award by up to 25 per cent.

Letter before claim

17.9   In cases under the EqA 2010 consideration should be given to using pre-action correspondence to establish points from which an ET may wish to draw inferences including the inference that discrimination etc has taken place. In dismissal cases, if disciplinary appeals and grievance procedures are unsuccessful, a clear indication of the likelihood of litigation can be effective in bringing the claim to a successful conclusion. The claimant should send the employer a letter before claim, setting out the basis for the claim and compensation sought. The letter needs to be clear and easy for the employer to understand. If the employer replies, that will probably give a preview of the defence.

17.10   The Enterprise and Regulatory Reform Bill clause 59, once it becomes law, removes the specific questionnaire procedure provided for by EqA 2010 s138 in relation to contraventions occurring on or after a date to be announced. Even after s138 is removed, the formal questionnaire procedure may still be used for questions about discrimination that had occurred beforehand. For discrimination occurring thereafter, correspondence such as a letter before claim can form the basis of inferences by the ET. A failure to answer requests for information may form the basis for an inference.[11] However, to be effective, it is suggested that the following approach is adopted:

---

11   ERR Bill Explanatory Notes para 424. See also *Dattani v Chief Constable of West Mercia Police* [2005] IRLR 327.

- The letter should make clear that it is something that, if proceedings are started, will be put before the ET.
- They will be invited to draw inferences that discrimination has occurred from the evidence including any failure to provide answers to the letter before claim.
- The letter should give a reasonable period of time in which the employer is invited to answer it. That period should reflect the complexity of the information sought.
- If documents are sought, the letter should make it clear that the ET can draw inferences from a failure to make proper disclosure of documents relating to the primary facts of the case.[12]

Questionnaires

17.11 For discriminatory acts occurring after EqA 2010 s138 is removed claimants will have to use the processes described above to probe the respondent's case and formulate their complaint. At present, and in relation to acts occurring before its removal, claimants may use the questioning process under EqA 2010 s138. If a person (P) thinks that another person (R) has contravened the Act,[13] P may ask R any question. The question and the answer are admissible as evidence in proceedings before the ET. An ET can draw an inference from a failure by R to answer P's questions within eight weeks of service of the question. It can also draw an inference if the answers are either equivocal or evasive. There may be more than one possible inference, but clearly this includes the inference that an act of discrimination has taken place. The EqA 2010 makes clear that the question or answer is admissible as evidence and that the question does not have to be contained in a prescribed form (neither does the answer).

17.12 An ET may not draw an inference from these matters[14] where:

- R reasonably asserts that answering (or to do so differently) might have prejudiced a criminal matter (or revealed the reason for not starting/continuing proceedings);
- the failure or equivocation is for the purpose of safeguarding national security.[15]

---

12 Case C-415/10 *Meister v Speech Design Carrier Systems GmbH* [2012] ICR 1006.
13 Including a breach of an equality clause or rule (see EqA 2010 s138(6)).
14 EqA 2010 s138(5).
15 Equality Act 2010 (Obtaining Information) Order 2010 SI No 2194 para 6; thus far this is the only other exception.

17.13   Generally R is not required to respond (at all or unequivocally) to a question but an ET may draw inferences from a failure to respond within eight weeks or from evasive or equivocal answers.[16] A failure to respond does not raise a presumption of discrimination. In direct discrimination cases an inference should only be drawn where the failure sheds light on the 'mental process' (which may not be conscious) of the decision-maker.[17] So the inference can be drawn if the answers shed light on the reason why the employer did the act about which complaint is made.

17.14   It is important to employ common sense in the drafting and interpretation of questions:[18]

> It is necessary in each case to consider whether in the particular circumstances of that case the failure in question is capable of constituting evidence supporting the inference that the respondent acted discriminatorily in the manner alleged; and if so whether in the light of any explanation supplied it does in fact justify that inference. There will be many cases where it should be clear from the start, or soon becomes evident, that any alleged failure of this kind, however reprehensible, can have no bearing on the reason why the respondents did the act complained of, which in cases of direct discrimination is what the employment tribunal has to decide. In such cases time and money should not be spent pursuing the point.

17.15   However, the questioning process may be used in all types of case in which a contravention of the EqA 2010 is suspected. Thus the question of when it is appropriate to draw an inference must be seen in the light of the range of cases that will arise, including indirect discrimination, victimisation and so on. The central question in each case will be whether the evasion, failure to answer or inaccuracy of answer supports the inference that a contravention of the Act has occurred. Claimants should point out to the ET how the question that was unanswered was relevant to the claim being made. This can be done by relating the questions to the specific elements of the statutory claim in the case when writing the questions. They should then retain these headings (which do not need to be part of the questionnaire) for later reference and if the respondent does not respond or responds evasively, the claimant should explain to the ET the relevance of the question and the effect of the failure to answer (or evasion in the answer).

---

16   EqA 2010 s138(4)
17   *D'Silva v NATFHE* [2008] IRLR 412.
18   *D'Silva v NATFHE* [2008] IRLR 412 at para 38.

17.16   The questioning process is useful because the claimant can ask broad questions to identify contraventions of the EqA 2010 and germane areas of evidence concerning whether the contravention has occurred. It also permits the claimant to see at an early stage whether or not there is an innocent explanation for what happened.

17.17   The purpose of the questionnaire procedure was to assist in the formulation of the claimant's case, and so questions may be asked to search for evidence, when the claimant does not know whether such evidence exists. It is a more powerful tool than discovery of documents in this respect.

17.18   If the questions are irrelevant to the issues or disproportionate, the respondent may legitimately refuse to answer some or all of them. They can be used to find out the explanation which the respondent may rely upon. Frequently at an early stage of the litigation the respondent does not consider its answers thoroughly and may be more frank than later, for example after litigation has started. Responses can be used to highlight inconsistencies in the respondent's account during cross-examination.

17.19   The Equality Act 2010 (Obtaining Information) Order 2010[19] provides a standard form for the questionnaire. Questions do not have to be on any prescribed form,[20] but it provides a useful structure and gives the respondent appropriate warnings about the inferential process (which should be included in any letter mirroring this process). The effect of the process of questions and answers is the same whether they are set out in the questionnaire form or not.[21] There is a process for serving the formal questionnaire:[22]

- delivering it to the respondent or by sending it by post to the respondent, at the respondent's usual or last-known address or place of business;
- serving it through electronic means (only if the respondent has indicated in writing that the respondent will accept electronic service);[23] or
- if the respondent is represented by a solicitor it can be delivered or posted to the solicitor, or sent by electronic means (with written agreement).

19 SI No 2194.
20 EqA 2010 s138(3).
21 *Dattani v Chief Constable of West Mercia Police* [2005] IRLR 327 under the RRA 1976. The principles in that case will apply to the EqA 2010.
22 Equality Act 2010 (Obtaining Information) Order 2010 SI No 2194 art 5 2.
23 Service by electronic means takes place on the day the questionnaire is sent so long as it is before 4.30 pm on a business day.

Discrimination in employment / chapter 17

The questionnaire must be served either before the start of proceedings, or within 28 days of their commencement or 'such later time as the court or tribunal specifies'.[24]

Tribunal procedure

17.20 The EqA 2010 gives ETs jurisdiction in discrimination matters relating to work.[25] The procedure is governed by the ET Regs 2004.[26] ETs have no powers outside of those set out in the legislation. The ET is required to deal with cases in the light of the 'overriding objective' and must seek to give effect to it when interpreting the ET Regulations or when exercising any powers under the Regulations.[27] The overriding objective is to 'deal with cases justly', which includes so far as practicable:

- ensuring the parties are on an equal footing;
- dealing with the case in ways which are proportionate to the complexity or importance of the issues;
- ensuring that it is dealt with expeditiously and fairly; and
- saving expense.

The parties must assist the ET or employment judge to further the overriding objective.[28]

Presenting a claim

17.21 The ERR Bill provides, from a date to be announced, for compulsory contact with ACAS before being able to present a claim in relevant proceedings, including those under EqA 2010 ss120 and 127. If settlement is not possible, or not achieved, the ACAS conciliation officer will issue a certificate to that effect. If a claim is already late, EqA 2010 s140B(3) disregards the time spent waiting for that certificate. Otherwise, the normal time-limit is extended to one month after the date the ACAS certificate is received, or treated as having been

---

24 The questionnaire must be served within the period set out in para 4 of the 2010 Order.
25 EqA 2010 s120.
26 Employment Tribunals (Constitution and Rules of Procedure) Regulations 2004 SI No 1861. The Rules of Procedure are found in Sch 1.
27 ET Regs 2004 r3.
28 ET Regs 2004 r3(4).

received. The claim must be on prescribed ET1 form[29] and presented to an ET office within the appropriate time-limit.[30] It can be posted, faxed, emailed or completed online. The whole of it must arrive at the ET office (or server if by electronic means) by midnight on the last day. It should be sent to the appropriate ET office dealing with the postcode of the place of work but presentation at the wrong office (within the deadline) is sufficient, but will cause delay while the case is transferred. The government also proposes a system of fees for presenting claims and for pursuing a case to a hearing. Final details, including the date fees will be introduced, had not been announced by the date this book went to press.

17.22 Contents of a discrimination claim form: The claim should include all the relevant facts relied on in support of the legal conclusion the claimant seeks to establish and if possible set the legal conclusion out by reference to the EqA 2010. It should identify which claims under the Act are being pursued. A final section setting out references to the sections on which the claimant bases the case can make the point clearly. The aim is to present as full and complete a claim as possible that does not require later amendment. As it is the first document the ET will read, it gives the claimant the opportunity to start fostering the confidence of the ET in the case. Usually there will be insufficient room on the form so the claimant can attach particulars of the claim as an attachment to the ET1. A template is provided in appendix A.

Time-limits

17.23 Time-limits should be viewed as strict. Proceedings may not be brought after the end of:

- three months[31] starting with the date of the act to which the complaint relates; or,
- such other period as the ET thinks just and equitable.[32]

17.24 When does time start? Time starts to run from the date of the act about which complaint is being made.[33] The three-month time-limit starts to run from the date of the act or omission so that the deadline

---

29 Forms can be obtained online at www.justice.gov.uk/forms/hmcts/ employment.
30 ET Regs 2004 r1.
31 Six months where the claim is against the armed forces: section 121.
32 EqA 2010 s123.
33 For which EqA 2010 s123(1) provides.

in respect of an act done on 15 April is 14 July and not 15 July. There are two additional principles dealing with:

- conduct extending over a period;
- failures to do something.[34]

17.25   **Acts**: If the claim relates to an act such as a decision, time starts from the date of that decision and not the date on which it was communicated to the claimant.[35] Reconsideration of a decision can amount to a further discriminatory act if it involves a true reconsideration of the matter and not simply a reference back to the earlier decision.[36] In the case of discriminatory dismissals, time does not run from the date on which the employee is given notice of dismissal but from the date on which the dismissal actually takes effect.[37] An internal appeal against dismissal does not stop the limitation period in respect of a claim following a discriminatory dismissal.[38]

17.26   **Conduct extending over a period**: Where the complaint relates to 'conduct extending over a period' it is to be treated as occurring at the end of that period of time for the purposes of limitation.[39] This will only apply where it is the discriminatory conduct that is continuing as opposed to a single discriminatory decision which has ongoing consequences. Thus a decision not to promote is a single act with ongoing consequences.[40] In contrast, a complaint against a manager relating to a series of unreasonable instructions would refer to conduct extending over a period. The House of Lords has held that an act extended over a period where there was a continuing discriminatory 'regime, rule, practice or principle'.[41] Under the EqA 2010 it is likely to be sufficient if the ET is satisfied that there was a continuing discriminatory state of affairs however constituted and the House of Lords' test has been applied quite liberally. The Court of Appeal has suggested that all a claimant need show is that the allegations of discrimination are linked and that they indicate a 'continuing discriminatory state of affairs.'[42]

---

34   EqA 2010 s123(3).
35   *Virdi v Commissioner of the Police of the Metropolis* [2007] IRLR 24.
36   *Cast v Croydon College* [1998] IRLR 318, CA.
37   *British Gas Services Ltd v McCaull* [2001] IRLR 60.
38   Confirmed in *Robinson v Post Office* [2000] IRLR 814.
39   EqA 2010 s123(3)(a).
40   See *Sougrin v Haringey Health Authority* [1992] IRLR 416.
41   *Barclays Bank plc v Kapur* [1991] IRLR 136.
42   *Hendricks v Metropolitan Police Comr* [2003] IRLR 96.

17.27 **Complaints of failure to do something:** Where the complaint is of omission, the act of discrimination is treated as occurring 'when the person in question decided on it'.[43] In the absence of evidence to the contrary, this is taken to be the date when:

- the person in question does an act inconsistent with any duty to act; or,
- if there is no inconsistent act, then on the expiry of the period in which the person might reasonably have been expected to act.

17.28 A failure to make reasonable adjustments[44] is an omission and not an act.[45]

Extension of time-limits

17.29 Where a claim has been brought outside the limitation period, the ET can extend time. A complaint may be brought after the end of three months if it is brought within 'such other period as the ET thinks just and equitable'.[46]

17.30 Up to 2010, it was thought that exercising the discretion is the exception rather than the rule.[47] However, the Court of Appeal has moved away from this extreme position: each case is to be considered on its merits with no restrictive or liberal policy to extend time.[48] It is a matter of weighing up all relevant factors, which the claimant should set out and give evidence upon. The Court of Appeal has encouraged ETs to consider the factors set out in s 33 of the Limitation Act 1980:[49]

> That section provides a broad discretion for the court to extend the limitation period of three years in cases of personal injury and death. It requires the court to consider the prejudice which each party would suffer as the result of the decision to be made and also to have regard to all the circumstances and in particular, [amongst other things], to –
> (a) the length of and reasons for the delay;
> (b) the extent to which the cogency of the evidence is likely to be affected by the delay;

43 EqA 2010 s123(3)(b).

44 Now under EqA 2010 s20 and Sch 8.

45 *Matuszowicz v Kingston upon Hull City Council* [2009] IRLR 288.

46 EqA 2010 s123(1)(b).

47 *Robertson v Bexley Community Centre* [2003] IRLR 434.

48 *Chief Constable of Lincolnshire Police v Caston* [2010] IRLR 327 per Sedley LJ.

49 *Coal Corporation v Keeble* [1997] IRLR 336. This approach was endorsed by the Court of Appeal in *Department of Constitutional Affairs v Jones* [2008] IRLR 128.

(c) the extent to which the party sued had cooperated with any request for information;

(d) the promptness with which the [claimant] acted once he or she knew of the facts giving rise to the cause of action;

(e) the steps taken by the [claimant] to obtain appropriate professional advice once he or she knew of the possibility of taking action.

However, the guidelines expressed in *Keeble* are a reminder of factors that may be taken into account. Their relevance depends on the facts of the particular case. The factors that have to be taken into account depend on the facts, and the self-directions that need to be given must be tailored to the facts of the case as found.[50]

17.31   The claimant should ensure that there is evidence available to the ET on all the factors it will need to consider. A claimant's mental impairment may be a relevant consideration.[51] In *London Borough of Southwark v Afolabi*[52] a claimant was allowed to proceed with his claim nine years out of time. He only became aware of the facts underpinning his claim when he was given access to his personnel file. The ET may have regard to all the material before it, including pleadings, correspondence and medical reports.[53] It is not confined solely to evidence from witness statements.

17.32   The claimant's ill-health or pressing personal issues that prevent the claimant from concentrating on making a claim are common grounds but the ET will need to be convinced by clear evidence.

17.33   Other grounds for extension have included:

• failure by the claimant's representatives to make the claim in time or to advise correctly on the time-limits;[54]

• a substantial overlap with a claim that was presented in time;[55]

• a delay while the claimant sought to resolve the dispute using the employer's internal grievance mechanisms;[56]

• where the claimant did not have grounds to believe that he had been the victim of discrimination until some evidence came to his attention after the expiry of the time-limit;[57]

---

50 *Department of Constitutional Affairs v Jones* [2008] IRLR 128.
51 See *Department of Constitutional Affairs v Jones* [2008] IRLR 128.
52 [2003] ICR 800.
53 *Accurist Watches Ltd v Wadher* UKEAT/102/09, 23 March 2009.
54 *Chohan v Derby Law Centre* [2004] IRLR 685.
55 *Berry v Ravensbourne NHS Trust* [1993] ICR 871.
56 *Apelogun-Gabriels v London Borough of Lambeth* [2002] IRLR 116.
57 *London Borough of Southwark v Afolabi* [2003] IRLR 220.

- where a judicial decision clarified the law and gave the claimant a right that he was not understood to have had previously.[58]

Equal pay time-limits

17.34 Where there is a complaint of breach of an equality clause that comes within the ET's jurisdiction, the time-limit is six months from the date when employment ended. The six months run from different dates in cases of concealment or incapacity.[59]

17.35 Different time-limits apply in cases involving the armed forces. Note also that it will not be an abuse of process to commence equal pay proceedings in the county court within the six-year limitation period proper to contractual disputes.[60]

The correct respondent

17.36 Individual respondents may need to be included where the claimant wants to be able to receive a remedy against:

- an individual employee or agent of the respondent who may be held liable for an act of discrimination;[61]
- a person who has instructed,[62] caused,[63] or induced[64] another to commit a contravention of the Act in relation to a third person;
- a person who has knowingly aided a contravention of the Act.[65]

Particulars/details of claim

17.37 The particulars or details of claim should (if possible) be self-contained so as to be understood without reference to other documents. They should be clear, succinct and persuasive. Templates or precedents can provide a claimant with inspiration but should not be rigidly followed. At the end of this book we have set out some recommendations on drafting particulars of claim. Here are some common omissions.

---

58 *Foster v South Glamorgan Health Authority* [1988] IRLR 277.
59 See paras 14.122–14.128.
60 *Birmingham City Council v Abdulla* [2012] ICR 20, [2011] EWCA Civ 1412.
61 EqA 2010 s110.
62 EqA 2010 s111(1).
63 EqA 2010 s111(2).
64 EqA 2010 s111(3).
65 EqA 2010 s112.

17.38   The claimant must address each part of the relevant legal test. Failing to provide proper details at the outset is likely to result in orders requiring the claimant to provide further particulars or similar additional information. The best way to approach this task is to look at the legal provision (or the Employment Code) and look at each element required to constitute the unlawful act under the EqA 2010.

- **The nature of the protected characteristic:** In certain types of case it is necessary to give details of the protected characteristic in some depth. Eg:
  - the impairment(s) relied upon by the claimant in certain claims for disability discrimination;[66]
  - in religion and belief cases the claimant should provide specific information about the religion or (particularly) belief;
  - identifying the relevant age group in age cases will be vital;
  - in race cases the claimant should specify which aspect of race is in issue if it is known (ie colour, ethnic origin, ethnicity, national origins or simply race). If the claimant is not sure this need not be done immediately.
- **Comparators:** Where reliance must be placed on a comparator, the comparator(s) should be identified. If the comparator is hypothetical, as is often the case, that should be stated.
- **Provisions, criteria and practices:** In claims for indirect discrimination[67] and for failure to make reasonable adjustments,[68] the relevant disadvantaging provision, criterion or practice should be specified together with the disadvantage.

The response

17.39   The respondent has 28 days to enter a response on the ET3 form.[69] An extension of time can be requested within those 28 days. If no response is submitted then the respondent will be debarred from taking any part in the proceedings and the ET may give judgment in default.[70] There are limited circumstances in which a respondent that wishes to enter a response out of time may do so and have the judgment in default set aside by way of a review.[71]

---

66 See paras 1.10–1.52.
67 EqA 2010 s19.
68 EqA 2010 s20.
69 ET Regs 2004 r4.
70 ET Regs 2004 r8.
71 ET Regs 2004 r33.

Case management

17.40 **Case management discussion:** ETs have the power to hold a case management discussion (CMD).[72] CMDs are held as a matter of routine in almost all claims of discrimination. The claimant should be prepared to:

- discuss what parts of the claim are and are not dispute, and to allow the ET to identify the issues to be decided in determining the claim;
- help the ET deal with directions for the case to proceed to trial; and,
- deal with any outstanding interlocutory (interim) applications (see below).

Claimants should list the points that arise under each of these headings before attending a CMD. What follows should assist in this process. Good CMD preparation, particularly in respect of identifying the issues, sets the stage for the trial and can bring the case to a speedy conclusion whether by trial or settlement.

Identifying the issues

17.41 The ET will often require the parties to provide more detailed information about their claim and response if it is lacking in the pleadings. Thus in a discrimination claim involving multiple allegations, it is sensible to prepare a list of issues[73] giving:

- details of each allegation such as what happened, when, where and who was involved;
- for each allegation, the legal nature of the allegation: ie is it direct/indirect discrimination and/or harassment etc and if possible identifying the section of the EqA 2010 that covers the complaint;
- in cases involving a comparator, the identity of any comparators or whether a hypothetical comparator is relied on;
- if all or part of the claim is out of time, whether the claimant is arguing that the allegations are a continuing act and/or whether the ET will be asked to extend time applying the 'just and equitable test'.

17.42 The respondent can be required to provide further details. In disability discrimination cases, the respondent will often be asked whether it is disputed that the claimant was a disabled person for the purposes

---

72 ET Regs 2004 r17.
73 See appendix A for a template of issues.

of the EqA 2010 at the material time. In a direct discrimination claim the respondent should be pressed to provide the non-discriminatory reason for the treatment. The claimant should go to the CMD with a list of points which the respondent should be asked to clarify. ETs expect the parties to have a clear understanding of the case. Using the legal framework for the claim will assist the claimant to have this understanding.

Directions

17.43   After the issues are identified, the ET will have an idea of the length and complexity of the final hearing. It will then give directions to the parties to prepare the case for trial. The claimant should consider how much time they will realistically need to do the things that the ET directs, and should also be realistic about how long the respondent will need to do the same. ETs usually make directions for:

- the claimant to provide a schedule of loss (see the example in appendix A);
- the parties to disclose by list all documents in their possession or control, whether supportive or adverse to their case;
- the parties to request inspection of the documents on the opposing party's list and for inspection to take place (usually by providing copies of the documents);
- the parties to agree a joint bundle for the final hearing, which will contain all of the documents that the parties wish to put before the ET;
- the parties (or sometimes one of the parties) to prepare the bundle and ensure there are sufficient copies for all of the parties, the members of the ET and one for use by witnesses;
- the parties to exchange witness statements in advance of the hearing containing all the evidence which the witness wishes to give;
- the matter to be set down for a full hearing.

17.44   In disability discrimination cases there will frequently be directions for medical or other experts given at the CMD. In preparation for a CMD at which issues involving experts are to be discussed, it is worth seeking to discuss with the respondent whether a joint expert could be instructed. In certain cases this will be the most appropriate way for the ET to obtain the expert's views. The following guidelines should be borne in mind:[74]

74 *De Keyser Ltd v Miss L Wilson* [2001] IRLR 324.

- Before instructing an expert, consider the need for the evidence carefully.[75] The evidence must be the independent product of the expert. It must be uninfluenced as to form or content by the exigencies of litigation.[76]
- Explore first with the ET in correspondence whether, in principle, expert evidence is likely to be acceptable or do this at the CMD.
- The joint instruction of a single expert is the preferred course that will be followed unless a party has already instructed an expert.
- The terms that the parties will need to agree include how payment of the expert's fees and expenses is to be divided. The ET cannot make an order concerning this aspect;.
- If the means available to one side or another are such that, in its view, it cannot agree to share or to risk any exposure to the expert's fees or expenses, or if, irrespective of its means, a party refuses to pay or share such costs, the other party or parties can be expected reasonably to prefer to require their own expert but even in such a case the weight to be attached to that expert's evidence (a matter entirely for the ET to judge) may be found to have been increased if the terms of his instruction shall have been submitted to the other side, if not for agreement then for comment, ahead of their being finalised for sending to the expert. Thus if this has not happened in a case it should be the subject of comment in submissions.
- In the case of a joint expert the ET generally fixes a period within which the parties are to seek to agree the expert's identity[77] and joint letter of instruction; it can direct a date by which the joint experts' report is to be made available.
- Any letter of instruction should specify in as much detail as can be given any particular questions the expert is to be invited to answer and all more general subjects that he is to be asked to address.
- Such instructions are as far as possible to avoid partisanship. There can often be an exchange of correspondence at this point in preparing joint instructions with the other parties' representatives. The letter itself should avoid being tendentious. Where assumptions of fact underlie the question being asked, they must be spelled out. The letter should emphasise that in preparing his

---

75 See remarks in *Whitehouse v Jordan* [1981] 1 WLR 246 at 256H.

76 Reference should be made to Civil Procedure Rules rr35.1–35.14 and the associated Practice Direction for further guidance (available at www.justice.gov. uk/courts/procedure-rules/civil).

77 If the parties cannot agree the ET may 'assist' them by holding a further CMD for this purpose.

evidence the expert's principal and overriding duty is to the ET rather than to any party.

- The ET can direct which issues the expert can (or cannot) address.

- If there are separate experts (absent the parties' agreement) the ET may specify a timetable for disclosure or exchange of experts' reports and, where there are two or more experts, for meetings of the experts.

- Timetables generally provide for the raising of supplementary questions with the expert or experts and disclosure or exchange of the answers in good time before the hearing.

- Separate experts should be encouraged to meet. The ET will encourage meeting on a without prejudice basis with a view to their seeking to resolve any conflict between them and, where possible, to their producing and disclosing a schedule of agreed issues and of points of dispute between them.

- If a party fails, without good reason, to follow these guidelines and if, in consequence, another party or parties suffer delay or are put to expense which a due performance of the guidelines would have been likely to avoid, then the ET may wish to consider whether, on that party's part, there has been unreasonable conduct within rules concerning costs.

17.45   When setting the case down for a full hearing, the ET will want to know how many witnesses (including the claimant and individual respondents) each party expects to call so that an estimate can be made of the length of the hearing. The ET will normally set a hearing date at the CMD so it is imperative that the parties are aware of any dates to avoid for their witnesses or representatives.

Pre-hearing review

17.46   Where there is a discrete issue which may be decisive to the claim, the ET may call a pre-hearing review (PHR). This will occur where there is an application for a strike out or deposit order, or where it is appropriate to decide an issue before embarking on a full trial. Sometimes in discrimination claims, a time-limit point can be considered at a PHR (if there is a discrete point for the ET to consider).

Applications

17.47 Case management powers are set out in ET rule 10. This provides that an employment judge may 'at any time either on the application of a party or on his own initiative make an order in relation to any matter which appears to him appropriate'. The rule gives examples of orders which may be made as orders:

(a) as to the manner in which the proceedings are to be conducted, including any time-limit to be observed;

(b) that a party provide additional information;

(c) requiring the attendance of any person in Great Britain either to give evidence or to produce documents or information;

(d) requiring any person in Great Britain to disclose documents or information to a party [or] to allow a party to inspect such material as might be ordered by a County Court (or in Scotland, by a sheriff);

(e) extending any time-limit, whether or not expired (subject to rules 4(4), 11(2), 25(5), 30(5), 33(1), 35(1), 38(7) and 42(5) of this Schedule, and to rule 3(4) of Schedule 2);

(f) requiring the provision of written answers to questions put by the tribunal or [employment judge];

(g) ...

(h) staying (in Scotland, sisting) the whole or part of any proceedings;

(i) that part of the proceedings be dealt with separately;

(j) that different claims be considered together;

(k) that any person who the [employment judge] or tribunal considers may be liable for the remedy claimed should be made a respondent in the proceedings;

(l) dismissing the claim against a respondent who is no longer directly interested in the claim;

(m) postponing or adjourning any hearing;

(n) varying or revoking other orders;

(o) giving notice to the parties of a pre-hearing review or the Hearing;

(p) giving notice under rule 19;

(q) giving leave to amend a claim or response;

(r) that any person who the [employment judge] or tribunal considers has an interest in the outcome of the proceedings may be joined as a party to the proceedings;

(s) that a witness statement be prepared or exchanged; or

(t) as to the use of experts or interpreters in the proceedings.

17.48 Rule 11 requires that applications must be in writing and state the case number. They must be made not less than 10 days before the date of the hearing at which they are to be considered.[78] They must state what order is sought and the reasons for the request and should include 'an explanation of how the order would assist the ET or employment judge in dealing with the proceedings efficiently and fairly.

17.49   A copy of the application should be sent to the other parties at the same time as it is sent to the ET providing details of the application and why it is being made[79] and state that any objection must be sent to the ET with seven days of receipt or before any hearing if that is sooner. The notice should state that any objections must be copied to all other parties. The covering letter to the ET for the application must state that the other parties have been served with the copy application and that the requirements of rule 11(4) have been met.

Electronically stored information: The disclosure obligations include disclosure of any documents held in electronic form, no matter whether they are stored on a smart phone, central server or in a back-up archive. As well as obvious documents, it includes data bases, audio files and text messages. Co-operation in agreeing proportionate ways to retain, identify and disclose potentially relevant documents is essential. As a starting point, it is helpful to consider the principles identified in the Civil Procedure Rules Practice Direction 31B *Disclosure of Electronic Documents*.[80]

Amendments

17.50   Applications to amend should be made as soon as possible but they do not take effect until the ET gives permission. In *Selkent Bus Co Ltd v Moore*[81] the EAT reviewed the practice of amending claims and stated that ETs should take into account all the circumstances and balance the injustice and hardship of allowing the amendment against the injustice and hardship of refusing it. The relevant circumstances include:

- the nature of the application: How substantial is it? Does it seek to (a) alter the basis of an existing claim; (b) introduce a new legal

78   Unless that is not reasonably practicable or an employment judge considers it in the interests of justice to allow shorter notice.
79   Unrepresented parties do not have to do this.
80   Available on www.justice.gov.uk/courts/procedure-rules/civil/rules/pd_part31b. For more resources on electronic disclosure, go to www.ediscosure.uk.com/wiki_new/index.php?title=Electronic_Disclosure.
81   [1996] ICR 836.

conclusion linked to the already pleaded facts (relabeling); or, (c) introduce a new claim?

- time-limits: If a new claim is out of time, the discretion to extend time must be considered;[82]
- timing and manner: An amendment can be allowed at any time but it would be relevant to consider the reason for any delay and whether the parties would be prejudiced.

17.51   In *Lehman Brothers Ltd v Smith*[83] and *TGWU v Safeway Stores Ltd*[84] the courts allowed amendments even where out of time, considering the balance of hardship and injustice as most important.

Additional information

17.52   The ET may require a party to provide additional information regarding its claim or response.[85] There is a related but separate power to request 'written answers to questions put by the ET'.[86] After the questionnaire procedure is abolished claimants may use this power instead. As the power to order answers is only available after the commencement of the claim, some consequential amendments may be needed.

17.53   If the claim and response have been properly pleaded, then a request for additional information (or 'further particulars') is not normally necessary. Where an allegation or counter-allegation has been made but without sufficient detail for a response, further particulars should be sought.[87] Thus, if the response says 'the claimant was dismissed for a fair reason', asking for the precise reason and details is appropriate. Further particulars are generally ordered to provide sufficient details of the case to enable the other parties to know the case they have to meet (factually and legally). In particular the breadth and basis of a defence can be established more clearly by obtaining an order. If there is a generalised complaint it is usually sensible to seek particulars of (a) dates, (b) places, (c) people, (d) the gist of what

---

82 Direct and indirect discrimination have been held to be separate causes of action: *Ali v Office of National Statistics* [2005] IRLR 201. A change to a named comparator in an equal pay case however was seen as a simple amendment to an existing cause of action in *Smith v Gwent District Health Authority* [1996] ICR 1044.

83 UKEAT/486/05, 13 October 2005.

84 UKEAT/92/07, 6 June 2007.

85 ET Regs 2004 r10(2)(b).

86 ET Regs 2004 r10(2)(f).

87 See *Byrne v Financial Times Ltd* [1991] IRLR 417.

happened. Likewise when pleading the claim it is sensible to make sure that this information is present whenever possible. When replying to a request, it is often most useful to provide the information in a tabular form. If the party is genuinely unable to provide these details, approximate dates can be used.

Disclosure

17.54   ETs have very broad powers to order a person to disclose documents to a party to the claim. They are the same powers as a county court.[88] The ET can exercise the power against anyone in Great Britain[89] even if they are not a party to the proceedings. Disclosure is a crucial step in discrimination claims because an ET relies on making inferences from secondary evidence. It is important therefore to seek and give full disclosure. ETs often make an order for disclosure under which the parties exchange lists of all documents in their possession that are relevant to the claim. They must disclose documents that are damaging to their case as well as favourable documents. The duty is a continuing duty so if further relevant documents come into a party's possession at any time before the end of the hearing they must be disclosed.[90] What is relevant depends on the case. The framework for relevance is the claim. Any documents that might assist a party to prove their case or defence must be disclosed. Typical examples of disclosable document categories in discrimination cases include: minutes of meetings; documents preparatory to meetings, emails and other notes, minutes or other memos that refer to a meeting or its consequences. When making a request the claimant should first consider the claim under the EqA 2010 being pursued. The claimant should look at the section of the EqA 2010 and look at each element of the legal claim and then ask in what way the document in question could help or hinder proof of any of the elements of the case.

17.55   The ET often makes an order for 'inspection' of documents to take place after disclosure.[91] This means that the parties can ask to

---

88   Under Civil Procedure Rules 1998 Part 31 by ET Regs 2004 r10(1)(d).

89   This restriction means that an order cannot be made for disclosure of documents held overseas by a foreign parent company of the respondent. See *Weatherford UK Ltd v Forbes* UKEATS/38/11, 21 December 2011.

90   *Scott v IRC* [2004] IRLR 713.

91   This gives the parties the right to see any documents from the other party's list. It is common for the parties to write to each other specifying which documents they require. This is then responded to by the other party sending photocopies of the requested documents. Very often parties will simply copy the documents which would otherwise be inspected.

come and look at (and potentially take copies of) documents listed by the other parties. If many documents are involved a respondent may insist on this process. In those circumstances a clear idea of the relevance principle may ensure that the claimant does not miss a vital document that forms part of one of the many boxes of barely relevant information supplied by the respondent and that may in effect conceal relevant and damaging information.

17.56   An example of the relevance principle at work is *West Midlands Passenger Transport Executive v Singh*.[92] There the Court of Appeal confirmed that statistical evidence would be relevant to many discrimination claims if it showed how different groups were treated and should therefore be disclosed.

17.57   **Limits on disclosure**: The ET will limit disclosure where it would otherwise be oppressive or disproportionate. In a case alleging discrimination in recruitment, an ET is unlikely to order a large employer to disclose copies of all job applications and related documents for every job applicant (the disclosure could be many thousands of files). It is more likely to require disclosure of applications for work in a particular role or department at a particular location over the last, say, three years.[93] The Court of Appeal in *Canadian Imperial Bank of Commerce v Beck*[94] stressed that the touchstone for disclosure was whether it was 'necessary for disposing fairly of the proceedings'. When making the application for an order therefore claimants should seek to demonstrate that the documents sought are necessary for fair disposal. Again, linking the document clearly to the statutory framework will assist. In *Beck* the Court of Appeal was unsympathetic to the defence that full disclosure would entail the recovery of over 500,000 emails. The key question is the ease of the search that is needed.

17.58   Confidentiality does not preclude disclosure if disclosure is necessary for a fair trial.[95] Where possible confidentiality should be preserved by redacting (blacking out) parts of the document or substituting letters or numbers for the names of individuals referred to. If there is any dispute over whether it is necessary to disclose a document or whether parts should be redacted then the ET should hold a hearing in private to decide how to proceed.[96] Respondents often cite

92 [1988] IRLR 186.
93 See *Perera v Civil Service Commission* [1980] IRLR 233 for an example of this practice.
94 [2009] IRLR 740, CA.
95 *Science Research Council v Nasse* [1979] IRLR 465, HL.
96 See for example *Asda Stores Ltd v Thompson (No 2)* [2004] IRLR 598.

the Data Protection Act 1998 as a reason for non-disclosure. In most cases the DPA makes no difference to whether there should be disclosure and, if ordered by an ET, the information becomes required by law to be provided.

17.59   Some common law principles restrict disclosure of certain classes of documents.[97] These rules apply equally in the ET as they do in any other court.[98] Every communication with a professional legal adviser is subject to professional legal privilege and is not disclosable unless the communication was made in furtherance of a fraud.[99] This rule only applies to communications with lawyers; it does not apply to communications with HR advisers or union representatives.[100] All communications by a party to litigation or proposed litigation that is of a confidential nature regarding the case are covered by litigation privilege and are not disclosable.[101]

17.60   Although privileged documents are immune from disclosure, a party can still disclose such documents if it wishes to do so. Once privilege is waived, either party can rely on the document. Whether there has been waiver depends on the nature of the information that has been revealed and the circumstances in which that information was revealed. The more complete the information provided about the legal advice, the higher the risk that waiver will have occurred. There must also be reliance on the legal advice to establish waiver.[102] Moreover if one party seeks to rely on advice from their solicitor to establish a point, this may waive privilege in the advice given. Disclosure could be ordered if that was the way to ensure fairness between the parties.[103]

17.61   **Specific disclosure:** If a party fails to disclose a particular document an application can be made. There should first be a written request specifying the document or type of document. Failing compliance, an application may be made to the ET for a 'specific disclosure' order for the document(s). The application should explain why it is believed the other party has the documents and how the

---

97   The rules regarding legal professional and litigation privilege were comprehensively set out by the House of Lords in *Three Bridges District Council v Governor and Company of the Bank of England* [2005] 4 All ER 948.

98   *Brennan v Sunderland City Council* [2009] ICR 479.

99   *Kuwait Airways Corporation v Iraq Airways Company* [2005] 1 WLR 2734, CA.

100   *New Victoria Hospital v Ryan* [1993] IRLR 202.

101   See *Howes v Hinckley BC* UKEAT/0213/08, 4 July 2008 for example.

102   *Brennan v Sunderland City Council* [2008] UKEAT/0349/08 and see *D (A Child)* [2011] EWCA Civ 684, endorsing the EAT's principles in *Brennan.*

103   *National Centre for Young People with Epilepsy v Boateng* UKEAT/0440/10.

document is relevant. Without this the request is a 'fishing expedition' made in the hope of finding within the documents some useful evidence.

17.62   The EAT has said that disputes regarding the admissibility of documents should be decided at a PHR in private.[104]

Settlement

17.63   All ET claims are sent to the Advice, Conciliation and Arbitration Service (ACAS), which has a duty to conciliate in ET claims.[105] ACAS can conciliate before a claim has been presented.[106] Discussions with an ACAS officer are 'without prejudice', meaning they cannot be relied on as evidence and should not be referred to in the ET.[107] Successful ACAS negotiation results in an agreement in a COT3 form, which may be enforced in the county court as if it were an ET judgment. An oral agreement reached through ACAS binds the parties.[108]

17.64   Without ACAS involvement an agreement will only settle statutory claims if the requirements for 'a qualifying compromise contract' are satisfied.[109] It must be in writing. The complainant must have received advice from an independent adviser[110] who is insured and is identified in the contract. The contract must state that the conditions for a qualifying compromise contract are met.

17.65   A settlement agreement that does not comply with the above requirements does not exclude any statutory claims. It is effective for contractual claims only so the claimant can enforce that aspect. The provisions for compromise agreements cannot be used to contract out of a legal right where a claim has not yet arisen but can validly

---

104 *Eversheds LLP v Gray* UKEAT/585/11, 29 November 2011.
105 Trade Union and Labour Relations (Consolidation) Act 1992 s211 and ETA 1996 s18.
106 ETA 1996 s18(3). Once section 18A is inserted into the Employment Tribunals Act 1996, pre-claim contract with ACAS becomes compulsory – see para 17.21 above.
107 ETA 1996 s18(7).
108 *Gilbert v Kembridge Fibres* [1984] ICR 188.
109 EqA 2010 s144. An invalid compromise agreement may still be an enforceable agreement preventing the party from bringing a common law claim: *Sutherland v Network Appliance Ltd* [2001] IRLR 12.
110 EqA 2010 s144(4) sets out who qualifies as an independent adviser. The list includes qualified lawyers, trade union officers, officials or employees (certified in writing by the union as competent to give advice). It also includes a worker or volunteer at an advice centre (certified in writing by the centre as competent to give advice).

apply to where there are threatened or anticipated proceedings which have not yet been presented.[111] If a public authority agrees to settle a claim for a sum of money without following its own internal procedures and/or where the sum offered is irrationally excessive, it may be acting ultra vires. In such circumstances, the settlement, whether by a compromise agreement or COT3 will be void.[112] Claimants settling large claims against public authorities will want to reassure themselves that the authority is acting lawfully in settling for the amount offered.[113]

'Without prejudice' communications

17.66   Discussions for the purpose of a genuine attempt to compromise a dispute are frequently 'without prejudice' to the parties' positions and may not be admitted in evidence. This means that a party can maintain before the ET something they might be prepared to concede for the purposes of reaching an agreement. 'Without prejudice' discussions may not be referred to before the ET. The rule avoids the ET being influenced by negotiations. A party can make an open offer of settlement or a 'without prejudice save as to costs' offer to which reference can be made should an application for costs be made. It is always safest to make the without prejudice status of a communication explicit. However, the application of the rule is not dependent upon the use of the phrase 'without prejudice' and if it is clear from the surrounding circumstances that the parties were seeking to compromise the action on a without prejudice basis the evidence will be excluded.[114] Claimants therefore should always ensure that if a communication is intended to be without prejudice it clearly states that this is the case. The ET will require the party claiming that an unlabelled document was without prejudice to rebut the inference that it was open given that it was not marked 'without prejudice'.[115]

17.67   Parties often say that a meeting is 'without prejudice' when it is not. So for the principle to apply:

111 *Hinton v University of East London* [2005] IRLR 552, CA.
112 *Gibb v Maidstone and Tunbridge Wells NHS Trust* [2010] EWCA Civ 678, [2010] IRLR 786; however, an authority seeking to rely on this principle will have a very difficult job of persuading the court.
113 However, the Localism Act 2011 now provides that a local authority has power to do anything that individuals generally may do (s1(1)). Therefore most settlements by public authorities will be lawful.
114 However, see *Schering Corporation v Cipla Ltd* [2004] EWHC 2587.
115 *Cadle Co v Hearley* [2002] 1 Lloyd's Rep 143 at para 29.

- there must be an actual or prospective legal dispute.
- what is said or done must be a genuine attempt to compromise that dispute.

Once section 111A is inserted into the Employment Rights Act 1996, it will exclude evidence in ordinary unfair dismissal claims of pre-termination negotiations. Such negotiations before a dispute was in prospect continue to be admissible in automatically unfair and discriminatory dismissals. However, evidence may not be excluded if the tribunal considers it 'improper' or connected to 'improper behaviour'. For example, what is said at a s111A or a without prejudice meeting may amount to harassment or discrimination in its own right so neither s111A nor common law principles should apply if the communication would prejudice the person to whom it is addressed, for example because it forms part of the basis of a claim against the employer of discrimination or harassment or victimisation. This last point covers any abuse of the privilege of 'without prejudice' and should also cover s111A negotiations.[116]

Preliminary hearing

17.68 The ET has the power to hold a preliminary hearing on any issue that must be determined before the case proceeds to trial, for example limitation issues. It is only appropriate if determination of the issue will end proceedings or substantially simplify them. The benefits must be clear. The following are examples of situations in which a preliminary hearing is unlikely to be appropriate:

- determining whether a lengthy series of acts constitutes a continuing discriminatory state of affairs for the purposes of determining when the limitation period starts.[117] If the claimant has a reasonably arguable basis for the contention that the various complaints are so linked as to be continuing acts or to constitute an ongoing state of affairs,[118] it should be determined as an issue at the full hearing. It is difficult to say in advance of the evidence that no such case exists;[119]

---

116 *BNP Paribas v Ms A Mezzotero* [2004] IRLR 508.

117 *Hendricks v Commissioner of Police for the Metropolis* [2003] ICR 530, [2003] IRLR 96: the preliminary issue was whether a lengthy list of allegations of race discrimination spanning 11 years could constitute a 'continuing act'. Now see EqA 2010 s123(3)(a) (conduct extending over a period).

118 *Ma v Merck Sharpe and Dohme Ltd* [2008] EWCA Civ 1426 at para 17.

119 See *Hendricks* at paras 48–52.

- it can be argued that ETs should generally not hold preliminary hearings in disability discrimination cases to establish whether the claimant is disabled and therefore covered by the legislation.[120] Preliminary issues often involve legal arguments that are susceptible to lengthy appeals, so there is a risk, which materialised in *Boyle*, that, by the time the preliminary issue is finally determined, many years will have elapsed before the substantive case can be heard.

Strike out

17.69   The ET has the power to make an order to strike out claims or responses at a pre-hearing review where:[121] (a) the claim or response is scandalous, vexatious or has no reasonable prospect of success;[122] (b) the manner in which the proceedings have been conducted by or on behalf of the claimant or respondent has been scandalous, unreasonable or vexatious; (c) the claim is not actively pursued; (d) there has been non-compliance with an order or practice direction; or (e) it is no longer possible to have a fair hearing.

17.70   Before striking out, the ET must notify the party in question that it is considering doing so and invite them to reply setting out reasons why the order should not be made.[123] A strike out can only be made at a pre-hearing review or a full hearing if requested by one of the parties.[124]

17.71   Where the central facts are in dispute the power to strike out should only rarely be used.[125] Discrimination cases should not be struck out as an abuse of process 'except in the most obvious and plainest cases.'[126] In *Anyanwu* the House of Lords stated:[127]

> Discrimination cases are generally fact-sensitive, and their proper determination is always vital in our pluralistic society. In this field perhaps more than any other the bias in favour of a claim being examined on the merits or demerits of its particular facts is a matter of high

---

120 *Boyle v SCA Packaging Ltd* [2009] IRLR 746.

121 ET Regs 2004 r18(7).

122 See *Tayside Public Transport v Reilly* [2012] IRLR 755, Court of Session; *Bolch v Chipman* [2004] IRLR 140.

123 ET Regs 2004 r19.

124 ET Regs 2004 r18(6).

125 *North Glamorgan NHS Trust v Ezsias* [2007] IRLR 603; *Tayside Public Transport v Reilly* [2012] IRLR 755, Court of Session.

126 Lord Steyn in *Anyanwu v South Bank Students' Union* [2001] IRLR 305.

127 [2001] IRLR 305 at para 24.

public interest. Against this background it is necessary to explain why on the allegations made by the appellants it would be wrong to strike out their claims against the university.

17.72   Respondents seeking a strike out will often rely on *ABN AMRO Management Service Ltd v Hogben*[128] where Underhill J struck out a claim of age discrimination that he found to be 'fanciful' because the claimant's comparator was only nine months younger. However, the preponderance of (higher) authority points to a different test. If the grounds of complaint indicate a dispute,[129]

> what one must be able to say ... is that the case is truly exceptional in the sense that the prospects of the claimant in establishing a connection between her dismissal and earlier events is utterly fanciful; in other words, this is such an extreme case that it falls within the exception that it should be struck out as having no reasonable prospects of success.

Lady Smith in *Balls v Downham Market High School*[130] stated:

> Where a strike out is sought or contemplated on the ground that the claim has no reasonable prospect of success, the structure of the exercise that the [ET] has to carry out is the same; the [ET] must first consider whether, on careful consideration of all the available material, it can properly conclude that has the claim has *no* reasonable prospect of success. I stress the word 'no' because it shows that the test is not whether the claimant's claim is likely to fail nor is it a matter of asking whether it is possible that the claim will fail. Nor is it a test which can be satisfied by considering what is put forward by the respondent either in the ET3 or in submissions and deciding whether their written or oral assertions regarding disputed matters are likely to be established facts. It is, in short, a high test. There must be *no* reasonable prospects.

17.73   Strike out for non-compliance with orders or for unreasonable behaviour is a last resort and will only be ordered where a party's behaviour has made a fair hearing impossible or amounts to a deliberate and

---

128   UKEAT/266/09, 20 November 2009.

129   *A v B and C* UKEAT/0450/08 (para 53) later upheld in [2010] EWCA Civ 1378. The claimant's claim for sex discrimination was struck out as having no reasonable prospects of success. A had brought a grievance about sexual harassment by the principal of her employer, a higher education institution, who subsequently dismissed her for academic fraud (purchasing academic qualifications and bringing it into disrepute). The ET said the case against A was supported by overwhelming documentary evidence. However, the EAT and Court of Appeal disagreed.

130   [2011] IRLR 217.

persistent disregard of the ET's procedures.[131] The case can normally be saved and the defaulting party appropriately punished by a lesser order, such as one for costs.[132]

17.74   Where one party has sought to intimidate the other in a way 'specifically designed to put the other in fear of the consequences of continuing with the action' and that has had the effect of putting the other party in fear, then a strike out will normally be appropriate[133] although the guilty party might still be allowed to take part in a hearing on remedies.

17.75   A non-compliance strike out should be considered in good time before the substantive hearing. The ET must consider whether there is a less draconian way of ensuring that a fair trial can take place, for example an unless order, an adjournment and/or costs.[134]

17.76   A claim can be struck out if it is not actively pursued and the delay is inordinate, inexcusable and will have caused the other party to be prejudiced.[135] It can also be struck out if the claimant has failed to take reasonable steps to progress his claim in a manner that shows disrespect or contempt for the ET and/or its procedures.[136]

17.77   The final ground for strike out, that a fair hearing is no longer possible, rarely arises. It may arise if a fair trial has been made impossible but neither party is at fault.[137]

Deposit order

17.78   A deposit order can be made if the judge considers that the contentions put forward by any party in relation to a matter required to be determined by an ET have 'little reasonable prospect of success'.[138] It requires a deposit not exceeding £1,000 as a condition of continuing

---

131 *Blockbuster Entertainment Ltd v James* [2006] IRLR 760; see also *Bolch v Chipman* [2004] IRLR 140; *Masood v Zahoor* [2010] 1 WLR 746, CA at para 71.
132 See also *De Keyser Ltd v Wilson* [2001] IRLR 324, where the respondent had acted scandalously.
133 *Force One Utilities Ltd v Hatfield* [2009] IRLR 45.
134 *Blockbuster Entertainment Ltd v James* [2006] IRLR 630, CA.
135 *Birkett v James* [1978] AC 297 and *Evans' Executors v Metropolitan Police Authority* [1992] IRLR 570.
136 *Rolls Royce Plc v Riddle* [2008] IRLR 873.
137 However, see *Abegaze v Shrewsbury College of Arts & Technology* [2009] IRLR 238: even a six-year delay and retirement of two ET members did not make a fair trial (on remedy) impossible.
138 ET Regs 2004 r20.

the proceedings.[139] The order can only be made at a pre-hearing review. There is some debate as to the extent that the ET is entitled to consider the likelihood of the claimant succeeding with any factual as well as legal assertions. In *JE Jansen Van Rensburg v Royal Borough of Kingston upon Thames*[140] the EAT said the facts could be assessed summarily and cases which were unlikely to succeed on the facts could be the subject of a deposit order. That approach gives some leeway in deciding whether or not to make a deposit. In *Spring v First Capital East Ltd*, Supperstone J held that a judge can consider both written and oral evidence as appropriate and that the test is as set out in rule 20(1).[141]

17.79 A discrete order is required for each matter where the test is satisfied. However, the ET must always take reasonable steps to ascertain the paying party's means so that the deposit can be met.[142] If the deposit is not paid within 21 days then the claim or response is automatically struck out. No member of the ET that considered whether to make a deposit order may sit on the ET at the final hearing.[143] Unless a costs order is made at the end of the proceedings it is returned. If a party continues litigating after a deposit order has been made and has been unsuccessful then the ET 'shall consider whether to make a costs or preparation time order against that party on the ground that he conducted the proceedings relating to the matter unreasonably in persisting to have the matter determined'.[144] Such costs orders can only be made if the party lost on substantially the same grounds as led the ET to make the earlier deposit order.

Withdrawal

17.80 A claimant may withdraw all or part of his claim at any time.[145] A claim can be withdrawn so that it can be pursued in the civil courts

---

139 Inserted by Employment Tribunals (Constitution and Rules of Procedure) (Amendment) Regulations 2012 SI No 468 in relation to claims presented from 6 April 2012.

140 UKEAT/096/07, 16 October 2007.

141 UKEAT/567/11, 20 July 2012. At para 17, the EAT finds that *Sharma v New College Nottingham* UKEAT/287/11, 1 December 2011, provides no support for the proposition that the test for making a deposit order was the same as for a strike-out.

142 ET Regs 2004 r20(2). County Court form EX140 should be used to assist determining the paying party's means: *Oni v NHS Leicester City* [2013] ICR 91.

143 ET Regs 2004 r18(9).

144 ET Regs 2004 r47.

145 In accordance with ET Regs 2004 r25.

provided that it would not be an abuse of process.[146] The withdrawal
of a claim cannot be reversed.[147]

17.81   Once a claim has been withdrawn, the respondent can apply for
the proceedings against him to be dismissed. The claimant cannot
then restart his claim either in the ET or in another court.[148]

Preparing for the hearing

17.82   The following is a checklist for hearing preparation:

- **Bundles:** Seek to agree a joint bundle containing all (and only) the
  documents that the ET will require at trial.
  - Include the documents (with pleadings and orders but not wit-
    ness statements).
  - Start with the pleadings and thereafter have documents fol-
    low a chronological order, with the earliest first, avoiding repe-
    tition. Rather than repeat a number of documents, include
    just the index pages to any internal grievance, disciplinary or
    appeal hearing bundles. Policy documents and medical docu-
    ments should have separate dividers.
  - Paginated starting with 1 at the start of the bundle and con-
    tinuing regardless of dividers.
  - Put an index of documents showing where documents are
    by reference to page number at the front. Respondents will
    generally prepare the four to six bundles necessary. The index
    should bring in all the relevant documents and exclude irrele-
    vant ones.
- **Witness statements:** Claimants often fail to exploit the opportunity their witness statement gives them, and thus can lose the case.
  Avoid verbosity, but note that the statement is the opportunity
  to ensure all the evidence gets before the ET (including relevant
  references to the pages and passages relied on in the bundle). An
  over-lengthy witness statement will alienate the ET. With very few
  exceptions, it is likely to be largely irrelevant. A witness statement
  must achieve the following objectives:
  - tell the ET who the witness is and the job the witness does or
    did;

---

146   *Verdin v Harrods Ltd* [2006] IRLR 339.
147   *Khan v Heywood & Middleton Primary Care Trust* [2006] IRLR 793, CA.
148   ET Regs 2004 r25(4).

- if the claimant, then to give evidence to describe the respondent accurately and neutrally (size, numbers of employees, locations, what the respondent does etc);
- provide information rather than opinion (unless the witness is an expert). However, the witness should say (if relevant) how they interpreted events. The witness can deal with normal practice;
- provide complete information, supplying all relevant detail. This can include hearsay. The weight of hearsay evidence is increased if the source and how the information was obtained is described;
- refer to the documents in the bundle by page number without quoting lengthy passages unless essential;
- be the witness's own words. It may have to be read out. Punctuate it clearly and use numbered paragraphs. Use sub-headings to help the ET review the evidence.

- **Schedule of loss**: Prepare a schedule of loss as it will allow the respondent to understand the value of the claim and may assist settlement negotiations.[149] The more articulated the justification for any heading of the schedule, the more likely it is to be awarded or conceded. It should therefore state why the sum claimed is justifiable.
- **List of issues/chronology/cast list**: These can be ordered but should be provided in any event. These documents can assist the ET in understanding the case before it. The parties should try to agree the document.[150]
- **Attendance of witnesses**: If a person has relevant information they can be called as a witness. First ask the witness to attend voluntarily. However, often a witness may require a witness order before he will attend. This is the case where the witness will not be released by his employer, where the witness is caught in an awkward position because he intends to give evidence against his current employer or where the witness is simply reluctant to give evidence. The ET has the power to order any person in Great Britain to either attend to give evidence or to produce any documents of information.[151] The ET has a discretion to order a witness to attend, so demonstrate in the application that:

149 See para 17.63. A sample schedule is included.
150 In *Price v Surrey CC* EAT, unreported, 27 October 2011, guidance was given on how a list of issues should be drafted. In particular, the ET should not accept a list of issues uncritically even if it is agreed between the parties.
151 ET Regs 2004 r10(1)(c).

– the witness has relevant evidence to give; and
– he will not attend without an order.[152]
The ET will consider whether the evidence the witness is likely to give is sufficiently relevant to justify making the order.[153] Therefore set out the name and (normally work) address of the proposed witness; a summary of the expected evidence; an explanation of why his evidence is of sufficient relevance to the proceedings. Give details of the steps taken to secure the witness's voluntary attendance and why it is believed that the witness will not attend voluntarily. It is a criminal offence for a person under a witness order to fail to comply with the order without reasonable excuse.[154]

Final hearing

Burden of proof

17.83 EqA 2010 s136 sets out the burden of proof using different language to the precursor legislation to express the same idea:

> (2) If there are facts from which the court could decide in the absence of any other explanation, that a person (A) contravened the provision concerned, the court must hold that the contravention occurred.
> (3) But subsection (2) does not apply if A shows that A did not contravene the provision.

17.84 If the claimant shows facts which suggest that he could have been discriminated against ('a prima facie case'), the respondent is liable for discrimination unless it can show that it did not discriminate. The provision applies to all proceedings for a contravention of the EqA 2010, so that it applies to victimisation cases[155] as well as claims for breach of an equality clause or rule.[156]

17.85 In *Igen Ltd v Wong*,[157] the Court of Appeal provided general guidance to ETs applying the shifting burden of proof which may still prove valuable. The case may be summarised as follows:

152 *Dada v Metal Box Co Ltd* [1974] IRLR 251, NIRC.
153 *Noorani v Merseyside TEC Ltd* [1999] IRLR 184.
154 ETA 1996 s7(4).
155 *Oyarce v Cheshire CC* [2008] EWCA Civ 434, [2008] ICR 1179 should no longer be followed.
156 EqA 2010 s136(4).
157 [2005] ICR 931.

(i) it is for the claimant who complains of discrimination to prove on the balance of probabilities facts from which the tribunal could conclude, in the absence of an adequate explanation, that the respondent has committed an act of discrimination against the claimant which is unlawful or which is to be treated as having been committed against the claimant.

(ii) If the claimant does not prove such facts the claim will fail.

(iii) In deciding whether the claimant has proved such facts it is important to emphasise that it is unusual to find direct evidence of discrimination. Few employers would be prepared to admit discrimination, even to themselves. In some cases the discrimination will not be an intention but merely based on the assumption that 'he or she would not have fitted in'.

(iv) The outcome at this stage of the analysis by the tribunal will usually depend on what inferences it is proper to draw from the primary facts found by the tribunal.

(v) the word 'could' in the legislation is important. At this stage the tribunal does not have to reach a definitive determination that such facts would lead it to the conclusion that there was an act of unlawful discrimination. It is looking at the primary facts before it to see what inferences of secondary fact could be drawn from them.

(vi) In considering what inferences or conclusions can be drawn from the primary facts, the tribunal must assume that there is no adequate explanation for those facts.

(vii) The inferences can include, in appropriate cases, any inferences that it is just and equitable to draw from an evasive or equivocal reply to a questionnaire or any other questions.

(viii) The tribunal must decide whether any provision of any relevant code of practice is relevant and if so, take it into account in determining such facts . This means that inferences may also be drawn from any failure to comply with any relevant code of practice.

(ix) Where the claimant has proved facts from which conclusions could be drawn that

– the respondent has treated the claimant less favourably (in a direct discrimination case),

– that a provision criterion or practice has placed the claimant at a substantial disadvantage and an indication of what adjustments should have been made (so that it could be inferred that the duty to make reasonable adjustments had been breached)[158]

– that the respondent has applied a provision criterion or practice which has placed the claimant at a particular disadvantage and which has (or would place those with a protected characteristic at a particular disadvantage (indirect discrimination cases)

---

158 In relation to disability claims for reasonable adjustment: *Project Management Institute v Latif* [2007] IRLR 579.

17.86   Then the burden of proof moves to the respondent:

> (x) Once the burden of proof has shifted it is for the respondent to prove that they did not commit, or as the case may be, is not to be treated as having committed, that act. Thus in reasonable adjustment cases the burden will be to show that the set of indicative adjustments suggested by the claimant were not reasonable for the respondent to have to take. In an indirect discrimination claim the respondent would have to show that the use of the provision criterion or practice was justified.
>
> (xi) To discharge that burden it is necessary for the respondent to prove, on the balance of probabilities, that the treatment was in no sense whatsoever on the grounds of sex, since 'no discrimination whatsoever' is what the EU Directives require.
>
> (x) In a direct discrimination claim that requires an ET to assess not merely whether the respondent has proved an explanation for the facts from which such inferences can be drawn, but further that it is adequate to discharge the burden of proof on the balance of probabilities that sex was not a ground for the treatment in question.
>
> (xi) Since the facts necessary to prove an explanation would normally be in the possession of the respondent, an ET would normally expect cogent evidence to discharge that burden of proof. In particular, the tribunal will need to examine carefully explanations for failure to deal with the questionnaire procedure and/or code of practice.

17.87   One issue that will need to be determined under the new formulation is whether the expression 'in the absence of any other explanation' has the same effect as the words 'in the absence of an adequate explanation'. In *Madarassy v Nomura International plc*[159] the Court of Appeal held that the latter (in a direct discrimination case) only became relevant once the burden had shifted. The wording of the EqA 2010 suggests that the burden shifts where there are facts (rather than that the claimant has proved facts) from which the court could decide in the absence of any other explanation that a contravention has occurred. It is suggested that this means that the ET is allowed to take account of the explanation of the employer at the stage of determining whether it could conclude that the employer had committed a contravention.[160]

17.88   Thus the new provision does not expressly or impliedly prevent the ET at the stage of determining the primary facts from hearing, accepting or drawing inferences from evidence adduced by the respondent disputing and rebutting the complainant's evidence of

---

159 [2007] EWCA Civ 33, [2007] ICR 867.

160 See further *Hewage v Grampian Health Board* [2012] UKSC 37, [2012] ICR 1054 which endorses this approach.

discrimination. 'The respondent may adduce evidence at the first stage to show that the acts that are alleged to be discriminatory never happened; or that, if they did, they were not less favourable treatment of the complainant; or that the comparators chosen by the complainant or the situations with which comparisons are made are not truly like the complainant or the situation of the complainant; or that, even if there has been less favourable treatment of the complainant, it was not ...'[161] because of the protected characteristic.

17.89   The burden of proof can shift to the respondent due to inadequate disclosure of documents.[162] Similarly it can shift if there have been inadequate answers to requests for information, for example in a questionnaire. It does not shift automatically in these circumstances however.

Hearings in public

17.90   Generally all hearings (save CMDs[163]) are in public.[164] A hearing can be held in private (in full or in part) where there is evidence or representations that are likely to involve information that could not be disclosed without contravening an enactment;[165] or that is subject to obligations of confidentiality, or, the disclosure of which would, for reasons other than its effect on negotiations over collective agreements, cause substantial injury to any undertaking which the relevant witness owns or works in.

Restricted reporting orders

17.91   In a case involving sexual misconduct allegations or in disability discrimination cases where evidence of a personal nature is likely to be heard, then a restricted reporting order may be made.[166] An order can be made for 14 days, and a full order can be made until liability and remedy have been determined. The order prohibits any publication or broadcast that identifies the alleged victim or the alleged trans-

---

161 See [2007] ICR 867 at paras 71–72.

162 Case C-415/10 *Meister v Speech Design Carrier Systems GmbH* [2012] ICR 1006.

163 ET Regs 2004 r17(1).

164 ET Regs 2004 rr18(1) and 26(3).

165 Under ET Regs 2004 r16; legislation includes the Human Rights Act 1998 and has been held to cover the right to respect for private and family life: *XXX v YYY* [2004] IRLR 137, [2004] IRLR 471, CA.

166 ET Regs 2004 r50.

gressor in a sexual misconduct case;[167] or the disabled person in a disability case.'[168]

17.92   The ET also has power to take necessary and proportionate measures to protect the parties' rights to privacy under Article 8 of the Concention (Human Rights Act 1998 Sch 1 Pt 1), where rule 49 or 50 does not apply or does not provide sufficient protection.[169] If required, these powers can be exercised to make a permanent anonymity order.

Order of proceedings

17.93   In short, procedure is a matter for the ET hearing the case. Often at the start of the hearing there is a short discussion to ensure that the issues are clear at the start. Theoretically the burden of proof determines who should start. In discrimination cases it is normally the claimant who has that burden initially. If the claimant can start the opportunity to do so should not be given up lightly as a well-drafted witness statement can set the tone of the hearing. The usual order is:

- claimant, claimant's witnesses
- respondent's witnesses.

17.94   However, the ET can ask witnesses questions at any point in the proceedings although they may reserve some questions to the end of the evidence for the witness.

Evidence-in-chief and supplementary questions

17.95   The witness statements are supposed to contain all the evidence that the witness wishes to put before the ET. Occasionally a witness may be allowed to read aloud to the ET some or all of their witness statement. The usual practice now is for ETs to read statements to themselves.[170] Statements often fail to contain all the information required; certain details are accidently left out, new points arise when the other side's statements are disclosed (or further instructions are received from a client). Sometimes the ET will permit supplementary questions (if asked to do so). These should be in the form of an

167 ETA 1996 s11.
168 ETA 1996 s12.
169 Under ET Regs 2004 r10: see *A v B* [2010] ICR 849 and *F v G* [2012] ICR 246, 21 September 2011.
170 ET Regs 2004 r27(2), adopting the guidance in *Mehta v Child* [2011] IRLR 305. The adoption of this guidance has been far from even.

open question, which should not suggest to the witness the 'correct' answer or restrict the witness into giving yes/no answers. In Scotland the practice is to lead the witness through the evidence-in-chief. Again, open questioning should be used.

Cross-examination

17.96   Cross-examination occurs after evidence-in-chief and in discrimination cases cross-examination should be firmly linked to the statutory framework. The ET can only make findings on liability in relation to issues that were set out in the claim form (ie pleaded), so that document should provide the framework for what the claimant seeks to establish. Cross-examine if there is a gap in the witness's evidence that needs filling, or if their version (or interpretation) of facts on a relevant issue is one which the claimant wishes to challenge. In cross-examination, questions can be open or closed. They must however be clear and relevant to the matters in issue. Only put one matter at a time to the witness, rather than asking complex questions where there may be an answer to each part separately.

Re-examination

17.97   After cross-examination there is an opportunity to ask questions arising out of the cross-examination. It should be used solely to deal with loose ends, answers which were cut short by an advocate or to clarify an ambiguous answer given in cross-examination. It should never be used as an opportunity to supplement examination-in-chief in the sense of raising something that does not arise out of cross-examination.

Submissions

17.98   When the evidence has been heard, the parties can make closing submissions. Usually whoever gives evidence first makes submissions last. They should:

• summarise the evidence (briefly) and tell the ET what findings of fact the claimant wishes the ET to make;
• invite the ET to draw inferences from evidence heard, indicating which evidence is relevant;
• give the relevant legal principles and to identify all of the legal arguments which are being relied on and highlight how the facts advanced fit the legal framework.

Many advocates prepare written submissions that they then expand on orally.

Non-attendance

17.99   If a party fails to attend or be represented at a hearing the ET may dismiss the proceedings, continue in the party's absence or adjourn to a later date. In considering which order to make, the ET must consider any information available to it.[171]

Judgment, review and appeal

17.100   At the end of the trial, the ET will consider its decision. It may give its decision directly to the parties immediately or it may 'reserve' it. If the judgment is reserved then it is sent to the parties by post at a later date.[172] ETs are not required to provide reasons for their judgments unless asked to by one of the parties. A request for reasons must be made either orally at the hearing or in writing within 14 days of the judgment. This time-limit can be extended.[173]

17.101   ETs have a very broad power to review their own decisions and sometimes this may be a better course to adopt than an appeal, although both may be pursued. The ETs can review default judgments.[174] The ET can review a decision not to accept a claim, response or counterclaim and a judgment (other than a default judgment but including an order for costs, expenses, preparation time or wasted costs).[175] If the decision was wrongly made due to administrative error or non-receipt of notice of proceedings then a review may be granted. If the decision was made in the absence of a party or new evidence has become available since the conclusion of the hearing to which the decision relates[176] or if the interests of justice require such a review, then a review may be sought and may be granted.[177]

17.102   The interests of justice include not only the interests of the party seeking the review but also the interests of the party resisting the review and the public interest in the finality in litigation.[178] Although it will be unusual for a case to be reopened by way of a review, there

---

171   ET Regs 2004 r27(5) and (6).
172   ET Regs 2004 r28(3).
173   ET Regs 2004 r30.
174   ET Regs 2004 r33.
175   ET Regs 2004 r34.
176   Provided that its existence could not reasonably have been known or foreseen at that time.
177   ET Regs 2004 r34(3).
178   *Lindsay v Ironsides Ray & Vials* [1994] IRLR 318.

is no requirement of showing 'exceptional circumstances' before a review is held. The power is exercised rarely. The application should be made at a hearing, or in writing to the ET, within 14 days of the date on which the decision is sent to the parties. The ET can extend time if it is 'just and equitable' to do so. The application should state the ground on which it is made by reference to rule 34(3).[179] It is considered on the papers by the original employment judge or ET unless that is not practicable. The ET must refuse the application at this stage if there are no grounds for a review or if the application has 'no reasonable prospect' of success.[180] Otherwise a review hearing is held before the same decision-makers. At the review hearing, the ET may confirm, vary or revoke the decision. If the decision is revoked, an order will be made for the decision to be taken again.[181]

17.103   The Employment Appeal Tribunal appeal process[182] is governed by the Employment Appeal Tribunal Rules 1993[183] and Practice Direction (Employment Appeal Tribunal – Procedure) 2008. Note the following points:

- **Time-limits**: Appeal must be made within 42 days of the order or judgment in question.[184] Under the Practice Direction an appeal is only presented on a particular day if it is received by the EAT before 4pm. The EAT does have the power to receive an appeal out of time, but it is exercised sparingly and only where a good excuse for the delay is shown.[185]
- **Grounds**: Appeals to the EAT must be on a point of law. An appeal lies to the EAT only on the grounds that:
    - the ET misdirected themselves as to the applicable law;
    - there was no evidence to support a particular finding of fact; or
    - the decision was perverse.[186]

179 ET Regs 2004 r35(1) and (2).
180 ET Regs 2004 r35(3).
181 ET Regs 2004 r36. There are further powers under rule 37 to correct clerical mistakes in any order, judgment or other ET document.
182 Under ETA 1996 s20.
183 SI No 2854.
184 If written reasons were requested orally at the ET or were requested in writing within 14 days of the judgment; or if the ET reserved its reasons and promulgated them in writing the deadline for appealing is 42 days from the date on which the written reasons were sent to the parties (Employment Appeal Tribunal Rules 1993 SI No 2854 r3(3)).
185 PD 3.7; *Jurkowska v Hlmad Ltd* [2008] IRLR 430.
186 *British Telecommunications plc v Sheridan* [1990] IRLR 27.

17.104   To be validly lodged, the notice of appeal must have with it copies of the:

- judgment or order appealed against and the ET's written reasons;
- ET1 and ET3 ;
- application that had been made to the ET for a review (if any) and review judgment, if received.

17.105   However, the Practice Direction provides for circumstances in which these documents are not available.[187]

17.106   **Error of law:** Two of the grounds above are straightforward conceptually: the ET must have got the law wrong or reached a conclusion for which there was no evidence (as opposed to a conclusion where there was a choice of whose evidence to accept on the point) or where it misunderstood a fact that the parties had agreed upon. However, perversity needs, even in this short exposition, some explanation. The Court of Appeal has indicated exactly how high the threshold for perversity is. Mummery LJ stated:[188]

> Such an appeal ought only to succeed where an overwhelming case is made out that the employment tribunal reached a decision which no reasonable tribunal, on a proper appreciation of the evidence and the law, would have reached. Even in cases where the Appeal Tribunal has 'grave doubts' about the decision of the Employment Tribunal, it must proceed with 'great care': *British Telecommunications plc v Sheridan* [1990] IRLR 27 at paragraph 34.

17.107   If an appeal is successful, the EAT may substitute its decision for that of the ET or remit the case (or a particular issue) to the same or a different ET to have the case or issue reconsidered.[189] The appellant should set out what order is sought in this respect. Appeals against the judgments of the EAT lie with the Court of Appeal.[190]

---

187 PD 2.3.
188 *Yeboah v Crofton* [2002] IRLR 634.
189 ETA 1996 s35.
190 ETA 1996 s37.

Enforcement of judgments and payment of allowances and costs

17.108　Under the Employment Tribunals Act 1996 s15 and the Civil Procedure Rules r70.5, the winning party can apply to a county court for enforcement.[191]

17.109　For claims made on or after 6 April 2012, fees and allowances are paid only for equal value reports ordered under EqA 2010 s131(2).[192] Other expenses are discretionary, eg for the cost of an essential medical report. Applications should explain why the cost is necessary to ensure a fair hearing.[193]

Costs and preparation time orders

17.110　The general rule in ETs, in contrast to most civil jurisdictions, is that no costs are awarded; the parties bear their own costs. The Rules do however allow ETs to award costs in certain prescribed circumstances. An order for costs can only be made where the receiving party has been legally represented at a hearing or when the proceedings are otherwise determined. Costs are defined as 'fees, charges, disbursements or expenses incurred by or on behalf of a party, in relation to the proceedings'.[194] Where a party is unrepresented, they are not entitled to costs, as none have been incurred, but they may receive a preparation time order.

17.111　A costs order must be made if a claimant is claiming unfair dismissal and has expressed his wish to be reinstated or reengaged at least seven days before the hearing but the hearing is postponed or adjourned because the respondent has failed, without special reason, to adduce reasonable evidence of appropriate jobs for the claimant to return to.[195]

17.112　A costs order may be made:

- as a result of the adjournment or postponement of a hearing (payment of costs wasted by the adjournment or postponement);[196]

191　Form N471 may be used. See also 18.156 for the Fast Track scheme.
192　ETA 1996 s5. Discretion, subject to the consent of the Treasury, is under s5(3).
193　Guidance is available on the ET website at: www.justice.gov.uk/tribunals/employment.
194　ET Regs 2004 r38(3).
195　ET Regs 2004 r39.
196　ET Regs 2004 r40(1).

- if a 'party has in bringing the proceeding, or he or his representative has in conducting the proceedings, acted vexatiously, abusively disruptively or otherwise unreasonably, or the bringing or conducting of the proceedings by the paying party was misconceived';[197]
- a party which has failed to comply with an order or practice direction.

17.113   Misconceived is defined as meaning 'having no reasonable prospect of success'.[198]

17.114   The ET may only award costs up to £20,000. If it wishes to permit a higher award to be made, it may refer the issue of costs to a county court for detailed assessment. The county court will then determine the costs in accordance with the Civil Procedure Rules 1998 and the amount of costs it may award is unlimited.[199]

17.115   Wasted costs: In certain circumstances, the ET may make an award of costs against a party's representative.[200] This is the case where a party's representative is found to have led to wasted costs as a result of 'any improper, unreasonable or negligent act or omission'. What counts as 'unreasonable' in this context is different and more rigorous than in an ordinary costs application.[201] The power is exercised in a similar manner to that under the Civil Procedure Rules[202] and can be exercised following a summary hearing, usually without the need to hear live evidence.[203] This procedure is suitable only for plain and obvious cases.[204] When an ET is considering whether to make an award of costs and the amount of any such award, it is required to consider the paying party's ability to pay.[205]

---

197 ET Regs 2004 r40(3).
198 ET Regs 2004 r2.
199 ET Regs 2004 r41. For claims made before 6 April 2012, an ET can award costs of up to £10,000 only.
200 ET Regs 2004 r48.
201 See *Mitchells v Funkwerk Information Technologies York Ltd* UKEAT/541/07 at para 28 and *Ratcliffe Duce and Gammer v Binns* UKEAT/100/08 at para 13.
202 *Jackson v Cambridgeshire County Council* UKEAT/402/09, 8 June 2011, referring to *Ridehalgh v Horefield* [1994] Ch 205 and *Medcalf v Mardell* [2003] AC 120.
203 *Godfrey Morgan Solicitors Ltd v Cobalt Systems Ltd* [2012] ICR 305.
204 *Gill v Humanware Europe Ltd* [2010] ICR 1343, CA at paras 27–30 and 39.
205 ET Regs 2004 r41(2). This includes an assessment not only of income and expenditure but also capital: *Shields Automotive Ltd v Greig* EAT, unreported, 15 July 2011.

17.116 **Practical points**

- Always use EqA 2010 to structure the claim and as a framework for relevance.
- The claimaint should use short, clear paragraphs in the details of the claim.
- Particular care should be taken to ensure all of the acts of unlawful treatment for which a remedy is sought are set out in the claims. If an event is relied on only as background, say this explicitly.
- A useful framework is a table with these headings:

Date	Event	Why unlawful

- Careful preparation for any CMD including setting out as a detailed list of issues will benefit the claimant.
- Once disclosure has occurred the claimant can add to the above framework a column named 'evidence' enabling the claimant to collect the relevant evidence for an allegation.
- The witness statements can be structured around this framework, in a chronological order.
- When provided with a bundle the claimant should become familiar with the location of documents in it. A litigant in person should use the index of the trial bundle for this.
- A litigant in person should always ask the tribunal if unsure about procedure.
- A professional representative should ensure that a litigant in person is not disadvantaged by ignorance of procedure.

CHAPTER 18

Remedies

continued

Key points

- The ET may award compensation for past and future loss of earnings, pension loss, loss of benefits, injury to feelings, personal injury, aggravated and exemplary damages.
- In addition the ET can make a declaration that a person has been subjected to unlawful discrimination.
- The ET can also make recommendations to obviate the effect of the discrimination.
- In an equal pay case, the ET can declare that the claimant is entitled to the benefit of an equality clause and order arrears of remuneration.

Statutory provisions

18.1   This chapter deals with the remedies that an ET can award if it makes a finding of discrimination.

The available remedies

18.2   When an ET upholds a complaint of discrimination, it may:

- make a declaration as to the rights of the complainant and the respondent in relation to the matters to which the proceedings relate;
- order the respondent to pay compensation to the complainant;
- make an appropriate recommendation to obviate the effect of the discrimination.[1]

18.3   The amount of compensation that may be awarded by the ET corresponds to the amount that could be awarded by a county court or sheriff court.[2] Consequently, it should be calculated in the same way as a claim in tort (or reparation). The provisions in the EqA 2010 relating to county court remedies expressly provide that an award of damages may include compensation for injury to feelings, whether or not it includes compensation on any other basis[3] and this applies equally in the ET.

---

1   EqA 2010 s124(2). See paras 18.145–18.155 for recommendations.
2   EqA 2010 s124(6), which refers back to EqA 2010 s119.
3   EqA 2010 s119(4), read together with EqA 2010 s124(6).

18.4   The ET's power to make a recommendation is broader under the EqA 2010 than under the previous legislation. An appropriate recommendation may now be made not only with reference to the individual claimant but also 'any other person'. This is dealt with in more detail at the end of this chapter.

18.5   The ET has no express power to order reinstatement or re-engagement, although if the claimant has also brought a successful unfair dismissal case, the ET may also exercise its power to make such an order under the Employment Rights Act 1996.[4] If the order is not complied with, compensation is likely to be restricted to ERA 1996 s117 and caught by the statutory cap. It is thus essential for an ET to state it has not made a final order on compensation for discrimination.

Remedies in equal pay cases

Non-pensions cases

18.6   If the ET finds a breach of an equality clause, it may:

- make a declaration as to the rights of the parties in relation to the matters to which the proceedings relate;
- order an award by way of arrears of pay or damages in relation to the complainant.[5]

18.7   When an ET upholds an equal pay claim, it may make a declaration that an equality clause is to be read into the worker's contract. Where a woman and a man are engaged on equal work, a 'sex equality clause'[6] operates so as to modify any term of the woman's contract that is less favourable to her than a corresponding term of the man's contract is to him; or alternatively to insert into the woman's contract any missing term that corresponds to a term in the man's contract and that benefits him.

18.8   The ET may also award arrears of remuneration. The amount awarded will be the difference in remuneration (including pay, benefits, bonus etc) between that of the claimant and the comparator employee from the relevant 'arrears day' onwards.[7]

- In a standard case, the arrears day is the day falling six years before the day on which the proceedings were instituted.

---

4   ERA 1996 ss114–115, s126(2) prevents awarding double compensation.
5   EqA 2010 s132(2).
6   EqA 2010 s66.
7   EqA 2010 s132(3).

- In a concealment and/or incapacity case, the arrears day is the day on which the breach first occurred.[8]

18.9 The position is different in Scotland.

- In a standard case, the arrears day is the first day of the period of five years ending with the day on which the proceedings were commenced.
- If the case involves a relevant incapacity, or a relevant fraud or error, the period of 20 years ending with the day on which the proceedings were commenced.[9]

18.10 Where a claim is based on the job having been rated as equivalent by the employer, the employee will be entitled to equal pay only from the date on which the job was rated as equivalent.[10]

18.11 In a case under the precursor legislation,[11] the EAT held that compensation for non-pecuniary loss, for example injury to feelings, cannot be awarded in an equal pay claim. This is because a claim for compensation for, say, direct race discrimination is by way of recovery for a statutory tort, whereas a claim under the equal pay provisions is a financial claim in contract. It is created by the statutory implication into the contract of employment of an equality clause. For the same reason, awards of aggravated or exemplary damages are not available in equal pay cases. This reasoning would appear to hold good under the new legislation. Unlike the provisions relating to remedies for discrimination claims,[12] Chapter 5 of Part 9 of the EqA 2010 makes no reference to the availability of an award for injury to feelings.

Pensions cases

18.12 Where an ET finds that there has been a breach of an equality rule or a breach of an equality clause that relates to the terms on which people become members of an occupational pension scheme, it may declare that the claimant has the right to be admitted to the scheme with effect from a specified date,[13] provided that the date is not before 8 April 1976.[14]

---

8 EqA 2010 s132(3)–(4). For the definition of standard, concealment and incapacity cases, see paras 14.115–14.127.
9 EqA 2010 s132(5).
10 *Bainbridge v Redcar and Cleveland Borough Council (No 2)* [2007] IRLR 494, EAT.
11 *Degnan v Redcar and Cleveland Borough Council* [2005] IRLR 504, EAT.
12 EqA 2010 ss119 and 124.
13 EqA 2010 s133(4).
14 EqA 2010 s133(5).

18.13   If the breach relates to the terms on which existing members are treated, the ET may declare that the claimant is entitled to secure the rights that would have accrued if the breach had not occurred[15] in respect of a specified period, which must not begin before 17 May 1990.[16] If the ET makes a declaration of this sort, the employer must provide the pension scheme with the resources to ensure that the claimant has the same accrued rights for the specified period as other members, without the claimant or other members of the scheme having to make further contribution.

18.14   Where there has been a breach of an equality clause or rule relating to the terms of a scheme, an ET may make an award to the pensioner member by way of arrears of benefits or damages. The same limits apply in cases of this sort as apply in non-pensions cases as to the maximum period for which the ET can award arrears (see above).[17]

Damages for indirect discrimination

18.15   In an indirect discrimination case, where the ET finds that the provision, criterion or practice was not applied with the intention of discriminating against the claimant, it must not make an award of damages unless it first considers whether to make a declaration or recommendation.[18] This would appear to give the ET a wide discretion to withhold or award compensation as it sees fit. There appears to be nothing in the language that prevents an ET from both making a recommendation and awarding compensation but respondents will probably argue that compensation ought to be a remedy of last resort. However, as with all legislation based on the EU Directives relating to discrimination, the ET should be reminded of the principle that sanctions for discrimination should be 'effective, proportionate and dissuasive'.[19] The United Kingdom has chosen to allow compensation as a sanction. In almost all cases compensation will be proportionate, dissuasive and or effective, and should therefore be awarded.

18.16   In any event the criteria for intentional indirect discrimination in UK law are fairly minimal. When the PCP is imposed, if the person imposing it wants to bring about the state of affairs that constitutes

15 EqA 2010 s133(6).
16 EqA 2010 s133(7).
17 EqA 2010 s134.
18 EqA 2010 s124(4)–(5).
19 See eg Art 17 of Directive 2000/78 of 27 November 2000, establishing a general framework for equal treatment in employment and occupation.

the prohibited result[20] and knows that the prohibited result will follow from imposing the PCP, the act of indirect discrimination will be held to be intentional.[21] The Employment Code clarifies the meaning of 'intentional' in this context:[22]

> Indirect discrimination will be intentional where the respondent knew that certain consequences would follow from their actions and they wanted those consequences to follow. A motive, for example, of promoting business efficiency, does not mean that the act of indirect discrimination is unintentional.

18.17 Clearly the motive of achieving business efficiency is wholly consistent with intending to impose a PCP which the person knows will place a group at a particular disadvantage. The person imposing the PCP may intend to discriminate in order to achieve that end. It is sufficient if the means (that disadvantage) are intended.

Compensation

Key legal principles

18.18 The claimant may be compensated under the following heads of loss:

- past and future financial loss;
- loss of pension;
- injury to feelings;
- personal injury;
- aggravated damages;
- exemplary damages;
- disadvantage on the labour market;
- stigma damages.

18.19 Unlike compensation for unfair dismissal, there is no statutory cap on the amount of compensation that the ET may award in a discrimination case.

18.20 Under the previous legislation, it was for the ET to decide, having regard to all the circumstances of the case, which of the available remedies it was 'just and equitable' to award to the claimant. 'Just and equitable' referred to the selection of the order, not the

---

20 Ie placing the disadvantaged group at a particular disadvantage.
21 See eg *London Underground v Edwards* [1995] ICR 574, [1995] IRLR 355, EAT and *MOD v Cannock* [1994] ICR 918, [1994] IRLR 509, EAT.
22 Employment Code para 4.45.

amount of the award. Once the ET decided to award compensation, the amount of compensation fell to be calculated on the basis of what damages would be recoverable in a county court in a successful claim in tort and not on the basis of what an ET thought to be just and equitable.[23]

18.21   The phrase 'just and equitable' no longer appears in this context but the language of EqA 2010 s124 ('the Tribunal ... may order the respondent to pay compensation to the complainant ...') suggests that it retains a discretion as to which, if any, of the available remedies it awards in any particular case. It would appear to leave open the option of not awarding damages at all, although any such discretion must always be exercised judicially.

18.22   If the ET is considering its discretion in this respect, its attention should be drawn to the relevant principles of EU law flowing from the directives and be reminded that sanctions should be 'effective, proportionate and dissuasive'.[24] In most cases an award of compensation will therefore be appropriate.

18.23   It is submitted that once the ET has decided to award compensation under EqA 2010 s124, the claimant is entitled to full compensation and the ET does not have a general discretion to increase or reduce it. The law of tort does provide for reductions in certain circumstances, for example where a claimant has failed to mitigate his losses or has contributed to those losses by his own conduct. The application of those principles is considered below.

18.24   Practitioners will sometimes have to deal with the suggestion that the ET's discretion should be exercised against making any award of compensation. An example of a case under the pre-existing legislation in which it was not considered 'just and equitable' to make an award is *Chief Constable of Greater Manchester Police v Hope*.[25] Although it is trite law that the discriminator's motives and intentions are irrelevant to the question of liability, a majority of the EAT (the two lay members) considered that motive may be relevant to the question of remedy and held that, in the absence of discriminatory intent, the ET should not have made an award of compensation. However, their view was based on some (obiter) remarks of the EAT in *O'Neill v Governors of St Thomas More Roman Catholic Voluntary Aided Upper School*,[26] and in that case the correct principles do not appear to have

23 *Hurley v Mustoe (No 2)* [1983] ICR 422, EAT and Directive 2000/78 Art 17.
24 For which see paras 19.140 and 19.146.
25 [1999] 1 ICR 338, EAT.
26 [1997] ICR 33 at 43C.

been drawn to the attention of the EAT, so the outcome in *Hope* was reached without regard to the correct principles.

18.25   Ordinarily, the complainant is entitled to the full measure of damages for the statutory tort of unlawful discrimination. As Morison J stated in *Ministry of Defence v Cannock*:[27] 'as best as money can do it, the [claimant] must be put into the position she would have been in but for the unlawful conduct'.

18.26   Thus, even where the discrimination claim arises out of a relationship governed by a contract of employment, the potential compensation is not confined to the damages that might have been recovered under that contract.

18.27   The burden of proof is on the claimant to prove his loss and to show that the loss has been caused by the discrimination. Conversely, the burden of proof is on the respondent if he contends that the claimant has acted unreasonably in failing to reduce his losses by seeking alternative work (has failed to mitigate his losses, for which see below). The respondent must lead evidence to show this; it is not for the ET to fill the evidential vacuum itself.[28]

18.28   In *Essa v Laing Ltd*,[29] the Court of Appeal held, by a majority, that if a claimant can establish that his loss was caused by the discrimination, he need not go on to prove that the particular type of loss (in that case psychiatric injury) was reasonably foreseeable. It is not entirely clear whether this principle is confined to cases of direct discrimination or harassment. Pill LJ suggests[30] that different considerations might apply where the discrimination takes forms other than the overt racial abuse in that case, although it is difficult to see why different rules on foreseeability should apply to different factual scenarios. Clarke LJ expressed the view[31] that, even if there were a requirement for foreseeability, if the claimant can show that a degree of injury to feelings is foreseeable (which it will be in most cases), then personal injury should also be regarded as foreseeable, since the two categories of injury are similar in kind.

18.29   The discriminator must take his victim as he finds him. He cannot complain if the loss or damage caused by the discrimination turns out to be more serious than might have been expected because of the

27 [1994] ICR 918 at 935H–936A, [1994] IRLR 509, EAT at para 60.
28 *Ministry of Defence v Hunt* [1996] ICR 554, [1996] IRLR 139, EAT.
29 [2004] EWCA Civ 2, [2004] ICR 746, [2004] IRLR 313.
30 *Essa* para 39.
31 *Essa* para 55.

victim's particular vulnerability. He is liable for the full extent of that loss or damage. This is known as the 'eggshell skull principle'.

18.30   An employer cannot rely upon a subsequent wrong that it has committed (for example an unfair dismissal) to argue that there has been a break in the chain of causation that ought to stem its liability for the loss flowing from its earlier act of discrimination.[32]

18.31   In *Chapman v Simon*[33] the Court of Appeal emphasised that the ET may only compensate the claimant in respect of the complaints of discrimination that have been properly raised in the course of proceedings. If those complaints are not upheld, it is not for the ET to find another act of discrimination of which complaint has not been made in order to give a remedy.[34]

18.32   Where an employer is found to be vicariously liable for its employee's discrimination, it will usually be ordered to make a payment in compensation. However, where the perpetrator has been named as an individual respondent, it has until recently been quite common for Tribunals to apportion the damages as between the two respondents: *Way v Crouch*.[35] Awards against individual respondents tended to be relatively modest, although for an example of a large award against an individual, see *Crofton v Yeboah*.[36]

18.33   However, in *London Borough of Hackney v Sivanandan*[37] the President of the EAT departed from *Way v Crouch* and held that there is no basis for the apportionment of 'indivisible' damages in discrimination cases. His approach was subsequently approved by the Court of Appeal.[38] The past practice of awarding a small sum against a named individual respondent, and a larger sum against his or her employer in respect of the same act, cannot now continue.

18.34   Compensation should follow the ordinary principles of the law of tort. Where the same, 'indivisible', damage is done to a claimant by concurrent tortfeasors – ie either tortfeasors who are liable for the same act (joint tortfeasors) or tortfeasors who separately contribute to the same damage – each is liable for the whole of that damage. As between any particular tortfeasor and the claimant no question

32 *HM Prison Service v Beart (No 2)* [2005] EWCA Civ 467, [2005] ICR 1206, [2005] IRLR 568.
33 [1994] IRLR 124, CA.
34 Although see *British Telecommunications v Reid* [2003] EWCA Civ 1675, [2004] IRLR 327 at para 19.59.
35 [2005] IRLR 603, EAT.
36 UKEAT/475/00, 15 April 2003.
37 [2011] ICR 1374, [2011] IRLR 740.
38 [2013] EWCA Civ 22.

of apportionment arises (leaving aside the question of contributory negligence). It is obviously potentially unjust that a single tortfeasor may find himself responsible to the claimant for the entirety of damage for which others may also be liable or to which they may have contributed. However, that issue is addressed by the provisions of the Civil Liability (Contribution) Act 1978 Act, which gives any person liable in respect of any damage the right to claim 'contribution' from concurrent tortfeasors to the extent of such proportion of the overall liability as the court considers just and equitable.[39]

18.35 Underhill P held in *Sivanandan*:[40]

It is important to emphasise that while this kind of 'apportionment', as it is often described (though that term is not used in the statute) determines the liability of concurrent tortfeasors as between themselves, it has no impact on the liability of any of them to the claimant. The claimant can recover in full against whichever tortfeasor he chooses, and that tortfeasor has the burden of recovery of any contribution from the others, and the risk that they may not be solvent.

Financial loss

18.36 Past losses are often a matter of record (subject to mitigation) and include any earnings lost or expenses incurred that are attributable to the discrimination. The basic guide is the amount being earned immediately prior to ceasing work, but if this is not representative, an average over the preceding (representative) period should be used. Evidence should be obtained of any increase in rates of pay post-termination.

18.37 'Earnings' may include additional benefits. For example, the claimant may be able to claim loss of:

- bonus;
- use of company car;
- insurance, for example health insurance;
- clothing allowance;
- free or subsidised goods;
- travel concessions;
- accommodation.

---

39 Although the view has been expressed obiter in *Brennan v Sunderland City Council* [2012] ICR 1183, that the Civil Liability (Contribution) Act 1978 Act does not apply at all in discrimination claims, so that contribution proceedings could not even be pursued in the County Court or High Court.

40 [2011] ICR 1374, [2011] IRLR 740.

18.38   An attempt should be made to put a monetary net value on the benefit and add that sum to the overall weekly loss.

18.39   Many claimants fall quickly into debt if they are unable to work. They should be asked to keep records in relation to any of the following:

- overdraft interest;
- credit card interest;
- loan interest;
- interest on arrears of mortgage or rent;
- interest on debts to creditors or suppliers.

18.40   A successful claimant is entitled only to net losses, so losses should be calculated net of tax and national insurance.

18.41   In a claim relating to a discriminatory dismissal, credit must be given for earnings received through alternative work, as well as for any sums saved in consequence of the discrimination. For example, if an employer discriminates against a woman by preventing her return to work after maternity leave, she must offset against her claim for loss of earnings the savings in respect of childcare not required during her period of unemployment. Similarly, an unemployed claimant may be saving on the expenses of going to work (eg travel, business clothing etc). There are important exceptions for charitable or other benevolent payments, and insurance payments (for a detailed analysis of the common law see *Gaca v Pirelli General plc*[41]). Disability and ex gratia pensions paid before retirement age are also disregarded.[42]

18.42   The fact that there is no loss of job as a result of the discriminatory treatment does not mean that there is no loss of earnings. In *Taylor v Dumfries and Galloway Citizen Advice Services*[43] the Court of Session held that failure by an employer to carry out reasonable adjustments to enable employees to take up an offer of higher paid employment should be compensated by a loss of earnings award based on the salary for the higher paid employment. In a recruitment case, the ET will assess the chance that the application would have been successful and assess losses accordingly.

18.43   Future losses raise more speculative questions. In the case of a discriminatory dismissal, the ET should treat what would have happened but for the dismissal as the evaluation of a loss of a chance.

---

41 [2004] EWCA Civ 373, [2004] 1 WLR 2683.
42 *Parry v Cleaver* [1970] AC 1.
43 [2007] CSIH 28, 2007 SLT 425.

Evaluation is likely to depend on the answers to the following questions.

- What would C have earned and what would C's career path have been but for the discrimination?
- What will C's earnings and career be post-discrimination?
- When would C have retired (but for discrimination), and with what pension entitlements?
- When will C now retire, and with what pension entitlements?
- What would or might have been the effect of other contingencies (such as disability or ill-health) in, for example, enforcing early retirement? Post-discrimination, have those contingencies loomed larger?

18.44   The Court of Appeal put it thus in *Vento v Chief Constable of West Yorkshire Police (No 2)*:[44]

> The question is: what were the chances, if Ms Vento had not been discriminated against and dismissed, of her remaining in the police force until the age of retirement at 55? ... It is not like an issue of primary fact, as when a court has to decide which of two differing recollections of past events is the more reliable. The question requires a forecast to be made about the course of future events. It has to be answered on the basis of the best assessment that can be made on the relevant material available to the court.

18.45   In *Abbey National plc v Chagger*,[45] the Court of Appeal rejected an argument that the employee's compensation should be limited to the period of time he would have remained in the respondent's employment. The proper approach is to ask when the employee is likely to find another job on an equivalent salary to his salary with the respondent and award compensation for the period between the date of dismissal and the estimated date he would start the new, equivalent, job. A 'loss of chance' approach should be adopted, if appropriate, in discrimination cases. The ET will assess the chance that the dismissal would have occurred in any event and reduce the damages accordingly to reflect that chance.

18.46   In *Ministry of Defence v Wheeler*[46] the female claimants were all dismissed from the armed forces when they became pregnant. The Ministry of Defence admitted liability for sex discrimination. The Court of Appeal held that the correct approach to calculating the compensation due to them was to take the sum they would have earned

44 [2002] EWCA Civ 1871, [2003] ICR 318, [2003] IRLR 102 at paras 32–33.
45 [2009] EWCA Civ 1202, [2010] ICR 397, [2010] IRLR 47.
46 [1998] 1 WLR 637, [1998] ICR 242, [1998] IRLR 23, CA.

had they remained in the forces, deduct from that sum the amount which they had, or should have, earned elsewhere, and then discount the net loss by a percentage to reflect the chance that they might have left the armed forces in any event.

18.47   In *O'Donoghue v Redcar and Cleveland Borough Council,*[47] the ET upheld the claimant's complaints of discrimination but found that her divisive and antagonistic approach to her colleagues was such that it would inevitably have led to her fair dismissal within a further period of six months. The Court of Appeal found that the ET was entitled to regard that as a cut-off point for the purposes of compensation for pecuniary loss but that it was wrong to reduce the award for injury to feelings on the same basis. To make a discount from those damages in respect of a separate (notional) future event, which would hardly have reduced her sense of outrage, was unjustified.

18.48   In 2011, in *Wardle v Credit Agricole Corporate and Investment Bank,* the Court of Appeal held[48] that it would be a 'rare case where it is appropriate for a court to assess compensation over a career lifetime'. When calculating future losses, ETs should assess the loss suffered up to a certain point in time when an employee would be likely to secure another job on similar terms, rather than award compensation up to the point when there was certainty that the employee would secure another job on equivalent terms. Losses after that date should be ignored. The ET's prediction may not be accurate but this is the best that can be achieved to bring finality to the assessment of compensation for future loss.

18.49   Other factors will be brought into play on each side. Employees will rely on the lost potential resulting from dismissal, such as promotion opportunities. Employers will rely on negative factors, which the employee would have had to face in any event, for example any downturn in market conditions, possible takeover or other redundancy risks. Issues such as local levels of unemployment may also be relevant.

18.50   Long-term future loss will usually be calculated using the multiplier/multiplicand approach.

- First, the multiplicand must be worked out. This is a lump sum representing the annual net loss.
- To this is applied the multiplier, which represents the number of years for which the loss will be suffered. The multiplier is an actuarial figure, which takes account of early ('accelerated') receipt and

47 [2001] EWCA Civ 701, [2001] IRLR 615.
48 [2011] EWCA Civ 545, [2011] ICR 1290, [2011] IRLR 604 at para 50.

the risk of early death, and so it is less than the actual number of years for which the claim is being made. It is conventionally taken from the Ogden Tables (now in their seventh edition). These are tables published by the Government Actuary as an aid to the calculation of damages in personal injury cases.[49]

18.51 The EAT has made clear that, in discrimination cases in the employment field, the Ogden Tables should be applied with care and with due regard for all the relevant contingencies:[50]

> For a claimant to be compensated in full (subject to accelerated receipt) for his assumed annual loss for every year and month of the rest of his career involves treating as a certainty the assumption that he would have continued for the rest of his career to receive his pre-dismissal earnings. But that cannot be a certainty. On the contrary, it is subject to a number of contingencies: he might have died or become too ill to work, or his employer might have gone out of business, or he might have been dismissed for some other good cause or have left voluntarily for any one of a number of reasons. The only one of those contingencies taken into account in the main Ogden Tables is the possibility of death (and even that may be inadequately represented if there is reason to believe that the claimant's risks are substantially worse than those of the general population from which the Ogden figures derive). Those other contingencies must be properly reflected in the ultimate multiplier used. There may be cases where a tribunal believes the contingencies in question are balanced by 'upside' contingencies not reflected in the multiplicand (eg promotion); but otherwise the multiplier will fall to be reduced.

18.52 Guidance on the various additional discounts that can be applied can be found in *Facts and Figures: Tables for the Calculation of Damages*,[51] as can the Ogden Tables themselves. The seventh edition of the Ogden Tables has greater differentiation between cases and, in particular, takes employment prospects for disabled people into account.

18.53 Damages for future loss of earnings tend to be higher in disability discrimination cases than in sex or race cases. This is because, where disabled claimants are dismissed on grounds of their disability, it can often be proved that it will be unusually difficult for them to gain other employment.

---

49 The Tables can be downloaded from: www.gad.gov.uk/Documents/ Other%20Services/Ogden%20Tables/Ogden_Tables_7th_edition.pdf

50 *Abbey National and Hopkins v Chagger* [2009] ICR 624, [2009] IRLR 86, EAT at paras 113–117, a point not disapproved by the Court of Appeal in the same case.

51 Published annually by Sweet and Maxwell.

18.54   In *Sheffield Forgemasters International Ltd v Fox*[52] the EAT held that the fact that a claimant is in receipt of disability benefit does not, in itself, preclude him from claiming compensation for loss of earnings during the same period. Although incapacity benefits are paid when somebody is 'incapable of work', those words are a deeming provision and the statutory phrase does not necessarily coincide with an individual's actual inability to work but it has a special meaning set out in the relevant legislation. The regulations relating to incapacity benefits have since been replaced but the underlying principles arguably still hold good, although in recent years the 'capability' tests have been made more onerous.

Discrimination and unfair dismissal

18.55   Where an ET finds a dismissal both unfair (within the meaning of the ERA 1996) and an act of discrimination, it will usually make the award under the discrimination legislation. This is advantageous to claimants for a number of reasons: there is no cap on the compensation which can be awarded and there is no general 'just and equitable' discretion to reduce the compensation.

18.56   However, as there is no express power in the EqA 2010 to make an order for reinstatement or re-engagement, such orders are made under ERA 1996 ss114–115. ERA 1996 s126(2) does not prevent this: it only prevents duplicate awards of compensation for matters or losses already taken into account. Re-employment orders include an element for loss of earnings for the period between dismissal and re-employment. In case the order is not complied with, a claimant should expressly reserve his right to return to the ET to seek further, uncapped, compensation under the EqA 2010 for the whole of his loss of earnings. If he does not, compensation is likely to be capped under ERA 1996 s117(3).[53]

Injury to feelings

18.57   Practitioners must be aware of the need to ensure that the ET has proper evidence in the witness statement of this element of the claim for compensation. Very often a claimant's witness statement does

---

52 [2009] ICR 333, [2009] IRLR 192, EAT.
53 See *Lambeth v D'Souza* [1999] IRLR 240, CA; *Selfridges Ltd v Malik* [1997] IRLR 577 and if compensation has been lost, para 19.141 and Directive 2000/78 Art 17.

not spell out this element and ETs are left to give a very rough estimate of what they conceive the injury to feelings may be. It is worth
spending some time taking proper instructions on this aspect of the
effect of discrimination as it is an important element in compensat-
ing the claimant.

18.58   The EAT in *Ministry of Defence v Cannock*[54] held that, although an
award for injury to feelings is not automatically to be made when a
discrimination complaint is upheld, no ET will take much persuasion
that the anger, distress and affront caused by the act of discrimination has injured the applicant's feelings. In some cases, for example
where the claimant has remained in the respondent's employment
or left and immediately found a new job on an equivalent salary, an
award for injury to feelings will be the only significant element of
compensation.

18.59   In *Coleman v Skyrail Oceanic Ltd*,[55] it was held that compensation
for injury to feelings must only be in relation to such injury as arose
directly from the act of discrimination that the ET has found to be
proven. However, in *British Telecommunications plc v Reid*,[56] the Court
of Appeal held that the ET had been entitled to take into account,
when making an award for injury to feelings in respect of a racially
abusive remark, that the claimant had subsequently been subjected
to a disciplinary investigation, transferred to another location and
that he had to wait a long time for his grievance to be dealt with.
There was no finding of discrimination in relation to those matters
but they arose directly out of the act of discrimination and they were
relevant to the inquiry into the extent of the injury to the claimant's
feelings.

18.60   In *Taylor v XLN Telecom Ltd*[57] the EAT held that *Skyrail* is not
binding authority precluding an award for injury to feelings where
the claimant did not know about the motivation of the discriminator.
The claimant was dismissed but did not know then that the dismissal
was in part prompted by a grievance he had raised relating to discrimination. The EAT held that it would be 'artificial and arbitrary' to
withhold compensation for proven distress and humiliation merely
because the victim did not know of the respondent's discriminatory
motivation. The EAT considered that it was still an injury attributable
to the discriminatory conduct.

54 [1994] ICR 918, [1994] IRLR 509, EAT.
55 [1981] ICR 864, [1981] IRLR 398, CA.
56 [2003] EWCA Civ 1675, [2004] IRLR 327.
57 [2010] ICR 656, [2010] IRLR 499.

18.61   In *Armitage and Marsden and HM Prison Service v Johnson*[58] the EAT gave guidance in relation to awards for injury to feelings. Awards should be:

- compensatory, not punitive;
- not so low as to diminish respect for the policy of the anti-discrimination legislation;
- restrained, as excessive awards could be seen as the way to untaxed riches;
- broadly similar to general damages awards for personal injury;
- in line with the value in everyday life of the sum to be awarded, by reference to purchasing power or earnings;
- command public respect; and
- relate to the degree of detriment suffered by the claimant, having regard to the claimant's own evidence.

18.62   The leading case on the assessment on awards for injury to feelings remains *Vento v Chief Constable of West Yorkshire Police*,[59] in which the Court of Appeal established three bands into which awards should generally fall. The limits of each band have subsequently been revised upwards by the EAT to reflect inflation.[60]

- Low band: between £600 and £6,000. This is appropriate for less serious cases, such as where the act of discrimination is an isolated occurrence. Awards lower than this are to be avoided altogether, as they risk being regarded as so low as not to be a proper recognition of injury to feelings.[61]
- Middle band: between £6,000 and £18,000. This should be used for serious cases, which do not merit an award in the highest band.
- Top band: between £18,000 and £30,000. This covers the most serious cases, such as where there has been a lengthy campaign of discriminatory harassment. Only in the most exceptional case should an award of compensation for injury to feelings exceed £30,000.

18.63   In some ways it is difficult to reconcile these bands with the tortious nature of compensation, focusing as they do on the nature of the dis-

---

58 [1997] ICR 275, [1997] IRLR 162, EAT.
59 [2002] EWCA Civ 1871, [2003] ICR 318, [2003] IRLR 102.
60 *Da'Bell v NSPCC* [2010] IRLR 19, EAT.
61 See, for example, *Assoukou v Select Service Partners Ltd* [2006] EWCA Civ 1442 (£500, which was then regarded as the minimum, awarded for feelings of anger and frustration).

criminatory conduct rather than the gravity of the injury to feelings. Of course, in many cases the two will go hand in hand but there are cases in which the discrimination is serious but the hurt feelings relatively minor, if the claimant is particularly robust. Nor is it unknown for an ostensibly minor discriminatory act to have a devastating effect on a vulnerable individual. Given that awards for injury to feelings are compensatory, not punitive, the size of the award ought really to reflect the nature of the injury rather than the nature of the conduct. ETs can only justify making larger awards if there is proper evidence of the effect on the claimant's feelings before it. The bands represent, in our view, the circumstances in which the correlative injury to feeling would ordinarily be expected.

18.64   ETs may have to assess compensation for acts of discrimination that occurred many years earlier, either because of procedural delay in the matter reaching the ET (for example, where interlocutory decisions have been appealed) or because the claimant is relying on a 'continuing act' reaching back in the employment relationship. An ET should always award the 'going rate' for compensation, even if it is more in real terms than it would have been at the date of the injury complained of, whether because of inflation or the greater appreciation of the distress and hurt which discrimination may cause.[62]

18.65   The size of the discriminator's undertaking should have no bearing on the size of the award for injury to feelings; nor should the ET's feelings of indignation at the conduct in question, however justified.[63]

18.66   Where more than one form of discrimination arises out of the same set of facts (for example disability discrimination and race discrimination), the EAT has held[64] that it would be artificial and unreal to ask to what extent each head of discrimination had contributed to injured feelings that an employee had consequently suffered. In a case where certain acts of discrimination fall into one category or another, however, the question of damages for injury to feelings has to be considered separately in respect to each incident of discrimination. Each incident has to be regarded as a separate wrong for which damages have to be provided.

18.67   In order to ensure that an appropriate award is made, the ET will require clear evidence as to the nature and extent of hurt feelings and this should be dealt with explicitly in a witness statement. 'Injury to

62 *Ministry of Defence v Cannock* [1994] ICR 918, [1994] IRLR 509, EAT.
63 *Corus Hotels plc v Woodward* UKEAT 0536/05, 17 March 2006.
64 *Al Jumard v Clywd Leisure Ltd* [2008] IRLR 345, EAT.

feelings' is a broad category, covering everything from frustration and embarrassment to humiliation and mental distress. It may be reflected in the impact on the complainant's social life, family life or sex life and, in more serious cases, it may extend to anxiety or depression. If the ET considers it appropriate to compensate the claimant for loss of congenial employment, this should not be awarded separately but should be reflected in the award for injury to feelings.[65]

18.68   Witness statements should be reasonably detailed, giving specific examples where possible, yet avoiding the sort of language that the respondent might seek to characterise as overly dramatic or exaggerated. In some cases, it helps to lead evidence from a third party, such as a family member, partner or friend, who has witnessed the impact of the discrimination on the claimant's feelings. It may also be relevant to adduce a GP letter or, in a more serious case, a psychiatric report to explain any impact on the complainant's health.

18.69   A trial judge's assessment of damages for injury to feelings will only be interfered with on appeal in certain circumstances: if the award is so much out of line as to amount to an error of law; because the trial judge has misdirected himself in principle or reached a decision which was plainly wrong; for some other reason, such as wrongly evaluating the facts. The court is not entitled to interfere simply on the ground that it would have awarded a higher amount, if it had been trying the case.[66] In practice, however, the appellate courts have shown themselves willing to step in to adjust an award they consider excessive or inadequate, although they are always careful to characterise the exercise as the correction of an error of law.

- *Doshoki v Draeger Ltd*[67] is an example of a case where the EAT considered an award of £750 compensation for injury to feelings by reason of racial taunts and insults as 'inadequate to a degree where it was wrong in law'. It considered that £4,000 would be an appropriate sum.
- In *Massey v Unifi*,[68] the Court of Appeal considered that the EAT had been wrong to assess the figure for injury to feelings so far down the bracket of the Vento medium range at £7,500. The medical evidence was suggestive of intensely injured feelings and their duration was amply established. It was a 'legal error' not to place

65 *Ministry of Defence v Cannock* [1994] ICR 918, [1994] IRLR 509, EAT.
66 *R (Elias) v Secretary of State for Defence* [2006] EWCA Civ 1293, [2006] 1 WLR 3213, [2006] IRLR 934.
67 [2002] IRLR 340, EAT.
68 [2007] EWCA Civ 800, [2008] ICR 62, [2007] IRLR 902.

the case at or near the top of the middle band, and the appropriate figure for injury to feelings was £12,500.

- Conversely, in *Zaiwalla & Co v Walia*[69] the EAT reduced the award from £15,000 to £10,000 on the basis that the ET had fallen into error by equating the injury to feelings with the symptoms of mid-range, moderately severe PTSD and had made an award that was 'plainly wrong' and 'outside the permissible bracket'.[70]

- In *Governing Body of St Andrew's Catholic Primary School v Blundell*[71] the EAT reduced an injury to feelings award from £22,000 to £14,000 on the basis that, although the victimisation was serious, it could not be characterised as being comparable to the campaigns of discrimination in cases such as *The Prison Service v Johnson*[72] or *HM Prison Service v Salmon*.[73] The EAT described these two cases as a 'benchmark' against which to measure whether an award in the top Vento bracket was merited.[74]

18.70   It will be more difficult for the appellate decision-makers to interfere with an ET's award if the ET's decision is based on well-articulated evidence concerning this element of compensation to which reference may be made in resisting any appeal.

Personal injury

18.71   A claimant may seek damages for personal injury caused by discrimination. This should not be confused with a freestanding claim for personal injury. In this context, it is an aspect of remedy, not a separate complaint or cause of action. It was confirmed in *Sheriff v Klyne Tugs (Lowestoft) Ltd*[75] that compensation under this head can be claimed in the ET. Indeed, in an employment case, if it is arguable that the discrimination is the material cause of the injury, the claim must be brought in the ET, the common law courts lacking any jurisdiction to determine employment discrimination claims.

18.72   Although the injury complained of may be physical, for example in a harassment claim where a complainant has been subjected to

---

69 [2002] IRLR 697, EAT.

70 *Zaiwalla* at para 21.

71 UKEAT/0330/09, 6 April 2010, at paras 15–18. This aspect of the decision did not form part of the subsequent appeal to the Court of Appeal.

72 [1997] ICR 275, EAT.

73 [2001] IRLR 425, EAT.

74 *Blundell* UKEAT/0330/09, [2010] EqLR 156 at para 18.

75 [1999] ICR 1170, [1999] IRLR 481, CA.

an assault, it is more common in discrimination cases for the claim to relate to psychiatric injury, for example anxiety or depression. A medical report will be required, usually from a consultant psychiatrist. It is particularly important that the report focuses carefully on the question of causation, as it is not uncommon for there to be more than one cause of a psychiatric injury. The expert must be supplied with all the medical notes.

18.73   The expert may have to attend court to give evidence, unless the contents of the report can be agreed with the other side. Joint instruction of an expert is preferable, although it may not always be possible in particularly hard-fought cases.

18.74   An award for pain, suffering and loss of amenity is usually made where a claim for personal injury succeeds. Reference should be made to the Judicial Studies Board *Guidelines for the Assessment of General Damages in Personal Injury Cases.*[76] These provide guidelines for appropriate level of awards by reference to injuries of different types and severity.

18.75   The claimant may also rely on other cases which are comparable to his own. These can be found in volumes such as *Kemp and Kemp: Quantum of Damages*[77] and the *Butterworths Personal Injury Litigation Service.* There are also online sources of PI quantum reports such as *Current Law* and *Lawtel.*

18.76   Apart from the pecuniary losses already discussed, the heads of damages listed below may sometimes arise where personal injury has been caused by discrimination. The same principles are relevant as in other personal injury claims and are covered in the leading PI texts referred to above:[78]

- cost of care, whether provided professionally or by family and friends;
- private medical treatment, eg to mitigate the effects of depressive illness;
- housing, equipment etc. Only in very rare cases will victims of discrimination require adapted or new accommodation or equipment.

---

76 Oxford University Press, 11th edn, 2012. Note that from 1 April 2013, general damages in tort cases, including damages for pain, suffering and loss of amenity, will be increased by 10 per cent – see *Simmons v Castle* [2012] EWCA Civ 1288.

77 A looseleaf publication, published by Sweet and Maxwell and updated annually.

78 See also Latimer-Sayer (ed) *Personal Injury Schedules* (3rd edn, Bloomsbury Professional, 2010).

18.77 Where an ET chooses to make separate awards for psychiatric injury and for injury to feelings, it must be careful not to compensate a claimant twice for what may essentially be the same injury.[79] Whilst in principle, awards for psychiatric injury and for injury to feelings are distinct, in practice they may not be so easily separable since it is not always possible to say when the distress suffered as a result of the unlawful discrimination becomes a recognised psychiatric illness such as depression.

Aggravated and exemplary damages

18.78 Where the respondent has behaved in a 'high-handed, malicious, insulting or oppressive manner' aggravated damages may be awarded.[80]

18.79 In *ICTS Ltd v Tchoula*,[81] the EAT emphasised that aggravated damages (like injury to feelings) are compensatory and not punitive, and that, whether they are awarded separately or as part of an award for injury to feelings is a matter of form, not substance. In *Scott v Comrs of Inland Revenue*[82] the Court of Appeal held that aggravated damages are distinct from damages for injury to feelings in the sense that they are not subsumed within the three *Vento* bands (see above). In *Virgo Fidelis Senior School v Boyle*[83] the EAT awarded a further £10,000 by way of aggravated damages in addition to the £25,000 already awarded by the ET for injury to feelings. Although this was a whistleblowing case, the approach to awards under this head is analogous. Advisers should, however, note that in a recent decision on the point, the EAT was somewhat dubious about the value of aggravated damages as a separate head of loss, and held that it would be a 'healthy reminder' of their non-punitive nature if they were to be awarded as a sub-heading of damages for injury to feelings.[84]

79 *HM Prison Service v Salmon* [2001] IRLR 425, EAT.
80 *Alexander v Home Office* [1988] 1 WLR 968, [1988] ICR 685, CA. See *Commissioner of Police of the Metropolis v Shaw* UKEAT/0125/11, [2012] IRLR 291 at paras 19–24 for a summary of the applicable legal principles.
81 [2000] ICR 1191, [2000] IRLR 643, EAT.
82 [2004] EWCA Civ 400, [2004] ICR 1410, [2004] IRLR 713 at paras 34–37.
83 [2004] ICR 1210, [2004] IRLR 268, EAT.
84 *Commissioner of Police of the Metropolis v Shaw* UKEAT/0125/11, 29 November 2011 at para 28. The EAT reduced the ET's award of £17,000 for injury to feelings plus £20,000 aggravated damages to a total award of £30,000 of which £7,500 was (if necessary) to be attributed to aggravated damages.

18.80   By way of example, aggravated damages have been awarded for:

- the failure to apologise or show remorse for the discriminatory conduct; [85]
- the manner in which the complaints of discrimination were investigated;[86]
- the promotion of the discriminator while he was still subject to disciplinary proceedings concerning the alleged discrimination.[87]

18.81   In principle, aggravated damages may be awarded where a respondent's oppressive conduct of the proceedings has aggravated the harm caused by the original discrimination.[88] If a respondent conducts himself badly in the defence of a discrimination case, it may amount to victimisation of the applicant in respect of the protected act of bringing the claim. The EAT considered that it would be regrettable if the claimant had to issue fresh proceedings to be compensated for the victimisation.

18.82   Unlike damages for injury to feelings and aggravated damages, exemplary damages are punitive rather than compensatory. In *Kuddus v Chief Constable of Leicestershire*,[89] the House of Lords confirmed that exemplary damages may be awarded in discrimination cases in two categories of case:

- where there has been oppressive, unconstitutional conduct by servants of the government; or
- where the conduct has been calculated to make a profit which may exceed the compensation to the complainant.

18.83   As for the first category, the ET must consider whether the respondent has acted as servant or agent of the government. *City of Bradford Metropolitan Council v Arora*[90] is the only reported discrimination case in which exemplary damages have been awarded and the only issue before the court was whether the council officials whose conduct was criticised were exercising private or public functions. The Court of Appeal rejected the suggestion that when the claimant was being interviewed for a job, the committee, consisting of senior employees of the council and a councillor, was carrying out a private function of the council. It restored the ET's award of £1,000 exemplary damages.

---

85   *Virgo Fidelis Senior School v Boyle* [2004] ICR 1210, [2004] IRLR 268, EAT.
86   *Armitage v Johnson* [1997] ICR 275, [1997] IRLR 162, EAT.
87   *British Telecommunications v Reid* [2003] EWCA Civ 1675, [2004] IRLR 327.
88   *Zaiwalla & Co v Walia* [2002] IRLR 697, EAT.
89   [2001] UKHL 29, [2002] 2 AC 122.
90   [1991] 2 QB 507, [1991] ICR 226, [1991] IRLR 165, CA.

The question of the type of misconduct which could attract an award of exemplary damages, however, was not before the court.

18.84   Most recently, in *Ministry of Defence v Fletcher*,[91] a case concerning a lesbian soldier who had suffered a campaign of sexual harassment and victimisation, the EAT overturned the ET's award of exemplary damages and held that these 'are to be reserved for the most serious abuses of governmental power' and, whilst the army's failure to operate adequate procedures of redress for the claimant's complaints was 'deplorable', this failure did not cross that high threshold.[92]

18.85   In *Virgo Fidelis Senior School v Boyle*,[93] the EAT confirmed that there was no reason in principle why exemplary damages should not be awarded in discrimination cases if the relevant conditions are met, although it added: 'clearly, in the majority of cases, aggravated damages would be sufficient to mark the employer's conduct'.

Damages for disadvantage on the labour market

18.86   This is a head of damage familiar in personal injury law, otherwise known as a *Smith v Manchester* award.[94] It is only rarely seen, however, in ET claims. This head is intended to compensate the claimant for his disadvantage (by reason of his injury or other effects of his discriminatory treatment) in competing for work on the open labour market.

18.87   There are two factual scenarios: firstly, although employed at the date of trial he is vulnerable to losing the job and will then be disadvantaged when competing for another job; secondly, he was unemployed at the date of trial and because of his disadvantage in the labour market cannot find a job, but is likely to do so at some point.

18.88   Because of the speculative nature of the loss in this type of case, the multiplier/multiplicand approach is not appropriate, and the compensation will be in the form of a lump sum.

18.89   In the case of an employed claimant, evidence is required that there is a real not a fanciful risk that they will in future lose their job. The assessment is necessarily speculative and depends on issues such as the claimant's skills and present job security, regional unemployment and industry conditions.

18.90   If the claimant is unemployed and likely to remain unemployed for a significant further period, the appropriate award is future loss of earnings for that period. But there may be additional vulnerability

91 [2010] IRLR 25, EAT.
92 [2010] IRLR 25, EAT at para 115.
93 [2004] ICR 1210, [2004] IRLR 268, EAT.
94 Named after the first case of its type: (1974) 17 KIR 1.

thereafter as well. So lost competitiveness on the open labour market can be compensated as an alternative to future loss of earnings or as an additional element, depending on the circumstances.

Stigma damages

18.91   In *Abbey National plc v Chagger*[95] the employee argued successfully in the ET that he had been refused employment by third parties because he had brought discrimination proceedings against the respondent and that he should be compensated for being permanently 'stigmatised'. The ET awarded him £1,325,322 for future loss on the basis that he would never again be able to obtain employment in his particular industry. The EAT overturned the award on the ground that, since the loss resulted from unlawful victimisation by third party employers, it was too remote to be attributed to the dismissing employer. The Court of Appeal, however, ruled that the original employer must remain liable for 'stigma loss', even where the actions of the third party employers are unlawful.[96]

18.92   However, in most cases there will be no need to consider this as a separate head of loss, since it can be properly factored into the consideration of whether the employee has taken reasonable steps to mitigate his loss.

18.93   There is one exceptional case where it could be necessary for an ET to award compensation specifically by reference to the impact of stigma on future job prospects. This is where this is the only head of future loss. An example would be where the ET has found that the claimant would definitely have been dismissed even had there been no discrimination. He would be on the labour market at exactly the same time and in the same circumstances as if he had been dismissed lawfully. Accordingly, the damage to his employment prospects from the stigma of taking proceedings would be the only potentially recoverable head of future loss.

Pension loss

18.94   The steps involved in determining the value of a pension claim are too complex to discuss in depth in this chapter. A useful starting

95   [2009] ICR 624 (EAT).
96   [2009] EWCA Civ 1202, [2010] ICR 397.

point is *Compensation for loss of pension rights: Employment Tribunals*[97] (the Guidelines).

18.95   In essence the Guidelines set out two different bases for calculation of pension loss: 'the simplified approach', which involves shorter-term calculations, and 'the substantial loss approach', which involves more complex longer-term calculations. The Guidelines include actuarial tables specifically for these purposes. They are similar but not identical to the Ogden Tables.

18.96   Although the assessment of pension losses is often difficult, it is important for the ET to give reasons as to why it prefers the 'simplified approach' or 'the substantial loss approach' or any other approach. It must set out its conclusions and explain the compensation it has arrived at in respect of each head of claim so that the parties and the EAT can identify an error.[98]

18.97   In *Orthet v Vince-Cain*[99] the EAT endorsed the suggestion[100] that where the period of loss is likely to be more than two years, the correct method of calculating future pension loss is the 'substantial loss approach'.

18.98   In *Sibbit v The Governing Body of St Cuthbert's Catholic Primary School*,[101] the EAT held that it was an error of principle for the ET to adopt the simplified approach in circumstances where the claimant had long service, had been in stable employment and was (as a teacher) unlikely to be affected by the economic cycle and less likely to be looking for new pastures. She was unlikely to find alternative employment before retirement and the loss was quantifiable. The substantial loss approach should have been applied as provided by the Guidelines.[102]

18.99   Claimants should be aware that, where they have suffered the loss of securely-pensioned employment but have future years of employability ahead, the respondent is likely to argue that they can at least partially mitigate their pension loss even if their future pension rights are inferior. This is because, as the Guidelines observe,[103] pension rights are a fringe benefit and may be compensated by an increase in

97 The Stationery Office, 3rd edn, 2003. Available at www.justice.gov.uk/tribunals/employment/claims/booklets.

98 *Greenhoff v Barnsley Metropolitan Borough Council* [2006] 1 ICR 1514, EAT.

99 [2005] ICR 374, [2004] IRLR 857, EAT.

100 The Guidelines para 7.1.

101 UKEAT/0070/10/ZT, 20 May 2010.

102 The Guidelines paras 4.13 and 4.14.

103 The Guidelines para 4.12.

salary. That higher salary could, in turn, be used by the claimant to fund a private pension or ISA.

18.100   In *Orthet*,[104] the EAT found that the ET had been wrong to award a sum for loss of pension covering a period of four and a half years on the basis that the employers were about to introduce a pension scheme at the time of the claimant's dismissal. The ET should have considered the nature of any pension scheme that would be available to her in new employment when she had retrained, and the effect that would have on the pension loss which she would have suffered. It also erred in failing to take account of the fact that the payment of compensation to the applicant ought to reflect early receipt.

18.101   As the Guidelines were last produced in 2003, when the economic outlook was somewhat different than today, there is an argument that the 'substantial loss' approach will no longer produce the correct outcome in some cases. This point was successfully argued by the respondent in *Chief Constable of West Midlands Police v Gardner*,[105] where the EAT held that an ET could properly adopt an approach to assessing pension loss that was in practice based on the Ogden Tables, in circumstances where it had found that those tables better reflected modern economic reality than the 2003 Guidelines. Guidance on applying the Ogden Tables approach to pension loss can be found in personal injury texts such as Personal Injury Schedules.[106]

Reductions to the award

18.102   The loss claimed must be caused by the discrimination. If the loss is partly a consequence of other factors, for example a pre-existing medical condition or other personal problems, the ET will apportion the damages accordingly and only award the amount which can properly be attributed to the discrimination. For example, in *HM Prison Service v Salmon*[107] the EAT approved the decision of the ET in assessing the applicant's damages for psychiatric injury resulting from sexual harassment at £15,000 and then discounting that by 25 per cent on the basis that her depressive illness was only caused to the extent of 75 per cent by the proven acts of discrimination.

18.103   An award of compensation will be reduced if the respondent persuades the ET that the claimant has failed to mitigate his losses,

---

104 [2005] ICR 374, [2004] IRLR 857, EAT.
105 UKEAT/0174/11 and UKEAT/0502/11, 19 October 2011, [2012] EqLR 20.
106 Latimer-Sayer (ed) (3rd edn, Bloomsbury Professional, 2010).
107 [2001] IRLR 425, EAT.

for example by seeking alternative work. However, the duty on the claimant to keep his losses to a minimum is only to act reasonably and the cases suggest that the standard of reasonableness is not high in view of the fact that the employer is a wrongdoer.[108] The court or ET must not be too stringent in its expectations of the injured party. As Sedley LJ put it in *Wilding v British Telecommunications plc:*[109]

> It is not enough for the wrongdoer to show that it would have been reasonable to take the steps he has proposed: he must show that it was unreasonable of the innocent party not to take them. This is a real distinction. It reflects the fact that if there is more than one reasonable response open to the wronged party, the wrongdoer has no right to determine his choice. It is where, and only where, the wrongdoer can show affirmatively that the other party has acted unreasonably in relation to his duty to mitigate that the defence will succeed.

18.104 Respondents usually try to prove a failure to mitigate by adducing evidence of adverts for jobs not applied for, evidence of the state of the job market more generally and through cross-examination. In meeting such evidence, practitioners should ask, for example, what the source of the advertisement was; whether it was at all likely that the claimant would normally have seen it and whether the evidence of the job market is truly representative of the environment in which the claimant reasonably could be expected to seek work. It is important for claimants to keep good records of all steps taken to find alternative work in order to resist a submission of this sort. This should take the form of copies of job advertisements, job applications and responses, evidence of contacts with job agencies and a clear note of phone calls made, along with the outcome. The question for the ET is not whether there were further steps that could have been taken to find work, but whether the claimant has taken reasonable steps to lessen the loss. Where an ET finds that a complainant has not acted reasonably, it will deduct a sum from his compensation equivalent to that which he would have saved had he acted reasonably. So, for example, if an ET finds that he ought to have found alternative employment at an equivalent salary within six months, the ET will award no loss of earnings after that point.

18.105 The situation is rather more complex when the claimant seeks to mitigate his losses by setting up his own business. In *Aon Training Ltd v Dore*,[110] the Court of Appeal held that the ET was wrong to

---

108 *Fyfe v Scientific Furnishings Ltd* [1989] ICR 648, [1989] IRLR 331, EAT.
109 [2002] EWCA Civ 349, [2002] ICR 1079, [2002] IRLR 524 at para 55.
110 [2005] EWCA Civ 411, [2005] IRLR 891.

quantify the claimant's losses arising from his dismissal (partly for reasons relating to his disability) solely on the basis of the interest on loans that he took out in order to set up his own business rather than seeking alternative employment. If the ET is satisfied that setting up his own business was reasonable mitigation, the ET must first calculate what sum represents the loss of remuneration; it should then consider the costs incurred in mitigating that loss and these, if reasonably incurred, should be added to the loss; from that sum should be deducted the earnings from the new business.

18.106   In determining the measure of a claimant's loss and assessing compensation, a tribunal may be invited by the employer to find that, had there been no unlawful discrimination, the dismissal would have occurred in any event for other, non-discriminatory reasons (for example, by reason of a subsequent redundancy exercise).[111] The Tribunal will adopt a percentage chance approach to this exercise (see paras 18.45–18.47 above).

18.107   Although there is no express provision allowing for a reduction of the award for contributory fault, an award of compensation in a discrimination case is subject to the Law Reform (Contributory Negligence) Act 1945, which allows for reduction in compensation in tortious claims where the claimant's conduct itself amounts to negligence or breach of a legal duty and it contributed to the loss or damage.[112]

Case management

18.108   A remedies hearing in almost any discrimination case requires careful advance analysis and preparation. If a claimant fails to lead evidence on a relevant issue, it may be impossible to appeal an unfavourable award.

18.109   The importance of a good schedule of loss is often overlooked. A key aim for claimant advisers is to put the respondent at risk. This aim is furthered by setting out all realistically arguable claims in a reasoned and transparent schedule, with calculations of tax and interest if applicable, to enable the respondent and its advisers to understand how much the case might be worth if things go badly for them. If no settlement ensues, the ET will at least have a coherent formulation of the claim, which it can adopt or modify.

---

111 *Abbey National plc v Chagger* [2009] EWCA Civ 1202, [2010] ICR 397.
112 *Way v Crouch* [2005] ICR 1362, [2005] IRLR 603, EAT.

18.110   In *Buxton v Equinox Design Ltd*,[113] the EAT affirmed that the remedies hearing in discrimination cases required careful management and might require further directions and exchange of witness statements on remedy. In all but the simplest cases a timetable for disclosure of documents and exchange of statements is appropriate.

18.111   As regards directions, it will usually facilitate negotiations for schedules of loss (see appendix A) and counter-schedules to be exchanged after the evidence, but well ahead of a hearing date. Sequential exchange is often best (ie schedule first). Following exchange of schedules and experts' discussions, the scope of the issues can usually be narrowed, or at least defined, by the time of the remedies hearing, even if settlement proves impossible.

18.112   Where expert evidence is necessary (for example as to the likely prognosis for recovery from psychiatric injury caused by discrimination), there are well-established case-management principles in the ET. In *De Keyser Ltd v Wilson*,[114] the EAT gave guidance (see para 17.44 above).

18.113   The same approach should be adopted if either party proposes to instruct an employment expert to comment on the claimant's future employment prospects. It is important that an employment consultant's report is not seen by the ET as usurping its function but, rather, providing assistance. A good report can persuade an ET of the real difficulty of mitigation faced by a particular claimant. They are particularly effective in cases where the loss of job or change of career will lead to a continuing reduced earning capacity.

18.114   The letter of instruction to such an expert should include instructions as to the factual circumstances and characteristics of the claimant including their known skills and qualifications. If there are any factors reasonably limiting ability to travel to work, for example, these should be set out. In the case of a joint expert, if the parties cannot agree on the factual circumstances alternatives reflecting what each states to be the circumstances of the claimant should be set out.

Interest

18.115   In discrimination claims the ET has jurisdiction to award interest and must consider doing so in all cases in which it makes an award.[115] A failure to include interest can be corrected as a 'slip' (on

---

113 [1999] ICR 269, EAT.
114 [2001] IRLR 324, EAT.
115 Employment Tribunals (Interest on Awards in Discrimination Cases) Regulations (ET Regs) 1996 SI No 2803 reg 2.

the ET's own motion or on application under the ET Rules of Procedure 2004 r37(1)). Interest should be awarded on the claimant's net, rather than gross, loss[116] and should be calculated as simple interest which accrues from day to day.[117]

18.116   The rate of interest is that prescribed under the Court Fund Rules 1987[118] r27(1) (the rate prescribed for the special investment account). For several years this was 6 per cent. Unsurprisingly, it has been substantially reduced in recent years. The rates applicable as of specific dates are as follows:

- from 1 August 1999: 7 per cent
- from 1 February 2002: 6 per cent
- from 1 February 2009: 3 per cent
- from 1 June 2009: 1.5 per cent
- from 1 July 2009: 0.5 per cent.

18.117   If the rate has varied over the relevant period, the ET may, in the interest of simplicity, apply an average of the applicable rates.[119]

18.118   Interest is calculated from the date of the act of discrimination on awards for injury to feelings and pain, suffering and loss of amenity.[120] For past pecuniary losses, interest is usually calculated from the point midway between the act of discrimination and the date of calculation, as is the practice of the civil courts in personal injury claims.[121]

18.119   The ET should give reasons if it decides not to award interest on the above basis. It has a discretion to calculate interest by reference to different periods in respect of different elements of the award, if it considers there are exceptional circumstances and a serious injustice would be caused if interest were awarded on the usual basis.[122]

18.120   If the judgment sum remains unpaid after 14 days, then interest is payable from the day after judgment at the Judgments Act 1838 rate[123] (currently 8 per cent) under the Employment Tribunals (Interest) Order 1990.[124]

---

116 *Bentwood Brothers (Manchester) Ltd v Shepherd* [2003] EWCA Civ 380, [2003] ICR 1000, [2003] IRLR 364.
117 ET Regs 1996 reg 3(1).
118 SI No 821.
119 ET Regs 1996 SI No 2803 r3(3). Alternatively, a useful cumulative interest table is to be found in *Facts & Figures: Tables for the Calculation of Damages*, published annually by Sweet & Maxwell.
120 ET Regs 1996 r6(1)(a).
121 ET Regs 1996 r4.
122 ET Regs 1996 r6(2).
123 ET Regs 1996 r8.
124 SI No 479.

Adjustments to awards for failures to comply with the ACAS Code

18.121 Awards of compensation may be adjusted to reflect a failure by either party to comply with the requirements of the ACAS Code on disciplinary and grievance procedures.[125] This applies to discrimination and equal pay claims brought by employees only; it does not apply to other kinds of worker.

18.122   If the employer or the employee has failed to comply with the Code and that failure was 'unreasonable' then the ET may, if it considers it just and equitable to do so, increase or decrease any award by up to 25 per cent.[126] The language of the new provision suggests that the ET has a wide discretion and that there is no presumption that an adjustment will be made in every case.

18.123   The summary below sets out only the key recommendations. These are amplified in the Code, which provides detailed guidance and should be carefully consulted. Further guidance and examples of how the procedures ought to work in practice is provided in the (non-statutory) ACAS Guide.[127]

18.124   In a disciplinary situation (which includes both misconduct and poor performance issues):

- The employer should establish the facts of the case without unreasonable delay.
- He should notify the employee in writing of the case to answer, giving sufficient information to allow the employee to prepare his case.
- This will normally include providing copies of any written evidence and may include witness statements.
- The employer should hold a meeting with the employee to discuss the problem, giving the employee a reasonable time to prepare his case.
- The meeting should usually be conducted by a different person from the person who conducted the investigation.
- The employer should allow the employee to be accompanied at the meeting in cases to which the statutory right to be accompanied applies.

---

125 ACAS Code of Practice 1 *Disciplinary and Grievance Procedures* (2009). This can be downloaded from the ACAS website (www.acas.org.uk).

126 TULRCA 1992 s207A.

127 ACAS Guide *Discipline and Grievances at Work* (2011).

- The employee should be given a reasonable opportunity to ask questions, present evidence and call relevant witnesses.
- The employer should then decide on the appropriate action.
- If an employee is persistently unable or unwilling to attend a disciplinary meeting without good cause, the employer should make a decision on the available evidence.
- He should provide the employee with an opportunity to appeal against the decision.

18.125   In a grievance situation:

- If it is not possible to resolve the grievance informally, the employee should raise the grievance formally.
- He should put the grievance in writing and set out its nature.
- The employer should hold a meeting with him to discuss the grievance.
- The employer should allow the employee to be accompanied at the meeting in cases to which the statutory right to be accompanied applies.
- The employer should decide on the appropriate action.
- The employer should provide the employee with an opportunity to appeal. Any appeal should be lodged by the employee, and heard by the employer, without unreasonable delay.

18.126   Under the Code both employer and employee may be in breach at the same time of its provisions. There is thus a very real prospect of an ET making adjustments upwards and downwards to reflect failures to comply by both parties.

Taxation and grossing-up

18.127   As has been pointed out above, losses are calculated on a net basis. However, the ET must ensure that, after tax, the claimant receives in her hands the full sum of her award, no less and no more. If the claimant finds herself having to pay tax on the net sums, she will end up with less than that full sum. In order to avoid this, if part of an award will be taxed, it must be 'grossed up' by the ET so that the respondent covers the tax liability. Two questions arise: which parts of awards are liable to tax; and how does the 'grossing-up' calculation work?

18.128   Subject to important exceptions, the Income Tax (Earnings and Pensions) Act (ITEPA) 2003 ss401–404 render an employee or ex-employee liable to income tax[128] on such

> payments and other benefits [as are] received directly or indirectly in consideration or in consequence of, or otherwise in connection with ... the termination of [his] employment'. Such payments or benefits are treated as 'employment income of the employee or former employee ... for the relevant tax year.

18.129   One exception relates to the first £30,000 of a termination payment, which is not taxable.[129] A contractual entitlement to pay in lieu of notice has been held to be an emolument of the employment: earnings coming within ITEPA 2003 s62, rather than a termination payment coming within section 403(1).[130] Another exception is a payment or other benefit provided '(a) in connection with the termination of the employment by the death of the employee or (b) on account of injury to or disability of the employee'.[131]

18.130   There is still some dispute as to whether awards for injury to feelings are taxable.

18.131   In *Orthet v Vince-Cain*[132] the EAT considered that the ET was correct to regard an injury to feelings award as non-taxable (because it fell within exception (b) above) and therefore to exclude it from the grossing-up calculation. However, the EAT itself recognised that its judgment is not binding on the Revenue and there is no guarantee that the position may not change. The Orthet judgment has been described in *Yorkshire Housing Ltd v Cuerden* by another division of the EAT (HHJ Peter Clark presiding) as obiter and 'controversial').[133] However, in the same case,[134] the EAT accepted counsel for the claimant's concession that awards for injury to feelings arising out of pre-termination acts of discrimination are not taxable and should not, therefore, be grossed-up.

18.132   The most recent word on the subject is the decision of the First-tier Tribunal, Tax Chamber in *Oti-Obihara v Comr for HM Revenue and Customs*,[135] from which the following points can be drawn.

---

128 Only income tax and not national insurance.
129 ITEPA 2003 s403(1).
130 *Goldman v HMRC* [2012] UKFTT 313 (TC).
131 ITEPA 2003 s406.
132 [2005] ICR 374, [2004] IRLR 857, EAT.
133 UKEAT/0397/09 at para 29.
134 At para 29.
135 [2010] UKFTT 568 (TC), [2011] IRLR 386.

- Counsel for the Revenue conceded that, to the extent that any part of the disputed settlement payment comprises damages for injury to feelings as a consequence of discrimination, it will not be taxable under either ITEPA 2003 s6 or s401, even if it is paid on the occasion of the termination of the employment.
- A compensation payment made by an employer to an employee for discrimination will be taxable under ITEPA 2003 s401 if the discrimination is the cause of the termination of the employment, but only to the extent that the compensation meets financial loss caused by the termination of the employment.
- Any other amount received by reason of discrimination represents compensation for the infringement of the right not to be discriminated against, not compensation for the termination of the employment.
- The Revenue's approach in such cases should be to take a figure representing the financial loss flowing from the termination of the employment and to tax that as a termination payment, rather than trying to isolate an injury to feelings payment and then taxing the remainder as a termination payment.[136]

18.133   *Oti-Obihara* provides the clearest indication yet that awards for injury to feelings will not be taxable. However, as the position has altered on a number of occasions over the years, advisers should approach the point with caution and check for any later decisions.

How is the calculation performed?

18.134   The correct approach is, we suggest, best illustrated by an example. Suppose the ET awards the claimant £10,000 for injury to feelings and £90,000 for pecuniary losses. Applying the *Orthet/Oti-Obihara* reasoning, only the £90,000 would be subject to grossing-up.

18.135   Of that sum the first £30,000 is exempt and £60,000 is taxable. Note that as only one termination of employment can be at issue, no more than £30,000 of such a payment is exempt, including where payments in relation to the same termination have been made in more than one tax year. A new tax year does not trigger entitlement to a further £30,000 exemption. In the simple case where the employment terminated and an award is made in the same tax year, then to the extent that it exceeds the £30,000 threshold, the payment counts as 'employment income' for the tax year in which it was received. So

---

136 See [2011] IRLR 386 at paras 18, 26, 31 and 43–44 respectively.

let us assume for simplicity that the money is paid today, and that the claimant has no other 'employment income' in this tax year.

18.136   The relevant tax bands are for 2013 – 2014[137] ie:

Up to £9,440   0%
On the next £32,010   20% ('basic rate tax')
On the rest[138]   40% ('higher rate tax')

18.137 So on the claimant's taxable £60,000, she will pay the following tax at the basic rate:

On the first £9,440   nil
On the next £32,010   £6,402

18.138 So an extra £6,402 in her hand would indemnify her against basic rate tax. But that sum will in turn be taxed at the higher rate because it too will be regarded as 'employment income'. So it has to be added in to produce the balance which is taxable at the higher rate:

$$(60,000 - 32,010 - 9,440) + 6,402 = £24,952$$

18.139 In order to receive that £24,952 balance in her hand after higher rate tax at 40 per cent, she should get:

$$100/60 \times 24,952 = £41,586.67$$

18.140 So her £90,000 becomes £113,036.67 after grossing up (ie £30,000 + £9,440 + £32,010 + £41,586.67), an extra £23,036.67. This is what the ET should award to ensure that she is indemnified against tax.

Provision for legal costs

18.141 ITEPA 2003 s413A, which applies to payments made on or after 6 April 2011,[139] provides that tax will not be levied, as it otherwise would under Chapter 3 of Part 6 ITEPA 2003, on a payment that meets the following conditions:

- the payment meets the whole or part of legal costs[140] incurred by an employee exclusively in connection with the termination of the employee's employment; and either:

---

137 For a person aged under 65 on 5 April 2013: different personal allowances apply to those aged 65 and over, which can be found at www.gov.uk/income-tax-rates.

138 Up to £150,000, where the 45% rate commences from 6 April 2013.

139 Payments made prior to this date would have been dealt with in accordance with the Inland Revenue's Extra-Statutory Concession A81.

140 Defined as 'fees payable for the services and disbursements of a lawyer'; see ITEPA 2003 s413A(4). Costs payable to, eg, an employment consultant who is not a qualified lawyer will not therefore be covered.

- the payment is made pursuant to an order of a court or ET, or
- the termination of the employee's employment results in a compromise agreement[141] between the employer and the employee and:
  - the compromise agreement provides for the payment to be made by the employer, and
  - the payment is made directly to the employee's lawyer.[142]

18.142 The strict terms of the statutory provision must be met if it is to apply. Thus, for example, agreements conciliated through ACAS will not be covered, as such agreements fall under ERA 1996 s203(2)(e) and not s203(3).[143] To ensure that the claimant has the benefit of ITEPA 2003 s413A, any agreement in which ACAS is involved should be concluded by means of a compromise agreement that complies with ERA 1996 s203(3).

18.143   In a pre-hearing settlement context, it is therefore important to record in the compromise agreement that payments are made in accordance with these requirements. More generally, if the compensation payment is structured this way, it will obviously reduce the overall sum that is subject to tax or other deductions.

Declarations

18.144 The ET has the power to make declarations. A declaration is a statement declaring the rights of the claimant and the respondent. In practice, this simply reflects the findings in the judgment of the ET, for example, that the respondent has directly discriminated against the claimant because of his race, or has failed to make reasonable adjustments in respect of his disability.

Recommendations

18.145 The pre-existing legislation limited ETs to making a recommendation that benefitted the individual claimant. This assumed they were still

141 As defined in Employment Rights Act 1996 s203(3) or Employment Rights (Northern Ireland) Order 1996 art 245(3); see ITEPA 2003 s413A(4).
142 The 'lawyer' must be a qualified lawyer within the meaning of ERA 1996 s203(4) or Employment Rights (Northern Ireland) Order 1996 art 245(4); see ITEPA 2003 s413A(4).
143 The position was different under the old Extra-Statutory Concession, which covered COT3 agreements.

in the workplace. Recommendations were, therefore, of limited value to the 70 per cent of claimants who had already left the workplace.

18.146 The EqA 2010 gives the ET the power to make an appropriate recommendation that, within a specified period, the respondent take specific steps for the purpose of obviating or reducing the adverse effect of any matter to which the proceedings relate on the claimant or on 'any other person'.[144]

18.147 This allows ETs to make recommendations in discrimination cases that benefit the whole workforce and not just the individual claimant. Indeed the use of the phrase 'any other person' suggests an even wider ambit, extending beyond employees or workers to applicants for jobs, independent contractors etc. This has the potential to be a useful tool in seeking to change the culture within offending organisations. Careful consideration needs to be given to framing draft recommendations to put before ETs.

18.148 By way of example, the Employment Statutory Code of Practice[145] (the Employment Code) suggests that an ET could recommend that the respondent:

- take steps to implement a harassment policy more effectively;
- provide equal opportunities training for staff involved in promotion procedures; or
- introduce more transparent selection criteria in recruitment, transfer or promotion processes.

18.149 The Employment Code[146] suggests that the following circumstances might lead to an ET making recommendations that affect the wider workforce:

- if the evidence in the case suggested that wider or structural issues were the cause of the discrimination and that they are likely to lead to further discrimination unless addressed; and
- it is commensurate (or 'proportionate') to the respondent's capacity to implement it.

18.150 In *The Governing Body of St Andrew's Catholic Primary School v Blundell*[147] the EAT found that the terms of a recommendation went too far. The ET had ordered that the school write to all parents making a general apology to the claimant and, specifically, apologising on behalf of an individual for criticisms of the claimant 'which she now

144 EqA 2010 s124(3).
145 At para 15.47.
146 At para 15.50.
147 UKEAT/0330/09, [2010] EqLR 156.

accepts were unfounded'. The EAT accepted a submission that, as a matter of fact, the individual in question ('however wrongheaded') accepted no such thing. It would be wrong to require her to make statements with which she did not agree and the EAT ordered that the recommendation be varied so as to delete those words.

18.151   The consequence for a respondent if it does not comply with a recommendation made which relates to the individual claimant is that the ET may increase the amount of compensation awarded (or, if no award was made, make one).[148]

18.152   There is no equivalent sanction where a respondent fails to comply with a recommendation relating to 'any other person'. No mechanism has been put in place in place to regulate how, and if, such recommendations are implemented. However, failure to comply with a recommendation applying more broadly than the claimant could be used as evidence to support subsequent similar discrimination claims against the same respondent. In certain circumstances it may be appropriate to draw the attention of the Equality and Human Rights Commission to such recommendations, as it has power to investigate in a situation in which there is evidence of such structural problems under the Equality Act 2006.

18.153   Some examples of recommendations.

- In a case where a reference had been provided that the ET found to be an act of victimisation: that the respondent write to each employer to whom the original reference had been sent acknowledging that the provision of such a reference had been found by an ET to amount to an unlawful act of discrimination and asking that the reference be deleted from all its files and systems, along with a copy of the communication to the claimant.[149]
- In a sex discrimination case, the ET recommended that the employer come to an agreement with the employee on a work roster that fitted in with her childcare commitments rather than the fixed shift pattern the respondent had sought to impose.[150]
- In a sex discrimination case, the ET recommended that the employer carry out an equal opportunities enquiry, to be concluded within two months of the hearing.[151]

---

148 EqA 2010 s124(7).
149 *Geraghty v (1) Age Concern (Luton) (2) McKeaveney*, ET Case No 1202329/07, unreported.
150 *Garcia-Bellow v Aviance*, ET Case No 2201476/07, unreported.
151 *Hylton v MOD*, ET Case No 2201476/07, unreported. Further examples, since 2010, may be found in the *Equality Law Reports*.

18.154 The ET's power to make recommendations is not without limits. In *Noone v North West Thames Regional Health Authority (No 2)*[152] the Court of Appeal held that it was not open to an ET to make a recommendation that the claimant (a doctor who had not been promoted because of unlawful discrimination) should be automatically appointed to the next such post to become available, without going through the normal selection procedure. Such a recommendation would, itself, have the effect of overriding statutory NHS recruitment procedures. The court substituted the more limited recommendation that the respondent should specifically draw the attention of all members of any appointments committee, considering any future application by the appellant, to the need for compliance with the Race Relations Act 1976 and that it should record and remind such committee members that the appellant's previous application for such a post had failed on racial grounds.

18.155 If a claimant is seeking a recommendation therefore it is worth seeking to make the proposal specific and precise in terms of actions to be taken and the time in which those actions are to be taken.

Enforcement of tribunal awards

18.156 If the respondent fails to comply with the ET's order to pay compensation, the position used to be that application had to be made to the county court for enforcement. That option is still open to claimants but, with effect from 6 April 2010, the Ministry of Justice introduced a new Employment Tribunal Fast Track scheme, which simplifies the process for successful ET claimants. They may now call on an extended service from the High Court enforcement officers if the other party fails to pay the award ordered by the ET. An Officer will complete the court processes for them and move on to enforcement as soon as possible. The only cost to the claimant is the £50 court fee needed to issue a writ to seize assets that will cover the amounts they are owed and this will be added to the debt owed by their employer. The £70.50 the High Court enforcement officer would normally charge the employee if the award could not be recovered will be waived.

152 [1988] ICR 813, [1988] IRLR 530, CA.

CHAPTER 19

International sources of discrimination law

continued

> ### Key points
> - Advisers should use this chapter to assist them in interpreting the concepts used in the EqA 2010.
> - In particular, the international instruments can be used to show the purpose of the anti-discrimination legislation.
> - The chapter can also be used when arguments concerning EU law arise – for example whether it is necessary to disapply any provision of domestic law or concerning the mandatory interpretation of domestic law to give effect to the underlying EU law.
> - For a more detailed treatment of the themes in this chapter, advisers should consult *Non-Discrimination in International Law: a Handbook for Practitioners.*[1]

19.1   The source of the concept of equality is rooted in the principle that persons in like situations should be treated alike and that persons in unlike situations should not be treated in the same manner. 'Thus to treat unequal matters differently according to their inequality is not merely permitted but required' by the principle of equality.[2] This idea underpins the principle of equality so that it encompasses non-discrimination, positive discrimination and reasonable accommodation.

19.2   Advisers will need to know something about the international context of the protected characteristic involved in their case, including the human rights context. We have therefore divided this chapter by the protected characteristics with which the EqA 2010 is concerned.

19.3   The domestic courts 'take no notice of treaties as such ... until they are embodied in laws enacted by Parliament, and then only to the extent that Parliament tells us'.[3] A treaty is not part of English law unless and until it has been incorporated into the law by legislation.[4] However, domestic law must be interpreted in line with the state's obligations under international law whenever possible to do so regardless of whether the treaty has been incorporated into domestic law. They may be referred to in order to develop the common law,

1   2011, Interights: www.interights.org/document/153/index.html.
2   See *South West Africa case* (ICJ Rep. 1966, 4) dissenting Opinion of Judge Tanaka.
3   *Blackburn v Att-Gen* [1971] 1 WLR 1037 at 1039G–H per Lord Denning MR.
4   *JH Rayner (Mincing Lane) Ltd v Dept of Trade and Industry* [1990] 2 AC 418 at 499F–500C.

and when interpreting statutes.[5] Where there is an ambiguity, or the law is otherwise unclear or so far undeclared by an appellate court, the English court is obliged to consider the implications. There is a prima facie presumption that Parliament does not intend to act in breach of international law and therefore ambiguous statutes are to be interpreted in line with international law.[6]

Race

19.4   The relevant international sources are:

- the International Convention on the Elimination of All Forms of Racial Discrimination (ICERD);[7]
- TFEU;
- Directive 2000/43 (the Race Directive).

19.5   ICERD provides in Article 1 that

> In this Convention, the term 'racial discrimination' shall mean any distinction, exclusion, restriction or preference based on race, colour, descent, or national or ethnic origin which has the purpose or effect of nullifying or impairing the recognition, enjoyment or exercise, on an equal footing, of human rights and fundamental freedoms in the political, economic, social, cultural or any other field of public life.

19.6   This definition does not appear to have the effect of blurring the line between direct and indirect race discrimination as two separate forms of legal wrong.[8] Preference based on descent[9] is part of the definition. This means that the concept of 'race' includes the concept of discrimination by reference to caste.[10] ICERD does not apply to

---

5   See *Derbyshire CC v Times Newspapers Ltd* [1993] AC 534, HL.

6   Diplock LJ *Salomon v Commissioners of Custom and Excise* [1967] 2 QB 116.

7   660 UNTS 195 adopted in 1965 and entered into force in 1969. Although Article 14, ICERD allows CERD to adjudicate complaints lodged by individuals and groups, the UK government has not yet granted CERD jurisdiction to perform this function.

8   See *R (Elias) v Secretary of State for Defence* [2006] EWCA Civ 1293, [2006] 1 WLR 3213, [2006] IRLR 934 at [100]–[115].

9   For a discussion of this point see *R (E) v Governing Body of JFS (United Synagogue and others intervening)* [2009] UKSC 15, [2010] 2 AC 728 at [81].

10   Thus rendering EqA 2010 s9(5) a merely clarifying provision concerning the means by which specific situations of caste discrimination should be dealt with. The provision itself is not required to ensure that a caste discrimination case may be brought as a race discrimination claim.

distinctions made by the state between citizens and non-citizens.[11] ICERD provides for positive action in appropriate cases. Special measures, taken for the sole purpose of securing adequate advancement of certain racial or ethnic groups or individuals requiring such protection as may be necessary in order to ensure such groups or individuals equal enjoyment or exercise of human rights and fundamental freedoms, shall not be deemed racial discrimination. However, these measures must not lead to the maintenance of separate rights for different racial groups and they may not be continued after the objectives for which they were taken have been achieved.

19.7   Article 5 provides that the states parties will prohibit and eliminate racial discrimination in all its forms, and guarantee the right of everyone, without distinction as to race, colour, or national or ethnic origin, to equality before the law. This applies particularly to (among others) the enjoyment of the right to work, to free choice of employment, to just and favourable conditions of work, to protection against unemployment, to equal pay for equal work and to just and favourable remuneration.

TFEU

19.8   Article 18 prohibits discrimination on the grounds of nationality within the scope of the Treaty and can be relied upon directly in cases before the national courts that are within the scope of the Treaty.[12]

Charter of the Fundamental Rights of the European Union ('Charter')

19.9   Article 21 prohibits 'any discrimination based on any ground such as sex, race, colour, ethnic or social origin, ... membership of a national minority ... birth, ...'

Directive 2000/43

19.10   Directive 2000/43[13] provides for a prohibition on discrimination on the basis of racial or ethnic origin. Article 2 defines direct and

---

11 Article 1.2 ICERD.

12 Contrast this with Article 19 TFEU (see para 1.89 below) which provides a legal basis on which action may be taken to combat discrimination based on prohibited grounds, but does not give rise directly to rights.

13 Directive 2000/43 of 29 June 2000 implementing the principle of equal treatment between persons irrespective of racial or ethnic origin.

indirect discrimination. Article 2.3 prohibits harassment. Article 2.4 provides that an instruction to discriminate shall itself be discrimination. Article 3 gives the scope of the Directive. It indicates the situations in which discrimination on racial grounds is unlawful under the Directive. As well as covering conditions for access to employment and occupation, and to self employment, employment and working conditions, including dismissals, it also covers membership of organisations; social protection, including social security and healthcare; social advantages; education and access to and supply of goods and services which are available to the public, including housing. Its scope is therefore considerably broader than employment and occupation. The basis for genuine occupational requirements in race discrimination cases is in Article 4.

Sex

CEDAW

19.11   The term 'discrimination against women' means:

any distinction, exclusion or restriction made on the basis of sex which has the effect or purpose of impairing or nullifying the recognition, enjoyment or exercise by women, irrespective of their marital status, on a basis of equality of men and women, of human rights and fundamental freedoms in the political, economic, social, cultural, civil or any other field.

19.12   In the field of employment, CEDAW provides at Article 11 that:

States Parties shall take all appropriate measures to eliminate discrimination against women in the field of employment in order to ensure, on a basis of equality of men and women, the same rights, in particular:
(a) the right to work as an inalienable right of all human beings;
(b) the right to the same employment opportunities, including the application of the same criteria for selection in matters of employment;
(c) the right to free choice of profession and employment, the right to promotion, job security and all benefits and conditions of service and the right to receive vocational training and retraining, including apprenticeships, advanced vocational training and recurrent training;
(d) the right to equal remuneration, including benefits, and to equal treatment in respect of work of equal value, as well as equality of treatment in the evaluation of the quality of work;

(e) the right to social security, particularly in cases of retirement, unemployment, sickness, invalidity and old age and other incapacity to work, as well as the right to paid leave;

(f) the right to protection of health and to safety in working conditions, including the safeguarding of the function of reproduction.

TEU and TFEU

19.13 Article 2 TEU provides:

> The Union is founded on the values of respect for human dignity, freedom, democracy, equality, the rule of law and respect for human rights, including the rights of persons belonging to minorities. These values are common to the Member States in a society in which pluralism, non-discrimination, tolerance, justice, solidarity and equality between women and men prevail.

The TFEU provides that in all its activities, the Union shall aim to eliminate inequalities, and to promote equality, between men and women.[14] When interpreting a piece of EU legislation, particular regard must be had to these aims.

TFEU, equal pay

19.14 Article 157[15] provides that member states shall ensure that the principle of equal pay for male and female workers for equal work or work of equal value is applied. For this purpose, 'pay' means the ordinary basic or minimum wage or salary and any other consideration, whether in cash or in kind, which the worker receives directly or indirectly, in respect of his employment, from his employer. Equal pay without discrimination based on sex means that:

- pay for the same work at piece rates shall be calculated on the basis of the same unit of measurement;
- pay for work at time rates shall be the same for the same job.

Directive 2006/54/EC

19.15 Directive 2006/54/EC,[16] known as the Gender Recast Directive (alternatively referred to as the Recast Equal Treatment Directive),

---

14 TFEU Art 8.

15 Ex TEC Art 141.

16 Directive 2006/54/EC of the European Parliament and of the Council of 5 July 2006 on the implementation of the principle of equal opportunities and equal treatment of men and women in matters of employment and occupation (recast).

effectively consolidates previous gender discrimination directives.[17] It took effect on 15 August 2006, and the earlier Equal Treatment Directive 76/207 was repealed with effect from 15 August 2009.[18] By recital 1, the Recast Directive was made for 'bringing together in a single text the main provisions existing in this field'. The aim of the Directive is to ensure the implementation of the principle of equal opportunities and equal treatment of men and women in matters of employment and occupation. It contains provisions to implement the principle of equal treatment in relation to:

- access to employment, including promotion, and to vocational training;
- working conditions, including pay;
- occupational social security schemes.[19]

19.16   The Recast Directive applies similar definitions of prohibited actions to those set out in Directive 2000/78, and considered in detail at para 19.61 below.

Equal pay under the Recast Directive

19.17   Chapter 1 of the Directive provides that 'for the same work or for work to which equal value is attributed, direct and indirect discrimination on grounds of sex with regard to all aspects and conditions of remuneration shall be eliminated'.[20] In particular, where a job classification system is used for determining pay, it must be based on the same criteria for both men and women and so drawn up as to exclude any discrimination on grounds of sex.

---

17   The Directive was a major consolidation. Where case-law refers to any of the following directives, advisers should now look to the Recast Directive: Council Directive 75/117/EEC OJ L 45, 19.2.1975, p19; Council Directive 76/207/EEC OJ L 39, 14.2.1976, p40; Directive 2002/73/EC of the European Parliament and of the Council OJ L 269, 5.10.2002, p15; Council Directive 86/378/EEC OJ L 225, 12.8.1986, p40; Council Directive 96/97/EC OJ L 46, 17.2.1997, p20; Council Directive 97/80/EC OJ L 14, 20.1.1998, p6; Council Directive 98/52/EC OJ L 205, 22.7.1998, p66. For a tabular explanation of where the principles contained in these Directives were consolidated in the Recast Directive see p34 of the Official Journal: 26.7.2006 EN Official Journal of the European Union L 204/35 (online reference http://eur-lex.europa.eu/LexUriServ/LexUriServ.do?uri=OJ:L:2006:204:0023:0036:en:PDF).
18   See Recast Directive Art 34.
19   Recast Directive Art 1.
20   Recast Directive Art 4.

Occupational Social Security Schemes under the Recast Directive

19.18 Chapter 2 of the Directive provides for equal treatment in relation to occupational social security schemes. This covers (a) the scope of such schemes and the conditions of access to them; (b) the obligation to contribute and the calculation of contributions; (c) the calculation of benefits, including supplementary benefits due in respect of a spouse or dependants, and the conditions governing the duration and retention of entitlement to benefits.[21]

19.19 Article 6 deals with the Chapter's personal scope.[22] Article 7 gives the material scope of the Chapter, providing that it applies to:[23]

- occupational social security schemes that provide protection against the risk of sickness; invalidity; old age, including early retirement; industrial accidents and occupational diseases; and unemployment.
- occupational social security schemes that provide for other social benefits, in cash or in kind, and in particular survivors' benefits and family allowances, if such benefits constitute a consideration paid by the employer to the worker by reason of the latter's employment.

19.20 Article 8 deals with the situations to which the Chapter does not apply (exclusions from the material scope). Article 9 gives 11 examples of provisions that are contrary to the principle of equal treatment.

Sex discrimination in employment and occupation

19.21 Equal treatment as regards access to employment, vocational training and promotion and working conditions is dealt with in Chapter 3[24] of the Recast Directive. Thus the Recast Directive provides that there

---

21 Recast Directive Art 5.
22 Ie members of the working population, including self-employed persons, persons whose activity is interrupted by illness, maternity, accident or involuntary unemployment and persons seeking employment and to retired and disabled workers, and to those claiming under them, in accordance with national law and/or practice.
23 By Article 7.2 the Chapter also applies to pension schemes for a particular category of worker such as that of public servants if the benefits payable under the scheme are paid by reason of the employment relationship with the public employer. The fact that such a scheme forms part of a general statutory scheme shall be without prejudice in that respect.
24 Recast Directive Arts 14–16.

must be no direct or indirect discrimination on grounds of sex in the public or private sectors, including public bodies, in relation to:

- conditions for access to employment, to self-employment or to occupation, including selection criteria and recruitment conditions, whatever the branch of activity and at all levels of the professional hierarchy, including promotion;
- access to all types and to all levels of vocational guidance, vocational training, advanced vocational training and retraining, including practical work experience;
- employment and working conditions, including dismissals, as well as pay as provided for in Article 141 (now Article 157) of the Treaty;
- membership of, and involvement in, an organisation of workers or employers, or any organisation whose members carry on a particular profession, including the benefits provided for by such organisations.[25]

19.22   Article 15 provides that a woman who is on maternity leave shall be entitled, after the end of her period of maternity leave, to return to her job or to an equivalent post on terms and conditions which are no less favourable to her and to benefit from any improvement in working conditions to which she would have been entitled during her absence.

19.23   Article 16 provides that the Recast Directive is without prejudice to the right of member states to recognise distinct rights to paternity and/or adoption leave. Those member states that recognise such rights shall take the necessary measures to protect working men and women against dismissal due to exercising those rights and ensure that, at the end of such leave, they are entitled to return to their jobs or to equivalent posts on terms and conditions that are no less favourable to them, and to benefit from any improvement in working conditions to which they would have been entitled during their absence.

19.24   Article 24 deals with victimisation, requiring states to introduce into their national legal systems such measures as are necessary to

---

25 However, Recast Directive Art 14.2 permits states to introduce 'genuine occupational requirements' in the context of access to employment including the training leading thereto. So a difference of treatment which is based on a characteristic related to sex shall not constitute discrimination where, by reason of the nature of the particular occupational activities concerned or of the context in which they are carried out, such a characteristic constitutes a genuine and determining occupational requirement, provided that its objective is legitimate and the requirement is proportionate.

protect employees, including those who are employees' representatives provided for by national laws and/or practices, against dismissal or other adverse treatment by the employer as a reaction to a complaint within the undertaking or to any legal proceedings aimed at enforcing compliance with the principle of equal treatment.

19.25 Other relevant Directives include Directive 2010/41/EU of the European Parliament and of the Council of 7 July 2010 on the application of the principle of equal treatment between men and women engaged in an activity in a self-employed capacity and repealing Council Directive 86/613/EEC.[26]

19.26 The additional EU law sources dealing with the related protected characteristic of pregnancy and maternity are set out at paras 7.40–7.47 above.

Sexual orientation

19.27 Sexual orientation is an 'other status' within the meaning of that term in international instruments such as Article 26 ICCPR, and Article 2(2) of the ICESCR. Many monitoring bodies have emphasised that their respective conventions cover discrimination based on sexual orientation in respect of their beneficiaries.[27] The ECtHR case-law on Article 14 has also developed a regional prohibition on discrimination based on sexual orientation in relation to the rights guaranteed under the ECHR.[28]

19.28 Sexual orientation is one of the protected grounds in Article 19 TFEU, and in Article 21 of the Charter. On that basis action in the

---

26 OJ 2010 L180/1.

27 Human Rights Committee (see among others, *Toonen v Australia*, 1994, *Young v Australia*, 2003, *Joslin v New Zealand*, 2002, and *X v Colombia*, 2007); Committee on Economic, Social and Cultural Rights (General Comment No 14 of 2000, General Comment No 15 of 2002, General Comment No 18 of 2005); Committee on the Rights of the Child (General Comment No 4 of 2003); Committee against Torture (General Comment No 2 of 2008); Committee on the Elimination of Discrimination against Women (General Comment No 28 of 2010).

28 See for example *Dudgeon v United Kingdom* (1982) 4 EHRR 149; *Norris v Ireland* (1991) 13 EHRR 186; *Modinos v Cyprus* (1993) 16 EHRR 485; *Smith v United Kingdom* (2000) 29 EHRR 493; *L v Austria* (2003) 36 EHRR 55; *Salgueiro da Silva Mouta v Portugal* (2001) 31 EHRR 47; *Fretté v France* (2004) 38 EHRR 21; *EB v France* (2008) 47 EHRR 21; *Karner* (2004) 38 EHRR 24; *Sibomana v Sweden* (Admissibility) (32010/09); (2012) 54 EHRR SE8 and *Dojan v Germany* (Admissibility) (319/08) (2011) 53 EHRR SE24.

form of Directive 2000/78 has been taken to prohibit discrimination on the basis of sexual orientation in employment and occupation.[29]

19.29   Cases involving sexual orientation in the ECJ have been rare, but present no conceptual difficulties. The characteristic of sexual orientation is capable of forming a symmetrical discrimination ground. This means that a person, C, can complain about discrimination on the grounds of a particular type of sexual orientation (homosexual, bisexual or heterosexual), and can be the subject of less favourable treatment either because of a specific sexual orientation or lack of it.[30]

Disability

19.30   Until the UNCRPD there were no major international human rights treaties that applied solely to persons with disabilities. However, those instruments that guarantee that the rights recognised in them will be exercised without distinction of any kind, 'such as race, colour, sex, language, religion, political or other opinion, national or social origin, property, birth or other status' are considered to apply to the situation of persons with disabilities, under the heading 'other status'.

ICESCR

19.31   The right to work (Article 6) may be violated when the state fails to adopt adequate regulations and policies to make the workplace accessible to disabled persons, to provide persons with disabilities with adequate technical and vocational guidance to improve their capabilities and skills or to support the integration of persons with disabilities in mainstream employment.

---

29   For a discussion of the operation of Directive 2000/78 see paras 19.105–19.146.

30   In Case C-267/06 *Maruko v Versorgungsanstalt der Deutschen Bühnen* [2008] ECR I-1757, [2008] All ER (on the application of EC) 977, [2008] IRLR 450, Ruiz-Jarabo Colomer A-G discusses the history of the treatment of sexual orientation in European Law in the context of Directive 2000/78 at paras 82–104. Ultimately the CJEU determined that the factual situation postulated by the referring court did not fall within EU law at that time. The analysis of how sexual orientation is to be treated under Directive 2000/78 does not differ from the analysis of how religion or belief is to be treated in any material respect.

CERD and CEDAW

19.32　Neither CERD or CEDAW has specific provisions relating to persons with disabilities. However, it is recognised that members of racial groups with disabilities, or members of a particular gender are more likely to suffer discrimination than members of those groups who are not disabled.[31]

UNCRPD

19.33　Unlike all of the other conventions to which reference may be made, the UN Convention on the Rights of Persons with Disabilities has the unique property that the groups of persons for whom it aims to make provision were involved in its construction. In addition, the EU is a signatory to the UNCRPD. It also contains fundamental principles of human rights interpreted so as to give those fundamental rights full and equal effect in the case of persons with disabilities.

19.34　　It is important to understand how the UNCRPD operates. It is used to interpret the existing framework of human rights so as to ensure equality for persons with disabilities. Thus the ECtHR, taking account of the view of the UN Commission on Human Rights that the term 'other status' in non-discrimination provisions in international legal instruments can be interpreted to cover health status, and the UN Convention on the Rights of Persons with Disabilities which imposes on its state parties a general prohibition of discrimination on the basis of disability, has held that:[32]

> ... a distinction made on account of one's health status, including such conditions as HIV infection, should be covered – either as a form of disability or alongside with it – by the term 'other status' in the text of art.14 of the Convention.

19.35　The UNCRPD aims to 'protect and ensure the full and equal enjoyment of all human rights and fundamental freedoms by all persons with disabilities, and to promote respect for their inherent dignity'.[33] 'Discrimination on the basis of disability' means any distinction, exclusion or restriction on the basis of disability which has the purpose or effect of impairing or nullifying the recognition, enjoyment

31　See eg General Recommendation No 18 (tenth session, 1991): *Disabled women: The Committee on the Elimination of Discrimination against Women*.

32　See *Kiyutin v Russia* (2011) 53 EHRR 26 and *Kiss v Hungary* [2010] MHLR 245; see also *Glor v Switzerland* (13444/04) 30 April 2009 at paras 53–56; and *GN v Italy* (43134/05) 1 December 2009 at para 119.

33　UNCRPD Art 1.

or exercise, on an equal basis with others, of all human rights and
fundamental freedoms in the political, economic, social, cultural,
civil or any other field. It includes all forms of discrimination, including denial of reasonable accommodation, meaning:[34]

> necessary and appropriate modification and adjustments not impos-
> ing a disproportionate or undue burden, where needed in a particular
> case, to ensure to persons with disabilities the enjoyment or exercise
> on an equal basis with others of all human rights and fundamental
> freedoms.

19.36   The UNCRPD sets out general principles;[35] makes special provision
for children,[36] and women[37] with disabilities, and sets out a principle
of equality and non-discrimination.[38] The UNCRPD requires the
state to be active in awareness-raising.[39]

19.37   The state's role in ensuring accessibility requires it to take appropriate measures to provide training for stakeholders on accessibility
issues facing persons with disabilities.[40] Article 12 deals with equality
of persons with disability before the law. They must have legal capacity on an equal basis with others. The state must take appropriate
measures to provide persons with disabilities with access to the support they need in exercising their legal capacity.

19.38   Such provisions may have an impact on the obligation of the state
to fund assistive support for a person who, with reasonable accommodations, could have sufficient understanding to have legal capacity
(eg to give instructions on litigation).[41]

19.39   The state must ensure effective access to justice for persons with
disabilities on an equal basis with others, including through the

---

34 UNCRPD Art 2; note that Article 2 also provides definitions of
    'communication', 'language' and 'universal design'.
35 UNCRPD Arts 3 and 4 .
36 UNCRPD Art 7.
37 UNCRPD Art 7.
38 UNCRPD Art 5: the principle of equality and non-discrimination requires
    recognition that all persons are equal before the law and entitled to equal
    protection from discrimination under it, which the state guarantees equal for
    persons with disabilities. The state is required to take all appropriate steps
    to ensure that reasonable accommodations are provided. Moreover, specific
    measures necessary to accelerate or achieve de facto equality of persons with
    disabilities are not to be considered discrimination for the purposes of the
    UNCRPD.
39 UNCRPD Art 8.
40 UNCRPD Art 9 (among other obligations relating to the built environment).
41 Such capacity issues must in the United Kingdom be determined under the
    Mental Capacity Act 2005.

provision of procedural and age-appropriate accommodations, in order to facilitate their effective role as direct and indirect participants, including as witnesses, in all legal proceedings, including at investigative and other preliminary stages.[42]

19.40 In order to help to ensure effective access to justice for persons with disabilities, states parties shall promote appropriate training for those working in the field of administration of justice, including police and prison staff.[43]

19.41 The UNCPRD provisions as to work are set out in Article 27:

States Parties recognize the right of persons with disabilities to work on an equal basis with others; this includes the right to the opportunity to gain a living by work freely chosen or accepted in a labour market and work environment that is open, inclusive and accessible to persons with disabilities. States Parties shall safeguard and promote the realization of the right to work, including for those who acquire a disability during the course of employment, by taking appropriate steps, including through legislation, to, inter alia:

(a) Prohibit discrimination on the basis of disability with regard to all matters concerning all forms of employment, including conditions of recruitment, hiring and employment, continuance of employment, career advancement and safe and healthy working conditions;

(b) Protect the rights of persons with disabilities, on an equal basis with others, to just and favourable conditions of work, including equal opportunities and equal remuneration for work of equal value, safe and healthy working conditions, including protection from harassment, and the redress of grievances;

(c) Ensure that persons with disabilities are able to exercise their labour and trade union rights on an equal basis with others;

(d) Enable persons with disabilities to have effective access to general technical and vocational guidance programmes, placement services and vocational and continuing training;

(e) Promote employment opportunities and career advancement for persons with disabilities in the labour market, as well as assistance in finding, obtaining, maintaining and returning to employment;

(f) Promote opportunities for self-employment, entrepreneurship, the development of cooperatives and starting one's own business;

(g) Employ persons with disabilities in the public sector;

(h) Promote the employment of persons with disabilities in the private sector through appropriate policies and measures, which may include affirmative action programmes, incentives and other measures;

42 UNCPRD Art 13(1).
43 UNCRPD Art 13.

(i) Ensure that reasonable accommodation is provided to persons with disabilities in the workplace;

(j) Promote the acquisition by persons with disabilities of work experience in the open labour market;

(k) Promote vocational and professional rehabilitation, job retention and return-to-work programmes for persons with disabilities.

TFEU and Charter

19.42   Disability is a protected characteristic under Article 19 TFEU. Article 21 of the Charter provides for non-discrimination against persons with disabilities and Article 26 provides for integration of persons with disabilities, on the basis that the Union recognises and respects the right of persons with disabilities to benefit from measures designed to ensure their independence, social and occupational integration and participation in the life of the community. Thus in determining policy and in the interpretation of EU law, this aim must be achieved.[44]

Religion and belief

UNDHR

19.43   It is important to remember that it is both religion and belief that are protected by international law norms. Article 18 of the UNDHR states

> Everyone has the right to freedom of thought, conscience and religion; this right includes freedom to change his religion or belief, and freedom, either alone or in community with others and in public or private, to manifest his religion or belief in teaching, practice, worship and observance.

19.44   The right includes various expressions of belief. It is difficult to prise apart the holding of a belief, which the law must gauge by observed behaviour including linguistic expression, from the manifestation of belief.

19.45   This difficulty often arises in the context of the conflict between the expression of one human right, freedom of expression, and belief

---

44   More generally TFEU Art 10 provides: 'In defining and implementing its policies and activities, the Union shall aim to combat discrimination based on sex, racial or ethnic origin, religion or belief, disability, age or sexual orientation.'

and religious freedoms. The ICCPR provides in Article 19 that everyone shall have the right to hold opinions without interference and shall have the right to freedom of expression. This right includes freedom to seek, receive and impart information and ideas of all kinds, regardless of frontiers, either orally, in writing or in print, in the form of art, or through any other media of his choice. The expression of information under Article 19 ICCPR carries with it special duties and responsibilities. It may therefore be subject to certain restrictions, but these shall only be such as are provided by law and are necessary: (a) for respect of the rights or reputations of others; (b) for the protection of national security or of public order, or of public health or morals. By Article 20(2) any advocacy of national, racial or religious hatred that constitutes incitement to discrimination, hostility or violence must be prohibited by law.

19.46 The rights relating to religion and belief (and those relating to free expression) are aimed at building a tolerant society. The Commission on Human Rights has emphasised 'the importance of a continued and strengthened dialogue among and within religions or beliefs, encompassed by the dialogue among civilizations, to promote greater tolerance, respect and mutual understanding'.[45]

19.47 Equally the rights relating to religion and belief must be exercised in tolerance. The Human Rights Committee general comment 22 makes this point clearly, at paragraph 7:

> In accordance with Article 20, no manifestation of religion or belief may amount to propaganda for war or advocacy of national, racial or religious hatred that constitutes incitement to discrimination, hostility or violence. As stated by the Committee in its general comment 11, States parties are under the obligation to enact laws to prohibit such acts.

ECHR and Charter

19.48 Article 9 ECHR provides that everyone has the right to freedom of thought, conscience and religion. This right includes freedom to change one's religion or belief and freedom, either alone or in community with others and in public or private, to manifest that religion or belief, in worship, teaching, practice and observance.[46]

---

45 Commission on Human Rights Resolution on Elimination of all forms of intolerance and of discrimination based on religion or belief, Resolution 2005/40 of 19 April 2005, para 10.

46 ECHR Art 9(1). The inclusion of the right to manifest the belief in community with others means that religious (or belief) communities will also have rights

19.49   By contrast, the freedom to manifest one's religion or beliefs shall be subject to such limitations as are prescribed by law and are necessary in a democratic society in the interests of public safety, for the protection of public order, health or morals, or for the protection of the rights and freedoms of others.

19.50   In *Leyla Sahin v Turkey*[47] the ECtHR held that Article 9 does not always guarantee the right to behave in a manner governed by a religious belief. It does not confer the right to disregard justified rules. The contracting states have a margin of appreciation in this area. The court found that the ban on the wearing of religious symbols (including headscarves by Muslim women) in universities had a legitimate aim, was prescribed by law, necessary in a democratic society, justified in principle and proportionate to the aim pursued. The Turkish constitution stressed the protection of the rights of women, and implicitly gender equality.[48] The ECtHR said that, when examining the question of the Islamic headscarf in the Turkish context, the impact that wearing such a symbol, which is presented or perceived as a compulsory religious duty, may have on those who choose not to wear it must be taken into account. Thus the protection of the 'rights and freedoms of others' and the 'maintenance of public order' were relevant to the question of justification of the ban. Those issues are particularly important where a symbol has taken on political significance as it had in Turkey in the years preceding the case. The existence of extremist political movements seeking to impose on society as a whole their religious symbols and conception of a society founded on religious precepts was also relevant to the existence of a pressing social need. The court held that every member state may, in accordance with the Convention provisions, take a stance against such political movements, based on its historical experience. The banning regulations viewed in context constituted a measure intended to achieve the legitimate aims referred to above and thereby to preserve pluralism and secularism in the university.

---

under Article 9; see eg *Church of Scientology Moscow v Russia* (2008) 46 EHRR 16, at, paras 72 and 81; *Biserica Adev rat Ortodox din Moldova v Moldova* (2009) 48 EHRR 20, at paras 24–38; and *The Moscow branch of the Salvation Army v Russia* (2007) 44 EHRR 46 at paras 57–98, all ECtHR.

47   Which concerned the wearing of headscarves by Muslim women at a university, (2007) 44 EHRR 5, 19 BHRC 590, [2006] ELR 73, at paras 75–123.

48   Gender equality has been recognised as one of the key principles underlying the ECHR and a goal to be achieved by member states of the Council of Europe.

19.51   Article 9 can protect proselytising.[49] A balance must be struck between the rights of those who want to convert others, and the rights of those who do not want to be converted. Thus it is permissible to ban improper proselytism.[50]

19.52   Where employment contractual obligations conflict with religious beliefs the ECtHR has favoured the contractual relationship. This is on the basis that the contractual requirements do not require a person to forsake their religion or belief, as the latter can be maintained by the employee leaving the employment.

19.53   Thus there was no interference with the Article 9 rights of a Muslim who complained that he had to leave his job because his contract of employment did not permit time off on Friday for religious observance, and his employer would not give him the time off. The Commission decided that when exercising this right, an individual may need to take account of his professional position and/or his contractual position. The obligations of his contract were accepted 'of his own free will'. When applying for the post, and for six years after taking it up, he had not stated that he might need this time for prayers at the mosque. The Commission regarded it as significant, in this context, that he could have resigned on discovering the conflict between his religion and his work. The Commission decision appears to suggest that it is only arbitrary interference that will be considered as an interference with the right. There was evidence from the state of the needs of its education system, based on which the interference could be shown not to be arbitrary.[51]

---

49 *Kokkinakis v Greece* (1994) 17 EHRR 397.

50 Eg offering material or social advantages with a view to gaining new members for a church, or exerting improper pressure on people in distress or in need; it may even entail the use of violence or brainwashing; more generally it is not compatible with respect for the freedom of thought, conscience or religion of others.

51 *Ahmad v UK* (1982) 4 EHRR 126. The significance of the ability of the individual to preserve his religious freedom by resignation was also stressed in *Konttinen v Finland* (1996) 87 DR 68. There the Commission distinguished between the dismissal of the applicant by the Finnish State Railways because of religious convictions and for failing to observe his contractual hours of work. The latter was not protected by Article 9(1), despite being a product of his religious persuasion. He did not respect his working hours because, as a member of the Seventh-Day Adventist Church, work after sunset on a Friday was forbidden. The Commission held that the applicant had failed to show that he was pressured to change his religious views or prevented from manifesting his religion or belief. See also *Stedman v UK* (1997) EHRLR 545, (1997) 23 EHRR CD168.

In 2013, in *Eweida and others v United Kingdom*,[52] the ECtHR reconsidered the point that the possibility of resignation from employment was sufficient to guarantee Article 9 rights. The court noted that no similar restriction is placed on the exercise of other rights under the ECtHR. Having considered some of the cases the ECtHR stated that 'where an individual complains of a restriction on freedom of religion in the workplace, rather than holding that the possibility of changing job would negate any interference with the right, the better approach would be to weigh that possibility in the overall balance when considering whether or not the restriction was proportionate'.[53] Now, therefore, the earlier position is unlikely to be influential, and the Courts are likely to adopt the balancing approach set out in *Eweida*. The same reasoning will apply to manifestations of all beliefs within the scope of Article 9, and not simply religious beliefs. The ECtHR considered the approach of the national judges to the question of the legality of the prohibition on wearing a Christian cross visibly on a work uniform (which had been considered under equality legislation using indirect discrimination techniques). It conducted its own examination of whether (under Article 9) a fair balance had been struck between Ms Eweida's rights and those of others. It concluded that a fair balance had not been struck. Ms Eweida sought to exercise a fundamental right to manifest her belief. As against that was the employer's wish to project a corporate image. Too much weight was given to this by the domestic courts. The particular cross could not have detracted from her professional appearance. Other items of religious clothing were not shown to have had any negative impact on BA's image. There was no evidence of any real encroachment on the rights of others, and the UK failed sufficiently to protect the right to manifest religion in breach of its positive obligations under Art 9 ECHR.[54] This analysis demonstrates that indirect discrimination cases related to manifestations of belief will have to be carefully analysed by tribunals placing due weight on the importance of the right to manifest beliefs, including religious ones. It does not follow, however, that such prohibitions may not be upheld where there is sufficient justification.

19.54   In *Thlimmenos v Greece*,[55] the applicant was able to establish that he had been discriminated against in the enjoyment of his right

52 [2013] ECHR 37, [2013] IRLR 231.
53 Para 83.
54 Paras 83–95.
55 (2001) 31 EHRR 15.

to manifest his religious beliefs. He was a Jehovah's Witness who refused, as a result, to wear a military uniform. He was sentenced to two years' imprisonment. On release he passed his accountancy exams. He was refused admission to the accountants' professional body due to his conviction. The ECtHR held that the rule prohibiting admission to those with convictions was ostensibly neutral. The rule discriminated against the applicant because his conviction emanated from the manifestation of his belief system.[56]

19.55   A difficult issue in relation to breach of Article 9 is whether the ET considering the case can preserve the balance that the Convention requires between respect for free speech and respect for beliefs of adherents to belief systems. Pluralism demands tolerance of views that are critical of religion and that there must be toleration and acceptance for the denial by others of faith and belief systems. A balance must be struck, such as that eg in *Otto Preminger Institut v Austria*.[57] Respect for religious feelings of believers could be violated by provocative portrayals of objects of religious veneration so that a breach of Article 9 could arise.[58] Portrayals that are extremely provocative violate the spirit of tolerance inherent in the Convention as a whole. The same reasoning will apply to those who seek to force their beliefs on others by abusing their position.

19.56   Unfettered power or discretion in matters relating to fundamental rights is contrary to the rule of law, so restrictions on them must be prescribed by law. The law must indicate with sufficient clarity the scope of any such discretion and the manner of its exercise.[59] The restriction must be justified by one of the aims recognised under the European Convention and must be shown to be 'necessary in a democratic society'. Finally any qualification to rights cannot be applied in a discriminatory fashion.

56 See also *Ivanova v Bulgaria* (2008) 47 EHRR 54, 23 BHRC 2008, [2007] ELR 612 at paras 77–86. The court was prepared to look beyond the ostensibly neutral reason for dismissal (amendment of the requirements for the post) to the motivation for the amendment and for the treatment of the applicant in particular (her religious beliefs and affiliation with the organisation Word of Life). The fact that the dismissal was procedurally flawless in domestic law made no difference to the conclusion that the dismissal was an infringement of her Article 9 rights. The substantive motive for dismissal was her belief system. In particular the court noted that there had been a meeting in which the applicant was pressured by two Government officials to renounce her religious beliefs in order to keep her job (a flagrant violation of Article 9).

57 (1995) 19 EHRR 34.

58 Contrast *Dubowska & Skup v Poland* (1997) 24 EHRR CD75.

59 See eg *Biserica Adevărat Ortodoxă din Moldova v Moldova* (2009) 48 EHRR 20, at paras 24–38).

19.57   The Charter provides for protection against discrimination on the basis of religion or belief[60] and for freedom of thought, conscience and religion.[61] The prohibition on discrimination under the Charter appears to be wider than that under the TFEU's call for action in Article 19[62] as it includes 'religion or belief, political or any other opinion'. If the TFEU concept of 'belief' does not include 'political opinion' for these purposes, then less favourable treatment of a person because of political opinion would not be covered by any existing provision of the Treaty. However, the Charter is clear that it does not extend the scope of the Treaty or give any new task to the EU. Therefore, Article 19 of the Treaty must be interpreted as including political opinion in the concept of belief. Hence Directive 2000/78 must also be interpreted so as to provide protection for political opinion.[63]

19.58   In relation to anti-democratic political opinions, Article 54 of the Charter mirrors Article 17 ECHR and states that:

> Nothing in this Charter shall be interpreted as implying any right to engage in any activity or to perform any act aimed at the destruction of any of the rights and freedoms recognised in this Charter or at their limitation to a greater extent than is provided for herein.

Article 17 ECHR was held to permit the Netherlands to convict people for distributing racist pamphlets and prevent them from standing in local elections on an explicitly racist platform.[64]

19.59   The Court of Appeal in *Hall v Bull*[65] rejected an argument that Articles 10 (freedom of thought, conscience and religion) and 15 (freedom to choose an occupation) of the Charter protected the reli-

---

60 Charter Art 21.
61 Charter Art 10.
62 Which refers only to combating discrimination based on 'religion or belief'
63 In domestic law, to qualify for protection a philosophical belief must: be genuinely held; be a belief and not an opinion or viewpoint based on information currently available; concern a weighty and substantial aspect of human life and behaviour; attain a certain level of cogency, seriousness, cohesion and importance and be worthy of respect in a democratic society and not incompatible with human dignity and the fundamental rights of others (*Grainger plc v Nicholson* [2010] ICR 360). It is not clear whether political opinions would satisfy this definition and in *Kelly v Unison* ET Case No 2203854/08, Marxist/Trotskyist beliefs were held not to be protected. World view political beliefs, such as socialism, Marxism, communism or free-market capitalism could all potentially qualify as philosophical beliefs under the *Grainger* test.
64 Commission's admissibility decisions in App Nos 8348/78, 4806/78, *Glimmerveen and Hagenbeek v the Netherlands*, 18 D & R 187; (1982) 4 EHRR 260 and see *Künen v Germany*, App No 9235/81, 29 D & R 194.
65 [2012] EWCA Civ 83.

gious beliefs of the hotel-owning appellants such as to allow them to discriminate against a gay couple seeking to use their services. In doing so the court observed that these articles could give no greater rights than those conferred under the ECHR Articles 14 and 9.

19.60   However, it was established in *Handyside v UK*[66] that the right to freedom of expression will protect not only "information' or 'ideas' that are favourably received or regarded as inoffensive or as a matter of indifference, but also to those that offend, shock or disturb the state or any sector of the population.[67] In the context of political expression in particular the ECtHR has stressed the need to protect free expression. Interference with it calls for the closest of scrutiny.[68]

Directive 2000/78

19.61   Religion and belief are treated in the same way as other grounds. However, under Article 4 special provision is made for a genuine and determining occupational requirement specific to religion and belief.[69] The text is set out in full here:

> 2. Member States may maintain national legislation in force at the date of adoption of this Directive or provide for future legislation incorporating national practices existing at the date of adoption of this Directive pursuant to which, in the case of occupational activities within churches and other public or private organisations the ethos of which is based on religion or belief, a difference of treatment based on a person's religion or belief shall not constitute discrimination where, by reason of the nature of these activities or of the context in which they are carried out, a person's religion or belief constitute a genuine, legitimate and justified occupational requirement, having regard to the organisation's ethos. This difference of treatment shall be implemented taking account of member States' constitutional provisions and principles, as well as the general principles of Community law, and should not justify discrimination on another ground. Provided

---

66 (1979–80) 1 EHRR 737, ECtHR.

67 See also ECtHR, *Steel and Morris v UK* (2005) 41 EHRR 22 where the applicants were sued by McDonalds for defamation. Free speech on matters of public interest deserved strong protection, said the court, and this was a case of a powerful corporate entity which had not proved that it had suffered harm as the result of the distribution of several thousand leaflets. The damages were relatively high compared to the applicants' income, so the interference with their freedom of expression (ECHR Art 10) was disproportionate.

68 *Castells v Spain* (1992) 14 EHRR 445, ECtHR.

69 See *R (Amicus-MSF Section) v Secretary of State for Trade and Industry (Christian Action Research Education and others intervening)* [2004] EWHC 860 (Admin), [2007] ICR 1176.

that its provisions are otherwise complied with, this Directive shall thus not prejudice the right of churches and other public or private organisations, the ethos of which is based on religion or belief, acting in conformity with national constitutions and laws, to require individuals working for them to act in good faith and with loyalty to the organisation's ethos.

19.62   A rigorous and strict approach must be adopted in determining whether this particular exception applies.[70] If the legitimacy or justification of a requirement were to be assessed purely by reference to the subjective view of the employer, this would add nothing to the stipulation that a requirement be genuine. Whether or not a particular religion or belief is a legitimate and justified requirement of an occupation is an objective question for the court. The question is whether, in all the circumstances of the case, the requirement is not only genuine, but legitimate and justified.

Age discrimination

International law

19.63   Ironically the youngest recognised protected characteristic – age – has the smallest number of international agreements. There is no settled convention on age discrimination. During the 65th session of the United Nations General Assembly in 2010, an Open Ended Working Group on Ageing was established to encourage governments to pay greater attention to protect the human rights of older persons.[71] There have been international agreements of principle and resolutions.

19.64   However, the absence of internationally agreed concepts in this area gives rise to a utilitarian view of age discrimination in which age distinctions are regarded as often useful and legitimate.

---

70 Case C-26/03 *Stadt Halle v Arbeitsgemeinschaft Thermische Restabfall-und Energieverwertungsanlage TREA Leuna* [2005] ECR I-1 and Case C-106/89 *Marleasing SA v La Comercial Internacional de Alimentación SA* [1990] ECR I-4135.

71 See Resolution A/RES/65/182 adopted by the General Assembly on 21 December 2010 for more detailed information. On 15 February, 2011 the Open Ended Working Group on Ageing had its first organisational session.

ECHR

19.65   Age is treated as 'other status' under Article 14. Justification of age discrimination under Article 14 may exist if there are utilitarian reasons for less favourable treatment based on age. In *R (Carson) v Secretary of State for Work and Pensions*,[72] age was viewed as a borderline case falling between those rights which are concerned with fundamental dignity and in relation to which discrimination can seldom be justified (race, sex etc), and those rights which can be justified by utilitarian justifications in respect of matters of social policy.

Directive 2000/78

19.66   Age receives a specific treatment in the Directive.[73] The general principle of direct discrimination applies. Thus a claimant (C) needs to show that C was treated less favourably than another person in the same situation (a real or hypothetical comparator) was, is or would have been treated.[74] In the case of indirect discrimination, C must show that that an apparently neutral provision criterion or practice puts or would put persons having a particular age at a particular disadvantage compared with other persons. However, in relation to direct discrimination Article 6(1) of the Directive says that member states may provide that differences of treatment on grounds of age shall not constitute discrimination if, within the context of national law, they are objectively and reasonably justified by a legitimate aim, including legitimate employment policy, labour market and vocational training objectives, and if the means of achieving that aim are appropriate and necessary. The Directive gives a non-exhaustive list of examples of differences of treatment that may be justified.

19.67   The CJEU has emphasised difficulties in dealing with age discrimination cases: 'It is ... a much more difficult task to determine the existence of discrimination on grounds of age than for example in the case of discrimination on grounds of sex, where the comparators are more clearly defined'.[75] Differentiating on this ground

---

72   [2005] UKHL 37, [2006] 1 AC 173, [2005] 2 WLR 1369. See also *R (British Gurkha Welfare Society) v Ministry of Defence* [2010] EWCA Civ 1098.

73   See O'Dempsey and Beale, *Age and Employment* (European Commission, 2011).

74   Directive 2000/78 Art 2.

75   C-411/05 *Félix Palacios de la Villa v Cortefiel Servicios SA* [2007] ECR I-8531, [2009] ICR 1111.

is socially and economically useful.[76] The member state has a wide discretion in identifying the means to achieve its social policy aims and also in the definition of the aims themselves.[77] The justifiable nature of direct age discrimination makes criticism of implementation difficult. The CJEU has stated that it is not for the member states to define age discrimination.

19.68   However, the need to draw a clear distinction between acceptable and unacceptable treatment is plain in Recital 25 to the Directive.

19.69   In *R (Incorporated Trustees of the National Council on Ageing (Age Concern England)) v Secretary of State for Business, Enterprise and Regulatory Reform*[78] the CJEU recognised that Article 6(1) of the Directive represents a scheme of derogation from the principle of equal treatment. As such it is to be construed narrowly.[79]

19.70   In the same case, the Court stated:[80]

> For its part, art.6 of Directive 2000/78 establishes a scheme of derogation specific to differences of treatment on grounds of age, on account of the recognised specificity of age among the grounds of discrimination prohibited by the Directive. Recital 25 in the preamble to that Directive makes clear that it is: 'essential to distinguish between differences in treatment which are justified, in particular by legitimate employment policy, labour market and vocational training objectives, and discrimination which must be prohibited'.

19.71   It went on:[81]

> It is apparent from Article 6(1) of Directive 2000/78 that the aims which may be considered 'legitimate' within the meaning of that provision, and, consequently, appropriate for the purposes of justifying derogation from the principle prohibiting discrimination on grounds of age, are social policy objectives, such as those related to employment policy, the labour market or vocational training. By their public interest nature, those legitimate aims are distinguishable from purely

---

76 C-388/07 *The Incorporated Trustees of the National Council on Ageing v Secretary of State for Business, Enterprise and Regulatory Reform (Age Concern England)* [2009] ECR I-1569, [2009] ICR 1080; see Mazák A-G's opinion at para 74.

77 See *Age Concern England*, Mazák A-G's opinion at paras 85–87, citing *Palacios*.

78 [2009] ECR I-1569, [2009] ICR 1080.

79 See also C-427/06 *Bartsch v Bosch und Siemens Hausgerate* [2009] All ER (EC) 113, [2008] ECR I-7245 at para 103: 'First, recital 25 makes it clear that age discrimination within the meaning of the Directive is a broad concept. That is also consistent with standard principles of interpretation, which dictate that the concept of discrimination in Article 2 should be read broadly, while the justifications and derogations under Article 2(2)(b)(i) and under Article 6 should be construed narrowly.'

80 See para 60 of the judgment.

81 At para 46 of the judgment.

individual reasons particular to the employer's situation, such as cost reduction or improving competitiveness, although it cannot be ruled out that a national rule may recognise, in the pursuit of those legitimate aims, a certain degree of flexibility for employers.

19.72   In the *Age UK* case before the High Court,[82] Blake J stated that there must be a reasonable relationship of proportionality between the means employed and the legitimate objectives pursued by the measure being contested. First, the measure must have an objective that is sufficiently important to justify limiting a fundamental right. Second, the measure designed to meet the legislative objective must be rationally connected to that objective. It must not be arbitrary, unfair or based on irrational considerations. Third, the means used to impair the fundamental right must be no more than is necessary to accomplish the legitimate objective. The more severe the detrimental effects of a measure are, the more important the objective must be if the measure is to be used in a democratic society.[83]

19.73   In subsequent cases the CJEU has re-emphasised the importance of the distinction between aims under Article 6(1) of the Directive in the case of direct age discrimination and those that can be used in indirect discrimination cases.[84] The Advocate-General in *Andersen*[85] expressly stated in the Opinion:

> The Court has indeed held that 'purely individual motives specific to the employer's situation, such as cost reduction or improving competitiveness', are not as such capable of justifying a direct difference in treatment on grounds of age. At the same time, however, it has not ruled out the possibility that employers' interests may be taken into account in the pursuit of employment and labour-market policy objectives in the general interest. It was therefore legitimate that, when formulating the entitlement to a severance allowance under para.2a of the FL, the Danish legislature also took into consideration the employers' interest in averting an excessive financial burden; see in this regard *Age Concern England* [2009] 3 CMLR 4 at [51]. In

82   *R (Age UK) v Secretary of State for Business, Innovation and Skills* [2009] EWHC 2336 (Admin), [2010] ICR 260.

83   *Age UK* at paras 35–41 of the judgment.

84   See C-159/10 *Fuchs v Land Hessen* [2011] 3 CMLR 47, [2012] ICR 93, [2011] IRLR 1043 at para 52; C-88/08 *Hutter v Technische Universitat Graz* [2009] ECR I/5325, [2009] All ER (on the application of EC) 1129 at para 41; C-499/08 *Ingeniorforeningen i Danmark v Region Syddanmark ('Andersen')* [2012] All ER (on the application of EC) 342, [2011] 1 CMLR 35 A-G Opinion paras 31 and 72; C-555/07 *Kucukdeveci v Swedex GmbH & Co KG* [2010] All ER (on the application of EC) 867, [2010] IRLR 346, A-G Opinion at paras 37 and 47 and C-447/09 *Prigge v Deutsche Lufthansa AG* [2011] IRLR 1052 at para 81.

85   [2012] All ER (on the application of EC) 342, [2011] 1 CMLR 35.

Kücükdeveci [2010] 2 CMLR 33 too, the Court by no means held to be insignificant objectives such as 'greater flexibility in personnel management' or alleviating the employer's burden in connection with the dismissal of certain categories of employee ([39]); rather, it considered that the legislation chosen by the legislature '[was] not appropriate for achieving that aim' ([40]).[86]

19.74   The Supreme Court, in the case of *Seldon v Clarkson Wright & Jakes*[87] considered the question of whether Article 6(1) of the Directive requires the concept of legitimate aim to be construed in this way in individual cases.

Using European law in the tribunals

19.75   Equality was a necessary component of the creation of a common market ensuring free movement of goods and services, labour and capital. What has become Article 157 of TFEU established the principle of equal pay for men and women for equal work with the aim of avoiding a situation in which undertakings established in states that had implemented the principle of equal pay might suffer a disadvantage in competition. It was one of the social objectives of the Community (to ensure social progress and the constant improvement of living and working conditions) and was therefore a part of the foundation of the Community.[88] The principle of equality then was described as a fundamental personal human right respect for which was one of the general principles of community law.[89]

19.76   The TFEU contains Article 19 which explains that the Council has competence in anti-discrimination issues:

> Without prejudice to the other provisions of this Treaty and within the limits of the powers conferred by it upon the Community, the Council, acting unanimously on a proposal from the Commission and after consulting the European Parliament, may take appropriate action to combat discrimination based on sex, racial or ethnic origin, religion or belief, disability, age or sexual orientation.

---

86   See fn 61, relating to para 72.
87   [2012] UKSC 16.
88   Case 43/75 *Defrenne v SABENA (No 2)* [1976] ECR 455.
89   Case 149/77 *Defrenne v SABENA (No 3)* [1978] ECR 1365.

19.77 Council Directive 2000/78 of 27 November 2000 establishing a general Framework for equal treatment in employment[90] ('the Directive') is a key part of the action that has been taken pursuant to that Article.

Using EU law

19.78 Section 2 of the European Communities Act 1972[91] makes European Community law part of domestic law. European Community law takes precedence over domestic law where the two are in conflict.[92] It is important to distinguish between provisions of Community legislation that may be relied upon in all circumstances, those that can only be relied upon against an emanation of the state and those which can only be relied upon for their interpretative effect. For reasons given below, this distinction becomes slightly unclear in discrimination cases.

The treaty provisions

19.79 There are two relevant treaties for the purposes of current anti-discrimination law: the Treaty on European Union (TEU) and the Treaty on the Functioning of the European Union (TFEU). Certain TFEU provisions create private rights and obligations for individuals, which are enforceable by those individuals before their national courts regardless of whether the member state has acted to implement the particular Community standard into its national law. Treaty provisions, such as Articles 157 and 45, are directly effective. If it has this 'direct effect' individuals may assert EU law before national courts in order to invoke their Community rights. The CJEU developed this concept in Van Gend en Loos.[93] Treaty articles can be invoked against a member state in national courts. Provisions such the principle of non-discrimination on the basis of nationality, are directly effective

---

90 OJL 303, 2.12.2000, p16.

91 As amended

92 *Van Duyn v Home Office (No 2)* [1975] Ch 358, [1975] 3 All ER 190, ECJ.

93 Case 26/62 [1963] ECR 1, [1963] 2 CMLR 105. The Van Gend & Loos company had imported chemicals from Germany into the Netherlands and was charged with an import duty. It argued the duty had been increased since the time of coming into force of the EEC Treaty, contrary to Article 12 of the EEC Treaty. The ECJ asserted that 'independently of the legislation of Member States, Community law ... not only imposes obligations on individuals but is also intended to confer upon them rights which become part of their legal heritage.'

within the scope of the matters dealt with in the treaty.[94] The treaties
have the status of primary legislation in all member states.[95]

The Charter

19.80   Advisers may be less used to using the Charter on Fundamental
Rights[96] than other provisions of EU law. Rights contained in the
Charter are enforceable.[97] By Article 6(1) TEU, the European Union
recognises the rights, freedoms and principles set out in the Charter,
'which shall have the same legal value as the Treaties'.[98]

19.81   The provisions of the charter are addressed to member states only
when they are implementing Union law.[99] The Charter provisions
are to be recognised by the courts and ETs of the member states only
in the interpretation of actions of the member states implementing Union law and when determining the legality of such actions[100]
– such as the EqA 2010, which implements Union law in respect
of all the protected characteristics in the field of employment and
occupation. Thus the Charter does not extend the field of application
of Union law beyond the powers of the Union or establish any new
power or task for the Union or modify powers and tasks as defined in
the treaties.[101] Rights recognised by the Charter for which provision
is made in the treaties shall be exercised under the conditions and
within the limits defined by those treaties.[102] In particular, in so far
as the Charter contains rights which correspond to rights guaranteed

---

94 Case 36/74 *Walrave and Koch v Association Union Cycliste Internationale* [1974]
ECR 1405.

95 They are the highest form of law for member states (see *Costa v ENEL* [1964]
ECR 585, [1964] CMLR 425).

96 2007/C 303/01 Charter of Fundamental Rights of the European Union 1 OJ
2007 C 303, p32: http://eur-lex.europa.eu/JOHtml.do?uri=OJ:C:2007:303:
SOM:en:HTML

97 See *R (NS) v Secretary of State for the Home Department* [2010] EWCA Civ 990
at para 7 and Case C-411/10 *N S v Secretary of State for the Home Department*
judgment 21 December 2011, ECJ at para 46. There is some doubt in relation
to the chapter dealing with solidarity and rights at work.

98 As noted in C-555/07 *Kücükdeveci v Swedex GmbH* [2010] All ER (on the
application of EC) 867, [2010] IRLR 346 at para 22 of the judgment, and see
30.3.2010 Official Journal of the European Union C 83/13 at 83/19 (http://eur-
lex.europa.eu/LexUriServ/LexUriServ.do?uri=OJ:C:2010:083:0013:0046:EN:
PDF).

99 Charter Art 51(1).

100 Charter Art 52(5).

101 Charter Art 51(2).

102 Charter Art 52(2).

by the ECHR, the meaning and scope of those rights is the same as those laid down by the ECHR.[103]

19.82 Recital 5 of the Preamble and Article 52(7) of the Charter provide that the Charter must be interpreted in accordance with the explanations provided by the praesidium of the Convention that drafted it.[104]

19.83 As yet there have been few cases in which the Charter has been invoked to deal with the scope of fundamental rights. It is clear that

---

103 Charter Art 52(3): The list of rights that may at the present stage, without precluding developments in the law, legislation and the treaties, be regarded as corresponding to rights in the ECHR within the meaning of the present paragraph is given hereafter. It does not include rights additional to those in the ECHR.

    1. Articles of the Charter where both the meaning and the scope are the same as the corresponding articles of the ECHR: Article 2 corresponds to ECHR Art 2; Article 4 corresponds to ECHR Art 3; Article 5(1) and (2) correspond to ECHR Art 4; Article 6 corresponds to ECHR Art 5; Article 7 corresponds to ECHR Art 8; Article 10(1) corresponds to ECHR Art 9; Article 11 corresponds to ECHR Art 10 without prejudice to any restrictions which Union law may impose on member states' right to introduce the licensing arrangements referred to in the third sentence of ECHR Art 10(1); Article 19(1) corresponds to Art 4 of Protocol No 4; Article 19(2) corresponds to ECHR Art 3 as interpreted by the ECtHR; Article 48 corresponds to ECHR Art 6(2) and(3); Article 49(1) (with the exception of the last sentence) and (2) correspond to ECHR Art 7.

    2. Charter articles where the meaning is the same as the corresponding articles in the ECHR, but where the scope is wider: Article 9 covers the same field as ECHR Art 12, but its scope may be extended to other forms of marriage if these are established by national legislation; Article 12(1) corresponds to ECHR Art 11, but its scope is extended to European Union level; Article 14(1) corresponds to Art 2 of the Protocol to the ECHR, but its scope is extended to cover access to vocational and continuing training; Article 14(3) corresponds to Art 2 of the Protocol to the ECHR as regards the rights of parents; Article 47(2) and (3) corresponds to ECHR Art 6(1), but the limitation to the determination of civil rights and obligations or criminal charges does not apply as regards Union law and its implementation; Article 50 corresponds to Art 4 of Protocol No 7 to the ECHR, but its scope is extended to European Union level between the courts of the member states. Finally, citizens of the European Union may not be considered as aliens in the scope of the application of Union law, because of the prohibition of any discrimination on grounds of nationality. The limitations provided for by ECHR Art 16 as regards the rights of aliens therefore do not apply to them in this context.

104 See OJ [2007] C 303/17 (http://eur-lex.europa.eu/LexUriServ/LexUriServ. do?uri=OJ:C:2007:303:0017:0035:EN:PDF). The Charter and these explanations on each article are also available (with other material) online via the Fundamental Rights Agency: http://infoportal.fra.europa.eu/InfoPortal/.

the CJEU will apply it for this purpose, among other materials.[105] The significance of the Charter provisions becomes acute where the member states have reserved a significant margin of appreciation to themselves.[106] In particular when seeking to test whether the member state's implementation frustrates the prohibition on discrimination, the prohibition must be read in the light of the rights (including the right to engage in work) recognised in Article 15(1) of the Charter. These must be recognised as fundamental rights, and the degree to which the state may curtail them is accordingly to be cut back.

19.84   The Charter was invoked in the *Test-Achats* case[107] where a provision of EU law, which enabled the member states in question to maintain without temporal limitation an exemption from the rule of unisex insurance premiums and benefits, was held to work against the achievement of the objective of equal treatment between men and women and was incompatible with Articles 21 and 23 of the Charter.[108]

19.85   *Regulations* are issued by the Council or Commission. They are directly applicable so an individual can rely upon them in domestic courts. They are binding in their entirety on member states and take precedence over all domestic law.

19.86   *Directives*, by contrast, are expressed in terms of policy aims and leave the member state with discretion as to how the objective is to be implemented into domestic law. They are also issued by the Council or Commission, and have a similar level of binding force to Regulations. An individual can rely directly on a provision of a Directive against the state or an emanation of the state if it satisfies the following conditions:

- it is sufficiently clear and precise;
- it is unconditional;[109]

105 In C-391/09 *Runevic-Vardyn and Wardyn v Vilniaus miesto savivaldybés administracija* [2011] 3 CMLR 13, the CJEU used Art 21 of the Charter as one of the factors in determining the scope of the Race Directive 2000/43, acknowledging that '... in the light of the objective of Directive 2000/43 and the nature of the rights which it seeks to safeguard, and in view of the fact that that directive is merely an expression, within the area under consideration, of the principle of equality, which is one of the general principles of European Union law, as recognised in Article 21 of the Charter of Fundamental Rights of the European Union, the scope of that directive cannot be defined restrictively.' (para 43).

106 See C-159/10 *Fuchs v Land Hessen* [2011] 3 CMLR 47, [2012] ICR 93 at paras 61–63.

107 C-236/09 *Association belge des Consommateurs Test-Achats ASBL and v Conseil des Ministers* [2011] 2 CMLR 38.

108 *Test-Achats* at paras 30–33.

109 See Case 4 1-74 *Van Duyn v Home Office (No 2)* [1975] Ch 358, [1975] 3 All ER 190, ECJ.

- the time-limit for the implementation of the Directive by the member state has expired;[110]
- the state has failed to implement the Directive correctly or at all.[111]

19.87 The CJEU expanded the doctrine of direct effect from the Treaty provisions by confirming that EC Regulations are directly applicable and also by establishing the direct effect of decisions and Directives.[112] The result of that development is that individuals can assert treaty provisions and these three forms of EC law in national courts directly against the state[113] and decisions, treaty articles and regulations can be invoked directly by an individual in a national court against other individuals (horizontally). Although Directives can give individuals rights that they can enforce against their respective governments, they generally do not have this 'horizontal' direct effect. The court has stated that Directives are only binding on the member state to whom they are addressed and therefore they cannot be used against individuals or non-state entities.[114]

---

110 Case 148/78 *Pubblico Ministero v Ratti* [1979] ECR 1629 at para 47. However, in *Mangold v Helm* [2005] ECR I-9981, [2006] All ER (on the application of EC) 383, [2006] IRLR 143, the ECJ ruled that it was not necessary to wait for the expiry of the implementation period in certain cases.

111 Case 8/81 *Ursula Becker v Finanzamt Münster-Innenstadt* [1982] ECR 53, [1982] 1 CMLR 499.

112 Case 39/72 *Commission v Italy* [1973] ECR 101, [1973] 3 CMLR 439 (regulations); Case 9/70 *Franz Grad v Finanzamt Traunstein* [1970] ECR 825, [1971] CMLR 1 (decisions) and *Van Gend & Loos* [1963] ECR 1 (directives). See also Cases C-6/90 & C-9/90 *Francovich v Italy* [1991] ECR 1-5357, 1-5408, [1991] 2 CMLR 66.

113 A concept known as vertical direct effect, which includes claims against emanations of the state such as the government, local authorities, NHS trusts, the police and other emergency organisations.

114 See Case 152/84 *Marshall v Southampton & South-West Hampshire Area Health Authority* [1986] ECR 723, 749, 1 CMLR 688. Ms Marshall, an employee of the health authority, was dismissed in 1980 on the ground that she had passed the normal age of retirement applicable to women. The authority's policy was that female employees were to retire at age 60 and males at 65. UK legislation did not impose any obligation on women to retire at 60, because payment of the state or occupational pension would be deferred until actual retirement. She complained that her dismissal violated the 1976 Equal Treatment Directive before the ET. The court held that the binding nature of a directive exists only as against the state or states to which it is addressed. It could therefore be used by Ms Marshall as against the health authority as it was an emanation of the state.

19.88   In *Foster v British Gas*[115] the CJEU stated that:[116]

> It follows from the foregoing that a body, whatever its legal form, which has been made responsible, pursuant to a measure adopted by the state, for providing a public service under the control of the state and has for that purpose special powers beyond those which result from the normal rules applicable in relations between individuals is included among the bodies against which the provisions of a Directive capable of having direct effect may be relied upon.

19.89   The underlying principle in Foster and other cases is that the state may not benefit from its default in respect of anything that lies within the sphere of responsibility that by its own free choice it has taken upon itself, irrespective of the person through whom that responsibility is exercised.

19.90   These principles were taken a step further in *Seda Kücükdeveci v Swedex GmbH & Co. KG*,[117] where the CJEU held that Directive 2000/78 was adopted on the basis of Article 13 EC and does not itself lay down the principle of equal treatment in the field of employment and occupation, which derives from various international instruments and from the constitutional traditions common to the member states, but has the sole purpose of laying down, in that field, a general framework for combating discrimination on various grounds including age.[118]

19.91   It is worth quoting the CJEU's judgment at some length on this point:

> 47 However, the Member States' obligation arising from a directive to achieve the result envisaged by that directive and their duty to take all appropriate measures, whether general or particular, to ensure the fulfilment of that obligation are binding on all the authorities of the Member States including, for matters within their jurisdiction, the courts (see, inter alia, to that effect, *von Colson v Land Nordrhein-Westfahlen* (14/83) [1984] ECR 1891; [1986] 2 CMLR 430 at [26]; *Marleasing SA v La Comercial Internacional de Alimentacion SA* (C-106/89) [1990] ECR 1-4135; [1992] 1 CMLR 305 at [8]; *Faccini Dori* [1995] 1 CMLR 665 at [26]; *Inter-Environnement Wallonie ASBL v Region Wallonie* (C-129/96) [1997] ECR 1-7411; [1998] 1 CMLR 1057 at [40]; *Pfeiffer* [2005] 1 CMLR 44 at [110]; and *Angelidaki v Organismos Nomarkhiaki Afiodikisi Rethimnis* (C-378-380/07) [2009] ECR I-3071; [2009] 3 CMLR 15 at [106]).

---

115 [1991] 1 QB 405, [1990] ECR I-3313, [1991] ICR 84, ECJ.
116 See para 20 of the judgment.
117 Case C-555/07 [2011] 2 CMLR 27.
118 See also Case C-144/04 *Mangold v Helm* [2005] ECR I-9981, [2006] IRLR 143 at para 74. The principle is a general principle of EU law: para 75.

48 It follows that, in applying national law, the national court called on to interpret it is required to do so, as far as possible, in the light of the wording and the purpose of the directive in question, in order to achieve the result pursued by the directive and thereby comply with the third paragraph of art 288 TFEU (see, to that effect, *von Colson* [1986] 2 CMLR 430 at [26]; *Marleasing* [1992] 1 CMLR 305 at [8]; *Faccini Dori* [1995] I CMLR 665 at [26]; and *Pfeiffer* [2005] 1 CMLR 44 at [113]). The requirement for national law to be interpreted in conformity with EU law is inherent in the system of the Treaty, since it permits the national court, within the limits of its jurisdiction, to ensure the full effectiveness of EU law when it determines the dispute before it (see, to that effect, *Pfeiffer* [2005] 1 CMLR 44 at [114]).

49 According to the national court, however, because of its clarity and precision, the second sentence of para.622(2) of the BGB is not open to an interpretation in conformity with Directive 2000/78.

50 It must be recalled here that, as stated in [20] above, Directive 2000/78 merely gives expression to, but does not lay down, the principle of equal treatment in employment and occupation, and that the principle of non-discrimination on grounds of age is a general principle of EU law in that it constitutes a specific application of the general principle of equal treatment (see, to that effect, *Mangold* [2006] I CMLR. 43 at [74]–[76]).

51 In those circumstances, it is for the national court, hearing a dispute involving the principle of non-discrimination on grounds of age as given expression in Directive 2000/78, to provide, within the limits of its jurisdiction, the legal protection which individuals derive from EU law and to ensure the full effectiveness of that law, disapplying if need be any provision of national legislation contrary to that principle (see, to that effect, *Mangold* [2006] I CMLR 43 at [77]).

19.92   Note that it is the principle of equality that is the general principle. The reasoning of the court cannot therefore be confined to Directives relating to age discrimination, or to the characteristic of age alone.

19.93   The court then addressed the application of the Directive in cases between private individuals (horizontal effect):

52 As regards, secondly, the obligation of the national court, hearing proceedings between individuals, to make a reference to the Court for a preliminary ruling on the interpretation of EU law before it can disapply a national provision which it considers to be contrary to that law, ...

53 The need to ensure the full effectiveness of the principle of non-discrimination on grounds of age, as given expression in Directive 2000/78, means that the national court, faced with a national provision falling within the scope of EU law which it considers to be incompatible with that principle, and which cannot be interpreted in

conformity with that principle, must decline to apply that provision, without being either compelled to make or prevented from making a reference to the Court for a preliminary ruling before doing so.

54 The possibility thus given to the national court by the second paragraph of art.267 TFEU of asking the Court for a preliminary ruling before disapplying the national provision that is contrary to EU law cannot, however, be transformed into an obligation because national law does not allow that court to disapply a provision it considers to be contrary to the constitution unless the provision has first been declared unconstitutional by the Constitutional Court. By reason of the principle of the primacy of EU law, which extends also to the principle of non-discrimination on grounds of age, contrary national legislation which falls within the scope of EU law must be disapplied (see, to that effect, *Mangold* [2006] I CMLR 43 at [77])

55 It follows that the national court, hearing proceedings between individuals, is not obliged but is entitled to make a reference to the Court for a preliminary ruling on the interpretation of the principle of non-discrimination on grounds of age, as given expression by Directive 2000/78, before disapplying a provision of national courts.

19.94 Advisers, therefore, confronted with a piece of legislation such as the EqA 2010, which is deficient in certain respects (such as its failure to protect against victimisation after the end of employment[119]) should examine the Directives to see whether the true interpretation of the Directive requires the ET to make good the deficit in UK law by disapplying the national provision that is contrary to EU law if it cannot be read in a manner that is consistent with the proper meaning of the Directive.

Duty to interpret national law

19.95 The ET has a duty to interpret national law in conformity with Community law because:[120]

- the member states' obligation arising from a Directive to achieve the result envisaged by the Directive, and their duty under the EC Treaty to take all appropriate measures, whether general or

119 See *Jessemey v Rowstock* ET/2700838/11 and ET/2701156/11. The ET in that case was not shown the earlier cases, eg, *Rhys-Harper v Relaxion Group plc; D'Souza v London Borough of Lambeth; Jones v 3M Healthcare Ltd* [2003] UKHL 33, [2003] ICR 867, in which the point was dealt with by reference to EU law. *Jessemey* was incorrectly decided as a result. See further on this point para 8.11.

120 Starting with Case 14/83 *Von Colson and Kamann v Land Nordrhein-Westfalen* [1984] ECR 1891 para 26.

particular, to ensure the fulfilment of that obligation, are binding on all the authorities of member states including, for matters within their jurisdiction, the courts;[121]

- in applying national law, in particular legislative provisions that were specially introduced in order to implement the Directive,[122] the national court is required to interpret its national law, so far as possible, in the light of the wording and the purpose of the Directive in order to achieve the result pursued by the Treaty.[123]

19.96   In relation to primary legislation, in *Pickstone v Freeman Plc*[124] Lord Oliver stated

> It must, I think, be recognised that so to construe a provision which, on its face, is unambiguous involves a departure from a number of well-established rules of construction. The intention of Parliament has, it is said, to be ascertained from the words which it has used and those words are to be construed according to their plain and ordinary meaning. The fact that a statute is passed to give effect to an international treaty does not, of itself, enable the treaty to be referred to in order to construe the words used other than in their plain and unambiguous sense. Moreover, even in the case of ambiguity, what is said in Parliament in the course of the passage of the Bill, cannot ordinarily be referred to to assist in construction. I think, however, that it has also to be recognised that a statute which is passed in order to give effect to the United Kingdom's obligations under the EEC Treaty falls into a special category and it does so because, unlike other treaty obligations, those obligations have, in effect, been incorporated into English law by the European Communities Act 1972.

19.97   He went on to indicate that if the relevant legislation can be interpreted to give effect to the obligations under the treaty, it should be.

19.98   An example of a court reading words into primary legislation can be found in *Coleman v Attridge Law*.[125] This was a case in which

---

121 This obligation derives from EC Treaty Arts 249(3) and 10 (see Case 105/03 *Criminal Proceedings against Pupino* [2006] QB 83, [2005] ECR I-5285).

122 As was the case with the Age Regulations 2006.

123 Case C-106/89 *Marleasing SA v La Comercial Internacional de Alimentacion SA* [1990] ECR I-4135, 4159 para 8; Case C-334/92 *Wagner Miret v Fondo de garantia salaria* [1993] ECR I-6911, 6932 para 20; Case C-91/92 *Faccini Dori v Recreb Srl* [1994] ECR I-3325, 3357 para 26 and Case C-462/99 *Connect Austria Gesellschaft fur Telekommunikation GmbH v Telekom-Control-Kommission* [2003] ECR I-5197, 5236 para 38.

124 [1989] 1 AC 66, HL at 126B–D.

125 C-303/06 [2008] IRLR 722, [2008] ICR 1128 (as applied by the EAT; *EBR Attridge Law LLP (formerly Attridge Law) v Coleman* [2010] ICR 242, [2010] IRLR 10).

the claimant argued that she had been subjected to discrimination because her son was disabled; so-called 'associative discrimination'. The EAT read the DDA 1995 to conform to the ECJ's judgment concerning the interpretation of the Directive 2000/78. Underhill P stated the principle of EU law that the ET should 'so far as possible' interpret domestic legislation in order to give effect to the state's obligations under EU law.[126] Pursuant to that obligation a court or ET can in some circumstances go beyond the traditional strict limits of statutory construction and can read words into a statute in order to give effect to EU legislation that the statute was evidently intended to implement.[127] In *Coleman*, the EAT held that 'the proscription of associative discrimination is an extension of the scope of the legislation as enacted, but it is in no sense repugnant to it. On the contrary, it is an extension fully in conformity with the aims of the legislation as drafted'.[128]

19.99   The Court of Appeal has held in relation to the Employment Equality (Sexual Orientation) Regulations 2003[129] that they have to be construed purposively so as to conform as far as possible with the Directive and any challenge to them has to be resolved in light of what the court considered to be the true construction of the relevant provisions.[130]

19.100   In discharging its duty to give a purposive construction to Directives (and to Regulations issued in order to comply with the obligations imposed by Directives) so as to achieve the intended outcome, a national court has the flexibility to supply into the national provision, by necessary implication, words appropriate to comply with those obligations.[131]

19.101   In *Litster* the House of Lords was prepared to insert words into domestic regulations. The House of Lords held that the courts of the United Kingdom were under a duty to give a purposive construction to the Transfer of Undertakings Regulations 1981 in a manner

---

126 *Marleasing SA v La Comercional Internacionial de Alimentación SA* [1990] ECR I-4135.

127 *Pickstone v Freemans plc* [1989] 1 AC 66, HL, [1988] ICR 697 and *Litster v Forth Dry Dock & Engineering Co Ltd* [1990] 1 AC 546, [1989] ICR 341, HL.

128 See [2010] ICR 242 at para 14.

129 SI No 1661.

130 *R (Amicus) v Secretary of State for Trade and Industry* [2004] EWHC 860, [2007] ICR 1176.

131 *Litster v Forth Dry Dock & Engineering Co Ltd* [1990] 1 AC 546, [1989] ICR 341, [1989] IRLR 161, HL.

that would accord with the decisions of the ECJ on the Directive and, where necessary, to imply words which would achieve that effect.

Claim against the state

19.102 If the individual cannot rely directly on the provisions of the Directive, and if the domestic provision cannot be interpreted to give effect to the Directive, they may have a claim against the state for compensation for the loss and damage suffered by the failure to implement the Directive.[132] The claim is for breach of statutory duty under the European Communities Act 1972 and is brought in the courts.

19.103 The claimant must show that:

- the relevant rule of law was intended to confer individual rights;
- breach of that rule was serious; and
- there was a direct causal link between the breach and the loss suffered by the individual.[133]

19.104 Public authorities may be liable for damages for breach of EU law in addition to or in substitution for member states themselves on the basis set out above.[134]

Interpreting the Equality Act 2010 by reference to the Directives

19.105 The underlying principles of Directive 2000/78 show the way in which the EqA 2010 should be interpreted or supplemented where it fails to implement Directives. We will use that Directive as an example of the technique that advisers should adopt in presenting a convincing argument for the consistent interpretation of the EqA 2010.

19.106 Whether a relevant provision of national law was made before or after a Directive, the national court must interpret the domestic provision so as to comply with the Directive.[135] The interpretative duty is a very strong one indeed.[136]

132 Cases C-6/90 and C-9/90 *Francovich and Bonifaci v Italy* [1991] ECR I-5357, [1992] IRLR 84, [1995] ICR 722, ECJ.
133 Case C-46/93 *Brasserie du Pecheur SA v Germany* [1996] QB 404, [1996] ECR I-1029.
134 Case C-424/97 *Haim v Kassenzahnarztliche Vereinigung Nordrhein* [2000] ECR I-5123, [2002] 1 CMLR 11.
135 Case C-106/89 *Marleasing SA v La Comercial Internacional de Alimentacion SA* [1990] ECR I-4135, [1992] 1 CMLR 305, ECJ and *Finnegan v Clowney Youth Training Programme Ltd* [1990] 2 AC 407.
136 See paras 1.109–1.115.

19.107   **Recitals**: ETs should be directed to the preamble of the Directive where necessary. The preamble sets out the purposes of the Directive that are to be achieved, and refers to relevant international instruments, policy objectives and treaty provisions. In particular the international instruments to which reference has already been made in this chapter are relevant for the interpretation of all of the Directives with which advisers will be concerned.

19.108   The aim of Directive 2000/78 is the establishment of a general framework for the respect of the principle of equal treatment between persons irrespective of religion or belief, disability, age, or sexual orientation within the European Union. The areas covered by the Directive are access to employment and occupation, promotion, vocational training, employment and working conditions and membership of certain bodies.[137] The existence of an aim in the Recitals of the Directive will point very strongly in some cases to the aim which the national legislation must achieve.

19.109   The preamble to a Directive provides an essential reference point, namely the social purpose of the Directive. The Directive is always to be interpreted so as to give effect to that social purpose. The starting point for Directive 2000/78 for example is that:

> (4) The right of all persons to equality before the law and protection against discrimination constitutes a universal right recognised by the Universal Declaration of Human Rights, the United Nations Convention on the Elimination of All Forms of Discrimination against Women, United Nations Covenants on Civil and Political Rights and on Economic, Social and Cultural Rights and by the European Convention for the Protection of Human Rights and Fundamental Freedoms, to which all Member States are signatories. Convention No 111 of the International Labour Organisation (ILO) prohibits discrimination in the field of employment and occupation.

19.110   The concept of equality set out in these instruments is examined above and aims at providing equality in practice. To that end, some measures of positive discrimination may be deemed not to be discrimination.[138]

19.111   The Recitals make reference to the Charter.[139] Paragraph 11 of the Recitals states that discrimination may:

---

137 By contrast the Race Equality Directive 2000/43 deals also with the provision of goods and services.

138 See ILO Convention 111 Art 5. This is the approach that is adopted in Article 7 of the Directive.

139 Charter Art 21.

undermine the achievement of the objectives of the EC Treaty, in particular the attainment of a high level of employment and social protection, raising the standard of living and the quality of life, economic and social cohesion and solidarity, and the free movement of persons.

19.112 Although these are high aims, a measure which restricts access to employment will have to be justified against the damage it does to those aims.

19.113 The Recitals may also be the key to an understanding of the way in which certain characteristics are to be treated. This is particularly the case in relation to age and disability in Directive 2000/78.

19.114 Thus Recital (20) gives a clear answer to whether the Directive intends that there should be a right to reasonable accommodations for persons with disabilities. It states:

> Appropriate measures should be provided, ie effective and practical measures to adapt the workplace to the disability, for example adapting premises and equipment, patterns of working time, the distribution of tasks or the provision of training or integration resources.

The relevant Article explains what a reasonable accommodation is, but it then appears that the provision of reasonable accommodations is a defence to an allegation of indirect discrimination because of a person's disability. Most states have introduced a right to reasonable accommodation, and the UK's concept of reasonable adjustments should be regarded as an implementation of the Directive concept.

19.115 Similarly, in paragraph 25 the Recitals provide that:

> the prohibition of age discrimination is an essential part of meeting the aims set out in the Employment Guidelines[140] and encouraging diversity in the workforce. However, differences in treatment in connection with age may be justified under certain circumstances and therefore require specific provisions which may vary in accordance with the situation in Member States. It is therefore essential to distinguish between differences in treatment which are justified, in particular by legitimate employment policy, labour market and vocational training objectives, and discrimination which must be prohibited.

19.116 Recital 37 provides a clear statement of the way in which the Directive is to operate. The objective of the Directive is to create within the Community a level playing field as regards equality in employment and occupation. Paragraph 37 records the policy agreement between

---

140 These are the aims of employability, entrepreneurship, adaptability and equal opportunities.

the member states that this objective cannot sufficiently be achieved by member states.

19.117   Article 1 of Directive 2000/78[141] sets out its purpose of providing a general framework for combating discrimination on the grounds of various protected characteristics as regards employment and occupation by putting into effect the principle of equal treatment. 'Equal treatment' means that there must be no direct or indirect discrimination whatsoever on the prohibited grounds.[142] The definition of the principle of equal treatment contained in Article 2.1 is consistent with the definition provided by Article 2.1 of Directive 76/207/EEC of 9 February 1976 and is intended to be interpreted in the same way. The requirement that there should be no discrimination whatsoever[143] indicates that even the smallest amount of influence by a discriminatory factor is to be taken into account.

Structure of the Directive

19.118   Article 2 contains the definitions of direct and indirect discrimination. In the case of direct discrimination it links the treatment with the protected ground rather than any personal status and is concerned to establish whether the protected characteristic has played any role whatsoever in the less favourable treatment. It requires a comparison be made between the situation of the claimant and that of either an actual or hypothetical person in a comparable situation. In respect of age it must is read as subject to article 6 which provides for justification of differences in treatment on the grounds of age. Indirect discrimination does require the person to have the protected characteristic in question.[144] In the case of disability

---

141   See Directive 2006/54 Art 1 (sex discrimination), and of 2000/43 Art 1 (race discrimination).

142   Directive 2000/78 Art 2(1), Directive 2006/54 Arts 2, 4 and 14 (Recast Sex Discrimination Directive) and Directive 2000/43 Art 2 (race directive).

143   This is interpreted in the United Kingdom as meaning that there should be no discrimination of a more than minor or trivial nature, see *Igen Ltd v Wong* [2005] EWCA Civ 142, [2005] 3 All ER 812, [2005] ICR 931. Guideline 10 in *Barton v Investec Securities Ltd* [2003] ICR 1205, EAT makes it clear that in order to discharge the burden of proof the respondent will have to prove, on the balance of probabilities, that the treatment was in no sense whatsoever on one of the protected grounds. The Court of Appeal held (*Igen* para 37) that this was the same as saying that discrimination must not have been a significant influence on the treatment (the test proposed in *Nagarajan v London Regional Transport* [2000] 1 AC 501, [1999] ICR 877).

144   See Directive 2000/78 Art 2(2)(b)(ii) , Directive 2006/54 Art 2(1)(b), and Directive 2000/43 Art 2(2)(b).

(ii) as regards persons with a particular disability, the employer or any person or organisation to whom this Directive applies, is obliged, under national legislation, to take appropriate measures in line with the principles contained in Article 5 in order to eliminate disadvantages entailed by such provision, criterion or practice.[145]

19.119 The test for indirect discrimination is inspired by the case-law of the ECJ on the free movement of workers.[146] An apparently neutral provision, criterion or practice will be regarded as indirectly discriminatory if it is *intrinsically liable* adversely to affect a person or persons on the grounds referred in Article 1. That it is intrinsically liable may be proven on the basis of statistical evidence or by any other means that demonstrate that a provision would be intrinsically disadvantageous for the person or persons concerned.

19.120 Objective justification requires examination of two elements (a) the aim of the provision, criterion or practice which establishes a difference of treatment must deserve protection and must be sufficiently substantial to justify it taking precedence over the principle of equal treatment; (b) the means employed to achieve that aim must be appropriate and necessary. The definition of indirect discrimination should be construed in conjunction with the general rules on the burden of proof set out in Article 10. It is for the claimant to prove the disadvantage, and intrinsic likelihood of such disadvantage; it is for the respondent to prove all the elements of justification.

19.121 Harassment is deemed to be a form of discrimination.[147] A comparator is not necessary to establish harassment. Similarly the Directive stipulates that an instruction to discriminate against persons on grounds of a protected characteristic is deemed to be discrimination.[148]

---

145 Directive 2000/78 Art 2(2)(b)(ii).

146 See C-237/94 *O'Flynn v Adjudication Officer*, judgment of 23 May 1996 [1996] ECR I-2617; [1998] ICR 608 at para 20 ff.

147 Directive 2000/78 Art 2(3), Directive 2000/43 Art 2(3), Directive 2006/54 Art 2(1)(c) '"harassment": where unwanted conduct related to the sex of a person occurs with the purpose or effect of violating the dignity of a person, and of creating an intimidating, hostile, degrading, humiliating or offensive environment;' and Art 2(1)(d) '"sexual harassment": where any form of unwanted verbal, non-verbal or physical conduct of a sexual nature occurs, with the purpose or effect of violating the dignity of a person, in particular when creating an intimidating, hostile, degrading, humiliating or offensive environment'.

148 Directive 2000/78 Article 2(4), Directive 2000/43 Art 2(4), Directive 2006/54 Art 2(2)(b).

Public order etc derogations

19.122   Directive 2000/78 is without prejudice to measures laid down by national law which, in a democratic society, are necessary for public security, for the maintenance of public order and the prevention of criminal offences, for the protection of health and for the protection of the rights and freedoms of others.[149] However no equivalent provision appears in the Race Equality Directive 2000/43 or the Gender Recast Directive 2006/54.

19.123   Any derogation from an individual right (equal treatment) laid down in the Directive must be interpreted narrowly[150] and a derogation from equal treatment must observe the principle of proportionality. It must remain within the limits of what is appropriate and necessary for achieving the aim in view, and the principle of equal treatment must be reconciled as far as possible with the requirements of whichever of the matters is relied upon in the particular case.[151]

19.124   In *Prigge v Deutsche Lufthansa AG*[152] the CJEU described Article 2(5) as follows:

> In adopting that provision, the EU legislature in the area of employment and occupation, intended to prevent and arbitrate a conflict between, on the one hand, the principle of equal treatment and, on the other hand, the necessity of ensuring public order, security and health, the prevention of criminal offences and the protection of individual rights and freedoms, which are necessary for the functioning of a democratic society. The legislature decided that, in certain cases set out in Article 2(5) of the Directive, the principles set out by that latter do not apply to measures containing differences in treatment on one of the grounds referred to in Article 1 of the Directive, on condition, however, that those measures are 'necessary' for the achievement of the abovementioned objective.

19.125   Those aims are the aims of the state, the setting of which can only rarely be delegated, for example, to the social partners.[153] Directives 2000/78 and 2000/43 do not cover differences of treatment based on nationality and are without prejudice to provisions and conditions relating to the entry into and residence of third-country nationals and stateless persons in the territory of Member States. They are

---

149 Directive 2000/78 Art 2(5).
150 See eg AG Sharpston in C-427/06 *Bartsch v Bosch und Siemens Hausgerate* [2009] All ER (EC) 113, [2008] ECR I-7245 at para 103.
151 *Johnston v Chief Constable of the Royal Ulster Constabulary* [1987] QB 129, [1987] ICR 83 at paras 36-38 of the judgment.
152 C-447/09, [2011] IRLR 1052, CJEU.
153 See *Prigge v Deutsche Lufthansa AG*, C-447/09, [2011] IRLR 1052, CJEU.

without prejudice to any treatment which arises from the legal status of the third-country nationals and stateless persons concerned.[154] In *Vakante v Addey and Stanhope School Governing Body*,[155] an asylum seeker whose immigration status did not permit him to work complained of race discrimination consisting of dismissal and a failure by the employer to permit him training opportunities and other benefits, facilities and services. The ET rejected the claim because the contract was illegal and the complaints were so closely bound up with the contract. The Court of Appeal upheld that view. The refusal of the ET to entertain such a complaint arose from the claimant's status as a third country national.[156]

19.126　　By Article 3.3, Directive 2000/78 does not apply to payments of any kind made by state schemes or similar, including state social security or social protection schemes. Article 3.4 provides that Member States may provide that the Directive, in so far as it relates to discrimination on the grounds of disability and age, shall not apply to the armed forces. Directive 2000/78 applies to all persons, as regards both the public and private sectors, including public bodies.[157]

Genuine occupational requirement

19.127　In very limited circumstances, a difference of treatment may be justified where a characteristic related to one of the protected characteristics constitutes a genuine and determining occupational requirement (GOR), when the objective is legitimate and the requirement is proportionate.[158] Article 4 provides that a difference of treatment which is based on a characteristic *related* to one of the protected characteristics will not constitute discrimination where, by reason of (a) the nature of the particular occupational activities concerned or (b) the context in which they are carried out, such a characteristic constitutes a genuine and determining occupational requirement.

154　Directive 2000/78 Art 3(2).

155　[2004] EWCA Civ 1065, [2005] ICR 231.

156　Mr Vakante sought to rely on the Race Directive, Directive 2000/43, but it was not in effect at the time of the events (nor of the tribunal's decision).

157　Within the limits of the areas of competence conferred on the Community (Directive 2000/78 Art 3.1 and Directive 2000/43 Art 3(1)); in the case of gender discrimination no reference is made to the areas of competence conferred on the community (see Directive 2006/54 Art 14).

158　Recital 23.

However the objective must be legitimate and the requirement must be proportionate.[159]

19.128   An example of the use of a GOR is *Wolf v Stadt Frankfurt am Main*.[160] The CJEU held that a rule limiting recruitment to persons of not more than 30 years to intermediate career posts in the professional fire service laid down rules relating to recruitment conditions within the meaning of Article 3(1)(a) of the Directive. It considered Article 4.To examine whether the difference of treatment based on age in national law was justified, it was necessary to establish whether physical fitness is a characteristic related to age. If so, does it constitute a genuine and determining occupational requirement for the occupational activities in question or for carrying them out? Is the objective pursued by the legislation legitimate and the requirement was proportionate. Some of the tasks of persons at the relevant stage in the fire service, such as fighting fires or rescuing people, required exceptionally high physical capacities and could be performed only by young officials. Scientific data deriving from studies in the field of industrial and sports medicine showed that respiratory capacity, musculature and endurance diminished with age. Very few officials over 45 years of age had sufficient physical capacity to perform the fire-fighting part of their activities. As for rescuing people, at the age of 50 the officials concerned no longer had that capacity. Officials who had passed those ages worked in other branches of activities. It followed that the need to possess full physical capacity to carry on intermediate career posts the occupation of a person in the intermediate career of in the fire services was related to the age of the persons in that career.

19.129   There is a further GOR available in Article 4.2 whereby member States can keep existing national legislation or provide for future legislation incorporating national practices existing at the date of adoption of the Directive. The laws or practices must relate to occupational activities within churches and other public or private organisations the ethos of which is based on religion or belief. The laws

---

159 Directive 2000/78 Art 4(1), Directive 2000/43 Art 4, and Directive 2006/54 Art 4(2) which provides: 'Member States may provide, as regards access to employment including the training leading thereto, that a difference of treatment which is based on a characteristic related to sex shall not constitute discrimination where, by reason of the nature of the particular occupational activities concerned or of the context in which they are carried out, such a characteristic constitutes a genuine and determining occupational requirement, provided that its objective is legitimate and the requirement is proportionate'.

160 Case C-229 08 [2010] 2 CMLR 32, [2010] All ER (EC) 939, [2010] IRLR 244.

or practices must provide that a difference of treatment based on a person's religion or belief will not constitute discrimination where, by reason of the nature of these activities or of the context in which they are carried out, a person's religion or belief constitutes a genuine, legitimate and justified occupational requirement, having regard to the organisation's ethos. The difference of treatment on the basis of religion or ethos must be implemented taking account of Member States' constitutional provisions and principles, as well as the general principles of Community law, and should not justify discrimination on another ground. Therefore it is not possible to use a religion and belief GOR to justify, for example, age discrimination.

19.130   In *R (Amicus) v Secretary of State for Trade and Industry*,[161] certain trade unions applied for the annulment of the certain provisions of the Employment Equality (Sexual Orientation) Regulations 2003, which implemented the sexual orientation aspects of the Directive. The relevant provisions permitted exceptions to the general prohibition of discrimination on the grounds of sexual orientation on the basis of GOR, including occupation for the purposes of an organised religion and benefits dependent on marital status. The implementation survived this challenge.

Age justification

19.131   Article 6.1 of the Directive deals with the special derogation relating to age.[162] Based on this UK law is now interpreted so as only to permit justification of direct age discrimination where the employer can show a legitimate aim which contains an element of public interest.

Positive action

19.132   Directive 2000/78 provides for positive action in very much stronger terms than is permitted in the UK.[163] Article 7 permits, but does not require, member states to maintain or adopt specific measures to prevent or compensate for disadvantages linked to one of the characteristics. Where this is to be done with a view to ensuring full equality

---

161 [2004] EWHC 860 (Admin), [2007] ICR 1176.

162 See *Seldon v Clarkson Jakes Wright* [2012] UKSC 16, [2012] ICR 716 paras 32–49.

163 Directive 2000/78 Art 7, Directive 2000/43 Art 5 and Directive 2006/54 Art 3 which provides: 'Member States may maintain or adopt measures within the meaning of Article 141(4) of the Treaty with a view to ensuring full equality in practice between men and women in working life'.

in practice, it does not breach the principle of equal treatment. The purpose of any such measures must be to achieve substantive equality, in the sense that the principle of equal treatment does not simply require that everyone is treated identically. Strong measures of positive discrimination will have to be justified as proportionate and necessary. The UK's version of positive action is restricted to training and encouragement.

Minimum standards

19.133   A technical, but highly important, article in Directive 2000/78 is Article 8 which provides that Member States may introduce or maintain provisions which are more favourable to the protection of the principle of equal treatment than those laid down in the Directive. It also stipulates that the implementation of the Directive shall under no circumstances constitute grounds for a reduction in the level of protection against discrimination already afforded by Member States in the fields covered by the Directive.[164]

Remedies and enforcement

19.134   There are two main conditions for effective legislation implementing equal treatment provisions. A victim of discrimination must have an effective personal remedy against the person or body who has perpetrated the discrimination. There must also be adequate mechanisms in each Member State to ensure adequate levels of enforcement. Thus persons who consider themselves wronged must have the possibility of pursuing their claims through an administrative and/or judicial procedure to enforce their right to equal treatment, even after the employment relationship has ended.[165] Article 9(2) of Directive 2000/78 provides that Member States must ensure that associations, organisations or other legal entities which have, in accordance with the criteria laid down by their national law, a legitimate interest in ensuring that the provisions of the Directive are complied with, can engage, either on behalf or in support of the complainant, with his or her approval, in any judicial and/or administrative procedure provided for the enforcement of obligations under the Directive. In the UK the EHRC has this role. Article 9(3) preserves national rules relating

---

164 Article 8(2).
165 Directive 2000/78 Art 9, Recast Directive 2006/54 Art 17; Directive 2000/43 Art 7.

to time-limits for bringing actions as regards the principle of equality of treatment.

Burden of proof

19.135 Article 10 dealing with the burden of proof sets out how the burden of proof shifts to the defendant in accordance with the case law of the ECJ.[166] Detailed guidance has been given on the application of the burden of proof provisions as they will apply in the UK.[167] Note that recital 31 in the preamble makes clear that it is not for the respondent to prove that the claimant is of a particular age. Similarly, it will be for the claimant to prove a particular impairment exists amounting to a disability if necessary.

Victimisation

19.136 Victimisation, under the Directives, is seen not as a species of discrimination, but as a necessary adjunct to enforcing the principle of equal treatment. Member states are required[168] to introduce such measures as are necessary to protect employees against dismissal or other adverse treatment by the employer as a reaction to a complaint within the undertaking or to any legal proceedings aimed at enforcing compliance with the principle of equal treatment.

19.137 The UK in the EqA 2010, requires only that the complainant be subjected to 'a detriment', without any need for less favourable treatment.

Information, bargaining and NGOs and final measures

19.138 The Directive requires governments to engage in ensuring the dissemination of information concerning rights, down to an appropriate level, for example the level of the workplace.[169] Governments are also

---

166 *Danfoss*, Case C-109/88, [1989] ECR 3199, [1991] ICR 74, para 16; *Enderby v Frenchay Health Authority*, Case C-127/92, [1993] ECR 5535, [1994] ICR 112, paras 13 and 14 and *Royal Copenhagen*, Case C-400/93, [1995] ECR 1275, para 24.

167 *Igen Ltd and others v Wong and other cases* [2005] EWCA Civ 142, [2005] All ER 812, [2005] ICR 931; in *Galina Meister v Speech Design Carrier Systems GmbH*, Case C-415/10, 12 January 2012, Advocate General Mengozzi adopted a similar approach to the burden of proof: Article 10 of Directive 2000/78, Article 8(1) of Directive 2000/43 and Article 19(1) of Directive 2006/54.

168 By Directive 2000/78 Art 11, Directive 2006/54 Art 24, Directive 2000/43 Art 9.

169 Directive 2000/78 Art 12, Directive 2006/54 Arts 21 and 22, and Directive 2000/43 Art 11.

enjoined to encourage social dialogue between the social partners.[170] They must engage in dialogue with non-governmental organisations concerning anti-discrimination measures.[171]

19.139   The final measures of a Directive are often overlooked because they appear to contain fairly high-level obligations on states. This is not the case. Member States have to carry out a review of their existing legislation and if existing legislation offends against the principle of equal treatment it must be made to conform. The Gender Recast Directive 2006/54 goes further and requires Member States actively to take into account the objective of equality between men and women when formulating and implementing laws, regulations, administrative provisions, policies and activities in the areas referred to in the Directive.[172] Thus gender equality must be part of policy making.

Penalties

19.140   Directive 2000/78 Article 17[173] deals with the nature of the laws that must be introduced. It provides:

> Member States shall lay down the rules on sanctions applicable to infringements of the national provisions adopted pursuant to this Directive and shall take all measures necessary to ensure that they are applied. The sanctions, which may comprise the payment of compensation to the victim, must be effective, proportionate and dissuasive ...

19.141   In order to comply with these Directives, national law must provide 'effective, proportionate and dissuasive' sanctions for violation of national anti-discrimination norms.[174] Sanctions 'may comprise the payment of compensation to the victim'. The requirement that sanctions must be effective, proportionate and dissuasive means that all forms of damages (including punitive damages) must be available to a person whose claim is well founded. The Court of Justice has stated

> ... it has been consistently held since *Marshall v Southampton and South West Hampshire Area Health Authority* ... that a Directive cannot

---

170 Directive 2000/78 Art 13, Directive 2006/54 Art 30, and Directive 2000/43 Art 10.

171 Art 14.

172 Directive 2006/54 Art 29.

173 See also Directive 2006/54 Art 25 and Directive 2000/43 Art 5.

174 See further Lila Farkas ,'How to present a discrimination claim', EU Commission July 2011, chapter VIII.

of itself impose obligations on an individual, in this case a private-sector employer, and thus cannot be relied upon as such against such a person. However, it has also been consistently held since [Case 14/83 *Von Colson and Kamann* [1984] ECR 1891] that the Member States' obligation arising from a Directive to achieve the result envisaged by the Directive and their duty under Article 5 of the Treaty of Rome [now Article 10 EC] to take all appropriate measures, whether general or particular, to ensure the fulfilment of that obligation are binding on all the authorities of Member States including, for matters within their jurisdiction, the courts. As follows from *Marleasing SA v La Comercial Internacional de Alimentación* 1990 ECR I-4135, paragraph 8, and *Wagner Miret v Fondo de Garantía Salarial* 1993 ECR I-6911, paragraphs 20 and 21, in applying national law, in particular legislative provisions which, as in the present case, were specially introduced in order to implement the Directive, the national court is required to interpret its national law, so far as possible, in the light of the wording and the purpose of the Directive in order to achieve the result pursued by the third paragraph of Article 189 of the Treaty.[175]

19.142 Further the Court stated in *Von Colson v Land Nordrhein-Westfahlen*:[176]

It follows from [Article 6] that Member States are required to adopt measures which are sufficiently effective to achieve the objective of the directive to ensure that those measures may in fact be relied upon before the national courts by the persons concerned.

19.143 It is the objective of the Directive which is the standard by which the effectiveness of the measure is to be judged. Any measure introduced must in practice be capable of being relied upon by the individual. This standard has implications for the clarity and accessibility of the law implementing the Directive. The ECJ stated:

Although .... full implementation of the directive does not require any specific form of sanction for unlawful discrimination, it does entail that the sanction be such as to guarantee real and effective judicial protection. Moreover it must also have a real deterrent effect on the employer.[177]

---

175 (C185/97) *Coote v Granada Hospitality Ltd* [1998] ECR I-5199, [1999] ICR 100. This principle is consistent with having a ceiling on recoverable damages but only where the employer can show (in an appointment case) that the candidate would certainly not have obtained the appointment. Otherwise caps are not lawful (C180/95) Draehmpaehl v Urania Immobilienservice OHG [1997] ECR I-2195, [1997] 3 CMLR 1107, [1998] ICR 164.

176 (C-14/83) [1984] ECR 1891 at p1907 para 18.

177 *Von Colson v Land Nordrhein-Westfahlen* (C-14/83) [1984] ECR 1891 at p1908 para 23.

19.144   A study of the various cases gives no constant idea of what the CJEU considers meets the requirement that remedies be 'effective proportionate and dissuasive'.[178] What seems to be a common concept may be used in a different way in different fields of application.[179] However it is clear from cases such as *Marshall II* that a proposed sanction or remedy can be tested for effectiveness by reference to the aim proposed under a Directive.

19.145   In the case of Directives aimed at equality, *Marshall II* provides useful guidance:

> ... Article 6 [of EC Directive 76/207] does not prescribe a specific measure to be taken in the event of a breach of the prohibition of discrimination, but leaves Member States free to choose between the different solutions suitable for achieving the objective of the Directive, depending on the different situations which may arise.
>
> 24. However, the objective is to arrive at real equality of opportunity and cannot therefore be attained in the absence of measures appropriate to restore such equality when it has not been observed. As the Court stated in paragraph 23 of the judgment in *Von Colson and Kamann*, cited above, those measures must be such as to guarantee real and effective judicial protection and have a real deterrent effect on the employer.
>
> 25. Such requirements necessarily entail that the particular circumstances of each breach of the principle of equal treatment should be taken into account. In the event of discriminatory dismissal contrary to Article 5(1) of the Directive, a situation of equality could not be restored without either reinstating the victim of discrimination or, in the alternative, granting financial compensation for the loss and damage sustained.
>
> 26. Where financial compensation is the measure adopted in order to achieve the objective indicated above, it must be adequate, in that it must enable the loss and damage actually sustained as a result of the discriminatory dismissal to be made good in full in accordance with the applicable national rules.[180]

19.146   The requirement that the remedy be proportionate must be seen in the context of the third requirement which is that the remedy must be dissuasive of discrimination. Where a person has suffered financial

---

178   See Christa Tobler, *Thematic Report Remedies and Sanctions in EC Non-Discrimination Law*, June 2005 para 2.3; www.migpolgroup.com or www.publications.eu.int.

179   See *Aknlagemynidgheden v Hansen & Soen I/S* [1990] ECR I-2911, *Italy v Commission* C 297/02 of 23 September 2003.

180   C 271/91 *Marshall v Southampton and South West Hampshire Area Health Authority (Marshall II)* [1994] QB 126, [1993] ECR I-4367, [1993] ICR 893.

loss from discrimination, a system of compensation for breach of an anti-discrimination measure cannot be capped. Where compensation is awarded to penalise breaches of the prohibition of discrimination, such compensation has to be more than nominal so as to guarantee effective protection and to provide a deterrent to employers.[181]

References to the European Court of Justice[182]

19.147 Where there is a question concerning the proper interpretation of a provision of Community law the ECJ can give a preliminary ruling.[183] The power of the ET to make references to the ECJ derives directly from the Treaty.[184] Any court may make a reference if it considers that a decision on the interpretation is necessary to enable it to give judgment. A distinction is drawn between courts of last instance, which must make a reference to the ECJ unless the EC law issues are acte clair,[185] and other courts and ETs. National courts have the widest discretion in referring matters to the ECJ if they consider that a case pending before them raises questions involving interpretation, or consideration of the validity, of provisions of Community law, necessitating a decision on their part.[186]

19.148 The ECJ has stated that 'a reference for a preliminary ruling may prove particularly useful, at an appropriate stage of the proceedings, when there is a new question of interpretation of general interest for the uniform application of Community law throughout the Union, or

181 *Von Colson v Land Nordrhein-Westfalen* (14/83) [1984] ECR 1891
182 More detailed information concerning the process of litigating preliminary questions is in 'Litigating before the European Court of Justice: practical issues to consider', available to download from www.cloisters.com by Declan O'Dempsey (paper originally presented to the ERA at Trier).
183 TFEU Art 267. Where a question of interpretation is raised before any court or tribunal of a member state, that court or tribunal may, if it considers that a decision on the question is necessary to enable it to give judgment, request the ECJ to give a ruling thereon. Where any such question is raised in a case pending before a court or tribunal of a member state, against whose decisions there is no judicial remedy under national law, that court or tribunal shall bring the matter before the ECJ.
184 Examples of ET-originated preliminary rulings requests are Case C-13/94 *P v S* [1996] ECR I-2143 and *Coleman v Attridge Law and Mr Steve Law*, ET2303745/2005, 17 February 2006 and Case C-303/06 *Coleman v Attridge Law* [2008] ICR 1128.
185 *Acte clair* means that the correct application of EC law is so obvious as to leave no scope for any reasonable doubt as to the manner in which the question raised is to be resolved.
186 Case 166/73 *Rheinmühlen-Düsseldorf v Einfuhr- und Vorratsstelle für Getreide und Futtermittel* [1974] ECR 33 para 4.

where the existing case-law does not appear to be applicable to a new set of facts'.[187] In the United Kingdom this discretion has been the subject of guidance from the Court of Appeal, set out below.

Is the reference 'necessary'?

19.149 The guidance of the Court of Appeal is as follows:

- The point of European law must be conclusive, in the sense that it is necessary for the ET to give judgment in the case before it in the sense that if the provision of European law bears one interpretation judgment will be given one way, and if it bears another, the judgment will go the other way.
- Is there a previous ruling of the ECJ on the same point? If so, a reference is not necessary, unless the court or ET considers that the previous ECJ ruling may have been wrong or if there are new factors that ought to be brought to the ECJ's notice.
- If the point is acte clair there is no need for a reference. This means that the point is reasonably clear and free from doubt, so that the court or tribunal simply needs to apply the European law provision.
- The facts of the case should be decided first. As a rule, the ET will not be able to tell whether it is necessary to decide a point until all the facts are ascertained. The rule is a general rule[188] and there will be some situations in which a reference will be appropriate before facts are found (as for example where it is not possible to determine what the relevant facts are without the interpretation of the European law provision).

187 See OJ C143/1, 11.6.2005, (2005/C143/01) information note on references from national courts for a preliminary ruling. It is for the national court to explain why the interpretation sought is necessary to enable it to give judgment (see para 14).

188 Particularly in discrimination cases there may be situations in which a reference can be seen to be necessary at an earlier stage (namely the stage at which the primary facts are established or agreed).

Should the discretion to make a reference be exercised?

19.150 The following factors should be taken into account:

- the length of time it will take to get a ruling. Very considerable delays are occurring in the ECJ. The time taken to obtain a judgment in a preliminary ruling case has been rising;[189]
- avoid overloading the court. The right to make a reference should be exercised sparingly;[190]
- the question should be formulated clearly and relate solely to the interpretation of the European law provision. The facts should be found and stated clearly before the question is referred;
- unless the point is really difficult and important the tribunal or court should determine it.[191] There is a sliding scale.
  Where the national court is not a court of last resort:
  - a reference will be most appropriate where:
    (a) the question is one of general importance; and
    (b) the ruling is likely to promote the uniform application of the law throughout the European Union;
  - a reference will be least appropriate where:
    (a) there is an established body of case-law which could readily be transposed to the facts of the specific instance case; or
    (b) where the question turns on a narrow point considered in the light of a very specific set of facts and the ruling is unlikely to have any application beyond the instant case.[192]

---

189 *Viking Line ABP v International Transport Workers Federation & The Finnish Seamen's Union* [2005] EWHC 1222 (Comm), [2005] 3 CMLR 29. See also *Viking Line ABP v International Transport Workers Federation* [2005] EWCA Civ 1299, [2006] 1 CMLR 27 and *International Transport Workers' Federation v Viking Line ABP* (C-438/05) [2007] ECR I-10779, [2008] 1 CMLR 51, [2008] ICR 741, [2008] IRLR 143 for the eventual preliminary ruling given 11 December 2007.

190 Jacobs A-G in Case C-338/95 *Wiener SI GmbH v Hauptzollamt Emmerich* [1997] ECR-I 6495 warned against overloading the ECJ with references.

191 After Case C-55-07 *Kücükdeveci v Swedex GmbH* [2011] 2 CMLR 27 at paras 52–6 the courts may exercise their own powers of interpretation more frequently in relation to matters of EU law. In an obvious case, however nothing in that case requires or should incline a court not to make a reference.

192 In *Trinity Mirror* [2001] EWCA Civ 65, [2001] 2 CMLR 33, Chadwick LJ applied the *Else* test (at para 51 of his judgment), but said that it was necessary to have regard also to the observations in *Wiener*. See also *R v Comrs of Inland Revenue ex p Professional Contractors' Group* [2001] EWCA Civ 1945, [2002] 1 CMLR 46 and *R (Federation of Technological Industries) v Customs and Excise Comrs* [2004] EWCA Civ 1020, [2004] 3 CMLR 41.

- the expense to the parties should be taken into account. This will particularly be a factor in a jurisdiction in which costs will not automatically follow the outcome of the case.
- if both parties want the point to be referred the could or tribunal should have regard to their wishes, but should not give them undue weight. There should be some hesitation if one of the parties does not want a reference to be made.[193]

19.151   In *R v International Stock Exchange ex p Else*,[194] Lord Bingham MR gave further guidance on the reference of questions to the ECJ which he regarded as giving the essence of the above guidelines:

> I understand the correct approach in principle of a national court (other than a final court of appeal) to be quite clear: if the facts have been found and the Community law issue is critical to the court's final decision, the appropriate course is ordinarily to refer the issue to the Court of Justice unless the national court can with complete confidence resolve the issue itself. In considering whether it can with complete confidence resolve the issue itself the national court must be fully mindful of the differences between national and Community legislation, of the pitfalls which face a national court venturing into what may be an unfamiliar field, for the need for uniform interpretation throughout the Community and of the great advantage enjoyed by the Court of Justice in construing the Community instruments. If the national court has any real doubt it should ordinarily refer.[195]

19.152   Where a court or tribunal decides to make a reference it may invite the parties to agree the terms of the questions to be referred. The court or tribunal can decide the final wording of the question. The order of reference will contain a judgment setting out the facts and identifying the issues of law. The order should explain why the reference is appropriate. The questions are attached to the order.

19.153   The decision by which a national court or tribunal refers a question to the ECJ for a preliminary ruling takes the form of an order of the tribunal. The secretary to the ET then sends a copy of the order to the registrar of that court.[196] This order serves as the basis of the proceedings before the court and must contain such information as will enable the CJEU to give a reply which is of assistance to the national court. Moreover, it is only the actual reference for a preliminary

193   *Bulmer v Bollinger* [1974] Ch 401 per Lord Denning MR at p 419–25.
194   [1993] QB 534.
195   [1993] QB 534 at 545D–F.
196   See Employment Tribunals (Constitution and Rules of Procedure) Regulations 2004 SI No 1861 reg 58.

ruling which is notified to the parties entitled to submit observations to the court, in particular the member states and the institutions, and which is translated.

19.154 Due to the need to translate the reference, it should be drafted simply, clearly and precisely, avoiding superfluous detail. A maximum of about ten pages is often sufficient to set out in a proper manner the context of a reference for a preliminary ruling. The order for reference must be succinct but sufficiently complete and must contain all the relevant information to give the court and the parties entitled to submit observations a clear understanding of the factual and legal context of the main proceedings.

19.155 In particular, the order for reference must:

- include a brief account of the subject-matter of the dispute and the relevant findings of fact, or, at least, set out the factual situation on which the question referred is based;
- set out the tenor of any applicable national provisions and identify, where necessary, the relevant national case-law, giving in each case precise references (eg page of an official journal or specific law report, with any internet reference);
- identify the Community provisions relevant to the case as accurately as possible;
- explain the reasons which prompted the national court to raise the question of the interpretation or validity of the Community provisions, and the relationship between those provisions and the national provisions applicable to the main proceedings;
- include, where appropriate, a summary of the main arguments of the parties.

19.156 In order to make it easier to read and refer to the document, it is helpful if the different points or paragraphs of the order for reference are numbered. The referring court may, if it considers itself to be in a position to do so, briefly state its view on the answer to be given to the questions referred for a preliminary ruling. The question or questions themselves should appear in a separate and clearly identified section of the order for reference, generally at the beginning or the end. It must be possible to understand them without referring to the statement of the grounds for the reference, which however provides the necessary background for a proper assessment.

19.157 The parties, the Commission and member state governments may give their written submissions to the court. This must be done within two months of the date on which the ECJ notifies them of the registration of the case. There may be an oral hearing, after which the Advocate-General gives an opinion and suggests to the court the answer that should be given. The opinion is very influential in terms of providing more reasoning than will appear in the judgment subsequently (if the Advocate-General's opinion is followed). It should be noted however that the Advocate-General's opinion does not bind the court and is sometimes rejected.

19.158   If a reference is made by the ET, it is possible to get exceptional funding from the Lord Chancellor. If the EAT, or any other court makes the reference, legal aid may be available. There is minimal legal aid available from the CJEU, which an applicant may be able to obtain by writing to the court setting out financial circumstances.

APPENDIX A

Templates

1 Equality Act 2010 questions

QUESTIONS FOR [state name of employer/individual to whom these questions are addressed][1]

These questions are addressed to [Name of employer (R1)] of [address] and to [Name of individual discriminator[s] (R2)] of [address].

Introduction

I, [name] of [address], think that you may have discriminated against me in a way which is unlawful under the Equality Act (EqA) 2010. I think that this treatment may have been unlawful under the Act because of [insert relevant protected characteristic: eg race and/or disability and/or...etc]. I think that the treatment I received amounted to [insert label(s) for the treatment: eg direct discrimination, victimisation, harassment, failure to make reasonable adjustments, and discrimination arising from disability].

The treatment

I am complaining about the following treatment: [outline complaint briefly; eg my qualifications and relevant work experience are greater than Jane Doe's but after we were both interviewed she was promoted. She is white and has no disabilities. I am of African-Caribbean origin and am disabled due to sickle-cell anaemia.][2]

The questions

I have the following questions for you. If I have to take my case before an Employment Tribunal, I will be asking them to notice if you fail to answer these questions or if you give evasive answers to them, so please answer them fully, frankly and carefully. I will be asking the Tribunal to draw inferences which may include the inference that an unlawful act has taken place under the Equality Act 2010 from any failure to answer or from an evasive answer.

My questions to you are:

1) Do you agree that the statement [referred to] under the heading 'The Treatment' is an accurate description of what happened?

2) If not, in what respect do you disagree, or what is your version of what happened?

---

1   These can be contained in a letter. Although EqA 2010 s38(3) and (4) has been removed, a court or tribunal may nevertheless draw an adverse inference from a failure by R to answer a question by C within a reasonable time, or from an evasive or equivocal answer. As an indicator of what has been seen as a reasonable time, EqA 2010 s138 gave a period of 8 weeks beginning with the day on which the question was served.

2   If proceedings have already been issued the claimant can say instead: 'Please refer to my Employment Tribunal application for my statement of the treatment received and of the circumstances leading up to the treatment. Please also refer to my Employment Tribunal application for why I think the treatment I received was unlawful under the Act'.

3) Do you agree that your treatment of me was unlawful under the Act as set out under the heading 'The Treatment' above? If not:

a) why not?
b) what was the reason for your treatment of me?
c) did considerations of the protected characteristics referred to above affect your treatment of me?

In what follows claimants should adapt the questions they have to the issues they wish to explore (so as to see whether to formulate a case or how to formulate it). If the claimant has drawn up a framework document, it will be easier for the claimant to identify relevant questions. This framework document does not need to form part of the questionnaire, but should (at least) be used as a reference point

Date	Event	Why I think the event may be unlawful under the Equality Act 2010

In considering the last column the claimant should look at the elements of the law and state eg I think this was unlawful because another person in the same circumstances (identifying them) was treated more favourably than me, but does not share [state what the protected characteristic is] with me. The questions can be used to find out details which will help the claimant to make relevant comparisons. Example questions are given here in relation to a race and disability case.

4) What is the breakdown of the employees at [   ] by the following categories: department; location; role / job title; grade band; disability; ethnicity (giving details of numbers of workers classified as: white; black – African origin; black – African-Caribbean origin; Asian origin; other ethnicities)?

5) In relation to any disabled employees identified in your answer to the above question, please provide details of each such employee's disability, ethnicity, grade band and the role / job he/she currently performs.

6) What is your policy in relation to the employment of (i) disabled people (ii) black and minority ethnic people?

7) Please provide full details of the steps taken to do each of the following: implement; monitor; and enforce (a) your own policy and (b) the statutory code and guidance and (c) the Equality and Human Rights Commission's current statutory Code on (i) the elimination of discrimination in the field of employment against disabled persons and (ii) the elimination of race discrimination.

8) What, if any, monitoring for (a) disability equality purposes and (b) race equality purposes takes place in respect of the following categories: disciplinaries for reasons of (i) conduct (ii) capability (iii) performance; and all grievances relating to the following:

• departmental or other work reorganisations;
• recruitment;
• acting up opportunities;
• training opportunities;

- appraisals;
- review of job descriptions;
- promotion;
- dismissal;
- resignation.

9) If in any instance, no monitoring is undertaken for these purposes please explain why it is not.

10) In respect of all equal opportunities monitoring concerning disciplinaries and grievances, describe:

- who undertakes this monitoring;
- with what frequency is it undertaken;
- what is/was the outcome of the monitoring undertaken in (i) 2013 (ii) 2012 (iii) 2011;
- what action was taken as a result of the monitoring in those periods? If no action was taken what was the reason for this;
- who is the monitoring reported to?

11) How many Employment Tribunal complaints have been presented against R1 for (i) disability discrimination; (ii) race discrimination and (iii) discrimination on the basis of any other protected characteristic in each of the 5 years to date? In each case, what was the nature of the complaint, against whom was it made and what was the outcome?

12) State the number of grievances which have been filed against (a) R1 and (b) [each named individual respondent] for (i) disability discrimination (ii) race discrimination (iii) matters which could be interpreted as disability discrimination or race discrimination during each of the 5 years to date. In each case, what was the nature of the complaint, against whom was it made and what was the outcome?

13) Describe any analysis conducted by R1 following the completion of any Employment Tribunal complaint or internal complaint raising (i) disability and (ii) race issues during each of the 5 years to date by reference to:

- who undertakes that analysis;
- the outcome of that analysis;
- what changes have taken place as a result;
- how those changes are monitored.

14) What monitoring and analysis takes place to identify the existence / incidence of any less favourable treatment following Employment Tribunal and internal complaints (which raise any of the protected characteristics)? If no monitoring and analysis takes place, why not? If it does take place, please describe it.

15) What (i) disability awareness training (ii) race awareness training and (iii) anti-victimisation training have the following received and when: [name each alleged discriminator and victimiser].

16) Have any complaints of (i) disability discrimination or (ii) race discrimination or of matters which could be interpreted as disability discrimination or as race

discrimination ever been made against any of the individuals specified in the previous question?

In cases involving a public authority such as the civil service or a local authority, the claimant may wish to seek details of the extent to which it has complied with its duty under the public sector equality duty.

17) You will be aware that the public sector equality duty under section 149 of the Equality Act 2010 applies to single decisions as well as to general policy decisions. In the light of that, what do you think the duty required in my case?

18) Please give any details you have of how your treatment of me complied with your public sector equality duties? If you cannot do so, do you admit that you failed to have due regard in relation to the exercise of your functions to the objectives contained in section 149? If not why do you not admit it?

19) What steps did you take to ensure that the exercise of your functions in relation to [the promotion exercise] complied with your public sector equality duties?

20) In what way (if you do) do you consider that [the promotion exercise] complied with your public sector equality duties?

21) Please describe the process of compliance you say occurred.

Please send your answers to: [name and address].

Signed .... Date.....................................

2 Claim form – non-disability cases

(Heading as in disability cases)

Direct/indirect discrimination/harassment/victimisation claim (age, belief, disability, race, religion, sex, sexual orientation) claims

Modelled on an employment termination claim.

ET1 grounds

Introduction

Use this paragraph(s) to show the right of the claimant to bring the case in the first place. It should be used to establish matters such as ' employment' , contract worker status, or that the claimant is any of the other persons who can bring a claim under the Equality Act (EqA) 2010.[3]

Thus ' The claimant was employed by R as [...] from [date of commencement of employment] to [date of termination of employment].'

The respondent

The respondent is [what the employer does – the business].[4]

The nature of the claimant's job

Use this paragraph to describe the claimant's job – if appropriate refer to the job description.[5]

The protected characteristic involved in this case

Use this paragraph to identify the protected characteristic on which the claimant relies, and in the case of discrimination by association, show the relationship giving rise to that association.

Thus The claimant is of Irish ethnic origin/male/Catholic/gay/25 years old/ etc

OR

The claimant is associated with Z who has the protected characteristic of [state characteristic relied upon]. The claimant is associated with Z in the following way: [explain why the claimant and Z are (or are considered by Y to be) associated].

---

3   See eg chapters 9–11.
4   The claimant should keep this as a neutral statement, and should avoid making prejudicial remarks about the respondent in this section.
5   The claimant's account should again be a neutral statement. If it is important that a particular evaluation of how the job was done is mentioned, this should be separated out into distinct paragraphs. If value judgments are mixed up in the description of the job, it is likely to cause the tribunal to mistrust what is being said by way of description.

The nature of these claims

The claimant claims under EqA 2010 s39 and/or s40 against the respondent for

(a) Direct [insert protected characteristic in issue here] discrimination contrary to EqA 2010 s13(1).
(b) Indirect [insert relevant protected characteristic here] discrimination contrary to EqA 2010 s19(1).
(c) Harassment related to [that protected characteristic] contrary to EqA 2010 s26(1).
(d) Victimisation contrary to EqA 2010 s27(1).
Etc

The claimant should also deal with any other claims e.g. under the Employment Rights Act 1996 for unfair dismissal, in the same way.

The facts on which these claims are based

The description of the facts that the claimant intends to rely upon should be set out according to the following guidelines:

1. *Paragraphs should be short. Sentences should be short and should avoid sub clauses. Paragraphs should be numbered: this will make it easier for the ET to understand what the claimant is saying and refer to what is being said quickly. Some claimants find it helpful to adopt the following table to assist them to prepare the particulars of the claim:*

Date	Event	Claim (eg direct etc...)

2. *The events must be given in chronological order.[6] It is helpful to the ET if the claimant indicates the date of the event(s) the paragraph deals with at the start of the paragraph eg '* On 1 January 2012' or ' **1 January 2012**' . If the date is not certain, then the claimant should put ' on or about [date] ...'. If the event took place over a period ' From [state the earliest known date of the event] to [state last date or say ' to date'] ...'.

3. *Keep in mind the legal structure to which these facts relate at all times. The claimant may wish to say (in a direct discrimination case) for example: '* I believe that I was less favourably treated than [state name of actual comparator or say ' a hypothetical comparator'] because on the following dates the events set out occurred in my case but did not occur in [state name]'s case.' The claimant can use the legal structures set out in the preceding chapters to assist.

a) *Direct discrimination [Chapter 2]*
b) *Indirect discrimination [Chapter 3]*
c) *Harassment [Chapter 5]*
d) *Victimisation [Chapter 6]*

---

6 The narrative should deal with the start of employment to its termination and any appeal.

4. *Identify perpetrators.[7]*

5. *The claimant should, if possible be concrete, rather than general in what is alleged. From reading what the claimant has written the ET should be able to understand whether a grievance was raised and if so what happened to it, as well as any criticisms that the claimant has of the respondent, the respondent's procedure or individuals within the organisation which are relevant to the case before the tribunal.*

6. *If any particular act or omission by the respondent is going to be relied upon as a separate act/omission constituting unlawful conduct under the Equality Act 2010, this should be said. Where possible the claimant should assign an allegation number to the allegation eg 'Allegation 1: because of [protected characteristic] the respondent dismissed the claimant for misconduct when X who was guilty of the same misconduct was not dismissed'.*

Why the claimant's treatment was unlawful

Set out here how the facts relate to the legal framework. Thus

(Direct discrimination claims)

'the claimant's treatment, set out above, was unlawful because it was direct discrimination because of [the protected characteristic]:'

Identify the comparators: this should state what the respective circumstances of the claimant and the comparators were and why (or that) they were not materially different from each other.

Identify the differences of treatment

(Indirect discrimination claims)

Identify the provision criterion or practice ('PCP') applied by the respondent.

Say how the PCP placed persons of the protected characteristic group at a particular disadvantage;[8]

Say how the PCP disadvantaged the claimant, showing that it is in the same way as it disadvantages the group.

If a justification for the PCP has been offered and there are alternative means of achieving the same result that could be explored by the ET, which the claimant is able to address, the claimant might wish to address justification here. If this is done, however, the claimant should make clear that these assertions are without prejudice to (a) the duty of the respondent to establish justification (b) the tribunal's critical evaluation of any justification put forward by the respondent subsequently.

(Harassment claims)

The claimant should identify

---

7   Consider whether individuals should be included as parties. See chapter 8.
8   See chapter 3 for the various ways in which this can be done (eg because the PCP is intrinsically liable to disadvantage this group, or because there are statistics showing the disadvantage).

(a) *the unwanted conduct showing why it was unwanted if it is not obviously unwanted conduct;*[9] *this should include a detailed description of how things were done or said, if that is what causes the harassment, as well as what was done or said.*

(b) *whether it had the purpose of creating an intimidating, hostile, degrading, humiliating or offensive environment; or*

(c) *whether it had the effect of creating an intimidating, hostile, degrading, humiliating or offensive environment.*

(d) *Any special features of the claimant which meant that the claimant's perception was that the treatment had this purpose or effect.*

(e) *Details of the environment that was created. This should include the effects on the claimant and others in the environment. If there is an issue as to whether there was a continuing act of harassment (when the ET considers time limits), the continuing nature of this environment may be of importance.*

(Victimisation claims)

Identify the protected act(s) on which the claimant relies;[10]

Identify the treatment which was given to the claimant because the claimant did the protected act(s). State that this treatment was given because the claimant engaged in these protected acts.

(All claims)

Finish by saying what the claimant wants the tribunal to do:

The claimant seeks

(a) A declaration that the respondent acted unlawfully contrary to the Equality Act 2010, and in particular [state the provisions referred to as the basis of the claim] in respect of the facts set out above.

(b) Compensation including damages for injury to feelings [and personal injury;[11] aggravated/exemplary damages[12]].

(c) Recommendations.[13]

(d) Interest on any compensation under (b).

---

9 See chapter 5.

10 See chapter 6.

11 If appropriate, see chapter 18.

12 If this is to be sought, the narrative should include facts which demonstrate the relevant behaviour: see para 18.78.

13 See para 18.145.

3 Disability Cases Particulars of Claim[14]

Case No

IN THE ... EMPLOYMENT TRIBUNAL

BETWEEN:

MS Y	Claimant
and	
X PLC	Respondent

GROUNDS

Introduction

1. The claimant ('C') began working for the respondent ('R') as [a marketing assistant on 10 July 2009].[15]

2. R is [a large retailer ... with eighteen branches and an annual turnover in 2011/12 of two million pounds]. C [worked in its head office in Hull].

3. C's duties consisted primarily of [working in R's office assisting the Senior Marketing Officer, Mr Dan B, who was also her line manager, in developing and implementing its seasonal marketing strategy, four times a year].[16]

The events leading to this claim

4. On 6 February 2012 C went off sick with depression. She had first been diagnosed with depression in June 2005. At that time she had been unable to work for a year and had been on medication for two years. She was unable to dress herself; had difficulty in preparing a meal, going out, socialising, talking to others and concentrating. C submitted certificates from her GP to R.

5. C was certified as being fit to return to work on 9 July 2012. Her fit note said that she required a phased return to work and that she needed adjustments in the workplace in the form of supervision and support; and altered working hours, as her medication made her drowsy in the mornings, so she needed to come into work later that the usual 9am start time.

6. When C returned to work, however, her manager advised her that he needed her to get ' back up to speed' very quickly; that she would need to be 'on top form' as soon as possible; and that she needed to get into the office 'as early as everyone else'. She was told by him that if she did not pull her weight, she

---

14 This is the heading format which should be used in all of the templates.

15 Use the first couple of paragraphs to introduce the claimant and respondent. You can begin by introducing the claimant and their disability; or the claimant as the employee. It is important to set out the respondent and the nature of their business, particularly if they are a large company with a big turnover/profit.

16 Set out in brief what the claimant's duties were, and tell again in brief if possible what led to the events of the claim.

'would be out'. C felt upset and pressurised by her manager's response to her return to work.[17]

7. C felt concerned that her job was at risk and so attempted to return to work under her usual working conditions. However her medication made her very drowsy and so she arrived at work three days in a row at 10am.

8. On Thursday, 12 July 2012, C's manager called her into his office. He told her that things were 'not working out'; that she was clearly 'not fit' to work; and said that it was better that she 'leave' now before the job did her any further 'damage'. He handed her a letter of dismissal which stated that she was being dismissed with 3 weeks notice on grounds of capability.

Disability

9. C is and was at all relevant times a disabled person within the meaning of section 6 of the Equality Act (EqA) 2010.

Why C's treatment was unlawful

10. By reason of the facts set out above, R has discriminated against C in breach of sections 39(2)(c) and (d) of the Equality Act 2010 ('the Act'), and within the meaning of sections 13, 15, 20 and 21 of the Act. R has also subjected C to harassment, contrary to section 40(1) (a) and within the meaning of section 26 of the Act.[18]

11. C also claims that she has been unfairly dismissed contrary to section contrary to section 98 of the Employment Rights Act (ERA) 1996.

12. [C is awaiting a response to the questions sent to R on [date] and reserves the right to amend her claim upon receipt of answers to those questions].

The nature of C's claims

13. The claims are:[19]

   (i) C has been subjected to direct discrimination within the meaning of section 13 in being dismissed, contrary to section 39(2)(c) of EqA 2010; and/or

   (ii) C has been subjected to discrimination arising from disability, consist-

---

17 If something has been said which is particularly important, as for example where harassment is being claimed, ensure that the exact words are set out and that they are accurate. Put them in quotation marks only if certain that these are the words used. If not, state that 'words to the effect of...' were used.

18 If you are in a position to set out all the relevant claims, do so at an early stage. If you are not, then set out in general that this is a claim of disability discrimination contrary to section 39 of EqA 2010. The respondent will then require the claim to be particularised and certainly by the time of a case management discussion the claim will need to be set out in full ie what types of discrimination being relied upon will need to be specified.

19 A claimant might want to say something to the effect that ' The claimant believes that the facts set out above give rise to the following claims. However the claimant will seek to clarify all the issues, including the legal issues, at a Case Management Discussion'.

ing of detriment and dismissal contrary to section 15 and section 39(2)(c) and/or (d); and/or

(iii) R failed to make reasonable adjustments in breach of its obligations under sections 20 and 21 of the Act, as applied by section 39(5) and Schedule 8, and contrary to section 39(2)(c) and (d) of the Act as follows:

   (a) R failed to provide C with supervision and support following her return to work on 9 July 2012

   (b) R failed to permit C to come in to work later than the usual 9am start time following her return to work on 9 July 2012; and/or

(iv) C has been subjected to harassment within the meaning of section 26 and contrary to section 40(1)(a) of the Act as follows:

   (a) C's line manager's comments upon her return to work on 9 July 2012 as set out above made her feel as though she was incapable of performing her role because of her disability, creating a humiliating and degrading environment for her.

Remedies

14. C has suffered, because of what is set out above, loss and damage, including injury to feelings and psychiatric injury.

15. C also seeks reinstatement/re-engagement.

4 Letter of instruction to consultant psychiatrist in respect of definition of disability and future loss[20]

The opening paragraph of the letter should include the reference details of the case (case name and ET reference number if any). It should then introduce the writer and the capacity of the writer (if not the claimant) to act for the claimant. (Eg We act on behalf of Ms Y ('C'[21]) in her claim to the employment tribunal of disability discrimination under the Equality Act (EqA) 2010 against her former employer, X PLC (' R'). *If the instructions are joint the representative of R should then be introduced. The letter should then say* 'These are joint instructions to you. We have enclosed with this letter a copy of the claim form and the grounds of resistance'.[22]

Background

The letter should then give the background to any relevant diagnosis, work history and history of sickness absence if relevant: e.g. C was diagnosed with depression in 2005 by her GP and was unable to work for a year. She began work with R in July 2009. She was signed off work on 6 February 2012 with a recurrence of her depression. She was certified as being fit to return to work on 9 July 2012 with certain adjustments. She returned to work but was dismissed on 12 July 2012. She claims disability discrimination and unfair dismissal.

In order to bring a claim under the disability provisions of the Act, C must be a disabled person within the meaning of EqA 2010 s6. C and R wish to instruct you to provide a report to assist in determining this matter.

Disability[23]

As you may be aware, the definition of 'disability' is set out at EqA 2010 s6 and provides that a person has a disability if he or she has a physical or mental

---

20 Note: medical evidence in a case where the disability relates to a person's mental health may come from a GP as well as from a consultant psychiatrist. Sometimes it is more appropriate that the treating doctor comments on the claimant as the treating doctor will have more experience of the patient and will be able to comment more fully than the expert who merely interviews the patient on one occasion to form an opinion.

21 These abbreviations are adopted for reasons of space in this book.

22 It is likely once a claim has begun that if there is a dispute about disability the tribunal will order joint medical evidence to be obtained with both parties jointly bearing the cost. This means that instructions to the medical expert will need to be joint instructions, and so will need to be as 'neutral' as possible in order to ensure that they are agreed. Parties can in some circumstances call their own medical evidence though. See *GCHQ v Bacchus* [2012] EqLR 1002 for the most recent discussion of the approach to medical evidence in disability cases. If the instruction is on behalf of the claimant only, the letter should still try to state the facts neutrally, and it is a good idea to include in the documents the claim form and the grounds of resistance. The expert should be informed of the fact that the instructions are on behalf of the claimant, but that he or she is instructed as an independent expert.

23 It is worth setting out the guidance sources for the doctor, who may not be familiar with the test to which the expert evidence may go. Note that the medical expert should not be encouraged to comment on whether the impairment has substantial

impairment and the impairment has a substantial long-term and adverse effect on his or her ability to carry out normal day-to-day activities. The Secretary of State has produced the Equality Act 2010 *Guidance on matters to be taken into account in determining questions relating to the definition of disability* (the Guidance) and this provides guidance on how the various terms are to be interpreted, including the requirement that the effects be long-term.

'Substantial' is defined in the Act itself as meaning more than minor or trivial. Further information on the meaning of 'substantial adverse effect' can be found in Section B of the Guidance.

Section D of the Guidance contains information regarding the meaning of 'normal day-to-day activities'. In addition, the appendix to the Guidance sets out a non-exhaustive list of factors which it would be reasonable to regard as having a substantial adverse effect on normal day-to-day activities and a separate non-exhaustive list of factors which it would not be reasonable to regard as having such an effect.

Please note that, in accordance with the Act and the Guidance, to the extent that C was receiving any treatment (including counselling), you should consider whether any impairment would have been likely to have had a substantial adverse effect on her ability to carry out normal day-to-day activities without the treatment. In this context, 'likely' should be interpreted as ' could well happen' .

Questions

1) Is it your opinion that C has a physical or mental impairment and if so what is it?

2) From your own observations of C carrying out day-to-day activities and from the information provided to you at examination by C can you comment on the ease or otherwise with which she [eg moves, concentrates on a task, speaks etc - these activities can be taken from the examples of activity set out at Section D of the Guidance but do not have to be confined to these examples].

3) The Tribunal will determine whether the effects identified by C are more than minor or trivial. In relation to the effects either identified on examination by you or reported to you please would you provide your view as to whether the adverse effect was long-term.

For the purposes of the Act, an effect is to be regarded as long-term if (i) it has lasted at least twelve months or (ii) the total period for which it will last, from the time of the first onset, is likely to be at least twelve months ('likely' is to be interpreted as meaning ' could well happen'). Please state at what point the effects became long term.

4) C is taking the following medication: [state the medication being taken]. If C ceased to take this medication what, in your opinion would be the effects of the

adverse effects on the person's ability to carry out normal day to day activities. Whether it does so is a matter for the ET and is a question of fact (see chapter 4).

impairment identified by you above on the aspects of functioning referred to in 2 above? In particular in your opinion would the effects be more adverse?

5) How long in your opinion will C continue to have the impairment identified by you?

6) When, if ever, do you consider that C will be well enough to return to employment?

7) Please provide your view as to the extent to which C's condition was caused by or exacerbated by the events set out at paragraph [x] onwards of the ET1.

Please include, with your report, a statement of your qualifications and relevant experience. We would emphasise that your overriding duty in preparing the report is to the Employment Tribunal and not to either party or their representatives.

5 List of issues[24]

[Heading identifying the parties and giving the case number]

Disability

1. Does the claimant (' C') have a disability within the meaning of section 6(1) EqA 2010? The disability relied upon by C is [*state disability or disabilities, e.g. diabetes/ depression/ Crohn's disease/ chronic back pain etc.*].

Direct disability discrimination (EqA 2010 ss13(1) and 39(2))[25]

2. Did the respondent ('R') treat C less favourably than it treated, or would have treated [*if C can point to another employee who is not disabled and who has been treated differently in similar circumstances, that person can be named here as well as referring to 'other persons'*] other persons because of C's disability?

3. C relies on the following acts of discrimination:

   Here set out all the acts of direct discrimination said to have occurred by C in as concise a form as possible. Give the date of the incident where C is able to remember the date, and if not, give an approximate date (eg 'in or around January 2012'). Here are some examples in a case involving humiliating language, failure to promote and dismissal:

   3.1 *On 14 October 2012, C's manager, Mr Z, described him to another manager, in C's hearing, as a 'lame duck'.*

   3.2 *On or around 28 October 2012, Mr Z failed to shortlist C for the grade 6 position of assistant manager.*

   3.3 *R failed, in or around October/November 2012, to promote C to the position of assistant manager.*

   3.4 *On 18 December 2012, R dismissed C, allegedly by reason of redundancy.*

Discrimination arising from disability (EqA 2010 ss15(1)(a)[26] and 39(2))

4. Did R treat C unfavourably because of something arising in consequence of C's disability, namely [*set out the disability-related problem or characteristic that caused the unfavourable treatment; for example ' C's absence from work between X and Y dates'*]?

---

24 This template list of issues is for a disability discrimination claim brought by an employee, covering all types of discrimination, failure to make reasonable adjustments, harassment and victimisation. The list of issues should be set out as a series of questions that the ET will have to answer. The questions should follow the structure of the Equality Act 2010 to give the ET its legal framework. Some ETs have pro forma documents to be used for case management discussions, which may have a section for the list of issues. It is always worth checking whether the ET in which the claimant's claim is brought has such a document.

25 EqA 2010 s13(1) is the section dealing with direct discrimination in respect of all protected characteristics. EqA 2010 s39(2) is the section prohibiting discrimination against employees.

26 EqA 2010 s15 is the section prohibiting discrimination arising from disability.

5. The unfavourable treatment alleged by C is as follows:

   [*Here set out each act of alleged unfavourable treatment, following the format given at paragraph 3 above for direct discrimination*].

6. Was any such unfavourable treatment a proportionate means of achieving a legitimate aim, within the meaning of EqA 2010 s15(1)(b)? The legitimate aim relied upon by R is [*R should be asked to be specific about the aim upon which it relies in the list of issues*].

Indirect discrimination (EqA 2010 ss19(1)[27] and 39(2))

7. Did R apply to C a provision, criterion or practice ('PCP'), namely [*set out the provision, criterion or practice applied; eg 'requiring employees to have a good attendance record in order to achieve promotion' or 'using the employee's attendance record as the primary selection criterion in determining who should be made redundant'*]?

8. Did, or would, R apply that PCP to persons other than C, who do not have C's disability?

9. Did the PCP put persons who share C's disability at a particular disadvantage when compared with persons who do not have his disability, namely [*set out the disadvantage relied upon; for example, in relation to the PCPs given above, the disadvantage could be that C's disability required him to take frequent days off to undergo medical procedures or attend hospital appointments, meaning that his attendance record was comparatively poor*].

10. Did the PCP put C at that disadvantage?

11. Can R show the PCP to be a proportionate means of achieving a legitimate aim? The legitimate aim relied upon by R is [*R should be asked to be specific about the aim upon which it relies in the list of issues*].

Reasonable adjustments (EqA 2010 ss20(2), 21[28] and 39(2))

There are three different types of duty to make reasonable adjustments set out in EqA 2010 s20. This example is based on the duty set out in section 20(3), but the same format can be used in respect of sections 20(4) (substantial disadvantage caused by a physical feature) and 20(5) (substantial disadvantage caused by failure to provide an auxiliary aid).

12. Did R apply a provision, criterion or practice ('PCP') to C, namely [*set out the provision, criterion or practice applied; eg 'requiring employees to have a good attendance record in order to achieve promotion' or ' using the employee's attendance record as the primary selection criterion in determining who should be made redundant'*]?

13. Did that PCP put C at a substantial disadvantage in comparison with persons who are not disabled namely [*set out the disadvantage relied upon; for example, in relation to the PCPs given above, the disadvantage could be that C's disability*

---

27 EqA 2010 s19 is the section dealing with indirect discrimination in respect of all protected characteristics.
28 EqA 2010 ss20 and 21 deal with the duty to make reasonable adjustments.

required him to take frequent days off to undergo medical procedures or attend hospital appointments, meaning that he did not secure promotion, or was selected for redundancy].[29]

14. Did R take such steps as it was reasonable to have to take in order to avoid that disadvantage? C contends that R should have taken the following steps [*here set out the adjustments that C says R should have made; eg:*

    14.1 *disregarding the comparative attendance records of the candidates in conducting the promotion/redundancy selection exercise;*

    14.2 *disregarding any days on which C was absent for reasons relating to his disability in conducting those exercises;*

    14.3 *disregarding any days on which C was absent because he was attending a medical appointment or undergoing a medical procedure in connection with his disability in conducting those exercises.*]

Harassment (EqA 2010 ss26(1)[30] and 39(2))

15. Did R engage in unwanted conduct related to C's disability, namely [*set out the unwanted conduct relied upon, eg ' on 14 October 2012, C's manager, Mr Z, described C as a 'lame duck' to another manager, in C's hearing'*]?

16. Did that conduct have the purpose or effect of violating C's dignity, or creating an intimidating, hostile, degrading, humiliating or offensive environment for C?

17. In considering whether the conduct had the relevant effect, the ET should take into account:

    17.1 C's perception;

    17.2 the other circumstances of the case;

    17.3 whether it was reasonable for the conduct to have that effect.

Victimisation (EqA 2010 ss27(1)[31] and 39(2))

18. Did R victimise C, [*here set out the conduct on which C relies as victimisation; eg 'by dismissing him, allegedly by reason of redundancy, on 18 December 2012'*] because C had done a protected act, namely [*here set out the protected act relied upon, e.g. ' on 21 November 2012, raising a grievance alleging that he had not been promoted because he was a disabled person'*]?

Time limits

In cases involving a series of events, there will often be an issue as to whether some or all of the complaints have been brought within the time limits set out in the Act.

29 In many cases the 'comparators' in a reasonable adjustments case will be obvious from the nature of the substantial disadvantage, eg here, the comparator would be a person who did not have to take time off to attend medical procedures or hospital appointments. In such cases it may not be necessary specifically to identify the characteristics of the comparator at this stage, but some tribunals may require this. For further information about identifying comparators in reasonable adjustments cases see paras 4.52–4.63.

30 EqA 2010 s26 prohibits harassment related to all protected characteristics.

31 EqA 2010 s27 prohibits victimisation.

The following format can be used to set out the time limit issues in such cases.

19. Does the conduct of R set out at paragraphs 2–18 above, or any part of that conduct, amount to ' conduct extending over a period' within the meaning of EqA 2010 s123(3)?

20. Were any of C's complaints brought outside the relevant time limit specified in EqA 2010 s23?

21. If so, is it just and equitable to extend time for the bringing of those complaints?

6 Schedule of Loss

[Heading identifying the parties and giving the case number]

SCHEDULE OF LOSS[32]

Relevant information

Claimant's date of birth	25/01/1975
Date of commencement of employment	06/08/2006
Date of termination of employment	17/09/2012
Net weekly salary	£515.00

Unfair dismissal[33]

	£
Basic award	
6 x £450.00[34]	2,700.00
Compensatory award	
Loss of statutory rights[35]	600.00
For other losses claimed under the heading of the compensatory award, namely loss of earnings and loss of pension, please see the sex discrimination claim below.[36]	
Total	**3,300.00**

32 This template Schedule of Loss is for a claim involving complaints of discriminatory and unfair dismissal.

33 These heads of loss may only be claimed if, in addition to the discrimination claim, there is a claim for unfair dismissal.

34 An explanation of the basic award is outside the scope of this text, but it is calculated based on the number of years over which the claimant has been employed, and the claimant's age during those years of employment. In the simplest cases (such as that set out above), the basic award will be one week's gross pay (subject to a statutory cap which is £450 in respect of employment ending on or after 1 February 2013) per full year of employment. Where the basic award covers years of employment when the claimant was under 22 or over 41, the amount awarded in respect of those years of employment will be ½ a week's pay or 1½ weeks' pay respectively. For a full explanation of how to calculate the basic award, please refer to *Employment Law: an adviser's handbook* (9th edition, LAG, 2011).

Sex discrimination

Past loss of earnings	£
The claimant has now obtained new employment, but has not, as of the date of this Schedule, started in her new post. The claimant therefore claims her full loss of earnings from the date of her dismissal to date. 17/9/2012 – 11/2/2013 21 x £515 =	10,815.00
Future loss of earnings	
The claimant's loss of earnings is currently continuing at a rate of £515.00 per week. The claimant will start new employment on 25/2/2013, at a net rate of pay of £400 per week. The claimant will therefore suffer ongoing loss of £115 net per week thereafter. 11/2/2013 – 25/2/2013 £515 x 2 = Ongoing loss of £115 per week	1,030.00 To be confirmed[37]
continued	

35 This is a standard sum awarded in unfair dismissal claims to compensate for loss of protection against unfair dismissal. When the qualifying period to bring an unfair dismissal claim was one year's employment, the standard award under this head was £200-£300; now the qualifying period has been increased to two years, a claim for £600 would be reasonable.

36 Where claims for both unfair dismissal and discrimination arise out of the termination of employment, any claims for loss of earnings and pension should be included in the Schedule of Loss under the heading of discrimination, as there is no statutory cap on compensation for discrimination as there is for unfair dismissal. However, the losses should also be referenced in the unfair dismissal claim, in case the discrimination claim is unsuccessful.

37 When an updated Schedule of Loss is ordered for the trial, it will be necessary to put a figure on the likely future loss of earnings, even if the claimant is still out of work, or employed in a lower-paying job, and does not know when he/she will get a new job at the same or a similar salary. Claimants should include a future loss figure that is their best guess of the further loss they will suffer before obtaining equivalent employment, taking into account the labour market in their area and field of work.

Loss of pension[38]	£
The claimant was a member of the respondent's occupational pension scheme (defined contribution), under which the respondent contributed 6% of her gross salary towards her pension. The claimant's new employer's pension scheme is equivalent to that of the respondent, and she will suffer no loss once she commences her new employment. The respondent's weekly contribution to the claimant's pension was £41.14 17/9/12 – 11/2/2013 £41.14 x 21 = 12/2/2013 – 25/2/2013 £41.14 x 2 =	 863.94 82.28
Injury to feelings[39]	
The claimant suffered significant distress as a result of her discriminatory dismissal. Over a period of 3 months, she was frequently tearful and lost confidence in her ability to do her job. She was unable to contemplate applying for new positions over this period, and required significant support from friends and family. The claimant claims an award at the lower end of the middle band of the *Vento* guidelines, as uprated in the case of *Da Bell*.	 10,000.00
Total[40]	To be confirmed

38 This calculation relates to a 'money purchase' or 'defined contribution' type pension scheme, which is the type that most private sector employees will now have. Public sector employees are more likely to have the benefit of a 'final salary' or 'defined benefit' pension scheme, which requires a more complicated pension calculation. See 18.94 – 18.101 above and further the government guidelines on calculating loss of pension in Employment Tribunal, to be found at www.justice.gov.uk/downloads/tribunals/employment/claims/guidance-booklets/LossOfPensionRights.pdf .

39 Whilst details as to any distress and upset caused by the discrimination should be set out in full in the claimant's witness statement, it is useful also to set out a short summary in the Schedule of Loss.

40 Any claims for aggravated damages, exemplary damages and personal injury should also be included in this section.

Interest

Injury to feelings	£
Interest on this head of loss is claimed at the special account rate of 0.5% from the date of dismissal, 17/09/12. $147^{41}/365 \times 0.005^{42} \times £10,000$	20.14
Past monetary losses[43]	
Interest on these heads of loss is claimed at the special account rate of 0.5% from the halfway point between the date of dismissal and the date of this Schedule of Loss. $74^{44}/365 \times 0.005 \times £11,678.94$	11.84
Total	**31.98[45]**

Statement of Truth

I believe that the facts stated in this Schedule of Loss are true.

Signed: _____

Dated: 11 February 2013

---

41 Number of days since dismissal.
42 0.5% expressed as a decimal.
43 These losses comprise the past loss of earnings and the past loss of pension contributions.
44 Number of days from the halfway point between dismissal and date of Schedule to date of Schedule.
45 These sums would need to be updated in any final Schedule of Loss produced for trial.

Index